International Trade

I. F. Pearce

UNIVERSITY OF SOUTHAMPTON

International Trade

 W·W·Norton & Company · Inc · NEW YORK

Copyright © 1970 by I. F. Pearce

SBN   393 09948 2

Library of Congress Catalog Card No. 72-122316

Printed in the United States of America

1 2 3 4 5 6 7 8 9 0

Contents

Preface and Acknowledgements

ONLY an infinitesimal part of any book can be held to be truly original. It is quite impossible therefore to name or even to know the names of more than a very few of those whose ideas are included here. There is, however, a very special sense in which students and colleagues of the writer have collaborated in the creation of this book.

First, some of the results now incorporated in Chapters 6 and 8 were originally worked out by Professor Ian McDougall and S. F. Harris when they were students of the writer in Canberra. Next, it should be made clear that the very important exercises 7, 8, 9 and 10 to Chapter 4 were taken from a Ph.D. thesis presented by Kathryn Morfey at the University of Southampton. This may indeed be a suitable point to express the hope that Dr Morfey's thesis will soon be published.

I am most grateful to Professor Arthur Bloomfield of the Wharton School for reading and commenting upon section 4.6. The general result from which exercise 10 to Chapter 7 was constructed was deduced in a joint paper, unpublished at the time of writing, by the present author and David Horwell. Exercise 8, Chapter 7, is based on work done by yet another student of the writer, K. P. V. Karunaratne. The particularly devastating conclusion implied by exercise 11, Chapter 7, resulted from collaboration between the present author, K. P. V. Karunaratne and Kathryn Morfey. Honours should go to Kathryn Morfey for discovering the very neat trick which makes the problem tractable and indeed for being the first to find the special case we were seeking.

In Chapter 12 I have made extensive use of an essentially three-dimensional diagram first introduced by Professor Lionel McKenzie to illustrate the basic theorem of section 12.7 [7]†. Parts of Chapter 15 owe much to Professor Don Katzner. Throughout the whole of the writing I have benefited from constant discussion with David Horwell. Professor John Black and David Pearce very kindly read much of the manuscript and drew my attention severally and jointly

† Figures in square brackets refer to the numbered items in the Bibliography.

to a prodigious number of slips and obscurities. Stephen Pearce planned and drew the flow chart (Fig. 19.1).

The willingness of the author to let other people do his work for him must now be apparent. It will be readily appreciated, therefore, that there will inevitably be others whose direct contribution has been overlooked. These will include generations of students who have so kindly received the notes I have from time to time presented to them and whose comments have encouraged me to continue. It is to be hoped that all of these students and others will feel entitled to share the author's satisfaction in whatever success, if any, this book may have in preserving, or even here and there adding a particle to, our knowledge of the processes of international trade.

My thanks are due to Miss Diana Marshallsay for bibliographical advice and for the preparation of the index.

I. F. PEARCE

Introduction

1. FOR EVERYONE

ONE of the many manifestations of the truth of the doctrine of original sin is that which dictates that whoever succumbs to the temptation to write a book is immediately beset by an even more grievous temptation to review it himself. And it could be that this accounts for the present Introduction. On the other hand we ought not to lay too much blame at the door of original sin; for the fact is that the construction of a text involves a series of difficult choices the logic of which may not always be obvious to the reader. A case can be made out for revealing something of the plot before the play opens. Indeed, I was encouraged in this belief by a kind but critical reader of the manuscript now forming Chapters 1–18 of this book who wrote, among other things, that 'it just sort of begins'. An Introduction enables us after all to begin with a beginning.

Let it be claimed first that, however dismally executed this work may turn out to be, it was at least conceived for the very best of all reasons. My primary purpose was, and is, to put before my students that material which they ought to know in the order in which considerable experience suggests that it is best taken. This last point bears some further explanation.

It is often the case that inexperienced students of economics, when they can be induced to offer critical comment, make remarks which, shorn of their trimmings, mean in effect that lectures should be (*a*) more interesting, and/or (*b*) less difficult.

To this of course it is tempting and easy to reply that if the subject has no interest, why read it, and if it is found too difficult, might the fault not lie in the ability or industry of the student himself? But there is almost certainly more to it than this. A reader of a book on mathematics usually undertakes this task quite simply because he wishes, or is required, to learn some mathematics. A student of economics on the other hand very often reads economics, not because he has any interest in economic theory *per se*, but because he is disturbed and distressed by certain social problems. He may in short be much less concerned with the argument than with the answers. It is natural for such a person to feel cheated if he is required to investigate the reasons why the production possibility set is convex when he really wants to know about the balance of payments; or if he is required to learn about Paasche and Laspeyre index numbers as a measure of the value of the national product when he really wants to know the cause of unemployment on Tyneside.

It is always true of course that the beginner must learn to walk before he can run and it is equally true that if there were facile answers to all social problems there would be no social problems. But there are more ways than one of learning to walk and difficult arguments somehow become easier when it is understood that they are necessary to the achievement of a much desired objective. With these ideas in mind, an attempt has been made in this book to proceed always from the social problems to the difficulties rather than from the difficulties to the social problems.

This does not mean that we have reverted to the 'once over lightly' first approach to the teaching of economics now held in general disfavour. On the contrary great care has been taken to create a text of progressive difficulty, at the same time treating in depth each question as it arises. The student is never asked to unlearn something previously learned. It is intended that the whole work, Books I and II, should provide material for each of the three years of an undergraduate honours course. Chapters 1–5 of Book I may be considered suitable for year one and indeed are already taught in year one at the University of Southampton. The remainder of Book I and perhaps selected parts of Book II can be introduced in year two. Other sections of Book II might be thought to be for the specialist.

The suggestion that Book II is largely for the specialist, however, has been made only after considerable hesitation, for the whole work does, it is hoped, carry an important message, the full impact of which may very well not be felt until Chapter 19 is reached. In fact it was my first impulse to call Book I 'What We Know' and Book II 'What We Do Not Know'. It could well be more important, in the present climate of scientific euphoria, to understand that there are some things we do not know than to propagandise what we think we do. This is particularly true of matters dealt with in Chapters 17 and 18, the contents of which would certainly have been included in Book I were it not for the difficulty of the argument.

The idea that the theory of the balance of payments can be taught to beginners with scarcely any other knowledge of economics, to the level to which it is carried in Chapters 1–5, may, in some quarters, appear revolutionary. If it is revolutionary, however, then in my view the revolution is long overdue for reasons implied in the remarks above. The model of Chapters 1–4 is quite self-contained. The notion that a shortage in supply of any commodity induces a rise in its price is a very familiar one and nothing more is needed to sustain the argument. If it is accepted that many commodities can be aggregated into a single class called 'importables', and if it is accepted that many countries can be called the 'rest of the world', the student will have no difficulty in believing that he is learning at all times something of life in the real world. Care has been taken also to introduce monetary and employment problems quite naturally and immediately so that the relevance of the model is always apparent. Nor is the logic of Chapters 1–5 particularly difficult.

What is even more important is the fact that, when the study of economics is approached in this way, and if the present writer's experience can be taken as a guide, there arises a spontaneous demand to discuss matters which, when presented out of context, may seem to be dull and irrelevant. Students are usually surprised to be told that it is not always a 'good' thing to introduce a policy even though that policy will increase the value of the national product. Thus they are induced actually to ask about Paasche and Laspeyre index numbers, although they will not identify the problem by its name. In the same way it is impossible to remain uninterested in our grounds for supposing the production possibility set to be convex as soon as it is understood that it is not possible to make a single positive valid statement about the consequence of policy in international trade unless the convexity condition is met. In short there is something after all to be said for putting the cart before the horse if it is the cart and not the horse which is initiating the forward movement.

The above remarks explain in part the order in which the work is taken. It seemed more sensible and much more interesting to begin with familiar problems like the balance of payments, tariffs, customs unions and international liquidity than with the so-called 'theory of comparative costs' which, since it underlies everything else, might be held logically to take precedence. But this is not all. The theory of comparative costs, properly treated, is an infinitely more complex subject than the balance of payments. It would simply not be possible to teach the content of Chapters 12 and 15 to first-year students except to the exclusion of all else. Either it would be necessary to abandon the principle of progressive difficulty or the argument would have to be simplified to the point where it became misleading. The second alternative is not one which should commend itself.

It will be noted that each problem of Book I is treated first verbally and diagrammatically and then algebraically. This has a twofold purpose. First, the arrangement allows for the algebra to be omitted if desired in the early stages. Second, the algebra itself consistently demonstrates the superiority of the method. Furthermore, the dual approach is designed to teach the required techniques which we insist must be mastered sooner or later if Book II, and even parts of Book I, are to be properly understood.

Whatever may be thought to the contrary on first glancing at some of the pages, *no knowledge of mathematics whatever is needed to read the whole of Book I beyond that required to solve a pair of linear equations such as every schoolboy encounters.* It is true that the notation of the differential calculus is freely employed, but the reader is taught the very few necessary results as he goes along. And by this we do not mean that the book includes within itself a mathematical text. On the contrary it is doubtful whether more than three or four pages in total are taken up in explanation of purely mathematical points; for the fact is that only a microscopic amount of mathematics is made use of in Book I. If it appears to be more, this is because the same simple idea is brought into use again and again in ever more complicated applications, each time confirming the extraordinary power of the method. It follows that the sooner the trick is learned the better and, as we have already suggested, the least painful way for any economist to acquire technique is in the context of a social problem in which he is interested. This book is not for, and will not interest, mathematicians seeking some field in which to exercise their art. It is a book for students of social problems provided they stand ready to accept the assurance of the writer that, with a very small amount of initial effort, they may save themselves a great deal of trouble in the end.

Book II calls for a little more knowledge of mathematics but not more than the ordinary honours economics student might reasonably be expected to have picked up in other classes by the time Book II is reached. In any case suitable easy references are given. These references have been selected so as to draw attention to the mathematical tricks rather than the theory underlying the tricks. Readers interested mainly in economics are strongly advised to accept and make use of mathematical theorems without worrying too much about proofs. Unsolved problems are usually much more interesting to work on than those for which we already have standard answers. In any case proofs are quickly forgotten even by practitioners making constant use of the theorems proved.

The coverage of the whole work will be clear from the table of contents. It may be felt on looking at this that there is a regrettable absence of factual matter throughout and that no attempt is made to give any consistent account of recent world history in the field of international trading relations. This is a deliberate omission. Tables showing the volume and composition of world trade are readily available in a hundred different publications and any reader who attempts the exercises at the end of each chapter will find himself directed to some of these. World economic history is another matter. It is hoped that at all times a feeling for history is preserved. On the other hand a detailed study of the rise and fall of the Sterling Area or the birth and (hopefully) early life of the I.M.F. is something which ought not to be undertaken until the theory of the subject is properly understood. Economic theory cannot be learned from descriptive accounts of the development of economic institutions even though it is true that economic institutions help to determine behaviour. In this book an attempt is made to isolate the essential part played by economic institutions in world affairs from the mass of detail which tends in some cases to obscure it. The aim is to limit description to the minimum required for this purpose consistent with the maintenance of a sense of reality in the argument.

A fairly lengthy though far from comprehensive bibliography is added to give direction to the student's further reading. For two reasons this additional reading has been put at the end and arranged under subject headings rather than assigned to each chapter. First, the view is taken that in the first instance a beginner will benefit very little from attempting to read articles written largely by academics for academics even though the topic may relate to a chapter he has just followed in a text. Second, the study of economics consists in a large degree of creating a mental model of a whole economy which serves as a framework within which to put each question as it arises. Once this is achieved, points made by other writers are then easily assimilated into what becomes the personal way of seeing things of the individual concerned. The present book, it is hoped, provides one such framework. Each chapter discusses part of the 'works', the whole being finally put together in Chapter 19. Every solution to every problem treated compares stationary states of the model of Chapter 19, either in aggregate (simplified) form or suitably disaggregated. There are few questions (whether or not they are mentioned below) which cannot be put to the model of Chapter 19 either as it stands or with some minor modification.

Finally, the exercises at the end of each chapter should be considered an integral part of the whole work, since they are frequently designed to give important insights which can be gained only by carrying out the prescribed manipulations. In most cases and wherever possible answers are included implicitly in the question. The working is seldom difficult in principle though it is sometimes very tedious in practice. For this reason, if for no other, frivolous exercises are avoided. In each case an important and necessary lesson is to be learned from the work undertaken. If difficulty is experienced in obtaining the answer quoted it should be remembered that, in view of the relationships set out in Chapter 4, exercise 5, there will usually be more than one form in which the same formula can be expressed. What looks like a wrong answer may very well be correct. If it is correct it will be found possible, using the relationships mentioned, to convert the one into the other. (Compare for example equations (4.4.14) and (4.4.15), which are essentially the same.)

The remaining sections of this Introduction are addressed primarily to professional economists who may wish to use this book either as a reference work or a text. The beginner therefore *should not expect to understand fully* all of the points raised. In fact the following remarks constitute what might be called an *ex ante* defence against likely criticism on certain points which are sometimes misunderstood.

NOT FOR BEGINNERS

2 THE WELFARE PROBLEM – LARGE OR SMALL CHANGES ?

Books on international economics often contain a section which attempts to justify the use of the concept of 'community indifference curves' in the belief that this is a necessary tool for the proper analysis of policy problems. For at least two reasons nothing on this topic will be found in the work below. First, my *Contribution to Demand Analysis* [10, chap. 3]† gives a very full account of the difficulty and its solution. This should be sufficient to satisfy the critic who might argue that the splitting of demand elasticities into income and (symmetric) substitution effects, a device we frequently employ, already implies the existence of community indifference curves. Second, it probably is not true that anything is gained by the explicit introduction of a community welfare function even where the

† Figures in square brackets refer to the numbered items in the Bibliography.

issue specifically concerns the usefulness or otherwise of a policy. We manage very well without it.

Our device for managing without community indifference curves does, however, raise a point which seems, not surprisingly since it is counterintuitive, to have been overlooked in some quarters. In fact we say quite simply that there is a gain in welfare if consumption, valued at base prices, is increased. (This is subject to qualification – see Chapter 13 below.) More formally we claim that a policy is good if

$$\sum_i q_i\, dX_i > 0$$

where q_i is the going market price of the ith commodity and dX_i is the change in consumption due to the policy. The rationale of this does of course come from the theory of demand with its implicit assumption of the existence of a welfare function, but only in this case *for each individual* (see also Chapter 13). What demand theory implies is

$$\lambda q_i = u_i$$

where u_i is the so-called marginal utility of the ith commodity and λ is the (positive) marginal utility of money. Thus

$$\sum_i q_i\, dX_i > 0$$

states that

$$\rho\sum u_i\, dX_i = \rho\, du > 0$$

where ρ is the reciprocal of λ, which means that the change du in total utility is greater than zero.

So much is familiar, but the objection is sometimes raised that this approach will do only for *small* changes in policy generating small changes dX_i since, as is well known, the differential du measures the 'true' change in utility only approximately for small changes dX_i. Some writers have gone so far therefore as to argue that the theory of customs unions, for example, as set out in Chapter 7 is not a theory of customs unions at all, for its results apply only to small changes whereas the formation of a customs union means, by definition, a policy which will induce large changes. The same objection may be raised in some measure to almost every problem treated in this book, for the same kind of approximation is consistently employed everywhere.

Two ways of escaping the difficulty are available. The first is to assume some particular form of functional relationship. For example one writer has argued, apropos of the theory of the customs union, that the *only* way to proceed is geometrically. The form of the utility function is then expressed by choosing some 'shape' for community indifference curves. Again, certain authors interested in the actual measurement of gains from policy have introduced a particular algebraic expression for utility. It might be supposed for example that utility is the logarithm of the value of consumption.

It is difficult to believe that proposals of this first kind would be made if the writers concerned understood that an alternative exists, for no one form of function is known to be more acceptable than any other. Ignorance simply leads to still more ignorance. On the other hand mathematicians have discovered a very remarkable theorem which permits us to say what the value of *any* function will be at any value (say X') of the argument solely from observation of rates of change taken in the neighbourhood of some value, say X^0, quite different from X'. This is the counterintuitive proposition mentioned above and it provides us with the second way out of our difficulty.

Let du^* be the actual change in utility between two possible consumption patterns. Then it is true that du is a first approximation to du^* however large the change when

$$du = \frac{\partial u}{\partial X_1} dX_1 + \frac{\partial u}{\partial X_2} dX_2.$$

But, as we have agreed, it is also true that this might not be a very good approximation if dX_1 and dX_2 are large. On the other hand mathematicians have shown that a much better approximation is given by du' where

$$du' = \frac{\partial u}{\partial X_1} dX_1 + \frac{\partial u}{\partial X_2} dX_2 + \frac{1}{2}\left(\frac{\partial^2 u}{\partial X_1 \partial X_1} dX_1^2 + 2\frac{\partial^2 u}{\partial X_1 \partial X_2} dX_1 dX_2 \right.$$
$$\left. + \frac{\partial^2 u}{\partial X_2 \partial X_2} dX_2^2 \right)$$

and where

$$\frac{\partial^2 u}{\partial X_i \partial X_j}$$

is the second derivative of the function u, again evaluated at the initial point. Better approximations still may be obtained if we can succeed in evaluating the third and fourth derivatives in the pre-policy position. There is no need to know the form of any function except in so far as a knowledge of the value of its derivatives at a point implies something about its form.

If it had been considered worth while, it would have been possible, though exceedingly tedious, to work every formula of this book so that it included not only elasticities but rates of change of elasticities and rates of change of rates of change and so on up to the required degree of accuracy. In this way it would be feasible to ensure that the formulae obtained applied with as great a degree of accuracy as we like for changes as large as we like.

Note that the assumption of a particular form of function is precisely equivalent to assuming a value for higher-order derivatives. Clearly, if it is considered essential to take account of special function forms other than the linear approximation used throughout this book, then the sensible thing to do would be to set about computing higher-order derivatives by statistical observation of the data. To assume a special form without prior knowledge is to replace higher derivatives by actual numbers drawn at random as if from a hat. But if higher derivatives are important, they should be left in the formulae as unknowns. If they are considered unimportant, they should be left out entirely. It is inconsistent to argue that they are so important that they must be put in but that the numbers to be put in can be chosen at random whether they are right or wrong.

With some exceptions (e.g. Chapter 14) where higher-order derivatives have been implicitly considered, the general method of this book has been to leave them out. The argument by which we justify this procedure is simply that they are not thought to be important enough in general to overturn our fundamental qualitative conclusions even when the policy change is big. In quantitative work of course it will often be necessary to put them in. The method of doing this will be clear to the reader by the time he has progressed a little, if it is not already clear.

3 MONOPOLY AND INCREASING RETURNS TO SCALE

Another feature of this book, which may in some quarters be considered a shortcoming, is the failure, except in passing, to mention the problem of monopoly. Wherever the pattern of production is supposed to vary it is usually assumed that no manufacturer will employ any technique other than one which gives lowest average cost at prevailing prices. Selling price is always cost plus the standard market rate of profit (except in the dynamic version of the model – see Chapter 19).

There are two reasons why we have chosen to make very little of

the monopoly problem. The first is a profound scepticism on the part
of the writer regarding the applicability of monopoly theory as it now
stands to the facts of the real world. The only businessmen who have
been willing to confess to the author that they knew of a technique for
producing their product more cheaply, were at the same time moving
heaven and earth to reorganise their business so that they could
employ precisely that technique. And this applies equally to those
where producing more cheaply meant exploiting economies of scale.
At the same time most businessmen, whilst conceding that price may
exceed cost plus normal profits for a while, are usually able to show
good reason why a competitor producing some kind of substitute will
erode their excess profits before long. And this seems to be true however unique and protected the product may seem to be.

But the second reason for leaving out monopoly is even more com-
pelling. It is simply that to include it does not seem to make very much
difference to the conclusions reached, provided, that is, that it is introduced in the only form known to the writer to be logically consistent.
The theory of monopoly in fact suggests that, whenever a producer
becomes conscious of the effect of his choice of output upon the price
at which he can sell that output, then the quantity manufactured will
be restricted so that market price will ordinarily exceed cost, giving
rise to 'monopoly' profit. In these circumstances it may also be the
case that economies of scale are not fully exploited. The cheapest
known technique of production may not be employed.

If this theory corresponded strictly to the facts, the supply function
(see Chapter 15 below) would be heavily dependent upon the extent
to which each businessman *thinks* that the level of his own sales
affects market price. We emphasise the word 'thinks', since it is not
difficult to show that the actual extent to which the level of sales
affects prices is quite undefined until the reactions of other producers
are taken into account. And these reactions must themselves be
determined by the same kind of theory.

But suppose we accept without further question that somehow or
other each businessman does come to believe in the existence of a
unique demand schedule for his product. It is not then hard to show
that a supply function will exist which may be written

$$S_i = S_i[(\mu_1 q_1), (\mu_2 q_2), \ldots, (\mu_n q_n)]$$

where qs are market prices and μs are factors determined by each
producer's subjective idea of the slope of his demand schedule.
Furthermore if we replace the product $\mu_i q_i$ with a new variable q_i^*

there is no reason to suppose that the monopoly supply function

$$S_i = S_i(q_1^*, q_2^*, \ldots, q_n^*)$$

will lack any of the usual properties.

Of course it is true that in the presence of monopoly there could exist increasing returns to scale in the neighbourhood of equilibrium in which case the sign conditions on supply elasticities no longer hold. The argument for a convex production possibility set (see Chapter 15) cannot be sustained. But in the view of the present writer this is not likely to be an important empirical possibility, and even if it were, it would only add to the uncertainties which are already sufficiently emphasised. The presence of monopoly, if it exists in the sense imagined, will quickly make itself felt if and when proper empirical inquiries are made within the framework of a model something like that of Chapter 19.

Failure of sign conditions on supply elasticities does not of course invalidate any formula in which they appear. It simply makes less certain some of the qualitative conclusions we derive from the formula itself. It is perhaps worth mentioning also that the presence of monopoly, with or without increasing returns to scale, will affect welfare problems. This is because the qs which appear in the crucial result (15.4.14) then become q^*, in which case small changes in the pattern of supply will affect welfare. But it is not difficult to adjust the various results to take account of this. No fundamental change in the method is involved.

4 ON FEW COUNTRIES AND MANY ELASTICITIES

A very distinguished teacher of the present writer, Professor H. D. Dickinson, once remarked that all his life he had nursed a prejudice in favour of simple economics. Unfortunately, each time he tried to simplify his arguments, almost without noticing, they somehow got complicated all over again. Some thirty years earlier Marshall had expressed the same idea rather differently. 'In this world', he wrote, '. . . every plain and simple doctrine as to the relations between cost of production, demand and value is necessarily false: and the greater the appearance of lucidity which is given to it by skilful exposition the more mischievous it is' [6, p. 368].

If the reader learns nothing else from this book let him at least reflect deeply upon these two remarks; for it is not easy to attain, without guidance and against our own inclinations, a complete appreciation of all that is implied in the passages quoted.

Whatever we may wish to believe to the contrary it is important to come to terms with the fact that economic relationships are immensely complex and inexpressibly tedious to untangle, even if they can be untangled at all. The need to accept and not be deterred by this unpalatable truth is all the more necessary since the reader will encounter a great deal of propaganda in favour of an opposite view, that is, there exists a widespread belief that long arguments and complicated answers in economics can and ought to be simplified. And the quest for simplification is often carried to curious and extraordinary lengths.

Consider for example the following. Suppose that we wished to examine the effect of currency depreciation upon the balance of trade of two countries each producing importables, exportables, and a non-traded commodity. Evidently in such a system there are three prices to consider in each country and hence three elasticities for each demand function. The simplifier who runs true to form will immediately observe that this can easily be reduced to a two-price system by imagining that, for the non-traded commodity, the 'demand equals supply' equation is solved in each country so that the price of each non-traded commodity may be written as a function of the two traded-commodity prices. These functions may then be substituted for the non-traded commodity price wherever it occurs. If this 'reduced' system is now solved for the change in the balance of trade, only two 'elasticities' will appear in the solution. Indeed, the solution when it is obtained will *look* exactly like the solution for a system where there are no non-traded commodities in existence at all, for the simplifier will almost certainly use the same symbol to denote elasticity in either case. He may even cry triumphantly as a result of his efforts that the introduction of a non-traded commodity makes no difference whatever to the problem, for the same answer is obtained. But nothing could be further from the truth.

The two answers would not be the same. All that happens is that they look the same because the same symbol is used for two different things. One elasticity means the response of sales to a change in, say, the price of importables with aggregate expenditure and all other prices held constant. The other 'elasticity' means the response of sales to a change in the price of importables after the price of non-traded goods is adjusted so as to maintain equality between supply and demand for non-traded goods. The 'simplified' answer is useless, for nothing is known *a priori* which will give us the slightest clue as to the sign or magnitude of the reduced-form 'elasticity'. The only way to get this information is to solve the original unreduced problem in all its complexity to obtain an expression for the reduced 'elasticity' in terms of parameters whose signs we do know. This is precisely the reverse of simplification. Self-delusion might be a better description.

The full absurdity of the 'simplified' approach becomes even more obvious if we extend the procedure to its logical conclusion. Why do we not imagine that we have used the remaining demand/supply equations to eliminate all the other variables of the system so that we have left no more than a single simple relationship between the balance of trade and the rate of exchange? This must be possible or the model could not be solved at all. Following this grand simplification, all that we then need is to introduce the concept of the elasticity of the balance of trade with respect to the exchange rate. A new and obviously ridiculous 'theorem' will accordingly tell us that currency depreciation will improve the balance of trade if and only if the elasticity of the balance of trade with respect to the exchange rate is negative in sign. We may even, if we wish, defend our newly invented elasticity. Its meaning, it may be claimed, is after all quite clear. It is the response of the balance of trade to currency depreciation after all prices have changed so as to equate supply and demand and after aggregate expenditure has changed so as to maintain full employment or to bring about whatever other adjustment the model (which we may not even have specified) is supposed to call for.

The words in parenthesis are not without importance, for it is actually not uncommon for certain writers to introduce 'elasticities' which suppose prior adjustments without explicitly specifying the prior adjustments assumed in the definition of the elasticity introduced. In such a case not only do we know nothing about the sign or magnitude of the crucial parameter but we are also left to guess what it is supposed to mean from the context in which it appears.

It could be perhaps that the ambiguity in, and superfluity of, meanings which are so frequently attributed to the concept of elasticity is what causes the irritation reflected by one writer's willingness to dismiss attempts at exact mathematical analysis as 'mental gymnasia with few countries and many elasticities'. If so, then it can be claimed that throughout the present book this source of irritation has been removed. Only two kinds of elasticity appear, supply and demand, and the meaning of these is quite clear, conventional and properly explained. Indeed it is possibly true that this is the only book on the theory of international trade which nowhere mentions (except to beg the student not to mention) import and export price elasticities (see section 11.8).

Of course, elasticities of supply and demand appear many times in ever more complicated formulae depending on the degree of dis-aggregation of the model. But this is just *because* we take care to avoid the pseudo-simplification criticised above and because, in consequence, we do restrict ourselves to those parameters which are computable in principle and about whose signs and magnitudes we have some *a priori* information. It may be worth pointing out also that, if the reader objects to 'few countries', then, by disaggregating the model appropriately, he may easily add as many more as he feels able or energetic enough to cope with, at the cost, of course, of still more frequent appearances of the basic elasticities. Indeed, in the work below the author has already developed the analysis in this direction as far as seems profitable without the aid of a computer.

All of this is intended to encourage the reader who may already have found himself contemplating with some dismay, say, the results quoted in exercises 8, 9 and 10 to Chapter 4. These formulae are complicated, first because economic theory is complicated and second because the meaning of each symbol is relatively simple. To simplify formulae by complicating the meaning of symbols makes economic theory more difficult rather than less. We remind the student also of the assurance already given that we never require him to work algebra for the sake of the algebra. From each of the formulae quoted, some important economic lesson is to be learned.

5 NOTATION

Throughout this book care has been taken to repeat definitions of symbols wherever there appears to be a danger that the reader may have forgotten. It is hoped that enough users of the book will be grateful for this to compensate for the irritation which may be felt by those for whom the repetition seems unnecessarily tedious. It follows that a formal list of symbol meanings in this section is hardly needed. On the other hand it may be helpful to point to two features of the notation which could lead to difficulty.

First, we draw attention to the fact that throughout Book I the symbol p is used for home *commodity* prices and q is used for world commodity prices. In Book II, where factor prices are introduced, p is reserved for factor prices and q for commodity prices. World prices are identified by a prime. Second, in Book I it is convenient for reasons given in the text, to work in terms of elasticities. Hence all formulae represent pure numbers free of units. From time to time elasticities are split into income and substitution parts, the symbol σ being used for the substitution part. Note especially that the σ here is an elasticity and is accordingly unit-free. Hence some of the relationships set out in exercise 5 to Chapter 4 may look a little odd to experienced readers.

In Book II on the other hand most of the formulae are designed as counter-examples rather than general results from which conclusions can be drawn. To turn these formulae into elasticities is both tedious and unnecessary. In Book II therefore elasticities (log derivatives) tend to be replaced by ordinary response rates (partial derivatives) which are *not* unit-free. Despite this, however, it was judged potentially less confusing to use in Book II the same symbol σ for the substitution part of the demand response even though it is no longer unit-free. The reader is properly warned when the symbol is first introduced in its revised meaning.

For easy reference, chapters are divided into numbered sections and equations are numbered within each section. Thus the reference (4.4.15) means Chapter 4, section 4, equation 15. Diagrams too are numbered by chapter.

The book proper now begins.

Book I

'Every man is a piece of the continent'
John Donne, *Devotions* XVII

1 The Simplest Possible Model

1.1 THE COST OF IGNORANCE

THE great paradox of economic science is that many of the intensely practical problems with which it is concerned would never arise but for the fact that the mechanism of the system is not sufficiently well understood by the individual persons who are involved in it. Nowhere is this more true than in the field of international trade. International economic policy is, at any moment of time, very closely prescribed by what is politically possible. And what is politically possible is in turn limited by the extent to which the issues concerned can be understood by the electorate. The impact upon the individual of economic regulation is apparently so obvious and so direct that the public is, in this case, unwilling to leave everything to the experts, despite the complexity of the subject.

The fundamental truth which is so often misunderstood is simply that no country is or ever can be 'an island entire of itself'. It is important to realise that any economic programme, designed by a single country to strengthen its own international position, will almost always create a problem for the rest of the world in proportion to the success of that programme from the point of view of the country applying it. The difficulties of one country can be finally settled only if the difficulties of every other are settled simultaneously. Failure to act in accordance with this prescription lies at the root of most of our troubles, although such failure is readily excusable. It is far from obvious that unemployment, inflation and economic crises of all kinds are as readily exportable as exports themselves, or that gains from tariffs imply losses for somebody else. To understand fully and deeply the simple point of this paragraph of necessity implies the simultaneous understanding of a great deal of economic theory.

Short-sightedness in economic affairs is not really a surprising phenomenon. As long as the individual person has the money, he is accustomed simply to buy whatever he wants in the nearest shop, and to him that is the end of the matter. It requires a considerable act of imagination to see through the veil of money and to realise that what society really wants of the shopper is not his money but the service which he performs to earn it. It requires an even greater act of imagination to apply this principle when the goods bought are produced in a foreign country.

Of course it is true that no one today can fail to be aware of the existence of serious international trade problems, for various experiments in international co-operation as they occur are among the principle items of news reported. But it is difficult to trace the long chain of causation which links the action of the housewife to, shall we say, British policy in regard to the European Common Market. Nor is the situation helped by the continuous intervention of commentators who often appear to understand the issues less well than their confident use of technical terminology would suggest.

The consequence of all this is a Gilbertian situation in which mutually exclusive objectives come to be set. It is logically impossible for example, in the face of changing world conditions, both to hold stable the level of prices at home and to maintain a fixed rate at which, say, dollars can be bought for £1. Yet there exists a wide-spread conviction that change in either is 'wrong'. Again, the current irrational belief that an excess of exports over imports is always a 'good thing' has led many governments to pursue this objective despite the fact that it is obviously impossible for any nation to have an export surplus with the rest of the world unless the rest of the world has an equal and opposite import surplus with it.

Of course it can be argued that the method in this madness lies in the hope that it will always be somebody else who suffers the deficit, but this is a game that at least one country is bound to lose. It must therefore result in a situation in which at least one country will wish to change. And this illustrates the point with which we began. No country can be an island unto itself unless it ceases to trade. Evidently it is a matter of the utmost importance that the consequences of trade and trade policy are as well understood as is humanly possible and as widely as possible. Experience suggests that the best way to gain this understanding is by studying what economists call a 'model', and this is what is attempted in the following pages.

By a 'model' we mean all that is implied by this word in its ordinary sense, except that it is not always necessary actually to set up a physical construction which can be examined in operation. It is frequently, indeed usually, possible to learn a great deal simply by imagining how a model could be constructed if desired, or by imagining how an economy with special simplifications might work *if it existed*.

On the other hand it is worth putting on record that, where the working of the imagined system is exceedingly complex, a physical construction can be valuable. It is for this reason that electronic and mechanical 'machines' have occasionally been built by economists to simulate the working of some imagined system so that they can more easily study the consequences of interference with it. Indeed, in some cases models which involve the participation of human operators have been set up to add further realism. But we shall not be concerned in this book with anything more than the simplest kind of economy. Even this will turn out to be complicated enough.

Of course there are obvious objections to the study of over-simplified models. The simpler the model, the less it is like the real world in which we live and, in consequence, the less we can be confident that conclusions obtained from it have any relevance to the real world. On the other hand there is reason to believe that more mistakes have been made by confidently plunging in at the deep end than by beginning, as it were, at the beginning. Study of a simple model demonstrates how easily mistakes can be made and reveals the weakness of superficial argument. Moreover, successively more realistic constructions can be developed only when the less compli-cated system is properly understood.

At the same time it is necessary to stress – and we shall stress it repeatedly – that conclusions derived from a model with no more than two trading countries and two classes of commodities do not *necessarily* hold in the real world. To prevent misunderstanding, therefore, we shall modify such conclusions wherever it is already known that the simple model might be misleading even though a complete and convincing explanation why it should be so must be postponed until the reader is more advanced.

It would be as well to make clear also, once and for all, that despite efforts of great ingenuity no economist has yet succeeded in describing a model which even remotely approaches the true com-plexity of the real world. An element of judgement is always involved in any passage from study of a model to policy prescription. The student must satisfy himself of the value of model-building by experience and by the gradual realisation first that this, combined with observation and measurement, is the method of all science, and second that the only alternative is uninformed guesswork.

1.2 The Basic Model

Consider first of all what might happen in a world of two countries in which all commodities can be divided into two classes, namely,

'exportables' and 'importables'. Throughout this book we shall refer
to the two countries as the 'home country' or 'us' and 'the rest of the
world'. Wherever it is necessary to identify the countries by a number,
the 'home country' will be 1 and the 'rest of the world' will be 2.

The home country manufactures only 'exportables' and the rest of
the world produces only 'importables'. Naturally both 'countries'
consume some of both commodities. For the moment we shall
suppose that each government is clever enough to maintain full
employment of the whole of the resources of labour and capital
available for the manufacture of its own 'commodity', so that there
can be no change in production whatever may happen otherwise.

We shall now represent this situation diagrammatically so that the
various possibilities can be better understood. In Fig. 1.1, from the
point *O* we measure along *OM* the total amount produced by the
home country of the class of goods 'exportables'. The line *OM* in
fact represents this quantity. We remind ourselves also that country 1
produces nothing else but exportables and that we make the measurement in units of the commodity, i.e. in 'tons' or 'gallons'. There is no
question as yet of money. Indeed, we take care for the time being to
exclude money specifically, for the very good reason that the habit
of expressing every economic transaction in terms of money often
makes the underlying reality more difficult to understand.

Total production of the commodity 'importables' which takes

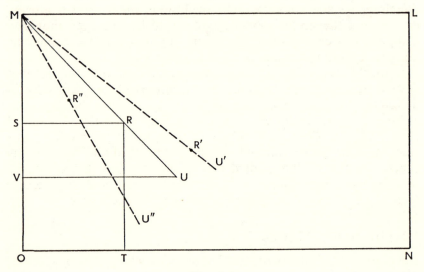

Fig. 1.1

place in country 2 – the rest of the world – is measured from *L* along *LM*, that is, *LM* represents the supposed quantity. We now have a total world production of *OM* units of exportables and *LM* units of importables to be shared between the two 'consumers', country 1 and country 2. The first question at once arises. How much will each consume and what mechanism determines the 'share-out'?

Let us for the moment concentrate our attention upon the lines *OM* and *ON*. We treat these as axes of an ordinary graph as encountered in elementary mathematics or physics. Quantities of commodities 1 and 2 are measured along *OM* and *ON* respectively. Any point such as *R* therefore, when referred to the axes, defines a certain pair of quantities of exportables and importables. For example, *R* determines *RS* of importables and *RT* of exportables. The reader will note that we shall always be consistent and measure exportables in the vertical direction and importables in the horizontal direction, and always in commodity units (tons or gallons). Clearly, *R* like any other point on the diagram could be a point representing the consumption of the home country. The home country could be consuming *RS* units of importables and *RT* units of exportables.

Now home production consists of *OM* units of exportables. To be able to enjoy the consumption pattern *R*, *SM* units of exportables must be exchanged for *SR* units of importables. This is only possible if country 2 is *willing* to make the exchange at the rate *SM* divided by *SR*. *SM/SR* will of course be a rate expressed, say, as so many gallons of exportables per ton of importables. If *SM* is a number of gallons and *SR* is a number of tons, *SM/SR* will be gallons per ton. *SM/SR* is a *real* price of importables different only from the ordinary price (pounds per ton) because it is expressed in gallons of the exportable commodity rather than in money. The steepness of the line *MU* in Fig. 1.1, therefore, measures the trade price level, which, because it is expressed in gallons rather than money, is called by economists the 'real terms of trade'.

We do not of course know as yet why the real terms of trade are what they are, or why country 2 should be willing to make an exchange at any particular rate. But let us suppose that country 1 does in fact find itself able to trade at the rate represented by *MU*. Evidently it is not bound to consume in the pattern defined by *R*. For example, it *need* not trade at all. It could consume its whole product *OM* and nothing of commodity 2; or it could push trade to the point *U* and give up *VM* gallons of exportables for *VU* tons of importables. Why does it choose *R* in particular?

The answer to this is simply that *R* represents the consumers' choice and we presume that, given prices, consumers know what they want. The real terms of trade appear to the individual shopper as a ratio of prices. £1 spent on exportables buys so many gallons. £1 spent on importables buys so many tons. In other words so many gallons of exportables are worth the same as so many tons of importables. The two quantities would exchange for one another in the market place at the same rate as the real terms of trade. If this were not so, it would be cheaper for the consumer who wants importables to buy exportables instead and to exchange them overseas for the importables he really wants. (In practice of course it would be some businessman who would carry out this operation on behalf of the consumer in order to earn a profit on the transaction.)

We can now set down more formally the relationship between money prices and the real terms of trade, since it is important that this should be thoroughly understood. The money price of exportables is written p_1, and the number of gallons which can be bought for £1 as x_1. Then the value of x_1 is p_1x_1, which is £1. Similarly, x_2 is the quantity of importables which can be purchased for £1 and p_2x_2 equals £1. Therefore

$$p_1x_1 = p_2x_2 = £1$$

and

$$\frac{p_1}{p_2} = \frac{x_2}{x_1}.$$

Evidently x_2/x_1 must be equal to *SR/SM* in Fig. 1.1, for *SR* units of importables are worth the same amount of money as the *SM* units of exportables which are used to pay for them, just as x_2 units of importables are worth x_1 units of exportables. The ratio of money prices p_1/p_2 is therefore another measure of the real terms of trade. The two are always the same.

But prices in the shops determine how people spend their incomes. The higher the price of imports, the less will be purchased. The point *R* is determined by consumers' choices at given prices, that is, given the real terms of trade. For each level of the real terms of trade there is a unique pattern of consumption which will be chosen. If, for example, imports become dearer and the terms of trade move to *MU''* (Fig. 1.1), then *R''* may be chosen. If they become cheaper and the terms of trade are *MU'*, then *R'* may be chosen. For obvious reasons a fall in import prices to *MU'* is called a 'favourable' movement in the terms of trade, whilst a rise is called an 'unfavourable' movement. A rise in import prices makes the consumer worse off.

To find out why a particular level of the terms of trade emerges, we have to consider what consumers might choose at every possible level. But before we turn to this it is necessary to draw attention to a very important point in connection with prices. p_1 and p_2 are money prices, that is, 10s a gallon or £20 per ton. When prices are expressed in this, the ordinary way, we are reminded that the consumer's pattern of spending must depend not only upon prices but also upon the amount of money income he has to spend. And on reflection it becomes clear that money income will also depend upon the level of prices. In fact income and spending are related in more ways than one.

Besides being a sum of money out of which spending takes place, income is also generated by that spending. In our very simple model an amount OM of exportables is produced and sold either at home or abroad. The businessmen who jointly produce OM receive in revenue therefore $p_1(OM)$ in money. This money is either paid in wages to employees or retained as profits. But profits and wages are the incomes out of which a new round of spending takes place. It follows therefore, since OM is constant, that incomes, $p_1(OM)$, rise when p_1 rises. Indeed, if p_1 is doubled, income is doubled. This is quite automatic.

Now common sense would suggest that if all prices are doubled, or multiplied by three or any other number, and if at the same time spending power is multiplied simultaneously, the consumers' choice will be unaffected. Goods cost more in the shops but just enough extra money is available to buy precisely what was bought before. The real situation is not changed. The ratio p_1/p_2, that is, the real terms of trade, remains exactly the same whenever all prices are increased proportionately. More generally, if the real terms of trade are, say, 1, prices being £1 and £1, they may be changed to, say, 1/2 either by doubling p_2 and keeping p_1 constant (which leaves income unchanged) or by doubling p_1 and multiplying p_2 by four (which doubles incomes). Clearly there are more ways than one of moving from R to R'', a fact which becomes important in later argument.

In the meantime we notice that if we are interested only in changes in the real situation, our simple model has only one 'real' price – the terms of trade. To put this another way, we can consider every possible real situation by supposing that the price p_1 never changes and that money incomes remain constant at $p_1(OM)$. In the simple model changes in p_2 are sufficient to attain every level of the real terms of trade, a procedure which is sometimes referred to as 'taking commodity 1 as numeraire', or 'measuring everything in terms of commodity 1'. This is the justification for identifying changes in the position of the line *MU* solely in terms of changes in import prices as we did above.

The reader is now reminded that our object is to try to discover why the real terms of trade are what they are and hence what determines the 'share-out' of world production between the two countries. To this end we examine first what country 1 would *want* to consume for *every* possible level of the real terms of trade. In Fig. 1.1 three levels only were illustrated giving rise to three patterns

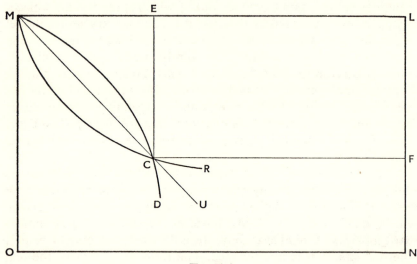

Fig. 1.2

of consumption R'', R and R'. If all possible levels had been included, the points R would mark out a continuous curve (MCR) as shown in Fig. 1.2. This curve is known to economists as an 'offer curve', and is so designated because it marks out the whole spectrum of offers which the home country might make to the rest of the world at various levels of the real terms of trade.

We now inquire whether the offer curve MCR shown in Fig. 1.2 might reasonably be supposed to take the form it does. Consider first the change from R' to R in Fig. 1.1. The price p_2 of importables has risen whilst p_1 and spending remain constant (commodity 1 is numeraire). In these circumstances country 1 must be worse off since it can now afford fewer imports. When the consumer is generally worse off, there is a tendency to buy less of everything, that is, a tendency for R' to move in the general direction of O. This tendency is called by economists the 'income effect'. But in addition exportables are now relatively cheaper than importables so that there will be a further tendency to substitute the cheaper commodity for the dearer, that is, to buy less of importables and more of exportables and so to move from R' towards M. This is the so-called 'substitution effect'. The joint result of both effects is seen, say, as a shift from R' to R as in Fig. 1.1.

If the substitution effect is small, that is, if importables and exportables are needed in relatively fixed proportions, the point R in Fig. 1.1 will be lower than is shown. If the substitution effect is large, that is, if both exportables and importables are, for example, food of some kind, being good substitutes one for the other, then R will be higher on Fig. 1.1. Finally, we note that there will usually be some import price high enough to discourage imports completely so that the offer curve will pass through M. At £1 million per ounce for importables, people will be inclined to live entirely on exportables. The curve MCR therefore is not unreasonably placed (Fig. 1.2).

The next step is to note that exactly the same considerations apply to the rest of the world. Production is LM and hence income is $q_2(LM)$ where q_2 is the price of importables expressed in terms of foreign currency (say dollars). The rest of the world will have an offer curve MCD corresponding to the home country's offer curve MCR. LM and LN are the axes of reference for the foreign country whose pattern of demand is measured with reference to them. At the point C, consumers in the rest of the world will demand CE of exportables (commodity 1) and CF of importables (commodity 2).

The reader may satisfy himself of the symmetry of the argument by turning the page on which Fig. 1.2 is presented on to its side and by looking at it in a mirror in such a way that, in the mirror, L appears in the bottom left-hand corner. It will be seen at once that all that has been said about the home country applies equally to the rest of the world.

The point of intersection C of the two offer curves MCR and MCD is of crucial importance. Only if the real terms of trade settle at MCU can world supply of commodities and world demand for commodities be equated. At any other terms of trade more of one commodity is produced than can be sold and less of another.

This can be checked at once by reference to Fig. 1.3. Suppose that MU represents the terms of trade. Then by definition of offer curves

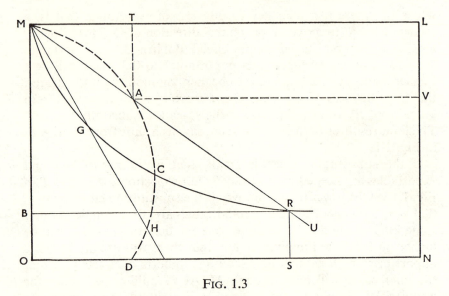

FIG. 1.3

the home country wishes to buy *RB* of importables and *RS* of exportables and the rest of the world *TL* of importables and *TA* of exportables. But *RB* + *TL* is greater than total production *ML* of importables and *TA* + *RS* is less than total production *MO* of exportables. Similar considerations apply whenever the terms of trade are different from *MC*. The reason why, in the diagram illustrating the model, we form world production into the 'box' *MONL*, is to make use of the convenient fact that only when points such as *A* and *R*, representing the patterns of demand at home and abroad, are coincident, as at *C*, is world demand just and only just satisfied by world supply. This is true each time the diagram appears in the rest of this book whatever the problem under discussion.

It is now clear that the position of the point *C*, and hence the 'equilibrium' terms of trade *MC* at which supply and demand are equated, are determined by the size of the box *OMLN* and the shapes and positions of the offer curves *MCR* and *MCD* (Fig. 1.2). And the position of the point *C* determines the share of each country in world production.

In turn the size of the box is governed by the productive resources available, and the positions of the offer curves are governed by the tastes of individual consumers. These are factors which, in the short run at any rate, are beyond the control of policy-makers. They represent the background of economic facts against which policy must be formulated.

Later we shall consider how the position of the point C might be influenced by policy to the advantage perhaps of one country or another. But for the moment we suppose that no such attempt is to be made. In these circumstances what is needed is some mechanism which will ensure that, if there is some change in the background conditions, i.e. some change in consumer preferences or techniques of production, the terms of trade will quickly and automatically reach their new equilibrium level whatever this might be.

It is not too strong an assertion to say that one of the major causes of economic disturbance is either the absence of such a mechanism or its failure in some respect. In the next chapter, therefore, we shall consider the various mechanisms as they are supposed to work and inquire in what ways they might break down and the probable consequences of breakdown. But before turning to this it is worth noting that already the study of even so simple a model permits us to dispose of at least one error of gigantic proportions constantly repeated in some form or another by successive generations of 'practical men'.

1.3 THE COMPETE OR PERISH FALLACY

In its modern form the argument goes something like this. Britain needs raw materials which must be imported since they cannot be produced at home at any cost (e.g. cotton). Unless Britain can maintain an engineering industry more efficient than that of, say the U.S.A., it will become impossible to export anything to pay for our necessary imports. It will be 'cheaper' for America to produce our 'exportables' for herself. Hence Britain must be 'technologically efficient' or die of raw-material starvation in the long run.

There are of course good arguments for aiming at technological efficiency, but this is not one of them. A technologically irefficient country can just as easily find something to trade as one which is super-efficient, for reasons simply explained in terms of our model. Clearly a box $OMLN$ can be formed however short the line OM and however long the line LM. If the two countries had identical resources of capital and labour, a relatively short line OM must represent relative technological inefficiency, for it means that country 1 is producing much less than country 2 with the same resources.

Let us suppose that this is the case. Offer curves may still be drawn and will intersect, demonstrating the possibility of mutually satisfactory trade as before. But there is a difference. We have so far assumed that country 2 produces no exportables at home. In terms of the argument above, America manufactures no engineering products. But if America is technologically efficient, why are no engineering products made? To answer this we must first inquire into the relative costs of engineering products and raw materials if they *were* both produced in America. Whenever labour and capital resources are directed into engineering, they cannot be used to extract raw materials. Something must be given up. Looking at Fig. 1.3, let us suppose that, if America produced TA units of engineering products, it would be necessary in consequence to give up producing MT units of raw materials, and proportionately for all other levels of production. Then relative costs in America are measured by the slope of the line MU. If the same resources can produce either TA or MT, the the total cost of MT equals the total cost of TA. All that this means is that America's offer curve $MACH$ (broken line) is irrelevant between A and M. If the real terms of trade were to move against America beyond the level MU, then America would of course cease to trade and produce her engineering products at home where they are now cheaper. But in fact we have argued above that the terms of trade can never in any case pass this point. They must settle at MC where the two offer curves intersect and trade will take place in the normal way.

It is pertinent of course to ask what would happen if the relative costs of producing the two commodities *in America* were measured by MH instead of MU. What would then happen to the argument? Evidently at terms of trade MC America would be unwilling to trade, since by producing at home she can consume the pattern H without trade. On the other hand it is a matter of indifference to America whether she produces in the pattern H or whether she carries on some trade provided the terms of trade are MH, the same as the internal relative costs. Britain could consume the pattern G by trading with America at the terms of trade MG whilst America produces only the balance of engineering products required to enable her to consume at the pattern H.

In other words America's offer curve is, in this second case, not the broken line $MACH$ determined entirely by demand, but the line MH (continuous line) continued broken to D. This is true quite generally of all offer curves wherever there is a possibility of producing at home when the relative price of imports rises above a certain critical level.

The intersection point of the modified offer curve with *MGC* is *G*, and as before this determines the point where the real terms of trade will settle. The rule is quite general. If America could produce at the relative cost *MA*, then her offer curve would be *MA* (continuous line) *CH* with the intersection point *C*. If she can produce at the relative cost *MH*, then her offer curve is *MHD* and *G* is the intersection point.

Evidently whatever the size of the box and whatever America's internal cost ratio, there will be some intersection with *MGC* and hence some level of trade except in the extreme case where the line *MH* is so steep that it nowhere intersects *MGC*. But this means that raw materials cost so much relative to engineering products that country 1 *prefers* to do without them. And the assumption of the practical argument is that we cannot do without raw materials however high their price, so that *MG* and *MC* must intersect somewhere. A further point to note in connection with this extreme case is that steepness of the line *MG* has nothing to do with America's *overall* technical efficiency (i.e. the length of *LM*) but only with her *relative* efficiency in producing engineering products. For *MG* to be steep, America has to be much more efficient in engineering than in raw-material production which is a very different situation from that of the original hypothesis.

Our study of the model has in fact revealed

(a) that absolute technological efficiency is not very relevant to the final trading position; rather it is relative technological efficiency that counts – that is, the steepness of the internal cost line *MA* is in a sense more important than the size of the box *MLNO*;

(b) that if no trade takes place it is because the inhabitants of the country prefer it that way, given the relative prices arising out of technological conditions;

(c) that if some raw material is technically a 'necessity', any country will get a share appropriate to its pattern of demand and bargaining power, whether generally efficient or generally inefficient; and

(d) that a country's bargaining power depends on the relative costs of production *within* countries and not on absolute technical efficiency.

1.4 THE 'SWEATED' LABOUR FALLACY

Ironically enough, the same basic mistake as that discussed in 1.3 is sometimes disguised under precisely the opposite argument. In a poor (presumably technologically inefficient) country labour is so cheap that if that country once enters into international competition it will be able to undercut everyone's price for exportables. Thus it would appear that both the technologically efficient and the technologically inefficient produce at the lower cost. 'Sweated' labour might be thought to provide an alternative advantage in trade to technological efficiency.

In fact we have already learned from our model that absolute cost has only limited meaning when making international comparisons. Indeed it has only limited meaning in the study of any economic phenomenon. The cost of anything can be measured only in terms of some other commodity or service for which it is exchanged. It is impossible therefore to make international comparisons without reference to the real terms of trade. And the real terms of trade are determined by demand conditions and relative cost conditions within the separate countries rather than by the extent to which one or other might be regarded as more technically advanced. In short it is as easy for a country with a well-paid labour force to find something to trade as it is for a country where labour is cheap.

1.5 ON THE ADEQUACY (?) OF CHAPTER 1

We have begun the present course of study by introducing a particularly simple model in which trade takes place between two countries for the elementary and obvious reason that each country wishes to consume something that it does not in fact produce for itself. On the other hand it was hinted in section 1.3 that in many cases an importing country may be quite capable of producing its own importables, perhaps even more efficiently than the exporter in a technical sense, and the reader will certainly be aware from his own observation that it is not at all unusual to find some items both imported and home-produced, e.g. agricultural products in the U.K.

In view of this, and in view of the fact that we do not fully develop the model beyond the one-commodity stage until well into Chapter 11, it may be felt that some of the explanations above are less than adequate. Indeed, the same view may be taken about later chapters, so that some word of assurance seems to be called for.

The pedagogical philosophy which underlies the construction of the present text is as follows. Although we sometimes refer loosely to the work of this or that chapter as the analysis of some naïve or over-simplified model, there is in fact in the mind of the author just one model. And this is as it should be, for there is but one world and only one model is needed to describe it. Specifically the geometry of Chapter 1 is no more than a diagrammatic representation of a special case of the equation systems of Chapters 17 and 18; and in turn the equation systems of Chapters 17 and 18 define a special case of a much more general, dynamic, computerised model which, as it happens, forms a focal point for research at the University of Southampton.† Our purpose in short is to bring the reader not to the point where he understands a great many models but to the point where he understands a great deal about one model.

On the other hand the obvious need to proceed from the simple to the more difficult does present problems. Some method of simplification must be found, and two devices have been employed in the present book. First, we aggregate, that is, we talk of many countries as if they were two, one country and the rest of the world. Second, we often begin with special cases such as that where one or both countries happen not to produce their own importables. The reader will find very little in the way of simplification which does not full into one or other of these categories.

In saying this, however, it is not intended to suggest that we have found some way of avoiding all the pitfalls referred to in the more general discussion of models set out in section 1.1. It remains true that, for some problems, aggregation obscures the issue rather than illuminates it, and the same applies to certain choices of special cases. Contrariwise, for other problems simplification of the model hardly affects conclusions at all. All the important points can be made within the framework of an aggregate version. In such cases the only real advantage to be derived from a study of the problem concerned in terms of a highly disaggregated system is the certainty thereby attained that aggregation does in fact make no difference. In this the present author has some advantage of hindsight.

In pursuit of the ideal of progressive difficulty, therefore, we have selected for discussion in early chapters precisely those topics where our chosen method of simplification does not matter, relegating those where it does matter in the main to Book II. This brings us back to the point from which we began this section.

The most obvious way to open a text on international trade is to attempt immediately to identify the underlying causes of trade, and

† A description of the complete model lies outside the scope of this book and in any case its development continues. Some hint of what is involved is given, however, in Chapter 19.

this is the usual practice. Thus we ordinarily learn early on of the 'Theory of Comparative Costs' or the 'Theory of Purchasing Power Parity'. Unfortunately these theories involve two separate and distinct points, one of which is hardly influenced by aggregation at all, whilst the other is not only influenced but might be said to be an integral part of the aggregation problem itself.

Essentially, any explanation of the phenomenon of trade must seek first to establish that the exchange of commodities is the natural consequence of differences in relative commodity prices *before* trade actually begins and at the same time that an *equilibrium level* of trade ordinarily exists at which relative prices are equalised in every region so that there is no pressure for further change. Here aggregation does not matter. But a complete explanation of the causes of trade must include also some account of why commodity prices should be *expected* to be different between regions before trade, and it turns out to be impossible to give this except in the context of a highly dis-aggregated model with many distinct commodities. The reader who follows the present work as far as Chapters 12 and 16 will find there a complete justification for these remarks. At a high level of aggregation all the problems and most of the interest disappear. We have chosen, therefore, to emphasise in Chapter 1 only point number one, leaving point number two until the reader has made more progress.

All of this still leaves a minor difficulty. The reader will no doubt be convinced by section 1.2 above that as far as the aggregate model is concerned an equilibrium position ordinarily exists and that equilibrium demands equal relative prices between regions; if relative prices are different between regions, it is impossible that both countries should wish to consume the pattern C (Fig. 1.3) as equilibrium requires. One and only one straight line connects M and C. It is a matter of common sense also that as long as relative prices are different before trade begins, then trade is a natural consequence, for if relative prices in the United Kingdom expressed in pounds are different from those in, say, the U.S.A. when U.S.A. prices are converted to pounds, then either it is cheaper for one country to buy *all* commodities abroad or it is cheaper for both countries to buy *some* commodities abroad. Only if relative prices are the same in both countries before trade could *all* prices be equal everywhere before trade. And only if all prices are the same everywhere will there be no trade. Nevertheless, the reader may fairly say that we have not yet demonstrated that equilibrium exists in the disaggregated case; we have merely suggested that no special problems arise.

The proper course to take, therefore, would be to return to all of the problems of Book I when sufficient progress has been made to permit us to prove what we have asserted. But this would be inexpressibly tedious. One of the major objects of this book is gradually to lead the student to give up diagrammatic methods and to encourage him to use much more powerful and useful algebraic techniques. Long before Chapter 18 is reached there will be no need any more to explain that equilibrium exists whenever the number of independent equations is equal to the number of unknowns. The reader will easily be able to settle for himself any doubts which may remain concerning the level of generality of any of the matters treated in Book I.

As a compromise, however, we have included among the exercises at the end of each chapter some which the student should attempt only after a first reading of the whole of both Books I *and* II. Such exercises should be regarded *as an integral part of the text*. In many cases they contain added information or are designed to give additional insights relevant to the subject matter of the chapter which could not be introduced in any more satisfactory order for reasons given above. Exercise 6 on p. 20 is the first of this kind. More will follow in later chapters.

Having shown that equilibrium in international trade exists, the next task is to inquire into the *stability* of the equilibrium, that is, we have to look for some mechanism whereby equilibrium will be attained and to show that it works smoothly and in the right direction. We turn to this problem in Chapter 2.

EXERCISES

1. (*a*) In the text the meaning of the 'real terms of trade' is explained. Study the relevant passage carefully and consider how we might define the 'real terms of trade' if our model admitted many imports and exports whose prices varied independently instead of just one 'importable' and one 'exportable' each with a single price.

   (*b*) Now turn to the statistics of imports and exports for the United Kingdom published by the Board of Trade and trace the movement in the real terms of trade during the past ten years.

2. Consider Fig. 1.2 (p. 10) and the accompanying text where 'income' and 'substitution' effects are defined. Speculate upon the probable shape of offer curves if:
    (*a*) Substitution effect is zero.
    (*b*) Importables and exportables are very good substitutes.
3. Suppose that 'importables' and 'exportables' are required by consumers in fixed proportions, that is, one is of no value without the other as in the case, say, of automobiles and petrol.
    (*a*) Will home and foreign offer curves still intersect?
    (*b*) Will offer curves still pass through M in this case?
4. Turn up the board of trade statistics showing the nature and extent of the United Kingdom's trade with India. How can it be that among the commodities exported by the U.K. to India we find items which are exported also to the United States, even though in the U.K. wages are higher than in India whilst in the United States they are higher still?
5. Carpets are woven by hand in India but by machinery in the U.K. In view, therefore, of India's 'technological inefficiency', how can we explain the importation into the U.K. and the relative cheapness of the Indian product?

To be attempted after a first reading of both Books I and II

6. Show, by setting out the relevant equations and thereafter checking the number of equations and variables to be determined, that an equilibrium exists with the prices of traded commodities (expressed in a common currency) everywhere equal when:
    (i) r countries are in a trading relationship;
    (ii) m commodities exist in the world, p of which are entirely excluded from trade;
    (iii) the rth country has a positive endowment of n_r basic factors of production, s_r of which are mobile.
Supply functions must be shown to exist, not simply postulated (see Chapter 15).

2 The Equilibrating Mechanism

2.1 SOME DOUBTS

THE equilibrating mechanism we have now to investigate is perhaps the hardest part of the theory of international trade to understand. It is hard to understand partly because it has never worked in practice in quite the same way as economists have, at various times, imagined that it might, so that in all probability no one knows, or ever will know, precisely how it did work in times past. It is hard to understand also because the method of operation subtly changes as economic institutions change. Finally, it is hard to understand because any equilibrating system must of necessity be what economists call a dynamic process. This means, briefly, that we are not only required to compare situations in which everyone is content with situations in which there is pressure to change, as we do in this chapter, but that we have also to be concerned with the exact speed and timing of the successive moves. In fact we know very little about the strength of the pressures to change in various circumstances despite their crucial importance to choice of policy. The nature of this difficulty will become clear as we develop the argument.

2.2 A FIRST LOOK AT THE PROBLEM

We begin from the simple notion that the real terms of trade in our model can be measured by the ratio of prices p_1/p_2. We remind ourselves that p is expressed as pounds per gallon or pounds per ton, i.e. it is written in terms of home currency units. In the foreign country there exists a parallel set of prices q_1 and q_2 which are this time expressed in foreign currency, say dollars. Now as only pounds are acceptable in the U.K. and only dollars are acceptable in America there must exist some price at which dollars can be bought for pounds. This price is called the 'rate of exchange'. For example, at the moment, about \$2·4 can be bought for £1. The price of the dollar is £1/2·4, that is, the rate of exchange is 1/2·4. We use the symbol e for the rate of exchange.

It is now clear that as long as the price q_2, expressed in foreign currency, retains the same commodity unit, we shall have

$$p_2 = eq_2.$$

By retaining the same commodity unit we mean that, if p_2 is pounds per *gallon*, then q_2 is dollars per *gallon* and not, say, dollars per *litre*. We assume that all foreign prices are so expressed. The operation of multiplying by e simply changes dollars to pounds. And prices abroad must be the same as prices at home in our model since commodity 2 is imported from abroad. (We suppose also, for the time being, that the actual work of importing costs only a negligible sum.)

It follows that if the real terms of trade are measured by p_1/p_2, they are equally well measured by p_1/eq_2. The advantage of writing the terms of trade in this way is that we now see at least three possible ways by which the terms of trade might be made to move against us. p_1/eq_2 will fall if

(a) p_1 falls, or
(b) e rises, or
(c) q_2 rises.

It is also true of course that any combination of these three changes will achieve the same result.

Consider a situation where the terms of trade are too much in favour of the home country, as in Fig. 2.1. Suppose in fact that the slope of MB measures the existing terms of trade. The home country will be attempting to buy the pattern of goods B (i.e. RB of importables and BS of exportables), whilst the rest of the world demands A (AT of exportables and AU of importables). Evidently more importables are in demand than the world is producing and fewer exportables are in demand than the world is producing. We have to discover whether in these circumstances some automatic mechanism will operate so as to shift the terms of trade from MB to MC where the two offer curves intersect and where, as we have seen, world supply equals world demand.

A simple and obvious argument suggests that when the world demand for importables exceeds world supply, producers will raise prices so as to earn more profits. Indeed, where shortages exist it is common practice for buyers to offer higher prices rather than go without. The price q_2 therefore rises; condition (c) above is met and the terms of trade move to MC.

But is this argument really convincing? We have already noted in

Chapter 1 that income and prices in our model are not independent. If q_2 rises, so do incomes abroad, for total income is precisely $q_2(ML)$. When money incomes rise, more will be spent on the home country's exportables, hence p_1 might rise. We have not yet shown that this price rise cannot offset the rise in q_2 and leave the terms of trade unchanged or even improved.

Of course the initial deficit in world demand for exportables

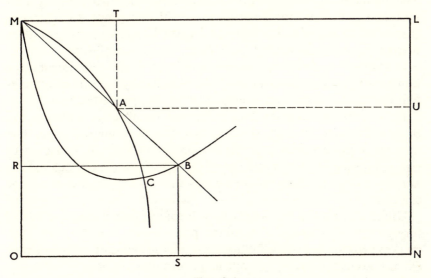

Fig. 2.1

suggests a fall in the price p_1 rather than a rise, for producers tend to cut prices when their output cannot be sold. But a cut in p_1 means a cut in money incomes, $p_1(OM)$, in country 1, which might be resisted. Manufacturers may be more willing to cut production than prices especially if trade unions refuse to accept wage cuts for their members, as is likely. Furthermore, even if wage cuts were acceptable, the fall in incomes in the home country would reduce the excess demand for importables and offset the pressure to raise the price q_2.

These doubts are reinforced if we recall that our model does not exclude the possibility that excess world demand for importables is met out of stocks accumulated by producers in past periods. Nor does it exclude the possibility that excess world production of exportables is used to build up stocks. Prices may not change at all.

If this occurred, pressure might build up on the exchange rate, e, as follows. The value of exports by country 1 is $p_1(TA)$; hence the foreign currency earned is $p_1(TA)/e$. But the demand for foreign currency is p_2RB/e. And the terms of trade p_1/p_2 is RB/MR; that is,

$$\frac{p_1}{p_2} = \frac{RB}{MR}$$

or
$$\frac{p_1(MR)}{e} = \frac{p_2(RB)}{e} .$$

The demand for foreign currency therefore is also measured by $p_1(MR)/e$. But from the diagram we see at once that MR is greater than TA so that foreign currency earned, $p_1(TA)/e$, is less than foreign currency demanded, $p_1(MR)/e$.

Similarly it is clear from the diagram that the foreign demand for home currency is less than the amount earned by the sale of importables in the home country. Indeed the two things are the same.

Now where there is an excess demand for foreign currency, the price of foreign currency will rise in terms of home currency. The number of dollars which can be bought for £1 will fall, hence e will rise. Condition (b) is met and the real terms of trade move against the home country. In these circumstances the prices p_1 and q_2 need not change.

Unfortunately the exchange rate will change only if free markets in foreign currency operate. At many periods in our history no such market existed, and indeed it does not exist today. The exchange rate cannot be changed except by official government order.

Enough has now been said to make it clear that a careful study of existing institutions must be undertaken before we can be sure that a satisfactory equilibrating mechanism is in operation. We have indirectly illustrated also the importance of the dynamic aspect of the problem earlier referred to. In considering adjustment through price changes it was shown that a great deal depends upon the effectiveness of pressures to reduce prices. Success or failure may very well rest also upon how quickly prices respond to pressures upwards or downwards. The existence of stocks can slow down the rate of response and lead to difficulties if no free market for foreign currency exists.

After a short but important digression on the nature of money, therefore, we shall mention very briefly some of the institutional arrangements which have operated in the past and speculate on how they might have worked or failed to work. This will lead to a description of the present organisation to set the background to more theoretical discussion.

2.3 A Digression On Money and 'Real' Money

At first sight the price of any object may appear to be one of its characteristics similar in principle to other features such as its weight or its length. Thus the pound sterling is simply the unit in which price is expressed, just as length is expressed in yards or weight in tons.

Up to a point this is a correct view, but only up to a point. The money problem is subtly different. It is easy in fact to tell whether an object is one yard or one and a half yards long, for by custom one single rod or bar is kept which it is agreed shall set the standard of length and all other objects are measured by direct or indirect comparison with it. To treat price in a similar way it would be necessary to identify some standard object whose price is always, by definition, £1. Unfortunately this is an exceedingly difficult thing to do, largely because of the inherent nature of a price as opposed to a size.

Any price is at bottom no more than the rate at which one object can be exchanged for another in the market. The fact that we express that rate by quoting *money* prices, that is, the rate at which each of two objects can be exchanged for a third object, money, is a matter of convenience, for the simplest way to enumerate every exchange rate between any two objects selected at random is to state the rate at which every object can be exchanged for some one of them. All other rates are then obvious.

It is convenient therefore to rid ourselves of any preconceived notions about the nature of money by imagining an economy without money. To be specific, suppose that all prices are expressed in terms of cigarettes. Beer is 10 cigarettes per pint and a television set costs 10 cartons of 1,000.† Now as long as cigarettes are used only for smoking and exchange is by barter only, it is a matter of indifference which commodity is used to express prices. By this we mean that as long as exchange is carried on by means of a physical market to which everyone brings a variety of objects, bartering them directly for whatever he wants, then the rate of exchange between beer and cigarettes depends only upon the supplies brought to

† Readers are invited to turn to a celebrated article by R. Radford entitled 'The Economics of a Prisoner of War Camp' [13] where events are described which actually occurred in practice similar to those imagined in this section.

market and the relative enjoyments which people derive from smoking or drinking beer. On the other hand we notice already an important difference between a price of beer measured in the 'imperial cigarette' and the length of a football pitch measured in 'imperial yards'. It is not that the price of beer can change over time, for after all many objects grow over time; rather it is that the price of beer can change for such a bewildering variety of reasons. It changes if our taste for beer develops or if the supply of beer falls off. Much more important, it can change if our taste for smoking develops or there is some increase or decrease in the supply of cigarettes or, for that matter, anything else whatever.

This might not be so bad were it not for another monstrous difficulty which appears as soon as we abandon in practice the pure barter economy. If it becomes the *custom* for all prices to be expressed in cigarettes and if, as a result, it becomes the *practice* to pay wages in cigarettes, and finally the practice for shopkeepers to accept cigarettes in exchange for any object they stock, then prices will be subject to many other influences. Cigarettes are now useful for quite another reason than smoking. Non-smokers will wish to carry a few packets with them to pay their bus fares, and the manufacturers of motor-cars will require stocks to pay their employees' wages. If there is no increased supply of cigarettes to meet this new stock requirement, their price must rise, which is to say the cigarette price of every other object must fall. Notice particularly that the extent of the new stock requirement, that is, the quantity of cigarette stocks needed to 'finance' transactions, is dependent upon contemporary habits in regard to the timing of payments and upon the level of activity. The level of activity is, in our model, the flow of output OM (Fig. 2.1) per period of time. By way of illustration you may recall that it is the present custom for businessmen to pay their workmen each week, but the workmen themselves make payments daily. Hence the need for a cigarette stock. If more payments per period of time are made, the need for cigarettes grows unless some change in the customary timing of payments is made.† Notice also that if the level of activity goes up, the rise in demand for cigarettes is a 'once for all' rise. The consequential rise in the price of cigarettes is temporary only. Since the new demand is for stock only and not for

† In the appendix to Chapter 15 (Book II), the timing phenomenon is treated much more fully in connection with the problem of computing the money capital required to sustain a productive process. The ordinary consumer is in much the same situation.

consumption, it could be met by a one-period increase in output, production thereafter falling to the old level. This well illustrates the dynamic nature of the problem. Timing is all-important.

Let us now suppose that there is a failure of the tobacco crop or a prolonged strike in the cigarette-producing industry. Stocks of cigarettes fall rapidly, including the stocks held by individuals to meet their bills as they fall due. The failure to understand properly the consequences of this fall in the cigarette stock and the impossibility of re-educating the entire population at short notice in their exchange customs will lead inevitably to a failure to switch to some more suitable commodity than cigarettes as the unit of account and means of exchange. All commodity prices expressed in cigarettes must fall rapidly, partly because supply for consumption has fallen and partly because of a tendency to consume the cigarette money stocks. But wage-earners may resist attempts to cut their wages in terms of cigarettes. Employers may be forced to cease some of their activity simply because it is impossible to secure enough cigarettes to 'finance' it.

It is also an uncomfortable fact (fortunately for society, but unfortunately for economists who seek to understand what is going on) that economic difficulties provoke evolutionary changes the significance of which is often not recognised until it is too late. The 'shortage' of cigarettes used to 'finance' transactions will, if history can be taken as a precedent, be met sooner or later by the creation of pieces of paper which would do part of the work of cigarettes.

If A owes B cigarettes for services rendered but has no cigarettes to pay, B may demand a firm promise in writing from A that he will pay at least within, say, three months. Now if B owes C money also, it is just possible that C would accept in settlement the promissory note which A delivered to B, provided it is suitably endorsed 'pay C'. The ready acceptance of notes of this kind in payment of debt will clearly lessen the need to hold cigarettes. Demand for cigarettes for finance is accordingly reduced so that activity is much less inhibited by shortage of cigarettes although commodity prices expressed in cigarettes remain heavily dependent on the supply and demand for cigarettes for consumption.

Again it seems almost certain that, as it is necessary for everyone to store their stock of cigarettes somewhere, specialists in cigarette storage would appear. 'Why risk your wealth in damp and airless dungeons?' reads the advertisement. 'We have air-conditioned storage space.' Sooner or later when A has to pay B he will simply advise the storage expert that *x* cigarettes which he holds are now the property of B; for both A and B store at the same 'bank'. As a next step the 'bank' manager will realise that he has in store a far greater quantity of cigarettes than anyone ever asks to withdraw. He would be less than human if he did not succumb to the temptation to lend some of them at a rate of interest to businessmen (or anyone else) in need. The businessman who borrows might very well then leave his cigarettes at the same bank, paying his bills simply by the transfer of rights exactly as if he had deposited cigarettes in the first place.

Evidently the bank is creating paper 'rights' not matched by cigarettes in stock, and such rights do the work of cigarettes in the same way as promissory notes. Little by little bank notes and other promissory notes become much the more important part of the stock of objects used to finance transactions. If the paper rights are created without restriction, it is clear that no shortage of actual cigarettes need ever inhibit activity, as earlier suggested, provided no general attempt is made to demand cigarettes to smoke in exchange for rights over cigarettes. A 'run' on cigarettes if it occurred would reveal the fact that titles to cigarettes far exceeded the number of cigarettes in existence, and the paper titles would lose value. Rights to one hundred cigarettes might then, paradoxically, exchange for no more than, say, two cigarettes, and all commodity prices must come to be expressed separately in terms both of cigarettes and cigarette rights.

On the other hand, as long as confidence in paper titles is maintained, these continue to exchange freely for their face value in cigarettes. This exemplifies an important conclusion. If no paper titles exist, cigarettes, when used as currency, can take on a value in exchange very different from that which they would have if used solely for consumption. At any moment of time it would be impossible to determine what part of the exchange value of cigarettes was due to their usefulness to smokers and what part due to their usefulness as currency.

Finally, we imagine that, in a country with a cigarette currency and no paper titles to wealth, the discovery of the link between smoking and lung cancer causes smoking in the community to be reduced to negligible proportions. In these circumstances there is a sense in which usefulness as currency could be said to be the only important determinant of the value of cigarettes. What can we now mean by the 'value of cigarettes'? In fact they have a negative value in any ordinary sense of the word, for all they can do, apart from representing titles to wealth, is to induce the occurrence of an unpleasant disease. What has happened almost imperceptibly is that the currency has ceased to be composed of objects of intrinsic value and has turned into a mere unit of account. The imperial cigarette has become little more than the measure by which we express the relative values of other commodities which do have intrinsic values. Notice that the value of work done (wages) or other services rendered is expressed also in the same units.

Consider alternatively the situation which would exist if cigarettes were almost entirely replaced by paper titles to wealth measured in cigarettes as explained above. Just because cigarettes proper have no intrinsic value, it no longer matters in the slightest whether we double or treble or halve the cigarette value of every commodity provided we do the same with all paper titles to wealth. The *relative* price of every commodity remains the same, including the *relative* price of labour and other services. But note that this is *not* true when the only recognised titles to wealth have an intrinsic value, as was the case with the pure cigarette barter economy, for the cigarette price of one cigarette is always *one*, so that doubling the price of some commodity alters the price ratio between it and cigarettes. And when the items exchanged *both* have intrinsic value, their price ratio cannot be arbitrary.

The loss of intrinsic value of the currency, added to the fact that titles to wealth can easily be created as indicated above, provided confidence in them can be sustained, means that the *general* price level is quite arbitrary. It can be anything we like. This would not matter too much were it not for the fact that economies grow and change. Intrinsic relative values of commodities and services do not remain constant, so that prices expressed in currency cannot remain constant. We have also the uncomfortable fact that a shortage of titles to wealth can inhibit business activity so that there is a continual tendency to create titles to wealth whenever a shortage seems to be acting in restraint of trade. The net effect is likely to be a rise in the general level of prices, expressed in currency, as well as changes in relative prices.

This again would not matter too much except for the fact that a general rise in prices operates with obvious inequity. Most contracts are expressed in terms of the unit of account, having regard to commodity prices existing at the date of the contract. But contracts take time to implement, and if commodity prices are continually changing, the contract may look very different when it comes to be settled. If, for example, A lends B 1,000 cigarettes when the price of labour is 1 cigarette per hour, A is lending 1,000 labour-hours. But if, when the time to repay comes, the price of labour is 2 cigarettes per hour, the repayment by B of 1,000 cigarettes is a repayment of 500 labour-hours only.

For these reasons those who seek to control the working of the economy have been caught between the Scylla of inhibited trade caused by currency shortage (high interest rates and unwillingness to create titles to wealth) and the Charybdis of ever rising prices (inflation) and consequent inequity. This problem is very much with us today, so much so indeed that government policy in the U.K. has been christened 'stop-go' in description of its attempts to avoid first one danger and then the other.

2.4 CONCLUSIONS

The following general conclusions emerge from the brief survey of section 2.3.

(i) A shortage of currency relative to the level of activity can bring about a general reduction in activity (unemployment of resources) with a possible pressure to reduce prices.

(ii) In cases where the currency has an intrinsic value of its own, a shortage of currency necessarily implies lower commodity prices, since less is available to meet non-monetary demand. Some reduction in activity is likely also, although this will, provided there is a desire to trade, tend to be offset by the invention of 'alternative' money leading eventually to a currency without intrinsic value.

(iii) When the main body of the currency has no intrinsic value, some control must be imposed on the quantity available to prevent inflation. This control may at times be in conflict with the need to provide sufficient currency and credit to sustain activity at the highest possible level.

(iv) When the currency has intrinsic value in all countries, the 'exchange rate' between currencies is fixed. Currencies must exchange at their relative intrinsic values.

(v) When the currencies of all countries have no intrinsic value, the general level of prices is arbitrary in each country. This implies that the exchange rate for currencies is arbitrary and may be set at any level as desired by governments. That is, if cigarettes are used for smoking *and* currency, then American and English cigarettes exchange at the rate at which they are valued for smoking. If on the other hand they are used only as currency, the exchange rate will tend to be set according to the relative general level of prices (in cigarettes) between countries.

(vi) A deliberate policy designed to reduce or increase the currency or quasi-currency may lead to a reduction or increase in activity or a reduction or increase in the general level of prices or to the invention of quasi-money according to rules which depend very heavily on the nature of existing institutions and even upon the expectation of businessmen and others regarding the future demand for commodities. Much depends also on the timing of events.

2.5 Some Historical Notes

We now have a convenient starting point for a discussion of actual world trading institutions.

In fact at an early stage in history the precious metals, gold and silver, came to be used as a price standard. The practice of minting coins developed simply as a matter of convenience to save weighing gold and silver against every transaction. Before the advent of coins, prices would be expressed in ounces of gold or some other unit of weight. As coins came into use, however, it became much more convenient to express prices in terms of the name given to the coin, e.g. the sovereign or the pound sterling. The coin name in fact defines a certain weight of gold or silver.

Suppose that our imaginary economy has reached this point of development but no further. How then would the international trade mechanism operate? Consider again Fig. 2.1, which illustrates a situation where the terms of trade are too much in favour of the home country. World demand for exportables is less than world supply. World demand for importables is in excess of world supply.

The rate of exchange e is fixed in a gold economy and can never be changed by any administrative procedure. Gold has intrinsic value, and both the home currency unit, say the pound sterling, and the foreign currency unit, the dollar, by definition represent a certain weight of gold. The exchange rate e must be simply the ratio of the two weights, for the exchange of currency in this context is no more than the exchange of one piece of gold for another. It follows that the real terms of trade cannot change unless either q_2 rises or p_1 falls or both.

At least four things may occur, or indeed any combination of the four. Thus:

(i) Excess demand for importables may induce businessmen abroad to mark up their prices in terms of gold in search of extra profits. At the same time surplus production at home might induce home suppliers to cut the gold price of exportables, taking a lower margin of profit. If this adjustment comes rapidly there will be no movement of gold abroad. The change in the terms of trade immediately equates world supply and demand.

(ii) Businessmen may be unwilling to change prices or unable to change them in the face of opposition to wage cuts. Excess demand for importables may be met out of stocks. Similarly excess production of exportables may be put into stock. In this case the demand for foreign coinage would exceed the supply coming in, as explained above (p. 24). Where the coinage consists of actual gold pieces, however, this does not matter, since gold pounds are as readily acceptable abroad as gold dollars. All that is necessary is to melt the gold sovereigns down and remint them as dollars. The exchange rate will not be affected. Indeed in the past it has often been the case that the reminting process has been considered not worth the trouble. 'Louis d'or' and 'pieces of eight' have circulated freely and simultaneously in England, with commodity prices separately expressed in terms of each.

The effect of the loss of gold currency abroad upon the country in deficit would be much the same as the smoking of cigarettes in the imaginary cigarette economy. Either commodity prices expressed in gold must fall, or the shortage of gold will create production difficulties. Suppose that prices fall in case (ii). It will be noted at the same time that the inflow of money into the foreign country could have the opposite effect and raise commodity prices. q_2 rises and p_1 falls, the real terms of trade are adjusted and the outflow of gold ceases.

The difference between case (i) and case (ii) is simply that in case (i) no outflow of gold is necessary whilst in case (ii) a significant gold loss actually occurs. In case (ii) the loss of gold is exactly balanced by an increase in commodity stocks and vice versa abroad.

It should be noticed that there is no necessary reason to expect the final (equilibrium) value of the absolute prices q_2 and p_1 to be the same in cases (i) and (ii) even though the exchange rate e remains

constant and the real terms of trade must always settle at *MC* in
Fig. 2.1 to equate world supply and world demand. This is because
already in the economy described the value of gold is only partly
'intrinsic'. There is no unique rate at which gold must exchange for
other commodities.

To make this point quite clear, suppose that initially $q_2 = \$10$ per
gallon and $p_1 = £10$ per ton. The real terms of trade must be

$$\frac{£10}{e\$10} = 2·4$$

given that $\$2·4$ can be bought for £1. Let the equilibrium level
MC(Fig. 2.1) be $2·4/1·5$. This may be attained either by raising the
dollar price q_2 to $12 and depressing p_1 to £8 per ton, so that the real
terms of trade are

$$\frac{£8}{e\$12} = \frac{2·4}{1·5}$$

with the exchange rate still at $\$2·4 = £1$; or by raising q_2 only to
$10·5, at the same time cutting p_1 to £7. As before, the real terms of
trade are

$$\frac{£7}{e\$10·5} = \frac{2·4}{1·5}$$

for $e = 1/2·4$. In both cases world supply equals world demand in the
equilibrium position.

It could be the case that if there were a gold loss, prices would fall
more at home than when adjustment takes place through a cut in
profit margins. If 'abroad' is the rest of the world, the effect on foreign
prices might be smaller since a large proportion of the home currency
is only a small proportion of all the currency of the rest of the world.

In fact economists have never had any really satisfactory theory
capable of predicting precisely what the final values of q_2 and p_1
would be or whether there would or would not be a gold loss in the
circumstances. A great deal may depend on chance circumstances of
the moment, even in the simple economy in which the only recognised money is gold. Nor have we any reliable statistics relevant to
times past which might enable us to find out what actually happened
in fact.

Possibilities (iii) and (iv) are:

(iii) The excess supply of exportables may cause businessmen to
cut their output and manufacture less. This might occur at the first

sign of a build-up of stocks without any price change – a possibility which was mentioned above (p. 23).

(iv) A gold loss may develop as in case (ii) which creates a shortage of money for new enterprises just as we imagined in the cigarette economy. Alternatively, the price of borrowing gold (i.e. the rate of interest) might rise owing to the overall shortage. Since interest is part of the cost of production, this again can discourage production.

Accordingly we have to trace the consequences of a cut in production of exportables which might take place as in cases (iii) and (iv), with or without an actual gold outflow. Once again the now familiar diagram will help. Fig. 2.2 repeats Fig. 2.1 except that the offer curves have been omitted for the sake of clarity. With full employment of all resources and real terms of trade *MB*, country 1 will try to consume the pattern *B* and country 2 will try to consume the pattern *A*. This is the initial position with excess demand for importables and a deficit in demand for exportables. Suppose now that at the first sign of a build-up of stocks of exportables home producers cut production.

In Chapter 1 we drew attention to the fact that profits and wages in country 1 come out of sales of exportables to consumers. If production, and consequently revenue, is reduced, so must spending be reduced, for businessmen and wage-earners cannot spend more than they receive in profits and wages. When spending is cut without any

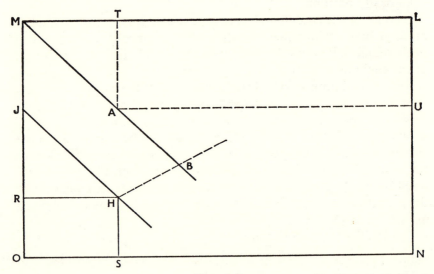

FIG. 2.2

change in prices, sales of both exportables and importables will fall. In particular, sales of exportables will fall, still further increasing the difference between maximum production, OM, and world demand. Production, and hence money spending, will again fall.

Suppose that the line BH in Fig. 2.2 marks out the locus of country 1's reducing pattern of expenditure as total spending falls. BH must point in the general direction of the corner O, indicating that demand for both importables and exportables is falling (prices constant). Eventually some demand pattern H which lies directly below A must be reached. At this point production of exportables is OJ instead of OM and since, by assumption, prices have not changed, JH is parallel to MB, the terms of trade line, and $AH = MJ$.

In this situation it is easy to see that world demand and world supply are equal. Home demand for exportables is HS and foreign demand is AT, and since $AH = MJ$,

$$TA + HS = OJ = \text{world production of exportables.}$$

Similarly home demand for importables is RH and foreign demand is TL, which, since H is directly below A, equals total world production ML.

This is a situation in which all prices remain unchanged. Changes in commodity stocks have been negligible and very little gold, if any, has moved. Nevertheless world supply and world demand have been equated *by a fall in the level of employment at home*. There is no automatic mechanism operating to restore the level of employment. If we drew a new 'box' as in Fig. 2.2 with sides OJ and ON instead of OM and ON, we should find that offer curves, which now begin at J, will intersect at H and we have an equilibrium position as in Fig. 1.2.

If a significant gold loss and build-up of stocks is the cause of the production cut as in case (iv), the same situation may result. Once again, however, the absolute prices q_2 and p_1 are likely to be different from case (iii) in equilibrium, even though their ratio q_2/p_1 must be the same.

2.6 A GOLD-BASED PAPER MONEY ECONOMY

The fable of the cigarette economy outlined above already suggests the most likely first step away from the simple system with gold coins as the sole means of exchange. As a matter of convenience, if not because of an actual gold shortage, bills of exchange came into use. An English exporter of wool to Europe in the fourteenth century would readily accept in payment a promise to pay at a given date a certain sum in foreign currency rather than carry home gold specie. This could easily be sold at home to an importer who needed foreign money to purchase goods abroad. Or it might be exchanged for a similar promise to pay sterling given by an English importer to a foreign seller.

These bills of exchange did not necessarily sell at their face value. By this we mean that a bill for £100 might be given up for a foreign promise to pay sometimes less and sometimes more than £100 worth of gold. This was partly because some waiting was involved, but also because at any moment of time there might be more sellers of sterling bills than buyers, or vice versa. The price of sterling bills in terms of foreign bills, and hence the rate of exchange, e, fluctuated within limits. Now we have already shown that, in general, changes in e operate as a stabilising mechanism, so that the introduction of bills of exchange might very well have lessened the danger of employment fluctuations.

On the other hand e could not fluctuate very widely as long as promises to pay gold had to be redeemed on demand at the due date. For if the price in foreign currency of a £100 bill fell very low, it would clearly pay the holder to collect in gold rather than sell. Indeed, the difference between the face value of a bill and its price expressed in gold could not be greater than the cost of shipping gold. The range of possible variation of e continued to be narrow. The limits of variation came to be known as 'gold points'.

Bills of exchange have, with various modifications, continued to be used in the settlement of international payments up to modern times. It is beyond the scope of this book to detail the exact procedures involved in their use throughout history, since the basic principle remains the same, but it is perhaps worth mentioning that as banking grew up it became the common practice to sell most bills at once to the banks. This is known as discounting the bill. The market for bills in consequence came to be concentrated in the banks. In the main, banks now arrange foreign payments of all kinds.

Parallel with the development of bills of exchange came various other types of coinage. The introduction of silver coins imposes an interesting strain on the system. Suppose at the time of first minting that $\frac{1}{8}$ oz of gold happens to exchange for 1 oz of silver. It is natural in these circumstances to call a silver coin of equal weight to £1 in gold by a name which means £$\frac{1}{8}$. If this occurs, prices expressed in pounds might be paid either in silver or gold without specification.

For example, if the silver crown by convention comes to be treated as one-quarter of a gold sovereign, four crowns and one sovereign become interchangeable. In this case, if there is any change in the rate at which gold bullion exchanges for silver bullion because of supply differences or changes in fashion in the use of gold and silver as ornaments, 'arbitrage' becomes possible. Arbitrage is a name given to operations of the following kind. A dealer notices that silver and gold bullion no longer exchange at the rate $1 : \frac{1}{8}$, even though eight silver half-crowns continue to exchange for one sovereign. It now pays to buy gold with silver coins and to have the gold minted into sovereigns. It follows that so long as arbitrage is possible, the bullion exchange rate can never depart far from or for long periods from the conventional relation between sovereigns and crowns. Curiously, it becomes impossible to tell whether bullion prices are sustained by the convention that the crown is $£\frac{1}{4}$ or whether the crown is sustained at $£\frac{1}{4}$ by gold and silver bullion prices.

On the other hand bullion prices do seem at various times to have differed slightly from those expected from the declared silver and gold content of the minted coins. This was partly due to the difficulty and inconvenience of trading in unminted precious metals and at other times due to restrictions in the right to mint coinage. If bullion cannot be minted on demand, then currency and bullion become, economically speaking, different objects commanding different prices even though both are in fact pieces of gold of equal weight and fineness. In these circumstances profits can be made on minting operations, a fact which led to still further government control. If it is possible to buy for nine sovereigns enough gold to mint ten sovereigns, the right to mint is a valuable prerogative.

Gradually names like pounds, shillings and pence ceased to be solely the names of coins. They took on the nature of abstract units of account in terms of which prices were expressed. The reader will best understand the nature of this subtle change by ridding his mind of the notion that one shilling must be one-twentieth of one pound. If the pound is the name of a gold sovereign and the shilling is the name of a piece of silver of given weight and fineness, then all prices must be expressed *both* in sovereigns *and* in shillings. A bale of wool costs either one sovereign or twenty shillings or twenty-one shillings. The rates at which sovereigns and shillings exchange are determined by the gold and silver bullion prices. But as soon as pounds, shillings and pence become units of account, the rate twenty shillings to the pound becomes fixed. Prices are expressed as £1 2s 6d per bale of wool instead of $1\frac{1}{8}$ gold sovereigns *or* $22\frac{1}{2}$ silver shillings. It is this development, combined with restrictions on the right to mint, which leads to the possibility of variations between the purchasing power of a coin and the purchasing power of the same weight of silver bullion.

The *exchange value* of the coin ceases to be determined by its silver content. It is sustained only by the willingness of the community to give a declared amount of bullion for it or more often by the central government's willingness to give bullion for it on demand. The coins now exchange for commodities at a rate different from their intrinsic value.

The successful introduction of coinage of low intrinsic value but high exchange value and the establishment of regular units of account encourages confidence. A much more general willingness arises to make use of bills of exchange or promissory notes as money. As banking developed for reasons closely parallel to those given in the cigarette fable, it became the practice for banks to issue notes even on those occasions when businessmen would ordinarily have required gold coins, that is, bank notes began to replace coinage. Even today the ordinary £1 note bears the legend 'I promise to pay ... the sum of one pound', although the time is long since gone when it could be exchanged for gold. Three kinds of money came commonly into use: coin, notes and instruments of transfer of rights to money deposited at banks. And as explained in the course of the cigarette fable, rights to money stored at the bank, because of bank lending, soon totalled a sum far in excess of the actual gold held at the bank. In time depositors no longer owned money stored at a bank. They simply owned a bank account which is the right to draw a cheque. Cheques now do the work of coins.

It is of course not the purpose of this book to describe the fascinating development of the banking and monetary system. This is a separate study on its own. The essential point to grasp for present purposes is that with the development of titles to wealth far in excess of actual gold in existence, the level of commodity prices expressed in pounds sterling came to depend more upon the supply of substitute money than upon the supply of gold. Moreover, it is not at all an easy thing to judge whether at any point in history the value of paper money was determined because it could be exchanged for gold or whether the value of gold was determined because of the willingness of governments and others to buy it for paper money at a fixed rate, and because that paper money gave valuable rights to other commodities. Such a situation is rather like the case in the cigarette fable where fear of lung cancer has destroyed the worth of cigarettes as a commodity in its own right. The only value in the currency lies in the fact that it *is* money and that it is everywhere accepted as such. We have now to reappraise the terms of trade-equilibrating mechanism as it might work in this new environment.

One further institutional feature must be explained, however, before we can begin. Originally the essence of any kind of paper 'money', whether bank notes, promissory notes or bank credit instruments of any kind, lay in the fact that it carried with it the ultimate right to a certain fixed weight of gold. On the other hand, as we have already seen, nothing like enough gold ever existed to meet the total liability represented by all paper in circulation at any one time. The system worked because in general most holders of paper money did not in fact demand the gold to which they were entitled.

The apparently precarious nature of this situation, coupled with a succession of failures of confidence in particular kinds of bank notes during the nineteenth century, led to the development of an especially vicious economic dogma, which, like most popular economic dogmas, consisted of little more than a half-truth. It came to be believed with an almost religious fervour that the quantity of paper money should not exceed a given fixed ratio to the quantity of gold held to 'back' the paper.

To give legislative effect to this rule, the right to issue notes was little by little confined to a single authority, namely the Bank of England,* and the national stock of gold came to be held by the bank. At the same time further rules were introduced to control the rights of the commercial banks and other institutions to grant credit in excess of their actual holdings of Bank of England notes or credits at the Bank of England. With such a tight hold upon the quantity of money, it is clear from our discussion so far that difficulties are likely to arise. If the population and the production of commodities increases at a faster rate than the gold supply, then sooner or later activity is checked. If at the same time there is resistance to price reductions, involuntary unemployment will appear. The only alternative is to invent some more ingenious form of money substitute which escapes the net of control. In practice a little of both occurred, and it is within this framework that we consider the exchange-equilibrating mechanism.

The important difference between the operation of the equilibrating mechanism in the institutional environment just described and

*Or the corresponding central banking authority in other countries.

its operation in a pure gold economy lies in the fact that in the latter the reduction in money supply due to loss of gold abroad is automatic, whereas in the former it can only be the result of deliberate activity on the part of the central banking authority. If the currency consists entirely of gold coins, when imports exceed exports the actual coins move abroad with consequences already noted. In a 'paper' economy, however, a market will develop in titles to various foreign 'currencies'. All of these currencies are of course paper rights to gold. They differ only in that they are freely exchangeable for commodities only in their country of origin. It follows that an English importer will seek to buy credits issued in terms of dollars by an American bank, whilst the American importer will want to buy titles to sterling issued by an English bank. On the other hand, since both are titles to gold, the exchange rate cannot differ from the declared gold content of the dollar and the pound by an amount greater than the cost of shipping gold, that is, e can fluctuate only between the gold points.

It follows that if the demand for dollars exceeds the demand for sterling for any length of time there must in the end be an outflow of gold as before. And if the legal ratio of total money to gold is fixed at ten to one, a loss of £1 million of gold demands action by the central bank to reduce paper money by approximately £10 million. But the required reduction in total money supply is not automatic. Banks must ordinarily be induced or instructed to call in loans, thereby reducing the rights of depositors to draw cheques, which is the same thing as reducing the quantity of quasi-money.

Provided the necessary action is taken, there is no difference in principle between the working of the exchange mechanism in the pure gold economy and the working under a gold-backed paper and credit economy. Against this there were probably a great many differences in the actual working-out.

We have already seen, for example, that whether prices fall or whether involuntary unemployment appears is a matter greatly influenced by the actions of businessmen, and these actions must depend upon whether businessmen feel confident or pessimistic about future prospects of sales. Confidence in turn is more likely to be undermined when it is known that the central authorities are deliberately restricting credit as a matter of policy than it is when the loss of gold is automatic and perhaps unnoticed. Again, the concentration of the foreign currency market into the hands of bankers (which is the natural consequence of the practice of discounting bills of exchange, as explained above) led naturally to the holding of stocks or 'reserves' of foreign money or titles to foreign money by the institutions which operate that market. These foreign currency holdings could take the form of notes, of bills of exchange drawn on foreign banks, or of credits held in banks abroad. Clearly, as long as banks are willing to run down stocks of foreign exchange it is quite possible to sustain an excess of imports over exports without any actual gold loss whatever. This might well happen if the excess of imports is thought to be seasonal or temporary. It could not of course continue indefinitely.

The practice of holding stocks of foreign currency had a further interesting consequence. One of the instruments used by the government to discourage the creation of credit when necessary is the rate of interest, which may be influenced by instructing banks to charge a higher rate on loans. A rise in interest rates, it was believed, would discourage borrowing and reduce the credit balances of customers, that is, the quantity of money substitutes. But a rise in interest rates in London might well lead holders (whether English or foreign) of dollar credits to exchange these for sterling credits in London, for by so doing higher interest rates might be earned. This movement of 'hot money' could go some way to check the loss of gold without any effect whatever on commodity prices or the level of employment, for such an inflow of foreign credits replaces, at least for a while, those lost by the imbalance of trade.

All in all, the development of a more complex institutional environment seems to have heightened rather than lessened the uncertainties which surround the operation of the exchange-equilibrating mechanism. The fundamental principles remained much the same, that is, any excess of imports over exports tended to be corrected either by price changes or changes in the level of employment in the long run. But the actual extent to which either influence operated at any moment of time cannot as yet be fully explained by any general theory.

2.7 THE EQUILIBRATING MECHANISM TODAY

The developments outlined above lead naturally to the next step. In times of crisis it is evidently possible to abandon or alter the legal ratio of gold to money substitutes. Stocks of gold could then be used consciously to finance an excess of imports over exports. But again this can only be a temporary expedient.

On the other hand experience (Britain for example abandoned gold on the outbreak of the 1914–18 war) has underlined the fact that, provided paper money is not created to excess, there is no real need to maintain a corresponding gold stock. Of course, as we have constantly reiterated, the general level of commodity prices is very much bound up with the quantity of money even though not entirely determined by it; but there is no reason at all today why the quantity of money should ever be subject to a control as arbitrary as that imposed by tying it to an uncertain gold supply.

Furthermore, it became clear that apart from the qualifications below, it is perfectly reasonable to allow the rate of exchange *e* to fluctuate freely according to the supply and demand for the currencies involved. Although there is evidence of a current resurgence of the myth, objections to freely fluctuating exchange rates had, by the 1930s, ceased to be based upon the quasi-superstitious belief that money must have an intrinsic (gold) value, for the universal practice of expressing all commodity prices in terms of common money units and the widespread understanding that the creation of money is closely controlled by the government had reduced the likelihood of a loss of confidence to negligible proportions.*

Thus the inter-war period saw many fascinating experiments in fluctuating exchange rates, although it is not the purpose of this book to attempt to describe these since we are interested in principles only. It is sufficient here to point out that fluctuating exchange rates do introduce an undesirable element of uncertainty in the fixing of long-term trading contracts. If an exporter contracts to supply a certain commodity at a future date at a given sterling price, the actual foreign price paid will depend upon the rate of exchange ruling at the time of payment. If the contract is made in terms of the foreign currency, the uncertainty is shifted on to the exporter.

Partly because of this and partly because of a fear that speculation or gambling on movements of exchange rates might cause even wider fluctuations, the majority of exchange rates are now once more fixed. But there is a difference. Most currencies are now pegged directly or indirectly to the United States dollar rather than to gold, although the gold content of the dollar is itself defined.

In principle this is very little different from a strict gold standard, but there may very well be political implications. It may for example be politically easier to announce a currency devaluation (i.e. to announce that fewer dollars can now be bought for £1) than to

---

* Since these words were written many economists, including the present writer, have become much less confident on this point.

announce that the gold content of the pound is now less. Indeed, 'once for all' changes in exchange rates are relatively commonplace events and are widely regarded as a proper instrument of policy in the correction of international trade disequilibria (subject to the qualifications below).

Another important institutional development is the almost universal monopolisation of the foreign exchange market by some arm of the national government. It is now usual for all foreign currency earned by exporters to be surrendered to a government-controlled central bank and for all applications for currency needed to pay for imports to be addressed, through the banking system, to the same central bank. This arrangement is the natural outcome of the more general realisation of the role of employment fluctuations in the equilibrating process which we have emphasised throughout.

As we have seen, the rise of paper and credit currency imposes an obligation to apply deliberate credit restriction where there is a gold loss. But as soon as it becomes understood that credit restriction can lead to involuntary unemployment, there is at once a reluctance to apply necessary remedies. The existence of currency stocks allows a breathing space whilst alternative policies are considered, and one natural alternative way to prevent loss of foreign currency is to apply some form of currency rationing. This is possible only if the sale of foreign currency is in the hands of a government monopoly.

The monopolising process was begun by experiments in the inter-war period in discriminating exchange rates. By this system different exchange rates were fixed for foreign currency required for different purposes. Obviously such experiments are impossible without close control of the right to buy and sell. Finally, the crisis created by the 1939–45 world war made it necessary for most of the important trading countries to control their imports. In practice, importing was prohibited except under government licence. The law was enforced by issuing foreign currency only against a licence, a practice which made it essential to monopolise the exchange market.

The present situation may now be summed up as follows. A fundamental imbalance in the trading position such as that illustrated in Fig. 2.1 leads either to a downward pressure on prices and employment or to a loss of national exchange reserves. This loss of reserves may be allowed to continue for some time but not indefinitely, for reserves would eventually be exhausted with obvious consequences. An outflow of reserves is in fact a signal that something must be done.

Two obvious policies are possible (*but do not overlook the caveat below in section 2.8*). The government may announce an appropriate change in the exchange rate, e, sufficient to correct the imbalance at once. Alternatively, some attempt must be made to reduce home prices p_1 by raising the rate of interest and/or restriction of credit (i.e. the quantity of money). Of the two policies the second is most commonly employed despite the danger of creating unemployment thereby. There are at least two reasons for this.

First, there is a widespread belief that currency depreciation by any one country would induce most other countries to devalue *pari passu*. Paradoxically this is because of the fear of being driven to employ the second policy. Every country believes that it is desirable to build up large stocks of foreign currency as an insurance against the necessity at some future date of restricting credit, thereby creating unemployment. To build up reserves by depreciating the home currency is regarded as 'unfair'. Attempts to depreciate may be met, therefore, by counter-depreciation.

Second, indiscriminate currency depreciation is contrary to international agreement. In recent years realisation of the need for buffer stocks of foreign currency has led to the development of what amounts to an international central bank called the International Monetary Fund or I.M.F. Again we do not propose to describe in detail the precise working of this system since it is complicated in practice. All that it is necessary to understand is that the I.M.F. makes loans in certain circumstances to countries running short of reserves. This is appropriate of course where the cause of the currency shortage is believed to be temporary only.

There has in fact been a great deal of evidence to suggest that world stocks of foreign currency are insufficient to meet temporary fluctuations in supply and demand, and the I.M.F. was set up to ease the problem. Naturally, however, I.M.F. members must agree to abide by reasonable rules, one of which is that no exchange rate adjustment can be made without prior permission of the Fund. Even then it must be shown that there is a long-term need for such adjustment.

Fortunately credit restriction might not today be as devastating an alternative as it could have been when the problem of maintaining full employment was less well understood. Since the nineteenth century the wheel has turned full circle and governments have now freed themselves from the idea that uncompromisingly strict control of the quantity of money is a *sine qua non* of economic well-being.

As a result, the danger today in most countries is of too fast an increase in the *general level of prices* rather than unemployment. Prices everywhere are rising at from 2 to 5 per cent per annum and the quantity of money is allowed to keep pace.

In these circumstances we note that we can change the real terms of trade p_1/q_2 *by ensuring that* p_1 *does not rise as fast as* q_2 just as well as by a reduction in the absolute value of p_1. And there is reason to believe that credit restrictions designed simply to slow up the rate of increase of prices in a world of generally rising prices are less likely to create serious unemployment than credit restrictions designed to reduce prices in a world of generally stable prices.

At this point the reader is warned that this review of international monetary experience has been kept to the absolute minimum necessary for a proper understanding of the very general problems which form the subject matter of this book. Many experiments in control have been omitted, and the full story is by no means as uncomplicated as the account given above would seem to suggest. Development has not been as steady or as unidirectional as might appear from the preceding pages, nor are the chains of cause and effect as clear-cut as we suggest. On the other hand care has been taken to explain the principles at the most general level possible, and the reader who understands the argument will have a firm base upon which to commence a detailed study of actual events.

2.8 A CAVEAT OF THE UTMOST IMPORTANCE

It would be a frightening thing if the reader were to infer, from the remarks in section 2.7, that whenever a loss of reserves of gold or foreign currency is actually observed, the proper course for a government to take is either to change the exchange rate or to restrict credit without further inquiry. The reference in section 2.7 to 'two possible policies' relates in fact to a highly special case. *Losses of reserves may be observed in practice for quite different reasons than those set out in section 2.2, in which case a policy of exchange depreciation might be quite the reverse of what is needed. Contrariwise, the situation described in section 2.2, which calls for depreciation, may exist without any visible loss of reserves at all.*

The reader should understand that we are discussing in section 2.2 a disequilibrium situation where what is actually observable is not defined or is defined only by implication. For example, suppose that prices and expenditures are apparently as specified in Fig. 2.1.

What Fig. 2.1 then illustrates is what consumers are *trying* to do and
not necessarily what they actually succeed in doing. In particular,
Fig. 2.1 shows both countries trying to spend exactly the value of
output OM and LM, thus demanding consumption patterns B and
A. But unless the foreign country carries stocks of importables and
is prepared to see them run down, it is *impossible* to consume in the
patterns B and A, for more would then be sold than can possibly be
produced.

In the text above, we have introduced, without special emphasis,
one or two plausible assumptions as to what in practice is likely to
occur. But consider another case. Suppose that there is no possibility
of meeting extra demand out of stocks and the foreign country
satisfies in full the demands of its own population. The home
country is now unofficially rationed and cannot consume the pattern
B. If there is no immediate price change in consequence, what we
should actually *observe* is a shortage of importables in the shops.
Furthermore, as TA is exported and only TM imported, *no loss of
gold or reserves* will actually be noticed. Even so, the correct policy
would be to depreciate the currency and all difficulties would
immediately disappear.

Against this in Chapter 4 we shall discuss at length the opposite
type of case. There we shall have a situation in which a loss of
reserves is *observed* but where the proper policy prescription is very
different from that of this chapter. In the situation of Chapter 4 there
must be a cut in aggregate spending and perhaps even an *appreciation*
of the exchange rate to attain the desired equilibrium.

Nothing could be more important than that the student should
grasp here and now the full implications of the examples quoted. The
real world is almost always in disequilibrium because of growth and
change. Nearly always something is wrong. There is unemployment,
and there is a balance of trade problem, or prices are rising too fast
and so on. In political circles and among popular journalists there is a
natural and powerful tendency to look at *just the one* variable in the
system which is going wrong and to ask what policy will put it right
with no reference whatever to what is happening to all the other
variables. It is but a short step from here to the development of
dogma or at least a use of language which implies that each separate
ill has its own unique cure. The only cure, for example, for unemployment may be thought to be an increase in aggregate spending. But we
have already described, in section 2.5 above, a case where a tendency
to unemployment is more properly cured by devaluation. In the same

way we must resist any dogmatic acceptance of a rule which says that loss of reserves calls for devaluation, or any other policy. The truth is that troublesome and persistent disequilibria occur for a variety of reasons and that, accordingly, no cure can ever be prescribed without careful diagnosis of the underlying causes. Such a diagnosis will ordinarily demand much more than a casual observation of the disequilibrium variable itself. In most cases a detailed study of the economy as a whole will be necessary. It would be as foolish for governments to react always in the same way to the same symptom of economic ill as it would be for a surgeon to operate in search of a brain tumour each time the patient complains of a headache. Indeed, like headaches, some disequilibria will disappear of their own accord.

2.9 On the Adequacy (?) of Chapter 2

In view of the remarks in 1.5, the reader will scarcely need reminding that the real world is infinitely more complex than the model as so far studied. In particular, even in the special case where trading countries produce none of their importables at home, there must be some manufacture or provision of goods and services which by their very nature cannot enter into trade (see Chapter 11, section 5). In consequence the total quantities available, of importables, exportables and non-traded goods, will not be fixed but will be dependent upon prices. In terms of Fig. 2.1, the size of the 'box' $MLNO$ is no longer constant even when full employment of all resources is maintained. Moreover, OM is not the total value of output of the country so that it no longer measures aggregate spending. Indeed, it does not even measure aggregate spending on traded goods alone unless spending on non-traded goods is exactly equal to the value of non-traded goods produced. Thus the offer curve MCB need not begin from M unless supply and demand are equal in the non-traded goods market. Finally, the positions and shapes of offer curves will usually be dependent upon the quantity of non-traded goods consumed, particularly if these are in any degree substitutes both for importables and exportables. The shapes of offer curves will therefore depend upon the relative prices of traded and non-traded commodities, which are themselves an added complication. The whole diagram (Fig. 2.1) moves as the equilibrating mechanism operates. In short, the geometric technique we have been using cannot cope with a less aggregated model. Algebraic methods later introduced are necessary for a deeper understanding.

Despite all this, however, the naïve model does demonstrate everything that is essential. We now understand the meaning of the currency exchange rate and we appreciate its role in adjusting the real terms of trade. Again, it has been possible to show how the ordinary working of the mechanism, whether under a gold system or a paper currency system, can lead to a quasi-equilibrium at something less than the full employment of all productive resources. Finally, we have seen something of the part played in the equilibrating process of the ordinary forces of supply and demand in the market, The only important point not brought out is the fact that there exists a crucial price ratio quite distinct from the real terms of trade, namely, the ratio of prices between traded and non-traded goods.

The attainment of equilibrium at full employment calls in general for the adjustment of *two* classes of prices, first the real terms of trade and second the ratio of prices between traded and non-traded commodities. A balance of trade deficit may be due to the one but it could equally well be due to the other or both. This point is taken up again in section 3.4 of the next chapter.

EXERCISES

1. From successive issues of *Economic Trends*, published by the U.K. Central Statistical Office, obtain quarterly figures from 1958 onwards of the U.K. *visible* balance of trade. Plot on a graph the visible balance against 'time'. On the same graph plot figures for the ratio of import prices to export prices and the level of unemployment, both obtainable from *Statistics on Incomes, Prices, Employment and Production*, published by the Ministry of Labour (now the Department of Employment and Productivity).

   Do you consider the terms of trade or the level of employment to have been the main determinant of the U.K. balance of trade?
2. Carry out the same exercise as above for the U.S.A. and France.
3. Compare the U.K. index of retail prices with a simple average of the index of import and export prices. Hence show that, since 1960, the price of non-traded goods in the U.K. has been rising relative to those traded. Compare these price movements with the U.K. visible trade balance over the same period.
4. Turn up, in *Financial Statistics*, published by the U.K. Central Statistical Office, figures for the total official gold and foreign

currency holdings between 1961 and 1968. Compare these holdings with the total U.K. money supply, also given in *Financial Statistics*. Explain why, in the circumstances now revealed, a £1 sterling note is worth anything at all on the international market.

5. Reconsider the argument associated with Fig. 2.2. What would occur if, simultaneously with the reduction of home production, foreign producers raised the price of importables because of the existing excess demand. Show that the more the increase in the price of importables, the less is the unemployment needed to attain equilibrium.

6. Reconsider the argument associated with Fig. 2.2. Assume that in the original situation the foreign government is alarmed by the loss of stocks and the danger of price rises associated with it. Suppose therefore it introduces an income tax the proceeds of which are not spent, so that the foreign country spends less than the value of its product even though it continues in full employment of all resources as before. Show diagrammatically that it is now impossible to attain full world equilibrium without price changes since there must always be a deficit in world demand for country 1's product.

3 The Stability of the Equilibrating Mechanism

3.1 INSTABILITY OF THE FIRST KIND

IN Chapter 1 it was shown that, in the general case, at least one position of equilibrium in international trade will exist where all countries will be satisfied. When such a position is attained there is no further pressure to change. In Chapter 2 we traced the main routes by which a situation that is not an equilibrium situation will usually be transformed into one that is. The word 'usually' reflects the fact that up to now we have not met pressures to change which operate in the wrong direction, that is, away from equilibrium rather than towards it. On the other hand it is not impossible for destabilising pressures to be generated quite automatically, for reasons into which we must now inquire.

In Chapter 2 we more than once drew attention to the fact that all economic mechanisms are necessarily dynamic in character. The timing of events is often as important a determinant of the final outcome as the character of the events themselves, as will now be simply demonstrated.

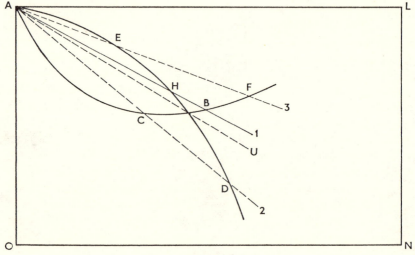

Fig. 3.1

First, reconsider the familiar situation depicted in Fig. 3.1 above. Suppose that initially the terms of trade stand at *AB* (position 1). As explained in Chapter 2 this implies an excess world demand for importables and a deficit in world demand for exportables. We now introduce timing quite explicitly into the argument. Choosing the simplest possible assumptions, let us imagine that in period 1 this month) producers in both countries maintain prices as before, meeting excess demand out of stocks or using excess production to build up stocks.

In period 2 (the following month), however, producers who have been building up stocks cut prices to increase sales whilst those who have been running down stocks seize the opportunity to increase prices. Since there is unlikely to be collusion between foreign and home price-fixers, there is no reason to suppose that the new prices will give rise exactly to the equilibrium terms of trade *AU*. It is not impossible that they will overshoot the mark and settle at position 2, where the excess demand for importables has turned into a deficit and the deficit demand for exportables has turned into an excess. In period 2, stocks build up where they formerly ran down and run down where they formerly built up. Furthermore, *CD* might very well be greater than *HB* so that the changes in stocks in period 2 are even greater than they were in period 1, but in the opposite direction.

Observing this, exporters might be encouraged to put up their prices in period 3 to a level actually greater than period 1 in the hope of regaining profits lost in period 2. Thus, although foreign producers of importables may be reluctant to reduce prices below the level of period 1, since this might mean giving up profits enjoyed in period 2, the real terms of trade in period 3 could move to position 3, which is further from equilibrium than the initial position 1. In turn this might induce a still wider movement in period 4. We have in fact illustrated a case of unstable 'explosive' fluctuation about an equilibrium *AU*. The terms of trade oscillate from period to period in ever-widening amplitude. The equilibrium *AU* is never attained.

This simple example demonstrates the fact that the stability or instability of an equilibrium position is not entierly determined by the underlying shapes of offer curves or the size of the production box *OALN*. For on the general argument of Chapter 2 the equilibrium of Fig. 3.1 would be stable, whereas in the particular case above it is unstable. As we have previously insisted, the strength and timing of reactions to each situation, as it makes itself felt, is also a determining factor.

This lesson should be well learned. In the real world of many prices disequilibrium is not necessarily *only* a matter of the 'wrong' terms of trade. Other prices also may need adjustment. In these circumstances the chain of causality is more complex and the possibility of instability correspondingly more difficult to assess. Moreover, the response of businessmen to given changes in the economic climate is very much conditioned by the prevailing state of optimism or pessimism, which in turn can depend upon prior events only distantly connected with economics. Evidently the study of our simple model does not answer all of the questions, and the reader is once again warned against indiscriminate use of argument based upon it.

3.2 Instability of the Second Kind

We next notice that instabilities of a rather different kind are possible. In the simple model and with the configuration of offer curves illustrated in Fig. 3.1, instability can arise only as a consequence of a timing pattern which may be thought to be unlikely. With a large number of independent producers it seems more probable that price adjustments will take place at many different times, depending on the particular circumstances of each firm, rather than simultaneously on the last day of the month. The terms of trade will not jump from position 1 to position 2; rather they will pass smoothly at a speed which depends upon the rates of change in stocks. As equilibrium AU is approached, the rate of change of the terms of trade will slow up. In these circumstances, overshooting is unlikely to occur or, if it does, oscillations will be 'damped' like those of a pendulum coming gradually to rest.

On the other hand, with certain not impossible shapes of offer curves instability can arise even with continuous price adjustment. Consider Fig. 3.2. Offer curves now cut three times at H, B and C so that AH, AB and AC are all possible equilibrium positions in which world supply equals world demand for all commodities. We now proceed to show that AH and AC can be stable positions whilst AB is unstable.

Suppose that the terms of trade stand at AS. Country 1 demands RT of exportables whilst country 2 demands SW. But RT plus SW is greater than world production OA so that there is an excess demand for exportables. Stocks are diminishing so that the price p_1 will tend to rise. On the other hand country 1 demands only UR of

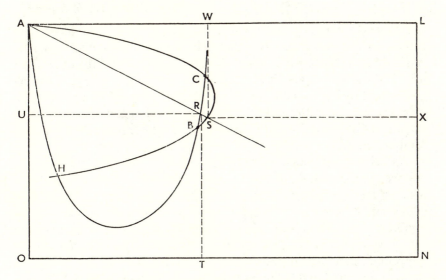

Fig 3.2.

importables whilst country 2 demands SX. This is less than world supply. Stocks are rising so that the price q_2 falls.

In this situation the real terms of trade tend to move away from AS towards AC. The reader may satisfy himself by similar argument that if AS lay on the other side of AB, the terms of trade would move towards AH. AB is a true equilibrium in the sense that at these terms of trade no pressure to change is generated; but the slightest displacement from the position AB will generate pressure to drive the terms of trade still further away. The equilibrium AB is unstable. Clearly it is desirable to know under what conditions of consumer tastes offer curves will cut three or more times as in Fig. 3.2.

Chapter 1 already gave a hint of these conditions when offer curves were originally introduced. Attention was drawn to two consequences of a rise in the price of, say, importables. First, the consumer is worse off, which means that less will be consumed of both exportables and importables. Second, since exportables are now relatively cheaper, they will be substituted for importables. Now in the region of the point B (Fig. 3.2), country 1's offer curve slopes sharply downward from right to left. This means that a price rise in importables leads to lower consumption of both importables and exportables despite the substitution effect. The substitution of exportables for importables must be very slight, for if it were greater we should expect more exportables to be demanded rather than less.

The necessary condition for instability is thus revealed. The reaction in consumption of importables to price changes must be small, since substitution is small. This will evidently be the case when importables and exportables tend to be consumed in fixed proportions whatever their relative prices, that is, when they are complementary commodities like motor-cars and petrol rather than substitutes like two different kinds of food. The same must be true of foreign demand.

Care should of course be taken in applying this conclusion to the real world, for with many commodities and many prices the problem is much more complex (see below for further comment on this). One lesson might be learned, however. Suppose that underlying consumer preferences are of the stable kind, as in Fig. 3.1, but that it takes time for housewives to adjust their patterns of spending to the new prices. Suppose in fact, that in the first three months after any price change they do not change their habits at all or they change them only very slightly. Imagine that the terms of trade are in position 1 (Fig. 3.1) and that an attempt is made to correct the situation by a change in exchange rates e. The price p_2 rises and the foreign price q_1 falls, but the housewife responds at once only to the change in the purchasing power of the family income and not to substitution possibilities. For three months the situation could be *as if* offer curves lay in the Fig. 3.2 shape, perhaps even intersecting to the 'north-east' of HB (Fig. 3.1). That is, Fig. 3.1 could look like Fig. 3.2 but with AS on the other side of AB. But in this case to worsen the terms of trade, i.e. to move still further in the direction of H (Fig. 3.2), will *increase* rather than decrease the building-up of stocks and the loss of currency reserves. This effect will only be temporary, however. As spending is gradually adjusted to the new pattern of prices, the situation will right itself. We have a temporary instability again due to the timing of responses.

3.3 On the Need for Algebra and a First Introduction to the Method

Many readers will remain dissatisfied with the account of the unstable case given in 3.2, for to say that a situation is stable if consumption response to price changes is high but unstable if it is low immediately invites the question 'How high is high?' It is impossible in fact to investigate this problem without a more exact numerical inquiry. An algebraic formulation of the problem is essential.

Instability of the second kind (section 3.2) is a property of the shapes of offer curves alone, so that it may be investigated as follows. Suppose first that excess and deficit demands for commodities are met always out of stocks. The balance of payments must then be the difference between the value of the foreign demand for exportables and the home demand for importables. What is demanded will be consumed and full employment is maintained.

Beginning from a state of balanced trade, we now imagine that the price of importables is raised. If a surplus on the home country's balance of trade is thereby created, this must be because foreign stocks of importables are increasing and home stocks of exportables are diminishing. In a model with fluctuating exchange rates the surplus on the balance of trade will raise the price of home currency in terms of foreign currency, cancelling the rise in p_2. In a model with a fixed exchange rate but where producers react by making smooth price reductions at the first sign of stock-building, p_2 will fall and p_1 rise, again cancelling the initial change. The equilibrium is stable.

If on the other hand the initial rise in p_2 creates a deficit on the home balance of payments, the reverse holds true. With fluctuating exchange rates the price of home currency will fall relatively, equivalent to a still further rise in p_2. Creation of a deficit means also that stocks are falling abroad and rising at home. Again the pressure is towards a further rise in p_2 relative to p_1. The equilibrium is unstable with either model.

To test for instability, therefore, all that is necessary is to inquire whether a rise in p_2, with everything else constant including the exchange rate, will create a surplus or a deficit on the balance of payments. In view of this we may very much simplify the problem by assuming the exchange rate, e, to be unity or, what amounts to the same thing, by measuring all prices in home currency. As e is to remain constant we can forget it for the time being. Thus in what follows we have no e and we write p_1 and p_2 for both home and foreign prices.

Let X_1 and X_2 be the quantities of exportables and importables consumed by the home country and X_1' and X_2' the quantities consumed abroad. We adopt in fact throughout this book the general convention that primes, as in X_1', indicate the foreign country. If trade is exactly balanced, that is, if equilibrium rules, then

$$p_1 X_1' - p_2 X_2 = B = 0 \qquad (3.3.1)$$

In words, the value of exports minus the value of imports (which equals the balance of payments, B) is zero. Note that if p_1 changes to $(p_1 + \Delta p_1)$ and X_1' changes to $(X_1' + \Delta X_1')$, then $p_1 X_1$ changes to

$$(p_1 + \Delta p_1)(X_1' + \Delta X_1') \tag{3.3.2}$$

where the symbol Δ is read 'a small change in'.

Multiplying out the expression (3.3.2) following ordinary algebraic rules, we obtain

$$p_1 X_1' + \Delta p_1 X_1' + p_1 \Delta X_1' + \Delta p_1 \Delta X_1' \tag{3.3.3}$$

But $\Delta(p\,X')$ which is the change in the value of exports is clearly

$$(p_1 + \Delta p_1)(X_1' + \Delta X_1') - p_1 X_1'$$

which, using (3.3.3) yields

$$\Delta(p_1 X_1') = \Delta p_1 X_1' + p_1 \Delta X_1' + \Delta p_1 \Delta X_1' \tag{3.3.4}$$

Applying the principle (3.3.4) to both terms in the left-hand side of (3.3.1) we can now write out in full the change in the balance of payments B which occurs when all ps and Xs change. Thus:

$$\Delta B = \Delta p_1 X_1' + p_1 \Delta X_1' + \Delta p_1 \Delta X_1' - \Delta p_2 X_2 - p_2 \Delta X_2 - \Delta p_2 \Delta X_2$$

If now we interpret the change in B as the consequence of a rise Δp_2 in the price of importables, Δp_1 being zero, we have at once

$$\Delta B = p_1 \Delta X_1' - \Delta p_2 X_2 - p_2 \Delta X_2 - \Delta p_2 \Delta X_2$$

Dividing both sides by Δp_2 we obtain an expression for $\Delta B/\Delta p_2$ which is the *rate* of change of the balance of payments per unit change in p_2, namely

$$\Delta B/\Delta p_2 = p_1(\Delta X_1'/\Delta p_2) - p_2(\Delta X_2/\Delta p_2) - X_2 - \Delta X_2 \tag{3.3.5}$$

We now recall that we are interested only in very small changes in Δp_2 and hence in ΔX_2. We can make Δp_2 as close to zero as we like without affecting the value of the rate $\Delta B/\Delta p_2$. As an aid to the understanding of this point reflect that it is commonplace to talk about the speed of a racing car at the point where it passes the winning post. The time that the tip of the front wheel takes to pass the winning post is almost zero, but the speed of the car is 100 m.p.h. In the same way the price change Δp_2 may be as near as we like to zero so that all actual changes are close to zero, but the response rates $\Delta B/\Delta p_2$ and $\Delta X_1'/\Delta p_2$, etc., are quite ordinary numbers. In these circumstances we can neglect the term ΔX_2 in (3.3.5). The problem now reduces to one of discovering the conditions under which the rate

$$\Delta B/\Delta p_2 = p_1(\Delta X_1'/\Delta p_2) - p_2(\Delta X_2/\Delta p_2) - X_2$$

is negative, that is, under which the balance of payments deficit increases with a rise in import prices. This, as indicated in the preamble to this section, is the unstable case.

We write the required condition as

$$p_1(\Delta X_1'/\Delta p_2) - p_2(\Delta X_2/\Delta p_2) - X_2 < 0 \qquad (3.3.6)$$

where $<$ is a symbol indicating 'less than'.

(3.3.6) with X_2 taken outside a bracket is

$$X_2\left(\frac{p_1 \Delta X_1'}{X_2 \Delta p_2} - \frac{p_2 \Delta X_2}{X_2 \Delta p_2} - 1\right) < 0$$

which, since X_2 is > 0, is equivalent to

$$\frac{p_1 \Delta X_1'}{X_2 \Delta p_2} - \frac{p_2 \Delta X_2}{X_2 \Delta p_2} - 1 < 0 \qquad (3.3.7)$$

We now recall from (3.3.1)

$$p_1 X_1' - p_2 X_2 = 0$$

or

$$X_2 = p_1 X_1'/p_2$$

Substituting this in (3.3.7) yields

$$\frac{p_2 \Delta X_1'}{X_1' \Delta p_2} - \frac{p_2 \Delta X_2}{X_2 \Delta p_2} - 1 < 0 \qquad (3.3.8)$$

for the condition of instability. Can this now be interpreted?

Consider what has occurred in country 1. Import prices p_2 have risen by an amount Δp_2 whilst export prices p_1 have remained unchanged. Furthermore, national production is also unchanged and, since the price, p_1, of the national product is constant, so is total expenditure in money terms. The change in consumption, ΔX_2, therefore, is the response in consumption of importables due to a change Δp_2 in their price with all other prices and money expenditure held constant.

The response rate, $\Delta X_2/\Delta p_2$, with all other prices and spending constant, is a fundamental magnitude which depends only upon the preference of consumers. In the form $\Delta X_2/\Delta p_2$, however, it is clear that this magnitude must depend upon the units in which X and p

are expressed. For example, if X is measured in gallons and p in shillings, the rate $\Delta X_2/\Delta p_2$ would be in gallons per shilling. Alternatively it might be measured in barrels per penny. In each case the fundamental number $\Delta X_2/\Delta p_2$ would be different even though both give expression to the same underlying pattern of consumer preferences.

To overcome this difficulty, economists have found it convenient in some cases to talk not of the response rate $\Delta X_2/\Delta p_2$ but of elasticity of demand

$$\frac{\Delta X_2}{X_2} \div \frac{\Delta p_2}{p_2}$$

which may be written $\dfrac{p_2}{X_2} \dfrac{\Delta X_2}{\Delta p_2}$. This is simply the *proportionate*

change in consumption due to a given proportionate change in price; or, what amounts to the same thing, the percentage change in consumption due to a 1 per cent change in price, all other prices and spending constant. We call this magnitude E_{22}, the subscripts 22 referring to commodity 2 and price 2 respectively.

Great efforts have been made in the past (and continue to be made) to measure as accurately as possible the elasticity of demand for various commodities and commodity groups and, within very broad limits, it is hoped that some of these numbers are now known. They will change as consumer tastes change of course, but it is assumed that they remain stable long enough to permit their use in prediction over short periods at any rate. We should in fact like to be able to say, for example, that a 1 per cent rise in the price of bread, other things being equal, will reduce bread consumption by 1 per cent or only $\frac{1}{2}$ per cent as the case may be. And there is evidence to suggest that the most recent estimates of some of these fundamental 'parameters' are not too far wrong, or at least not so far wrong as to be useless.

This being the case, it is obviously desirable that we should be able to express the stability condition in terms of the numbers E_{22}, etc., which we either know or have some hope of being able to discover. It might then be possible to say whether the system under examination is stable or unstable.

Looking at the condition (3.3.8), we notice that the second term is precisely E_{22} so that this may be substituted in. The first term, however, is more difficult. In country 2 the price of importables (foreign exports) has risen. It follows that the value of output, and hence aggregate money expenditure in country 2, has risen in the same proportion. The reader is reminded that the convention whereby we measure prices and incomes in country 2 in units of currency of country 1 means that the prices p_1 and p_2 apply equally in both countries. The interpretation of

$$\frac{p_2}{X'_1} \frac{\Delta X'_1}{\Delta p_2}$$

therefore must be the percentage change in consumption, of X'_1, due to a 1 per cent rise in the price of commodity 2 accompanied by a 1 per cent rise in total money expenditure. This is not immediately translatable into an elasticity. But in Chapter 1 it was explained that if *all* prices rise proportionately and if total expenditure rises in the same proportion there will be no change whatever in the sales of any commodity, for this implies no change in relative prices and the increased absolute prices just exhaust the increased incomes. Now suppose that the equal proportionate changes in p_2 and expenditure are arrived at in two stages. First, both prices p_1 and p_2 and total expenditure are raised in the proportion $\Delta p_2/p_2$. This will not occasion any change at all in purchases of exportables. Now let the price p_1 be *reduced* in the proportion $\Delta p_2/p_2 = \Delta p_1/p_1$. The response in consumption of exportables is bound to be $\Delta X'_1/X'_1$ since the final position is exactly that which, by definition, generates this change. It follows that putting *down* the price P_1, keeping the price p_2 and expenditure constant, brings about exactly the same changes in consumption which would occur if instead the price p_2 and expenditure were both put up in the same proportion with p_1 constant. Thus

$$\frac{p_2 \, \Delta X'_1}{X'_1 \Delta p_2} = -\frac{p_1 \, \Delta X'_1}{X'_1 \Delta p_1}$$

where the right-hand expression is, again by definition, minus the foreign elasticity of demand for exportables E'_{11}. Thus we write the condition for instability (3.3.8) in the final form,

$$-E'_{11} - E_{22} - 1 < 0 \tag{3.3.9}$$

Now elasticities of demand are inherently negative numbers, since a *rise* in price leads to a *fall* in demand and a positive change in price gives rise to a negative change in demand. $-E$ is therefore positive. The left-hand side of (3.3.9) will accordingly be positive (i.e. > 0) when the numbers E are together *numerically* greater than 1.

The unstable case occurs when they are numerically less than 1.

This is exactly in accordance with the results suggested by Fig. 3.2. Small responses are associated with instability. The algebra has, however, enabled us to state precisely how small is small – which was the object of the exercise.

3.4 ON WHAT WE DO NOT KNOW

At this point it seems proper to confess that the algebra of section 3.3 was introduced as much for purposes of subversion as for purposes of instruction. The result (3.3.9) is a very celebrated formula sometimes known as the 'Marshall–Lerner condition for exchange stability'. It is often presented in such a way that the ordinary reader might legitimately take it to be intended as a practical rule ready for the immediate guidance of the policy-maker. If elasticities are small, a free floating exchange rate would not work. If they are large, a free floating exchange is to be recommended. It is presumably to be inferred also that, even when exchange rates are pegged, the 'stability condition' is equally informative. The implication is that when we have a balance of payments deficit, a deliberate adjustment of the exchange rate in the direction in which it would move if not pegged will correct the imbalance in the stable case. If elasticities are low, however, the deliberate adjustment must, paradoxically, be in the opposite direction.

All of this would be fine if we could be sure that

1. aggregate spending could *never* be different from the value of output;
2. building-up of stocks *never* induces a cut in production;
3. supplies of all products are fixed whatever the prices;
4. there is no home production of importables or foreign production of exportables;
5. no class of goods excluded from trade exists (see section 2.9 above); and
6. neither depreciation nor a fluctuating exchange rate can ever induce a change in the general level of prices (inflation) within a country as opposed to the desired change in relative prices.

It is perhaps a pity that the world does not meet the requirements 1 – 6, if only because the present book need then contain fewer pages. But since it does not, the reader should be deeply aware of how little we have in fact learned from section 3.3. This is best illustrated by looking briefly and inadequately at the case where all conditions above are met except 5, thus fulfilling a promise made in section 2.9. Where non-traded goods exist, it is not only clear that the methods of 3.3 do not apply; we find that the entire question we are trying to answer ceases even to be properly specified.

In section 3.3 we let the price of importables rise to test whether a balance of trade surplus or deficit would be thereby generated. Note that it would not have mattered if we had reduced the price of exportables instead. The terms of trade movement would have been indistinguishable (Fig. 3.1) in either case. But when there exists a class of goods excluded from trade we have another quite distinct price to manipulate. Suppose that the price of non-traded goods is raised, leaving the real terms of trade unchanged, would we then expect a surplus or deficit on the balance of trade? The answer to this is that one or the other must appear, for money formerly spent on traded goods is now spent on non-traded goods or vice versa. The offer curve shifts and the equilibrium point is displaced. Can we now correct the imbalance by a movement in the real terms of trade? Obviously yes, but only at the cost of an imbalance in the supply/ demand position for the non-traded goods.

Now put the question the other way round. If we observe an imbalance in the trade position, is this due to 'wrong' terms of trade or a 'wrong' price ratio between traded and non-traded commodities? It might of course be either or both. In such a case will a freely fluctuating exchange rate correct the imbalance, or, if the rate is pegged, should the currency be depreciated or appreciated? Evidently the answer to this depends entirely on what is wrong and why and what relative price changes are likely to follow a currency depreciation.

As an example consider the case of Australia. It is commonly said that Australian import and export prices are entirely determined in world markets. Nothing that Australia can do will affect her terms of trade, since the quantities of traded goods bought and sold by that country are so small that changes in supply do not affect the world prices paid or charged. Notice that this situation is in contradiction with assumption 6 above, for it implies that if Australia depreciated her currency, the price of exportables in terms of Australian dollars must rise by the same percentage as the percentage depreciation, that is, the world price remains constant. Thus if no non-traded goods existed, any Australian devaluation would be immediately nullified by a general inflation exactly restoring the pre-devaluation real position.

But as non-traded goods are present in Australia, the most likely effect of currency depreciation would be to reduce the home price of non-traded goods relative to those traded. This might of course be precisely what is needed, for if traded goods' prices are immovable, the underlying cause of any Australian trade deficit *must* be a 'wrong' ratio of traded to non-traded goods prices, and this is just what is corrected by depreciation.

The lesson to be learned from all this is the same as that spelt out in section 2.9. The limited information, derived more from 'common sense' than extensive empirical inquiry, which we have used to build up the model so far, is *insufficient* to enable us to reach any general conclusions as to the stability of the international economic system under flexible exchange rates. For the same reason it is insufficient to tell us whether, under pegged exchange rates, the proper cure for a persistent trade deficit is to change the rate in the direction it would move if allowed to float.

What is required is more knowledge of how prices react and why. This must be introduced into the system in the form of so called 'difference' equations and the implications worked out. For example, we may discover that for a certain class of commodities producers invariably raise their prices by, say, 2 per cent for each 1 per cent fall in their stocks. Thus we could write as a 'law of the market':

$$\frac{(p_t - p_{t-1})}{p_{t-1}} = - \frac{2(S_t - S_{t-1})}{S_{t-1}} \tag{3.4.1}$$

where p_t is price in period t and S_t is stock in period t. In certain cases equation systems of this kind can be solved to determine the path of prices. In other cases it may be possible to specify conditions under which prices will approach their equilibrium value and whether or not the approach will be oscillatory around the equilibrium as in section 3.1. But for two reasons we cannot in this book develop this kind of argument further.

In the first place the mathematics involved is far from simple. Second, even if the mathematics were explained and suitable hypotheses introduced we should simply be led to conclude that almost anything can happen according to the value of the numbers such as the number 2 in (3.4.1). As long as the true value of these numbers applicable to the real world remains unknown, as they do, we learn nothing more than we have already discovered from the simple examples quoted in this and the previous chapter. There is no point in developing even more complicated examples just to exhibit the same old problem in a more tedious form.

In time, as more statistical evidence is acquired, the missing information will be filled in and the number of possibilities reduced. Work of this kind goes on continuously and indeed one of the primary purposes of the computerised model referred to in section 1.5 is to test various hypotheses and to attempt to add to our knowledge in this field (see Chapter 19 below).

In the meantime the student should not feel that he has gained nothing. As indicated in section 2.9, even the simplest model draws our attention to the most important features of the exchange mechanism. Furthermore, historical evidence suggests that in the immediate past a great deal of automatic adjustment did take place. Whatever the conditions for stability may be it seems likely that they must have been met, although possibly at the cost of fluctuations in employment levels.

Persistent balance of payment problems are a feature of the present rather than the past and this could be the consequence, not so much of instability, as of a new kind of institutional development interfering with the old mechanism. This will be the subject of the next chapter, but before we pass on to it an explanatory postscript must be added to avoid possible misunderstanding.

3.5 A Postscript

The following remarks have been relegated to a postscript because they lie outside the main stream of the argument and refer only to a matter of interpretation. Experienced readers of section 3.4 might wish to claim that the Marshall–Lerner condition for stability is much more general than is implied by the conditions 1–6. Such a claim might be justified as follows.

If in equation (3.3.1) above we interpret the quantities X_1' and X_2 as imports into countries 2 and 1 respectively rather than total consumption of commodities 1 and 2, then the algebra right up to the inequality (3.3.8) may be considered to apply to the most complicated model as well as the simplest. The difficulty arises only when we come to interpret the terms like

$$\frac{p \, \Delta X}{X \, \Delta p} \tag{3.5.1}$$

which appear in the answer. In order to identify this expression as an elasticity it was necessary to consider carefully all the changes which might have occurred in all of the variables in the model. An exact definition of the model is essential. The reader should understand that to move from a position like 1 in Fig. 3.1 to an equilibrium may, in the more complicated case, involve changes in other prices than p_2 and also changes in quantities supplied. Again, in the more general case the quantity of a commodity imported is not the same as the quantity consumed. Some may be produced at home. Indeed, if the foreign country is supposed to be the rest of the world it would be close to a logical contradiction to imagine that it produces nothing of the class of goods it imports. It follows that imports depend on a great many things besides prices and total consumption, for they depend also on how much is produced at home. In such a case it is quite wrong to call the terms like (3.5.1) 'elasticity of demand'. The reader in fact need only turn to Chapter 11, section 6, or even Chapter 4, section 4, to discover something of the complexities covered up by the portmanteau expression (3.5.1).

To be quite fair of course we should make it clear that those who quote the Marshall–Lerner condition usually refer to the E_{22} of (3.3.9) as the elasticity of demand *for imports* and not for *importables*, thereby confirming explicitly that what they intend is (3.5.1) and not E_{22} at all. The trouble with this is that we do not know how (3.5.1) is defined until we specify what is supposed to change and what remains constant. It has no existence independent of the model. We do not know its sign or its magnitude or anything else about it whatever. It follows that until we do define (3.5.1) in terms of known or calculable numbers, the Marshall–Lerner condition is nothing more than a 'disguised' way of saying that the exchange mechanism is stable if it is stable. Theory is useless unless it relates observable and measurable variables with other observable and measurable variables. Any attempt to transform the Marshall–Lerner condition until it meets this requirement simply leads back to all of the problems to which we have drawn attention.

EXERCISES

1. Reconsider the argument associated with Fig. 2.2. Suppose that offer curves take the shape illustrated in Fig. 3.2. Show that, to be consistent with consumption patterns B and A for countries 1 and 2 (Fig. 2.2), the terms of trade must be too unfavourable to

country 1 relative to the unstable equilibrium position. Show that nevertheless it is still possible to attain equilibrium at the cost of some unemployment by cutting production in country 1. Is the unemployment equilibrium so attained likely to be better or worse for country 1 than the stable equilibrium H (Fig. 3.2)?

2. Reconsider the argument of section 3.1 applied to the case where offer curves take the shape illustrated in Fig. 3.2. Show that although it is easy to introduce dynamic assumptions which imply instability of the first kind when elasticities are small, there is no plausible dynamic assumption which can turn the unstable equilibrium B (Fig. 3.2) into one which is stable.

3. Quantify the argument of section 3.1 as follows. Let price changes be determined by the following dynamic rule (see section 3.4)

$$p_1(t) = \left[p_1(t-1) \right] \left[\left(\frac{p_1 X_1'}{p_2 X_2} \right)(t-1) \right]$$

which says that the price of exportables for time period t is obtained by multiplying the price in the previous period, $(t-1)$, by the ratio of the value of exports to the value of imports in period $(t-1)$. Thus, if exports exceed imports so that stocks are falling, prices are raised in the following period and vice versa. Now, for convenience, we choose to measure all prices and quantities in the logarithm of the actual figures, so that the rule above implies two equations

$$p_1(t) = p_1(t-1) + p_1(t-1) - p_2(t-1) + X_1'(t-1) - X_2(t-1)$$
$$= 2p_1(t-1) - p_2(t-1) + X_1'(t-1) - X_2(t-1)$$

and similarly for country 2

$$p_2(t) = 2p_2(t-1) - p_1(t-1) - X_1'(t-1) + X_2(t-1).$$

Let $X_1'(t)$ and $X_2(t)$ be given by demand equations

$$X_1'(t) = E_{11}'(p_1(t) - p_2(t)) + 100$$

and $\qquad X_2(t) = E_{22}(p_2(t) - p_1(t)) + 98$

where Es are *constant* elasticities. Note that in the model Y/p_1 and Y'/p_2 remain constant so that the effect of expenditure on demand may be assumed to be incorporated in the constants 100 and 98 which appear in the given equations.

Choose numbers for E'_{11} and E_{22}

(i) such that $(1 + E'_{11} + E_{22})$ is negative and numerically greater than 1;

(ii) such that $(1 + E'_{11} + E_{22})$ is negative but numerically less than 1; and

(iii) such that $(1 + E'_{11} + E_{22})$ is positive and, of course, since Es must be negative, numerically less than 1.

Now choose suitable initial values for p_1 and p_2 and compute their time paths from the given equations for each of the cases (i)–(iii). From these computations show that, in case (i) ps oscillate more and more violently for ever, in case (ii) they oscillate but less and less, coming finally to rest at an equilibrium where

$$(p_1 - p_2) = -\frac{2}{1 + E'_{11} + E_{22}}$$

and in case (iii) no equilibrium can be attained although no oscillations will be observed. Hence confirm numerically what we learned from the diagram (see exercise 2).

4. Suppose that all home producers believe that their stocks are too low. Accordingly they raise prices above the 'equilibrium' level with the twofold objective of earning higher profits and at the same time allowing production to overtake sales. What would happen in these circumstances if the government, alarmed by the balance of payments deficit created, depreciated the currency? Treat this problem for both the high elasticity and the low elasticity case.

5. The United Kingdom devalued its currency both in 1949 and in 1967. Examine the behaviour of price indices of exports and imports at these times. Did the real terms of trade improve or worsen? What are the implications of the published figures for the price-setting behaviour of producers?

6. Currency revaluations occurred in France (Dec 1958), in Canada (May 1962) in Germany (Mar 1961) and Holland (Mar 1961). Examine movements of import/export price indices around these dates as in exercise 5. Extend your inquiries to at least two years after the given dates. Again consider the implications for price-fixing.

7. Investigate changes in the level of employment following the French, British and Canadian devaluations and the German and Dutch appreciations (see exercise 6). How far do you consider these changes accord with the theory set out in Chapters 2 and 3?

4 The Balance of Payments in the Twentieth Century

4.1 ON THE UNPLEASANT NECESSITY FOR CHANGE

IN this chapter we come to a difficulty which, as hinted in section 3.4, is in all probability peculiar to the twentieth century. As an introduction to this it has seemed worth while to reflect for a moment upon an odd and distressing feature of the continuing story of economic evolution. The solution of one problem seems often to give rise to another which is both unexpected and as painful as that just escaped. The explanation of this is not too difficult.

The one consistent feature of modern society is development and growth. Technical change and increases in production per head inevitably mean changes in relative prices, in techniques of production, and in the distribution of the work force. This in turn imposes economic pressures upon individuals which are unpleasant. They involve businessmen in capital losses where equipment becomes obsolete and require some workers to move from their place of employment or suffer a reduction in real income, either relatively or absolutely. Railway employees, for example, are at present among the lowest paid in the community, not necessarily because they are the least skilled but because their sector of the economy is a declining sector. Railways as a means of transport are tending to be displaced.

Individuals who suffer as a consequence of economic development naturally appeal in one way or another for relief. And the relief provided usually takes the form of half-hearted government regulation to stem the economic tide. Unemployment benefits inhibit necessary labour mobility rather then encourage it. Subsidies are offered to declining industries, or industries are nationalised and allowed to continue in production at a loss. Undesirably large differences in earnings between individuals are corrected through the tax system rather than by the provision of more equal education and training opportunities. Seldom, if ever, do we find positive attempts to induce individuals to move *with* the pull of economic forces instead of against them. This is partly because of a human tendency to resist change in personal habits and to object to government 'direction', and partly because economic difficulties are not always immediately recognised for what they are. That is, they are not seen simply as signals indicating that our own inventions and changes in tastes *require* us to change our production habits whether we like it or not, but as mysterious ailments whose symptoms have to be treated. It is hardly surprising than any 'solution' of the problem of a declining industry which relieves the industry of the need to decline inevitably leads to another 'crisis' somewhere else in the economy. It is the same with all economic change which is resisted. Let us consider how this applies to international trade.

Growth induces change in the equilibrium level of the real terms of trade. The box in Fig. 1.2 gets larger, not necessarily in proportion. The offer curves move and the real terms of trade line must change if no difficulties are to arise. In earlier chapters we have seen what this implies.

With the simplest model either the home price of exportables must alter, or the foreign price of importables q_2, or the exchange rate e. On the other hand experience of wage cuts has taught labour how to combine into trade unions to fight against reductions in money wages. The argument that wage cuts must be imposed solely to permit necessary reductions in price has never been found sufficiently impressive by labour to influence their resistance, even though such a policy might leave *real* welfare unchanged. The obvious 'solution' to the problem of labour unrest is 'no wage cuts' and *ipso facto* no price cuts. Similarly experience of the disruptive consequences of rising prices (inflation) has taught governments the importance of maintaining the value of money. The 'solution' to the problem of inflation is a tight control on money supply. Thus p_1 may not fall and q_2 may not rise.

Finally, experiments in fluctuating exchange rates have demonstrated inconveniences and difficulties already touched upon. Pegged exchange rates are now the rule; indeed they have become not only the rule but in banking circles an object of almost mystical reverence. The only possible adjusting mechanism left is the employment mechanism described in Chapter 2 see Fig. 2.2.† Remembering that the development of trade unionism ran parallel with the growing

† Some readers may be tempted to suspect that this dilemma is an imaginary one, being only a consequence of the over-simplified model. In the real world there is more than one relative price. But the argument above still applies. If trade unions prevent every price from falling, relative price adjustment can take place only if all prices are rising (not proportionately). But this is inflation on any interpretation of the word!

understanding of the way in which the money supply should be controlled, both being well established by the 1920s, it would not seem difficult, with our present hindsight, to have predicted the incredible unemployment situation which followed.

We should expect today that any solution to the unemployment problem would lead us back to inflation or balance of payments difficulties, and up to a point, since 1945, this has been our experience. On the other hand it is usually the case that old difficulties when they reappear do so in a form sufficiently different to render them not immediately recognisable. The economic environment is not the same. In the present case the struggle with unemployment left its mark both upon our ideas and upon our institutions, with consequences which we attempt to explain in the next section.

4.2 An 'Equilibrium' Balance of Payments Problem

So far in the whole of our argument we have supposed that, in any given time period, the total spending of the community is precisely equal to the value of its production. In all of the diagrams (Figs. 1.2– 3.2) offer curves began from the top left-hand corner of the box. It is important to understand that this need not be so.

In a general way, of course, the proceeds of sales of a firm's product are used to pay the incomes of the individuals who co-operate in the production process. To be specific,

total revenue from product = costs plus profits.

Costs are payments to raw-material producers plus wages and rents to property owners. Payments to raw-material producers are in turn used to pay wages and rents, so that

total revenue = wages + rents + profits = incomes.

This means that if all incomes are spent in any period, then total spending equals the value of production, which justifies the assumption we have used up to this point.

In practice, however, all income need not be spent in the time period in which it is earned. Conversely, some spending may come out of titles to wealth accumulated in past periods. This applies to the government, to industry and to individuals. The government may spend less than it collects in taxation during the period, in which case it is said to have a budget *surplus*; or it may spend more than it collects in taxation, either by borrowing funds accumulated in past periods or by creating money for the purpose,† in which case there is a budget *deficit*. Similarly businesses may withhold profits due to shareholders, thereby saving, or they may borrow and spend, or spend their own savings. Finally, individuals may save or dis-save. If total spending by all sectors from titles to wealth, accumulated in past periods (or newly created), exceeds current earnings not spent, then total spending will be greater than the value of total production and vice versa.

The reader with some knowledge of employment theory who is perhaps puzzled by this unconventional way of putting the matter should recall that, in our simple model, total production includes both the production of final consumer goods and of capital (investment) goods. That is, either or both of the composite commodities 'exportables' and 'importables' of the box diagram might very well be made up not only of items like food, which we consume, but also of the machinery which we use to produce food. Sales of machinery depend just as much upon price as sales of food, so that there is no contradiction involved in our treatment so far.

One of the great achievements of economists in the past thirty years is a notable improvement in their understanding of the ways in which the government can influence the extent to which total spending out of accumulated titles to wealth exceeds or falls short of new accumulation – in other words, in their understanding of ways to influence total spending in the period. Fiscal policy (i.e. taxation policy) can be used as a weapon, either directly by running a budget surplus or deficit, or indirectly by controlling the average amount of individual saving. As an alternative or a complement, monetary policy, i.e. manipulation of the rate of interest and/or control of the money supply, will have an effect upon the willingness of businessmen to spend on capital equipment. Today it is the common practice of governments to bring about an increase in total spending when stocks are piling up and production falling, and to discourage spending when stocks are running down or prices rising.

Suppose now that we have a situation of disequilibrium with the terms of trade too much in our favour, as *MU* in Fig. 1.3. Fig. 4.1 below depicts this situation except that, to simplify the diagram, offer curves from the corner of the box *M* have not been drawn. As

† When the borrowing is from the banks it is not always easy to distinguish exactly between these two operations, as students of monetary theory will understand.

we begin from disequilibrium the offer curves, if drawn, would intersect at some point *C* below the line *MU* (see Fig. 1.3). Suppose, in fact, that the offer curve for country 1 cuts *MU* at *R* and that for country 2 cuts *MU* at *A*, as in Figs. 1.3 and 4.1. This is of course consistent only with the two curves intersecting below *MU*. The points *A* and *R* are marked on Fig. 4.1.

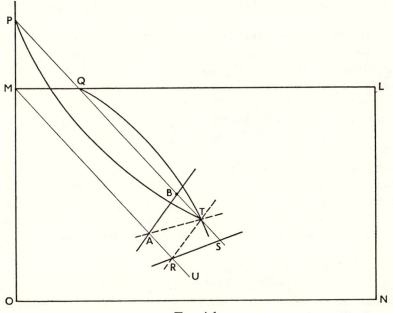

FIG. 4.1

As previously explained (Chapter 1), in the initial position there is a deficit in world demand for exportables and a surplus world demand for importables. Stocks of exportables are rising whilst stocks of importables are falling.

This, according to modern doctrine, is exactly the circumstance in which the home government will take action to increase spending, although it should of course simply devalue the currency. The foreign government on the other hand will be tempted to decrease total spending. Ironically this is the *opposite* action to that envisaged in the classical exchange adjustment mechanism described in Chapter 2.

If the excess world demand for importables is met out of stocks and if the deficit demand for exportables is countered by increasing stocks rather than by cutting employment, then there will be a drain of gold and/or foreign currency reserves abroad. A nineteenth-century government, anxious to avoid loss of confidence in the home currency, would seek to maintain the ratio between gold reserves and paper money. It would raise the rate of interest and take steps to reduce the supply of paper money to match the fall in reserves. This, it was supposed, would bring about a fall in home prices and hence the right movement in the real terms of trade, although in many cases it probably led to equilibrium by a cut in employment, as explained in section 2.6.

A modern government, however, fearing unemployment rather than loss of confidence in the currency, would do just the opposite. The building-up of stocks (i.e. the failure of demand for exportables) would suggest a *reduction* in the rate of interest and the creation of more money. This will induce more spending on the part of business-men and, if the creation of more money is associated with a reduction in taxation and a budget deficit, more spending on the part of individuals.

But total spending was initially equal to the value of total production. If spending increases as a consequence of government policy it will become greater than the value of total production. Abroad, the foreign government, worried by the excess world demand for its product, may reduce total spending below the value of production.

In Fig. 4.1 the offer curve for the home country is shown commencing from the point P. Total spending, measured in units of the product, is OP rather than OM. There is excess spending amounting to MP. The offer curve for the foreign country on the other hand begins from Q, indicating that total spending abroad LQ is less than total production abroad LM.

As drawn, the offer curves conveniently intersect at a point T which lies on the straight line $PQTS$. This means that

(i) Measured in terms of the home country's money unit, the excess spending over production in country 1 is exactly equal to the underspending in the rest of the world. This must be so since the ratio PM/MQ is equal to the real terms of trade ratio PT which is the ratio of prices p_2/p_1 in country 1.

Hence $$PM/MQ = p_2/p_1$$

or $$p_1(PM) = p_2(MQ)$$

(ii) World demand and world supply are exactly matched at the pattern of consumption *T*. This is indicated, as usual, by the co-incidence of the terms of trade lines *PT* and *QT* passing through the total expenditure points *P* and *Q*, and the point *T* of intersection of offer curves. The reader should not allow his understanding of this to be made more difficult by the fact that the terms of trade lines (or budget possibility lines) *PT* and *QT* for the two countries are now clearly distinct. This has not been the case previously only because both offer curves have commenced from the same point, namely, the top left-hand corner of the box.

The fact that in Fig. 4.1 the terms of trade line *PS* lies parallel to the old terms of trade line *MU* means also that:

(iii) No money price need have changed in either country and no relative price *can* have changed.

In practice none of the events implied by (i), (ii) and (iii) need occur. There is no reason at all why, in the first instance, the underspending abroad should exactly match the overspending. The offer curve for country 2 need not begin from the point *Q* which is the point of intersection of *PT* and *ML*. On the other hand the real terms of trade *must* be the same for both countries so that the lines *PT* and *QT* must be parallel even if they are not coincident as drawn. But if they are parallel and *not* coincident it is impossible that world supply and world demand should be equal for both commodities, for supply and demand to be equal requires that both budget lines should pass through the unique point of intersection of offer curves. The reader should satisfy himself on this point by constructing and interpreting a diagram in which *PT* and *QT* are not coincident.

On the other hand if world supply and world demand are not equal we should expect further adjustments in total spending to be induced until they are, that is, until *PT* and *QT are* coincident and conditions (i) and (ii) above are satisfied. We have also assumed (iii) that relative prices remain unchanged so that Fig. 4.1 will apply as drawn.

Attention is now drawn to the line *RT* on Fig. 4.1. This passes through the point *R* on *MU* which represents the pattern of demand in country 1 at relative prices *MU* and total spending *OM*. It also passes through *T* which is the pattern of demand with the *same* relative prices but with total spending *OP*. In the same way other points on the line *RT* are intended to mark out the patterns of demand generated as total spending increases from *OM* to *OP* with prices constant. The line *RT* is known to economists as an 'Engel' curve. The slope, or steepness, of the Engel curve is closely associated with the 'income effect' on consumption referred to in section 1.2. It measures the ratio of the increased quantities of importables and exportables consumed when total spending is increased with prices constant.

In the same way we have an Engel curve for country 2 shown on Fig. 4.1 as *TA*. It will be noticed that a great deal depends on the slopes of Engel curves, for in order to find a point *T* satisfying the conditions (i), (ii) and (iii) above it is necessary to assume that *AT* and *RT* converge as drawn. On the other hand there is no reason to suppose that they should. Country 2's offer curve might very well cut *QT* at *B* and country 1's offer curve might cut *PT* at *S*, yielding Engel curves *RS* and *BA*.

In this latter case it is easy to see that government reactions to approaching unemployment at home and inflation abroad have achieved quite the wrong result. In the initial position stocks of exportables were rising, which induced an increase in home spending. Abroad stocks of importables were falling calling for a cut in spending, say, to *LQ* (Fig. 4.1). But if the new demand patterns are *S* and *B* instead of *T* it is easy to see that stocks of exportables will rise even faster and stocks of importables fall even faster as a result of the action taken. Still more changes in total spending will be called for leading to an even worse situation.

The reason for this is simple. The rise in home demand for exportables caused by increased spending has been more than offset by the fall in foreign demand caused by the cut in spending abroad. This will occur if the foreign country spends a larger proportion of any increase in income on exportables than the home country, or, as economists say, if the foreign 'marginal propensity to consume' exportables is greater than the home marginal propensity to consume the same commodity. We shall later derive an exact algebraic result which demonstrates even more precisely the crucial role of the slope of Engel curves.

In practice it seems likely that government manipulation of total spending in the unstable case would alter the real terms of trade. In the home country, despite the best efforts of the government to stimulate spending, the excess of production over sales grows worse. Abroad demand increases despite attempts to restrict it. Prices at home will fall and prices abroad will rise. If this occurs the pressure may be removed. Offer curves from *P* and *Q* through *S* and *B* respectively will in all probability intersect somewhere between the parallel lines *MU* and *PS*. As the terms of trade move against the home country and *PS* becomes steeper, world demand for importables will fall. The foreign government will react by increasing spending so that Q and the offer curve beginning from Q move to the left together. A common point of intersection of PS and the two offer curves will soon be found. The reader should again construct his own diagram on the lines of Fig. 4.1 to test this.

We now observe that even in the stable case the real terms of trade may change, for the same pressures are there. The only difference between the stable and the unstable case is that in the former the terms of trade need not change. In either case a position where total world supply equals total world demand can be found, as illustrated in Fig. 4.2, with implications which require very careful consideration.

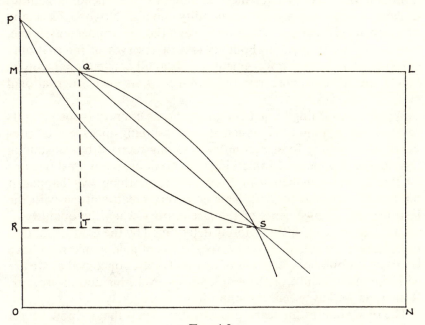

FIG. 4.2

World supply, as we have seen, is equal to world demand in both commodities. Employment is full and there is no pressure to change prices. There is, however, an excess of imports over exports from the point of view of country 1. Country 1 is also spending more than the value of its production. But there is no *automatic* pressure to adjust the balance of payments.

Country 1 is producing OM. Of this it exports $MR = QT$ of exportables in exchange for *TS* units of importables at the real terms of trade *PS*. The balance, $RT = MQ$, of its total consumption of importables, *RS*, is paid for in gold or foreign currency out of foreign currency reserves. *PM* measures the loss of gold in units of the exportable commodity. In other words, *PM* units of exportables could be bought with the amount of gold loss at current prices. Clearly, in money terms, the excess consumption is equal to the deficit on the balance of payments which is equal to the gold loss.

In the foreign country exactly the opposite situation prevails. Country 2 is consuming less than it produces by the amount of its export surplus which is equal in money terms to its receipts of gold or its equivalent. All this means that there are commodities to buy in both countries exactly equivalent in value to total spending without drawing on or adding to commodity stocks. No one feels any pressure to change the situation except the government at home, which will be concerned about its loss of reserves of international currency. The foreign government, if it is at all conventional, will be highly gratified to note the building-up of its own international currency reserves.

What is happening in fact is that the home country is spending its reserves on commodities which it is consuming in excess of production, whilst the foreign country is saving reserves by consuming less than its production. Something must be done, but it must be done *by the positive application of some policy*. Nothing will happen if matters are allowed to drift. This is in very great contrast with the institutional arrangements of the last century when the quantity of money was, by convention, closely determined by the gold stock, that is, by the international currency stock. Loss of gold would then have led to an automatic restriction of credit. Today, concerned as we are with the maintenance of the employment level, this does not occur. Rather, as we have seen, the opposite is more likely.

The really interesting feature of this situation is that we now have a deficit on the balance of payments to which the analysis of Chapters 2 and 3 does not apply. *It is no longer true that a deficit on the balance of payments is the immediate signal for an exchange-rate depreciation* even in the simplest case and even though the stability condition (3.3.9) of Chapter 3 may be met. We have come in fact to the example promised in section 2.8.

This is easily seen as follows. First, we note from Fig. 4.2 that it is no use simply to depreciate the currency by itself. This would do no more than steepen the real terms of trade lines *PS* and *QS* and upset the equilibrium in world supply and demand. What is needed, first and foremost, is a cut in home spending equal to the deficit, and an increase in spending abroad equal to the foreign surplus. This brings total spending at home and abroad into line with total production. As we have seen, *no balance of payments equilibrium with full employment is possible unless this condition is met*, whatever the real terms of trade.

We notice in passing that a cut in home spending of itself induces an increase in spending abroad if the foreign government is pledged to maintain full employment. For a cut in home spending means a cut in imports, which implies a failure of world demand for importables. Spending abroad must be increased in compensation.

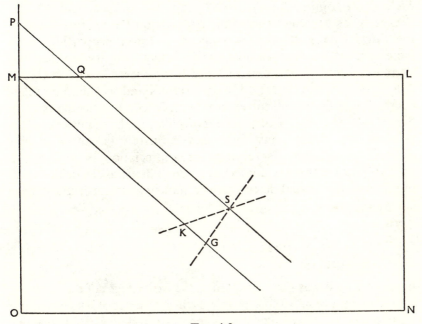

FIG. 4.3

In Fig. 4.3 we illustrate the position when total spending has been adjusted. *PS* in Fig. 4.3 is precisely the *PS* of Fig. 4.2. Offer curves from *P* and *Q* intersect at *S*. The adjustment of total spending to total production implies that both offer curves now begin from *M*. For the moment the terms of trade are unchanged so that *MG* is parallel to *PS*. Suppose, as case (i), that offer curve 1 cuts *MG* in *K* and offer curve 2 cuts *MG* in *G*. Then the intersection point of the offer curves must lie to the north-east of *MG* in the figure. The terms of trade must move *in favour* of country 1 to achieve an equilibrium. The proper government policy would be to cut spending and to *increase* the price of the home currency in terms of the foreign, that is, to *appreciate* the currency rather than depreciate it.

Case (i) implies that *KS* is the Engel curve of country 1 and *SG* the Engel curve of country 2. But consider now a case (ii). Suppose, as is quite possible, that the offer curve for country 1 cuts *MG* in *G* instead of *K*, and that the offer curve for country 2 cuts *MG* in *K* instead of *G*. The offer curves must now intersect to the south-west of *MG*, and the terms of trade must move against country 1 to find an equilibrium. In this case the proper policy is to cut spending and to *depreciate* the currency. *GS* is now the Engel curve for country 1 and *SK* that for country 2.

Clearly, as expected, everything depends on the relative slopes of the Engel curves. If country 1 spends a lower proportion of an increment of income on importables than country 2, then the decreased spending at home matched by increased spending abroad will increase world demand for importables and by the same token decrease world demand for exportables. To correct this the price of exportables must fall relative to importables. In the opposite case the price of importables must fall. These adjustments can be quickly effected by currency depreciation or appreciation respectively. It should be noted that the numerical value of demand elasticities is *not* in this case the crucial determinant of policy as it appeared to be in Chapter 3.

4.3 THE SAME PROBLEM WITH A CLASS OF NON-TRADED COMMODITIES

In section 1.5 it was promised that in the early stages of this book we should introduce only those problems the character of which does not change out of all recognition when the model is disaggregated. Although the work of the present chapter for the most part satisfies this criterion, attention must be drawn to one rather important feature of the more general case.

Suppose that we do observe a balance of payments deficit, with total world supply equal to total world demand for each commodity, just as in the previous section. But suppose at the same time that there exists in each country a class of goods excluded from trade, with prices p_3 and q_3 respectively. Precisely as before there is no hope of adjusting the deficit unless the country in deficit reduces aggregate expenditure until it equals the value of output (including the value of non-traded goods produced), and until the foreign country increases its expenditure in the same way. These changes in expenditure (all prices constant) will, according to the relative magnitudes of the home and foreign marginal propensities to consume, leave either an excess world demand or a deficit world demand for exportables, but we do not know which without measurement of the crucial marginal propensities. The same applies to importables. Up to this point the problem is the same as that of section 4.2. The expenditure changes must ordinarily be accompanied by some change in the real terms of trade.

But we now have an added complication. The cut in home expenditure (prices constant) necessarily implies a deficit world demand for the home non-traded commodity. This must be so, for the cut in home demand is not offset by any increase in the foreign demand as is the case for traded goods. To put the matter another way, the foreign marginal propensity to consume home non-traded goods must be zero by definition of a non-traded good. Only the home demand reduction is relevant.

Not only therefore do we have to adjust the real terms of trade, but we have also to find some way of adjusting the relative prices of traded and non-traded commodities so that supply and demand are once again equated in the non-traded sector. How is this to be done?

The theoretical attractiveness of currency depreciation as a policy stems from the fact that it is an easy and convenient way of adjusting the real terms of trade in whatever direction is required, provided we know the direction. But it is not immediately obvious that either appreciation or depreciation will help to attain the required change in the non-traded commodity price. Furthermore, even the direction of this change is not as obvious as it might seem. It is true that we know that the expenditure cut without price changes must of necessity create a deficit demand for commodity 3 at home. One would expect therefore that its price must fall relatively. On the other hand when the real terms of trade change both the demand for and the supply of the non-traded commodity will be affected. If the price of importables falls relative to exportables and importables are a good substitute for non-traded commodities, demand may shift from commodity 3 towards importables. How do we know that this shift may not invalidate and reverse the argument previously used to establish that p_3 must fall?

The truth of the matter is that international disequilibrium, like any other kind of disequilibrium, involves an adjustment of expenditures and prices in directions which are not always obvious. Ordinary competitive forces are usually supposed to operate to adjust prices through a supply/demand mechanism. The foreign exchange market is but one part of that system and must not be expected to do the whole of the work. On the other hand it is of the utmost importance to trace the part it might play, and the present author's inquiries in this direction have led to conclusions in some ways different from those of many classical writers on the subject.

To begin with we are not entirely ignorant of the probable necessary price changes, and we should know them precisely if we knew the numerical values of the relevant demand and supply responses (see section 4.4 below). As a first step therefore it is worth while calculating algebraically the crucial price changes in terms of these responses whose magnitudes we might hope to discover independently. This is in effect what we did diagrammatically in section 4.2 for the simple case, and it is what we shall do explicitly in section 4.4 for the same case. If we could do the algebra more generally it might be possible to learn much more than the literary argument above suggests is possible. In the very simple case, for example, we are clearly able to say that appreciation or depreciation is appropriate according to the numerical values of marginal propensities to consume. If the simple model could be presumed to be reasonably realistic in some particular case, even the relatively trivial work of section 4.2 already gives us a most valuable and immediate policy conclusion. We need no more than the roughest estimate of the *relative* magnitudes of the relevant marginal propensities.

Unfortunately, to work the algebra of the more general case is beyond the capacity of the student who has read only thus far. On the other hand by the time Chapter 19 is reached no further guidance will be needed and the reader will find it a simple matter to do the calculations for himself. Accordingly, the problem has been left as exercises (5 and 6, pp. 112–14). In the meantime, however, we shall give the conclusions and consider what they imply.

To avoid any misunderstanding we restate the problem. It is supposed that each of two countries produce both importables and exportables and its own class of non-traded goods, and that the supplies coming forward are dependent on prices. We observe a balance of trade deficit for the home country at a time when there is full employment of all resources everywhere. It is observed also that there is no running-down or building-up of stocks, so that world supply equals world demand everywhere. We wish to know what changes in expenditure and relative prices, at home and abroad, will correct the deficit, given that full employment is not to be disturbed. When we know what these changes are we may then inquire whether currency appreciation or depreciation is the more likely to bring them about. The algebra indicates that what is necessary is:

(i) A cut in money spending. This must be just, and only just, sufficient to equate total money spending with the total value of all production at home.

(ii) An equivalent increase in total spending abroad.

(iii) A fall in the price of home non-traded commodities relative to the average price of traded commodities.

(iv) A rise in the price of foreign non-traded commodities relative to the average price of traded commodities.

(v) Some change in the real terms of trade which is likely to be small relative to the price changes (iii) and (iv).

The first thing to be noted is that the intuitive argument of the third and fourth paragraphs of this section, suggesting the need for (iii) and (iv), is substantially justified despite the later doubts cast upon it. We observe also that the necessary terms of trade change is as indeterminate as it was in the simpler case and that the need for expenditure adjustment remains as before.

Now consider very carefully the dynamics of the problem. Suppose that, whatever the desired direction of the real terms of trade change, the home country depreciates its currency. Evidently the home price of importables must immediately rise, unless the foreign country is willing to reduce prices in foreign currency, which is unlikely. The foreign price of exportables could be reduced, since a given quantity of foreign currency now converts into a larger sum than before when expressed in home currency. But will producers reduce price? Not necessarily, since there is no failure of demand for their product abroad at the given foreign price.

On the other hand there may be a failure of demand for exportables at home partly because of (i) but also because of the real income loss due to the rise in the home price of importables. Hence the home producer will try to sell more exportables abroad, first because of the higher earnings per unit in terms of home currency and second, because of rising demand abroad. Rising demand abroad may come about as a consequence of the foreign country's extra spending (ii) undertaken to offset unemployment, which in turn is due to reduced sales of importables in the home country.

Suppose that in view of all this there is no immediate reduction in the foreign price of exportables. The real terms of trade do not immediately change. Furthermore, the switch of exportables away from the home market might easily raise their price in the home market. Indeed, it must do if prices are to be the same everywhere in the world when expressed in the same currency.

Notice now that, parodoxically, depreciation has, in the home country, left the real terms of trade unchanged, at the same time raising the price of all traded commodities relative to non-traded as required by (iii). Abroad the increased spending might very well raise the price of non-traded goods, so inducing the necessary change (iv). Ordinary market mechanisms could then conceivably operate to bring about the real terms of trade adjustment (v) which is in any case small relative to (iii) and (iv).

We have now discovered a case where currency depreciation could work even though the desired change seems to call for currency appreciation, exactly the reverse policy to that applied. But clearly the story outlined depends very heavily upon the assumed timing of events. It would not be hard to make dynamic assumptions leading to almost any result we care to choose.

Finally, it is important to draw yet another moral from the argument we have set out. All static algebraic and diagrammatic treatments of our subject must of necessity operate in terms of *relative* prices. Diagrammatically, we have price ratios as the slope of a line (e.g. *MG* in Fig. 4.3), whilst with the algebra it is necessary to keep one price – the numeraire price – constant (or two prices if we change the exchange rate). On the other hand in a dynamic story and in the real world *all* prices may change and, as previously explained, any rise in the general level of prices at home relative to abroad will act as the precise equivalent of an exchange appreciation whenever it occurs. It is this fact which makes the dynamics so complex.

In the example of this section exchange depreciation failed to move the real terms of trade against the depreciating country because it encouraged an offsetting or more than offsetting rise in the home price of exportables. In a dynamic setting this could occur even with the simple type of economy envisaged by the naïve aggregate version of the model. On the other hand it makes no sense to allow offsetting of this kind when we are looking only at different 'equilibrium' positions, since these imply different relative prices. If, despite exchange depreciation, no change in the real terms of trade takes place (in, say, the model of Fig. 3.1), because the depreciation is offset by a home price rise, then nothing happens in the model for us to observe. In short, treatments which are not dynamic have only limited (but nevertheless important) value. We can learn what *relative* price changes are necessary to move from some undesirable situation to one more desirable, and we may, by algebraic methods, evaluate these changes numerically in terms of standard demand responses as in section 3.3; but we do not thereby learn very much about how such changes are to be attained. The algebraic results may, and usually do, aid speculation on the probable dynamics, but they do not represent any substitute for the dynamic argument itself. The dynamics must always be an implicit or explicit addition.

This book is largely concerned with static versions of the model, not because dynamics is unimportant, but because it is not really possible usefully to study dynamics away from the computer. Very few dynamic results of any real value can be obtained by algebraic methods. Nevertheless, the first step required if we wish to get from *A* to *B* is to find out where *B* is, and this is the object of comparative static inquiry.

In the next section we present an algebraic version of the work of section 4.2, partly as a training for more important work to come, but partly also to show how we express numerically the conditions which demand a favourable or unfavourable movement of the real terms of trade to correct an imbalance of trade, as the case may be. For the time being we revert to the more simple model, but the reader should take care not to miss the concluding remarks of section 4.5.

4.4 MORE ALGEBRA

The reader will recall that the problem of section 4.2 was essentially the same as that of section 4.3, but without a non-traded goods sector in either country. Beginning from a position of trade deficit with full employment and world supply equal to world demand, we wish to correct this without at the same time either upsetting full employment or creating excess demand or supply for any commodity.

We proceed at first very much as in Chapter 3, supposing that any required change in the real terms of trade is achieved by changing p_2 and q_2 (where q_i is the ith foreign price), leaving p_1, q_1 and the exchange rate e unaltered. At the risk of unnecessary repetition we remind the student once again that the numerical result obtained will be exactly the same whether we adopt this course, whether we keep p_1 and q_2 constant changing e, or whether we hold p_2 and q_2 constant changing p_1 and q_1. Choice of numeraire does not matter when interest is centred on *relative* price changes only.

As in (3.3.6) we have

$$\frac{\Delta B}{\Delta p_2} = p_1\left(\frac{\Delta X_1'}{\Delta p_2}\right) - p_2\left(\frac{\Delta X_2}{\Delta p_2}\right) - X_2 \qquad (4.4.1)$$

Up to this point the steps are the same. The difference occurs when we come to interpret expressions like $\Delta X/\Delta p$. And this is a complicated matter which we must digress to explain.

The quantity sold, X, of any commodity is dependent on the prices p_1 and p_2 *and* on the total spending Y. Symbolically we express this

$$X_1 = X_1(p_1, p_2, Y) \qquad (4.4.2)$$

which is read X_1 is a function of p_1, p_2 and Y. This means simply that if p_1 changes X_1 changes, if p_2 changes X_1 changes, and if Y changes X_1 changes. Or, to put it yet another way, X_1 is determined by some formula, the exact form of which we do not know. It might be for example that

$$X_1 = 6p_1 + p_2 + 3Y$$

or

$$X_1 = p_1 p_2 + Y.$$

Once p_1, p_2 and Y are known we could work out the actual value of X_1 if we knew the formula.

The fact that we do not know the formula is fortunately not a matter for concern, since we are less interested in predicting what X_1 will be when prices and income have changed considerably than we are in predicting what it will be at the next moment of time. This is equivalent to saying that we are more interested in rates of change at the present moment than we are in the values which X_1, p_1, p_2 and Y will take at some distant time, when they are very different from now.

Because of this it is more convenient to write the functions (4.4.2) in a different form making use of the symbolic language ordinarily employed by mathematicians. Symbols are introduced not because we are about to appeal to some profound mathematical theorem, but simply to save time in exposition. We use the common mathematical notation first because, if we did not, it would be necessary to invent new words unnecessarily, and second because the reader may at a later stage find it of great value to have met and understood the language now in ordinary use in advanced work.

Given any relationship or function such as (4.4.2), we might equally well write

$$dX_1 = \frac{\partial X_1}{\partial p_1} dp_1 + \frac{\partial X_1}{\partial p_2} dp_2 + \frac{\partial X_1}{\partial Y} dY \qquad (4.4.3)$$

where dX_1 means the total *change* in X_1 due to the changes dp_1, dp_2 and dY in p_1, p_2 and Y respectively. The symbol $\frac{\partial X_1}{\partial p_1}$ means the *rate* of change of X_1 as p_1 changes *with* p_2 *and* Y *held constant*. $\frac{\partial X_1}{\partial p_2}$ is the rate of change of X_1 as p_2 changes with p_1 and Y constant. $\frac{\partial X_1}{\partial Y}$ is the rate of change of X_1 as Y changes with p_1 and p_2 held constant.

Clearly, if p_1 changes X_1 at the *rate* $\frac{\partial X_1}{\partial p_1}$, and if p_1 itself changes by an amount dp_1, then $\frac{\partial X_1}{\partial p_1} dp_1$ is the total change in X_1 due to the change dp_1 in p_1. The remaining two terms in (4.4.3) are the total changes in X_1 due to the changes dp_2 and dY on the same principle. The sum of the three terms is the grand total of all the changes in X_1, i.e. dX_1.

The reader may find it helpful to think of a three-dimensional example which can be visualised geometrically. Suppose that X_1 measures height above sea level and that p_1 and p_2 measure latitude and longitude respectively. Since height depends on location, X_1 is a function of p_1 and p_2, for p_1 and p_2 determine the position of a point on the earth's surface which has a given height above sea level. The corresponding expression (4.4.3) (without the third term) may now be interpreted as the total change in height dX_1 due to a movement dp_1 units due west, together with a movement dp_2 units due north. Any shift from any point on a map to any other can, of course, be expressed as a displacement of so many feet west and so many feet north, provided a negative number of feet west is treated as a positive move east and a negative move north is treated as a positive move south. Using this principle it is easy to see that, if we begin from a point on a hill and move to any other point on the hill, the change in height between the two points can be worked out by multiplying the slope of the hill in a westerly direction by the westerly component of the displacement and adding the slope of the hill in a northerly direction multiplied by the northerly component of the displacement. $\dfrac{\partial X_1}{\partial p_1}$ and $\dfrac{\partial X_1}{\partial p_2}$ are simply the slopes of the hill in the westerly and northerly direction. This is a particular interpretation of the general principle which enables us to write an expression like (4.4.3) for *any* function whatever.

In the case of consumer demand functions it is sometimes useful to divide both sides of the form (4.4.3) by X_1 and rewrite it as

$$\frac{dX_1}{X_1} = \left(\frac{p_1}{X_1}\frac{\partial X_1}{\partial p_1}\right)\frac{dp_1}{p_1} + \left(\frac{p_2}{X_1}\frac{\partial X_1}{\partial p_2}\right)\frac{dp_2}{p_2} + \left(\frac{Y}{X_1}\frac{\partial X_1}{\partial Y}\right)\frac{dY}{Y} \quad (4.4.4)$$

(Observe that this, in effect, is how we wrote demand equations in exercise 3 to Chapter 3.)

The object of the manipulation (4.4.4) is to get rid of units for reasons explained in Chapter 3 (p. 58). The reader will note that the $\left(\dfrac{p_1}{X_1}\dfrac{\partial X_1}{\partial p_1}\right)$ which occurs in the first term is the fundamental elasticity of demand referred to in Chapter 3 (p. 58). $\left(\dfrac{p_2}{X_1}\dfrac{\partial X_1}{\partial p_2}\right)$ in term 2 is the so-called *cross* elasticity of demand, i.e. the proportionate response of X_1 to change in p_2. Similarly $\dfrac{Y}{X_1}\dfrac{\partial X_1}{\partial Y}$ is known as income elasticity.

It is important now to understand the distinction between an elasticity, which is a fundamental number describing the feelings and actions of the community whose behaviour is under examination, and the changes $\dfrac{dX_1}{X_1}, \dfrac{dp_1}{p_1}, \dfrac{dp_2}{p_2}$ and $\dfrac{dY}{Y}$ which are the changes as they occur in the problem under review. For example the latter may be the changes which we note following a currency depreciation or a cut in spending. On the other hand the elasticities which we shall write E_{11}, E_{12} and E_Y are invariant.[†] As long as consumers' tastes remain

† But see Chapter 13, section 2, especially footnote (p. 370).

the same it is reasonable to suppose that they will always respond in the same way to given price changes. This remains true whatever policy is followed. Price responses are like the steepness of the hill in the north and west directions, which remain the same whether we walk north-east or north-west. The changes dX_1, dp_1, dp_2 and dY, however, are analogous to the direction we choose to move and are dependent on what we are trying to do at any moment, that is, on whether we are trying to get up the hill or down, or diagonally across.

The reader should now try to understand that the essential method of all economics, whether the approach is by literary argument, by the use of diagrams or by explicit algebra, is as follows. A set of equations like the consumer demand equation (4.4.4) is postulated. These equations define an 'equilibrium' position. For example, we may have a supply function indicating how much will be supplied at a given price together with a demand function, like (4.4.2), and an equilibrium rule saying that supply must be equal to demand. This is a 'model'. Provided we have enough equations the model determines a set of equilibrium values of the variables, e.g. prices, quantity supplied and quantity demanded. Solving these equations means finding values of the variables at which all equations are satisfied. Usually in economics we have also a dynamic story to explain how the system *moves* towards its unique equilibrium, but this is not important to the procedure here described.

Having defined the model we now ask questions of it. A question ordinarily involves a disturbance of the equilibrium, brought about by some policy change. For example, in the model of section 4.2 we have, implicitly, two demand equations, a balance of payments equation, and equations defining expenditure, all of which determine the initial equilibrium, T, in Fig. 4.1. Equilibrium is then disturbed by exchange-rate changes, from T (Fig. 4.1) to the desired position of balanced trade.

In a case of this kind the equations of the model may just as easily be used to solve for the *changes* in the variables between one equilibrium and another as they may be for solving for the actual values of the variables themselves. To solve for *changes*, however, we have first to take changes in the equations of the model, that is, we have to set out the model in the form (4.4.3) or (4.4.4) rather than in the form (4.4.2). As it happens, equations (4.4.1) and (4.4.4) are two of those which we shall need for the solution of the present system. We now see that the problem of interpreting the $\Delta X/\Delta p$ of equation

(4.4.1) is really the problem of *finding a solution for the equations of change*. The ΔXs and Δps of (4.4.1) are in reality the very same dXs and dps which occur in (4.4.4), and we shall henceforth use the notation dX for them rather than ΔX. A 'solution' expresses the values of dp or dX in terms of the fundamental elasticities E_{11}, E_{12}, and E_Y, etc. The reader should note that, in section 3.3, we were able to identify the changes $\Delta X/\Delta p$ with fundamental elasticities without apparently solving equations only because of the extreme simplicity of the problem under review. In a general way this is not possible.

One more point now remains to be emphasised before we proceed with the actual work. It may still be not entirely clear to the reader, in algebraic terms, why it should be considered an advantage to be able to solve for 'total' changes dp, dX, in terms of elasticities E_{11}, E_{12}, etc. We repeat therefore that it is only the E_{11}, E_{12}, etc., about which we have any *a priori* information. We do not know whether the dp, dX are large or small or positive or negative *until* we can express them in terms of Es. And we know something then only *because* we have expressed them in terms of Es and because we know something about the Es.

Consider why we can observe the value of the Es. The equation (4.4.4) holds *whatever* the changes dp and dY. In each time period statisticians can record changes dp, dY which occur in the real world. Given enough data so collected, we may calculate the most likely values of the Es by putting the observed dps and dYs in a set of equations like (4.4.4), one for each observation, and solving. The reader is reminded that the Es are constants (sometimes referred to as parameters). Note especially that we cannot do the same with dps since they will be *different* each time according to the nature of the disturbances affecting the economy we observe. Indeed the dp has no meaning apart from the particular disturbance with which we are concerned.

It is a fact also that we do have a certain amount of information about Es even in the absence of statistical inquiry. For example, we know that E_{11} is negative since common experience suggests that putting up a price, other things being equal, reduces sales. Furthermore, in Chapter 3 we deduced another interesting property of elasticities although it was not explicitly exhibited as such. We showed in fact that

$$E_{11} + E_{12} + E_Y = 0 \qquad (4.4.5)$$

for we argued that, if all prices and spending are changed in the same proportion, there will be no change in sales. The increased purchasing power is just absorbed by increases in prices and there is no change in relative prices. This intuitive argument applied to (4.4.4) says that

$$0 = \frac{dX_1}{X_1} = E_{11}\frac{dp_1}{p_1} + E_{12}\frac{dp_2}{p_2} + E_Y\frac{dY}{Y} \qquad (4.4.6)$$

whenever
$$\frac{dp_1}{p_1} = \frac{dp_2}{p_2} = \frac{dY}{Y}$$

Dividing (4.4.6) by dp_1/p_1 immediately gives (4.4.5).

Following the principles now clarified we proceed with our inquiry. The first step is always to write down the functional dependencies such as (4.4.2) and to ask ourselves precisely what has changed and what has not changed in the context of the problem. In our model we have four demand functions like (4.4.2), one for each commodity for each country. We know that sales depend on prices and spending and on nothing else. But we know also that total spending, Y, in each country depends on production and upon government action to influence the spending of titles to wealth amassed in past periods. Furthermore, we have specified that the objective of policy is to move from a position as in Fig. 4.2, where world supply equals world demand but there is overspending, to a position of full equilibrium. In this case we know that the actual overspending is precisely equal to the deficit in money terms on the balance of payments (*PM* in Fig. 4.2). In country 1, therefore, Y equals the value of output p_1O minus the balance of payments B which is negative.

$$Y = p_1O - B$$

where O is the physical quantity of exportables produced.

For country 2 we have

$$Y' = q_2O' + B/e$$

where O' is the physical quantity of importables produced abroad. B is of course defined in terms of country 1's currency (3.3.1) so that it is necessary to divide by e, the exchange rate, to convert to the currency of country 2. The positive sign preceding arises because the effect of an imbalance of payments is opposite in the two countries. A surplus in 1 is a deficit in 2 and vice versa.

We have assumed that as an act of policy we are to change home spending by an amount B (equal to the balance of payments surplus or deficit) and to change the price p_2 by an amount dp_2 so as to adjust the real terms of trade. p_1 and e and hence q_1 remain constant. We wish to discover what the change dp_2 is in terms of elasticities. Solution of the equations of the model proceeds as follows.

In the present case, from the demand equation, the change $\Delta X_1'$ of (4.4.1), now written dX_1', is given by

$$dX_1' = \frac{\partial X_1'}{\partial q_2} dq_2 + \frac{\partial X_1'}{\partial Y} dY'$$

since q_1 remains unchanged by specification of the problem. This implies that

$$\frac{dX_1'}{dp_2} = \frac{\partial X_1'}{\partial q_2} \frac{dq_2}{dp_2} + \frac{\partial X_1'}{\partial Y} \frac{dY'}{dp_2} \qquad (4.4.7)$$

but

$$Y' = q_2 O' + B/e$$

Remembering that O' does not change because full employment is maintained and constant employment gives constant output, and that e does not change by assumption, we have, taking the changes in Y, q_2 and B

$$dY' = dq_2 O' + \frac{1}{e} dB \qquad (4.4.8)$$

(The reader is here reminded of the principles for taking changes set out in section 3.3.)

Substituting for dY' in (4.4.7) we obtain

$$\frac{dX_1'}{dp_2} = \frac{\partial X_1'}{\partial q_2} \frac{dq_2}{dp_2} + \frac{\partial X_1'}{\partial Y} \left(\frac{dq_2}{dp_2} O' + \frac{1}{e} \frac{dB}{dp_2} \right) \qquad (4.4.9)$$

but

$$p_2 = e q_2$$

which, since e does not change, implies

$$dp_2 = e dq_2$$

Hence

$$e = p_2/q_2 = \frac{dp_2}{dq_2} = \frac{p_1}{q_1}$$

Substituting in (4.4.9) we have

$$\frac{dX'}{dp_2} = \frac{q_2}{p_2} \frac{\partial X_1'}{\partial q_2} + \frac{q_2}{p_2} \frac{\partial X_1'}{\partial Y} O' + \frac{q_1}{p_1} \frac{\partial X_1'}{\partial Y} \frac{dB}{dp_2}$$

$$= \frac{X_1'}{p_2} E_{12}' + \frac{q_2 O' X_1'}{p_2 Y'} E_Y' + \frac{q_1}{p_1} \frac{\partial X_1'}{\partial Y} \frac{dB}{dp_2}$$

At this point we introduce the assumption that the balance of payments is very nearly in equilibrium, i.e. that B is initially very close to zero. So close in fact that we can say that the ratio $\frac{q_2 O'}{Y'}$ is not appreciably different from 1 and, from

$$B = p_1 X_1' - p_2 X_2$$

that the ratio $p_1 X_1' / p_2 X_2$ is not appreciably different from 1. Hence

$$p_1 \frac{dX_1'}{dp_2} = X_2 E_{12}' + X_2 E_Y' + q_1 \frac{\partial X_1'}{\partial Y} \frac{dB}{dp_2} \tag{4.4.10}$$

These assumptions mean, of course, that our result will not be fully general. But the reader will see that the step we have taken does not destroy the validity of the method used. It implies only that the particular result we obtain is no more than approximately true for a relatively small area close to full equilibrium. The most general result is easily derived but is more complicated and can be left until the reader is more experienced in handling this kind of work.

We can now use the elasticity relation (4.4.5) to write finally from (4.4.10)

$$p_1 \frac{dX_1'}{dp_2} = X_2 (-E_{11}') + q_1 \frac{\partial X_1'}{\partial Y} \frac{dB}{dp_2} \tag{4.4.11}$$

Turning to ΔX_2 in equation (4.4.1), now written dX_2, we have from the demand dependency for country 1, following the usual principle, recalling that p_1 does not change,

$$dX_2 = \frac{\partial X_2}{\partial p_2} dp_2 + \frac{\partial X_2}{\partial Y} dY$$

or

$$\frac{dX_2}{dp_2} = \frac{\partial X_2}{\partial p_2} + \frac{\partial X_2}{\partial Y} \frac{dY}{dp_2} \tag{4.4.12}$$

But

$$Y = p_1 O - B$$

hence, taking changes,

$$dY = -dB$$

since neither O nor p_1 changes by specification of the problem. Thus

$$\frac{dY}{dp_2} = -\frac{dB}{dp_2}$$

which, substituted in (4.4.12), gives

$$\frac{dX_2}{dp_2} = \frac{\partial X_2}{\partial p_2} - \frac{\partial X_2}{\partial Y}\frac{dB}{dp_2}$$

or

$$p_2\frac{dX_2}{dp_2} = X_2(E_{22}) - p_2\frac{\partial X_2}{\partial Y}\frac{dB}{dp_2} \tag{4.4.13}$$

Equations (4.4.11) and (4.4.13) may now be substituted into (4.4.1) to obtain

$$\frac{dB}{dp_2} = X_2(-E'_{11} - E_{22} - 1) + q_1\frac{\partial X'_1}{\partial Y}\frac{dB}{dp_2} + p_2\frac{\partial X_2}{\partial Y}\frac{dB}{dp_2}$$

or

$$\frac{dB}{dp_2} = \frac{-X_2(E'_{11} + E_{22} + 1)}{1 - C'_1 - C_2} \tag{4.4.14}$$

where

$$C'_1 = q_1\frac{\partial X'_1}{\partial Y} \text{ and } C_2 = p_2\frac{\partial X_2}{\partial Y}$$

The reader will note that C'_1 is that proportion of unit increase in money expenditure which would be spent by the foreign country on commodity 1. Similarly, C_2 is that proportion of unit increase in expenditure which would be spent by the home country on importables. These Cs are obviously related to income elasticities and are of course fundamental magnitudes not dependent on the problem under review. Indeed, the ratio C_1/C_2 is the slope of the Engel curve AT of Fig. 4.1. We remind ourselves also that

$$C_1 + C_2 = 1$$

since what is not spent on commodity 1 must be spent on commodity 2.

Consider now what can be learned from the final result (4.4.14). $\frac{dB}{dp_2}$ is, by definition, the rate of change of the balance of payments as p_2 changes (p_1 constant), that is, as the real terms of trade change, when at the same time total spending is adjusted so as to maintain full employment at all times. From the *sign* of $\frac{dB}{dp_2}$, therefore, we know whether the real terms of trade must be made to change in favour of or against the home country in order to *improve* that country's trade balance. For by writing (4.4.14) as

$$dB = \left[\frac{-X_2(E'_{11} + E_{22} + 1)}{C'_2 - C_2}\right] dp_2 \qquad (4.4.15)$$

that is, multiplying both sides of (4.4.14) by dp_2 and using the fact that

$$1 - C'_1 = C'_2$$

we see that, for dB to be positive (an improvement in the balance), dp_2 must be positive if $\frac{dB}{dp_2}$ is positive, and negative if it is negative.

Assume first the stable case (section 3.2), where $(E'_{11} + E_{22} + 1)$ is negative, then $\frac{dB}{dp_2}$ will be positive if $C'_2 > C_2$ and negative if $C'_2 < C_2$. The sign of dp_2 depends therefore upon the relative magnitudes of C'_2 and C_2. This was the important conclusion derived from the geometry (section 4.2), but as usual the algebra teaches us more. The result just obtained is obviously reversed in the unstable case where elasticities are small and where $(E'_{11} + E_{22} + 1) > 0$. Once again care must be taken not to be deceived by events in the short run if there is a time lag in the response of consumers to price changes.

Much more important still, the formula (4.4.15), unlike the geometry, tells us *how large* the price change dp_2 must be to correct any known imbalance dB as long as elasticities are known. The exact numerical value may immediately be calculated. The larger is $\frac{dB}{dp_2}$ the smaller dp_2 needs to be. We notice that if $C'_2 = C_2$ then no change at all is necessary in dp_2 (the real terms of trade), for $\frac{dB}{dp_2}$ is infinitely great. On the other hand, if $(E'_{11} + E_{22} + 1)$ were zero, adjustment would be impossible.

It is important finally to notice that the value dp_2 is not the only consequence of policy which can be calculated from the system of equations comprising the model. On the contrary all of the changes dY, dY', dX_1, dX'_1, dX_2, and dX'_2, may be similarly worked out in terms of elasticities. In particular, we know that dY and dY' are equal to $-dB$ and dB, where dB is the known imbalance of trade we have to correct. Hence we know expenditure and price changes in each country so that changes in consumption can be computed from demand equations. As an example, we use (4.4.12) to inquire whether home imports increase or decrease and by how much. Thus from (4.4.12)

$$\frac{dX_2}{dp_2} = \frac{\partial X_2}{\partial p_2} + \frac{\partial X_2}{\partial Y}\frac{dY}{dp_2}$$

$$= \frac{\partial X_2}{\partial p_2} - \frac{\partial X_2}{\partial Y}\frac{dB}{dp_2}$$

Hence, using (4.4.15), we have

$$\frac{dX_2}{dp_2} = \frac{\partial X_2}{\partial p_2} + X_2\frac{\partial X_2}{\partial Y}\left(\frac{E'_{11} + E_{22} + 1}{C'_2 - C_2}\right)$$

$$= \frac{X_2}{p_2}E_{22} + \frac{X_2}{p_2}C_2(E'_{11} + E_{22} + 1)/(C'_2 - C_2)$$

$$= \frac{X_2}{p_2}(C_2E'_{11} + C'_2E_{22} + C_2)/(C'_2 - C_2) \qquad (4.4.16)$$

It is clear from this result that once again we do not know whether imports must increase or decrease to attain a balance. We may quite ordinarily have a case where a trade deficit demands, among other things, an increase in imports for its correction. This is of course quite the opposite to anything which might be expected intuitively.

4.5 A SUMMING-UP ON CURRENCY DEPRECIATION

Two major difficulties inhibit a proper understanding of the role of exchange-rate adjustments in a present-day context. First, all public discussion of the subject takes place in a highly emotionally charged atmosphere, so that we read daily of 'defence' of the pound sterling, as if this were a matter of honour, currency depreciation being both immoral and a national calamity involving loss of face. Second institutional developments of the past seventy years seem to have transformed the whole problem to the point where the consequences of exchange depreciation become infinitely more subtle than the straightforward worsening of the real terms of trade envisaged in classical writings on the subject.

On the emotional point not much need be said beyond the fact that the arguments used are not always entirely without justification. It *is* immoral for governments to announce that there will be no devaluation whatever happens and then to follow the announcement by doing immediately what they have promised they would not. If the object of the proclamation is attained and individuals are thereby induced, against their better judgement, to enter contracts which, because promises are not kept, later involve them in a real loss, then the proclamation at least is immoral. And a real loss must occur whenever debts to foreigners are expressed in terms of the depreciated currency.

On the other hand exchange depreciation is not immoral of itself. On the contrary it is both natural and inevitable, and even honest, that exchange rates should be adjusted whenever the *general level* of prices (as opposed to individual prices) in one country changes at a rate different from that of its trading partner.

When all currencies have intrinsic worth it is impossible for the general level of prices in any one country to change relative to that in any other, for the general level of prices simply reflects the intrinsic worth of the money commodity. History has taught us again and again, however, that with such a currency the problem of maintaining full employment becomes more difficult. Similarly, if the quantity of money and credit is maintained, by law, in a rigid fixed proportion to a fixed reserve of objects (say gold) of intrinsic worth there can again be no difference between countries in the rates of change of the general level of prices, but then the employment problem becomes almost intractable. Shortage of credit and attempts to depress the general level of prices in conformity have been shown to be capable of creating unemployment of monumental proportions far more deserving of the title 'immoral' than exchange depreciation.

The discovery that a currency need not have intrinsic worth and the development of means to maintain public confidence in such a currency system represents a major breakthrough in economic development. Governments now have one more degree of freedom. The general level of prices may be adjusted to suit the special needs of each individual country according to the developmental changes going on within it. One more weapon is added to the armoury of control, and the almost complete absence of serious unemployment throughout the world since 1945 is an indication of just how powerful that weapon is. It could only be described as a form of insanity to abandon its use.

The new weapon is, however, not costless. There are in fact two elements of cost. First, we are now faced with the *absolute* necessity to make exchange-rate adjustments whenever the general level of prices gets out of line. This is not a matter of choice but an inevitable consequence of the use of the new degree of freedom now available to governments. If we are prepared to tolerate a balance of payments problem of the kind analysed in this chapter, exchange adjustment may be avoided for a while. But in the end adjustment must come or there must be a return to the more rigid control of the general price level with all the old difficulties.

The second element of cost in the use of more flexible credit control is much more subtle. We are led in fact to the second problem referred to in the first paragraph of this section. As soon as we add one more degree of freedom to the exchange adjustment mechanism we introduce a manyfold increase in the complexity of the *dynamic* processes involved. It is now infinitely more difficult to find out just what an actual exchange adjustment will accomplish in any particular case. Indeed, it will be recalled that we have already suggested examples where an exchange depreciation might serve, not only to shift the *real* terms of trade in precisely the opposite direction to that which might be expected, but also to bring about a very considerable adjustment in the relative prices of traded and non-traded commodities.

The reason why this last point is so often overlooked is precisely because of the very importance of exchange-rate adjustments as an alternative to control of the general level of prices exactly as discussed above. To demonstrate this it is natural to present a model where the general level of prices remains fixed (by assumption) in terms of each national currency and where exchange-rate changes operate as a perfect alternative equilibrating mechanism without the need for supplementary relative price changes of any sort. And this is the kind of model set out in most elementary texts.

But notice that exchange-rate changes are only a perfect alternative, in a many-commodity world, to changes in the *general* level of prices with *relative* prices unchanged. Whenever a balance of trade problem is only partly due to a wrong general level of prices, that is, when disequilibrium *relative* prices are also a cause, then exchange adjustment is no longer a perfect alternative to price adjustments. The same is true when unemployment is a partial cause. Notice also the consequence of the preoccupation of governments with unemployment. There are two kinds of unemployment just as there are two kinds of price changes, general and relative. We have general unemployment, when it occurs in all sectors of the economy, and sectoral unemployment when it occurs just in one sector. Sectoral unemployment is not general whenever there exists sufficient overall demand to sustain full employment but where, because of 'wrong' price ratios, there is excess demand for one group of commodities and deficient demand for another. In one sector stocks may be running down and prices rising whilst in another stocks may be building up and production falling. If a government happens to be more sensitive to rising unemployment in one sector than it is to excess demand in another it may well apply the remedy for general unemployment to a situation where only sectoral unemployment exists. The consequence is bound to be a rise in the general level of prices and hence a need for exchange-rate adjustment. On the other hand exchange adjustment will not by itself correct the situation, for the underlying wrong prices which gave rise to the original difficulty remain.

It is the complex dynamical system, created by the new twentieth-century freedom to manipulate the general level of prices in the interests of a managed economy, which exacerbates present-day balance of trade problems. It is not that the mechanism has broken down or that it is unstable but that it has been deliberately tampered with. Exchange rates are kept pegged in circumstances where logic demands they should be freed. But if they were completely freed the reckless use of credit creation to combat purely sectoral failure of demand could lead to undesirably large movements in the general level of prices and correspondingly large movements in the exchange rates.

This brings us back to the moral problem of exchange-rate adjustments. There can be no immorality in this if it is known and if it is common practice to have flexible rates. Allowance can be made accordingly in the ordinary course of business. If, however, there is any risk that exchange rates, left to find their own level according to the supply/demand position for various currencies, will in fact fluctuate widely and rapidly then there is a case for fixed rates with occasional adjustment as necessary. If this course is chosen there is almost irresistible pressure upon the authorities to act immorally. The date of the exchange adjustment cannot be announced, for if it were speculators could buy, say, dollars before the change and use these to buy back sterling at a handsome profit after devaluation. Because of the certainty of speculation, rumours of exchange adjustment have to be denied until the very moment of its actual enforcement.

The moral difficulty is not, however, insurmountable. It is perfectly possible to offer compensation to foreign holders of a devalued currency and/or to tax the resident holders of foreign assets. This would both discourage speculation and operate equitably where no element of speculation is involved. Alternatively, small adjustments of the exchanges might be made frequently, without compensation, provided that by 'small' we mean small enough both to make speculation not worth while and not to act as a deterrent to ordinary business. Thus it might be announced that exchange rates will be adjusted monthly, a guarantee being given that the change will not exceed $\frac{1}{4}$ per cent. Speculative gains would then scarcely exceed the cost of speculating, and businessmen drawing contracts could be assured of at least a measure of certainty in arranging their affairs.

In truth the difficulty is not really one of morality but of determining, from the facts, the direction and extent of the exchange adjustment required. And this is the lesson of Chapters 2–4. Balance of trade deficits may be observed in circumstances very different in character. What appears on the surface to be the same disease is not always the same and different diseases need different treatment for their cure. Enough examples of this have been given both to illustrate the point and to make it clear that many more examples could be constructed.

If a balance of payments crisis arises, no policy prescription can be dictated without first checking for excess or deficit demand in every sector and without estimating very carefully what changes in aggregate spending and prices are likely to follow an exchange-rate change. Furthermore, our models tell us that we need this information not only for the country in deficit but for the rest of the world as well. No country can, in this matter, be an 'island unto itself'. Unilateral action taken on the basis of home statistics could be worse than useless. Currency depreciation is sometimes necessary but it is not always the only or even the certain cure for a trade imbalance. It is hoped that the student now understands that if currency depreciation works at all it probably does so for reasons more complicated than those commonly used as an excuse for applying it. We have learned a great deal but a great deal more remains still to be learned. Once again the next step is measurement and experiment within the framework of a model explicitly incorporating the timed reactions of producers, consumers and governments to the various events as they occur.

A hint of the kind of model necessary is given in Chapter 19. In the meantime, however, the understanding of the reader can be deepened by a careful study of exercises 7 and 8 at the end of this chapter. In these exercises we abandon the idea of a 'numeraire' commodity and introduce two new quasi-dynamic assumptions. First, we compute the consequences of currency depreciation when the act of devaluation itself is supposed to cause a rise in the general level of prices of some given amount (zero in exercise 7) or when the rise is controlled by policy. Second, we allow aggregate expenditure to be dependent upon absolute price changes in accordance with some rule which may, for example, reflect trade union bargaining success in the face of changing real welfare (see exercise 8). In each case new unknown parameters are introduced measuring the strength of the forces operating or indicating the chosen government policy as the case may be. The reader will note that whether devaluation improves or worsens the trade balance will now depend heavily on the values of the new parameters as well as the elasticities with which he is familiar. *A great deal will be missed by failure to work these exercises and by failure to work at a later stage exercises 9 and 10.*

Notice especially that although the form of words used in exercises 7–10 implies that we are asked to find the consequences of a joint policy of currency depreciation plus control of prices or expenditure, this interpretation is not essential. The given changes in the index of prices or expenditure may simply reflect the natural consequences of currency depreciation, in which case the policy may be thought of as one of devaluation alone. The difficulty which we face is simply that we know very little as yet about what the 'natural consequences' of devaluation may be so far as aggregate expenditure is concerned (see Chapter 19), and hence so far as its effect on a price index is concerned. It is for this reason that we have in the present chapter concentrated the greater part of our attention on identifying necessary changes rather than on specifying in full the precise policy which will bring about the changes shown to be necessary. The reader will understand this point more exactly by the time Chapter 19 is reached. In the meantime insights can be gained by comparing the list of conditions (i)–(v) for the correction of a trade imbalance set out in section 4.3 with the problem of exercise 8. Here, condition (i) is replaced by a specified change in aggregate spending which could of course simply be the *consequence* of currency depreciation. As a result there is a question whether the trade balance will be improved or not, which exercise 8 seeks to answer.

4.6 MORE ABOUT MONEY – THE PROBLEM OF INTERNATIONAL LIQUIDITY

We have now reached a point where reference may be made to the so-called 'problem of international liquidity', widely believed at the present time to be a matter for grave concern. Discussion of this purely monetary phenomenon has been put off until now since it cannot be understood without a full grasp of the work of the earlier sections of this chapter.

Very few difficulties in economics are new. What is often new, however, is the context in which the old difficulties reappear. The producer of the drama of economic history seems to be short of players. The same actors are sent back time and time again wearing a succession of disguises. The game is to spot actors despite the make-up. We shall try to recognise the international liquidity problem as the inverse of the banking problem of the early nineteenth century.

The reader should first recall the description in Chapter 2 of the way in which gold disappeared as a currency, gradually being replaced by paper documents of one kind or another (i.e. notes or bank accounts) giving titles to wealth. Gold when used as money is not wanted. It is a nuisance to carry and a nuisance to store. What is wanted is ownership of gold or more properly ownership of a certain quantity of rights to receive goods.

Early bankers were the goldsmiths who stored gold for its owners, giving in exchange certificates of ownership. Certificates of ownership could be used as money without disturbing the stocks of gold itself. In consequence goldsmith bankers could lend other people's gold at interest or, what amounts to the same thing, they could lend new certificates of ownership without limit. In other words they issued more bank notes than they possessed stocks of gold to back them.

If a rumour started that a banker had issued too many notes or if he did in fact lend too many notes, holders sometimes lost confidence and rushed to demand the payment in gold to which their notes entitled them. Since gold cover did not exist, banks were forced to close and loss to the holders of claims followed.

As explained in Chapter 2, concern over this problem led to the concentration of the right to issue notes in one way or another into government hands. The confidence thus engendered made it possible actually to withdraw the right to demand gold for government notes, thereby turning the currency into a purely documentary system recording the rights of individuals to commodities, rights being measured in a standard unit of account.

Now consider what is currently happening in the international sphere. The basic international currency continues to be gold. By this we mean that in the last analysis the only acceptable way of settling an international payment is with gold or with some document that gives a *real* right to gold. In practice anyone who gains rights to foreign currency by exports or by borrowing money abroad will, if he does not wish simply to hold them, exchange these rights at the ruling official rate for corresponding titles measured in home currency units. This exchange is ordinarily effected through some government-controlled central bank, so that, although private holders do exist, titles to foreign currency tend to become concentrated in the hands of central banks. And *de jure* central banks have the right, subject to certain unimportant limitations, to exchange any currency for any other at, or close to, the ruling official rate. Thus since U.S.A. dollars are *de jure* convertible into gold at a fixed rate it follows that directly or indirectly any currency is convertible into gold at a fixed rate, for a holder of sterling, say, may first claim dollars for sterling and then gold for dollars. *De jure*, therefore, international payments are made in gold, but *de facto* the situation is different.

Simply *because* rights to foreign currencies are *de jure* convertible, many private holders and central banks are content to hold paper titles *instead* of gold. The central banking authorities in each country are behaving rather like the early goldsmiths. Titles to home currency held by foreigners are certificates of ownership of the home central bank's stock of gold. Home holders of bank notes or bank accounts no longer have the right to demand gold from the central bank, but foreign holders of titles to home currency do. A country's stock of gold acts as a guarantee, not to all home currency any more, but only to that part of the home currency which is held abroad. Any country's reserves therefore consist of its gold stocks *plus* its holding of foreign currency rights which are *de jure* as good as gold.

The student of monetary history, having seen the analogy between the goldsmith bankers and modern central banks *vis-à-vis* foreign holders of home currency, will *ipso facto* be tempted to wonder whether there is any risk that central banks may have issued more rights to gold than they have gold and hence whether there is any risk of a run on the bank. The answer to both of these questions is 'Yes, but with a difference'.

Unlike the goldsmiths, central banks do not directly 'lend' titles to gold for their own profit. If foreigners own more titles to gold than there exists home gold stock, this must be for a number of reasons outside the control of the bank. Foreign rights (i.e. foreign-held bank balances in the home country) build up for at least three reasons. First, there may be a home deficit on the balance of payments of the type described in sections 4.2 and 4.3. At the same time actual payment in gold may not be demanded by the foreign country, since the foreign banker may very well be willing simply to allow his credit balance at the home central bank to accumulate. After all, titles to home currency are just as good as gold so that one might as well accumulate titles as go to the trouble of organising a local 'Fort Knox' complete with security guards and burglar alarms, especially when someone else is prepared to pay interest on the accumulating bank balance as well as look after the gold. Notice that this behaviour tends to remove all pressure on the home government to do anything about the imbalance of trade, for in the recent past it has been only the ratio of the trade imbalance to the stock of gold which has been a cause for concern. If the gold stock and the trade deficit remain constant, the total of titles to gold owned by foreigners may creep up unnoticed.

The second cause of build-up of foreign titles to the gold stock is home lending abroad. When private investors acquire assets abroad, foreign currency must be purchased to pay for them. If, to obtain this currency, the home central bank simply increases the foreign banker's credit balance in exchange for an increase in its own rights to foreign currency at the foreign bank, and if the foreign bank is content to allow its balance to grow, then there need be no diminution in the home gold stocks although foreign rights to gold are accumulating.

Finally, it has in the past been the practice of many gold-producing countries to sell the greater part of their output to the U.K. at once, in exchange for sterling credits in London. If more notice is taken of the extra gold so acquired than the corresponding extra titles to gold held by foreigners, then there is a greater risk that the total of foreign rights to the home gold stock, accruing for reasons one and two, may eventually come to exceed the total stock of gold held.

In fact this has occurred in both the U.K. and the U.S.A. According to F. Machlup, writing in October 1966, foreign titles to the U.K. gold stock exceeded that stock (including U.K. titles to foreign gold stocks) by $4,700 million. For the U.S.A. the corresponding figure was given as $650 million.

Following the goldsmith analogy the stage is clearly set for a 'run' on sterling, and this has been one of the causes of recurrent post-war crises. On the other hand Britain is not bankrupt nor is there really all that much cause for alarm. £2,000 million sterling sounds like, and is, a very large sum of money. But it is hardly 7 per cent of the total value of goods and services produced in the U.K. in one year.† Furthermore it could be argued that foreign claims on London are simply the counterpart of the foreign investment undertaken by the U.K. in the past twenty years. If foreigners would accept titles to ownership of factories and machinery located abroad instead of gold they could be paid at once. Indeed, in the case of the U.S.A. it seems certain that foreign investment is a major cause of the present situation, since U.S. exports regularly exceed imports.

Against this, foreign holders of sterling from a narrower point of view do have some grounds for concern; for whilst it is true that Britain is not bankrupt it is not true that Britain's creditors cannot lose. Indeed, as we have already seen, in the present institutional environment it is inevitable that sooner or later some currencies must be revalued if order is to be maintained in international trade. And, since foreign-held sterling credits must in the nature of things be built up by British balance of payments deficits, it is likely that the currency revaluation will be a depreciation of sterling rather than an appreciation.

A devaluation is of course a unilateral declaration on the part of the country issuing titles to gold that it intends only partially to honour these titles. It is as if the goldsmiths should announce, without waiting for a run on the bank, that henceforth certificates of

† Unlike goldsmith's notes sterling can always be used to buy British goods even though its gold counterpart does not exist in full. Hence it is sometimes said that sterling is fully covered by the U.K. national product even if it is not fully covered by gold.

ownership of 1 oz. of gold are to be regarded only as certificates of ownership of, say, $\frac{1}{2}$ oz. of gold. Even the goldsmiths, who were masters of the art of 'clipping' and 'sweating'† gold coins, never thought of this. And if they had, no doubt some suitable medieval punishment would have been devised as a deterrent. Respectability is attached to the modern confidence trick only because, so long as foreigners hold no *stocks* of currency or rights to currency other than their own, changes in currency exchange rates involve no loss and represent therefore a perfectly acceptable way of bringing the level of prices into line in the manner earlier described. And large stocks of paper rights to foreign currency are a relatively modern phenomenon the significance of which is only just now coming to be appreciated.

The problem is that, like the bank notes of the early banks, dollar and sterling credits have become an essential form of international currency in the absence of any alternative. Money is needed to finance international transactions just as money is needed to finance transactions within a country. The world stock of gold alone is now quite insufficient for this purpose.

Notice that, if foreign holders of sterling bank accounts in London could be paid off by, say, gold from the Bank of England, there would be no change in the world stock of gold but at the same time there would be a complete disappearance of the foreign rights to gold held in the form of London bank accounts. It would no longer be possible for, say, Australia to pay for her imports from the U.S.A. by transferring part of the credit balance in Australia's account in London to that of the U.S.A. The only way in which the payment could be made would be in gold. And we have already seen that the total of foreign credits in London and New York exceeds the total of gold stocks in Britain and the U.S.A. by something like £2,500 million sterling. Paying off sterling credits, even if it were possible, would diminish the world's money supply.

In truth economic developments on the international scene have left the world in more than its usual muddle. More by accident than design a fair proportion (perhaps one-quarter) of what might be called internationally acceptable money now consists of sterling and dollar credits, which closely parallel the notes of the goldsmiths. Since these credits represent, in the last analysis, liabilities of the U.K. and the U.S.A. *alone* to pay gold, and since neither the U.S.A. nor the U.K. have the gold to meet all their liabilities, there is a constant

† Small boys were employed to shake bags of coins, collecting the gold dust abraded in the bottom of the bag.

risk of a 'panic' demand for gold in exchange for dollar and sterling credits. Furthermore, it is a fact that countries faced with a loss of their gold stock will, according to custom, ordinarily depreciate their currency in terms of gold. The panic, once begun, brings about the very event fear of which created the panic in the first place.

Holders of sterling accounts in London are torn between a desire to get rid of these accounts and so escape the risk of loss and a desire to keep them as a necessary means of financing trade. The British Government on the other hand is equally torn between the need to adjust the official exchange rate so as to bring the general level of U.K. prices into line with world prices in the interest of trade equilibrium and the wish not to repudiate its full liability to pay in gold.

Notice also that sterling liabilities have been built up over a number of years as a consequence of repeated deficits on the balance of payments of the type described in section 4.2. Even if some other form of international currency were devised, British liabilities can be repaid only by a corresponding series of surpluses on the balance of payments. The reader is reminded that a deficit of the section 4.2 type is possible only if individuals are allowed to spend or invest in real assets an amount greater than the value of the national product. To create a surplus therefore demands a cut in individual disposable incomes which is unlikely to be politically popular.

A further dilemma arises out of the fact that any country which, by accident or design, issues a large quantity of rights to its currency to foreigners naturally becomes world banker just as the goldsmith who issued the most notes found himself in the biggest way of business. Acting as world banker means receiving income on this account. Banking services represent a kind of export which might have to be given up if an alternative world currency is created.

Reluctance on the part of Britain to give up her role as world banker necessarily implies a reluctance to change the sterling/gold exchange rate. But, as we have seen also, reluctance to change the exchange rate, for whatever reason, takes away one degree of freedom (section 4.5) in the control of the economy. In the absence of exchange-rate adjustment a balance of payments deficit can be corrected only by measures leading to serious risk of unemployment. The British Government therefore, and indeed most governments, have come to see large reserves of international currency as desirable insurance. If a country has large reserves it need not worry too much about a balance of trade deficit. But large reserves for every country means a larger stock of international currency. Accordingly there is a widespread belief in the need for a greater quantity of internationally acceptable money (liquidity). This is the problem of international liquidity – a growing loss of confidence in sterling accounts in London (and even dollar accounts) combined with a growing demand for still more international money.

It would be both confusing and unnecessary to attempt to outline in detail the various proposals which are being put forward at the present time to meet this difficulty. All that is necessary is to expand a little upon what is needed and leave the reader himself to assess the likely worth of the different schemes as they are described in the Press and at the innumerable international conferences and discussions currently devoted to the topic.

4.7 ON WHAT IS NEEDED

The natural approach to the international monetary problem, once it is recognised as the national monetary problem in disguise, is to look for a solution along familiar lines. We have observed that national central banks are behaving rather like the many private banks of the eighteenth century, each issuing its own notes insufficiently backed in some cases by its own private stock of gold. Every national central bank deals in titles to its own national currency in the form of accounts held by foreigners, i.e. dollar or sterling credits, etc., usually expecting these to have some degree of acceptability as international currency. On the basis of past experience we should therefore expect loss of confidence in one or other of these (many) international currencies and hence from time to time bouts of panic selling. This is in accord with what we currently observe.

The nineteenth-century cure for loss of confidence at the national level was to restrict the note issue to just one authority, e.g. the Bank of England in the U.K. The international analogue of this would be to have a single separate international currency created and issued by, say, the present International Monetary Fund and to insist that this currency be the only 'legal tender' for international transactions. A new unit of account, say 'the World Thaler' (W.T.), might facilitate this.

The first practical step would be to set a rate of exchange between each national currency and W.T.s which incidentally determines all commodity prices in terms of W.T.s. All private titles to foreign currency should be transferred to the national government (the central bank, if any) in exchange for equivalent credits in home currency. Each national government might then open an account with the International Monetary Fund (I.M.F.), depositing all its titles to the currency of the rest of the world and having charged against it all titles to home currency held by the rest of the world. Notice that by this act the sum of the balances of all national accounts must be zero, for a double entry is made of each title, one crediting the account of the owner of the title and one charging the account of the country in whose currency the title was held. As an example, consider two countries A and B. A holds titles to 1,000 W.T.s worth of B's currency and B holds titles to 500 W.T.s worth of A's currency either in the form of notes or credits at central banks. All notes and credits held will be eliminated and in exchange an I.M.F. account showing a credit balance of $(1000 - 500)$ W.T.s is opened for A and a balance owing, i.e. $(500 - 1000)$ W.T.s, for B. These balances sum to zero.

Notice that gold holdings have been ignored. Gold is after all a commodity, presumably of intrinsic worth. In the proposed system gold would no longer be required to give value to the international currency so that it may be sold for industrial purposes. On the other hand it should be understood that this might operate in some degree inequitably since it is impossible to say to what extent the present price of gold is due to its use as currency and how much is due to its value when used for industrial purposes. If, on demonetisation as proposed, the price of gold fell markedly, holders and producers of gold may have reason to feel aggrieved. But this is in a sense irrelevant to the problem of finding a satisfactory international monetary system; for the loss, if it occurred, would be a once-for-all loss and not a continuing malfunction of the mechanism.

If each nation has an account in W.T.s at the I.M.F., all international transactions may be settled by charging the account of each country with any deficit on its balance of payments and crediting any surplus. Notice that this still leaves the sum of all balances equal to zero as before.

Observe that no country need now hold a stock of any other country's currency. Currency reserves, where they exist, take the form of a credit balance at the I.M.F. which is measured in W.T.s. Any country may depreciate its currency at will without involving any other country in a loss. In this connection we remark that only governments will hold W.T. accounts, so that any individual expecting currency depreciation would not be able to buy W.T.s to hold so as to be able to repurchase his own currency at a profit after the exchange-rate change. This means that no unwanted currency depreciation could be forced upon a country simply because of an expectation of such depreciation.

It is true of course that it would be difficult to prevent individuals who expect currency depreciation (say in the U.K.) from buying, say, dollar assets (shares in U.S.A. companies) with the expectation of selling them again at a profit after currency depreciation. But there is an important distinction in degree between a positive speculative action involving both buying and selling and the present situation where holders of sterling credits fear a loss on what is after all the international currency which they need to conduct their day-to-day business. Positive speculative action may be controlled by making the exchange-rate changes small and frequent so that brokers' commission on buying and selling makes the gain hardly worth the cost. (The remarks in section 4.5 are relevant here.)

In short, proposals so far give *confidence* in the international currency. Notice also that it would give *liquidity*, that is, there can be no shortage of international currency. This is because the I.M.F. gives unlimited overdraft facilities. The fact that a country has a negative balance does not mean that W.T.s are not available to it. Indeed, since balances must sum to zero there will ordinarily exist many countries with a negative balance. If such a country is in deficit on its payments balance, its negative balance would be allowed to grow larger automatically. This brings us to the problem of *adjustment*.

Naturally enough there must be some penalty for running a negative balance. Nineteenth-century governments discovered that the penalty for allowing the central bank to issue too many notes is inflation. If purchasing power is unlimited but commodities are scarce, prices will rise. Control of the quantity of money is essential. In the same way any country with unlimited overdraft facilities at the I.M.F. could go on indefinitely with a payments deficit of the type described in section 4.2, thereby allowing its people to consume for ever in excess of the value of their product. Indeed, the inhabitants of such a country would have no need to work. All needs could be imported. If all countries attempted the same thing, excess expenditure in every country would compete up world prices.

Ideally, therefore, we should wish to keep all W.T. balances at the I.M.F. as close to zero as possible. Any country with a credit balance should be running a deficit on the balance of payments and vice versa. The obvious mechanism would be to charge interest on *both* credit balances and negative balances. This imposes a penalty on countries which have earned too many trade surpluses as well as on those which have lived beyond their means. As we have previously pointed out, the successful attainment of a trade surplus means that someone must be in deficit. Adjustment must be mutual.

Of course an interest charge is not by itself a penalty if the I.M.F. stands always prepared to give credit, for the interest charge can be paid out of the credit itself so that any country may in theory allow its negative balance to grow indefinitely. But in practice this is unlikely to happen if the interest charge is made to rise very steeply with the absolute size of the balance, whether positive or negative, and if some more drastic form of sanction is imposed jointly by all countries if the balance is allowed to grow beyond some previously agreed absolute level.

Notice that the system has removed the *need* for continuing trade surpluses, since it has removed the need for reserves. Hence penalties on credit balances should be acceptable as well as penalties on debit balances. The need for reserves is removed since imbalance may be corrected by currency revaluation, thereby avoiding the risk of unemployment. Imports may always be obtained if the importing country is prepared to pay the price. There can never be any 'shortage' of international currency since however great the level of international trade, finance for it is automatic. 'Liquidity' is preserved.

To avoid misunderstanding we hasten to add here that the skeleton suggestions above are not intended as properly thought-out proposals for immediate application without modification, nor would the present writer be qualified without a good deal more careful research and inquiry to make serious practical proposals. Innumerable minor difficulties are bound to arise in practice as a consequence of the very great variation in the details of current practice throughout the world.

We have chosen to make proposals simply to illustrate the nature of the problem. The words 'liquidity', 'confidence' and 'adjustment' used above occupy a prominent place in the literature of the subject. The final solution, whatever it turns out to be, must satisfy these three needs. It is of course unlikely that anything even faintly resembling the simple system above will eventually emerge. The prejudices and beliefs, justified or unjustified, of world bankers and others actually operating the present system are bound to play an important part in moulding the future system whatever it may turn out to be.

At the time of writing we note attempts to preserve confidence in sterling by the offer of stand-by credits made available by a consortium of world bankers.† In the event of 'panic' selling of titles to sterling, gold and other world currencies will be lent to London to bolster actual reserves. It is amusing to note the similarity between these arrangements and the mutual efforts of nineteenth-century bankers to tackle the same problem in the same way. And it is perhaps instructive to note that all of these efforts failed in the end and to compare the U.K. final solution with that, say, in the U.S.A.

At the same time proposals to increase the quantity of international currency tend to take the form, in effect, of proposals to allow the International Monetary Fund to issue still more 'rights to currency' backed by gold – a practice which already is in operation. On the other hand those countries which have ample reserves are more inclined to oppose the creation of more money, which they claim (rightly) will simply allow countries without reserves to continue to live beyond their means. Countries with reserves argue for a more effective adjusting mechanism, in particular for a return to settlement by genuine payment in gold or its equivalent.

In this last connection we meet the argument that world reserves could be effectively increased by depreciating *every* currency in terms of gold, i.e. raising the price of gold. This move would of course give a handsome free bonus to gold-holding and gold-producing countries. Note also that whenever more international currency is created by whatever method, there is always the problem of how the new currency should be 'shared out'. This difficulty is not present in the scheme outlined above.

It is to be hoped that the reader is now in a position to follow developments in this field as they occur, as suggested at the end of the previous section.

EXERCISES

1. Construct a diagram on the lines of Fig. 4.1 but this time assume that spending abroad exceeds LQ. Show that there must now be

† As much to protect the gold value of their own sterling accounts as anything else.

world excess demand for at least one commodity. In the same way show that if the foreign country spends less than LQ there must be a deficit in world demand for at least one commodity. Show also that when foreign spending is different from LQ the intersection point of offer curves has no special significance. Pay special attention to the case where elasticities are low, i.e. where $(E'_{11} + E_{22} + 1)$ is positive and offer curves intersect more than once.

2. Reconsider the argument relating to Figs. 4.2 and 4.3 for the case where $(E'_{11} + E_{22} + 1)$ is positive. Hence demonstrate the consistency of the diagrammatic treatment and the algebra leading to (4.4.15).

3. The equations of the model of section 4.4 are

$$B = p_1 X'_1 - p_2 X_2$$
$$X'_1 = X'_1(p_1, p_2, Y')$$
$$X_2 = X_2(p_1, p_2, Y)$$
$$Y = p_1 O - B$$
$$Y' = p_2 O' + B$$
$$p_1 = \text{constant}$$

The system has been solved for a policy change dp_2 in p_2 to give the result (4.4.15). Rewrite the model, substituting q_1 and q_2 for foreign prices and adding the equations

$$p_1 = eq_1$$
$$p_2 = eq_2$$

(where e is the exchange rate) which indicate that world prices are everywhere the same. Assume that policy is arranged at home and abroad so as to keep *both* p_1 and q_2 constant but that the exchange rate e is adjusted by an amount de. Solve for dB and show that the result obtained is precisely the same as (4.4.15).

4. The result (4.4.15) is based upon the assumption that the initial imbalance of trade B is negligible. Assume that it is not after all negligible and rework the equation system of exercise 3 to show that (4.4.15) must now be amended to read

$$dB = \left[\frac{-X_2(\lambda E'_{11} + E_{22} + \dfrac{B}{p_2 X_2} C'_1 + 1)}{C'_2 - C_2} \right] dp_2$$

where $\lambda = p_1 X'_1 / p_2 X_2$.

Hence justify the assumption of section 4.4 as a first approximation.

5. For many problems (see sections 1.2 and 6.5) it is convenient to make use of the fact that E_{ij} breaks up into two parts, the income part and the substitution part, as under

$$E_{ij} = -\frac{p_j X_j}{p_i X_i} C_i + \sigma_{ij}$$

Note that if i is the same as j we have

$$E_{ii} = -C_i + \sigma_{ii}$$

The following properties of σ_{ij} are well known [10, section 1.4] for three commodities:

(i) $\sigma_{i1} + \sigma_{i2} + \sigma_{i3} = 0$

(ii) σ_{ii} is negative

(iii) $\sigma_{ii}\sigma_{jj} - \sigma_{ij}\sigma_{ji}$ is positive

(iv) and $\sigma_{ji} = (p_i X_i / p_j X_j) \sigma_{ij}$

In exercises we shall make use of the following definitions:

$$\psi_{23} = \left(\sigma_{22} - \frac{S_2}{X_2} S_{22}\right) - \left(\sigma_{23} - \frac{S_2}{X_2} S_{23}\right)\left(\frac{\sigma_{32} - S_{32}}{\sigma_{33} - S_{33}}\right)$$

$$\text{and } \phi_{23} = \left[C_2 - C_3\left(\frac{\sigma_{32} - S_{32}}{\sigma_{33} - S_{33}}\right)\right].$$

For convenience we include in these definitions supply responses S_{ij} which the student has not yet met. If we write S_i for the amount supplied (produced) of the ith commodity, then we have a supply equation

$$S_i = S_i(p_1, p_2, p_3)$$

analogous to the demand equation, stating that the amount produced is dependent upon prices. S_{ij} is the elasticity $p_j \dfrac{\partial S_i}{\partial p_j} \bigg/ S_i$ analogous to the demand elasticity. Notice that in all problems where supply is assumed to be fixed (as in most of the problems of Book I), terms in S_{ij} are all zero and hence do not appear in ψ_{23} and ϕ_{23}. Hence we see from conditions (ii) and (iii) above that ψ_{23} must be negative. ψ_{23} behaves in fact rather like a substitution part, σ_{ii}. It is well known also [10, chap. 4] that σ_{ij}, where i is different from j, is positive in the usual case where the commodities i and j are not complementary. If all σ_{ij} are positive $(i \neq j)$, then from condition (i) above each σ_{ij} must be numerically less than σ_{ii}. Hence ϕ_{23} must be positive in sign (since σ_{32} and σ_{33} are of opposite sign) and less than unity. ϕ_{23} behaves therefore rather like C_i. Note also that $\phi_{13} + \phi_{23} = 1$ by condition (i), again like C_1 and C_2. The reader will discover that for many problems we may pass from the simple two-commodity model to a model with variable supplies and non-traded commodities by replacing σ_{ii} with ψ_{i3} and C_i with ϕ_{i3} in all algebraic results. It is significant, therefore, that the signs and magnitudes of σ and ψ and C and ϕ are ordinarily much the same. Note especially the word *ordinarily*, however. If σ_{ij} is ever negative, that is, if commodities i and j tend to be closely related in the satisfaction of some special need, say petrol and motor-cars, then ϕ may be negative and indefinitely large numerically.

As an introduction to a more general model the reader should now extend the algebra of section 4.4 as follows. In the equation system of exercise 3 add to the demand equations two new prices p_3 and q_3 representing home and foreign prices of a class of non-traded goods. Add two new demand equations

$$X_3 = X_3(p_1, p_2, p_3, Y)$$

$$X'_3 = X'_3(p_1, p_2, q_3, Y')$$

and amend the expenditure equations to read

$$Y = p_1 S_1 + p_3 S_3$$

$$\text{and } Y' = p_2 S'_1 + q_3 S'_3$$

to indicate that the home country produces S_1 of exportables and S_3 of non-traded goods and the foreign country produces S'_2 of importables and S'_3 of non-traded goods.

Now assume that supplies are given and fixed and that supply equals demand ($S_3 = X_3$ and $S'_3 = X'_3$) and so prove that, using the new notation, the result (4.4.15) must be amended to read

$$dB = \left[\frac{- X_2(\psi'_{13} - \phi'_{13} + \psi_{23} - \phi_{23} + 1)}{\phi'_{23} - \phi_{23}} \right] dp_2$$

Hence justify relevant comments in section 4.3.

6. Solve the expanded system of exercise 5 to show that, for the home country,

$$\frac{dp_3}{p_3} = \left[\frac{-\sigma_{32} - C_3 \dfrac{p_2 X_2}{p_3 X_3}\left(\dfrac{\psi'_{13} + \psi_{23}}{\phi'_{23} - \phi_{23}}\right)}{\sigma_{33}} \right] \frac{dp_2}{p_2}$$

where ψ and ϕ have the meaning of exercise 5.

Observe from exercise 5 that, if dB is to be positive, an improvement in the trade balance, dp_2/p_2 must ordinarily be of the same sign as $\phi'_{23} - \phi_{23}$. Observe also that as ϕ'_{23} and ϕ_{23} are ordinarily both positive and less than unity, their difference is likely to be very small. Hence, using conditions (i) and (ii) of exercise 5, show that the magnitude of the expression in square brackets will ordinarily be dominated by the magnitude and sign of the second term in the numerator. Hence show that dp_3/p_3 must be negative so that non-traded goods' prices will ordinarily fall relative to the price of exportables if the trade balance is to improve.

By deducting dp_2/p_2 from both sides of the result given in this exercise, at the same time making use of condition (i) of exercise 5, show further that non-traded goods' prices must fall also relative to the price of importables to improve the balance of payments. Hence justify the argument of section 4.3.

Consider the possibility of exceptions to the argument of section 4.3. In what circumstances could such exceptions arise? Speculate upon the value of currency depreciation as a policy in such a case.

7. Reflect very carefully upon the arguments of sections 4.3 and 4.5 and consider the role of the 'numeraire' price in the algebra of section 4.4. Note that formula (4.4.15) measures the effect of currency depreciation on the balance of payments only if prices p_1 and q_2 are held constant. If p_1 and/or q_2 change following currency depreciation, the consequences might be quite different.

Suppose that instead of holding p_1 and q_2 constant, steps were taken in each country to ensure that some *index* of *all* prices was held constant. Thus we might have

$$\beta_1 dp_1 + \beta_2 dp_2 = 0$$

for country 1 and

$$\beta'_1 dq_1 + \beta'_2 dq_2 = 0$$

for country 2, where βs are 'weights' considered by each country to be appropriate. Show now that the effect on the balance of trade of a currency depreciation de/e is given by

$$dB = \left\{ \frac{-q_1 X_1'(E_{11}' + E_{22} + 1)}{(C_2' - C_2)\left[\dfrac{p_1 \beta_1}{p_1 \beta_1 + p_2 \beta_2} - \dfrac{p_1 \beta_1'}{e(q_1 \beta_1' + q_2 \beta_2')}\right]} \right\} de$$

Hence show that if both countries have the same idea of what constitutes the general level of prices and if both countries attempt to hold this constant, the resulting situation is unstable (but see exercise 9).

Show that the stabilisation of an arbitrary price index in both countries is insufficient to ensure that currency depreciation will improve the balance of payments.

8. Assume that the attention of the government is now concentrated upon aggregate expenditure rather than a stable price index at the moment of currency depreciation. Suppose that trade union pressures and government real expenditure programmes are such that aggregate money spending at home and abroad changes in response to price changes according to the following rules

$$dY = \alpha_1 dp_1 + \alpha_2 dp_2$$

$$dY' = \alpha_1' dq_1 + \alpha_2' dq_2$$

where αs are weights determined by 'cost push' of trade union attitudes.

Use the new equations to replace $p_i = e q_i = $ constant in the system of exercise 3 and thereby deduce the following relation between the change in the balance of trade and currency adjustment de:

$$dB = \left[\frac{-q_1 X_1'(E_{11}' + E_{22} + 1)}{(C_2' - C_2)\left(\dfrac{p_1 X_1 - p_1 \alpha_1}{Y - p_1 \alpha_1 - p_2 \alpha_2} - \dfrac{q_1 X_1' - q_1 \alpha_1'}{Y' - q_1 \alpha_1' - q_2 \alpha_2'}\right) - (\sigma_{22} + \sigma_{11}')\left(\dfrac{p_1 X_1'}{Y - p_1 \alpha_1 - p_2 \alpha_2} + \dfrac{q_1 X_1'}{Y' - q_1 \alpha_2' - q_2 \alpha_2'}\right)} \right] de$$

Hence show

1. That if aggregate money spending is held constant in both countries (i.e. if $\alpha_1 = \alpha_2 = \alpha_1' = \alpha_2' = $ zero), then currency

depreciation will usually improve the balance of payments provided elasticities of demand are not very small.

2. That if trade unions insist upon full compensation for price changes (i.e. if $\alpha_1 = X_1$, $\alpha_2 = X_2$, $\alpha_1' = X_1'$ and $\alpha_2' = X_2'$), then currency depreciation will have no effect at all upon the balance of payments.

Exercises to be attempted only after first reading of Books I and II

9. Extend the problem of exercise 7 to include the possibility that both countries produce both exportables, importables and a class of non-traded commodities. Let supplies be dependent on prices. Show that we now have:

$$dB = \left[\frac{-q_1(X_1' - S_1')\left(\dfrac{X_2}{X_2 - S_2}\psi_{23} + \dfrac{X_1'}{X_1' - S_1'}\psi_{13}' - \phi_{23} - \phi_{13}' + 1 \right)}{(\phi_{23}' - \phi_{23})(\pi - \pi') + \left(\dfrac{X_2}{X_2 - S_2}\psi_{23} + \dfrac{X_1'}{X_1' - S_1'}\psi_{13}' \right)(\Gamma + \Gamma')} \right] de$$

where

$$\pi = \frac{\sigma_{33}\, p_1 \beta_1 - \sigma_{31}\, p_3 \beta}{\sigma_{33}\sum p_i \beta_i}$$

π' has the obvious meaning:

$$\Gamma = \left[\frac{C_3 p_1 (X_1' - S_1')}{\sigma_{33} p_3 X_3} \right]\left(\frac{p_3 \beta_3}{\sum p_i \beta_i} \right)$$

$$\Gamma' = \left[\frac{C_3' q_1 (X_1' - S_1')}{\sigma_{33}' q_3 X_3'} \right]\left(\frac{q_3 \beta_3'}{\sum q_i \beta_i'} \right)$$

and ϕ and ψ have the usual meaning.

Hence show that if elasticities differ between countries the same price index may be held constant in both countries without the instability noted in exercise 7.

Consider the case where

$$\beta_1 = \beta_2 = \beta_1' = \beta_2' = \text{zero}$$

that is, the case where the prices of non-traded goods must remain unaffected by currency depreciation in both countries in order to ensure that $\sum \beta_i dp_i = 0$. Show that in these circumstances

term two of the denominator, which must be positive in sign, will almost certainly outweigh term one. Hence show that a policy of stabilisation of the prices of non-traded goods at home and abroad combined with currency depreciation will almost certainly result in an improvement of the trade balance.
Now set

$$\beta_2 = \beta_3 = \beta_1' = \beta_3' = 0$$

and show

(i) that the result now obtained is a generalisation of (4.4.15), and
(ii) that dB is now of uncertain sign when the home currency is depreciated.

Hence prove *that even for the three-commodity case the stabilisation of an arbitrary price index at home and abroad is insufficient to ensure that currency depreciation will bring about an improvement in the trade balance.*

10. Extend the model of exercise 8 to the most general case (exercise 9). Show that we now have

$$dB = \begin{bmatrix} -q_1(X_1' - S_1')\left(\dfrac{X_2}{X_2 - S_2}\psi_{23} + \dfrac{X_1'}{X_1' - S_1'}\psi_{13}' - \phi_{23} - \phi_{13}' + 1\right) \\[2ex] (\phi_{23}' - \phi_{23})(\pi - \pi') - \left(\dfrac{X_2}{X_2 - S_2}\psi_{23} + \dfrac{X_1'}{X_1' - S_1'}\psi_{13}'\right) \\[2ex] (X_1' - S_1')(\Gamma + \Gamma') \end{bmatrix} de$$

where ϕ and ψ have the meaning of exercise 5 above,

$$\pi = \frac{p_1(X_1 - \alpha_1)}{Y - \sum p_i \alpha_i} - \frac{\sigma_{31} p_3(X_3 - \alpha_3)}{\sigma_{33}(Y - \sum p_i \alpha_i)}$$

and

$$\Gamma = \frac{p_1[X_3 \sigma_{33} - C_3(X_3 - \alpha_3)]}{X_3 \sigma_{33}(Y - \sum p_i \alpha_i)}$$

and primes mean 'pertaining to the foreign country' as usual. Note that last three bracketed expressions in denominator are multiplicative.

Hence show that the results (1) and (2) of exercise 8 continue to hold in the most general case.

5 The Balance of Payments – Cure by Deflation?

5.1 The Problem Introduced

In earlier chapters two classes of balance of payments problems were identified. First, a deficit on the trade balance may be observed when world production and world demand are not equal, excess demand being met out of stocks; second, a deficit will be observed when world production and world demand are equal, but when the home country consumes more, and its trading partner less, than the value of their respective products.

These two situations should not of course be regarded as mutually exclusive. In any particular case elements of both may be present so that an observed imbalance may in part be due to overspending and in part due to a 'wrong' price structure leading to excess or deficit world demand. We distinguish carefully between the two possibilities not because they cannot both occur simultaneously but because they represent two distinct economic imbalances each demanding its own separate and different adjustment. This fact is immediately brought out as soon as we recall that, so long as each country is consuming just and only just the value of its product, no imbalance of trade is possible *unless* there is world excess demand and supply in some commodities as described in Chapters 2 and 3. Conversely, it was shown in Chapter 4 that as long as any one country is consuming at a rate different from the value of its product there can never be equilibrium in the balance of trade even though world supply may be equal to world demand.†

As explained in Chapter 4, trade imbalance arising out of over-spending is almost certainly a recent phenomenon made possible on a significant scale only by modern institutional developments, and this no doubt is the reason why we find little reference to the overspending problem except in the literature of the last twenty years. On the other hand it could be that the new lesson has been a little too well learned. There is evidence that in some quarters a cut in real spending may

† Exceptions to this rule appear later in this book, but such exceptions arise only on account of tariffs, which modify the ordinary competitive arguments of Chapter 4.

now be regarded as an alternative to currency revaluation instead of its complement. There is even evidence of the existence of a converse school of thought which looks upon currency depreciation as an alternative to an unpleasant cut in spending which would otherwise be necessary.

The second of these views is of course disastrously wrong whenever the observed imbalance is due to excess spending, for no amount of price adjustment can ever succeed in reducing aggregate spending to the value of output when aggregate money incomes and the value of output are themselves determined by the very prices we are adjusting (see Chapter 2). The belief that it can do so is disastrous, not only because it is wrong but also because it will often appear to offer a politically attractive alternative to reduction of disposable incomes by direct taxation.

By contrast the claim that a trade imbalance can be corrected by a cut in spending alone without currency revaluation bears much closer investigation. This is partly because a cut in spending alone might very well succeed in practice in correcting the imbalance, even without any change in relative prices, whenever some degree of unemployment of resources is tolerated, and partly because a spending cut without currency depreciation will in all probability create pressures to change prices in the direction they must go for full equilibrium, and might, in consequence, actually bring about the desired result. Indeed, consideration of the argument of Chapter 4 makes it clear that a reduction in spending at home, plus a corresponding increase in expenditure abroad, will at once convert a balance of trade problem of the overspending type into one of the excess demand type. It is only the extreme difficulty in practice of reducing prices in absolute terms which inhibits the automatic operation of the adjusting mechanism of Chapter 2 and which accordingly creates a need for currency revaluation. Wherever absolute prices fail to adjust in response to pressure, sectoral or overall unemployment must appear.

The fact that a cut in spending alone can, by itself, correct an imbalance makes it worth while to set our model to work on this problem. The reader may then see for himself what cost in terms of unemployment either at home or abroad must be paid. To focus attention upon the main point we shall assume throughout that no prices ever change whether there is excess demand or supply or not. All adjustments both at home and abroad will be in aggregate spending and/or the level of employment.

In practice of course there would almost certainly be some change in relative prices wherever there is excess demand for one commodity and a deficit world demand for another, even though prices may be sticky in a downward direction. But it is not possible to take this into consideration within the framework of a 'static' model which takes no account of the timing of the various changes,† nor do we need to do so for present purposes, which are simply illustrative.

Notice first that the problem of the present chapter is not really new. As early as section 2.5 (Fig. 2.2) attention was drawn to the possibility of correcting the trade imbalance by a cut in production and hence in spending. The case treated in section 2.5, however, was a particularly simple one. At that stage very little had been said about the means which governments might use to influence aggregate spending. On the contrary it was implicitly assumed that total spending must be exactly equal to the value of output at all times, no mention having been made of the existence of accumulated titles to wealth. In these circumstances spending can be cut only by reducing production and we did not allow this to happen except in the country experiencing the trade deficit.

Unfortunately life is not as simple as this. Nor is it even as simple as we pretended in section 4.2 where the possibility of saving and dis-saving was first introduced. As long as all governments are pledged to maintain spending at a level sufficient to sustain the full employment of all resources, the proportion of saving undertaken by individuals is irrelevant, for if private saving increases, say, as a result of some policy change, then government saving must decrease by an equal offsetting amount so as to maintain full employment. On the other hand, whenever governments show willingness to tolerate some degree of unemployment as part of a balance of payments policy, then the response of individual saving to changes in the level of income does become important. It is imperative therefore to develop still further the ideas set out in Chapter 4 describing the determinants of total expenditure, a task we undertake in section 5.2 below.

By contrast with the work of section 2.5, we shall, in the present chapter, assume that all producers maintain their stocks at a constant level, that is, they cut production at the first sign of a deficit demand and increase production at the first sign of excess demand. Thus a balance of trade problem can arise only when one country is spending more than the value of its output whilst its trading partner spends

† But see Chapter 19.

less. Excess spending or deficit spending may occur as a consequence of attempts by one or other country to maintain full employment. Notice that, since there is one and only one set of prices consistent with full employment, balanced trade, and no change in stocks, our assumption of constant 'wrong' prices and no change in stocks means that balanced trade is possible only with some degree of unemployment. From this it follows that attempts to correct a home trade imbalance must induce either a change in policy abroad or some change in the level of employment abroad. Thus we have another example of the essential interdependence of economic policies.

If the home government seeks to correct its balance of payments deficit by restricting spending (which may be a necessary step) without *at the same time* taking steps to encourage the essential ancillary price adjustment, an obvious conflict of interests will arise. When total spending is cut, spending on imports will be cut. In the absence of a countervailing government policy abroad, this must mean that production, and hence incomes and spending abroad, are cut. The fall in spending in country 2 leads to a fall in demand for exportables and a fall in production at home. The consequent cut in incomes means a further cut in spending and a further reduction in imports and so on in an infinite series of repercussions back and forth. Employment will fall in both countries. Even if a country in deficit is prepared to tolerate some unemployment to avoid a balance of payments crisis, the country with a surplus might not. There could be no agreement on such a policy.

At least two questions of some importance arise. These are:
(i) Will the process come to an end and if so will the balance of payments problem have disappeared if country 2 takes no action? And if so, in view of the repercussions, how large should the initial cut in spending be?
(ii) What will happen if country 2 reacts by increasing total spending abroad at the first sign of unemployment? Can the balance of payments problem be solved in this case?

As a preliminary to the construction of a formal model to treat these questions, we turn to the promised further explanation of the determinants of aggregate expenditure.

5.2 THE CONTROL OF TOTAL SPENDING

In Fig. 5.1 a diagram is presented illustrating the flow of money from firms to factors of production (i.e. wages to labour, profits to the owners of capital and rents to property owners), from factors of production to commodities (the spending of income) and from commodities back to firms (sales revenue). This is the basic money flow described in Chapter 4. The purpose of the diagram is to demonstrate how extra money may be infused into the stream and in what ways the money might 'leak' away.

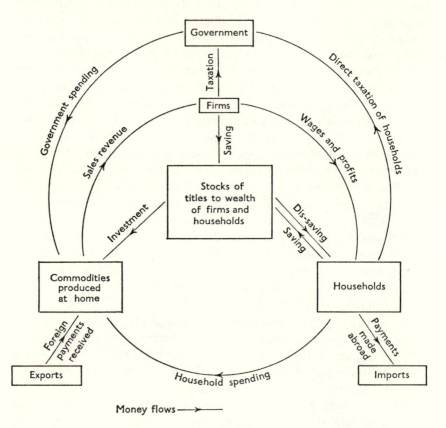

Fig. 5.1

If there were no opportunities for the carrying forward of titles to wealth accumulated in past periods, and no imports or exports, all money flows in Fig. 5.1 would disappear except for the basic circular movement from firms to factors, to commodities and back to firms. The pool of commodities, which represents the total production of the community in the period, would be just and only just sold. This, as explained in Chapter 4, is because all revenue of firms (value of sales) is paid out in income which, if there is no saving, must be spent on commodities and become revenue once again. No money is lost from the flow.

All complications which arise do so because of the leaks and influxes of money shown in Fig. 5.1 as tributaries of the basic flow. Firms can save by paying less than total profits to shareholders and by holding reserves of titles to wealth in various forms. Alternatively firms may buy commodities (machinery, etc.) produced by other firms by 'spending' accumulated titles to wealth. They may use their own accumulated savings for this purpose or they may borrow titles accumulated by individuals. If in any period firms spend on capital equipment more than they save, then there is said to be net investment and the pool of accumulated saving is that much depleted. Notice here that the words 'net investment' are used simply to indicate changes in the stock of money held by firms. The fact that we speak as if the stock of money is spent only on fixed equipment is really an irrelevant and perhaps dangerous concession to common usage. Fig. 5.1 is strictly about money flows. What the money buys does not matter. The word 'investment' therefore has a technical meaning in the present context much narrower than its ordinary everyday meaning.

Readers who have already studied some monetary and employment theory will be aware, and others should be warned, of the intolerable confusion in the literature occasioned by attempts to distinguish 'investment' from day-to-day spending by reference to the class of commodity bought (e.g. fixed equipment or, say, raw materials). Thus when, in any time period, less money is spent on commodities than the value of commodities produced, then stocks of finished goods will build up. On the commodity definition of investment there is a temptation to regard the building-up of stocks as well as purchases of new machinery as investment by firms, for the building-up of stocks could be deliberate and purposive as well as involuntary. If such a definition is accepted, investment in stocks becomes simply a balancing item exactly equal to the difference between the value of production and sales. The equation (5.2.1) introduced below must then always be true by definition of the word 'investment'. It ceases to be a condition of equilibrium, that is, a condition for a stationary level of employment as explained below, and becomes an empty tautology satisfied even when the level of employment is changing.

Saving by firms is shown on Fig. 5.1 as money flowing into a central pool of accumulated saving. Gross investment is the money flow out of accumulated saving used to purchase commodities (perhaps, but not necessarily, machinery, buildings, etc.) on behalf of firms, over and above those purchased out of the flow of sales revenue in the time period. Net investment is the diminution, positive or negative, of the stock of money held by firms.

The ambiguity of the more usual definition of investment is still further emphasised by reflection on the fact that firms may pay wages to labour engaged in preparing sites for new buildings and machinery. Conversely they may buy machinery to replace worn-out items without any intention of increasing plant capacity to produce, a type of activity not ordinarily referred to as investment.

We are fortunate indeed that no distinction is necessary between the different kinds of purchase. The two essential points to grasp are, first, that firms, like individuals, may set aside some of their revenue as saving or may spend out of the revenue earned in past periods. And the flow of new saving is not necessarily equal to the spending out of past revenue. Secondly, it must be understood that this type of activity can be influenced by government policy. A lower rate of interest, encouragement of lending by individuals to firms, or special tax concessions can speed up the flow of spending by firms out of accumulated saving and perhaps decrease saving by firms. In short the central box of Fig. 5.1 is a container for money, filled and emptied at varying rates by the saving and spending activities of both firms and households. It does not matter that it is not always easy to decide whether a particular purchase by a firm should be regarded as a flow from firms to commodities and back to firms via saving and investment or whether it should be regarded as part of the basic circular flow. What does matter is that both flows exist and that there is reason to believe that the saving investment flow can be controlled by policy.

Saving and dis-saving by individuals is shown on Fig. 5.1 as a flow of money from factors into accumulated saving and back to factors. Saving is simply not spending in the period, whilst dis-saving is the spending by persons of titles to wealth accumulated in past periods. Here it is obvious that the two activities need not be equal. The pool of accumulated titles to wealth may be increasing or diminishing.

The reason why we distinguish between investment (saving and dis-saving by firms) and saving (positive or negative) by individuals is not that they are any different in their effects but that they represent two activities governed by separate and distinct principles. Gross investment is influenced by the availability of funds and the expectation of a profit. Saving on the other hand is determined partly by commodity prices and the rate of interest, but also, to a considerable (perhaps greater) extent, by the level of individual incomes (i.e. by the level of production in the period). The higher the level of income the greater the amount saved.

Two other important interruptions to the flow of money have to be considered. First, money is taken both from firms and individuals by taxation and spent by the government on commodities (or returned to individuals as old-age pensions, etc.). If more is collected in the period than is spent, there is said to be a budget surplus. If less is collected than is spent, there is a budget deficit. Obviously the government has complete control of the size of the surplus or deficit, which is automatically fixed by 'fiscal' (i.e. taxation) policy.

Second, some money is spent by individuals and firms on commodities produced abroad (imports). Conversely there is a flow of money directed to the purchase of home commodities coming from abroad (exports). These import/export flows have of course been the focus of our inquiries in earlier chapters and, as we have seen, will be determined by prices both at home and abroad. If exports exceed imports money is added to the main flow and vice versa.

In sum, Fig. 5.1 represents a convenient classification of causes of leaks or infusions into the basic money flow. These are imports, exports, saving, investment and budget imbalance. Depending on the strength of these activities in any period the flow of money available for the purchase of commodities may be greater than, equal to, or less than the value of commodities produced. If it is greater there will be a tendency for output, or prices, or both, to rise. If it is less the tendency is for output, or prices, or both, to fall.

It follows that, if there is to be no pressure to change either the general level of prices or employment or commodity stocks, we must have

$$\text{exports} - \text{imports} = \text{saving} - \text{gross investment} + \text{budget surplus}$$

$$(5.2.1)$$

or, to put it another way, the sum of the money infusions, exports and investment, must equal the sum of the money leaks, saving, imports and budget surplus. The condition (5.2.1) must hold exactly both before and after the correction of a trade imbalance whenever we assume that there is no building-up or depletion of stocks at any time. Indeed saving, investment and budget imbalance are the three channels whereby the government may influence total expenditure as explained in Chapter 4, so that (5.2.1) is only another way of saying that, when stocks are constant, any loss of international currency (exports less imports) must be offset by spending in excess of the value of output. Thus aggregate spending, (Y), is given by (5.2.2):

$$Y = p_1 O - \text{saving} + \text{investment} - \text{budget surplus} \qquad (5.2.2)$$

which simply indicates that the home population, people, firms and government, spend the value of production (current incomes) plus the net amount withdrawn from past titles to wealth. In the form (5.2.2), spending is broken down into constituent parts in such a way that we are able to consider how the various elements may be affected by policy. This is done as the occasion arises.

5.3 CORRECTING AN IMBALANCE WHERE THERE IS NO POLICY REACTION ABROAD

Our primary problem is, how far can the government adjust a trade imbalance by policies designed to reduce investment and/or create a budget surplus, given that no relative prices are to change? Changes in output, O, are to be permitted but no pressure to change stocks or prices is to be present either before or after. That is, supply and demand are equated by adjustments in production.

In this section we assume no policy reaction on the part of the foreign country. We take it also that changes in output (employment), which are permitted, do not themselves affect either the level of investment or the budget imbalance. In fact we shall suppose that investment and the budget surplus together (g), are entirely controlled by the government, which determines that the total expenditure change on both items together is to be dg. This is reasonable since both may be influenced by fiscal policy and the object of the exercise is to discover the consequences of some policy which may be identified as a change dg in g.

As (5.2.1) must hold both before and after the changes envisaged, then changes in the left-hand and right-hand side of (5.2.1) must be equal. We have therefore,

$$dB = dE - dI = dS - dg \qquad (5.3.1)$$

which says simply that the change in the balance of payments must be equal to the change in exports less the change in imports, which in turn must be equal to the change in saving less dg, the infusion of money by government policy.

Since prices do not change, changes in exports and imports depend on changes in total expenditure alone, at home and abroad. In fact we have

$$dE = C_1' dY' \tag{5.3.2}$$

and

$$dI = C_2 dY \tag{5.3.3}$$

(5.3.2) says that the change in exports equals the foreign marginal propensity to consume exportables (exactly in the sense of Chapter 4) multiplied by the change in total expenditure abroad dY'. (5.3.3) expresses the change in imports as the home marginal propensity to consume importables multiplied by the change in total expenditure at home.

Private saving, S, as we have indicated, depends upon prices and income $p_1 O$, that is, since prices do not change, upon $p_1 O$ alone. Hence we write

$$dS = sp_1 dO \tag{5.3.4}$$

and abroad

$$dS' = s' q_2 dO' \tag{5.3.5}$$

where s and s' are the proportions saved of unit increase in money incomes at home and abroad respectively. s is called the marginal propensity to save. Thus from (5.2.2) we deduce that

$$dY = p_1 dO - sp_1 dO + dg \tag{5.3.6}$$

and abroad

$$dY' = q_2 dO' - s' q_2 dO' \tag{5.3.7}$$

No dg' appears in (5.3.7) since we have assumed that foreign government policy leaves investment and the budget imbalance unchanged abroad. Substituting all these results in (5.3.1) and converting to home currency units gives

$$dB = e[C_1'(q_2 dO' - s' q_2 dO')] - C_2(p_1 dO - sp_1 dO + dg) = sp_1 dO - dg$$

or

$$C_1'(1 - s')p_2 dO' - [C_2(1 - s) + s] p_1 dO = (C_2 - 1) dg$$

or, dividing by dg,

$$C_1'(1 - s') p_2 \frac{dO'}{dg} - [C_2(1 - s) + s] \frac{p_1 dO}{dg} = C_2 - 1 \tag{5.3.8}$$

For the foreign country we have a similar equation since, in the foreign country also, (5.2.1) and (5.3.1) must hold. Hence

$$C_2(1 - s) \frac{p_1 dO}{dg} - [C_1'(1 - s') + s'] \frac{p_2 dO'}{dg} = - C_2 \tag{5.3.9}$$

(5.3.8) and (5.3.9) are two simple linear equations in two unknowns, $\dfrac{p_1 dO}{dg}$ and $\dfrac{p_2 dO'}{dg}$, which can easily be solved by the usual elementary method to give

$$\frac{p_2 dO'}{dg} = \frac{C_2}{s'C_2(1 - s) + sC_1'(1 - s') + ss'} \qquad (5.3.10)$$

and

$$\frac{p_1 dO}{dg} = \frac{s'(1 - C_2) + C_1'(1 - s')}{s'C_2(1 - s) + sC_1'(1 - s') + ss'} \qquad (5.3.11)$$

$\dfrac{p_1 dO}{dg}$ is the rate of change of the value of output in country 1 as spending is cut by government policy, given no change in prices. Similarly $\dfrac{p_2 dO'}{dg}$ is the rate of change of output in country 2 as spending is cut by government policy in country 1, assuming that no retaliatory policy is instituted by the government in country 2.

The first thing to notice is that the expressions (5.3.10) and (5.3.11) are both positive since all s and C must be positive and less than 1. This follows from the fact that both s and C are proportions by definition. Hence output will be cut in *both* countries if dg is negative, i.e. dO' and dO will both be negative. We have also an estimate of the magnitude† of the fall in employment, since from (5.3.11)

$$dO = \frac{1}{p_1} \left[\frac{s'(1 - C_2) + C_1'(1 - s')}{s'C_2(1 - s) + sC_1'(1 - s') + ss'} \right] dg$$

A similar expression for dO' is given by (5.3.10).

The fact that the employment changes in both countries are necessarily negative means first of all that the infinite series of repercussions on employment described in section 5.1 are quite realistic and will come to an end in the sense that they eventually become so small as to be imperceptible. When this occurs the final changes in employment will be the dO and dO' above. If any dO

† Readers who have already encountered the idea of the international trade multiplier in their studies of employment theory elsewhere should not be puzzled by a slight apparent difference between the results developed here and those in the literature. Our marginal propensities to consume C are the proportions of changes in *expenditure* Y going to the respective commodities and not the proportions of changes in income, pO. We implicitly also make the further reasonable, but apparently original, assumption that some part of any excess spending (above the value of production) is spent on importables. The general conclusions are not materially affected.

were positive, requiring an increase in employment, the process would not have been possible if the exercise had been begun from a position of full employment. As, however, both the verbal description and the algebra show that unemployment must be expected, the result is quite general. And the most superficial study of the history of international economic relations makes it plain that something of the kind demonstrated must have occurred many times in the past.

It is perhaps worth remarking in passing that there is no reason to suppose that the degree of unemployment exported abroad will be any less than that created at home. This is easily seen by noting that $(1 - C_2)$ and $(1 - s')$ are both less than 1 by the meaning of C and s, so that the numerator of (5.3.11) is necessarily less than $s' + C_1'$. And $s' + C_1'$ could easily be less than C_2 so that *a fortiori* the numerator of (5.3.11) would be less than the numerator of (5.3.10). On the other hand it is quite clear also that it could be larger.

Of course, if the home country is small relative to the foreign country (the rest of the world), then the *same* amount of unemployment will be a relatively large percentage of the home work force and a relatively small percentage of the world work force. But it is as well to remember that 50,000 unemployed will be equally unhappy whether they live at home or abroad. Their plight is in no way relieved by the fact that it might be less conspicuous.

We have now to confirm that some government policy (i.e. some dg) can be chosen so that any balance of payments deficit is corrected and that such a policy must be a *cut* in spending for the country in deficit. To this end we note first that, for the foreign country, the change in saving must be equal to minus the change in the balance of payments. This follows from the fact that, by assumption, neither investment nor the budget imbalance, have changed in the foreign country. We have in fact an equation like (5.3.1) for the foreign country which we write

$$- dB = dI - dE = edS' \qquad (5.3.12)$$

bearing in mind that we are measuring in units of home currency and that imports for the home country are exports for the foreign country. From (5.3.12) and (5.3.5) we have

$$dB = - s'p_2 dO'$$

or

$$\frac{dB}{dg} = - s'\frac{p_2 dO'}{dg} = \frac{- s'C_2}{s'C_2(1 - s) + sC_1'(1 - s') + ss'}, \qquad (5.3.13)$$

The expression (5.3.13) is bound to be negative, from which it follows that a negative change dg in total spending is necessary to change the balance B in a positive direction, for (5.3.13) implies that

$$dB = -\left[\frac{s'C_2}{s'C_2(1-s) + sC_1'(1-s') + ss'}\right] dg \quad (5.3.14)$$

In other words we have shown that a cut in spending in the home country leads to a fall in employment at home and abroad and an improvement in the balance of payments from the home country's point of view.

Finally, from (5.3.14), if dB is to equal the deficit B on the balance of payments, then

$$dg = \frac{-B[s'C_2(1-s) + sC_1'(1-s') + ss']}{s'C_2}$$

which gives a measure of the cut in spending required to correct a given imbalance B.

5.4 Correcting an Imbalance with a Positive Policy Reaction Abroad

We need now to discover what will occur if the foreign country reacts to a fall in employment with a policy designed to restore the situation. This problem is most easily studied by rewriting the two equations (5.3.8) and (5.3.9), remembering

(i) that there is now to be a change, dg', in the investment and/or the budget imbalance in the foreign country. Hence edg' will appear in (5.3.7) and dg' (without e) in (5.3.8) and (5.3.9), and

(ii) that the change dg' is *chosen* as a matter of policy to keep dO' zero (full employment abroad) so that dO' will *not* appear in the amended (5.3.7), (5.3.8) and (5.3.9).

We shall have in fact

$$- [C_2(1-s) + s]\frac{p_1 dO}{dg} + C_1'\frac{edg'}{dg} = C_2 - 1 \quad (5.4.1)$$

as the counterpart of (5.3.8) and

$$C_2(1-s)\frac{p_1 dO}{dg} - (C_1' - 1)\frac{edg'}{dg} = -C_2 \quad (5.4.2)$$

as the counterpart of (5.3.9).

Again this is a case of two equations in two unknowns, $\dfrac{p_1 dO}{dg}$ and

$\dfrac{edg'}{dg}$, which may be solved by the usual methods.

The result turns out to be

$$\frac{p_1 dO}{dg} = \frac{1 - C_2 - C_1'}{C_2(1 - s) + s(1 - C_1')} \qquad (5.4.3)$$

and

$$\frac{edg'}{dg} = \frac{- C_2}{C_2(1 - s) + s(1 - C_1')} \qquad (5.4.4)$$

Notice first that the numerator of (5.4.3) is not necessarily positive, although the denominator must be. It follows, paradoxically, that a cut, dg, in home expenditure could lead to a rise dO in output provided we begin from a position of less than full employment so that some increase in output is possible. This curiosity arises because of our assumption of a foreign reaction. If home consumption is cut, so are imports. Accordingly spending abroad must be increased to maintain full employment, some of this spending being directed to exportables. The cut in home spending is replaced, in this case more than replaced, by foreign demand.

It is worth noting, conversely, that if the attention of the government happened to be directed more to existing unemployment than to an imbalance in the balance of payments, and if the change dg in expenditure represented an *increase* designed to alleviate unemployment, the policy could fail if $1 - C_2 - C_1'$ were negative. In such a case (5.4.3) equally well indicates that a rise in expenditure will be followed by a *fall* in employment despite the efforts to increase it. This is because the foreign country, on our assumptions, will meet the inflationary pressure arising from the increased demand for importables by a cut dg' in spending leading to a cut in world demand for exportables.

Against all this the reader is reminded that a negative $1 - C_2 - C_1'$ is not very likely to be observed in the real world, where a high proportion of expenditure is directed towards commodities which do not enter into trade. In the U.K., for example, only about one-sixth of national income is spent on importables, and the U.K. is often represented as a country more than usually dependent upon trade.

Remarks on the interpretation of C which appear below and in section 5.5 are also relevant.

Assuming therefore that $1 - C_2 - C_1'$ is positive, (5.4.3) implies that a cut in expenditure will reduce output. Similarly, (5.4.4) implies that dg' and dg must be of opposite sign, since $-C_2$ is necessarily negative. Thus the foreign country is bound to react to a negative dg with an increase in spending. Consider then the effect of all this on the balance of payments.

From (5.3.1)

$$dB = dS - dg$$

or

$$dB = sp_1 dO - dg$$

or

$$\frac{dB}{dg} = \frac{sp_1 dO}{dg} - 1$$

which, with (5.4.3), gives

$$\frac{dB}{dg} = \frac{s(1 - C_2 - C_1')}{C_2(1 - s) + s(1 - C_1')} - 1 = \frac{s - sC_2 - sC_1' - C_2 + C_2 s - s + sC_1'}{C_2(1 - s) + s(1 - C_1')}$$

$$= -\frac{C_2}{C_2(1 - s) + s(1 - C_1')} \tag{5.4.5}$$

which is bound to be negative in sign.

The negative sign of $\frac{dB}{dg}$ means, as in section 5.3, that if the balance of payments is to be *improved* (i.e. dB positive) then dg must be negative (i.e. spending must be cut). Note especially that the sign of (5.4.5) is not in any way dependent on the sign of $1 - C_2 - C_1'$. An improvement in the trade balance *always* demands a cut in spending even though when $1 - C_2 - C_1'$ is negative this implies a rise in employment.

Too much should not be made of the obvious analogy between the result (5.4.3) and its consequences, and the fundamental result of Chapter 4 where again the sign of $1 - C_2 - C_1'$ was crucial. There is of course an immediate connection which is seen at once if we assume $1 - C_2 - C_1'$ to be zero. In such a case dO would be zero (from (5.4.3)) and the balance of payments could be corrected without unemployment in either country, simply by cutting spending at home and increasing it abroad. We see in fact from (5.4.4) that, if $1 - C_1' = C_2$, as it must if $1 - C_1' - C_2 = O$, then $\dfrac{edg'}{dg} = -1$ or

$$edg' = -dg$$

which is exactly in line with all that was said in Chapter 4. The similarity is more apparent than real, however, for as soon as we introduce employment changes as an alternative to changes in the real terms of trade, the problem is in fact quite different, particularly when we face the fact that goods excluded from trade exist. In Chapter 4 the crucial magnitude is the difference between C_1 and C_1', which is the same as the numerator of (5.4.3) only because $C_1 = 1 - C_2$ in a two-commodity world. In the problem of this chapter it is the value of $1 - C_2 - C_1'$ which remains critical even in a world with non-traded goods. This is easily seen by the fact that we have made no direct use in this chapter of the assumption that only importables and exportables exist.

Finally we see that, as before, we can write down from (5.4.5) the usual measure of the required magnitude of the policy change. If dB is to equal B, the imbalance, then

$$dg = -\frac{B[C_2(1 - s) + s(1 - C_1')]}{C_2} \tag{5.4.6}$$

which is necessarily negative, as we have already noticed.

5.5 THE PROBLEM OF 5.4 WITH A CLASS OF NON-TRADED COMMODITIES

As indicated earlier, there is, in the present chapter, no explicit appeal to the assumption that only one class of commodities, namely exportables, is produced at home and only one class, importables, produced abroad. Before we claim that the results above hold equally in the more general case, however, attention must be drawn to at least two important points.

First, the letter O is used throughout to designate output, and accordingly $p_1 O$ is the value of output at home. This of course implies that only commodity 1 at price p_1 is manufactured at home. On the other hand the argument is in no way changed if we assume that, say, three commodities, importables, exportables and non-traded commodities, are produced at home. All that is necessary is to write for the value of output wherever it occurs

$$\sum_i p_i O_i = p_1 O_1 + p_2 O_2 + p_3 O_3 \tag{5.5.1}$$

and each result stands as before. In (5.5.1), of course, O_1, O_2 and O_3 are the quantities produced at home of commodities 1, 2 and 3 and p_1, p_2 and p_3 are their prices respectively.

In this more general version we should have

$$\frac{\sum p_i dO_i'}{dg} = \frac{C_2}{s'C_2(1-s) + sC_1'(1-s') + ss'} \qquad (5.5.2)$$

corresponding to (5.3.10) and similarly throughout. The right-hand side of (5.5.2) measures the rate of change in the *value* of output in country 2 as spending is changed in country 1 exactly as in the simpler case. Since prices do not change, a cut in the value of output must imply a cut in employment of resources even though more than one commodity is produced.

Great care must now be taken, however, in interpreting the meaning of the C_2 and C_1' which appear in the various formulae. As long as there was no home production of importables and no foreign production of exportables, no ambiguity arose. The Cs were marginal propensities to consume which depend solely upon tastes just as in Chapter 4. In such a case the magnitudes of the Cs do not vary in any special way with the sizes of the countries concerned. There is no *a priori* reason to suppose that the marginal propensity to consume importables of the United Kingdom should be larger or smaller than the rest of the world's marginal propensity to consume exportables. Both represent a proportion of a single-unit increase in spending.

But in this section we have supposed (more realistically) that some part of the rest of the world's consumption of exportables is actually manufactured in countries other than the home country, so that we have a complication. C_1' must now be interpreted not as the foreign marginal propensity to consume exportables but as the foreign marginal propensity to consume exportables multiplied by that proportion actually produced in the home country. This is so since we want $C_1' dY'$ to represent the change in exports and not the change in total foreign consumption of exportables, which is a different thing.

In most cases we should expect the proportion of foreign consumption of exportables manufactured abroad to be large for a small exporter and small for the rest of the world. Thus we have an *a priori* reason for expecting C_2 to be larger than C_1'. Indeed the problem is more serious than this, for when there is unemployment at home and abroad, the proportion of the world market secured by the two classes of sellers might well be indeterminate, depending as it does upon chance and/or the energy of rival salesmen.

Fortunately, however, most of the qualitative results of this chapter do not depend for their validity upon the magnitudes of the Cs but upon their signs. And these must always be positive whatever the situation. The warning of this section therefore refers primarily to inferences about magnitudes of effects and not about their direction. Most of our conclusions will remain valid in the real world subject to the provisos of the paragraphs following whatever the numbers of commodities produced.

The second important point to be noted in this section concerns the foreign reaction assumption of section 5.4. The results of section 5.4 depend crucially upon the expectation that the foreign country will respond to a cut in spending in the home country by increasing its own spending so as to restore the value of production (employment) to the same level at which it originally stood. This works perfectly well even in the case where a non-traded commodity is produced *provided resources are not fully employed initially*.

To illustrate the difficulty which otherwise arises, let us suppose that there is full employment abroad at the moment when the home country cuts its expenditure. The impact effect upon the foreign country will be a cut in the demand for the importables which it supplies. But note especially that there will be no cut in the demand for the foreign non-traded commodity, since by definition no demand for this originates in the home country. If therefore the foreign government raises its aggregate expenditure to compensate for the fall in demand for importables, it will necessarily create excess demand for non-traded goods. Contrary to assumption this excess demand cannot be met by increased production (because of the initial full employment) unless resources are moved from production of importables, where there is deficit demand, to the production of non-traded goods.

Actually of course, a movement of productive resources is precisely what will occur, but there are good reasons for supposing that such a movement cannot take place unless encouraged by an appropriate change in relative prices. And if we admit changes in relative prices we are simply back to the problem of Chapter 4. Indeed, the difficulty we have before us illustrates very well the impossibility of sustaining the distinction between the economics of employment and the economics of prices despite our present wish to do so.

One way out of the dilemma is to imagine what would happen *if* productive resources (labour and capital) *could* move from one industry to another even though there are no price changes. If this could happen, all of the formulae of this chapter would stand without amendment whatever the numbers and location of commodities produced. We should have a fully general theory. We may think of the theory not as an exact account of the consequence of policy, but as a description of the underlying mechanism which would operate upon the level of employment and the balance of payments were it not for the effect of price changes which interfere in some degree.

The reader who may feel this is an unsatisfactory way to leave the argument is reminded once again that no proper fusion of employment effects and price effects is possible on present information.[†] Until we are able to discover the empirical laws governing the timing and magnitude of the changes in prices and production which producers introduce in response to involuntary stock changes, nothing further can be said. Knowledge of the direction alone of responses is not enough.

5.6 Conclusions

We learn from this chapter that, even when we begin from a position where world demand is equal to world production, it is always possible to correct a trade imbalance by a cut in expenditure by the country in deficit. But we note that this will usually be accompanied by the appearance of involuntary unemployment of resources either at home or abroad or in both places.

Comparison of equations (5.3.13) and (5.4.5) reveals that a smaller cut in expenditure is sufficient whenever the country in surplus can be relied upon to take action to maintain full employment. Note that dividing the top and bottom of (5.3.13) by s' equates numerators of both (5.3.13) and (5.4.5) and the denominator of (5.3.13) may be written

$$C_2(1 - s) + s(1 - C_1') + \frac{s}{s'} C_1' \qquad (5.6.1)$$

Inspection now shows the denominator of (5.3.13) to be numerically greater than that of (5.4.5) by the last term of (5.6.1), which is necessarily positive. This justifies the claim which begins this paragraph and which accords with our understanding that unemployment wherever it appears will be 'exported' in some degree. If the country in surplus permits some degree of unemployment, part of this will be transferred to the country in deficit.

† But see Chapter 19.

It is well worth remarking also that the conclusions of this section underline the fundamental importance of the cut in spending which is necessary even when currency depreciation takes place (see Chapter 4). It is not an exaggeration to insist that the basic cause of modern balance of payments difficulties is over and underspending. Price adjustments are necessary only to clear markets and prevent the accumulation or depletion of stocks and/or unemployment.

EXERCISES

1. In the problem of section 5.4 explain from first principles why the foreign policy change in expenditure edg' must equal the change in the balance of payments. Hence without actually solving the equations justify the similarity of the results (5.4.4) and (5.4.5).
2. Show diagrammatically or otherwise that even though in both cases the foreign country maintains full employment at all times, the problem of section 5.4 is very different from that of section 2.5 (Fig. 2.2). In what ways, if any, does the final equilibrium differ between the two cases?
3. Suppose that businessmen are induced to increase their investment activity by increases in the level of production, O, according to the rule

$$dZ = idO$$

   at home and

$$dZ' = i'dO'$$

   abroad, where dZ is the change in investment and i and i' are constants. Rework the problem of section 5.3 to show that (5.3.11) becomes

$$\frac{p_2 dO'}{dg} = \frac{C_2}{(s'-i')C_2(1-s-i)+(s-i)C_1'(1-s'-i')+(s-i)(s'-i')}$$

   and analagously for other results.
4. Show that a once-for-all change dZ in investment activity has exactly the same effect as an equal change dg in government policy spending.
5. Suppose that in each time period the government of the home country tries, by adjusting g, to correct any imbalance of the

previous period using the formula (5.3.14) to determine g, that is

$$dg(t) = - B(t - 1)\left[\frac{s'C_2(1 - s) + sC_1'(1 - s') + ss'}{s'C_2}\right]$$

where t is the time period. Suppose at the same time that, unknown to the government, businessmen at home and abroad adjust their investment activity according to changes in the level of output in the previous period following the rule

$$dZ(t) = idO(t - 1)$$

Select suitable values for the various parameters s and C and some initial trade imbalance and output change at time zero minus one and calculate the changes dB for twenty time periods. (Assume no policy reaction abroad.)

Show by example that this model may generate fluctuations in the level of employment and the balance of trade, that is, show that it may spontaneously give rise to successive booms and slumps.

6 The Transfer Problem

6.1 UNREQUITED CAPITAL MOVEMENTS

IT is now possible to turn to a question which has, at various times and in various contexts, been the centre of a storm of debate both political and academic. Transactions between countries are not always confined to the exchange of commodities; there is sometimes a deliberate intention to give or lend titles to wealth for reasons very different from the usual straightforward payment for goods or services received. For example, it has for a long time past been common practice for a government to sell bonds to private investors abroad, a practice which is equivalent to private lending by foreigners to the home government. This in turn gives rise to 'debt servicing', that is, to payments of interest on the loan by the home country to foreign nationals

Again, after the war of 1914–18 Germany was required to pay compensation to other countries, the amount being expressed in money terms. The circumstances surrounding these reparation payments provided material for endless controversy among contemporary economists and other commentators.

More recently we have witnessed the somewhat odd spectacle of the victors paying sums of money to the vanquished, either in the form of loans or outright gifts, simply in order to restore a war-shattered economy. It is an ironic but not surprising fact that this may have proved to be a more beneficial policy than the imposition of reparations even from the point of view of the giver, for the gains from trade thereby developed could very well have been worth more than any compensation which might have been paid.

Unrequited money payments of all kinds, similar to those mentioned above, are called 'transfers', and the general problem of effecting them is usually referred to as the 'transfer problem'. It may perhaps be useful therefore to begin by asking why we should expect there to be a 'problem' at all? Why is it not as straightforward to make an international loan as it is, say, for a millionaire to leave his fortune to his son?

The essential complication arises partly out of the scale of the operation but mainly out of the fact that two or more countries are involved in the one case whereas only one country is concerned in the other. Most loans or gifts are made in terms of money. The underlying intention, however, is to transfer real wealth, that is, commodities, so that it should not really matter whether the payment is made in money or aspirin tablets – which is not unknown – provided the 'value' of the transfer can be determined. Unfortunately, where two countries are involved, a shift in aggregate expenditure from one country to another will almost certainly affect prices. In particular it will alter the real terms of trade and so affect the purchasing power of the money (or aspirin tablets) transferred. Alternatively, or at the same time, the level of employment may be affected creating difficulties in implementing the transfer itself. Analysis of these secondary effects forms the subject matter of this chapter.

6.2 THE TRANSFER PROBLEM AS THE INVERSION OF THE BALANCE OF PAYMENTS PROBLEM

Before we proceed to more detailed comment the reader must understand that the transfer problem is really nothing more than the balance of payments problem of Chapters 4 and 5 slightly disguised. A proper appreciation of this point immediately lays bare the muddle and confusion which bedevils much of the literature on the subject.

First, it is necessary to be quite clear about the question we are trying to put. Although we have not yet emphasised the point, the concept of a transfer is, *by definition*, an activity which raises expenditure in the receiving country and reduces it in the giving country. Not every money payment is a transfer in this sense; indeed it is quite easy to imagine circumstances where foreign exchange is transferred in such a way that nothing happens at all, except a flow of money. For example, suppose that reserves of gold and foreign currency were high enough in the U.S.A. for the government there not to be concerned over some reduction in their level. Suppose further that in the U.K. reserves are so low that it is thought essential to increase them and that the government has been successful in engineering a surplus of exports over imports. Given that supply and demand are everywhere equal, there must be a flow of gold from the U.S.A. to the U.K. But this is not a transfer in the sense in which we wish to use the word. There is no *intention* that the flow of reserves should be used to raise spending in Britain and cut spending in the U.S.A. On the contrary, as we have seen in Chapters 4 and 5, increased spending in the U.S.A. and decreased spending in the U.K. would simply cut off the flow of gold which we are supposing to occur, for it would remove the U.K. balance of trade surplus which gave rise to it.

On the other hand when Germany was ordered to pay reparations to France the *intention* was that Germany should consume less and France should consume more. The same applies when aid is offered to a country in need. Paradoxically, a money transfer which is intended to transfer real spending must be accompanied by measures which render the transfer of money unnecessary, or at least returns the money transferred back to the country of origin in exchange for commodities.

The point we have just made is usually brought out only indirectly in discussions of the transfer problem as such. If the transfer is made on account of aid or reparations, there is an implicit or explicit assumption that the titles to wealth to be transferred have first to be obtained by increased taxation in the home country. This is presumed to reduce spending at home and increase it abroad. But if the initiative for the transfer comes from individual investors lending abroad, there may or may not be an automatic cut in spending to correspond. If the lending is out of current personal saving which would otherwise be lent to producers at home for the purchase of machinery and buildings, then there will be a cut in home spending. But if the lending is out of money balances which would otherwise lie idle, then home spending might be unaffected or at least be affected only in an unpredictable degree due to changes in the rate of interest.

All of this lends point to the definition of a transfer with which we began this section. To succeed in its objective the transfer policy must be one which, on impact, raises expenditure abroad and diminishes it at home by the amount of the transfer. Otherwise the money payment is not a transfer. The only exception to this is an act which might be called a quasi-transfer. It could be that the intention of the transferor is simply to pass on gold or reserves themselves to the transferee, both countries being content to leave their spending unchanged. This may be thought of as the case where the 'commodity' to be transferred is 'reserves'. Since no side-effects are generated by such a policy, we do not comment further on this possibility. In short if we introduce the assumption that the two countries concerned are content with the level of their reserves and do not wish their reserves to be affected by the transfer policy, then there is one and only one way to affect that transfer. Country 1 must create a balance of payments surplus and country 2 must create a balance of payments deficit equal in value to the amount to be transferred. In the absence of a money transfer, country 1's trade surplus would bring in a flow of gold or foreign currency whilst country 2's deficit would lead to a currency loss. This will be just sufficient to allow country 1 to pay country 2 the amount of the transfer without any actual change in the level of reserves in either country.

Put this way it is clear that it does not much matter whether the amount of the transfer is expressed in gold or aspirin tablets. If the country making the transfer ordinarily exports aspirin tablets to the transferee, it might as well meet its liabilities by saying that the aspirin tablets are given free as by insisting that they be solemnly paid for in gold which is then to be returned as a transfer. As long as supply and demand are everywhere equated and reserves are to stay constant, the problem of making a transfer is nothing more than the problem of creating a balance of payments surplus.

Looking back at Chapters 4 and 5 we recall that this may be achieved in one of two ways or a mixture of both. In either case expenditure at home must be cut and expenditure abroad increased in compensation. In the context of the transfer problem we see this as brought about by increased taxation at home and the transfer of the titles to wealth so raised to the foreign country. If prices remain unchanged, the transfer of expenditure will bring about changes in employment thus creating a balance of payments surplus by precisely the mechanism of Chapter 5 where a balance of payments deficit was corrected. Alternatively, world supply and demand may be adjusted after the transfer of expenditure by suitable price changes after the manner of Chapter 4.

The problems which remain are really numerical. In case one we should like to know how much change in the level of employment would be necessary to achieve a given monetary transfer. In case two the question reduces to one of finding out what changes in prices are necessary or, what amounts to the same thing, what is the 'real burden' of a given monetary transfer. All of these questions are implicitly answered in the algebra of Chapters 4 and 5. We shall present explicit answers below.

One more point is relevant to this section. It is convenient now to make a distinction, so far not introduced, between the balance of *trade*, which is the difference between exports and imports, and the balance of *payments*, which is the *net* movement of reserves. If a capital transfer is being made, *trade* will not be balanced even though *payments* are. This is the essence of the desired position for a transfer. Indeed, a definition of a transfer might well be a *desired* imbalance of trade consistent with a *balanced* payments account.

6.3 SOME COMMENTS ON THE LITERATURE

The reader who is planning a study of the very extensive literature of the transfer problem should not expect to find there any very clear exposition of the main point of section 6.2. For quite understandable reasons earlier writers were slow to recognise the formal similarity between the requirements for a transfer and the requirements for the correction of a trade imbalance. Discussion of the two topics proceeded in fact in precisely opposite directions. The trade-equilibrating mechanism was originally seen as a *price* mechanism with adjustments in the real terms of trade as the key element. Only gradually did it come to be realised that overspending could be a cause of imbalance and that, when overspending is corrected, the direction of the necessary residual change in the real terms of trade is not obvious.

In considering a transfer on the other hand, attention is naturally focused upon the shift of expenditure between countries rather than the need to create a trade surplus. Indeed, much of the debate, arising as it did out of the post 1914–18 war reparation agreements, centred on the probable effects of the expenditure shifts on the levels of employment at home and abroad. In some quarters it was felt that the cut in spending demanded would reduce employment in the country making the transfer to such an extent that the whole operation would turn out to be impossible. This may now be seen as a question which can be put to the model of Chapter 5. On the other hand it is also clear from the work of Chapter 4 that appropriate price adjustments could perfectly easily sustain full employment at all times and in all countries, and this later came to be appreciated in the context of a transfer. Curiously enough the realisation that the change in the terms of trade needed to sustain full employment is not necessarily unfavourable to the transferor considerably antedated the realisation that the same is true of a country needing to improve its balance of trade.

Of course this is a tidy view of the development of economic thought and, like most tidy views of any human activity, it is not entirely accurate. At a quite early stage some writers, thinking in terms of a transfer of gold, argued as follows. Given that exports are not increased and imports not diminished, the transfer must imply a loss of gold from the country making the payment. This will create a downward pressure on home prices and so bring about an unfavourable movement in the real terms of trade. Thus a transfer automatically ensures that the money paid will eventually be worth more to the transferee than could have been anticipated when the agreement to transfer was originally made. Or, looked at the other way, the unfavourable movement of the real terms of trade imposes an 'added burden' on the transferor over and above the sum of money lent or given.

The same argument has been presented in different form in connection with the case where the transfer is attempted by the sale of foreign government bonds to private individuals in the home country. The first effect of this activity might well be the appearance of a deficit on the balance of payments due to the purchase by individuals of the foreign currency needed to buy the foreign bonds. In such a case the identity with the trade imbalance problem becomes quite clear and no one would dispute, in this context, the need to change prices, perhaps by currency depreciation. Hence the 'added burden' argument reappears.

The reader who has thoroughly understood section 4.2 and worked the algebra of sections 6.4 and 6.5 below should have no difficulty either in identifying the element of truth which underlies the various suggestions above or in rejecting what is false. Before turning to the more serious analysis, however, one further matter calls for comment in this section.

Because of the interest in spending and employment, a great deal of the early literature on transfers missed the point by focusing too much attention upon the method of raising the money to finance the payment. It was argued for example that if the money is obtained by borrowing, it might have less effect upon aggregate spending than if it is raised by taxation of incomes direct. It is important to realise that all of this dispute is largely irrelevant except in so far as the sharing out of wealth between individuals is a matter for concern (see below).

In order to make a transfer, aggregate spending must be cut by an amount precisely determined by the sum to be transferred. Indeed, the sum actually transferred is exactly equal to the balance of payments surplus created which, as we have seen in Chapters 4 and 5, cannot be different from the change in aggregate spending. It is simply not true that the *same* transfer can be affected by *different* expenditure cuts, given price changes necessary to maintain full employment, or that the *same* transfer can be effected by *different* changes in the level of employment, given constant prices and the foreign government reaction dg' (see Chapter 5).

To be quite sure that there can be no misunderstanding on this last point, consider again equation (5.3.1), which we repeat below (6.3.1) for easy reference:

$$dB = dS - dg \qquad (6.3.1)$$

This says that the change in the balance of payments must be equal to the change in saving minus the effect dg of government action upon investment and the budget surplus. In Chapter 5 we found it convenient to assume that personal savings, S, depend upon the level of production alone, that is upon incomes alone, from which we deduced (5.3.4), i.e.

$$dS = sp_1 dO \qquad (6.3.2)$$

But suppose that we had instead accepted the contention that government taxation policy can affect personal saving. It would then have been necessary to divide the change dS in saving into two parts, the dS of (6.3.2) which is due to the change $p_1 dO$ in incomes and some other change dS^* due to government taxation policy. On the other hand the dS^* could, in equation (6.3.1) be perfectly easily assimilated into the dg on which interpretation (6.3.1) stands as before. The dS in (6.3.1) is precisely the dS of (6.3.2). No other modification to Chapter 5 is necessary.

Note now that, by (5.3.14), dg is determined uniquely as soon as dB is given. That is, if we are told the amount to be transferred, then dg is given, for dB is the amount of the transfer. Once we have dg, then by (5.3.10) and (5.3.11) the changes in employment are uniquely given. The same arguments apply to the more general model of section 5.4.

Note also that, by (5.3.6), dg and dO uniquely determine dY which is the change in aggregate spending. A unique change in employment and aggregate spending is associated with a given transfer dB.

What we have done in adding the impact effect of policy on saving into the effect of policy on investment and budget surplus is simply to say that if the policy affects saving it must be arranged so as to have an equal and opposite effect upon investment and the budget surplus. An even simpler way to put the matter is to say that government policy must be arranged so as to change aggregate spending by a unique amount dY. This may be achieved by borrowing, by interest-rate manipulation or by taxation policy or by any other means operating on saving, investment or the budget surplus or all three together, provided only that the net effect is the change dg in aggregate spending due to policy as determined by equation (5.3.14) or its analogue (5.4.6).

Of course the manner of achieving a given dg does matter to individuals in the community just as any taxation policy matters. Questions of justice and injustice arise and these considerations are important in policy-making. But we are at the moment less concerned with the distribution between individuals of a given aggregate real income than we are with the determination of the aggregate itself. On the other hand mention of distribution does raise a general problem, not specific to capital transfers, which it may be desirable to refer to at once.

It is perfectly possible that the redistribution of any given real income could make a difference to the saving and spending habits of the community taken as a whole. In terms of the diagrams of this book, such a change would alter the shape of offer curves. That is, from the algebraic point of view, it would alter the numerical values of the various elasticities of demand and/or marginal propensities to save or consume whose signs and magnitudes we are supposed to know.

We have not made the point earlier, but it is ordinarily true that any policy designed to cut spending, indeed any policy whatever involving price changes, must lead to changes in the distribution of the aggregate, which could in turn mean a shift in offer curves. We have not faced this question partly because it is not difficult to deal with in general, but mostly because it is unlikely to affect materially the conclusions we have drawn. To treat it at the present time would simply obscure issues thought to be more important. For the time being we assume therefore that income distribution is random with respect to tastes. This means simply that by and large, for every individual who spends an unusually high proportion of his income on, say, golf clubs and whose income is affected adversely by any policy, there is another individual with the same tastes who is favoured by the redistribution. In short the shape of offer curves is assumed not to change as a result of any relative income redistributions which might occur.

We are now in a position to turn to a rather more formal discussion.

6.4 THE TRANSFER WITH CONSTANT PRICES

In practice of course a transfer usually begins with some political or other decision to raise a sum of money in one country and hand the foreign exchange equivalent to another. If this is all the action which is taken, a chain of consequences will ensue involving, in all probability, changes in prices, in the balance of payments and in the level of employment, in a manner which it is impossible to predict without further information regarding likely government reactions, at home and abroad, to the appearance of unemployment or a trade deficit. Since we do not know what governments will in fact do, we cannot make sense of the question before us until we introduce assumptions as appropriate. We deal here only with two or three possible cases. Following the pattern set in Chapter 5 we begin by supposing that producers will adjust output to demand, keeping prices constant, and that the government is prepared to tolerate any degree of unemployment and any balance of trade surplus or deficit consistent with no change in currency reserves. This is the model of Chapter 5.

Imagine to begin with that the two governments concerned approach the problem of making a transfer in only a partially sophisticated way. They have sufficiently good economic advisers to be able to understand that it is impossible to make a transfer without a loss of currency reserves unless expenditure is cut in the one country and increased in the other. They understand also that to cut expenditure it is necessary to create an excess of government and private saving over investment and vice versa. Suppose therefore that to effect the transfer government 1 introduces a policy designed to reduce expenditure by dg, the amount of the intended transfer, whilst the foreign government aims to increase expenditure by the same amount. At the same time the sum of money dg is transferred in cash.

Very conveniently it is now possible, using the theory of section 5.3, to write down at once the consequences for the balance of trade of the attempted transfer. (5.3.14) tells us that the cut in spending in country 1, in the absence of any change in spending abroad, would change the trade balance by

$$-\left[\frac{s'C_2}{s'C_2(1-s) + sC_1'(1-s') + ss'}\right] dg \qquad (6.4.1)$$

Similarly, by pretending that country 2 is country 1 and applying the same formula, remembering that the change in spending abroad is an increase and therefore of opposite sign and that the change in the trade balance for one country is of opposite sign to that of the other, the change in the home balance due to the foreign policy by itself would be

$$-\left[\frac{sC_1'}{s'C_2(1 - s) + sC_1'(1 - s') + ss'}\right] dg \qquad (6.4.2)$$

The full change dB in the home trade balance brought about by the attempted transfer, therefore, will be the sum of (6.4.1) and (6.4.2), that is,

$$dB = -\left[\frac{s'C_2 + sC_1'}{s'C_2(1 - s) + sC_1'(1 - s') + ss'}\right] dg \qquad (6.4.3)$$

It is convenient to rearrange the denominator of (6.4.3) to put it in the form

$$dB = -\left[\frac{s'C_2 + sC_1'}{s'C_2 + sC_1' + ss'(1 - C_1' - C_2)}\right] dg \qquad (6.4.4)$$

When the result is written this way it is easy to see that, except in the coincidental circumstance where $(1 - C_1' - C_2)$ is zero, dg and dB cannot be equal in magnitude. The policy introduced has failed. The transfer of dg in cash (measured in home currency units) has led to a balance of trade surplus at home, and hence an inflow of currency, equal to dB. If dB is greater than dg there will be a net gain in reserves contrary to the defined objective. If dB is less than dg there will be a net loss of reserves.

Following the arguments of Chapter 5 (especially section 5.4), we recall that ordinarily we should expect $(1 - C_1' - C_2)$ to be positive in sign. Hence the expression in the square bracket on the right-hand side of (6.4.4) will be less than unity, so that dg must be expected to be greater than dB and there would be a loss of reserves by the home country in the usual case.

All that these results tell us, of course, amounts to little more than we had already noted in earlier sections. If we wish to make a transfer with no change in reserves we must choose some dg such that dB is equal to the amount to be transferred and not set dg itself equal to the transfer.

Partly for the sake of completeness and partly to emphasise once again the fact that levels of employment must change, we write down from equations (5.3.10) and (5.3.11), using the principle employed to derive (6.4.3), the solutions for changes in the value of output at home and abroad when the transfer is attempted on the wrong principles as described. We should in fact have

$$p_1 dO = \left[\frac{s'(1 - C_1' - C_2)}{s'C_2(1 - s) + sC_1'(1 - s') + s's} \right] dg \qquad (6.4.5)$$

for the change in value of output at home and

$$p_2 dO' = - \left[\frac{s(1 - C_1' - C_2)}{s'C_2(1 - s) + sC_1'(1 - s') + s's} \right] dg \qquad (6.4.6)$$

for the change in the value of output abroad. Note that, with $(1 - C_1' - C_2)$ positive, employment will fall at home and rise abroad.

At this point we have to face the fact that any government sophisticated enough to understand that, to effect the real transfer of commodities of a given value, it is necessary to look at the balance of trade rather than the expenditure change, is likely to be sophisticated enough also to understand the employment problem thereby created. If it tries to correct the employment fall by an increase in spending as an integral part of the operation, further changes are induced. We have in fact dg different from dg' in the analysis above, and anything can happen.

From Chapter 5, however, we learn that, whatever values are put on dg, we cannot have simultaneously

(a) full employment in both countries; and
(b) a given level of the balance of trade (i.e. an effective transfer without a loss of gold).

One or other or all must go. If (*b*) is met, full employment is possible in one country but not in both. But this is only another way of saying that a gold loss can be corrected by changes in the level of employment in one or both countries just as we learned in Chapter 5.

These considerations simply reflect the absurdity of any attempt to make a transfer without at the same time engineering an appropriate change in relative prices, which brings us back to the problem of the 'added burden'. We treat this in the next section.

6.5 THE WELFARE EFFECT OF A TRANSFER WITH FULL EMPLOYMENT

At this point we leave behind the partially sophisticated governments and assume that the economic advisers of the two countries have read this book and, accordingly, fully understand what must be done to make a money transfer of a sum dB expressed in home currency units, at the same time preserving full employment and the balance of payments.

The problem before us is simply to compute the 'added burden' of the transfer. The sum of money paid is dB, but the act of paying has changed prices. We should like to know whether the change in welfare, measured in money, is less than, equal to, or greater than the agreed transfer dB.

The importance of this inquiry is obvious and has already been touched upon. If the transfer is on account of reparations, the paying country may complain that the receiving country is gaining more than the amount of the transfer. If, on the other hand, the transfer is of capital for foreign investment, the community at large may object that the actions of a small number of investors seeking private profit impose a burden on everyone else by raising the price of imports. Indeed, there may be a situation in which it would be worth while to offer a payment to investors to induce them to keep their funds at home.

One of the great advantages of the algebraic methods developed in this book as an alternative to the diagrams is that it permits us to make quantitative statements in answer to welfare questions such as that raised above. We proceed in the following way.

First we note that a suitable measure of the change in welfare following any change in policy is given by valuing the change in total consumption at existing prices. It should be noted that this is not the same thing as looking simply at the total change in money expenditure, for, in the usual case some prices will have changed as well as money expenditure. For example, we might double money expenditure, but if at the same time we double prices, no one can be any better off. It is for this reason that we choose to measure increases in real spending by valuing the actual changes in physical quantities of goods consumed. In the case where there is no change in physical consumption we then get the result 'no change in real income' even though a change in money expenditure may have occurred.

One qualification is necessary, however. There is a very real sense in which a community could be said to be worse off even when it is consuming more. This might be the case if incomes were 'badly' distributed between individuals and if the 'bad' distribution were the consequence of an increase in consumption. For example, it might be held that a country enjoys a higher welfare when all are reasonably well off than it would if its total output were much greater but if the greater part of that output fell into the hands of a minority. We assume therefore in what follows that increases in wealth will be reasonably distributed. Accordingly, in symbols, we have

$$p_1 dX_1 + p_2 dX_2$$

as a measure of the change in welfare in country 1 consequent upon any policy change, assuming as usual that only two commodities are consumed.

Again, whatever policy is under consideration, it must always be true that

$$p_1 X_1 + p_2 X_2 = Y \qquad (6.5.1)$$

for this simply says that the value of consumption equals total spending. (6.5.1) must hold for all possible values of ps, Xs, and Y so that, taking changes, we have

$$p_1 dX_1 + p_2 dX_2 + X_1 dp_1 + X_2 dp_2 = dY \qquad (6.5.2)$$

In deriving (6.5.2) we have of course followed the principles of Chapter 3, writing changes in $p_1 X_1$ as $p_1 dX_1 + X_1 dp_1$. This ignores terms like $dp_1 dX_1$ which are negligible when compared with the included items, given that dX and dp are themselves small (see section 3.3). The problem of measuring the welfare change dw now reduces to one of finding the values of dp_1, dp_2 and dY, for from (6.5.2) and the definition of dw we have

$$dw = dY - X_1 dp_1 - X_2 dp_2 \qquad (6.5.3)$$

Note that if we were interested in the welfare change when the transfer is attained by permitting unemployment, with prices constant, the answer is immediately given by (6.5.3), for dp_1 and dp_2 are zero by assumption so that the welfare change is dY. And by (5.3.6)

$$dY = (1 - s)p_1 dO + dg \qquad (6.5.4)$$

Using (5.3.14) and (5.3.11) or their analogues in section 5.4, according to the assumptions made about policy reactions abroad, values of dg and dO for insertion in (6.5.4) may easily be worked out.

There is little point in deriving the formula in full, however, for the result we shall get is quite trivial. Indeed it must be true that

$$dw = p_1 dO - dB \qquad (6.5.5)$$

which simply says that the change in welfare is equal to the transfer plus the change in the value of output. Since prices have not changed, there is no problem. The 'added burden' is the value lost by increased unemployment and to calculate it we have only to calculate the unemployment, as we have already done.

Returning, however, to the main problem of this section, we have to consider what changes in dY, dp_1 and dp_2 must have occurred to achieve the balance of trade surplus, dB, equal to the transfer, when full employment is everywhere maintained.

Again there is no need for very much algebra, since this has already been worked in full in section 4.4 for the simple model with no non-traded commodities. We know in fact from Chapter 4, and indeed from the more complex definitions (5.2.1) and (5.2.2), that

$$Y = p_1 O - B$$

which, since output remains constant, and since, following section 4.4, we keep p_1 constant, measuring the real terms of trade change by dp_2, implies

$$dY = - dB$$

Thus the welfare change dw is, from (6.5.3),

$$dw = - dB - X_2 dp_2 \qquad (6.5.6)$$

that is, the added burden is $- X_2 dp_2$.

And from section 4.4 we have a measure of this, for by (4.4.14)

$$dB = \left[\frac{- X_2(E'_{11} + E_{22} + 1)}{1 - C'_1 - C_2} \right] dp_2 \qquad (6.5.7)$$

Hence

$$- X_2 dp_2 = \left[\frac{(1 - C'_1 - C_2)}{(E'_{11} + E_{22} + 1)} \right] dB \qquad (6.5.8)$$

dB is of course a positive trade surplus equal to the sum of money it is desired to transfer. Hence, assuming

$$(E'_{11} + E_{22} + 1) < 0$$

which is the condition for stability (see section 3.3), it is clear that the added burden will be a negative burden (i.e. dw positive) if

$$(1 - C'_1 - C_2) < 0 \qquad (6.5.9)$$

It is of the utmost importance to understand that the condition (6.5.9) is perfectly possible in the context of the present model. The reader should not be misled by our earlier argument that $(1 - C_1' - C_2)$ will ordinarily be positive (see section 5.4). It is true that in the real world (6.5.9) is not likely to be met, for C_1' and C_2 are the proportions of an increment of expenditure spent on importables by the home country and on exportables by the foreign country, and if there exists a large class of non-traded commodities neither C_1' nor C_2 is likely to be greater than one-half. But the result (6.5.8) is *not* a proposition about the real world. It is a proposition about a model from which non-traded commodities are excluded. As a matter of logic we must have

$$1 - C =_1' C_2'$$

so that

$$1 - C_1' - C_2 = C_2' - C_2 \qquad (6.5.10)$$

Put this way the proposition (6.5.9) is equivalent to the much more plausible proposition that C_2' might be less than C_2. It now seems quite clear that the necessary change in the real terms of trade could be in favour of the country making the transfer. Instead of an added burden we find that, in certain circumstances, the burden of the transfer might be lightened by the secondary effects. Nor should this surprise us, for we have already encountered in Chapter 4 cases where the correction of a trade imbalance demands a favourable rather than an unfavourable movement of the terms of trade.

A further interesting point concerns the *magnitude* of the secondary burden or relief. We know that each elasticity E is the percentage response in consumption to a price change. In Chapter 1 it was explained that this response has two parts, an 'income' effect which arises because a rise in price is equivalent to a diminution of real income, and a substitution effect which is due to the change in relative prices. The cheaper commodity is 'substituted' for the dearer.

Consider the measure of the income effect if price rises by an amount dp. If X is the quantity purchased, the additional cost of buying X will be Xdp units of money. The income effect on the purchase of X will therefore be

$$- Xdp \, \frac{\partial X}{\partial Y}$$

which is the product of the loss, measured in money, times the income response rate $\partial X / \partial Y$. If we turn this into an elasticity by multiplying by p/X as required, we obtain the result

$$- Cdp$$

for the income effect, where C, as before, is $p(\partial X/\partial Y)$. The number E therefore contains $- C$ plus a substitution effect which must also be negative. E is always negative and numerically greater than, or at least equal in magnitude to, C.

It follows that the denominator of (6.5.8) contains within it the number $1 - C_1' - C_2$ which is the numerator. If (6.5.9) holds, the expression in the square bracket (6.5.8) is positive and numerically less than one. If $1 - C_1' - C_2$ is positive, however, the square bracket of (6.5.8) will be negative and less than unity where Es are large but could be very large indeed and either negative or positive if the sum of the Es is of the order of magnitude unity.

Note that the numerical value of the square bracket could easily be as high as unity when $(1 - C_1' - C_2)$ is positive. This would be the case if the negative substitution parts of the Es added to not more than twice $(1 - C_1' - C_2)$. In such a case the secondary effect of the transfer would be as great a burden as the transfer itself. This at first sight surprising and at second sight disturbing result confirms that the added burden argument is an important one. On the other hand in its classical form it is quite false when it claims that the burden is always a burden. A relief is not at all unlikely, and if the substitution part of the Es were relatively small it is at least conceivable that a transfer could be made at a real cost of something of the order of one-half of the sum transferred. This is not a matter to be overlooked in any political negotiations.

6.6 ON THE PROBLEM OF 6.5 WITH NON-TRADED COMMODITIES

It is, unfortunately, not convenient to work the more general version of the problem of section 4.4 at this stage since the manipulations are especially tedious (refer however to exercise 5, Chapter 4). On the other hand the assurance is given that the principles set out in section 1.5 continue to be strictly adhered to. All of the important conclusions of section 6.5 stand, with very little modification, even in the most general case, a fact which justifies the treatment of the problem at this stage. However, for the student who may find the author's glib assurances less convincing than his own doubts, some intuitively plausible argument can be given, and this we now attempt.

First, suppose that all prices, including the real terms of trade, are given and fixed for some one country. Whatever the number of commodities produced, consumed and traded, it seems reasonable to suppose that the level of all three activities will be chosen, by self-interest, so that welfare is maximised. The argument used by economists to justify free competition has always been precisely this. It follows that any small adjustments which might occur when maximum welfare has been found would have no effect on welfare. The principle, in fact, of seeking a maximum demands that changes should take place until it is found to be impossible to discover any other change which would make a further contribution to welfare, that is, until all possible moves add nothing.

The reader will accept therefore that any gain or loss in welfare which occurs as a result of policy must come, as it were, from outside. It must represent a change which the competitive system could not have made of itself. Obviously a transfer is an act of this kind. Another possibility is a change in the real terms of trade. If there is a favourable movement in the terms of trade, there is a real loss to the foreign country and a real gain at home.

If a transfer is made there is a loss dB of the sum transferred. The transfer will also change the real terms of trade by an amount dp_2 (p_1 constant). Imports are now purchased at a cost $x_2 dp_2$ different from the old cost. All other changes have zero welfare effect since they represent adjustments which *could* have been made without the external stimulus of the policy. Hence whatever is produced or traded, the total welfare change will be

$$dw = - dB - x_2 dp_2 \qquad (6.6.1)$$

The only difference between (6.6.1) and (6.5.6) is that x_2 now represents the quantity of imports as distinct from X_2, the quantity of importables consumed. The two will not be the same if there is any home production of importables.

The reader will now recall the work of section 4.3, where reasons were given why, even where non-traded commodities exist, the creation of a trade surplus or the annihilation of a deficit may just as easily call for a favourable movement of the terms of trade as an unfavourable one. Hence dp_2 may be negative and the added 'burden' may be a 'relief' just as in section 6.5.

Of course the formula for dp_2 will look very different in the more general case, as will the formula for dB. We are not excused the necessity of working it by the argument above, although the actual work will be left as an exercise to be completed after reading the whole book.

EXERCISES

1. Interpret Fig. 4.1 to show that it is consistent with balanced payments provided the foreign country is making a transfer to the home country of a sum of money (in foreign currency) equal to $(MQ)q_2$. Hence show that the problem of making a transfer is precisely the reverse of that of section 4.2 where the home country is required to balance its trade beginning from the position illustrated in Fig. 4.1.

2. Examine the Balance of Payments Accounts published by the Central Statistical Office in the journal *Financial Statistics*. Find what proportion of U.K. payments and receipts to and from abroad are on account of capital transfers. Carry out the same exercise for the U.S.A.

3. Consider the argument leading to (6.5.6). Suppose that country 1 produces S_1 of exportables and S_3 of non-traded goods in fixed quantities. Show that the added burden of a transfer is still measured by the quantity

$$- X_2 dp_2$$

and hence justify in part the assertion (6.6.1).

4. Write down (in elasticity form) from the result of exercise 5, Chapter 4, the added burden corresponding to the more general model of exercise 3 above. Show that no new problem arises consequent upon this generalisation.

5. Show from the results of exercise 6, Chapter 4, that a transfer ordinarily requires a relative fall in the home price of non-traded goods.

Exercises to be attempted only after a first reading of Books I and II

6. Allow home production of importables and non-traded goods and correspondingly abroad. Let supplies be dependent on prices. Prove the result (6.6.1) and show that the most general version of (6.5.8) is

$$- x_2 dp_2 = \left[\frac{\phi'_{23} - \phi_{23}}{\dfrac{X_2}{X_2 - S_2}\psi_{23} + \dfrac{X'_1}{x'_1 - S'_1}\psi'_{13} - \phi_{23} - \phi'_{13} + 1} \right] dB$$

Hence show that once again the generalisation adds little to our qualitative conclusions.

7 Tariffs and Subsidies

7.1 THE FIVE SHEEPSKINS OF THE WOLF

GOVERNMENT and taxation are virtually synonymous; and almost since government began, inter-regional trade has been a favourite object of taxation. Tariffs on imports have, in the past, been imposed for at least five general reasons, and all but one of these has been, and continues to be, the subject of unending controversy. The forms which the arguments take differ according to the circumstances of the day. They range from the Mercantilist (and even modern) passion to protect the stock of 'wealth' (i.e. gold) of the country to the controversy over the desirability of U.K. entry into the European Common Market, but the essential issues remain unchanged. It is convenient to begin our discussion by listing the five possible motives referred to.

Import duties may be imposed:

1. To raise revenue for the government;
2. To correct a balance of payments deficit;
3. To 'protect' the home producer against foreign competition;
4. To 'protect' the home labour force against foreign competition; and
5. To exploit the foreign country (i.e. to shift the real burden of taxation under (1) on to the foreign supplier).

We shall not treat (1) explicitly since it is obviously necessary for any government to raise revenue, and the question whether it is best to raise it by taxes on imports is simply a matter of balancing considerations (2)–(5) with other aspects of public finance which lie outside the scope of this book. The more important problems connected with (4) must also be left until a more suitable model has been developed (see Book II, Chapter 14), whilst (3) and (2) are deferred to Chapter 8. In the main, therefore, we shall be concerned, in this chapter, with various facets of (5).

7.2 TARIFFS AND THE REAL TERMS OF TRADE

Motive (5), the deliberate exploitation of the foreign country, has seldom been invoked explicitly as a reason for the imposition of a tariff, partly, perhaps, because of the apparent ethical overtones, but mostly since it is not intuitively obvious, and therefore not widely understood, why a tariff should in fact 'exploit' the foreign country. (It should be explained in parenthesis that what we mean by 'exploit' is that the country imposing the tariff should be better off, with the exporting country worse off. It is *not* implied that one situation is any 'fairer' than the other. The well-being of a country is determined partly by accident of history and partly by endowment of natural resources, and there is no economic principle upon which to decide whether any particular distribution of the world's resources is 'fair' or otherwise.)

When a tariff is imposed it is apparently paid by the buyers of the imports, not by the sellers. There is no obvious reason why the sellers should be worse off. On the other hand economists have long been aware that tariffs ordinarily do change the *real* terms of trade in favour of the importing country and that some of the burden of the tax is therefore shifted on to the foreigner. The model developed in earlier chapters permits us to see at once why this should be so.

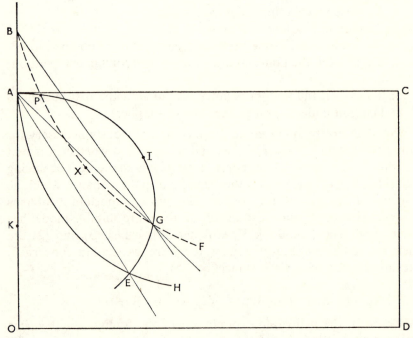

FIG. 7.1

Fig. 7.1 represents the familiar box with offer curves initially *AEH* for country 1 and *AGE* for country 2. Equilibrium before the imposition of a tariff is at *E*, the point of intersection of the two offer curves. *AE* is the original real terms of trade line.

A tariff is now imposed yielding a revenue to the government equal to *AB*, measured in units of country 1's exportables. Consider now the level of total spending in country 1. First of all the community receives an income of *AO* equal to its total production. No doubt the government will take some of this in taxation and spend it on essential services, but this does not alter the fact that the total *AO* is spent, for the offer curve *AEH* takes into account government demand for commodities as well as demand by consumers and by firms for new plant and machinery.

When the tariff is imposed, government income is increased by *AB*. Either government spending must be increased or other taxation remitted in which case consumer expenditure increases. In both cases total spending *must* increase by the amount *AB* of tariff revenue

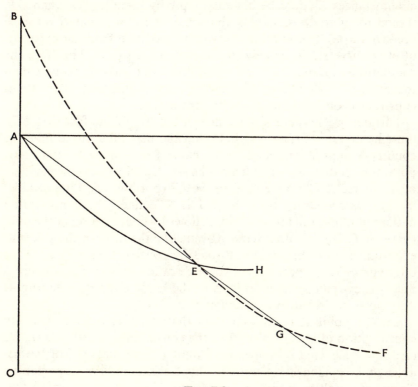

FIG. 7.2

collected. Accordingly we draw a new offer curve, the broken line *BGF*. We notice also that *BGF* cannot cut *AEH* but must lie above it. This can be shown as follows. Suppose that the two offer curves *AEH* and *BGF* do cut at *E*, as in Fig. 7.2.

Let *AEG* be the real terms of trade line appropriate to the total expenditure *OA* and consumption pattern *E* and let this cut *BGF* in *G*. First, we reflect that the community must prefer the consumption pattern *E* to the consumption pattern *G*. This follows from the fact that, by definition of an offer curve, *E* is preferred (chosen) before all points on the terms of trade line *AEG*. At the real terms of trade *AG*, by trading more or less, country 1 can consume any combination of exportables and importables represented by any point on *AG*. Since it chooses *E* rather than *G* we presume it will do so always, provided *E* and *G* are *possible* consumption points.

Suppose now that total consumption were *OB* and the terms of trade *BG* (not drawn in on Fig. 7.2). By definition of the dotted offer curve *BGF*, *G* would be the chosen consumption pattern. But in these circumstances *E* could be bought simply by spending less than *OB*, the terms of trade remaining the same. It follows that *G* must be preferred to *E*. This contradicts what we deduced from the existence of offer curve *AEH*, namely that *E* is preferred to *G*. Therefore the configuration of Fig. 7.2 is impossible and offer curves constructed on the basis of higher total expenditure cannot intersect offer curves constructed on the basis of lower expenditure.

Turning back to Fig. 7.1 we now make use of the fact that *BGF* must lie above *AEH* to conclude that the new offer curve *BGF* for country 1 must intersect the offer curve for country 2, *AGE*, at a point *G* such that *AG* is less steep than *AE*. Consider now the meaning of the line *AG*. The price ratio between exportables and importables in the *home* country must be *BG* if *G* defines the consumption pattern at home and abroad. This follows by construction of the offer curve *BGF*. On the other hand *AG* must be the ratio of the prices of exportables and importables abroad by construction of the *foreign* offer curve. We expect these two price ratios to be different since a duty is now paid on importables in the home country. The import duty must be added to the foreign price.

Let the point *K* be chosen such that *AK* measures the foreign consumption of exportables when the consumption pattern is *G*. We can now trace what is happening. Country 1 produces *OA* of exportables and exchanges *KA* units of this for *KG* units of importables. These importables, however, have a duty imposed on them so that they are sold in the shops at a price higher than the import price. Total expenditure on *KG* of importables measured in units of exportables is *BK*, not the *AK* which is paid to the foreign country. This is consistent with the idea that the slope of the line *BG* (= *BK/KG*) measures the home price ratio between exportables and importables. The amount of import duty collected is *AB*, again measured in units of exportables. Both countries are content to consume at the pattern *G*, i.e. country 1 buys *KG* of importables and *KO* of exportables whilst country 2 buys *AK* of exportables and (*AC – KG*) of importables. World consumption is just equal to world production. Total spending in country 1 equals the value of total output *OA* plus the tariff revenue *AB*, as previously explained. Total spending abroad is equal to the value of the foreign production.

AG therefore is the new real terms of trade line. And by the argument which showed that *AG* must be *less* steep than *AE*, it follows that the real terms of trade have moved in favour of country 1. Fewer exportables are now given up per unit of importables. Country 1 has gained at country 2's expense. The import duty 'exploits' the foreign country as required by (5).

7.3 A TECHNICAL POINT ON OFFER CURVES

The reader inspecting Fig. 7.1 may possibly have some difficulty over a new feature of the 'equilibrium' position, *G*, arising after the imposition of the tariff. Up to section 7.2 there has been no problem in identifying equilibrium as the point of intersection of offer curves. In Fig. 7.1, however, the broken curve *BGF* and the foreign offer curve *AGE* intersect twice, once at *G* and once at *P*.

It is as well to understand that *both* of these intersections are possible equilibrium points. Two positions exist because there are two distinct tariff rates which give rise to the *same* total revenue *BA*. If the tariff rate had been set sufficiently higher than it is at *G*, an equilibrium at *P* could have been attained, with real terms of trade *AP*, with home relative prices *BP*, and the same total tariff revenue *BA*.

Note that, as the tariff rate is raised above that existing at *G*, total revenue from the tariff increases shifting the point *B*, and hence the offer curve *BGF*, upwards. Eventually the home offer curve will cease to intersect the foreign offer curve *AGE* at any point. The critical level of tariff where the two offer curves are tangential identifies the rate which yields maximum total revenue. At higher tariff rates the falling-off in the quantity of importables demanded outweighs the effect on duty collected of the increase in the tariff rate. Total revenue falls. At lower levels of total revenue the home offer curve moves inwards until once more it begins at B (Fig. 7.1), the level of tariff yielding BA being measured by the difference between the real terms of trade AP and the home price ratio BP.

These remarks underline the meaning of the offer curve as drawn in Fig. 7.1. Each point on the home offer curve, say X, defines what the home country would wish to consume if the real terms of trade were AX *and* home prices were BX. In these circumstances it follows automatically that the revenue collected would be BA if demands were actually supplied. Note that where tariffs and/or subsidies are involved, at least two of home prices, the real terms of trade or revenue collected must be specified before a point like X on the offer curve can be identified.†

7.4 A Warning

It may be helpful, at this point, to draw the attention of the reader to the fact that a fair proportion of the literature on tariffs has been concerned to show that the expected improvement in the real terms of trade might not occur if the object of the exercise is to raise additional revenue for some particular project dear perhaps to the hearts of reigning politicians.

Some writers, for example, make the assumption that total *government* spending will rise by the amount of the tariff revenue, private spending remaining constant at the total value of output. In these circumstances, of course, everything depends upon the way in which the tariff revenue is actually spent by the government, that is, upon the purpose for which the tariff was imposed. If the intention is to buy commodities produced at home, the terms of trade must move favourably since world demand for exportables will be that much more intensified. If, on the other hand, the object is to secure importables for government use, then demand will be diverted to importables and the terms of trade movement may be unfavourable.

All this, in our model, can be interpreted to mean that, associated with the imposition of the tariff, there has been a change in the way

---

† In many texts (perhaps most) offer curves are constructed on the basis of constant tariff rates and hence variable revenue collected. The reader should take note of this when comparing the approach above with more orthodox treatments.

in which the community as a whole *wishes* to allocate its expenditure. Such a change in preferences invalidates the argument of section 7.2 which showed that the new offer curve *BGF* must lie above the old, *AEH*.

To see this even more clearly suppose that, instead of an import duty, the government imposed an income tax. It does so because it has decided that the community as a whole would be better advised to spend its money on roads than upon, say, refrigerators. Money is therefore taken forcibly from individuals and handed to the government. There has been a redistribution of spending power away from individuals towards the government, which has different ideas about the desirable pattern of spending. The pattern of consumption which emerges, therefore, for any given price ratio and total expenditure, will have changed. Our offer curve, which includes government preferences as well as individual preferences, will have shifted. Indeed we have already remarked in Chapter 6 that in a quite general way the position of offer curves as we have defined them must depend not only upon the preferences of individual consumers and the government but also upon the distribution of spending power between them. It was pointed out in connection with the transfer problem that if the method of raising the money to transfer imposes a specially heavy burden on one section of the community, where tastes are different from the rest, then there may be a shift in the shape of offer curves.

We justify the work of section 7.3, therefore, on exactly the same grounds as that of Chapter 6. When we say that a tariff ordinarily improves the real terms of trade of the country imposing it, it should be understood that this assumes no redistribution of spending power away from the community as a whole to the government. If such a redistribution (or any other kind of redistribution) is thought to be a likely consequence of the import duty, then separate consideration must be given to the effect of this. Any shift in the position of offer curves will in general change the real terms of trade quite independently of the tariff effect, and we have no reason to suppose that either one of these influences will or will not outweigh the other. When there is an income redistribution which is not random with respect to tastes, we cannot be sure that the *net* effects of a tariff on the terms of trade will be favourable.

On the other hand there is very little point in attempting to work out in detail the consequences of all the various assumptions which might be made. The reader who has thoroughly understood the argument so far is not likely to be misled into supposing that we are attempting to establish anything more profound than the simple rule that a tariff will improve the real terms of trade, provided its imposition is not associated with some other activity with opposite effects.

7.5 QUANTITATIVE ASPECTS

As usual, the diagrammatic treatment of the tariff problem yields only a qualitative result. It tells us that the terms of trade will be improved but not by *how much*. From the point of view of the policy-maker this is helpful but not helpful enough, for the international game of tariff bargaining cannot be played unless the participants have some notion of the magnitudes of the *quid* and the *quo*. Or more strictly the game can be (and probably is) played, but only as a sort of blind-man's-buff.

To be more precise, consider the recent controversy over the desirability or otherwise of Britain's entry into the Common Market. As far as the issues concerned are economic issues they may be summed up as a reorganisation of the rates of import duties charged between Britain and the rest of the world. Very seldom in the whole debate is any serious attempt made to show what proportion of the national income might be involved annually and, accordingly, what weight should be given to purely economic arguments against the political.

To calculate the gain in terms of welfare of an import duty, it is necessary to express our model algebraically. Of course the results we get have no greater validity than the model from which we derive them, but the exercise will be worth while, partly as a training in method, and partly as an indication of *orders* of magnitude.

To begin with, it is necessary to work out the rate of change of the foreign price of importables, q_2, with respect to a change in the tariff rate t. As a preliminary, we recall two important principles already well established which we shall repeatedly apply. The first is the rule for the expression of the change in any variable, functionally related to other variables, in terms of the fundamental responses (parameters) of the relationship and the given changes in the related variables. Thus, as usual, if demand X_1 is a function of prices and spending

$$X_1 = X_1(p_1, p_2, Y)$$

then for the change in X_1 we shall write

$$dX_1 = \frac{\partial X_1}{\partial p_1} dp_1 + \frac{\partial X_1}{\partial p_2} dp_2 + \frac{\partial X_1}{\partial Y} dY$$

The second principle is that which says that, for small changes, the change in a product $\pi = X_1 p_1$ may be written

$$d\pi = X_1 dp_1 + p_1 dX_1$$

This is the method of section 3.3 as applied when we set out equation (3.3.4) and later neglected the term ΔX_2 in (3.3.5) to obtain the left-hand side of (3.3.6).

We now write down an equation which says simply that the balance of trade is balanced:

$$p_1 X_1' - q_2 X_2 = B = 0 \qquad (7.5.1)$$

It should be noticed that we use q_2 for the foreign price of importables since this may now be different from p_2 by the amount t of the import duty. From this point, for convenience, we suppose foreign prices and home prices to be measured in a common currency. This is equivalent to taking the exchange rate e as equal to unity. As there is no intention to consider exchange-rate changes, we lose nothing by leaving it out. Trade is balanced when the amount of money $p_1 X_1'$ received for exports is equal to the amount of money $q_2 X_2$ which is actually paid to the foreign country.

Since p_2 and q_2 differ only by the amount of the duty, we have also

$$p_2 = q_2(1 + t) \qquad (7.5.2)$$

where t is the proportion of q_2 added to the foreign price by way of tariff.

Since (7.5.1) holds both before and after the change dt in the tariff rate, changes in the left-hand side of (7.5.1) must be zero, if the balance of trade is to remain zero. Thus, following principle two,

$$p_1 dX_1' - q_2 dX_2 + X_1' dp_1 - X_2 dq_2 = 0 \qquad (7.5.3)$$

We now suppose that, as in section 4.4, we measure the change in the real terms of trade by observing the change dq_2 in q_2, keeping p_1 constant. The reader is again reminded that the exchange rate e is taken to be unity so that $p_1 = q_1$. Thus dp_1 is zero and (7.5.3) becomes

$$p_1 dX_1' - q_2 dX_2 - X_2 dq_2 = 0$$

or

$$dq_2 = p_1 \frac{dX_1'}{X_2} - q_2 \frac{dX_2}{X_2} \qquad (7.5.4)$$

We now set out to find dX_1' and dX_2 following principle one. First, we know that

$$X_1' = X_1'(q_1, q_2, Y')$$

which says simply that consumption of exportables abroad is dependent on prices and total expenditure in the usual way. Principle one therefore gives us

$$dX_1' = \frac{\partial X_1'}{\partial q_1} dq_1 + \frac{\partial X_1'}{\partial q_2} dq_2 + \frac{\partial X_1'}{\partial Y} dY' \qquad (7.5.5)$$

which, when we remember that q_1 is constant and equal to p_1, reduces to

$$dX_1' = \frac{\partial X_1'}{\partial q_2} dq_2 + \frac{\partial X_1'}{\partial Y} dY' \qquad (7.5.6)$$

But total spending Y' abroad is the total output of importables O_2' multiplied by the price of importables q_2, i.e.

$$Y' = O_2' q_2$$

Taking changes in the usual way, remembering that O_2' does not change, by the full-employment assumption we have

$$dY' = O_2' dq_2 \qquad (7.5.7)$$

Putting (7.5.7) in (7.5.6) gives

$$dX_1' = \frac{\partial X_1'}{\partial q_2} dq_2 + \frac{\partial X_1'}{\partial Y} (O_2' dq_2) \qquad (7.5.8)$$

and multiplying (7.5.8) by q_2, remembering $Y' = O_2' q_2$,

$$q_2 dX_1' = \left(q_2 \frac{\partial X_1'}{\partial q_2} + Y' \frac{\partial X_1'}{\partial Y} \right) dq_2 \qquad (7.5.9)$$

Now look again at (7.5.5). This is an identity which must be true for any values whatever of dq_1, dq_2 and dY'. It is true therefore for values

$$dq_1 = \frac{1}{100} q_1$$

$$dq_2 = \frac{1}{100} q_2$$

$$dY' = \frac{1}{100} Y'$$

so that

$$dX_1' = \frac{\partial X_1'}{\partial q_1}\left(\frac{1}{100}q_1\right) + \frac{\partial X_1'}{\partial q_2}\left(\frac{1}{100}q_2\right) + \frac{\partial X_1'}{\partial Y}\left(\frac{1}{100}Y'\right) \quad (7.5.10)$$

But common sense tells us that if we raise prices by 1 per cent and total spending also by 1 per cent, there will be no change in the actual quantity consumed of any commodity. The increase in spending is just absorbed by the increased prices. It follows that dX_1' in (7.5.10) is zero so that

$$\frac{\partial X_1'}{\partial q_1}\left(\frac{1}{100}q_1\right) + \frac{\partial X_1'}{\partial q_2}\left(\frac{1}{100}q_2\right) + \frac{\partial X_1'}{\partial Y}\left(\frac{1}{100}Y'\right) = 0$$

or, multiplying by 100,

$$\frac{\partial X_1'}{\partial q_1}q_1 + \frac{\partial X_1'}{\partial q_2}q_2 + \frac{\partial X_1'}{\partial Y}Y' = 0$$

or

$$\left(\frac{\partial X_1'}{\partial q_2}q_2 + \frac{\partial X_1'}{\partial Y}Y'\right) = -\frac{\partial X_1'}{\partial q_1}q_1 \quad (7.5.11)$$

The reader will note in passing that (7.5.11) is a proposition which we arrived at intuitively towards the end of section 3.3. The argument above is a more formal proof.

The result (7.5.11) should now be substituted in (7.5.9) to give

$$q_2 dX_1' = \left(-\frac{\partial X_1'}{\partial q_1}q_1\right)dq_2 \quad (7.5.12)$$

To find dX_2 is not so difficult. We proceed as before, writing

$$X_2 = X_2(p_1, p_2, Y)$$

hence

$$dX_2 = \frac{\partial X_2}{\partial p_2}dp_2 + \frac{\partial X_2}{\partial Y}dY \quad (7.5.13)$$

remembering p_1 is constant.

Total spending Y in country 1 is, as we have seen, the value of total output of exportables $O_1 p_1$ plus the tariff revenue $q_2 X_2 t$. Thus

$$Y = O_1 p_1 + q_2 X_2 t$$

and

$$dY = (q_2 X_2)dt + t[d(q_2 X_2)]$$

$$= (q_2 X_2)dt + tX_2 dq_2 + q_2 t dX_2$$

We now assume, as we did in Fig. 7.1, that initially the tariff t is zero. We are in fact imposing a tariff dt for the first time. Thus

$$dY = (q_2 X_2)dt$$

which when put in (7.5.13) yields

$$dX_2 = \frac{\partial X_2}{\partial p_2} dp_2 + \frac{\partial X_2}{\partial Y} q_2 X_2 dt \qquad (7.5.14)$$

Equation (7.5.2) sets out the identity relation between q_2 and p_2 which, taking changes, gives

$$dp_2 = dq_2(1 + t) + q_2 d(1 + t)$$

$$= dq_2(1 + t) + q_2 dt$$

or, when $t = 0$,

$$dp_2 = dq_2 + q_2 dt \qquad (7.5.15)$$

Putting (7.5.15) in (7.5.14) gives

$$dX_2 = \frac{\partial X_2}{\partial p_2} dq_2 + \left(q_2 \frac{\partial X_2}{\partial p_2} + q_2 X_2 \frac{\partial X_2}{\partial Y} \right)dt \qquad (7.5.16)$$

We now substitute (7.5.12) and (7.5.16) in (7.5.4) to obtain the required relation between dq_2 and dt, namely,

$$dq_2 = \frac{p_1}{X_2}\left(-\frac{q_1}{q_2} \frac{\partial X_1'}{\partial q_1} \right) dq_2 - \frac{q_2}{X_2}\left[\frac{\partial X_2}{\partial p_2} dq_2 + \left(q_2 \frac{\partial X_2}{\partial p_2} + q_2 X_2 \frac{\partial X_2}{\partial Y} \right) dt \right]$$

$$(7.5.17)$$

It follows also from the fact that the balance of trade is always zero (see (7.5.1)) that

$$X_2 = \frac{p_1}{q_2} X_1'$$

This enables us to write for (7.5.17), remembering $p_1 = q_1$ and $p_2 = q_2(t = 0)$,

$$dq_2 = -(E_{11}')dq_2 - (E_{22})dq_2 - q_2(E_{22})dt - q_2(C_2)dt \qquad (7.5.18)$$

where the Es, as before, are the fundamental elasticities $\frac{\partial X}{\partial p} \frac{p}{X}$ and C_2 is the marginal propensity to consume importables $p_2 \frac{\partial X_2}{\partial Y}$.

Collecting terms in (7.5.18) gives

$$(1 + E'_{11} + E_{22})dq_2 = - q_2(E_{22} + C_2)dt$$

or
$$\frac{dq_2}{q_2} = -\left(\frac{E_{22} + C_2}{1 + E'_{11} + E_{22}}\right) dt \qquad (7.5.19)$$

This is our final result. It expresses, in terms of the fundamental parameters E and C, the proportional change in the foreign price (i.e. the real terms of trade) consequent upon the imposition of a tariff of dt per cent on the foreign price.

We notice that the requirement that $(1 + E'_{11} + E_{22})$ shall be negative is the familiar stability condition of Chapter 3 (see Fig. 3.2). Assuming that this condition is met, it follows that the 'multiplier' of dt in (7.5.19) must be negative in sign, for E_{22} is negative (demand falls when price rises), and although C_2 is positive it must be numerically less than or equal to E_{22}. This is because the elasticity (income and substitution effects together) already contains the income effect C_2 (section 6.5). It follows that when a tariff is imposed, dt positive, dq_2/q_2 must be negative, q_2 falls and the real terms of trade are improved for country 1.

Note that the algebra does a great deal more than confirm the validity of the result deduced from the diagrams. First of all it warns us to be on the look-out for the perverse case where $(1 + E'_{11} + E_{22})$ is positive, which it may be when elasticities are numerically low. In this case the conclusion above is reversed. The reader is invited as an exercise to attempt to construct a diagram with offer curves as in Fig. 3.2 to illustrate the possibility. On the other hand he is warned again not to make too much of the result. With a more realistic model the chances of the perverse case are very much reduced.

Second, and much more important, the algebraic result enables us to say something about the probable numerical limits of the change in q_2. Of course the exercise we are about to attempt by itself is of very little practical value since our model is hopelessly over-simplified for quantitative work. Nothing really useful can be said until we have studied a much more complex model. On the other hand the principle remains the same and, oddly enough, the conclusion is not so very different. Unfortunately for the student this is something which cannot be demonstrated until a great deal more work has been done.

Suppose none the less that the marginal propensity to consume exportables in the foreign country is not so very different from the marginal propensity to consume exportables in the home country, i.e. C_1 is not so very different from C_1'. But $C_1 + C_2 = 1$ so that $1 - C_1' - C_2$ is not so very different from zero. We also recall that E_{11}' and E_{22} are negative and *include* the income effects C_1' and C_2. The whole of the denominator of the multiplier of dt in (7.5.19), therefore, might not be very different from the sum of the two *substitution* parts of the elasticities E_{11}' and E_{22}. And we have already seen that the C_2 in the numerator cancels with the income part in the elasticity E_{22} leaving the substitution part of E_{22} only. Now substitution parts of elasticities must be negative and, in a two-commodity world, not very different.† For substitutions out of commodity 1 can only be into commodity 2 and vice versa. If 2 is a good substitute for 1, then 1 is equally a good substitute for 2. It follows that the expression,

$$\sigma_{22}/(\sigma_{11}' + \sigma_{22})$$

where σ is a symbol representing substitution parts of elasticities, might not be too different from $+\frac{1}{2}$ in magnitude.

It follows that if dt is $\frac{1}{10}$ (i.e. a 10 per cent tariff), then $\dfrac{dq_2}{q_2}$ is $-\frac{1}{20}$ or a 5 per cent fall in the price q_2. This kind of calculation permits us now to say something about the total real effect of the imposition of a tariff.

We have already noted in section 6.5 that a useful measure of the welfare effect of any policy change can be obtained by valuing changes in total consumption at the going prices. We need in this case therefore to compute

$$dw = p_1 dX_1 + p_2 dX_2$$

for country 1, where dw is the welfare change.

As in section 6.5, we write

$$p_1 X_1 + p_2 X_2 = Y$$

which simply says that the value of total consumption is equal to total spending Y. This must be true for all patterns of consumption so, taking changes due to the tariff, again as in section 6.5, we have

$$p_1 dX_1 + p_2 dX_2 + X_1 dp_1 + X_2 dp_2 = dY$$

or
$$p_1 dX_1 + p_2 dX_2 = dY - X_1 dp_1 - X_2 dp_2 \tag{7.5.20}$$

† As a matter of fact the values of σ_{11} and σ_{22} stand in the same ratio as the total expenditures on each commodity.

But p_1 does not change, so dp_1 is zero and at the same time $t = 0$ and

$$Y = O_1 p_1 + q_2 X_2 t$$

Thus $$dY = (q_2 X_2) \, dt$$

to give, from (7.5.20),

$$p_1 dX_1 + p_2 dX_2 = dw = (q_2 X_2)dt - X_2 dp_2 \qquad (7.5.21)$$

but (7.5.15) tells us that

$$dp_2 = dq_2 + q_2 dt$$

which substituted in (7.5.21) gives

$$dw = (q_2 X_2)dt - X_2(dq_2 + q_2 dt)$$
$$= - X_2 dq_2$$

Hence from (7.5.19)

$$dw = X_2 q_2 \left[\frac{E_{22} + C_2}{1 + E'_{11} + E_{22}} \right] dt \qquad (7.5.22)$$

By the argument above, the right-hand side of (7.5.22) is positive for a positive tariff, dt, so that a tariff improves welfare. But we can take the argument still further, for we have shown that the order of magnitude of the expression in square brackets in (7.5.22) is around one-half. If, say, a 20 per cent tariff is imposed so that $dt = \frac{1}{5}$, then dw will be $\frac{1}{10}$ (or 10 per cent) of the total value of imports $q_2 X_2$.

In the U.K., therefore, if we could take the figures above as roughly the right order of magnitude, we should gain, with a 20 per cent tariff, something like 10 per cent of £5,000 million per annum or say $1\frac{1}{2}$ per cent of the total national income. This is what is at stake when issues such as entry or non-entry into the Common Market are under review. Viewed as a sum of money, $1\frac{1}{2}$ per cent of the national income is far from negligible. On the other hand, if integration in Europe offered the prospect of an increase in the annual rate of growth of, say, $\frac{1}{2}$ per cent, then in less than three years any loss due to the removal of tariffs would be recovered and subsequent increases would be pure gain.

It is furthermore stressed that we should not be too impressed by the prospect of gain from the retention of tariffs, for the imposition of a tariff almost always provokes retaliation by the foreign country which in most cases cancels out or more than cancels out the gain. This point is worth further study.

7.6 TARIFFS AND RETALIATION

It is a curious fact that, in matters of economics, society often has a way of being right for the wrong reasons. This only ceases to be surprising when we reflect that to most questions there are but two answers – yes or no, up or down, etc. A random choice yields 50 per cent correct results.

From earliest times it has been argued that international trade is a 'good' thing and leads to the accumulation of wealth (i.e. gold). 'Treasure' by 'foreign trade' has always been a commonplace notion, based probably on the simple observation of the fact that exporters obtain gold from abroad for their sales – and gold is wealth. By the same token impediments to trade imposed by the foreign country (i.e. tariffs) inhibit the accumulation of treasure and are to be opposed. The natural reaction to a foreign duty on exportables is to retaliate by the raising of a similar levy on home imports of foreign goods, if only to prevent the foreign country drawing off home gold. From earliest times, therefore, tariffs have ordinarily provoked opposing tariffs.

On the other hand the more sophisticated student of the problem will not be impressed by arguments which point only to the size of the gold hoard. A country which is losing gold does so, in a general way, because it is enjoying more consumption at the expense of the foreign country, and vice versa; and this is not axiomatically bad. Furthermore it is far from obvious why a tariff should necessarily lead to gain, and indeed we have already seen in the low-elasticity case, and will see again below (section 7.7), that it may not. It is easy to accept the false view that, after all, a tariff is paid by the importer, not the foreign supplier, being passed on by the importer as a levy on the home consumer. What does the foreign country lose?

It requires all of the argument of section 7.5 to *prove* that indeed the tariff-imposing country will in many cases gain at the foreign country's expense, and to show by how much. Nor can we really be certain that the foreign country loses until we have looked carefully at the diagram (Fig. 7.1), or computed the value of

$$q_1 dX_1' + q_2 dX_2'$$

as we did for country 1.

Were it not for the coincidental accord, therefore, between the results of intuitive, false reasoning and the economists' more correct argument, a great deal more unconscious exploitation by tariffs might take place. As it is, however, there is very little possibility that changes in the structure of import duties will escape the notice of foreign countries, and perhaps this is just as well. In fact the ordinarily well-informed reader will already be aware that there exists an international organisation, the General Agreement on Tariffs and Trade (G.A.T.T.), whose main object is to negotiate multilateral tariff reduction bargains wherever possible. For this and other reasons it would be wrong to leave the argument of the previous sections without proper consideration of the consequences of retaliation or mutual tariff abolition.

Fortunately, a very straightforward extension of Fig. 7.1 is all that is required to demonstrate the major lesson to be learned.

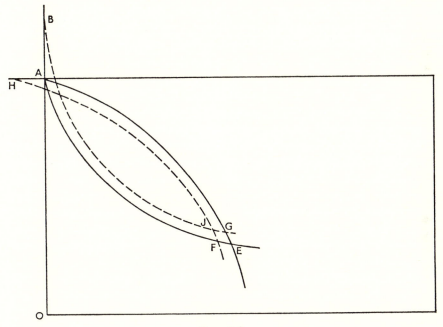

FIG. 7.3

In Fig. 7.3, country 1 has imposed a tariff to yield a revenue of *AB*, so that total spending increases by this amount. Accordingly the offer curve *AFE* shifts up to *BJG* in the usual way. We have already shown (see Fig. 7.2 and accompanying text) that *BJG* cannot cut *AFE*.

In retaliation, country 2 imposes a tariff to yield *AH* (measured in units of importables) so that offer curve *AGE* shifts to *HJF*. Applying the argument of Fig. 7.2, this time to country 2, we again reach the conclusion that *HJF* cannot cut *AGE*. The new equilibrium pattern of consumption *J* must therefore lie *inside* the region *AFEGA* bounded by the original offer curves.

Lines whose slopes represent relative price ratios have not been drawn in on the figure, but the reader will easily see that the new real terms of trade are measured by *AJ*, the home relative prices (p_1/p_2) by *BJ*, and the foreign relative prices (q_1/q_2) by *HJ*.

If Figs. 7.3 and 7.1 are compared, it will be seen that the effect of the retaliatory tariff is, as we should expect, to move the real terms of trade back again from *AG* towards the original level *AE*. It should also be clear that, if country 2 knew the shape of its own and the home country's offer curve, it could *choose* exactly that level of retaliatory tariff which would cause the point *J* to settle on the straight line *AE*. The real terms of trade would be restored to their original level.

It is easy to see that this is possible by noting that an increase in tariff rates moves *HJF* to the left whilst a decrease moves it to the right, leaving the position of *BJG* unchanged. There is no difficulty therefore in finding that position where *J* is coincident with the intersection of *AE* and *BJG*.

It is a simple matter to derive a corresponding algebraic result direct from equation (7.5.19). To this end we imagine the two tariffs separately imposed. If country 1 introduces a levy at the rate dt, the proportionate change dq_2/q_2 in q_2 is given by (7.5.19). The real terms of trade are of course defined as p_1/q_2. If p_1 is held constant and q_2 is *reduced* by the tariff in the proportion dq_2/q_2, then p_1/q_2 increases in that proportion.

Note now that if we had carried out our analysis in reverse, treating the foreign country as the home country, putting the tariff on exportables instead of importables, and keeping q_2 constant instead of q_1, we should have, by analogy with (7.5.19),

$$\frac{dp_1}{p_1} = -\left(\frac{E'_{11} + C'_1}{1 + E'_{11} + E_{22}}\right) dt'$$

where dt' is the foreign tariff rate on exportables. It is clear also that if the tariff dt' causes p_1 to fall in the proportion dp_1/p_1, p_1/q_2 is this time reduced. Thus, if we think of both tariffs simultaneously applied, for the real terms of trade to remain constant all that is necessary is to choose dt and dt' so that,

$$\frac{dp_1}{p_1} = \frac{dq_2}{q_2}$$

or $$\left(\frac{E_{11}' + C_1'}{1 + E_{11}' + E_{22}}\right) dt' = \left(\frac{E_{22} + C_2}{1 + E_{11}' + E_{22}}\right) dt$$

or $$\frac{dt'}{dt} = \frac{E_{22} + C_2}{E_{11}' + C_1'}$$

$$(7.6.1)$$

that is, dt' must be chosen so that the ratio of tariff rates is the same as the ratio of the substitution parts of the demand elasticities for the commodity imported by each of the two countries. It should be noticed that whatever the value dt, dt' can be chosen appropriately.

Of course, the fact that a pair of tariffs can be fixed so as to leave the real terms of trade unchanged is unimportant in itself, for the object is always to improve the real terms of trade, not to leave them unchanged. The interest in the special case derives from the now obvious conclusion that if

$$\frac{dt'}{dt} > \text{(is greater than)} \ \frac{E_{22} + C_2}{E_{11}' + C_1'}$$

the real terms of trade move against the home country. If, on the other hand, it is less, they move in favour of the home country.

An important qualitative result seems now to follow immediately. A 10 per cent import tariff, say, can improve welfare in the sense of equation (7.5.22) even though the foreign country retaliates with a 10 per cent import tariff on exportables if and only if

$$1 < \frac{E_{22} + C_2}{E_{11}' + C_1'}$$

$$(7.6.2)$$

If $<$ becomes $>$ welfare is diminished. These conclusions may be deduced from the work leading to (7.5.22) where it was shown that a measure of the change in welfare for the home country is given by

$$- q_2 X_2 \left(\frac{dq_2}{q_2}\right)$$

that is, the value of imports multiplied by the proportionate change in the real terms of trade. The sign of the welfare change depends only on the direction of the change in the real terms of trade – only, that is, on whether the real terms of trade improve or worsen.

The reader who fully understands the diagrammatic model may, however, anxiously assert that something has now gone seriously wrong. We seem to have proved that, if the real terms of trade do not change, the tariffs have had no effect whatever upon welfare in either country. On the other hand inspection of Fig. 7.3 suggests that both countries must be worse off if J is a point on the line AE. We argue this as follows.

If AFE is an offer curve, the pattern of consumption E must be preferred to all other possible consumption patterns on the line AE. Country 1 can consume anywhere along the line AE when the slope of this line measures the real terms of trade, and it chooses E out of all the possibilities. Therefore it prefers E to J. Similarly, country 2 prefers E to J by definition of its offer curve. It follows that any change which drives both countries from E to J must leave both countries worse off.

This apparent contradiction leads us to a subtle and difficult point which demonstrates still further the superiority of algebraic over diagrammatic methods. Consider the reasons why country 1 chooses the point E on AE rather than any other. Suppose, to fix our ideas, that the real terms of trade are 2:1, that is, one unit of exportables can be exchanged for two units of importables. Country 1 can trade 1 for 2, 2 for 4, 3 for 6, or n for $2n$. It chooses to exchange say k for $2k$ – why? The answer is that it gets more satisfaction out of the first two units of importables than it gives up with one unit of exportables. Similarly it gets more satisfaction from the third and fourth units of importables than it gives up with the second unit of exportables. Similarly for the third and fourth and fifth units of exportables given up until it reaches the kth. It does *not* offer the $(k+1)$th unit of exportables for the $(2k+1)$th and the $(2k+2)$th units of importables because it is not thought to be worth it. More satisfaction is gained by holding on to the $(k+1)$th unit. Before the number k is reached there is a gain in trading another unit. After k there is a loss. It follows that *at k* one unit of exportables is just and only just 'worth' two units of importables – there is no gain or loss in welfare in trading.

We now see why the algebra shows no loss in moving from E to J. Both countries are failing to trade as it were the last or kth unit on which there is no gain. And if there is no gain from trading, there can be no loss from not trading. Of course if the move E to J represented more than the last unit some loss will be involved, for there is a loss if the $(k-1)$th unit is not traded. Immediately the question arises: how big is a unit and how much trade can be sacrificed before a loss is felt? The strict answer to this is that only a very small amount indeed can be sacrificed. There is always some loss for any finite loss of trade so that in any practical case both countries lose, as reflected in the diagram. What the diagram fails to show, however, is how crucially the argument for a welfare loss in both countries depends upon the fact that at *E* (Fig. 7.3) the gains from the final infinitesimal unit of trade are zero. It is illuminating to write (7.5.22) in the form

$$\frac{dw}{dt} = - X_2 \frac{dq}{dt} \qquad (7.6.3)$$

obtained by dividing both sides of (7.5.22) by dt. It does not now matter how small we choose dt; the numbers dw/dt and dq/dt need not be small. Indeed dw/dt must now be interpreted not as a quantity of welfare but as the *rate of change* of welfare with respect to tariff changes. It is analogous to the steepness of a hill at a point, or the speed of a motor-car as it passes a radar check point. Speed may be very great even though distance travelled in a very short time is small.

What the algebra leading to (7.6.1) really tells us is that when two tariffs dt and dt' are imposed in a ratio satisfying (7.6.1), then the *rate* of change of welfare is zero at the point *E*, where tariffs are zero. In an analogous way the condition (7.6.2) says that whenever a tariff is met by a retaliatory tariff *at the same rate*, the rate of change of welfare in the home country, at *E*, is positive if and only if (7.6.2) is satisfied and negative if and only if the 'less than' symbol $<$ is replaced by 'greater than'. It follows that for sufficiently small tariff changes it is possible either to improve or worsen welfare. In other words a tariff can improve welfare even though there is retaliation at a matching rate. The diagram fails to make this clear.

To put it another way, we can be sure that, for sufficiently small tariff changes, the terms of trade effect will outweigh the loss of trade effect which is so obvious diagrammatically *provided* we begin from the point *E* and provided (7.6.2) holds. We do not of course know how big the tariffs can be before the approximations inherent in the method lead us into error (see Book II, Chapter 13, for a solution to this), but we do know that for some tariff rate the algebraic result is qualitatively correct. An analogy may perhaps make this clear.

If we are certain that, at the moment, we are walking uphill, we can be sure that, if we take a sufficiently small step forward, we are bound to finish up higher up the hill. On the other hand, if we are very near the summit and we take a large step we may pass over the top of the hill and find ourselves lower than we were. But unless we *are* exactly at the top it is always possible to choose a small enough step to be sure of being higher. And if of course we are, as is most likely, a long way from the top, we can walk some distance and continue to rise.

The work above tells us that if we are at the point E (Fig. 7.3) we are *not* at the summit, unless, in (7.6.2), $<$ is replaced by $=$. As long as $<$ holds, the tariff policy carries us uphill. This is an important result since it is not widely understood that the terms of trade improvement effect will, for relatively low tariffs, outweigh the loss of trade effect, so that in the tariff-bargaining game it is usually the change in the terms of trade which is crucial. On the other hand it might not be socially desirable to publicise too widely such a result. The belief that everybody is bound to lose may be a myth worth preserving even though it is nevertheless a myth.

At this point it might be wise to emphasise once again that, so far, we have worked only the simplest case. In particular we have considered the situation only at the point E (Fig. 7.3), that is, where there are no tariffs initially. In the case where some tariff already exists, either at home or abroad, and we are contemplating adjustment of the rate, the argument above does not hold. Algebraically we should not be able to set $t = 0$ as we did to derive (7.5.15). If t is initially different from zero, both the working and the final formula become more complicated.

In fact it would no longer be necessarily true that the terms of trade effect must outweigh the loss of trade effect. The reverse might very well be the case. We shall demonstrate this in the next section by finding a point at which the two effects are equal. The reader will no doubt be readily convinced that if there exists a point where an increase in the tariff rate will improve the real terms of trade but leave welfare unchanged notwithstanding, then there is likely to be a point where a tariff increase will *reduce* welfare. If such a point exists then it will exist *a fortiori* if there is tariff retaliation, for retaliation reduces the extent of the favourable movement in the real terms of trade.

The most general working of the welfare effect of a tariff change would of course give a relationship between the change in welfare and elasticities of demand, for *any* initial level of tariff in either country. The algebra of this case is not difficult, but it is tedious and space-consuming without adding a great deal to our basic understanding of the issues. It should be worked by the student, however, after reading section 7.10. In the meantime we shall assume a zero tariff abroad and no retaliation and proceed to find what level of tariff t we reach before it becomes apparent that any further increase will cease to improve welfare (because of the loss of trade effect). This is known to economists as the 'optimum tariff problem', the solution of which answers the question 'What is the best tariff rate assuming no retaliation?'

7.7 THE OPTIMUM TARIFF

It is useful to begin the present inquiry by asking in rather a different way why it is that the loss of trade effect makes a community worse off. Loss of trade is of course the intuitively obvious way of putting it. But why should trade be lost? Consider again Fig. 7.3. If *J* lies on *AE* so that tariff and retaliation leave the real terms of trade unchanged, why do we not trade up to the point *E* as before? Why stop at *J*? To move to *E* is perfectly possible and would make everyone better off.

The answer is simply that the community, in choosing what it wishes to buy, is being misled by prices which now differ from the real terms of trade. Because of the tariffs, imports in both countries *look* much more expensive than they really are. In country 1 the home price ratio is *BJ*, steeper than the real terms of trade *AJ*. In country 2 it is *HJ*, less steep than the real terms of trade. It is the artificially raised prices of imports in both countries which restrict trade, not any change in the real situation on either the supply or the demand side. The community makes a wrong choice because money prices do not truly reflect the real cost of production or importation. It is a general rule of economics that when this occurs there is a loss of welfare caused by the 'wrong' choice on the part of the consumer.

Now refer to Fig. 7.1. Any point within the box *ACDO* can be regarded as defining a possible consumption pattern for country 1. In particular every point on the *foreign* offer curve *AIGE* is a possible consumption pattern for country 1. Moreover, we have seen from the construction of Fig. 7.1 that the point of equilibrium *G*, following the imposition of a tariff, lies always on the foreign offer curve. By choosing an appropriate tariff rate country 1 can fix its own consumption pattern at any point it chooses on the foreign offer curve. A higher tariff rate moves *G* towards *A*, a lower rate moves it towards *E* along *AIGE*. We wish to determine the 'best' position of *G* from the point of view of country 1.

Now by definition of an offer curve, *E* on *AIGE* must be preferred to *A*, where only exportables are consumed, for *E* is chosen when *A* could be chosen. We have also shown that, for a small enough tariff implying a change, say, to *G*, there is an improvement in welfare over

E. Hence in moving from *E* through *G* to *I* and *A* welfare must first rise above *E* and then fall to *A*. Hence there must be a point of maximum welfare, say at *I.*

As a matter of fact it is easy to see diagrammatically where this optimum position must be. It will be the point where the home price ratio *BG* just touches but does not cut the foreign offer curve *AIGE* (see Fig. 7.1). This may be proved as follows. Any move, say from *G* to *I*, involves country 1 giving up a small quantity of importables

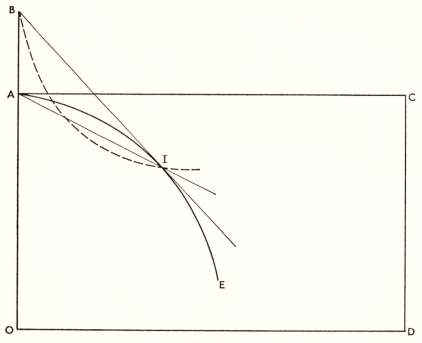

FIG. 7.4

(say dX_2) in exchange for a small quantity (dX_1) of exportables. Trade is reduced by these amounts. And since both *G* and *I* are on the foreign offer curve, the ratio dX_1/dX_2 is approximately equal to the average steepness of the foreign offer curve over the range *G* to *I*. The condition of tangency illustrated in Fig. 7.4 is the condition that for very small reductions dX_1 and dX_2 in trade the slope dX_1/dX_2 of the offer curve is equal to the ratio of home money prices p_2/p_1 represented by the line *BI*. Remembering that dX_2 is negative (imports given up) and dX_1 is positive, the condition of tangency may be written algebraically as

$$-\frac{dX_1}{dX_2} = \frac{p_2}{p_1}$$

which, cross-multiplying and carrying over, gives

$$p_1 dX_1 + p_2 dX_2 = 0 \tag{7.7.1}$$

This is immediately recognisable as the condition for zero change in welfare (section 6.5). The changes in consumption, valued at going prices, sum to zero, that is, the money value of the change in physical consumption is nothing. No small change is worth anything to the community. The crucial point, where the rate of change of welfare with respect to the tariff change is zero, has been found. To the right of I country 1 will gain from raising the tariff, to the left it will lose. Hence the tariff which leads to consumption at I is optimum.

A minor point of interest, perhaps, to students who have encountered elsewhere the idea of monopoly behaviour, is the analogy between the choice of an optimal tariff and the maximisation of monopoly profits. If we assume for convenience that p_2 is the constant (numeraire) price and that the home price ratio is changed by changing p_1 only, it is then appropriate to think of country 1 as if it were a monopolist selling a product X_1 at a price equal to $p_2 X_2 / X_1$. The monopolist is aware that if he sells more of X_1 the price which he can get from the foreign country will fall. In order to maximise profits, therefore, he will continue to offer X_1 for sale only as long as the increment of total receipts is equal to unit cost p_1 of X_1. A competitive producer on the other hand would continue to offer X_1 as long as the price $p_2 X_2 / X_1$ received covers cost p_1.

Note that the total revenue received from sales of X_1 is $p_2 X_2$, that is, price $p_2 X_2 / X_1$ times X_1. Since p_2 is constant, the increment of revenue gained from selling an extra dX_1 units of X_1 will be $p_2 dX_2$. The cost of dX_1 is of course $p_1 dX_1$. Profit is maximised where

$$p_1 dX_1 = p_2 dX_2$$

which, remembering that changes in sales dX_1 are counted as negative, is the same as (7.7.1).

The competitive position would be where

$$p_2 X_2 = p_1 X_1$$

that is, where price $p_2 X_2 / X_1$ is equal to cost p_1. Clearly the competitive profit maximisation position is that attained where the tariff rate is zero and accordingly

$$p_2 = q_2$$

for balanced trade implies

$$p_1 X_1 = q_2 X_2$$

which for zero tariff is the same as the competitive condition.

7.8 THE ALGEBRA OF THE OPTIMUM TARIFF

Once again the diagrammatic treatment of the problem under review does not tell us all we would like to know. We can deduce very little from Fig. 7.4 about the *size* of the optimum tariff. Is it 20 per cent, 100 per cent or 500 per cent? Quantitative conclusions are impossible without the algebra which now follows.

First we have, as before,

$$p_1 X_1 + p_2 X_2 = Y$$

which says that the value of purchases equals total spending.

Taking changes by the now familiar principle

$$p_1 dX_1 + p_2 dX_2 + X_1 dp_1 + X_2 dp_2 = dY \qquad (7.8.1)$$

Using now the condition for the optimum tariff,

$$p_1 dX_1 + p_2 dX_2 = 0$$

we write (7.8.1) in the form

$$X_1 dp_1 + X_2 dp_2 = dY \qquad (7.8.2)$$

as an alternative condition.

Again as before we have

$$Y = p_1 O_1 + X_2 q_2 t \qquad (7.8.3)$$

that is, total spending in country 1 is equal to the value of the total output of exportables O_1 plus the tariff revenue on the value $q_2 X_2$ of imports. Taking changes,

$$dY = O_1 dp_1 + X_2 d(q_2 t) + q_2 t dX_2$$
$$= O_1 dp_1 + X_2 t dq_2 + X_2 q_2 dt + q_2 t dX_2 \qquad (7.8.4)$$

It is now convenient to make a slight change in the procedure which, apart from section 7.7, has been followed so far. Up to the present, for reasons given in Chapter 1 (p. 9), we have assumed the price p_1 to be unchanged, measuring the change in the real terms of trade by changes in q_2. But we could equally well have assumed q_2 to be constant, measuring changes in the real terms of trade by changes in p_1. As it happens we save a great deal of algebraic manipulation by adopting this second convention in the present case. Thus dp_1 is not zero but dq_2 is. (7.8.4), therefore, now becomes

$$dY = O_1 dp_1 + X_2 q_2 dt + q_2 t dX_2 \tag{7.8.5}$$

Putting this result in (7.8.2) gives

$$X_1 dp_1 + X_2 dp_2 = O_1 dp_1 + X_2 q_2 dt + q_2 t dX_2 \tag{7.8.6}$$

as the new condition for an optimum tariff.

But

$$p_2 = q_2(1 + t)$$

since the two prices differ only by the proportionate tariff t. Taking changes,

$$dp_2 = q_2 d(1 + t) + (1 + t)dq_2$$

$$= q_2 dt \tag{7.8.7}$$

since dq_2 is zero and $d(1 + t) = dt$.

The result (7.8.7) put in the condition (7.8.6) gives a new condition

$$X_1 dp_1 + X_2 q_2 dt = O_1 dp_1 + q_2 t dX_2 + X_2 q_2 dt$$

or $\qquad (O_1 - X_1)dp_1 + q_2 t dX_2 = 0 \tag{7.8.8}$

But

$$O_1 = X_1 + X_1'$$

being the total production of exportables, so that (7.8.8) becomes

$$X_1' dp_1 + q_2 t dX_2 = 0$$

or $\qquad q_2 \dfrac{dX_2}{dp_1} = -\dfrac{X_1'}{t} \tag{7.8.9}$

We now make use of the fact that the balance of trade must always be balanced so that

$$q_2 X_2 = p_1 X_1'$$

for all possible quantities and prices. Taking changes gives

$$q_2 dX_2 + X_2 dq_2 = p_1 dX_1' + X_1' dp_1$$

which, recalling that dq_2 is zero, is equivalent to

$$q_2 dX_2 = p_1 dX_1' + X_1' dp_1$$

or dividing by dp_1

$$q_2 \frac{dX_2}{dp_1} = p_1 \frac{dX_1'}{dp_1} + X_1' \tag{7.8.10}$$

But (7.8.9), the condition for an optimum, is also an expression for $q_2(dX_2/dp_1)$ so that for an optimum tariff

$$-\frac{X_1'}{t} = p_1 \frac{dX_1'}{dp_1} + X_1' \tag{7.8.11}$$

Again foreign consumption of exportables X_1' depends only on the foreign prices q_1 and q_2 and foreign total expenditure Y_1'. Hence

$$dX_1' = \frac{\partial X_1'}{\partial q_1} dq_1 + \frac{\partial X_1'}{\partial q_2} dq_2 + \frac{\partial X_1'}{\partial Y} dY'$$

where $\frac{\partial X_1'}{\partial q_1}, \frac{\partial X_1'}{\partial q_2}$ and $\frac{\partial X_1'}{\partial Y}$ are the fundamental responses of consumers.

But dY' does not change, for

$$Y' = O_2' q_2$$

and neither O_2' nor q_2 change by the assumption of full employment and constant q_2. Hence

$$dX_1' = \frac{\partial X_1'}{\partial q_1} dq_1$$

which, since $dq_1 = dp_1$ (no tariff on exportables), gives

$$\frac{dX_1'}{dp_1} = \frac{\partial X_1'}{\partial q_1} \tag{7.8.12}$$

Putting this in (7.8.11), remembering $p_1 = q_1$, the optimum tariff condition reads

$$-\frac{X_1'}{t} = q_1 \frac{\partial X_1'}{\partial q_1} + X_1'$$

Dividing by X_1' gives

$$-\left(1 + \frac{1}{t}\right) = \frac{q_1}{X_1'} \frac{\partial X_1'}{\partial q_1} = E_{11}' \tag{7.8.13}$$

where E_{11}' is the foreign elasticity of demand for exportables.

The first lesson to be learned from (7.8.13) is that the optimal tariff t can never, in this aggregate form of the model, be negative.

That is, it can never be a good thing from the point of view of the home country to offer a subsidy on imports.

To see that t can never be negative, consider first the possibility that t might be less than -1. Since

$$p_2 = q_2(1 + t)$$

it must follow that p_2 is negative, which is impossible. Now suppose that t lies between -1 and zero. In such a case the left-hand side of (7.8.13) must be greater than or equal to zero. To satisfy (7.8.13) therefore, E'_{11} must be positive or at least zero, and a positive E'_{11} is impossible. Hence t must be positive or zero, except that it could conceivably be -1. But note that if t is -1 then p_2 must be zero.

The fact that t can never be negative and at the same time satisfy (7.8.13) might at first sight puzzle the reader who has properly understood section 7.5. This is because, by (7.5.19) it is clear that a subsidy (negative dt) will improve the real terms of trade in the exceptional low-elasticity case when

$$1 + E'_{11} + E_{22} > 0$$

and an improvement in the real terms of trade must improve welfare by (7.5.22). Why is it that a subsidy can (rarely) improve welfare although an optimal subsidy can never exist?

The answer to this becomes clear when we understand that (7.8.13) is merely a condition for a best tariff, not a rule which asserts that a best tariff is feasible or even that only one tariff satisfying (7.8.13) is possible. If E'_{11} is very low as well as E_{22}, welfare will be improved by subsidising right up to the point where $t = -1$ and p_2 is zero. What (7.8.13) tells us in this case is that it will always pay to go on subsidising as long as p_2 is positive, whatever the actual value of the (low) E'_{11}. Thus (7.8.13) is not in contradiction with (7.5.22).

Furthermore, the necessary shape of offer curves implying low elasticities in the zero tariff position (see Fig. 3.2) suggests that the higher the foreign cost of exportables, the higher the elasticity E'_{11}. Even in the case where a small positive tariff causes an unfavourable movement of the terms of trade, a very large tariff could have the opposite effect. In particular the reader will note that Fig. 3.2 shows three possible positions of trade equilibrium, namely H, B, and C. It is true that a tariff, if imposed, would raise the offer curve $AHBC$ (Fig. 3.2) and so move the point B to the left, creating an unfavourable terms of trade movement. But the same tariff would shift equilibrium C to the left also, which would imply a favourable movement of the terms of trade had these been measured by AC initially. It is easy to see also, comparing Figs. 3.2 and 7.4, that a position of optimal tariff might be attained somewhere in the region of C (Fig. 3.2) where the elasticity E'_{11} is much higher than it is at B.

If a subsidy were offered (Fig. 3.2) beginning from equilibrium B, total expenditure would fall since taxation would be necessary to raise the subsidy. Note that equation (7.8.3) still holds as before. t is negative so that Y is less than $p_1 O_1$ by the amount of the subsidy. Hence the offer curve $AHBC$ would begin from a point nearer O. The intersection B would move to the right and the real terms of trade would improve in accordance with (7.5.19). If the subsidy is increased still further, the points of equilibrium B and C will come together, the home offer curve now being tangential to the foreign offer curve. When offer curves are tangential, this is a sign that

$$1 + E'_{11} + E_{22} = 0$$

a condition which renders equation (7.5.19) meaningless. If the subsidy is further increased, the equilibrium possibilities B and C disappear, leaving only H somewhat to the left of its position in Fig. 3.2. The real terms of trade begin by improving, but later, if there is to be equilibrium at all, they jump to a level much less favourable than AB from which they began.

If on the other hand a positive tariff is imposed, it will be the equilibrium possibilities H and B which come together and disappear, leaving only C representing much more favourable terms of trade. Thus a positive tariff will end by improving the terms of trade when it is large enough even though it begins by doing the opposite. Notice carefully that all these possibilities arise not because there is anything wrong with the algebra but because it is sometimes unreasonable to suppose that elasticities will remain constant for large tariff changes.

The second point to be made about the result (7.8.13) concerns magnitudes. It is natural to wonder just how large the optimal tariff is likely to be. From the work of economists who carry out statistical analysis of data on consumer demand there is good reason to believe that, for broad categories of commodities like 'exportables', E'_{11} is not likely to be very large numerically. In most cases -2 would be the lower limit, and something greater than -1 is not impossible. It is interesting to note therefore that if E'_{11} is greater than -1 the optimal tariff is indefinitely high. It can in fact never be attained, for the left-hand side of (7.8.13) is bound to be less than -1 as long as t is positive however large we make t.

Of course, we have already noted that E'_{11} must be expected to become numerically larger as t increases, and the statistical measures referred to have been made only at relatively low tariff rates. But even if the imposition of a tariff raises E'_{11} numerically to, say, -2, the tariff will not be optimal until it reaches the 100 per cent level. For an optimal tariff as low as 20 per cent it would be necessary for E'_{11} to be -6, which does not look very probable.

We emphasise again, however, that remarks about magnitudes cannot be applied to situations other than those which the model properly incorporates. In the world in which we find ourselves today most countries have tariffs. It would be wrong therefore to speculate upon the further scope for exploitation through tariffs on the basis of formula (7.8.13), which explicitly assumes no existing tariff in the foreign country. For this reason we introduce now, without proof, a formula which will be the subject of later comment, and which is the generalisation of the result (7.8.13) to the case where a foreign tariff on exportables is already in existence. Where there is a foreign tariff t', the home optimal tariff, t, on imports is given by

$$- \left(1 + \frac{1}{t} \right) = E'_{11} \bigg/ \left(1 - \frac{t'}{(1 + t')} C'_1 \right) \qquad (7.8.14)$$

Notice that the amendment makes some difference, but not a great deal. However large t' may be, $t'/1 + t'$ must be less than unity. Even if the foreign marginal propensity to consume, C'_1, were as high as one-half, the effect of introducing the foreign tariff cannot multiply E'_{11} by more than two. For an optimal tariff as low as 20 per cent, E'_{11} must be numerically larger than -3, which again does not look plausible. On the other hand, when non-traded commodities and changes in the patterns of production are admitted, the optimal tariff need not be so high, as we now explain.

7.9 Tariffs and the Optimal Tariff when Non-Traded Goods are Present

We shall not, either in this book or in Book II, present the actual working of the algebra of tariffs in the context of any less aggregative version of the model than that of earlier sections. This task is left to the student, some of the more important results being given in the exercises at the end of this chapter.

Naturally the formulae obtained look quite different in the more general case. When non-traded goods are present and where there is some home production of importables at home ard exportables abroad, the patterns of production will be affected by price changes. Supply responses as well as demand responses therefore appear, and these the reader will not meet until Chapter 11. Even so it is possible to give assurances that, apart from magnitudes, nothing fundamental is changed by disaggregation. All of the issues raised in earlier sections stand with undiminished importance.

The reason why it has been thought worth while to comment here upon disaggregation is that there exists the possibility that too much might be read into the concluding remarks of section 7.8 on the subject of magnitudes. It seems to be a general rule of disaggregation that each supply response, where it exists, appears in an additive way with its corresponding demand response (see Chapter 11). It is also true that whenever some part of the consumption of a commodity imported is produced at home, the elasticity of demand is multiplied by the ratio of total consumption to the quantity imported. If the foreign country is taken to be 'the rest of the world', as it must in any attempt to be realistic, the ratio of consumption to imports may very well be quite large.

Neither of these peculiarities of disaggregation has any obvious influence, one way or the other, upon the formula (7.5.19) for the effect of a tariff on the terms of trade. And since the corresponding welfare change is determined by the terms of trade change, it will be accepted that the same must apply to (7.5.22). But the reverse is true of the optimum tariff condition (7.8.13). In this case the addition of supply elasticities and the 'weight' attached to the demand elasticity tends to reduce the size of the optimal tariff in any given situation in the same way as the existence of a foreign tariff on exportables (see section 7.8).

It remains possible that in a world where the 'foreign country' is large relative to the home country and where non-traded commodities are important, the optimal tariff could be very high just as in section 7.8. But the likelihood of this seems rather lower in the more general case than it did in a world with just two countries specialising in exportables and importables respectively.

7.10 TARIFF WARS

The fact that it is possible to identify the optimal tariff for *any* given, existing, foreign tariff (see (7.8.14)) opens up the fascinating theoretical possibility of a formal tariff war, with a determinate solution, the properties of which can be studied.

Beginning from a position where no tariffs at all exist, country 1 could impose its optimal tariff, say t, on imports from country 2. Country 2 might then retaliate by imposing its optimal tariff t', on exportables from country 1, given the existing duty t imposed by country 1. As the imposition of t' shifts the offer curve for country 2, the import tariff, t, levied in country 1 is no longer optimal. Thus it would be profitable for country 1 to answer the challenge of country 2 by changing its tariff rate t to some new value, say t_1, which is optimal when country 2 levies a duty t' on its imports. But this in turn moves country 1's offer curve so that t' is no longer optimal for country 2. Country 2 will be tempted to make a change and so on in infinite regression.

At least two interesting points now arise. First, do there exist 'equilibrium' tariff rates which, if they were imposed simultaneously by country 1 and country 2, would call for no further change? That is, can both be optimal tariffs given that both are in operation? And if such equilibrium tariff rates do exist, will the successive acts described in the previous paragraph guide the two countries towards equilibrium or away from it? In short, does a tariff war have a solution, is it unique, and is it a stable process?

If the tariff war is known to have a stable solution a second question immediately becomes relevant. In the final equilibrium, must both countries be worse off, or can one be better off, than in the free-trade position? If it is known, say, that the home country would be better off, it is clearly in the home country's interest to begin a tariff war. The best that the foreign country can do is to find the final equilibrium and stay there. But this is a position advantageous to the home country. Of course the foreign country could spoil country 1's game by setting a tariff so high that both are bound to lose, perhaps in the hope that a free-trade agreement can be reached. But such behaviour by the foreign country must be at some added cost to its own welfare and, in any case, it is still open to the home country to refuse to be hustled, or to answer bluff with counter-bluff.

Happily, so far as we know, a formal tariff war has never been waged at this level of sophistication. On the other hand, in these days of electronic computers and common markets, such a war is not beyond the bounds of possibility. It is as well therefore to know the rules.

The condition for the *existence* of a solution to the tariff war is easily written down from (7.8.14). We shall not, even here, prove this result (this is left as an exercise – p. 224), but we note that if (7.8.14) gives the solution for an optimal tariff in the face of an existing foreign tariff, t', the condition for t' to be optimal for the foreign country in the face of t follows by symmetry. In order that there should be no misunderstanding we set this out in full. For t' to be optimal we must have

$$- \left(1 + \frac{1}{t'} \right) = E_{22} \bigg/ \left(1 - \frac{t}{1+t} C_2 \right) \qquad (7.10.1)$$

It is now convenient to define

$$T = \frac{t}{1+t}$$

and

$$T' = \frac{t'}{1+t'} = 1 \bigg/ \left(1 + \frac{1}{t'} \right)$$

so that (7.8.14) may be written

$$- \frac{1}{T} = \frac{E'_{11}}{1 - T'C'_1}$$

or

$$T'C'_1 - TE'_{11} = 1 \qquad (7.10.2)$$

and similarly (7.10.1) is

$$- T'E_{22} + TC_2 = 1 \qquad (7.10.3)$$

If *both* T and T' are to be optimal, the equations (7.10.2) and (7.10.3) must be satisfied simultaneously. Values of T' and T meeting this requirement are easily found by solving the two equations in the usual way. Thus we arrive at the following necessary conditions for the existence of a solution to a tariff war:

$$T = - \frac{E_{22} + C'_1}{E'_{11}E_{22} - C_2 C'_1} \qquad (7.10.4)$$

and

$$T' = - \frac{E'_{11} + C_2}{E'_{11}E_{22} - C_2 C'_1} \qquad (7.10.5)$$

It is easy to see from these results that an equilibrium may or may not exist. By the work of section 7.8 we know that t is positive, and all arguments apply equally to (7.8.14), given that t' is positive by assumption. Hence, as

$$T = \frac{t}{1+t}$$

T must be positive and less than unity. Clearly, feasible values of E'_{11}, E_{22}, C'_1 and C_2 exist, which will satisfy both (7.10.4) and (7.10.5) at the same time yielding T positive and less than unity. For example, if both Es were large relative to Cs and greater than 1 numerically, the values of T and T' would be not so very different from $-1/E'_{11}$ and $-1/E_{22}$, both of which are positive and less than unity.

On the other hand if we separate E'_{11} and E_{22} into their income and substitution parts, writing

$$E'_{11} E_{22} = (\sigma'_{11} - C'_1)(\sigma_{22} - C_2) = \sigma'_{11}\sigma_{22} - C'_1\sigma_{22} - C_2\sigma'_{11} + C_2 C'_1$$

we observe that the denominator of (7.10.4) is necessarily positive in sign, for Cs are positive and σs negative. Hence if we allow C'_1 to be numerically larger than E_{22}, which it may be for small elasticities, then T must be negative to satisfy (7.10.4) which is impossible.

Notice that if *both* σ'_{11} and σ_{22} are small enough there positively *cannot* be a trade-war equilibrium, for the numerators of (7.10.4) and (7.10.5) may be written $\sigma_{22} + C'_1 - C_2$ and $\sigma'_{11} - (C'_1 - C_2)$ respectively, which implies, when σs are small enough, that either T or T' must be negative. Against this it may be thought that substitution effects are likely to be greater than the difference between income effects so that the balance of probabilities lies in favour of the existence of solutions to (7.10.4) and (7.10.5), and this holds true with equal force when we work the algebra of a more disaggregate case.

The question of the stability and uniqueness of the tariff-war solution, if it exists, is a much more complex matter which cannot be treated here. But in this connection the reader should take cognisance of the fact that, in the ordinary way, elasticities, E, will be dependent upon the chosen values of T and T' and not simply constants. There may therefore be many more than one pair of values T and T' satisfying (7.10.4) and (7.10.5) for the same two countries. The progress of a tariff war in these circumstances might be both amusing and complicated.

It remains now to show that a tariff war might be worth waging. There is no need of course to establish that it might *not* be since we already know that somebody must lose. All that we need is a particular case in which one country might gain.

To find such a case, let us suppose that the optimal tariffs defined by (7.10.4) and (7.10.5) are relatively small, so small in fact that it makes little difference whether we use the formula (7.5.22) to measure the change in welfare or the analogue of (7.5.22) applicable when a foreign tariff already exists (see exercise 7). If both countries apply the optimal tariffs t and t', the total change in welfare in country 1 will be

$$dw = \frac{dw}{dt} t + \frac{dw}{dt'} t' \qquad (7.10.6)$$

As an estimate of dw/dt we may use (7.5.22), dividing both sides by dt. And since for small t the loss in the foreign country is equal to the gain in the home country, we have

$$\frac{dw'}{dt} = -X_2 q_2 \left(\frac{E_{22} + C_2}{1 + E'_{11} + E_{22}} \right)$$

from which, by the symmetry of the problem,

$$\frac{dw}{dt'} = -p_1 X'_1 \left(\frac{E'_{11} + C'_1}{1 + E'_{11} + E_{22}} \right) \qquad (7.10.7)$$

As long as trade is balanced,

$$p_1 X'_1 = q_2 X_2$$

so that substitution in (7.10.6) yields

$$dw = X_2 q_2 \left[\frac{(E_{22} + C_2)t - (E'_{11} + C'_1)t'}{1 + E'_{11} + E_{22}} \right] \qquad (7.10.8)$$

To find the simplest case where country 1 might gain, let us suppose that the Es are numerically large enough to allow us to ignore the Cs. This is an allowable procedure, since Cs are by definition less than unity, whereas Es may be assumed to be as large as we please.†
Dropping the Cs therefore in (7.10.4), (7.10.5) and (7.10.8), and using

$$T = \frac{t}{1 + t}$$

to find ts, we deduce that

$$dw = X_2 q_2 \left[\frac{-E_{22} - (E_{22})^2 + E'_{11} + (E'_{11})^2}{(1 + E'_{11})(1 + E_{22})(1 + E'_{11} + E_{22})} \right] \qquad (7.10.9)$$

Taking the case where all Es are numerically greater than unity (consistent with the assumption that Es are numerically fairly large), the denominator of (7.10.9) must be negative. Country 1 will gain or lose from the tariff war according as E'_{11} is numerically larger or smaller than E_{22}. Moreover, since (7.10.9) is symmetric with respect to countries, it is clear that the corresponding result for country 2 would differ only by sign from (7.10.9). If country 1 gains, country 2 must lose and vice versa.

† Note that in any case Es must be large to give small optimal T.

It follows that the assumptions leading to (7.10.9) provide us with a large class of possible situations where it would be advantageous for either one country or the other to engage in a tariff war. And all that is needed to justify the argument is just one example.

As a matter of fact we could have established a single example much more simply, almost by intuition, and it may strengthen the reader's confidence in the algebra if we do this. Suppose that, for consumers in the foreign country, one unit of importables and one unit of exportables are perfect substitutes. If the price q_1 of exportables is greater than the price of importables, q_2, the foreign country will consume all importables and offer nothing for export. If on the other hand q_2 is greater than q_1, the foreign country will offer all of its production for export and try to consume all exportables. Only if prices abroad are equal can there be equilibrium in trade. In terms of Fig. 7.4, the foreign offer curve AI must be a straight line of slope 45°. The foreign offer curve and the terms of trade line will be coincident.

It follows that the optimal tariff for country 1 must be zero, for if the foreign offer curve and the terms of trade line are coincident the best position on the foreign offer curve for the home country is the 'best' position on the terms of trade line, that is, the point where the home offer curve cuts the terms of trade line. And this is the zero tariff equilibrium position.

Inspection of the condition (7.8.14) reveals that zero tariff is optimal for very high E'_{11} even when the foreign country has an existing tariff, for $1 + \dfrac{1}{t}$ will be very large only when t approaches zero. Thus the solution to a tariff war will find country 1 with zero tariff and country 2 with a tariff equal to

$$t' = -\frac{1}{E_{22} + 1}$$

by (7.8.13). This must mean a gain in welfare by country 2 and a loss by country 1. It would be in the interests of country 2 to engage in a tariff war.

The work above is sufficient to establish that a tariff war may be a feasible exercise and that someone *might* gain from it. It does not, however, prove that someone *must* gain from it; nor does it present any general rule to identify the probable winner. To find out what would happen in any practical case it would be necessary first to develop a much more realistic model and second to measure the relevant elasticities. We emphasise this in order to prevent too much being made of the formula (7.10.9) in the form in which it appears.

On the other hand, by the time he has completed a study of this book the reader will have little difficulty in working the algebra of the more general version of the model where flexible production possibilities and non-traded commodities exist. Certain further results are included also among the exercises. It might not be impossible, with very little more knowledge, at least to find which of two countries stands to gain. The qualitative question 'Who gains?' can often be answered by very imperfect estimates of elasticities even if the question 'By how much?' cannot. For example, looking at (7.10.9), we see that the sign of dw depends only upon whether E'_{11} is or is not greater than E_{22}, the amount by which it is greater being irrelevant.

7.11 THE SUPPOSED SYMMETRY OF IMPORT AND EXPORT TAXES

It is sometimes said by economists that import and export taxes have precisely the same effect, that is, a 10 per cent tax on exports would change prices and welfare both at home and abroad, in exactly the same way as a 10 per cent duty on imports. To the lay person who understands only the meaning of the words used this must seem a bewildering pronouncement, for in one case it is clearly sales at home which are being taxed, whilst in the other it is sales abroad.

Similarly the student who believes in the symmetry of import and export taxes and who has learned that subsidies are simply negative taxes may be equally bewildered when he comes to read that a 10 per cent import duty combined with a 10 per cent export subsidy has the same effect as exchange-rate depreciation, for the symmetry theorem implies that the tax and subsidy must cancel one another out, whereas no one ordinarily claims that currency depreciation has zero effect. It seems obvious in fact that currency depreciation adds to the price of imports and cheapens exports just as a tax and subsidy would.

A brief inquiry into this apparent paradox will ensure that no misunderstanding remains concerning the questions put and answered in this chapter and elsewhere in this book.

Consider what we mean by the 'effect' of an export tax. Throughout this chapter we have been concerned with positions of 'equilibrium' where supply and demand are always equal and where there is never any imbalance of trade. This is reasonable since we are putting questions about the 'welfare' associated with various tax structures. It is not sensible to confuse this issue with the dynamic problem of actually attaining equilibrium.

With this in mind, we define the 'effect' of a tax to be the long-term residual effect *after* equilibrium has been found. In the case of an export tax there will be permanent changes in expenditure and in prices at home and abroad. Let us find out what these will be. First, aggregate expenditure at home is determined by the value of output plus the tax revenue which must, of course, be spent by someone. Thus we write

$$Y = p_1 O_1 + t p_1 X_1' \qquad (7.11.1)$$

In the foreign country there is no tax collected, so that aggregate expenditure is

$$Y' = O_2' q_2 \qquad (7.11.2)$$

In addition we have the following price equations:

$$\left. \begin{array}{l} q_1 = p_1(1 + t) \\ \text{and} \qquad q_2 = p_2 \end{array} \right\} \qquad (7.11.3)$$

where t is the export duty as in (7.11.1).

Now compare (7.11.1) with the definition of expenditure given in the working leading to (7.5.14). As in section 7.5 balanced trade implies that at all times

$$p_1 X_1' = q_2 X_2 \qquad (7.11.4)$$

the Y of 7.5 might just as well be written

$$Y = p_1 O_1 + t p_1 X_1'$$

which is the same as (7.11.1) above. Similarly the Y' of (7.11.2) is the same as the Y' of 7.5.

Again, if we compare the equations

$$p_1 = q_1$$

$$p_2 = q_2(1 + t)$$

of 7.5 with (7.11.3), we note that both imply that

$$\frac{p_1}{p_2} = \frac{q_1}{q_2(1 + t)}$$

so that price ratios change in the same relative way in both section 7.5 and in the present exercise. It follows, since all the equations are the same, that the solutions must be the same. Import and export taxes have the same 'effect'.

This may be made clearer by looking again at Fig. 7.1 which was drawn originally to illustrate the effect of an import duty. But it will do equally well for the export tax. Beginning from the initial equilibrium E, suppose that an export tax is levied. As long as the rate of tax is the same as that of the supposed import duty it follows from (7.11.1) and (7.11.4) that the new expenditure is OB, the same as it would have been for the import duty. Hence the new offer curve is BGF and the new equilibrium is G. The new home price ratio is BG and the new foreign price ratio is AG. In a real sense the two kinds of tax are indistinguishable in their final effects.

Notice also that we can simultaneously impose a subsidy on exports of $-t$ and a tax $+t$ on imports so that the expenditure equation (7.11.1) reads

$$Y = p_1 O_1 - t q_1 X_1' + t q_2 X_2 \qquad (7.11.5)$$

Particular attention should be paid to the fact that the rate of subsidy t is expressed this time as a fraction of q_1, the selling price abroad, and not p_1, the selling price at home, as in the case of a tax. The reason for this convention is that whenever p_1 and q_1 differ, the trade balance must be expressed

$$B = q_1 X_1' - q_2 X_2 = 0$$

and not as (7.11.4), for the foreign currency earned is $q_1 X_1'$ and not $p_1 X_1$. Hence (7.11.5) is equivalent to

$$Y = p_1 O_1$$

which in terms of Fig. 7.1 means that the 'new' offer curve also begins at A (Fig. 7.1) and is therefore the same as the old. This confirms the statement with which we began the section, namely that an equal export subsidy and import tax has zero real 'effect', subject of course to the proviso that by 'equal' we mean when expressed as a fraction of the foreign price. The final equilibrium is the same, in terms of real consumption and real trading and relative prices, as the initial equilibrium before the imposition of the tax/subsidy structure.

Having demonstrated the element of symmetry in the effects of import and export taxes, it is of the utmost importance now to emphasise that this symmetry is more apparent than real. Suppose that all taxes are immediately passed on by the supplier to the consumer. It follows that a tax imposed by the home country on exports will raise the price of exportables abroad relative to importables. Relative prices at home will be unaffected. By contrast a duty on imports will raise the price of importables relative to exportables at home, prices abroad being unaffected. In short, far from being symmetric, the impact effects of import and export duties are just about as asymmetric as they could possibly be. One changes only home

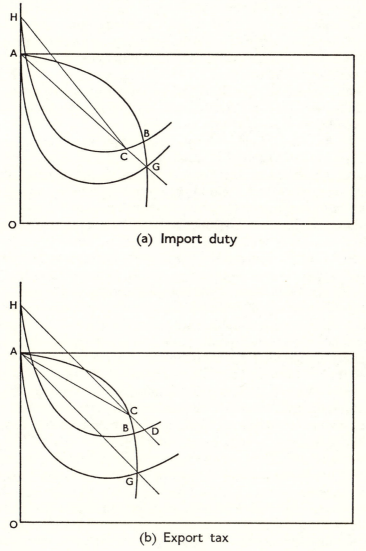

(a) Import duty

(b) Export tax

FIG. 7.5

prices and the other only foreign prices; one raises exportable prices relatively whilst the other raises importable prices.

It is instructive to follow the dynamics of the two taxes, tracing the path to equilibrium in each case. To this end we introduce Figs. 7.5 (*a*) and (*b*). Both (*a*) and (*b*) show the same initial equilibrium, with foreign offer curve *ABG* and home offer curve *AG* intersecting at *G*. In the first instance, therefore, the real terms of trade are given by *AG* and world supply equals world demand.

The remainder of Fig. 7.5 (*a*) illustrates the impact effect of an import duty. The foreign price *AG* and foreign aggregate expenditure remain unchanged so that the foreign country continues to demand commodities in the pattern *G*. The home country, however, experiences an increase in expenditure of *AH*, equal to the duty collected, so that a new offer curve *HCB* appears. At the same time the price of importables rises so that the new relative prices are given by the slope of *HC*. Accordingly the consumption pattern *C* is demanded.

Of course world supply and demand are not now equal, but let us suppose that excess demand is met out of stocks and that deficit demand leads to a stock build-up, production remaining constant. In these circumstances amounts demanded will actually be consumed. The difference between the slopes *AC* and *HC* measures the tax rate and the diagram is consistent with a tax revenue receipt of *HA*.

But note that the action taken has created a balance of trade surplus for the home country just as one would intuitively expect. This surplus is a trade imbalance precisely as described in Chapter 2, and its presence should set off some equilibrating mechanism. Let us suppose that the equilibrating mechanism is a currency exchange appreciation looked at from the point of view of the home country. The effect of this would be to raise the price of exportables relative to importables in both countries. Points *C* and *G* would move towards *B*, eventually coming to rest at *B*. Of course, in the process, the total tax revenue collected would change so that the point *H* and hence the home offer curve must move. But as soon as the system does come to rest, the diagram must look exactly like Fig. 7.1.

Now turn to Fig. 7.5 (*b*). Here we illustrate the impact of an export tax. This time it is the home price ratio which is unaffected although home aggregate spending is. As before spending goes to *H*, leading to a new offer curve *HBD*, but the price ratio line *HD* remains parallel to the original price ratio line *AG*, indicating no change. The new consumption demand for country 1 is *D*. In country 2 exportables become dearer so that the price ratio line is less steep at *AC*, although the offer curve remains fixed at *ACBG*. The new foreign consumption demand pattern is *C*.

If, as before, demand is met, where necessary, out of stocks, the amounts traded indicate that *AH* of revenue will actually be collected. But note that this time the deficit demand appears for the product of country 1. It is country 2's product for which excess demand exists. What is now called for therefore is a currency *depreciation*, not a currency *appreciation* as in the case of the import duty. As intuition would suggest, an export tax is likely to cause, on impact, a deficit on the balance of trade, not a surplus.

On the other hand if the currency is suitably depreciated after the imposition of the export tax the equilibrium *B* will at once be attained. And this, as we see, must be precisely the same equilibrium *B* illustrated in Fig. 7.5 (*a*), for the position of offer curves is determined only by the preferences of consumers, which remain unaffected by taxation policy. The points *B* and *G* therefore occur in precisely the same position in both (*a*) and (*b*) of Fig. 7.5.

It is now clear that there is a powerful sense in which the symmetry of import and export taxes is an illusion. It might be more accurate to say that an import duty plus a currency appreciation has exactly the same effect as an export tax plus a currency depreciation rather than that import and export taxes by themselves are symmetric in their effects.

On the other hand the student who has read Chapter 2 will understand that exchange-rate adjustment is not absolutely essential to the attainment of equilibrium. The necessary price changes might equally well be brought about by the ordinary operation of market forces. Indeed, currency depreciation should, strictly speaking, never be thought of as a *policy* in the same sense as a tax or a quota. Exchange-rate adjustments are simply an alternative, and often more convenient and quick-operating, method of bringing about price adjustment which supply/demand pressures would otherwise be expected to generate, provided that at the same time money and credit are controlled in such a way that the *general* level of prices remains constant between countries. Alternatively of course it is a way of bringing international general price levels into line in a way which the market mechanism never could.

Most economists, asked to comment upon the long-run effects of any tax policy, would naturally seek to discover the final patterns of trade and consumption which emerge after the restoration of equilibrium and not those at some intermediate position such as at (*a*) or (*b*) of Fig. 7.5. It is for this reason that we tend to say, perhaps rather loosely, that the 'effects' of import and export taxes are the same. The dynamics of taxation policy become important only when we are using taxation as a weapon to re-create equilibrium and not when its purpose is to redistribute or protect welfare. We shall return to the dynamics in a later chapter.

In the meantime we observe that our earlier statement to the effect that a combined export and import tax is equivalent to currency depreciation is essentially a statement about the impact effect and not the final effect. Attention has already been drawn to the fact that a subsidy is a negative tax. We should expect therefore that, if an export tax creates a trade deficit as in Fig. 7.5 (*b*) (assuming excess demands are met out of stocks), then an export subsidy would create a surplus. Currency appreciation would be demanded to restore equilibrium. The import duty according to Fig. 7.5 (*a*) creates a still further surplus demanding still further currency appreciation.

The final (after currency appreciation) equilibrium of an equal subsidy and tax must be the same as the initial equilibrium, since we have shown that one cancels the other. But before the currency appreciation demanded by the two taxes, the economy must be in a position equivalent to that created by a currency depreciation. Hence the claim that the two taxes are equivalent to currency depreciation. Indeed, a subsidy cheapens exportables abroad and an import duty raises the price of importables at home just like a currency depreciation. If an attempt were made to develop a diagram like Fig. 7.5 to show the impact of an equal export subsidy and import tax, we should end up with something very like Fig. 2.1 where it would be seen that a currency appreciation would immediately restore the free-trade equilibrium. This simultaneously illustrates both halves of the paradox with which we have been concerned in this section.

It should perhaps be said that the words 'very like' in the previous sentence were chosen with some care, for in a situation where trade is not balanced, a tax on imports will yield either more or less than the amount needed to pay a subsidy at the same rate. This is because $q_1 X_1'$ is no longer equal to $q_2 X_2$ (see 7.11.5). The proper offer curve will not be *exactly* that appropriate to the free-trade equilibrium. But as long as the imbalance is small, the approximation of Fig. 2.1 is near enough. This brings us to an important matter.

In a way, the theroem which shows import and export taxes to be symmetric has very little real content. The symmetry rests heavily, first upon the trivial fact that both taxes cause the real terms of trade to move in the same direction, and second upon the rather special assumption that trade is balanced. Indeed, it rests also upon the even more unlikely assumption that there are no previously existing export or import duties either at home or abroad. In short, for the two taxes to be symmetric in their effects it must be true that the amount of the tax collected, measured in units of the home commodity, must be the same. This is not ordinarily true for equal tax rates, a fact which gives rise to the problem of the next section.

7.12 THE OPTIMAL STRUCTURE OF IMPORT AND EXPORT TAXES

In an earlier section it was shown that there may exist an optimal import duty. But as import and export duties are symmetric in their final effect, we might as well say that there exists an optimal export tax. Alternatively we would expect that the very same trading advantage might be gained by various combinations of import and export taxes. It would seem, for example, that one-half of the desired 'exploitation' could be achieved by an import duty and the other half by an equal export tax, and so on.

Actually this supposition is only partly true for reasons which have already emerged in the previous section. Equal changes in tax rates, either import or export, do not have the same welfare effect if taxes already exist. It follows that there is a powerful sense in which it is 'better' to have *both* import and export taxes rather than one or the other. We study this problem by extending the model as follows.

The reader will already appreciate that, if we had been ready to face the tedious complications, we could have worked the algebra of section 7.5 assuming that both import and export taxes already exist. The essential amendments would be, first, to write the balance of payments equation as

$$q_1 X_1' = q_2 X_2$$

since, in the presence of a tax, t_1, on exports, q_1 and not p_1 is received by the home country for each unit of exportables. Second, aggregate expenditure at home will include both kinds of revenue, so that

$$Y = p_1 O_1 + t_1 p_1 X_1' + t_2 q_2 X_2$$

where t_2 is the import duty. Finally, the price identities are now

$$q_1 = p_1(1 + t_1)$$

and

$$p_2 = q_2(1 + t_2)$$

In all other respects the algebra is the same as in section 7.5 so that it need not be reworked in the text.

Solving the amended system to find the welfare consequence dw of an import duty change dt_2 yields

$$dw = q_2 X_2 \left\{ \frac{(E_{22} + C_2)\,[1 + E'_{11}\,(t_1 + t_1 t_2 + t_2)/(t_1 + 1)\,(t_2 + 1)]}{1 + E_{22} + [1 - C_2\,(t_1 + t_1 t_2 + t_2)/(t_1 + 1)\,(t_2 + 1)]\,E'_{11}} \right\} dt_2$$

$$(7.12.1)$$

which of course reduces to (7.5.22) when both t_1 and t_2 are initially zero.

If now we were to begin again and find the welfare effect of a change dt_1 in the *export* duty, this time with the import duty held constant, we should obtain a result precisely the same as (7.12.1) *except* that $q_2 X_2$ is multiplied by the ratio $(1 + t_2)/(1 + t_1)$. This conclusion is of course not obvious and should be checked by the student as an exercise. The working is not given here only because it would be repetitive to do so.

Comparing the two measures of welfare change reveals that

$$dw/dt_2 = (dw/dt_1)\,[(1 + t_1)/(1 + t_2)]   (7.12.2)$$

a relationship which expresses conclusively the asymmetry of import and export taxes in the general case. It simply is not true that an increase of, say, 10 per cent in an export tax has the same effect as a 10 per cent increase in import duty except in the case where t_1 equals t_2. Similar considerations apply when the foreign country has a non-zero tax structure.

Notice also that the differences in welfare (and other) effects may be quite significant in magnitude. Suppose, for example, that import duty stood at 20 per cent ($t_2 = \frac{1}{5}$) and a proposal to increase this duty by a further 10 per cent were under consideration. If no export tax existed, dw/dt_1 would be, by (7.12.2), 20 per cent higher than dw/dt_2. Accepting now the rough orders of magnitude of section 7.5, the choice between an import or export duty could be a choice between having or not having an annual addition to the U.K. real national income of something like £100 million. Expressed as a percentage of the national income this is not a large sum. But it might help to make a point if the present writer, here and now, revealed how very satisfied he would be to accept 1 per cent of the possible saving in exchange for the helpful advice implicit in this section.

Of course it can always be argued that there is *some* level of export tax which is equivalent in its effect to a given import duty. For example, in the case above, a 12 per cent import duty would have the same real effect as a 10 per cent export tax. But this statement says no more than that the welfare effect of both taxes has the same sign. Both either improve welfare or worsen it.

This point brings us to the question of an optimal tax structure, a problem which may be approached as follows. Evidently the level of welfare is dependent upon the chosen pattern of taxation, so that we may give expression to this relation by writing a function

$$w = w(t_1, t_2) \tag{7.12.3}$$

in every way analogous to the demand functions with which we are now familiar. Suppose that we wished to choose t_1 and t_2 so that w is maximised. Following the usual rule we might write

$$dw = \frac{\partial w}{\partial t_1} dt_1 + \frac{\partial w}{\partial t_2} dt_2 \tag{7.12.4}$$

Clearly w can be maximised only if it is impossible to choose any tax change dt_1 or dt_2 or any combination such that the change in welfare dw is positive. Indeed it is necessary also that we should not be able to choose tax changes dt_1 or dt_2 so that dw is negative either, for in such a case $(-dt_1)$ and $(-dt_2)$ would make dw positive. It follows that both

$$\frac{\partial w}{\partial t_1} \text{ and } \frac{\partial w}{\partial t_2}$$

must be zero. Only this way can we make sure that dw is zero for all possible dt. This of course is only a way of saying that at the top of the hill we find level ground in all directions.

Now note that by dividing both sides of (7.12.1) by dt_2 we obtain an expression for $\partial w/\partial t_2$, for (7.12.1) was derived by changing dt_2 *holding* t_1 *constant*. Thus for $\partial w/\partial t_2$ zero we require

$$-1 = E'_{11} (t_1 + t_1 t_2 + t_2)/(t_1 + 1) (t_2 + 1) \tag{7.12.5}$$

which is an equation relating t_1, t_2 and a known elasticity. A similar equation can be obtained by setting $\partial w/\partial t_1$ equal to zero, having found an expression for this by the usual method. We now have two equations like (7.12.5) in two unknowns t_1 and t_2 so that we should expect to be able to find values of t_1 and t_2 such that both equations are satisfied. The values t_1 and t_2 so found represent therefore the *optimal tariff structure*.

This approach to the problem of the optimal tariff structure raises an interesting point. In the ordinary way we should not expect there to be a very large number of solutions to two equations in two unknowns. Furthermore, even if there were, only one of these could represent the true optimum tariff structure, for a hill has only one summit even though we may encounter subsidiary 'peaks' on the way to the top.

On the other hand inspection of (7.12.2) reveals that *whenever* $\partial w/\partial t_2$ is zero, so is $\partial w/\partial t_1$. Indeed, the second equation which we need to solve for *both* t_1 and t_2 must turn out to be exactly the same as (7.12.5). As long as (7.12.5) is satisfied we have an optimal tariff structure and we see that, within limits, a value of t_1 can be chosen to satisfy (7.12.5) *whatever* the value of t_2.

The following really important question now arises. Suppose that we were to disaggregate the model, separating importables and exportables into their many different commodity components. Evidently we should then be free to consider the effects of distinct and separate export and import taxes, one on each commodity not necessarily at the same rate. If, say, m commodities were involved, we should have m tax rates $t_1, t_2, \ldots, t_m$ and a welfare function

$$w = w(t_1, t_2, \ldots, t_m) \qquad (7.12.6)$$

to be maximised. Hence we should have m $\partial w/\partial t$s to equate to zero and m equations to solve. It would be of great interest to know whether these m equations are all like (7.12.5) or whether they have new and unexpected properties.

To clarify this point, let us write the optimal import duty condition (7.8.13) in the form

$$-1 = E'_{11} \frac{t}{1+t} \qquad (7.12.7)$$

and compare with (7.12.5) which is the condition for an optimal combined export tax and import duty. Notice that the denominator of the multiplier of E'_{11} is in each case the product of 1 plus each tax rate, which may be written

$$\prod(1 + t_i)$$

and the numerator is

$$\prod(1 + t_i) - 1.$$

If it could be proved that this same rule extends to the many-commodity case and that the formula for the optimal tariff structure retains the form

$$- 1 = E \frac{\prod(1 + t_i) - 1}{\prod(1 + t_i)}$$

where E is some kind of average elasticity of all imports, we should have a result of considerable practical value.

For an optimal tariff structure all that would be necessary would be to attain a particular value of

$$\frac{\prod(1 + t_i) - 1}{\prod(1 + t_i)}$$

And one way of achieving this would be to impose one single across-the-board tax on imports or exports or both. There would be no need whatever to distinguish between commodities. The same rate on all imports would do.

The thoughtful reader will, however, already be protesting that our conjecture is highly unlikely to be correct. The odd result which we get in the single-importable/single-exportable case is entirely due to the troublesome fact, encountered again and again in economics, that doubling all prices and doubling expenditure has no effect upon production or consumption patterns. There are infinitely many ways of attaining the same real equilibrium position.

What is important is not prices but price ratios. Notice also that our model demands

$$q_1 = p_1 (1 + t_1)$$

and

$$p_2 = q_2 (1 + t_2)$$

from which we deduce that

$$\frac{p_2}{p_1} = \frac{q_2}{q_1} (1 + t_1) (1 + t_2) \tag{7.12.8}$$

The problem of setting an optimal tariff structure is the problem of choosing the best disparity between home and foreign relative prices, that is, the best value of $\prod(1 + t_i)$. And as we have found, the given best value can be attained by some t_1 whatever the value of t_2. But with many commodities there are many price ratios.

Moreover, we have not said all that might be said about two goods. It is to be recalled that we found earlier that $\partial w / \partial t_1$ is numerically greater than $\partial w / \partial t_2$ (by (7.12.2)) whenever t_2 is greater than t_1 and vice versa, provided of course that both are not zero. Quite apart then from our observation that, if a given percentage tax is to be imposed, it had better be imposed on whichever class of commodities is taxed least, there is an important sense in which the optimal tariff structure demands, in the two-commodity case, equal rates of tax on both imports and exports.

For political reasons, if for none other, it may be thought desirable to attain a given value of the product $(1 + t_1)(1 + t_2)$ with the lowest tax rates, that is, with the lowest $t_1 + t_2$. This is the same thing as asking how we can attain the highest

$$(1 + t_1)(1 + t_2) = 1 + (t_1 + t_2) + t_1 t_2 \qquad (7.12.9)$$

with a given $t_1 + t_2$ which, from (7.12.9) we see is in turn the same as attaining the greatest $t_1 t_2$ with a given $t_1 + t_2$.

A few moments' experimentation with figures will easily convince the reader that the required maximum demands $t_1 = t_2$, a result consistent with all that we deduced from (7.12.1) and (7.12.2). Even with the simple two-commodity model the infinity of optimal tariff structures disappears if we insist that our exploitation of the foreign country be carried out with the greatest possible degree of tact.

We now emphasise again that the disaggregated problem is vastly different. Recall that (7.12.8), if t_1 and t_2 are in optimal combination, measures the best difference between just *one* pair of prices. We have already observed that where many commodities are to be considered there are many price ratios each with its own best difference. For m commodities there are $m - 1$ equations like (7.12.8), not just one. Moreover, the crucial price ratios will be between pairs of importables and pairs of exportables as well as pairs including both importables and exportables.

In order that no misunderstanding can remain on these points we shall write down the solution for the optimal tariff structure when there are many exports and many imports so that the reader may inspect it. In fact the desired set of tariffs and export duties may be determined by solving the equations

$$\left. \begin{array}{l} q_1 R_{11} m_1 + q_2 R_{21} m_2, \ldots, \quad q_n R_{n1} m_n = 0 \\ q_1 R_{12} m_1 \hspace{5.5cm} = 0 \\ \hspace{0.6cm} \vdots \\ q_1 R_{1n} m_1 \hspace{0.4cm} \cdots\cdots\cdots\cdots \hspace{0.4cm} q_n R_{nn} m_n = 0 \end{array} \right\} \qquad (7.12.10)$$

for the n ms in terms of Rs and the foreign prices q. The ith m, m_i, so found will be $(1 + t_i)$ if the ith commodity is an import and $1/(1 + t_i)$ if the ith commodity is an export. The general R_{ij} is defined by

$$R_{ij} = \frac{\partial X'_i}{\partial q_j} - \frac{\partial S'_i}{\partial a_j} + S'_j \frac{\partial X'_i}{\partial Y} \qquad (7.12.11)$$

that is, the foreign demand response minus an analogous supply response plus the amount of the jth commodity supplied abroad times the foreign income response. (The reader has not yet encountered supply responses, although he will do so in Chapter 11.)

It is beyond the scope of this chapter to prove (7.12.10), but the general method has already been outlined. Furthermore the student who has completed a first reading of Book II will find himself in a position to face the complications involved without strain (see exercise 10).

The point to be made in regard to (7.12.10) will be obvious if the reader understands the special problems of homogeneous equations but otherwise not. Even so it is easy to see that if m_1^0, m_2^0, ..., m_n^0 is a solution then so is λm_1^0, λm_2^0, ..., λm_n^0 where λ is any arbitrary number whatever – for inserting λ simply multiplies the left-hand side of each equation by λ leaving it zero as before. Thus, just as in the two-commodity case, we have infinitely many tariff structures.

On the other hand if we assign just one m arbitrarily and leave out one equation, one and only one solution exists for the remaining $n - 1$ ms. For example, suppose we set m_1 at unity, that is, no tax or tariff on commodity 1. The first term on the left-hand side of the first $n - 1$ equations of (7.12.10) may now be shifted to the right-hand side, the variable m_1 having disappeared. These new equations have no difficult form, so they may be solved uniquely.†

All of this confirms what was said above. *An optimal tariff structure cannot be attained by a given across-the-board tax rate even if it is applied both to imports and exports except in the case where only two commodities are traded.* For an across-the-board tax t to be optimal, we should require the impossible multiple coincidence where the solutions to (7.12.10) turned out to be

$$m = (1 + t)$$

for an import and

$$m = 1/(1 + t)$$

for an export with t the same in each case. It is hard to believe that we should ever encounter such a coincidence in the real world.

† For more experienced readers we remark that this does not mean that given $m_1 = 1$ only one set of optimal tariffs exists on the remaining commodities. It should be recalled that the actual values of R_{ij} may depend on the tariff rates and more than one set of values R_{ij} and t_i may satisfy (7.12.10). The word 'uniquely', above, means a unique relation between ts and Rs.

We emphasise again that an optimal tariff structure will ordinarily call for taxes on exports as well as taxes on imports. All that is left of the symmetry of import and export taxes is the fact that in choosing an optimal tariff structure one rate may be arbitrarily chosen. And even this is not true if we impose the political criterion, that is, if we choose the optimal structure which satisfies the condition that the sum of all tax rates should be minimised as we did in the two-commodity case. Note that this will not give equal import and export duties but equal import and export duties *on the average*.

Finally in this section we remark that where non-traded commodities exist these also may be taxed or subsidised, leading possibly to a net gain. The same may be said of any kind of tax anywhere in the economy. A tax change is a policy change and welfare depends on policy. In a trading economy any policy change may 'exploit' the trading partner even though the trading partner is not directly concerned. Taxes on trade enjoy no monopoly in this respect. The general method of finding out whether a tax creates a net gain or loss is precisely the method of this section. The whole system must be solved for $\partial w / \partial t$, the tax being 'good' if $\partial w / \partial t$ is positive in sign. An optimal fiscal system is one where $\partial w / \partial t$ is zero for all possible taxes wherever they may fall.

7.13 TARIFF WARS IN THE LIGHT OF 7.12

The careful reader of section 7.10 on tariff wars who may have concluded that he had at last learned the rudiments of the game is unlikely, after section 7.12, to feel quite so confident. The object of this short section is to restore perspective on the matter, if possible.

There is no difference of principle involved in waging a tariff war with an optimal fiscal policy than there is with a single import duty on a single commodity. Any tax, or group of taxes, which lead to a gain by the home country at the expense of its trading partner might provoke retaliation abroad. The computation of the various steps to be taken at each stage of the war are more complicated when many commodities are involved, but the methods have already been established.

Furthermore, the same game could be played with a single across-the-board import duty even though perhaps with less efficiency. If we insist upon the same proportional import tariff on all commodities it is still possible to find a best tariff rate. For example, a 20 per cent import duty may be too high to be optimal for some commodities and too low to be optimal for others. In these circumstances a rise to, say, 21 per cent would produce a loss on account of those commodities where 20 per cent was already too high but a gain where it was too small. If these losses and gains just balance each other, then there is a sense in which 20 per cent is optimal. A greater gain could be made but only at the cost of varying between commodities. Application of this principle could lead to a modified tariff war.

The really important point to be made in this section, however, is to confirm the basic lesson of section 7.10. By whatever rules the tariff-war game is played, there is always a *possibility* that one country could be the gainer even in the final equilibrium. However sophisticated our economic computation may become, there exists, so far as we know, a real chance that someone may find long-run profit in a tariff war.

7.14 The Welfare Effect of an Export Subsidy

A subsidy is, of course a negative tax so that its welfare effect is equal but of opposite sign to the welfare effect of a tax. Indeed we have already commented upon the fact that the very same formula for the welfare effect of a tax will do also for a subsidy without modification.

It follows therefore that an export subsidy will, by (7.12.1) and (7.12.2), setting t_1 and t_2 at zero and remembering that dt_1 is now negative, have a negative welfare effect in the usual case.

We make this point under a separate heading simply because in the eyes of some commentators import duties and export subsidies appear as alternative ways of correcting an imbalance of trade. It should be understood that if either of these policies should turn out to be successful, the net welfare result must be precisely equivalent to

(a) correcting the imbalance by more conventional means, and

(b) imposing the duty or subsidy as the case may be.

In view of (b) and the relative welfare effect of duties and subsidies, it is clear that there are powerful arguments for using an import duty rather than an export subsidy. Indeed, there seems to be very few occasions indeed on which it is ever desirable to recommend an export subsidy, and the reason is intuitively obvious. A subsidy is bad *both* because it disguises true costs from the consumer *and* because it gives better terms to the foreign buyer. An import duty disguises true costs from the consumer and is bad in this respect; but at least it improves rather than worsens our terms of trade.

This last remark raises an interesting point in connection with the optimal tariff structure. We have earlier argued at length in the two-commodity case that the optimal tariff can never be negative, i.e. that it can never be a subsidy. And this is consistent with the claim that subsidies are always bad.

On the other hand the question arises 'Is the same true in the disaggregate, many-commodity world?' The answer has been shown to be a rather hesitant 'no'. Here and there there may be a case for a subsidy on a particular commodity, but only on a particular commodity. It is always true that, on the average, the optimal tariff structure is positive on both imports and exports and the balance of probability tends towards an all-positive structure. Before accepting a proposal to subsidise any exportable at all, for any reason, the burden of proving numerically that the welfare effects are positive should be imposed upon the proposer. The computational method is known and understood and can be carried out up to a certain degree of approximation. Subsidies should be regarded as guilty until proved innocent. Import duties are innocent until proved guilty.

7.15 CUSTOMS UNIONS

A 'customs union' or 'free-trade area' is formed when a group of countries enter into an agreement to operate a common tariff policy. In extreme cases tariff barriers between members will be removed entirely and a common duty fixed for all imports from non-members. The common import duty is of course essential since otherwise all imports from the outside would tend to enter the area via the member with the lowest tariff. In some cases also more extended economic co-operation is envisaged, designed to control aggregate expenditure of the group as a whole and/or to avoid the development of internal balance of payments problems between members. Recent years have seen a great revival of interest in this kind of co-operation and indeed a number of such groups currently exist. The European Free Trade Association and the European Common Market are examples.

As almost every conceivable argument, consistent or mutually contradictory, honest or dishonest, has at some time been invoked either for or against particular customs unions, it is hardly possible to give any reasoned explanation of recently observed events. Indeed it may not be too far from the truth to hazard the guess that at least one free-trade area was formed largely because its members found themselves (accidentally) excluded from another, and thought accordingly, that they had better do something. (There is, after all, great comfort to be derived from following the crowd even when the crowd is not quite sure where it is going.)

On the other hand it is probably true that at least two powerful ideas do lie somewhere among the root causes of the present pro-customs union movement. The first of these is the notion that 'free' trade is economically efficient, that is, that it creates an environment where more welfare can be produced with a given input. The second, perhaps currently more influential, dogma, is that which equates efficiency with size. The bigger the market the more cheaply market demand can be met. We shall deal with these ideas in turn.

But first the reader should understand that in identifying only two kinds of argument we do exclude all those which are purely political, having no economic content. To those who feel that it is a 'good' thing to have 'influence' in world affairs *per se*, a political union may appear to be desirable or, for a small country, even essential. Indeed, if we equate 'influence' with the absolute size of the economic reserves available for government spending, as we are entitled to do on some interpretations of the meaning of the word 'influence', then it is hard to dispute the logic of this suggestion however much we may wish to disagree with the premisses. More can be done with 40 per cent of the income of 200 million people than with 40 per cent of the income of 10 million.

Alternatively, if one sees a customs union as the first step to political union and the political union of a few countries as the first step towards ultimate rational world government, the first step itself might be worth many sacrifices. There would be no need to look for economic gain. The fact that no emphasis is placed upon issues of this kind in the present book does not mean that they are not important. It means only that they concern economists as citizens rather than as economists.

Of the two essentially economic arguments in favour of customs unions it is convenient to take first that which holds that it is impossible to be technically efficient unless production can take place on a large scale. The purpose of the customs union is first to remove tariffs between member countries so that manufacturers are not hindered by trade impediments from selling anywhere within the enlarged market, and second to raise tariff barriers against the outside world so as to prevent penetration of the common market by outside producers. Economies of scale are thus gained to the benefit of the union.

This suggestion is of course very simple and unsubtle. The reader should take careful note, however, of what it implies. First, if it were really true that the larger the total output of any given industry the lower the cost of production, then we ought to observe that small countries, by and large, have lower standards of living than larger ones. Canada should have a very much lower standard of living than the U.S.A. and indeed than, say, Italy. The U.S.A. should have a lower standard than Russia. Australia should have a lower standard than Germany and Sweden a lower standard than Spain. Clearly it is almost easier to find cases where the expected rule is contradicted than where it is met.

Of course the fact that smaller countries do not always have lower living standards is not a conclusive argument. Other factors may intervene to complicate the issue. It is worth while therefore to reflect upon certain further implications of the assumption that massive gains from scale are ready and waiting to be exploited. If it were really true that the removal of tariff barriers alone is of itself sufficient to make possible gains from scale, it must be that existing producers within a country are already operating at something greater than the lowest possible cost, being restricted only by the smallness of the market. But this could only be true if the whole of the home demand for each product was met by a single manufacturer. Otherwise whichever manufacturer produces more cheaply, or has the courage to increase his sales by reducing price, can take over at least the whole of the home market, thereby forcing his competitors out of business. Needless to say we do not observe just one producer for each commodity in the usual sense of that word.

The reader who is familiar with other branches of economic theory may object at this point that it is not always profitable to increase sales by reducing price even though economies of scale are present. Gains from lower costs might well be outweighed by losses due to the price reduction necessary to secure larger sales. But increased sales do not necessarily imply reduced prices if they are gained at the expense of a competitor producing the same commodity or a close substitute. The presence of market economies of scale therefore necessarily implies one producer, one commodity, and, except in the sense below, we do not observe this in the real world.

It is quite possible, and indeed likely, that the widespread belief that there exists scope for economies of scale finds its origin in the observations of producers themselves who see the situation somewhat as follows. *A* produces motor-car brand *A* whilst *B* produces motor-car brand *B*. *A* and *B* are different machines each demanding different equipment for their production and different design staffs to plan that production. Obviously a cheaper motor-car could be manufactured if a merger were arranged. No one would dispute that 200,000 Ford cars could be produced more cheaply than 100,000 Fords and 100,000 Austins. It is easy to observe the possibility of economies of scale. Why therefore are these not exploited?

The answer to this is that the two cars concerned are in a narrower sense quite different products. Each type has its own adherents. Each manufacturer believes that it would be necessary to reduce prices to increase sales by at least as much as the cost advantage derived from these increased sales.

We now have a situation in which some possibility of gain from increased size is present in a certain sense. But it is a situation quite different from that envisaged by the advocates of a customs union. Gains from scale of the type we are now considering can be exploited without any customs union, and conversely there is not the slightest reason why the creation of a customs union should induce their exploitation. If the forces of competition do not eliminate either Ford or Austin behind a tariff barrier, why should they do so if the tariff barrier is removed? The same techniques of advertising and gimmickry which presently persuade people that an Austin is different from a Ford will continue to be present whether there is a customs union or not. Nor should it be thought that the removal of tariff barriers will present Austins with a greater chance of winning some of the Opel market, say, than it will offer Opel the chance to win Austin's.

In short, the only kind of economy of scale likely to be realised by economic union is the one where the economies are so marked that it is obviously not sensible to have more than one plant or organisation producing the whole of the needs of the country contemplating the union and where, despite the single-producer situation, the full extent of the economies remains unrealised. It is unlikely that, at the present time, many countries find much of their industry in this position.

In thinking about this type of problem the reader should not confuse 'firms' and 'plants'. A firm is identified by its name – say Lever Brothers or General Motors. A plant is a collection of machines and buildings in a given location. The fact that a 'firm' wishes to grow and control more plants does not by itself imply that economies of scale are available at the plant level. It is interesting to note that many companies wishing to extend their markets do so by setting up more plants abroad, that is *within* the country where they hope to sell. This may in part be due to a desire to escape import duties, but even so it does not encourage the belief that there can be any very great economies to be gained from having larger plants in any one location. Such economies as there are must arise from standardisation, that is, the spreading of design and planning costs over a larger number of units of output. Against this must be set the cost of co-ordination of activity, which must be considerable, and, much more important, the simple fact that consumers show little sign of *wanting* standardisation unless this is offset by price reductions which are quite marked. It is this last fact which opens the door to 'product differentiation', that is to the creation of an artificial distinction between units of what is essentially the same commodity (e.g. Ford and Austin), a phenomenon which simultaneously prevents the exploitation of certain relatively minor economies and at the same time gives rise to a belief that such economies are more important than in all probability they really are.

To sum up, a closer look at the full implications of the 'large market' argument and at the facts of the world around us gives rise to doubts whether there is very much in it except perhaps in the rare case. It is not really surprising that a country like Sweden can enjoy low-cost production despite the relatively small size of her home market. After all, 7 million consumers is a not inconsiderable number which may well afford all the opportunities for large-scale production that any single producer might find profitable.

Finally, the reader should take care not to be misled by apparently spectacular special cases. It would seem, for example, that immense economies of scale are present in the computer industry and it could be argued that the international activities of, say, the International Business Machines Co. lend weight to this observation. But it may well be that these economies are simply a feature of very rapid technological change. There could come a time when the majority of the world's computers are fairly standard objects with no very great obsolescence rate and with their technology widely understood. In such a case there are obvious reasons why economies of scale should disappear. We note for example that it is still possible for small firms to produce saleable aircraft (e.g. the Islander) despite the apparent economies of scale in the development of 'prestige' machines.

We may not be too far wrong, therefore, in continuing our inquiry into the virtues of the customs union within the framework of our model so far, which, since output and hence world sales are always constant, cannot take account of economies of scale. This brings us to the second economic argument for the customs union, namely that which sees free trade as a good thing. We continue the discussion of this point in the next section.

7.16 THE WELFARE EFFECTS OF A CUSTOMS UNION

As indicated in section 7.15, the present customs union movement was born in part out of the idea that, if world tariffs cannot be swept away, at least it may be possible to create a free-trade 'bloc' of neighbouring states. Once it is accepted, if it is accepted, that completely free trade is efficient, it is natural to feel that half-way to free trade is at least half-way to full efficiency.

On the other hand it is easier to be led into talking nonsense on the lines of the previous paragraph than it is in almost any other branch of economics, and the reader will no doubt already be aware that it is not difficult to make economic nonsense sound plausible whatever the topic. Consider first of all what might possibly be the meaning of economic efficiency in the present context. It is a fact, of course, that if tariffs exist relative market prices will ordinarily be different in different countries even after a flow of trade is established. Indeed, in our present model we are already accustomed to write

$$\frac{p_1(1 + t')}{p_2} = \frac{q_1}{q_2(1 + t)} \tag{7.16.1}$$

This immediately implies that some further exchange of commodities could improve welfare in both countries, a fact which may be explained as follows. For both countries to be better off we must have both

$$p_1 dX_1 + p_2 dX_2 > 0$$

and $\qquad q_1(- dX_1) + q_2(- dX_2) > 0 \quad \Big\}$ $\qquad\qquad$ (7.16.2)

by our usual criterion. Note that any change dX_1 in consumption of country 1 must be matched by a change $- dX_1$ in consumption of country 2, since we are considering an exchange of commodities between the two. Dividing the inequalities (7.16.2) by dX_2 and minus dX_2 respectively, we restate the required condition as

$$\frac{dX_1}{dX_2} p_1 + p_2 > 0$$

and $\qquad \dfrac{dX_1}{dX_2} q_1 + q_2 < 0 \quad \Bigg\}$ $\qquad\qquad$ (7.16.3)

Clearly we may choose dX_1/dX_2 equal to minus p_2/p_1, in which case the left-hand side of the first inequality in (7.16.3) will be zero. Furthermore, by (7.16.1) the second inequality in (7.16.3) may be written

$$\frac{dX_1}{dX_2} p_1 (1 + t') + \frac{p_2}{(1 + t)} < 0 \qquad (7.16.4)$$

which, if dX_1/dX_2 equals minus p_2/p_1, is obviously satisfied, for we then have the left-hand side of (7.16.4) equal to

$$- p_2(1 + t') + \frac{p_2}{(1 + t)}$$

which is negative as long as either t' or t is greater than zero.

It is now easy to see that by choosing dX_1/dX_2 slightly smaller than p_2/p_1 we have the first inequality of (7.16.3) satisfied and, provided at the same time dX_1/dX_2 is not made too small, the second is satisfied also.

In short we have proved that, whenever tariffs t' and/or t exist at all, some exchange of dX_1 between the two countries can be chosen so as to make both countries better off. It is for this reason that economists have often argued that tariffs are inefficient and should be abolished. Whenever tariffs exist, further beneficial exchanges are possible but will not take place.

Against this, however, it is of the *utmost importance* to understand that the removal of the tariff barriers does *not*, repeat *not*, mean that beneficial exchanges which must be possible will in fact take place. The exchange which actually will be provoked is something quite different. *Efficient* behaviour is not necessarily *desirable*.

Intuitively this is easy to see. Consider a country which operates an optimum tariff. By definition of an optimum that country will be made worse off by the removal of such a tariff. Thus the changes dX_1 and dX_2 in consumption which actually occur *cannot* satisfy the rule

$$p_1 dX_1 + p_2 dX_2 > 0$$

In our model world production is assumed to be constant throughout. Hence any changes in consumption dX_1 and dX_2 can only be the consequence of some change in the pattern of trade. The abolition of tariffs will certainly bring about some readjustment of consumption but not necessarily one which makes everyone better off. Indeed, in the case under review the new exchanges cannot be beneficial to the country abolishing the tariff.

All that we are saying in fact is that whilst it is true that two countries which have reached equilibrium after engaging in a tariff war could enter into an agreement to exchange which would make both better off, the simple abolition of tariffs would not necessarily have the desired effect. This is obvious since we have shown that one country might gain from a tariff war; accordingly it must lose by restoring the *status quo*.

The strength and weakness of the idea of economic efficiency should now be clear. If tariffs exist, the *world* as opposed to individual countries may be said to be acting inefficiently. This is because some exchange is possible which will make *everyone* better off. If on the other hand no tariffs exist, the world *cannot* be said to be acting inefficiently since obviously it is impossible to satisfy (7.16.2) with any set of dXs if the ps are equal to the qs. None of this means, however, that it can never be in the interests of any one country to act inefficiently, for we have shown that a tariff can improve the welfare of one country even though it may reduce that of another.

Curiously enough the thinking of economists on the subject of customs unions has been much more influenced by the idea of economic efficiency than it has by the more practical desire to find out, in any particular instance, precisely who gains and precisely who loses from any proposed policy. The result of this preoccupation has been to introduce into the literature a number of arguments which are at best misleading half-truths and at worst just plain nonsense.

Notice that the concept of efficiency is very difficult to quantify in the present context. It is easy to identify full efficiency; this is simply a situation where it is impossible to make one country better off without making another worse off. But it is a very different matter to have to say, of two inefficient situations A and B, which is the *more* inefficient. It is nonsense, for example, to compute the world welfare change induced by a shift from A to B by summing the separate country welfare changes. In particular we cannot say that there is a world loss from a change in some tariff rate just because

$$dw + dw' = p_1 dX_1 + p_2 dX_2 + q_1 dX_1' + q_2 dX_2' < 0.$$

There are at least two reasons for this.

First, when ps are different from qs, the valuation put upon a unit of each commodity is different in the two countries. It does not make sense therefore to add them up. Second, and much more important, if one country gains and one country loses, how do we measure the loss against the gain so as to conclude that the *world* has gained or lost? Indeed, how do we even attribute a meaning to 'world welfare'?

The reader is reminded that *within* any country our measure of welfare change is the change in the total value of the national product priced at initial prices. As prices are the same for everyone, each individual valuation of one more unit of each good is the same. We are assuming also that the home government will take steps through adjustments of income tax or other means to share equitably any increase in the value of national consumption (see Chapter 13 on this point). The country is better off because everyone is better off. In the international sphere, however, no mechanism exists to share between countries any increase in the value of world consumption even if some meaning and measure could be attached to the idea of such an increase as the consequence of a policy change. On the contrary, one of the prime objectives of a customs union, or any tariff policy, is precisely a redistribution of world welfare in favour of the country initiating the policy. The policy would be unnecessary if a valid sharing mechanism existed.

Economists are of course well aware of these difficulties. Attempts have been made to develop a criterion for ranking situations *A* and *B*, say, from a world welfare point of view, in terms of a compensation principle. *B* is said to be better than *A* if the countries gaining by a change from *A* to *B* could compensate the countries losing without entirely eliminating their gain. Even this, however, turns out to be useless from the point of view of reaching world agreement upon what is or is not a 'good' trade policy.

In the first place, as we shall show at greater length in Chapter 13 (Book II), the compensation criterion does not always permit us to put *A* and *B* in order. It is easy to develop examples where a move from *A* to *B* could, with compensation, make everyone better off and where, paradoxically, a move from *B* to *A* satisfies the same condition (see Chapter 13).

And even if we could *sometimes* rank *A* and *B* by the compensation criterion, such a ranking could have no more than academic significance unless the compensation is actually made. France is unlikely to agree to remove her tariff on British-manufactured goods just because United Kingdom economists can prove that France could be compensated for any loss if only the Treasury would pay up. And if governments ever become so sophisticated that they showed willingness to offer compensation abroad for the effects of their policies, there seems no reason why we should not go the whole way and agree upon what is a proper distribution of world welfare between countries. Anything else is nonsense. To imagine that one country can go to another and demand compensation for not carrying out all conceivable policies that it might carry out borders on the fantastic.

We have made much of the world welfare problem primarily because pursuit of this will-o'-the-wisp has led, as indicated above, to the appearance in the literature of at least two propositions which are open to criticism and call for comment.

First, it has been suggested that, as a general rule, a reduction in the highest tariff will, in a many-country world, improve world welfare; that is, if country 1 has a 50 per cent import duty and countries 2 and 3 have each a 20 per cent import duty, then it is in some sense a 'good' thing for the world as a whole to reduce the 50 per cent tariff to, say, 40 per cent. The writer of a recent survey of international trade theory presents this proposition as having 'interesting policy implications'.

Obviously the argument referred to cannot mean that every country will be better off individually, for we already have a counter-example. In a world of two countries, one with an optimal tariff and one with a zero tariff, a reduction of the higher tariff is bound, by definition of an optimum, to make at least the tariff-reducing country worse off. And we lose no generality by taking two countries rather than three, for the country with no tariff could easily be taken to be two separate but identical countries with similar tastes.

This example does not of course disprove the proposition under review. It simply illustrates the fact that the 'gain' in world welfare, if it exists, must rest upon a definition of 'gain' which appeals to the compensation principle. But in this case it is both trivial and certainly no guide to policy. It is most obviously trivial when it is applied, as it has been, to an imaginary situation where production in each country is given and fixed, that is, when there is only a given quantity of each commodity available in the whole world for distribution and this quantity does not change whatever the policy. For whatever the policy, the gainers can always compensate the losers provided only we begin from a position which is not full efficiency. This is a proposition which requires no proof. For if we begin from a position, say A, where some further exchange to a second position, B, can make everyone better off (and this is the definition of an inefficient state A), then any country which wishes to move to C, where the total quantity of all commodities available for distribution is the same as at A, can offer compensation so that the total move amounts to a move to B. This is true whatever the policy C. Thus if country 1 has a high tariff and country 2 has low tariffs, it is just as 'good' by the compensation principle to raise the high tariff still further as it is to reduce it as long as no production changes are involved, for compensation could be arranged so as to allow precisely the same consumption pattern for each country in either case, and that consumption pattern will be one which allows increased welfare for all.

Nor can it be said that, in the context, the compensation principle is any less vacuous even when we suppose that changes in production patterns may be induced by the proposed policy, at least if we extend the principle in what would seem to be the only rational way. For if we are to accept as a definition of an improvement in world welfare the simple statement that in the new position everyone could be made better off by some hypothetical redistribution to be attained nobody knows how, then it is equally sensible to say that the new position is better if by some combination of *both* expenditure redistribution *and* production pattern change everyone could be made better off. By this criterion any policy is 'good'. Whatever the world situation, if it is not efficient, anyone who wishes to make a change can show that, after the change, there exists the possibility of arriving, by unspecified means, at a further position which is efficient and hence where everyone is better off than initially. The nature of this absurdity becomes still more obvious when we reflect that the hypothetical possibility of attaining the 'best' position is there equally before and after the implementation of the policy the argument seeks to justify. It follows that by the proposed criterion it is equally 'good' to move back to the original position and so on *ad infinitum*.

All of this reveals why the compensation principle can never be a guide to policy, at least in the world as it is presently organised. It is impossible in a general way to reach agreement upon what is good or bad from a world point of view until we have a supra-national government ready to determine and implement a 'fair' distribution of the world's wealth. And with a fair distribution of wealth there would be no need for tariffs, for the object of a tariff is to gain for the imposing country some advantage which would either be judged to be unfair or which, if justified, could be attained by some more efficient means. We now turn to the second, less precise, argument which arises out of the world welfare idea.

There exists throughout the literature a strong tradition that whatever inhibits trade is 'bad' and whatever promotes trade is 'good'.

Some part of this tradition finds its origin in the proposition noted above that, whenever tariffs exist, some further exchange could be advantageous to all parties. Tariffs prevent this exchange from taking place by misleading the consumer into believing that the real cost of one unit of importables is the home price p_2 and not the foreign price q_2 which is lower. In the same way the opening-up of trade allows the production of each commodity to develop in those areas where it can be most cheaply manufactured. Thus there are advantages of trade in the areas of both production and exchange.

There is of course an element of (imprecise) truth in all this. But the reader must understand that it is *not* possible to measure the gains from trade by measuring the *amount* of trade. It does not follow that the more we export and import the better off we are or the better off the world is.

Consider the simplest example. Examine our very first tariff diagram, Fig. 7.1 on p. 158. Suppose that we remove the tariff in the interests of 'free trade', believing this to be 'good'. Notice first that in the case illustrated the physical quantity of imports into country 1 must *fall* as equilibrium moves from G to E. The removal of the trade impediment reduces trade instead of increasing it. Furthermore, if we take the foreign price q_2 of importables as numeraire, the *value* of exports will have fallen even though the quantity of exports has risen. Of course we could show the value of trade to have risen if we choose some other price as constant, but this serves only to underline still further the danger of associating free trade necessarily with more trade in every case.

Furthermore, we already know that the removal of a tariff may make one country worse off even if it makes another better off. And we have, as we have argued at length, no means of saying whether this result improves world welfare or worsens it. Thus even if the removal of impediments did increase trade, we have no reason to accept that this is necessarily a 'good' thing for the world.

The main point which emerges from this discussion is that it is on all counts improper to try to guess probable gains and losses from proposed tariff policy by guessing the probable changes in the level of trade. This point is important since some writers have attempted to create a theory of customs unions based entirely on the idea we have here brought into question. As an example we quote the following typical argument. Consider a three-country world in which countries 1 and 2 form a customs union with country 3 as the outsider; that is, countries 1 and 2 abolish their tariffs on one another's products but raise a common tariff against country 3. Such a union will 'create' trade between countries 1 and 2 but will 'divert' trade away from country 3. Whether the union is 'good' or 'bad' for the world is then supposed to depend upon whether or not the 'trade creation' effect outweighs the 'trade diversion' effect, that is, upon whether the net consequence is more world trade or less. Thus it might be argued that if country 3 is sole producer of a commodity which countries 1 and 2 find it necessary to have at all costs, there can be little trade diversion. If at the same time countries 1 and 2 trade in commodities the demand elasticities for which are high, the removal of tariffs will be trade-creating (see for example Fig. 7.3 (p. 173), where the removal of tariffs shifts the equilibrium position from J to E). The net effect therefore would be trade-creating so that a customs union in these circumstances must be 'good'.

In view of all that has been said above it is hoped that the reader will now be ready to share the alarm of the present writer when he comes to read, in a recent survey of international trade theory, that 'the familiarity of government and international officials around the world with the key concepts of trade creation and trade diversion testifies to the timeliness of [this] theory'. It simply is not true that changes in the level of trade measure welfare changes either within a country or for the world as a whole. Nor can any significant meaning be attached to any proposition about world welfare except in the case where *every* country experiences an increase in welfare or *every* country experiences a fall.

7.17 A SUMMING-UP ON CUSTOMS UNIONS

In view of the rather tedious argument of sections 7.15 and 7.16, it has seemed desirable to sum up briefly the main conclusions which emerge. These are:

1. The economic theory of the customs union is no more than a particular application of the general theory of tariffs set out in this chapter. It is particular only because it envisages coalitions between groups of countries in the setting of tariff rates rather than a 'free for all' in which each country separately plays the tariff game 'against' every other.

2. The principles for computing the gains and losses from tariff policy remain the same whether there is a customs union or not. It is a simple matter to extend the analysis of this chapter to many countries so as to be able to analyse the effects of combinations of

tariff changes rather than of one single tariff change (see exercise 8 at the conclusion of this chapter).

3. Any decision whether or not to form a customs union can only be made on the basis of proper consideration of the individual gains which are expected to accrue to the participants, and ideally of course after equal consideration of the losses or gains which will be felt by other members of the world community of nations. No sensible meaning can be attributed to the idea of a 'world' gain or loss.

4. No general principles enable us to predict on *a priori* grounds what the individual losses or gains may be. In the absence of proper measurement on the lines indicated in this chapter it is impossible even to guess at the outcome of any tariff adjustment, whether such adjustment is unilateral or the consequence of a customs agreement. Inspection of the results given in exercises 3 and 6 at the end of this chapter are sufficient to show that, of two countries, both might lose by the imposition of a tariff, and at least one country might lose from the reduction of a tariff. The result of exercise 8 is sufficient to show that in a three-country world the reduction of a tariff could make two countries out of three worse off. Indeed, there is no reason to suppose that a case might not be devised where the reduction of a tariff serves to make *everyone* worse off (see exercise 11). In these circumstances there is little point in producing more and more complicated algebra. Empirical studies are urgently awaited.

5. Whilst it is true that, wherever a tariff structure exists, further beneficial exchange is possible, it is equally true that the removal of tariffs will not necessarily bring about the desired exchange. This conclusion is of course one of the immediate implications of (4) and indeed of all tariff theory. No situation should be called inefficient until a policy which will bring about certain improvement can be defined.

6. In view of the calculations of section 7.5, the order of magnitude of gains or losses due to the formation of customs unions might not be more than say 2 or 3 per cent of the value of the national product of the participating nations.

We now leave this subject with a reminder to the reader of certain comments in section 7.15. In focusing attention upon the material gains and losses attendant upon the creation of a customs union we should not lose sight of other, perhaps infinitely more important, features of the movement. Seen as a first step along the road to world government, a customs union might very well be worth any amount of material loss. Indeed, one of the interesting features of tariff wars is the analogy with warfare proper. If tribal battles lead to national governments, then tariff wars might lead to world government. Perhaps we should pursue them with and without coalitions!

EXERCISES

1. Construct a diagram on the lines of Fig. 7.1 but with offer curves satisfying $(E'_{11} + E_{22} + 1) > 0$. Show that in this case the imposition of a tariff will cause the real terms of trade to move unfavourably and hence confirm diagrammatically the algebraic result (7.5.19).

2. Introduce into the algebra of section 7.5 a third (non-traded) commodity produced and consumed by each country. The quantities produced of each commodity traded or non-traded remain fixed. Commodity 2 is not produced in country 1 and commodity 1 is not produced in country 2. Show that in this case the algebraic result corresponding to (7.5.19) is

$$\frac{dq_2}{q_2} = -\frac{\psi_{23}}{1 + \psi'_{13} + \psi_{23} - \phi'_{13} - \phi_{23}} \, dt$$

where ψ and ϕ have the usual meanings (see exercise 5, Chapter 4). Hence show that the introduction of a third commodity leaves the conclusion of 7.5 fundamentally unchanged.

3. Extend the algebra of section 7.5 to show that the rate of change dw/dt of welfare in the home country in the case where a foreign import duty t' exists and the home import duty t is different from zero initially, is given by

$$\frac{dw}{dt} =$$

$$q_2 X_2 \left[\frac{\left(E_{22} + C_2\right)\left(1 - \frac{t'}{1+t'} \, C'_1 + \frac{t}{1+t} \, E'_{11}\right)}{\left(1 - \frac{t'}{1+t'} \, C'_1\right)E_{22} + \left(1 - \frac{t}{1+t} \, C_2\right)E'_{11} + \left(1 - \frac{t'}{1+t'} \, C'_1\right)} \right]$$

4. By setting dw/dt in exercise 3 equal to zero, prove the optimal tariff formula (7.8.14) in the text.

5. Introduce into the problem of exercises 3 and 4 a third (non-traded) commodity as before. Under the conditions of exercise 2 show that the optimum tariff condition must now become

$$-\left(1 + \frac{1}{t}\right) = \psi_{13}' - \phi_{13}'.$$

6. In the problem of exercise 3 above show that the rate of change of welfare abroad, dw'/dt, with respect to a change in *home* import duty is given by

$$\frac{dw'}{dt} = -\frac{q_2 X_2}{1+t}\left[\frac{\left(E_{22} + C_2\right)\left(1 - \frac{t'}{1+t'} - t'E_{11}'\right)}{\left(1 - \frac{t'}{1+t'}\,C_1'\right)E_{22} + \left(1 - \frac{t}{1+t}\,C_2\right)E_{11}'} + \left(1 - \frac{t'}{1+t'}\right)C_1'\right]$$

Hence show that it is never possible for both countries to lose from the removal of a tariff although it is possible for both countries to lose from the imposition of a tariff.

7. Prove the results (7.12.1) and (7.12.2).

8. Construct a model with three countries A, B and C. Let A produce only commodity 1 and let B and C produce only commodity 2. Let t_1' be a tariff imposed by B on imports from A and let no other tariffs exist. Show that a reduction dt_1' in t_1' will change welfare in each of the three countries at the rates

$$\frac{dw}{dt_1'} = -\frac{p_1 X_1'(E_{11}' + C_1')/(1 + C_2't_1')}{D}$$

where

$$D = \left[1 + E_{22} + \frac{E_{11}' + t_1'\,(E_{11}' - C_1')}{(1 + C_2't_1')} \cdot \frac{X_1'}{X_1' + X_1''} + \frac{E_{11}''\,X_1''}{X_1' + X_1''}\right]$$

$$\frac{dw'}{dt_1'} = p_1 X_1'\left[t_1'(1 + E_{22}) + \frac{X_1'}{X_1' + X_1''}\right.$$
$$\left. + \frac{t_1'\,E_{11}'\,X_1''}{X_1' + X_1''}\right]\left[\frac{(E_{11}' + C_1')/(1 + C_2't_1')}{D}\right]$$

and

$$\frac{dw''}{dt_1'} = p_1 X_1'\left[\frac{(E_{11}' + C_1')/(1 + C_2't_1')}{D} \cdot \frac{X_1''}{X_1' + X_1''}\right]$$

where primes identify variables or parameters belonging to country B and double primes those belonging to country C.

From the results given, show that a *reduction* in the tariff rate t_1' may make two out of the three countries worse off. Consider how far this example is in contradiction with the argument that a unilateral reduction in the highest tariff rate is bound to make the world as a whole better off (see section 7.16).

Hint: Note that for three countries we must have a balance of payments equation

$$B = p_1(X_1' + X_1'') - p_2 X_2.$$

It is assumed that countries B and C neither export nor import to or from each other.

To be attempted only after a reading of both Books I and II

9. Introduce into the problem of exercise 5 non-zero supply elasticities and allow the manufacture of importables and exportables both at home and abroad. Show that the optimal tariff formula is now:

$$-\left(1 + \frac{1}{t}\right) = \frac{X_1'}{x_1}\,\psi_{13}' - \phi_{13}'$$

where ψ_{13}' now contains supply elasticities (see exercise 5, Chapter 4), and $x_1 = X_1' - S_1'$. Hence defend the argument of section 7.9.

10. Construct a model with two 'importable' commodities and two 'exportable' commodities. Find the value of dw/dt_i where t_i is the tax on the ith import or export. Show that $dw/dt_i = 0$ is satisfied simultaneously for all commodities if and only if (7.12.10) is satisfied. Hence defend the argument of section 7.12.

11. When world supply and demand are equated, a country's imports must be equal to home consumption less home supply. Use this fact to show that the change in welfare at home due to the reduction of an import duty abroad can be expressed entirely in terms of home elasticities of supply and demand and the change in the terms of trade. Prove in particular that if country 1 in, say, a three-country world produces commodity 2 which it also imports, together with commodity 1, which it exports, and a non-traded commodity (3), and if country 2 reduces its

import duty on commodity 1, then the change in welfare in country 1 is given by

$$dw = \frac{-\left(X_2 - S_2\right)\left(1 + \frac{t_2^2}{1 + t_2}\phi_{23} - t_2 \frac{X_2}{(X_2 - S_2)}\psi_{23}\right)}{1 + t_2 - t_2\phi_{23}} dp_2$$

where ϕ_{23} and ψ_{23} have the meanings of exercise 5, Chapter 4, and where p_1 is the numeraire price and t_2 the import duty of country 2.

Hence show that if $\sigma_{31} - S_{31}$ is negative in sign (as it may be if commodities 1 and 3 are complementary goods), dw may be negative even though the real terms of trade for country 2 improve.

Hence justify the claim in (4), (7.17) that a case may be devised such that a unilateral reduction in the highest tariff rate in the world economy could make *every* country worse off.

8 Tariff Protection and the Balance of Payments Again

8.1 Do Tariffs Protect?

So far we have concentrated upon the more positive effects of import duties, that is, upon their power to exploit the foreign country. In recent times, however, the tariff has been thought of more as a defence mechanism than an aggressive instrument. It protects the home country from 'unfair' competition or it discourages imports when the balance of trade is unfavourable. These are objectives (2) and (3) in the list at the beginning of Chapter 7.

We begin with the argument for protection. This has two main bases, first the preservation of the *status quo*, and second the so-called 'case for the infant industry'. To justify a tariff imposed to preserve the *status quo*, it is necessary to argue that foreign competition is 'unfair' or for some other reason undesirable, for in a general way it is accepted that competition ensures both efficiency and cheapness whether the source of competition is home or foreign. Obviously it is in the interests of the consumer to buy wherever it is cheapest.

On the other hand, the suggestion that competition is in fact unfair is one which is made frequently, and for obvious reasons, by any home producer who discovers that, because of some change in relative prices due to growth, technical change or exchange-rate adjustment, he no longer manufactures at a cost equal to or less than that at which his product can be imported. Such a producer will immediately compare labour costs or raw material or capital costs in the foreign country, making currency conversions at the going rate of exchange, and say, quite rightly, that his foreign competitors have the advantage of cheap labour or a low rate of interest. From there it is a short step to emotive expressions like 'sweated labour' or a claim that the foreign government subsidises production by keeping interest rates down. The final stage is to argue that by protecting the industry the home worker will in turn be protected against competition by labour which can exist on a 'handful of rice'.

This last suggestion looks particularly silly if it is believed at the same time that trade ordinarily increases welfare whoever is the trading partner, and if it is understood that it is precisely the competitive process which leads the foreign country to specialise in that which it can produce more cheaply. It is clearly inconsistent to argue, on the one hand, that free competition in a capitalist society is a good thing but that it is unfair when the same mechanism involves the scrapping of valuable specialised equipment or when it leads to all the unpleasantness associated with changing a way of life.

Against all this it has to be recognised that valid reasons for imposing protective tariffs can exist. If sudden and unexpected changes occur exposing an existing industry to particularly distressing pressures, there may be a case for temporary shielding to allow time for adjustment. The same kind of thinking underlies the infant industry argument mentioned above. Thus it may be felt by some businessman that whilst he could not manufacture at a competitive cost currently, he could, after experience had been gained in some new field and when the industry had grown, do without the temporary protection which would be needed to start him off. In principle the tariff can give time to establish or time to adjust. In practice of course it is easier to impose a tariff than it is to remove it when the 'infant' is fully grown or when the period of adjustment is over.

Even more important, it might be thought desirable to protect an industry permanently if it were considered necessary for reasons of national security that it should not be allowed to die. A country which is dependent on imports for some essential commodity, without which it could not exist, is very vulnerable to political and military pressure. There may be good reasons for encouraging home production, whatever the cost.

Fortunately we are not required in this book to define the circumstances in which a tariff should or should not be imposed. This is a matter which involves political and ethical judgements which lie outside the realm of our subject. The object of the present inquiry is more simply to describe the *economic* consequences of import duties and to show how far, if at all, such duties are likely to achieve the declared end for which they are to be imposed. We have listed possible objectives only so that we might consider whether they will be attained as claimed.

Whether the protective intent is to eliminate competition based on natural advantage as opposed to efficiency, or whether it is to avoid temporary embarrassment or to permit permanent development of a relatively high-cost industry, one common feature is present. The tariff must 'protect', that is, it must raise the home price of the protected commodity relative to all other prices, or, what may or may not amount to the same thing, permit an increase in home supply.

The reader who has progressed thus far will already understand that it is far from obvious that an import duty will result in an increase in the home price p_2, for although the home price after the change includes a new tax element, the foreign price q_2 will have fallen. If the percentage improvement in the real terms of trade is greater than the percentage tariff imposed, then the home price will fall instead of rise.

A possibility of this kind looks very surprising at first glance and is one not likely to be considered by persons untrained in economics. It will seem obvious to the casual observer that a tariff must protect. The consumer is required to pay more for the imported commodity by the amount of the tariff, so that a prospective home producer will be in a position himself to charge more. And even when attention is drawn to the real terms of trade effect, intuition suggests that it ought not to be large enough to outweigh the price rise due to the tax. It is important therefore to examine the problem with some care.

We note first of all that the simplicity of our model at once restricts the scope of our inquiry. We have assumed at the outset that there is no home production of importables. It follows that we cannot show how far a tariff can help an *existing* producer. All that can be done is to find the circumstances in which a prospective manufacturer who cannot compete without protection might be helped by a tariff to *enter the market*.

In the simple two-commodity case there is no difficulty. If the home price of importables rises relatively to a sufficient degree, home production can begin. In the real world, however, the problem is not so easy. If there is some home production, both of exportables and of a class of non-traded goods, the imposition of a tariff will almost certainly change their relative prices even though it is only importables which are taxed. The production pattern will change and with it the relative prices of capital and labour. Even though the price of importables may have risen relatively, it is not at all clear whether the change in input prices (capital and labour) has or has not improved the chances of a home producer of importables entering the market.

Furthermore, if there already exists some home production of importables, there may be more than one problem to solve. We may suppose first of all that the home manufacturer can produce a given quantity competitively but that his costs rise with increased output. We may wish to know whether a protective tariff will enable him to produce more and still remain competitive. For example, it may be thought that a community which grows, say, 40 per cent of its own food competitively ought, for security reasons, to grow 50 per cent. It is by no means obvious that a tariff will make this possible even if the price of foodstuffs at home rises relatively, for if the relative price of exportables and non-traded goods change also, as they will in general, then we cannot say with certainty that the total effect upon the supply of foodstuffs will lead to an increase. This is a matter for investigation within the framework of a much more complex model.

Alternatively the following question might arise. Suppose that some technical change abroad reduces the foreign price of importables relatively to the foreign price of exportables. Will a tariff now protect the home industry in the sense of preventing a *reduction* in its output of importables in the face of new competition? The answer to this is no less complicated than that to the question of the previous paragraph.

As it happens, however, most of the difficulties disappear as far as the naive model is concerned. When one commodity only is produced with the total resources of the community (capital and labour), and when employment remains full, there can be no change in the relative prices of capital and labour. Only when the new commodity (importables) is actually in production can there be such a change. All that we need at present to investigate is whether or not the tariff does indeed raise the home importables price. If it does, at least the beginnings of an importables industry may be created.

Of course the reader may now ask quite rightly what is the use of an exercise which has so little applicability to the real world. There are two answers to this. First, we shall demonstrate that even in the simplest case the protection argument is not as obvious as it might appear at first sight to the untrained observer. Second, to work the simple case is the first step in the training required to understand the more complex problem.

Another fortunate fact about the simple case which will commend itself to the student is that we do not really have to work it. The answer has already been obtained implicitly in Chapter 7. Consider Fig. 7.1. The question we have to answer is simply whether the home price ratio after the tariff (*BG*) is steeper or less steep than the home price ratio before the tariff (*AE*). If it is steeper, the price of importables has risen relatively. If it is less steep, the tariff does not protect.

From the diagram there seems to be no reason why a construction either way should not be possible. It would appear to depend on the shapes of offer curves whether the tariff protects or not. In such a case it is necessary to turn as usual to the algebra and to find conditions upon the fundamental response rates sufficient to ensure that the import duty is effective. We shall discover that the *qualitative* result we seek will depend, as we have seen before, on the numerical magnitude of certain elasticities.

8.2 SOME ALGEBRA OF PROTECTION

Throughout the algebraic analysis of section 7.5 we assumed p_1 to be constant. We wish to know therefore the conditions under which dp_2 will be positive. Equation (7.5.19) gives us the change in the real terms of trade q_2 which we repeat below:

$$\frac{dq_2}{q_2} = - \left[\frac{E_{22} + C_2}{1 + E'_{11} + E_{22}} \right] dt \qquad (8.2.1)$$

From (7.5.15) we deduce

$$dp_2 = dq_2 + q_2\, dt$$

or

$$\frac{dp_2}{p_2} = \frac{dq_2}{q_2} + dt \qquad (8.2.2)$$

since $p_2 = q_2$ with zero tariff initially.
Substituting in (8.2.1) we have

$$\frac{dp_2}{p_2} = \frac{dq_2}{q_2} + dt = - \left[\frac{E_{22} + C_2}{1 + E'_{11} + E_{22}} \right] dt + dt$$

$$= \left(1 - \frac{E_{22} + C_2}{1 + E'_{11} + E_{22}} \right) dt$$

$$= \left(\frac{1 + E'_{11} - C_2}{1 + E'_{11} + E_{22}} \right) dt \qquad (8.2.3)$$

At first sight the result (8.2.3) seems to confirm what we already suspect, namely that it is possible that the tariff may not protect. The negative change in the real terms of trade dq_2/q_2 may outweigh the positive change dt in the tariff, that is, p_2 may fall.

But a little manipulation of our result shows that such a conclusion is unlikely almost to the point of impossibility. We recall first that every elasticity E contains a negative income effect, $-C$, equal to minus the marginal propensity to consume and a negative substitution part previously written σ (see exercise 5, Chapter 4). Writing (8.2.3) in full, breaking down the Es, we have

$$\frac{dp_2}{p_2} = \left(\frac{1 - C_2 - C_1' + \sigma_{11}'}{1 - C_2 - C_1' + \sigma_{11}' + \sigma_{22}}\right) dt$$

It is also a fact that in a two-good world

$$C_1 + C_2 = 1$$

since unit increase in total spending must be directed either to commodity 1 or to commodity 2. Hence

$$1 - C_2 = C_1$$

Thus

$$\frac{dp_2}{p_2} = \left(\frac{C_1 - C_1' + \sigma_{11}'}{C_1 - C_1' + \sigma_{11}' + \sigma_{22}}\right) dt \qquad (8.2.4)$$

But both C_1 and C_1' must be positive and less than unity, so that $C_1 - C_1'$ is less than unity *a fortiori*. Indeed, if consumer tastes are the same in both countries, $C_1 - C_1'$ is zero. And since all σ are negative in sign, the right-hand side of (8.2.4) must be positive for a positive tariff dt. The tariff protects.

Of course, if σ_{11}' is very small and C_1 is greater than C_1' by an amount less than σ_{22}, then dp_2 may be negative since the numerator of (8.2.4) will then be positive whilst the denominator is negative. But this is impossible if C_1' is greater than C_1 or if, as seems likely, the coefficient of dt in (8.2.4) is dominated by the substitution effects.

This last consideration should warn us that it must never be taken for granted that a tariff will protect an industry in any sense of the word. On the other hand we have not in this section gone very far towards a solution of the problem which is likely to be of value in the real world. We have learned only enough to justify investigation of a much more complex model.

Furthermore, we have not yet begun to examine how a tariff might protect *employees* rather than *employers*, if at all, that is, (4) in the list at the head of Chapter 7. All of this must be left until the student is more advanced (see exercises 1, 2 and 8 to this chapter).

8.3 TARIFFS AND THE BALANCE OF PAYMENTS

In this section we turn to motive (2) of Chapter 7, that is, the use of the tariff as a means of controlling the balance of trade. Intuitively it seems obvious that if a country is importing more than it can pay for by exports, one possible policy is to reduce imports by means of a tariff. On the other hand, will a tariff improve the trade balance when we bear in mind that the real terms of trade may move favourably? Inspection of Fig. 7.1 reveals that when the foreign elasticity of demand is low, as drawn, the quantity of imports may *increase* as a result of the duty. G in Fig. 7.1 lies to the right of E, which indicates that physical consumption of importables has gone up. It is evidently desirable to check carefully upon what might happen to the balance of payments if an import duty is imposed.

So far of course, in treating the tariff problem, we have assumed that the balance of payments will always remain balanced. It has been supposed that whatever change in the real terms of trade is necessary to secure this will actually take place. These assumptions have been made not because it is believed that in practice the imposition of a tariff will automatically be followed by a change in the real terms of trade but because, up to this point, it is the effect on the real terms of trade which has been the centre of interest. To put it another way, we have been concerned with the welfare effects of a *combined* tariff and balanced trade policy.

The work of section 7.11 will, however, have warned the reader that it can sometimes be misleading to look only at the narrower question. If a tariff gives rise to a balance of trade difficulty, either for the home or foreign country, something will have to be done about it in the long run. The real terms of trade and non-traded goods' prices must be adjusted in one of the ways described in Chapters 2–4. It might even be argued that, to reach an equilibrium situation as quickly as possible, the imposition of a general tariff should be accompanied by an appreciation of the exchange rate, or other measures, to adjust relative prices as required. In such a way necessary changes might be helped along. The work of Chapter 7 tells us implicitly by how much the exchange rate should be appreciated for any given tariff change. In particular, equation (7.5.19) can be interpreted this way if desired. In short, apart from section 7.11, our previous analysis leaves out the 'dynamics' of the problem, that is, we no not consider the mechanism necessary to induce the secondary changes required to attain equilibrium, although this mechanism is often of paramount importance.

All this suggests that we might reconsider the problem of tariffs the other way round. If a balance of trade deficit exists initially, or, what is an equivalent problem, if it is desired to create a trade surplus, can this be done *without changing the real terms of trade* simply by means of a tariff? In a general way the answer is 'yes'. This may be demon-strated as follows.

Suppose that we begin from a position exactly as in Fig. 2.1. We have offer curves *ASF* and *AES* (Fig. 8.1) for countries 1 and 2, inter-secting at *S*. Prices and exchange rates are such that the real terms of trade stand at *AF*. Comparison with Fig. 2.1 shows that there will be a deficit in world demand for exportables and an excess world demand for importables. As in Chapter 2 we assume that production

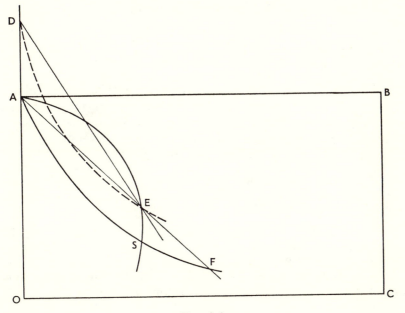

FIG. 8.1

in both countries continues at the full-employment level. Country 1 is building up stocks of exportables whilst country 2 is running down stocks to meet excess demand. There is an excess of imports over exports equal in value to the stocks building up. The difference must be paid for in gold.

Obviously this situation cannot continue indefinitely, and in Chapters 2 and 3 we considered various things which might occur to set matters right. We did not, however, envisage the consequences of an import duty if such were imposed. Suppose in fact that a tariff yielding *AD* (Fig. 8.1) were levied, the proceeds being used to reduce general taxation. Total spending increases to *OD* and a new offer curve *DE* emerges. If the level of tariff has been correctly chosen, the new offer curve will cut the foreign offer curve at *E*, the point of intersection of *AES* with the terms of trade line *AF*.

The home country's pattern of consumption is now shifted from *F* to *E*, which also defines the foreign consumption pattern. World consumption is now equal to world production and the gold loss ceases. Stocks of exportables cease to grow and stocks of importables cease to fall. No further adjustment is necessary for full equilibrium and the terms of trade have *not* moved against the home country as would be required in the absence of the tariff.

8.4 Trade Imbalance Adjustment by Tariff – The Algebra

The algebra of section 8.3 is exceedingly simple, indeed almost trivial, for neither total expenditure nor prices change in the foreign country if the real terms of trade remain constant. The price of exportables p_1 in the home country is of course kept constant as a 'numeraire' in the now familiar way. First we have

$$B = p_1 X_1' - q_2 X_2$$

as the definition of the balance of trade so that

$$dB = p_1 dX_1' - q_2 dX_2 \qquad (8.4.1)$$

(p_1 and q_2 are constant).

But X_1' depends on q_1, q_2 and Y' which do not change, since foreign output does not change. Therefore $dX_1' = 0$ so that

$$dB = -q_2 dX_2 \qquad (8.4.2)$$

This result is obvious from inspection of Fig. 8.1.

Following the usual principle

$$X_2 = X_2(p_1, p_2, Y)$$

hence

$$dX_2 = \frac{\partial X_2}{\partial p_1} dp_1 + \frac{\partial X_2}{\partial p_2} dp_2 + \frac{\partial X_2}{\partial Y} dY$$

which, since p_1 is constant, reduces to

$$dX_2 = \frac{\partial X_2}{\partial p_2} dp_2 + \frac{\partial X_2}{\partial Y} dY \qquad (8.4.3)$$

Again, the change dY is simply total imports multiplied by the change in tariff dt, that is,

$$dY = q_2 X_2 dt$$

as long as neither output nor the price of exportables changes and as long as the initial tariff is zero. Hence from (8.4.3)

$$dX_2 = \frac{\partial X_2}{\partial p_2} dp_2 + \frac{\partial X_2}{\partial Y} q_2 X_2 dt$$

and since

$$p_2 = q_2(1 + t)$$
$$dp_2 = q_2 dt$$

for q_2 constant and hence

$$dX_2 = \frac{\partial X_2}{\partial p_2} q_2 dt + \frac{\partial X_2}{\partial Y} q_2 X_2 dt.$$

From (8.4.2), therefore,

$$dB = - q_2 dX_2$$
$$= - p_2 dX_2 \text{ (for } t = 0)$$
$$= - q_2 X_2 \left(\frac{p_2}{X_2} \frac{\partial X_2}{\partial p_2} + p_2 \frac{\partial X_2}{\partial Y} \right) dt$$
$$= - q_2 X_2 (E_{22} + C_2) dt \qquad (8.4.4)$$

Since E_{22} consists of two parts, the substitution part σ_{22} and $-C_{22}$ (8.4.4) may be reduced to

$$dB = - q_2 X_2 (\sigma_{22}) dt \qquad (8.4.5)$$

which, since σ_{22} is negative, must be positive for positive dt.

We conclude that it is always possible to choose some positive tariff dt which will correct any given imbalance of trade dB except in the unusual case where there are no possibilities of substitution in consumption between exportables and importables, that is, when country 1 requires both commodities in the same fixed proportion whatever the price, so that $\sigma_{22} = 0$.

Care should be taken in interpreting the above result. We have not proved that whenever an imbalance of trade is observed all that is necessary is to impose an import duty at an appropriately chosen level. The reader is reminded that the exercise above was begun from a situation in which world supply and world demand for importables and exportables were not equated. Stocks of exportables were supposed to be building up and stocks of importables running down. The demands X_1' and X_2 of the balance of payments equation leading to (8.4.1) were assumed to be met even though they sum to more or less than world production. In any other case, B would not be an *observed* imbalance of trade. The tariff remedy imposed can succeed as explained only if the underlying causes of the imbalance are those specified.

Obviously it is necessary to reconsider the problem in other contexts, but before we pass on to this two points must be made. First, the reader is referred to exercise 3 at the end of this chapter which is designed to demonstrate that the problem is not materially different when non-traded commodities are present, except for a subsidiary need to change the relative prices of traded and non-traded goods. The second point merits a sub-heading of its own although the text will be brief.

8.5 TRADE IMBALANCE ADJUSTMENT BY EXPORT SUBSIDY

As intuitively one would expect export subsidies to be just as effective in the adjustment of a trade imbalance as import duties, it is worth pointing out that there are some important asymmetries. In the first place it is not possible to correct a trade imbalance as in section 8.4 with an export subsidy without at the same time inducing an adverse movement of the real terms of trade. We shall not attempt to prove this here since it is not difficult. The reader is simply referred to exercise 4 at the end of this chapter.

The second point to be made in connection with export subsidies is a consequence of the first. The import duty of section 8.4 corrects the trade imbalance with *no loss of welfare*. When the imbalance is corrected by an export subsidy, however, a loss of welfare is necessarily involved because of the adverse movement of the terms of trade. Exercise 5 at the end of this chapter is relevant (see also section 7.14).

We now turn to the case where trade imbalance is due to overspending.

8.6 ADJUSTMENT BY TARIFFS OF TRADE IMBALANCE DUE TO OVERSPENDING

Suppose that we begin with a trade deficit of the kind illustrated in Fig. 4.2.

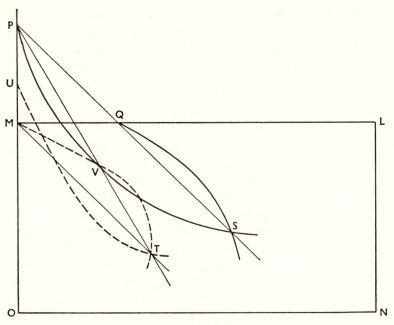

Fig. 8.2

In Fig. 8.2 the home country is spending OP, more than the value of its product OM. Country 2 is spending LQ, less than the value of its product LM. On the other hand there is no running-down or building-up of commodity stocks. S defines the pattern of spending both for country 1 and country 2 so that world supply equals world demand. Country 2 is in effect buying MP worth of foreign reserves for MQ of importables. MP is a measure of the trade deficit for the home country.

The problem now is, can this deficit be removed by means of a tariff without any change in the real terms of trade? The answer is again 'yes, with reservations'.

First of all we remind ourselves, from the work of Chapter 5, that the initial situation cannot exist without either

(a) an excess of government spending over government receipts, or
(b) an excess of private spending or industry spending above current receipts, or
(c) a combination of (a) and (b).

In any case the excess spending must total exactly MP, the trade deficit (see equation (5.2.1)). No balance of payments equilibrium is possible unless this excess spending is eliminated, for equation (5.2.1) must always hold if we are to avoid any pressure on the level of employment. Indeed, in the work of sections 8.3 and 8.4 we were bound to recognise commodity stocks to be changing precisely because the balance of trade was not balanced, yet no excess or deficit spending was present. The basic equation (5.2.1) did not hold.

One way to eliminate excess real spending at home is to use the proceeds of a tariff to run a government budget surplus. Unlike all previous cases the government should save and not spend the tariff revenue – nor should it adjust the level of direct taxation to compensate. If of course the excess spending MP were initially due to a government budget deficit, that is (*a*) above, then the tariff revenue will simply wipe out that deficit. Getting rid of a deficit implies precisely the same change in the budget imbalance as creating a surplus when the initial imbalance is zero.

If the tariff is first of all chosen to yield a revenue MP, then total money spending remains constant but total *real* spending is reduced. Purchasing power is taken out of the hands of consumers not by taking money from them directly but by taking it indirectly through a rise in price p_2 of importables following the tax. We now note that the rise in price of importables with other prices and income constant is bound to reduce demand for importables so that the foreign country will experience unemployment or at least failure of demand for its product. Indeed, the new pattern of home demand is V, which, with foreign demand, S, reveals the deficit.

To combat this, the foreign country can be expected to increase spending by means of a budget deficit or by otherwise operating on the spending of individuals or firms. The foreign offer curve will move to the left (Fig. 8.2). Eventually, if the foreign deficit demand is to be eliminated, as it must be if trade is to be balanced with equation (5.2.1) satisfied abroad, total spending abroad must be raised to LM. Let T be the point on the new foreign offer curve such that MT is parallel to QS, foreign prices q_2 and q_1 remaining unchanged. T represents the new foreign demand pattern at the old prices q_2 and q_1 but at the new spending level ML.

If the original home offer curve intersected the new foreign offer curve at T no further adjustment would be necessary. World supply and demand would be equated with the real terms of trade unchanged. The tariff revenue would be MP, the home price ratio p_2/p_1 would have risen to PT and the loss of gold halted. Exports would now exactly pay for imports.

But this could only occur by coincidence. In general the home offer curve through *P* will intersect *MT* either above or below *T* necessitating some actual change in the real terms of trade or some secondary adjustment of the tariff rate if the real terms of trade are to be held constant. On the other hand, apart from the existence of the initial tariff, the position as it now stands is simply that of section 8.4 in reverse. With home demand at *V* and foreign demand at *T* we have an excess of demand for exports over imports. We are interested to know whether equilibrium can be reached by a further adjustment of the tariff rate alone.

The answer to this is again 'yes', for the situation is just as if, in an attempt to solve the problem of section 8.3, the tariff had been set too high, that is as if, in Fig. 8.1, the offer curve *DE* cut *AES* above *E*. All that is necessary is to reduce the tariff slightly. At the same time the tariff taken off must be replaced by direct taxation, the proceeds being used for the same purpose as the lost tariff revenue.

This last proviso may at first seem puzzling, but this is only because we previously used the tariff to adjust excess spending exactly. No further adjustment is necessary so that any change in government revenue due to secondary tariff changes must be offset by corresponding taxation changes elsewhere precisely as described above (p. 159). This might be easier to understand if the whole process is looked at as two separate operations. First, get rid of excess spending by direct taxation on incomes (i.e. create a budget surplus or remove a deficit). Next, the tariff is imposed at the desired level, the tariff revenue being handed back as tax relief elsewhere, as described in earlier sections. The reader should note especially that the elimination of excess spending does not mean that total money spending must equal the total money value of output when a tariff is operative. For varying levels of the tariff, total spending may be *OP*, *OU* or *OM* or anything else in Fig. 8.2, even though *real* excess spending in the sense of (5.2.1) is zero.

To reach a final equilibrium it is necessary to reset the tariff so that the new offer curve *UT* cuts the foreign offer curve at *T*, the intersection of the line *MT* parallel to *QS*, and the foreign offer curve. Total spending at home is now *OU*, the proceeds of the new tariff being *MU*. World supply equals world demand and the real terms of trade remain unchanged at *MT*. The gold loss has been arrested and all excess or deficit demand eliminated.

The somewhat complicated description of the steps involved will demonstrate, however, the difficulties likely to be encountered in practice in any attempt to apply a policy of this kind. We have described what must be done but nothing more than a hint has been given as to how we might hit upon the right timing of the various moves. The initial tariff will probably lead to an increased spending abroad as explained, but there is no guarantee of any automatic mechanism of adjustment from there on. Nor would it be easy to hit upon the precise level of tariff.

Against this it is clear that if we knew all the elasticities of demand involved and could work out, as we can, the final level of tariff in terms of these elasticities, the ideal tariff for the purpose could be imposed at once. Adjustment of the budget imbalance in both countries so as to attain full employment would then lead to the equilibrium T provided prices were held constant.

8.7 THE ALGEBRA OF 8.6

The reader will by now have worked a sufficient number of cases to be able to set out for himself from first principles the algebra corresponding to the diagrammatic treatment of the previous section. We suggest that, as an exercise, this is now attempted. Such an exercise is proposed since we shall here take the opportunity to demonstrate a new and important principle which considerably lightens the task of working more complicated cases as they occur. The result which we obtain below may be checked against that derived as suggested from first principles.

Many adjustment problems can be treated as a combination of adjustments in two or more stages. This is convenient if any of the component steps have been previously worked as problems in their own right.

Consider for example the algebraic result (4.4.15) giving the relation between the balance of trade change and the real terms of trade change in the case where it is first necessary to remove the excess spending at home and the deficit in spending abroad. Knowing that we have already shown (in Chapter 3) that, for the case where no excess spending is present initially, the change in the balance is given by

$$dB = - X_2(E'_{11} + E_{22} + 1)\, dp_2 \qquad (8.7.1)$$

(see (3.3.9) and preceding argument), we need only to add the change in the balance due to the removal of excess spending at home and underspending abroad.

Write the balance of payments definition

$$B = p_1 X_1' - q_2 X_2$$

and take changes, assuming only that total spending abroad and at home have changed by amounts dY' and dY respectively, prices remaining constant; then

$$dB^* = p_1 \frac{\partial X_1'}{\partial Y} dY' - q_2 \frac{\partial X_2}{\partial Y} dY$$

$$= C_1' dY' - C_2 dY \tag{8.7.2}$$

(given of course that $p_1 = q_1$ and $p_2 = q_2$).

The notation dB^* is chosen to distinguish this from dB in (8.7.1).

We now think of the adjustment of Chapter 4 as the sum of two parts, first the spending adjustment (8.7.2) and next the terms of trade adjustment (8.7.1). The total is given by

$$dB^0 = dB^* + dB = -X_2(E_{11}' + E_{22} + 1)dp_2 + C_1' dY' - C_2 dY \tag{8.7.3}$$

But the required changes in spending at home and abroad must be equal to the total change in the balance of payments dB^0 as long as we are to avoid running down or building up of stocks. Therefore

$$dY' = dB^0$$

and $$dY = -dB^0$$

Substituting in (8.7.3) gives

$$dB^0 = -X_2(E_{11}' + E_{22} + 1)dp_2 + C_1' dB^0 + C_2 dB^0$$

or $$dB^0(1 - C_1' - C_2) = -X_2(E_{11}' + E_{22} + 1)dp_2$$

$$dB^0 = -X_2 \frac{(E_{11}' + E_{22} + 1)}{1 - C_1' - C_2} dp_2 \tag{8.7.4}$$

(8.7.4) is of course the result (4.4.15) obtained much more simply by using the work of Chapter 3.

The same principle may be used in many other contexts, and in particular we shall apply it to the problem of section 8.6. Beginning from the situation of full equilibrium (that is, balanced trade, world supply equals world demand, and zero tariff), we are required to find what tariff dt will create a given trade surplus dB, without an adverse movement in the terms of trade. The adjustment is thought of as consisting of two stages:

1. Reduction of home demand and increase in foreign demand by changes in total spending dY and dY' equal in magnitude to the desired trade surplus dB.
2. Imposition of tariff required as an alternative to real terms of trade adjustment.

As before, we write

$$dB^* = C_1'dY' - C_2dY \qquad (8.7.5)$$

as the adjustment under (1). Adjustment (2) is given by (8.4.5) as explained in section 8.6. That is

$$dB^{**} = -q_2 X_2(\sigma_{22})dt \qquad (8.7.6)$$

The final change is given by

$$dB = dB^* + dB^{**}$$

$$= -q_2 X_2(\sigma_{22})dt + C_1'dY' - C_2dY$$

which, remembering that the spending changes must be equal in magnitude to dB to prevent pressure on the employment level, gives

$$dB = -q_2 X_2(\sigma_{22})dt + C_1'dB + C_2dB$$

or $\qquad dB(1 - C_1' - C_2) = -q_2 X_2 \sigma_{22} dt$

or

$$dB = -\frac{q_2 X_2 \sigma_{22}}{1 - C_1' - C_2} dt \qquad (8.7.7)$$

This is a particularly interesting result since it shows that if

$$1 - C_1' = C_2' < C_2$$

the tariff change dt will have to be negative for a positive dB (i.e. to create a trade surplus). σ_{22} is of course negative in sign.

Such a possibility is far from obvious looking only at Fig. 8.2, although the results of Chapter 4 do prepare us for it. If the correction of a trade imbalance calls for an adjustment of the real terms of trade, which could be favourable, we should not be surprised that a subsidy, which causes an adverse terms of trade movement, might be required in the present case to restore the *status quo*.

In short it is perfectly possible in all cases to adjust a trade deficit by some budget adjustment through direct taxation combined with a tariff without any real terms of trade change and hence without any loss of welfare. But the tariff may have to be negative, that is, may have to be an import subsidy. Given the required surplus dB, equation (8.7.7) tells us precisely the tariff or subsidy dt required to achieve that surplus in terms of substitution elasticity, σ_{22}, and marginal propensities to consume.

We should perhaps draw attention to the fact that, as in Chapter 4, the algebra treats a slightly different case from the diagram. In the diagram we begin from a trade deficit and correct it to equilibrium. In the algebra we begin from equilibrium and create a surplus. For small deviations from equilibrium, however, the algebra will apply to both cases and the reader is invited to manipulate the diagram so as to be able to see how the negative tariff case might arise.

8.8 CORRECTION OF A TRADE IMBALANCE BY A TARIFF WITH NO DIRECT ADJUSTMENT OF AGGREGATE SPENDING

It is interesting to consider very briefly a third alternative. Suppose that we wish to create a trade surplus by means of a tariff. We may be willing to see the real terms of trade change but not willing to alter aggregate spending except to withhold the tariff revenue.

In this case the tariff must be chosen to yield a revenue exactly equal to the desired trade surplus. The tariff revenue must be applied to create the budget surplus needed to sustain the trade surplus. It is assumed that the various changes do not affect private or business spending plans and that the foreign country is willing or can be induced to increase its spending by the amount of the desired trade surplus as in section 8.7 (see also Chapter 9, section 4).

Finally, relative prices must be adjusted or some other means must be found to adjust the real terms of trade to an equilibrium position. A policy of this kind might be thought desirable as an alternative to cutting home spending by direct means. In such a case it would be necessary to find out what change in the real terms of trade must be achieved to obtain any given trade surplus.

Again the adjustment can be thought of in three steps:
1. Real terms of trade adjustment, as in Chapters 2 and 3.
2. Imposition of a tariff to yield required level of revenue.
3. A reduction in aggregate spending equal to the desired change dB in the trade balance.

The separate effects on the balance of trade will be:

$dB^* = -X_2(E'_{11} + E_{22} + 1)dq_2$ (terms of trade adjustment – equation (8.7.1) above with $p_2 = q_2$)

$$dB^{**} = -q_2 X_2 \sigma_{22} dt \text{ (tariff – equation (8.4.5) above)}$$

and $dB^{***} = C'_1 dB + C_2 dB$ (where dB is the desired improvement, as in section 8.7).

Adding these three we have

$$dB = dB^* + dB^{**} + dB^{***} = -q_2 X_2 \sigma_{22} dt - X_2(E'_{11} + E_{22} + 1)\, dq_2$$

$$+ C'_1 dB + C_2 dB \qquad (8.8.1)$$

But the tariff revenue $q_2 X_2 dt$ is chosen so as to equal the desired trade surplus dB, so that

$$q_2 X_2 dt = dB$$

Substituting in (8.8.1) yields

$$dB = -\sigma_{22} dB - X_2(E'_{11} + E_{22} + 1)dq_2 + C'_1 dB + C_2 dB$$

or $\qquad dB = -\left[\dfrac{X_2(E'_{11} + E_{22} + 1)}{1 - C'_1 - C_2 + \sigma_{22}}\right] dq_2 \qquad (8.8.2)$

The sign of the coefficient of dq_2 in (8.8.2) will normally depend upon the magnitude of σ_{22}, which is negative in sign, for, assuming stability, $(E'_{11} + E_{22} + 1)$ must be negative. But there is no reason to suppose that σ_{22} will be either greater or less than $(1 - C'_1 - C_2)$, so that a movement of the terms of trade either way is possible.

The result (8.8.2) of course does little more than prove that there can be no general rule even as to the direction of the required terms of trade changes. To estimate the magnitude of the change we should naturally need to set up a more realistic and hence more complicated model.

We make the point again also that *combined* policies of the kind analysed in this chapter are introduced only to draw attention to what might be politically more acceptable dynamic paths to some desired equilibrium situation. The final position attained will be one of balanced trade with a tariff or subsidy no different from those described in Chapter 7.

EXERCISES

1. Introduce into the algebra of section 7.5 the possibility of some
   home production S_2 of importables and some foreign production
   S_1' of exportables. The balance of payments equation (7.5.1) must
   now be written

   $$p_1(X_1' - S_1') - q_2(X_2 - S_2) = 0$$

   and the expenditure equations

   $$Y = p_1 S_1 + p_2 S_2$$

   and
   $$Y' = q_1 S_1' + q_2 S_2'.$$

   Assuming that the quantities produced S_1, S_2, S_1' and S_2' remain
   constant, show that the result equivalent to (8.2.3) is now

   $$\frac{dp_2}{p_2} = \frac{1 - C_2 + (X_1' E_{11}') / (X_1' - S_1')}{1 + (X_1' E_{11}') / (X_1' - S_1') + (X_2 E_{22}) / (X_2 - S_2)} \, dt.$$

   Hence consider whether it is more likely that a tariff will protect
   an existing industry than that it will create conditions favourable
   to the introduction of a new industry where none previously
   existed. Consider the likely magnitude of $X' / (X' - S')$ if the foreign
   country is the 'rest of the world'.
2. Use the result of exercise 2, Chapter 7, to show that the presence of
   non-traded commodities modifies the formula (8.2.3) as under,
   provided there is no home production of importables and no
   foreign production of exportables:

   $$\frac{dp_2}{p_2} = \frac{1 + \psi_{13}' - \phi_{13}' - \phi_{23}}{1 + \psi_{13}' + \psi_{23} - \phi_{13}' - \phi_{23}} \, dt.$$

   Hence show that, as far as price is concerned, the problem
   remains essentially unchanged by the introduction of non-traded
   commodities (but see exercise 8 below).
3. Introduce into the problem of section 8.4 non-traded commodities
   produced both at home and abroad. Assume as usual that all
   supplies S_i of the ith commodity are fixed and that the price of
   non-traded commodities is at all times set so that stocks of non-
   traded commodities are neither building up nor running down.
   Show that the correction of the trade imbalance dB of section 8.4
   now demands a tariff dt such that

   $$dB = - q_2 X_2 [\psi_{23}] dt$$

where ψ_{23} has the usual meaning of exercise 5, Chapter 4. Show also that the price p_3 of non-traded commodities must be adjusted by an amount

$$dp_3 = -\left(q_3 \frac{\sigma_{32}}{\sigma_{33}}\right) dt$$

4. Construct a diagram on the lines of Fig. 8.1 to show that a balance of trade problem of the type referred to in section 8.4 *cannot* be adjusted by a subsidy on exports without inducing a movement in the real terms of trade against the home country.

    Hint: Remember that a subsidy implies that the home country must spend *less* than the value of its production by the amount of the subsidy paid.

5. Show that in the problem of section 8.4 the home country settles its balance of trade deficit with no loss of welfare. Show that, in contrast, if an export subsidy is used to correct the imbalance there will be a loss in welfare equal to

$$-q_2 X_2 dq_2$$

given that q_1 is held constant. Set up a model and compute the value of dq_2 in terms of elasticities.

6. Introduce into the problem of section 8.7 non-traded commodities produced both at home and abroad. Assume, as usual, that all supplies S_i are fixed. Show that the tariff (subsidy) now required to correct the imbalance dB is given by

$$dt = \left(\frac{C_1' + C_2 - 1}{q_2 X_2 \psi_{23}}\right) dB$$

where ψ_{23} has the meaning of exercise 5, Chapter 4. Show further that the price p_3 of the non-traded commodity must be adjusted by

$$dp_3 = -\left[\frac{q_3 \sigma_{32}}{\sigma_{33}} - \frac{C_3(q_2 X_2 \psi_{23})}{X_3 \sigma_{33}(C_1' + C_2 - 1)}\right] dt$$

7. Construct a diagram on the lines of Fig. 8.2 to illustrate the result (8.8.2). Consider especially the case where $E_{11}' + E_{22} + 1 > 0$.

To be attempted only after a reading of Books I and II

8. Construct a model with importables, exportables and a class of non-traded commodities and determine the rate of change dS_2/dt

of the home production of importables with respect to a rise in the tariff rate on imports. Show that even if the home price of importables rises, the home production of importables may fall. Hence justify the following intuitive argument: 'The increase in real expenditure induced by a tariff will increase the demand for non-traded commodities and hence raise their price. The rise in price of non-traded commodities will in turn induce a movement of productive resources into their manufacture and away from the manufacture of importables.' Confirm the truth of the remarks in section 8.1.

9. Construct a model as in the previous question except that there is no home production of importables. Show that a tariff on importables could affect factor prices in such a way that the cost of production of importables in the home country rises relatively rather than falls so as to discourage rather than encourage the creation of an importables industry.

9 Quantitative Trade Restrictions

9.1 THE MECHANICS OF IMPORT QUOTAS

WHEN any country is experiencing a balance of payments difficulty, one obvious remedy, not so far discussed, is to apply quantitative restrictions upon imports. By this we mean that in one way or another importers are restrained from buying abroad even though it would be profitable to do so at going prices. The reason why the technique of physical control was not considered earlier, together with other methods of balance of payments control, is because of a close analogy with the tariff. The tariff restricts imports through the price mechanism leaving quantities free to find their own level. The import quota restricts imports quantitatively leaving prices to find their own level. We shall show that, with some reservations, the two methods amount to the same thing.

Any technique for restricting imports will of course achieve the desired result. In practice, however, one or other, or some combination of two distinct methods, has been most commonly applied in recent times. All importing may be forbidden except under government licence, licences being granted to importers up to a quota equal to a proportion of their normal business. Alternatively, foreign currency to pay for imports may be rationed. The rationing of foreign currency is possible of course only if one central authority is ultimately responsible for all foreign transactions. In the United Kingdom control can be effected by requiring all banks to pay all receipts of foreign currency to the Bank of England and to make all foreign payments through the Bank of England.

As is to be expected, both the licensing of imports and the rationing of foreign currency are difficult to operate in practice, although for obvious reasons currency control is the most easily evaded. However 'illegal' it may be there is no way of preventing any exporter from leaving his foreign currency receipts abroad, lodged with a foreign bank. He is then in a position to pay the bills of an importer who has been refused foreign currency by the central bank. The importer can reimburse the exporter in home currency at a rate of exchange favourable to the exporter and raise the selling price of his imports accordingly. The fact that imports are rationed means that they are in short supply from the point of view of the consumer at home. The consumer therefore is ready to pay a higher price. Evading currency control is accordingly a profitable exercise both for exporters and importers.

Quota restrictions are less easily evaded since, for other reasons, an efficient customs organisation is usually already in existence. As long as import licences cannot be forged, the only alternative facing an importer without a licence is somehow to evade customs inspection. This is virtually impossible except with small, highly valuable items. On the other hand, where, as is commonly the case, the quota is imposed, not on particular commodities without qualification, but on commodities from certain defined countries of origin, it may be evaded by first shipping imports from a restricted country to a non-restricted country. For example, if imports from the U.S.A. were officially rationed because of a shortage of dollars whilst imports from France were free, it may be possible to arrange for goods from the U.S.A. first to be imported into France and thereafter re-exported to England, the true country of origin being disguised.

An even more important difficulty with the quota lies in its inefficient and unfair operation as between importers. Quotas tend to be determined in proportion to the pattern of trade at a fixed base period during which trade was free. In practice this arrangement rapidly becomes out of date. It tends to prevent expansion of business by a new and perhaps more efficient firm by granting the equivalent of a monopoly to old-established importers. The right to a quota, or a position or reputation or history, which increases the likelihood that an application for a licence will be granted is a valuable asset. As with all assets there immediately arise pressures to buy and sell such rights. A new expanding firm might be tempted to bid for control of an existing firm solely because it has a right to a quota.

Moreover, as time goes on and tastes change, it becomes impossible to guess what the pattern of trade *would* be if quotas were removed. Importers cease to apply for licences not because they would not use them if they could be obtained but simply because they expect to be refused. The number of applications for licences to import ceases to be a measure of the strength of demand. In Australia, for example, in February 1960, when import controls were finally lifted, the quantity of imports in all lines went up to an extent far greater than anticipated despite the best efforts to predict from all available evidence.

In consequence of all this the arrangements for the granting of licences has to be made as flexible as possible. It is usual to combine both licence and currency rationing into a single system designed to give maximum security, reducing evasion to a minimum. The importer applies for permission to import and makes a special claim for currency against each licence granted. The licence in fact is both a permit to import and a permit to claim foreign currency. The importer who attempts to disguise the country of origin is forced to reveal it when he applies for the appropriate currency. And the importer who buys abroad with the proceeds from unreported exports is unable to pass his goods through the customs without a licence. The scope for the exercise of business 'ingenuity' remains considerable, however.

The need for flexibility means that the granting of licences must not be too closely tied to specified quotas. A compromise must be sought between efficiency and justice to old-established importers, whose livelihood may be threatened, not by their own inefficiency, but by deliberately chosen government policy. On the other hand, lack of clear-cut rules as to who is entitled to a licence places a great deal of power in the hands of the officials responsible for administering the scheme. The danger of corruption is obvious.

There are probably two main reasons why it has from time to time been thought desirable to introduce the quota rather than tariffs or other means of import control. These are, first, its intuitive appeal (it seems the obvious thing to do), and second its political acceptability.

When imports are to be restricted, the first instinct is to hold back the inflow of luxury goods rather than necessities. In this way it is felt that welfare is in some sense less affected. Alternatively, the import/export imbalance may be particularly large with one or more overseas countries taken separately, so that there is a case for reducing imports from these countries only. Accordingly the quota sometimes comes to be applied in a discriminatory manner. Particular commodities or countries are singled out.

Discrimination is of course possible with a tariff and indeed it is often applied in this way. Differential rates exist between commodities and between countries of origin. On the other hand tariff rates receive publicity and the element of discrimination is made obvious. Partly as a result of this, and partly because of a consciousness of the element of exploitation in the tariff, discriminatory rates have come to be widely regarded as 'unfair'. In tariff negotiations it is commonplace to introduce a 'most favoured nation' clause granting in effect equal rights to all countries, and what might be termed 'international economic law' generally looks on discrimination with disfavour.

Against this the issue of licences is a confidential matter between the importer and the trade authorities. Discrimination can be practised without attracting attention, so much so in fact that it might be very difficult for any third party to prove that it was in fact being practised. Furthermore, with quotas, the pattern of prices is not being interfered with in any very obvious way. All that seems to be happening is that the restricting country is very reasonably preventing her citizens from buying goods for which they cannot pay.

We shall now attempt to show that many of the reasons given for the use of quotas rather than tariffs are illusory and that 'common sense' is not always an infallible guide to what is best.

9.2 THE EFFECTS OF IMPORT QUOTAS

Consider first of all the situation depicted in Fig. 9.1. We have initially the usual balance of payments disequilibrium with stocks of commodities running down abroad and building up at home. The real terms of trade stand at *AF* instead of at the equilibrium level *AS*;

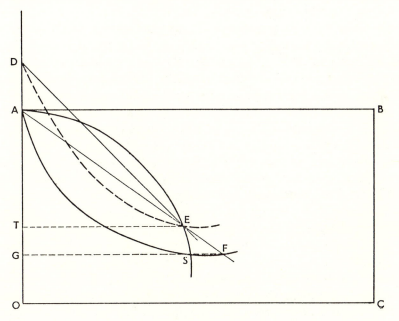

Fig. 9.1

that is, they stand too much in favour of country 1. Country 1 consumes the quantities of importables and exportables defined by the point F, whilst country 2 consumes E. World demand for exportables is less than world supply OA, whilst world demand for importables is in excess of world supply AB; hence the changes in stock levels. Country 1 is losing exchange reserves.

A quota is now imposed by country 1 designed to reduce imports from GF, at which it is running, to TE, which is the amount that can be paid for by the exports AT demanded by the rest of the world. The immediate consequence is a shortage of importables in the shops *in the home country*. It should be noted that there is no corresponding shortage abroad of either commodity. There is no pressure to change the foreign prices q_1 and q_2. World demand for importables, as far as the foreign country is concerned, has been brought into equality with world supply, for TE is the balance of world production after foreign requirements have been met.

In the home country, however, the shortage of importables will lead to a rise in their price. A rise in the price p_2 means excess profits for importers or retailers. It is worth while to reflect for a moment upon the causes of this price rise since it is sometimes denied that it is likely to take place. First of all, notice the essential difference between the initial situation and that after the quota is imposed. In the world as a whole before the quota, it is true that there was a shortage of importables in the sense that stocks are being run down. We have earlier suggested that, in spite of this shortage, producers abroad may not be immediately ready to raise prices. If they were, the real terms of trade would move against country 1 to the equilibrium position AS, excess world demand would disappear and our whole problem with it. The reason why this may not happen is simply that stocks exist. The excess demand can be met out of stocks, in which case consumers are able to buy all that they want at the going prices. There is no pool of unspent money. The only pressure to raise prices is that on the *producer* who sees his stocks diminishing. And as the producer is accustomed in the real world to fluctuating demand, he may well feel that the situation is temporary, calling for no immediate action.

After the import quota has been imposed, however, the situation is quite different. Importers may have stocks to meet the excess demand now concentrated entirely in the home country, but they have been made forcibly aware that their source of *supply* has been partially cut off for reasons of government policy. If they felt that the quota would soon be removed they may not raise prices, but there is no reason to

think this. It is immediately obvious that a permanent and unreliev-
able shortage has been artificially created. As a result importers
will *expect* prices to rise and in consequence be less willing to release
stocks even if they have them.

Moreover, when sales to consumers are reduced, excess money will
be available in consumers' pockets. In this situation pressure to raise
prices will come from consumers themselves. Shortages give rise to
queues at the shops. Lucky purchasers will receive offers from
disappointed consumers to resell at a higher price than that charged
in shops. Consumers will make offers to shopkeepers of higher prices
if the supplier will agree to reserve the next available supplies for
them. A strong incentive arises for criminals to steal or bribe
warehousemen to 'lose' commodities in their charge which are in
short supply. These will be sold at high prices to consumers who,
because of the shortage, are willing not to ask too many questions
about sources of origin.

In the face of these pressures it is hardly believable that importers
and other middlemen will not raise their prices. Indeed, all experience
suggests that they do despite protestations that they do not. Excess
profits may be spread along the line of supply but they none the less
exist. Moreover, as the quota arrangements continue and prices edge
up, the excess profits come to be concentrated in the hands of the
persons granted importing rights. It is the quota holders who gain. As
we have already indicated, the right to a licence is a right to excess profits.

Consider the effect of all this upon total community spending
measured in terms of commodity 1 as in Fig. 9.1. The community as a
whole produces OA of commodity 1, and since production creates
incomes it has OA to spend. But the community engages in a trading
activity as well as a producing activity and this also creates incomes.
If home relative prices are the same as the real terms of trade, no
additional income is created by the trading activity. But if home
relative prices p_2/p_1 are greater than foreign relative prices q_2/q_1, the
trading activity yields a profit, i.e. it yields additional income which
is available for spending. As soon as the price p_2 rises, total spending
must rise. Accordingly, the home offer curve shifts upwards becoming
DE in Fig. 9.1. As the price p_2 continues to rise, the additional
spending AD will increase until the new offer curve DE cuts the
foreign offer curve at E – the point where the foreign offer curve cuts
the real terms of trade line AF, that is, the point to which imports
were restricted.

The new position is one of full equilibrium. E is now a point defining the pattern of consumption simultaneously in both countries, as it must if world supply is to equal world demand in both commodities. The real terms of trade remain unchanged at *AF*. Commodity stocks have ceased to increase at home and decrease abroad and the outflow of currency reserves or gold is checked.

The reader will now notice that the diagram Fig. 9.1 is precisely the same as Fig. 8.1, which we developed to illustrate the effect of a tariff. Assuming that the original offer curves *ASF* and *AES* are the same in both diagrams, as they must be if the same two countries are involved, and assuming also that the real terms of trade are the same in both initial positions, then the point *E* must equally be in the same position in both diagrams. And we earlier proved, in section 7.2, that one and only one offer curve for one country can pass through any point on the diagram, such as *E*. It follows that the offer curve *DE* must be the same in both diagrams and hence the point *D* must be the same.

We have now shown that the imposition of a tariff which raises revenue equal to the excess profits of Fig. 9.1 restricts imports to the point *E*. Conversely we have shown that restriction of imports to the point *E* raises the price of imports by precisely the amount of the tariff required to restrict imports to *E* if the tariff weapon were used. The two policies are equivalent in their effects both at home and abroad with one qualification, to which we shall now turn.

In the case of the tariff, the revenue *AD* accrues directly to the government which then hands back its receipts to the community as a whole by remitting some other form of taxation or by direct distribution. With a tariff, therefore, the government is able to determine, according to some principle agreed to be fair, precisely who is to receive the extra spending money. When quantitative restrictions are applied, on the other hand, the extra spending power *AD* takes the form of 'windfall' profits which accrue to whoever is lucky enough to own the right to a licence, or to whoever is unscrupulous enough to profit from the shortage if the licence holder does not.

In other words the *distribution* of spending power is different in the two cases. And since different people have different tastes it could be that the shape and position of offer curves depend upon the distribution of spending power, in which event the two offer curves *DE* in Figs. 8.1 and 9.1 may not be the same. This in turn may destroy our conclusion that the excess profits *AD* of Fig. 9.1 sum to the tariff revenue *AD* of Fig. 8.1; but it does not destroy the conclusion that the trade imbalance can be corrected by either means.

If we knew precisely the differences in income distribution which would result in the two cases, and if at the same time we knew individual consumer tastes, it would be a simple matter to work out the exact consequences for the theory. No new ideas would be involved. We shall not therefore attempt here to do more than warn the reader of the possibility that some income redistribution effect might be felt in practice. It is also a fact, as we have previously noted on more than one occasion, that income redistribution effects may be associated with any kind of price change whatsoever. There is nothing different in principle in assuming no income redistribution effects when comparing tariffs and quantitative controls than there is in assuming no income redistribution effects when commodity prices change, leading inevitably to a different share-out of the national income between wages and profits. As long as the redistribution of spending is not mainly towards the government or some particular class of individuals likely to have markedly different spending habits, it is not unreasonable to suppose that the net effect is zero as a first approximation. And this assumption is made consistently throughout this book.

On the other hand the differences in income distribution which we have noted in the two present cases, tariffs versus quantitative controls, do have considerable ethical significance. In the tariff case the income changes are government-controlled; in the other they are a matter of chance. This aspect of the problem has in the past attracted some attention and various proposals have been put forward to meet the difficulty. It has been suggested, for example, that import licences should be auctioned by the government to the highest bidder rather than distributed free according to quotas assigned on the basis of 'normal' business as earlier explained.

If excess profits above the normal required to induce a businessman to trade can be earned by licence holders, then importers would be prepared to pay for their privilege. Competition at the auction would ensure that the price paid was sufficient to allow only normal profit to the most efficient importer. Hence the total price paid for all licences issued would be just equal to total excess profits AD in Fig. 9.1. This would accrue to the government in precisely the same way as the tariff and could be redistributed to the community, this time on government-determined principles.

The only difference now remaining between import controls and the tariff is in the administrative machinery required to operate it. The labour involved in issuing a separate licence and foreign currency allocation for every overseas order and/or in holding auctions for the right to claim such licences, together with the cost of the necessary control at the customs, is obviously much greater than that of collecting a tariff at the port of entry. It is probably because of this, and because of the natural resistance of established importers to the suggestion that they should compete in an auction for the right to carry on their own business, that the official sale of licences has never been attempted. The private sale of importing rights between businessmen is of course a natural consequence of physical controls which has already been commented on.

We sum up by remarking on the fact that in quarters where there continues to be dispute over the relative merits of tariffs and quantitative controls, the argument too often turns on imagined rather than real differences in their economic consequences. We have here another good example of the kind of misunderstanding which leads to the widespread acceptance of irrational and undesirable prohibitions upon certain kinds of policy. If quantitative controls are regarded as an acceptable means of adjusting a trade deficit then so should tariffs be – and vice versa.

9.3 The Algebra of 9.2

From the diagrammatic treatment of our problem above it is clear that we could, if we chose, extract all the required algebraic results direct from the working of the tariff problem in Chapters 7 and 8. On the other hand it is illuminating to find from first principles the excess profits which will arise from a restriction of imports designed to create a balance of trade surplus of dB. Comparison with the results of section 8.4 will then show this to be precisely equal to the revenue from the tariff required to achieve the same result. Thus we shall prove algebraically the result derived from the diagram of the previous section.

First we have the balance of payments equation

$$B = p_1 X_1' - q_2 X_2 \qquad (9.3.1)$$

The policy is to raise B by an amount dB by restricting imports X_2, at the same time holding the real terms of trade constant, that is, no price is to change except p_2, the home price of importables. It is convenient to assume that B is negative so that country 1 has a balance of trade deficit. As in section 9.2, aggregate expenditure is equal to the value of output in both countries initially and in country 2 it remains unchanged. Excess and deficit demands are of course met out of stocks.

From (9.3.1), dX_2, the given import restriction, must be chosen so that

$$dB = p_1 dX_1' - q_2 dX_2 \qquad (9.3.2)$$

where dB is the desired trade improvement. Thus, to bring country 1 into balance dB must equal minus the initial imbalance. We note also that dX_1' must be zero since X_1' depends only on foreign prices and spending, each of which is bound to remain unchanged throughout. Total foreign spending depends of course on total output O_2' and q_2, both of which are constant.

Hence from (9.3.2), remembering p_1 is the constant numeraire price,

$$dB = -q_2 dX_2 \qquad (9.3.3)$$

But
$$X_2 = X_2(p_1, p_2, Y)$$

so that
$$dX_2 = \frac{\partial X_2}{\partial p_1} dp_1 + \frac{\partial X_2}{\partial p_2} dp_2 + \frac{\partial X_2}{\partial Y} dY$$

which, since p_1 does not change, reduces to

$$dX_2 = \frac{\partial X_2}{\partial p_2} dp_2 + \frac{\partial X_2}{\partial Y} dY \qquad (9.3.4)$$

Now total spending Y is given by

$$Y = O_1 p_1 + (p_2 - q_2) X_2 \qquad (9.3.5)$$

where $(p_2 - q_2)$ is excess profits per unit of imports.

Hence
$$dY = X_2 dp_2 - X_2 dq + p_2 dX_2 - q_2 dX_2$$

since neither output O_1 nor price p_1 changes.

Furthermore, if imports are unrestricted initially, $p_2 = q_2$ and

$$p_2 dX_2 - q_2 dX_2 = (p_2 - q_2) dX_2 = 0$$

so that, remembering q_2 is constant,

$$dY = X_2 dp_2 \qquad (9.3.6)$$

Putting (9.3.6) in (9.3.4) we have

$$dX_2 = \frac{\partial X_2}{\partial p_2} dp_2 + \frac{\partial X_2}{\partial Y} X_2 dp_2$$

or $\quad \dfrac{dp_2}{p_2} = \dfrac{dX_2}{p_2 \dfrac{\partial X_2}{\partial p_2} + p_2 \dfrac{\partial X_2}{\partial Y} X_2} = \dfrac{dX_2/X_2}{E_{22} + C_2} = \dfrac{dX_2/X_2}{\sigma_{22}}$ $\qquad$ (9.3.7)

where σ_{22} is, as usual, the substitution part of the demand elasticity. This result gives us the percentage excess profit due to a given percentage import restriction dX_2/X_2.

Alternatively, using (9.3.3) in (9.3.7), we may write the percentage excess profit due to import restrictions designed to achieve a given trade surplus as we set out to do. Thus

$$\frac{dp_2}{p_2} = -\frac{1}{q_2 X_2 \sigma_{22}} dB \qquad (9.3.8)$$

This result should now be compared with (8.4.5), which we set out again for easy reference:

$$dB = -q_2 X_2 (\sigma_{22}) dt \qquad (9.3.9)$$

(9.3.9) gives the tariff dt required to achieve the trade surplus dB as under

$$dt = -\frac{1}{q_2 X_2 \sigma_{22}} dB$$

so that for given dB

$$dt = \frac{dp_2}{p_2} \qquad (9.3.10)$$

which proves our original assertion that the tariff dt, defined as a proportion of the import price q_2, is precisely the proportion of excess profits which would arise if import restrictions were used.

9.4 Adjustment by Import Quotas of Trade Imbalance Due to Overspending

We began this chapter with a statement suggesting that the government of any country experiencing a balance of trade deficit would be led quite naturally to consider import quotas as a means of adjustment. It is of the utmost importance to understand, therefore, that quantitative restriction alone cannot succeed in this except on the assumptions of sections 9.2 and 9.3. As so often emphasised in Chapters 2 to 5, the fundamental cause of a trade imbalance is usually over and/or underspending on the part of the home country and its trading partner. Like currency depreciation, the restriction of imports can do nothing by itself to correct a trade imbalance. Quotas must be combined with suitable adjustment of aggregate expenditure.

In sections 9.2 and 9.3 we evaded this problem by *assuming* that aggregate money spending did not initially exceed or fall short of the value of the national product. And after the imposition of the quota it was likewise taken for granted that aggregate spending could not exceed the value of the national product by more than the excess profits from imports created by the artificially high price of imports. In the same way, in sections 8.6 and 8.8 it was found necessary to specify carefully the uses to which tariff revenue might be put so as to adjust the level of aggregate spending as required. We have now reached a point where it is both convenient and possible to present the algebra of the model in a more systematic way so as to reveal more precisely what we mean when we say that import restrictions cannot be a policy *by itself*.

The essence of our most simple model is contained in the following set of equations.

$$B = p_1 X_1' - q_2 X_2 \tag{9.4.1}$$

$$X_1' = X_1'(q_1, q_2, Y') \tag{9.4.2}$$

$$X_2 = X_2(p_1, p_2, Y) \tag{9.4.3}$$

$$Y' = q_2 O_2' + M' \tag{9.4.4}$$

$$Y = p_1 O_1 + M + (p_2 - q_2) X_2 \tag{9.4.5}$$

$$p_1 = q_1 = \text{constant} \tag{9.4.6}$$

where M' and M measure excess spending over and above the money value of output abroad and at home. No change of notation is otherwise introduced.

Notice first that, by definition of the symbols used,

$$Y = p_1 X_1 + p_2 X_2 \tag{9.4.7}$$

and $$Y' = q_1 X_1' + q_2 X_2' \tag{9.4.8}$$

for Y and Y' mean total expenditure on commodities. Accordingly, using (9.4.4) and (9.4.5), we must have

$$q_2 O_2' + M' = q_1 X_1' + q_2 X_2'$$

and

$$p_1 O_1 + M + (p_2 - q_2) X_2 = p_1 X_1 + p_2 X_2$$

From which we deduce that

$$M' = q_1 X_1' - q_2(O_2' - X_2') = p_1 X_1' - q_2(O_2' - X_2') \qquad (9.4.9)$$

and $M = p_2 X_2 - p_1(O_1 - X_1) - (p_2 - q_2)X_2 = q_2 X_2 - p_1(O_1 - X_1)$
$$(9.4.10)$$

But O_2' is the world supply of commodity 2 and O_1 the world supply of commodity 1. If we *assume* that world supply and demand are equated, it follows that

$$O_2' - X_2' = X_2$$

and
$$O_1 - X_1 = X_1'$$

Comparison of (9.4.9) and (9.4.10) with (9.4.1) now reveals that *if* supply and demand are equated

$$M' = B = -M \qquad (9.4.11)$$

Only if world supply and world demand are not equated are we free to set M and M' according to government policy as explained in Chapter 5.

With all this in mind, consider the system of equations (9.4.1)–(9.4.6). Ignoring (9.4.6), which simply identifies the numeraire commodity, we have five equations in nine variables, B, Y, Y', p_2, q_2, M, M', X_1' and X_2. Total supplies O_1 and O_2' and the numeraire prices p_1 and q_1 are, of course, given constants. Now it is well known that, in a general way, five equations will determine five variables, that is, if all equations are to be satisfied simultaneously, the arbitrary selection of values for four of the variables will determine the other five. The reader will now note that, in general, p_2 and q_2 must, in the absence of tariffs, be the same and we shall ordinarily require the trade balance B to be zero. On these conditions selection of two variables will determine the remainder; thus selection of M and M' is sufficient to determine equilibrium.

Consider now the problem of section 9.2. Here we do not take it for granted that supply and demand are equated. On the contrary we assume that excess demand is met out of stocks. We have therefore to specify M and M', which we do by supposing that the government is pledged to maintain aggregate spending equal at all times to the value of output. That is, M and M' are maintained at zero. On the other hand B is not necessarily zero, nor is p_2 necessarily the same as q_2. It is plausible in the context, however, to assume that country 1 can act without affecting country 2, for aggregate spending abroad is constant, demand abroad is met at constant price p_1 and world demand for commodity 2 is met out of stocks without changing the price q_2. Hence we assume that q_2 does not change. We now have a system with five equations and six variables, B, Y, Y', p_2, X_1' and X_2, which are free to change. If the government influences any one of these as an act of policy, it will determine the rest. Thus the problem of section 9.2 can be seen as the arbitrary choice of some import level X_2 (quota) which thus determines all the remaining variables. In particular the home government wishes to choose a level of X_2 which gives zero B, that is, no payments imbalance. Note also that this will automatically equate supply and demand, since M and M' are both held at zero, thus satisfying (9.4.9) and (9.4.10). Finally, the reader should observe that the fixing of X_2 equally fixes p_2 so that we are free to solve for the change in p_2 due to the change in X_2 or the change in B due to the change in X_2 according to the interest of the moment. (9.3.7) is in fact the solution for the change in p_2. In the tariff problem of section 8.4, on the other hand, we looked at the problem the other way round, treating p_2 as the policy variable (via the tariff on q_2), solving the same system for the change in B due to the change in the tariff rate.

Now consider the case analogous to that of sections 4.2 and 8.8 where the initial trade imbalance is due to overspending. Here M and M' are not zero, but we do assume that prices are adjusted at all times so as to equate world supply and world demand. Accordingly (9.4.11) must be satisfied so that B and $-B$ may be substituted for M' and M in (9.4.4) and (9.4.5), reducing the number of free variables by two.

We now have five equations and seven variables making it necessary to select two as 'policy' variables instead of one. This is what we mean when we say that import restriction cannot be a policy *by itself*; something else must be taken under control by the government, the most obvious candidate being aggregate spending Y. If the system is disturbed by changing X_2 (import restriction), the mere fact that equations (9.4.1)–(9.4.6) must be satisfied is not sufficient to secure a determinate equilibrium. The new value of B could be anything we like if X_2 is the only controlled variable. To determine B we need two instruments of policy, not just one.

If we believe that in the real world prices are set so as to equate supply and demand at all times, and if at the same time we observe a trade imbalance, the government must be advised not only to restrict imports but also to control aggregate expenditure. Suppose accordingly that we recommend that, however the value of B changes, Y is to be held constant.

One convenient way to secure this would be to auction licences for the restricted imports at the same time ensuring that the proceeds of the auction are not spent. Since (9.4.5) must be satisfied at all times, any change in the trade balance $B = -M$ must be exactly offset by an equal and opposite change in $(p_2 - q_2)X_2$ which is the revenue from the sale of import licences. From the point of view of a solution to the system it matters little whether the government allows importers to earn and spend excess profits at the same time reducing expenditure through direct taxation by an amount equal to the desired improvement in the balance of trade, or whether it simply collects and saves the excess profits by the auction of licences. Either policy will serve to keep Y constant, but the one may be politically more acceptable than the other.

The reader should note especially that the aggregate spending policy appropriate to import controls is much less deflationary than that associated with cure by exchange-rate adjustment. In the former case it is not necessary to cut spending. All that is necessary is to prevent an increase. With exchange-rate adjustment on the other hand a definite cut in spending is essential. The reason for this difference is easily seen intuitively if we recall that import restrictions have much in common with a tariff. Correction of a trade imbalance by import restriction is equivalent to the combined effect of correcting the imbalance by exchange adjustment and deflation together with the subsequent imposition of a suitably chosen tariff. Since a tariff brings a welfare gain, a lesser reduction of real expenditure is necessary when it is applied than when it is not.

What we have now established is that it may be possible to adjust a trade imbalance due to overspending by import controls if at the same time steps are taken to hold home aggregate expenditure constant. The word 'may' is introduced first because of the underlying assumption that the foreign country will adjust its home expenditure and prices to maintain full employment and equilibrate supply and demand, and second because we have not yet shown that a reduction of imports will necessarily improve rather than worsen a trade imbalance. To investigate this last problem it is necessary to take changes in the equation system (9.4.1)–(9.4.6), remembering that dY is zero and dX_2 is fixed as an act of policy by the quota imposed. Given dX_2, therefore, we may solve the system for dB.

It would be tedious and, it is to be hoped, unnecessary to set out the algebra. We simply give the result:

$$dB = \frac{p_2(1 + E_{22} + E'_{11})}{E_{22}(E'_{11} + C'_1)} \, dX_2 \qquad (9.4.12)$$

and remark that dB could be negative for negative dX_2 if $(1 + E_{22} + E'_{11}) > 0$. Because of this possibility it is important to understand that low elasticities do not imply that a restriction of imports will worsen the balance of payments. On the contrary it means only that equilibrium cannot be found at a *lower* level of imports than that from which the exercise began.† This will become clear if a diagram representing this case is drawn on the usual lines (see exercise 2 below).

One more point only remains to be made. We have insisted throughout that tariffs and import quotas have much in common. To check this, the reader should solve the system (9.4.1)–(9.4.6) for dq_2/dX_2 as well as dB/dX_2. By dividing dq_2/dX_2 into (9.4.12) we obtain dB/dq_2, which should be the same as dB/dq_2 taken from (8.8.2) (see exercise 5).

EXERCISES

1. Construct a diagram on the lines of Fig. 9.1 to illustrate the case where $E'_{11} + E_{22} + 1 > 0$. Show that even in this case a properly chosen quota can correct a balance of trade deficit without change in the real terms of trade.
2. Construct a diagram on the usual lines to illustrate the meaning of the result (9.4.12) in the case where $E'_{11} + E_{22} + 1 > 0$.
3. Add to the system (9.4.1)–(9.4.6) the variable X_1 and the demand equation

$$X_1 = X_1(p_1, p_2, Y).$$

Solve for dX_1 and hence for

$$dw = p_1 dX_1 + p_2 dX_2$$

show that

$$dw = \frac{-p_2(E'_{11} + C'_1)}{E_{22}(E'_{11} + C'_1 - 1)} \, dX_2$$

† That is, it cannot be found for small changes. But see section 7.8 (pp. 185–7).

4. Replace the system (9.4.1)–(9.4.6) with one in which S_3 and S_3' units of some non-traded commodity are produced at home and abroad respectively. The home country produces at the same time S_1 units of exportables and the foreign country S_2 units of importables. Add the equations

$$S_3 = X_3(p_1, p_2, Y)$$

and
$$S_3' = X_3'(q_1, q_2, Y')$$

indicating that supply and demand for the non-traded commodities are equal.

Prove that the result (9.4.12) must now be written

$$dB = \frac{p_2(1 + \psi_{23} + \psi_{13}' - \phi_{13}' - \phi_{23})}{(\psi_{23} - \phi_{23})(\psi_{13}')} dX_2$$

where ψ_{23}, ψ_{13}', etc., have the meaning of exercise 5, Chapter 4. Show that this does not introduce anything fundamentally new into the problem.

5. Solve the system (9.4.1)–(9.4.6) for dq_2 in terms of dX_2 and hence prove that

$$dq_2 = -\frac{p_2(E_{22} + 1 - C_1')}{X_2 E_{22}(E_{11}' + C_1')} dX_2$$

Using this result together with (9.4.12) obtain a relation between dB and dq_2 and show that this is the same as (8.8.2). Hence justify the remarks at the end of section 9.4.

6. Solve the system of exercise 4 for the change dp_3 in the home price of non-traded commodities and hence show that the price of non-traded commodities must ordinarily fall relative to the price of traded goods in the home country when a trade imbalance is corrected by import restrictions.

7. Solve the system (9.4.1)–(9.4.6) for dB on the assumption that foreign money spending Y' is held constant and home money expenditure is varied so as to prevent the money price p_1 of home output from changing. Show that

$$dB = \frac{q_2 O_2'}{X_2' E_{22}'} dX_2$$

where dX_2 is an arbitrary import restriction. With the aid of a diagram try to devise a dynamic story showing how the new equilibrium might be reached.

8. Show, within the framework of the model (9.4.1)–(9.4.6), that it is impossible to correct a trade imbalance due to overspending by import restrictions unless the foreign country is prepared to allow either the foreign price of importables q_2, or aggregate spending Y', or both, to change.

To be attempted only after reading Books I and II

9. Introduce into the problem of exercise 4 some variability in the supply S_i of each commodity, adding supply functions to the equation system (9.4.1)–(9.4.6) where necessary. Show that (9.4.12) now becomes

$$dB = \frac{p_2 \left[1 + \left(\dfrac{X_2}{X_2 - S_2} \right) \psi_{23} + \left(\dfrac{X_1'}{X_1' - S_1'} \right) \psi_{13}' - \phi_{13}' - \phi_{23} \right]}{\left[\left(\dfrac{X_2}{X_2 - S_2} \right) \text{ as } \psi_{23} - \phi_{23} \right] \left[\left(\dfrac{X_1'}{X_1' - S_1'} \right) \psi_{13}' \right]} \, dX_2$$

where ψ_{ij} now contain supply elasticities (see exercise 5, Chapter 4).

Show that once again the problem is fundamentally unaltered.

10. If import taxes and export taxes are symmetric in their effects (see section 7.11), and if import quotas and import taxes are also equivalent, what would you expect to be the effect of an export quota?

Consider algebraically or otherwise the effect of an export quota imposed by a country with a balance of payments surplus where $M = M' = 0$. If initial excess demand for exportables is exactly matched by the export quota reduction, and if home prices therefore remain unchanged, show that the final effect will be equivalent to a foreign import quota. What would be the consequence of assuming that home exporters rather than foreign importers expropriated the excess profits?

Show as a result of your various arguments that it is improper to speak of the 'consequences of quota restrictions' in anything but a carefully specified dynamic context.

10 Economic Growth in an International Trade Context

10.1 THE PROBLEM STATED

IN this chapter we shall introduce in the simplest possible way some of the problems connected with economic change and growth. The reader is warned, however, that all the results obtained are severely modified when they are reworked in the context of a more realistic model. In particular it should not be concluded from what follows that in the real world the terms of trade are most likely to move against that country with the fastest rate of growth, even though the simple model may suggest this. We continue our study at the naïve level only for practice in manipulation and to create an awareness in the mind of the reader of the kind of difficulties which technological change creates.

It is a fact of economic life that year by year the productive capacity per head of population tends to change. If it did not, the task of the economist would be a great deal simpler. If the growth of resources, capital and working population continued at the same rate in all countries, exactly matching one another, and if the average consumer with an average income chose to spend his income in the same way for ever, the diagrams of previous chapters would remain essentially unmodified. They would in fact expand proportionately over time in such a way that the crucial slopes of the various curves remain unchanged. Once an equilibrium position is reached no force would be present to alter it. Prices and real income per head would remain constant.

Fortunately for the world but unfortunately for economists this does not happen. Rates of population growth are different in different areas. Moreover, output per head of working population changes for at least two reasons. First, output per head depends very much upon the ratio of 'capital' to the labour force. By 'capital' we mean here the actual tools of production, machines, buildings, roads and even educational institutions. These tools are bequeathed by each generation to the next. What we have is in large measure due to the efforts of our forefathers who for various reasons chose to save some of their earnings and to invest their savings in real capital. In the same way the *growth* of our stock of capital depends upon our own willingness not to seek to buy consumer goods with all of our income but to lend, directly or indirectly, a proportion of that income to businessmen who wish to buy machines.

Meanwhile population is growing throughout the world and, if the growth of our stock of machines does not keep pace with population growth, capital per head declines. This could lead to a decline in output per head, and it has been suggested that in some countries this might very well happen or be happening at the present time. Alternatively, if the stock of machines grows faster than population, output per head may rise on this account.

The second reason why output per head may grow is because we are continually finding new and more efficient ways to use the resources that we have. There is a more or less continuous technological advance. Even if capital per head were falling it is possible that output per head may rise. If on the other hand capital per head is rising, technological advance will lead to an even faster rise in output per head.

It is sometimes suggested that the rate of growth of capital stock and the rate of technical change are very much dependent upon one another, and this may be true. It may be that new inventions are more easily exploited when many new machines are being added to the capital stock, but it is probably true also, for at least two reasons, that technological change can take place with no change at all in the capital stock.

First of all, the same machines may be better utilised as a result of some new organisational device. But more important, a fixed capital stock does not mean that precisely the same machines are kept for ever. Every piece of productive equipment has a limited life. It does not last for ever. But every owner of every piece of equipment, or the owner's agent, takes care to charge in the hire price collected from the user (which may be himself) enough to replace each part with a new one at the end of its life. A constant stock of machines implies a continuous replacement of each item as it wears out. And each machine can be replaced with a more advanced version technologically as it wears out, thus permitting technical advance. Provided the stock of machines is not being run down as fast as they wear out, some technological change, even of the new-invention type, is possible.

Evidently the rate of population growth, the rate of capital accumulation and the rate of technological change are all intimately connected in a way which is scarcely as yet understood. But two things at least are clear. However much the one may be dependent upon the other, there is no reason to suppose that change will be such as to lead, even in the long run, to a constant output per head; nor is there any reason to suppose that changes in output per head will be the same in all countries. It is upon these two facts that many of our international trade difficulties rest.

Obviously, within the framework of the simplest model, it is impossible even to consider some of the most important consequences of growth. If, for example, in any country the ratio of labour to capital stock changes, then the relative efficiency of that country in the production of importables or exportables may change. If importables require much labour and little capital and exportables require much capital and little labour, the relative costs of producing importables and exportables may change in favour of importables in those countries where the labour force is growing faster than the capital stock, with obvious consequences for trade. But in our model so far we have not distinguished between different kinds of input. We have supposed only that all resources are put into one class of product, namely those exported. Nevertheless some effects of growth can be traced, as we shall now show.

10.2 GROWTH AND THE TERMS OF TRADE

Consider an initial position of trading equilibrium at a time we shall call t, represented by the 'box' $O_t BCD_t$ (Fig. 10.1) and the offer curves BMN and BMK. Suppose now that between time t and time $(t+1)$ there is growth in country 1 but no growth in country 2. We wish to examine the consequences for the real terms of trade and for community welfare at home and abroad.

First, it is necessary to say precisely what we mean by growth in this case. The length $O_t B$ in Fig. 10.1 measures the *total* output of exportables in country 1 at time t. $O_t B$ will grow if either population grows or capital grows or if technical advance takes place or any combination of these events occurs.

The model so far cannot identify different causes of the increase in output, nor can it distinguish between the differing consequences of such causes. For example, if capital per head were falling despite the growth of total output, the proportion of national income accruing to wage-earners and profit-earners may change, and this, as we have previously seen, might affect the shapes of offer curves corresponding to any given total expenditure. We escape these difficulties as usual by

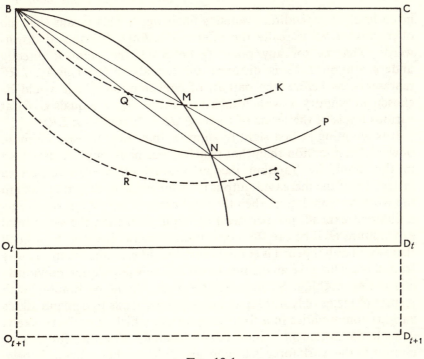

FIG. 10.1

assuming that any income redistribution is random with respect to individual tastes. In this case all that is implied by growth is an increase in total production with no change in the basic consumption demands of the community as a whole for any *given* level of total expenditure.

We represent the increase in output of exportables at time $(t+1)$ over time t by an increase in the 'height' of the box from $O_t B$ to $O_{t+1} B$. There is no change in the 'width' BC since there is no growth in country 2. It is convenient to build the added height $O_t O_{t+1}$ on to the bottom of the box rather than the top to avoid the necessity of shifting the position of the foreign offer curve BMN. Since nothing has happened in country 2, this remains in its original position.

For country 1 the point of origin O_t from which all measurements are taken falls to O_{t+1} and accordingly the old offer curve BMK corresponding to a total expenditure of $O_t B$ falls to the position LRS, where BL equals $O_t O_{t+1}$. We remind ourselves now of the assumption that any redistribution of income is random with respect to tastes so that the shape of the offer curve corresponding to any given level of expenditure remains unchanged. This means that the offer curve *LRS* is really the offer curve *BMK* transposed downwards. That is, for any point *Q* on *BMK* the point *R* directly underneath on *LRS* is distance *BL* (equals $O_t O_{t+1}$) away. *LRS* represents, as before, the pattern of consumption which would be chosen in country 1 with total expenditure $O_{t+1}L$ (equals $O_t B$) at various levels of the terms of trade. *BMK* is 'parallel' to *LRS*.

It is tempting at first sight to suppose that this represents a more powerful assumption than that which is normally implied elsewhere in this book by 'random income redistribution with respect to tastes', for if the increased output is to some extent due to growth in the working population, then the total expenditure $O_{t+1}L$ represents a different expenditure per head of population than the same total expenditure $O_t B$ before the population increase. It could be argued that what has happened is something rather like a redistribution away from those who have an income towards a new population previously consuming nothing. Such a redistribution would be random with respect to tastes only if the average consumer tends to demand all his various commodities in a fixed proportion, which is not very likely.

Such an argument might be misleading, however, for a new entrant to the work force is usually an adult who has previously been maintained out of the income of his parents. If family income were reduced, after the entry of a new member into employment, to the pre-existing level, then it is not unlikely that the family as a whole would demand very much the same pattern of consumption as before. The change may imply a redistribution of earning power away from the parent to other working members of the family, but this will be offset by the reduced demand on the parent to provide for his family's needs. The assumption that *BMK* (Fig. 10.1) is 'parallel' to *LRS* is therefore not at all unreasonable.†

We now show that the parallel relation between *BMK* and *LRS* provides us with information which helps to fix the relative position of the offer curve *BNP* which is associated with the after-growth total expenditure $O_{t+1}B$ of country 1. If *BNP* lies below *BMK*, then the real terms of trade, *BM*, must move against country 1 as a result of growth. If *BNP* could lie above *BMK*, then the intersection *N* of *BNP* and *BMN* would lie above *M* and the real terms of trade could show an improvement from country 1's point of view following growth. We shall show that the former must be the case in general.

† The reader who doubts this argument is free to do so, for it leads only to a conclusion which cannot be sustained in general (see sections 10.4 and 18.6).

Suppose that *BNP* could lie above *BMK*. Then it must cut the terms of trade line *BQN* at a point to the left of *Q* instead of to the right. Hence at real terms of trade *BN* country 1 would seek to import less than it would if its pattern of consumption were defined by *R*, which is directly below *Q*. But by the relationship between *BQK* and *LRS* earlier established, *R* is precisely the pattern of demand which would emerge if total expenditure were $O_{t+1}L$ and the real terms of trade were *LR* (parallel to *BQ*). In fact the move from *R* to *N* is precisely the change in demand which would result from increased expenditure *LB* with prices unchanged. In the usual case *N* will lie to the north-east of *R*.

To suppose that *BNP* could lie above *BMK* is to suppose that *N* lies to the left of *Q*, that is, to suppose that an *increase* in expenditure (prices constant) leads to a *lower* consumption of importables, i.e. a negative marginal propensity to consume. This is unlikely. If *N* must lie north-east of *R*, *BNP* must lie below and not above *BMK*. It follows that in the ordinary case growth will induce the real terms of trade to move *against* country 1.

One interesting conclusion of this analysis is that any gain in welfare due to growth will be passed on in some degree to the rest of the world, which benefits from an improvement in the real terms of trade. The question at once arises, can the welfare lost abroad be greater than the value of the growth, leaving a net loss of welfare to the home country? In order to show that this might very well happen, it is necessary as usual to work the algebra.

10.3 SOME ALGEBRA OF GROWTH

Again as usual it is a simple matter to treat algebraically a more general problem than that of the previous section. We shall therefore allow both countries to grow at different rates in the time period and attempt to determine the net effect upon welfare and the real terms of trade.

We begin with the balance of payments equation

$$B = p_1 X_1' - q_2 X_2 \tag{10.3.1}$$

As a consequence of growth it is necessary to change prices and quantities if the balance of payments is to be kept balanced, i.e. $B = 0$. Taking changes in (10.3.1), therefore,

$$dB = p_1 dX_1' - q_2 dX_2 + X_1' dp_1 - X_2 dq_2 \tag{10.3.2}$$

Now if B is zero both before and after growth then the change dB must be zero. We choose also to suppose that p_1 is kept constant in the usual way so that changes in the real terms of trade are measured by dp_2. Thus (10.3.2) becomes

$$0 = p_1 dX_1' - q_2 dX_2 - X_2 dq_2 \qquad (10.3.3)$$

Total expenditure in country 1 is

$$Y = p_1 O_1.$$

The change in Y, dY, therefore is

$$dY = dp_1 O_1 + p_1 dO_1. \qquad (10.3.4)$$

The change dO_1 in O_1 is the change in output due to growth. Also, p_1 does not change, so that

$$dY = p_1 dO_1 \qquad (10.3.5)$$

Similarly in country 2

$$dY' = O_2' dq_2 + q_2 dO_2' \qquad (10.3.6)$$

although in this case dq_2 is not zero.

Now X_1' depends upon prices and expenditure abroad, so that

$$dX_1' = \frac{\partial X_1'}{\partial q_1} dq_1 + \frac{\partial X_1'}{\partial q_2} dq_2 + \frac{\partial X_1'}{\partial Y} dY'.$$

Furthermore, since p_1 does not change and there is no tariff or change in the exchange rate, dq_1 is zero and

$$dX_1' = \frac{\partial X_1'}{\partial q_2} dq_2 + (O_2' dq_2 + q_2 dO_2') \frac{\partial X_1'}{\partial Y} \qquad (10.3.7)$$

when we make use of (10.3.6).

Similarly

$$dX_2 = \frac{\partial X_2}{\partial p_2} dp_2 + \frac{\partial X_2}{\partial Y} (p_1 dO_1) \qquad (10.3.8)$$

We now put (10.3.7) and (10.3.8) in (10.3.3) to give

$$p_1 \frac{\partial X_1'}{\partial q_2} dq_2 + p_1 \frac{\partial X_1'}{\partial Y} (O_2' dq_2 + q_2 dO_2') - q_2 \frac{\partial X_2}{\partial p_2} dp_2$$

$$- q_2 \frac{\partial X_2}{\partial Y} (p_1 dO_1) - X_2 dq_2 = 0 \qquad (10.3.9)$$

Or, using $dp_2 = dq_2$, again because there is no tariff and the exchange rate does not change, and collecting terms in (10.3.9), we have

$$\left[p_1 \frac{\partial X_1'}{\partial q_2} + p_1 \frac{\partial X_1'}{\partial Y} O_2' - q_2 \frac{\partial X_2}{\partial p_2} - X_2 \right] dq_2$$

$$= q_2 \frac{\partial X_2}{\partial Y} p_1 dO_1 - p_1 \frac{\partial X_1'}{\partial Y} q_2 dO_2' \qquad (10.3.10)$$

We now use the principle previously explained above (section 7.5), which says that

$$\frac{\partial X_1'}{\partial q_2} q_2 + \frac{\partial X_1'}{\partial Y} Y' = - \frac{\partial X_1'}{\partial q_1} q_1$$

which when multiplied by p_1/q_2 using $Y' = q_2 O_2'$ yields

$$p_1 \frac{\partial X_1'}{\partial q_2} + p_1 \frac{\partial X_1'}{\partial Y} O_2' = - \frac{p_1 q_1}{q_2} \frac{\partial X_1'}{\partial q_1}$$

Putting this last result in (10.3.10) we obtain

$$\left[- \frac{p_1 q_1}{q_2} \frac{\partial X_1'}{\partial q_1} - q_2 \frac{\partial X_2}{\partial p_2} - X_2 \right] dq_2 = q_2 \frac{\partial X_2}{\partial Y} p_1 dO_1 - p_1 \frac{\partial X_1'}{\partial Y} q_2 dO_2'$$

$$(10.3.11)$$

and taking X_2 outside of the square bracket gives

$$X_2 \left[- \frac{p_1}{q_2 X_2} q_1 \frac{\partial X_1'}{\partial q_1} - \frac{q_2 \partial X_2}{X_2 \partial p_2} - 1 \right] dq_2 = q_2 \frac{\partial X_2}{\partial Y} p_1 dO_1 - p_1 \frac{\partial X_1'}{\partial Y} q_2 dO_2'$$

$$(10.3.12)$$

But if the balance of payments is balanced (i.e. $B = 0$), we have from (10.3.1)

$$q_2 X_2 = p_1 X_1'$$

and we recall that $p_1 = q_1$ and $p_2 = q_2$. Thus (10.3.12) becomes

$$X_2 \left[- \frac{q_1}{X_1'} \frac{\partial X_1'}{\partial q_1} - \frac{q_2 \partial X_2}{X_2 \partial p_2} - 1 \right] dq_2 = \left(q_2 \frac{\partial X_2}{\partial Y} \right) p_1 dO_1 - \left(p_1 \frac{\partial X_1'}{\partial Y} \right) q_2 dO_2'$$

which, using the elasticity notation E, and the marginal propensity to consume notation C, is written

$$- X_2 [E_{11}' + E_{22} + 1] dq_2 = C_2 (p_1 dO_1) - C_1' (q_2 dO_2')$$

or $$dq_2 = - \frac{C_2 (p_1 dO_1) - C_1' (q_2 dO_2')}{X_2 (E_{11}' + E_{22} + 1)} \qquad (10.3.13)$$

which is the required expression for the change in the real terms of trade due to growth in the value of output of country 1, $p_1 dO_1$, together with growth in country 2 valued at $q_2 dO_2'$.

We are now in a position to confirm at once the result obtained diagrammatically in the previous section. It was there supposed that country 2 did not grow so that dO_2' could be taken as zero.

In this case formula (10.3.13) reduces to

$$dq_2 = - \frac{C_2(p_1 dO_1)}{X_2(E_{11}' + E_{22} + 1)} \qquad (10.3.14)$$

Now we know that in the ordinary 'stable' case $(E_{11}' + E_{22} + 1)$ is negative, and that C_2 and X_2 are positive. If dO_1 is positive, therefore, as when growth occurs, dq_2 will be positive. Import prices will rise, and since the price of exportables is fixed, the real terms of trade must move against the growing country.

Consider now the change in welfare dw in the home country. Following the usual principles we measure the change in welfare by valuing the change in consumption in the home country at initial prices. Hence

$$dw = p_1 dX_1 + p_2 dX_2 \qquad (10.3.15)$$

But

$$p_1 X_1 + p_2 X_2 = Y \qquad (10.3.16)$$

since the value of purchases of importables and exportables must equal total expenditure. Taking changes in (10.3.16), remembering to add the increased value of output due to growth, we have

$$p_1 dX_1 + p_2 dX_2 + X_1 dp_1 + X_2 dp_2 = p_1 dO_1$$

which from (10.3.15), remembering dp_1 is zero, gives

$$dw = p_1 dO_1 - X_2 dp_2 \qquad (10.3.17)$$

But dp_2 equals dq_2, so that by using (10.3.14)

$$dw = p_1 dO_1 + \frac{X_2 C_2(p_1 dO_1)}{X_2(E_{11}' + E_{22} + 1)}$$

$$= \left[1 + \frac{C_2}{(E_{11}' + E_{22} + 1)} \right] p_1 dO_1 \qquad (10.3.18)$$

From this result it is easy to see that dw might very well be negative if elasticities of demand are small. The value of $(E_{11}' + E_{22} + 1)$ could be negative but numerically less than C_2 so that the second term inside the bracket in (10.3.18) is less than -1.

This curious possibility suggests that it might be better for a country not to grow at all if demand elasticities are low. All of the benefit, and more, of its technical improvements and/or capital accumulations are transferred abroad via the adverse movement of the real terms of trade. It should be noted, however, that this conclusion is based upon the assumption of very low elasticities of demand. C_2 is of course bound to be small – less than unity, and probably less than, say, one-third. If elasticities are together numerically greater than 2, less than one-third of the value of growth is lost. On the other hand one-third is not a negligible proportion. Clearly the terms of trade effect could be of great practical importance.

10.4 A WARNING

The reader should take note that, in this chapter, we have done little more than introduce ideas which demand careful attention. We are still a long way from satisfactory answers.

In particular we have excluded from consideration by the over-simplified model any possibility that growth might affect the competitive position of the various commodities. If, for example, the accumulation of capital meant that the home producer of exportables is thereby able to compete in the manufacture of importables, there is no reason at all why the terms of trade should necessarily move against the growing country. The whole problem appears quite different as soon as we admit the production of many commodities calling for varied inputs of resources. In Chapter 18 we return to this question and demonstrate the great variety of possibilities.

The essential point we wish to make at this stage is that here again we have an example of an apparently obvious economic truth which, as it turns out, is neither obvious nor true.

EXERCISES

1. Construct a diagram on the lines of Fig. 10.1 illustrating growth in the case where $E_{22} + E'_{11} + 1 > 0$. Show that terms of trade must, in this case, move in favour of country 1. Hence confirm diagrammatically the algebraic result (10.3.14).

2. Show that the algebra of section 10.3 is developed essentially by solving a system of equations:

(i) $p_1 X_1' - p_2 X_2 = 0$ Trade balanced

$\left.\begin{array}{l} \text{(ii)} \;\; Y' = p_2 O_2' \\[6pt] \text{(iii)} \;\; Y = p_1 O_1 \end{array}\right\}$ Aggregate spending

$\left.\begin{array}{l} \text{(iv)} \;\; X_2 = X_2(p_1, p_2, Y) \\[6pt] \text{(v)} \;\; X_1' = X_1'(p_1, p_2, Y') \end{array}\right\}$ Demand equations

(vi) $p_1 = $ constant

where O_2' and O_1 are exogenous (i.e. independently fixed). Solve this sytem in your own way for dX_2 when changes dO_2' and dO_1 due to growth are given. Using a new demand equation

$$X_1 = X_1(p_1, p_2, Y) \text{ or } dX_1 = \frac{\partial X_1}{\partial p_1} dp_1 + \frac{\partial X_1}{\partial p_2} dp_2 + \frac{\partial X_1}{\partial Y} dY$$

for country 1, find dX_1, and hence show that

$$dw = p_1 dX_1 + p_2 dX_2$$

is given by

$$dw = \frac{(1 + \sigma_{11}' + \sigma_{22}) p_1 dO_1 - C_1'(p_1 dO_1 + p_2 dO_2')}{1 + E_{11}' + E_{22}}$$

where σ_{ii} is the substitution part of E_{ii}. Hence prove that growth abroad reduces the likelihood of a fall in welfare due to growth at home.

3. Extend the problem of exercise 2 as follows. Let country 1 produce S_1 units of commodity 1 and S_3 units of a non-traded commodity. Let country 2 produce S_2' units of commodity 2 and S_3' units of a non-traded commodity. Production is fixed whatever the pattern of prices. Aggregate spending equations thus become

$$Y' = p_2 S_2' + p_3' S_3'$$

and $$Y = p_1 S_1 + p_3 S_3$$

Prices p_3 and p_3' will appear in demand equations (iv) and (v), and two further equations

$$S_3 = X_3(p_1, p_2, p_3, Y)$$

$$S_3' = X_3'(p_1, p_2, p_3', Y')$$

must be added to express the fact that supply and demand for the third commodity must be equated.

Let supplies of all commodities grow by amounts dS_1, dS_3, dS_2' and dS_3'. Show that the change in the terms of trade is given by

$$dp_2 = \frac{\phi_{13}'(p_2' dS_2' + p_3' dS_3') - \phi_{23}(p_1 dS_1 + p_3 dS_3) - \dfrac{\sigma_{32}}{\sigma_{33}} p_3 dS_3 - \dfrac{\sigma_{31}'}{\sigma_{33}'} p_3' dS_3'}{X_2(1 + \psi_{13}' + \psi_{23} - \phi_{13}' - \phi_{23})}$$

where σ_{ij} is the substitution part of E_{ij}.

Compare this result with (10.3.13) and comment. ϕ_{ij} and ψ_{ij} have the meaning of exercise 5 to Chapter 4.

4. Show that, in the problem of exercise 3, the change in welfare in country 1 is given by

$$dw = \frac{\begin{aligned}(1 + \psi_{13}' + \psi_{23})(p_1 dS_1 + p_3 dS_3) - \phi_{13}'(p_1 dS_1 + p_3 dS_3 \\ + p_2 dS_2' + p_3 dS_3') - \frac{\sigma_{32}}{\sigma_{33}} p_3 dS_3 - \frac{\sigma_{31}'}{\sigma_{33}'} p_3' dS_3'\end{aligned}}{(1 + \psi_{13}' + \psi_{23} - \phi_{13}' - \phi_{23})}$$

Compare this result with that of exercise 2.

5. Solve the system of exercise 3 for the change dp_3 in the home price of non-traded commodities. Show that if dS_3 is zero, dp_3 will ordinarily be negative in sign.

To be attempted only after reading Books I and II

6. Introduce home production of importables and foreign production of exportables into the problem of exercise 3 and allow the quantities produced to depend upon prices. Show that, as usual, this generalisation modifies the results of exercises 3 and 4 only by bringing supply elasticities into ϕ_{ij} and ψ_{ij}, at the same time multiplying these parameters by a weight equal to the ratio of total consumption to imports. In addition σ_{ij}, wherever it occurs, will appear as $\sigma_{ij} - S_{ij}$ where S_{ij} is the cross-elasticity of supply.

11 Many Countries, Transport Costs and the Production Sector

WE have now all but exhausted the potentialities of the most simple system which has served as a framework for the greater part of the work so far. This is a suitable point, therefore, for a further brief review of the philosophy of model-building in general. In particular, two questions might very well now be in the mind of the reader.

First, in view of repeated warnings of the dangers of over-aggregation, and after comparison of some of the results in the text with those of the less aggregative exercises, it is tempting to ask, of what use is the most simple model? If we have, in any case, to study more complicated structures before our conclusions can be applied to practical problems, why not begin at once with the most realistic analogue that human intelligence can devise? Secondly, the student who has persevered so far may be justified in asking how he might distinguish in a general way between results derived from the most naïve model which have some practical significance and those which do not.

Neither of these questions admits of an easy answer. Obviously if we could describe the ultimate model nothing more would be needed. All our questions *could* be put to it just as all our questions would *have* to be put to it. But in practice no agreed ultimate model has ever been described, and even if it had, it would certainly be far too complex for anyone but the most expert economist to understand fully. Furthermore, the best way to an understanding of such a model would probably be through sequential study of successively more difficult simplifications.

Herein lies the dilemma. Not everyone with a legitimate interest in the outcome of economic policy is endowed with either the time or the wish to bring himself to the frontiers of knowledge wherever they may be. A powerful temptation exists to assume, without proof or on the basis of some kind of 'hunch', that whatever simple model it seems convenient to examine at the moment both correctly simulates tendencies which operate in the real world and at the same time parallels within itself *all* the most interesting and important features of the actual economy. It is all too easy to be convinced by some analytical construct, not only that certain problems are now understood, but even that no more problems exist. On the other hand, as matters at present stand, the greater part of the knowledge which we have – perhaps all – comes from the study of models simplified in some degree.

This brings us to question two. Given that we do make use of simplified models, how can we avoid being misled, and, more especially, how can the student avoid being misled when almost certainly his view of the economy will be a drastically simplified one?

One answer to question two is, of course, that economists do not study models to the exclusion of all else. They also look at the facts of the real world. If, for example, a model suggests that a general tariff will improve the real terms of trade, the next step is to test, as far as possible, whether this is true. In so far as it turns out to be true we have some confirmation that the model does simulate the real world even though it is aggregative; or, more accurately, we have no evidence to the contrary. Experienced economists therefore already know something of the strength and weaknesses of their models even before they have worked more complicated versions. Nor is this all.

In addition to the direct empirical test it is sometimes possible, without the complete description of the more complex case, to form some impression as to where a naïve model might be misleading simply by reviewing the assumptions upon which it is based. This is a difficult and dangerous exercise although it is certainly better that it should be undertaken than not. The purpose of the present chapter is to introduce the reader to this method, which is consciously or unconsciously used in all branches of economics. It is of the utmost importance that the student should at all times be aware of any differences between the facts of the real world and the assumptions of his model and that he should never accept any conclusion without first asking at least whether it is reasonable in the light of what can be observed.

11.2 MANY COUNTRIES

Consider our own model as specified up to this point. All our work so far has been based upon an elementary notion of one country trading with the rest of the world. How much confidence can we have in such a simple view, and in what respects are our conclusions likely to be modified when we recognise that the real world consists of many countries trading one with another?

To explore this question, suppose for the moment that we have three countries instead of two. The home country produces export-ables only and countries 2 and 3 produce importables only. As before, we can construct a box *OABC* (Fig. 11.1) representing total world production of importables and exportables together. *OA* units of exportables are produced by the home country. Country 2 manu-factures *BE* of importables and country 3 *EA* of importables making a world total of *BA*.

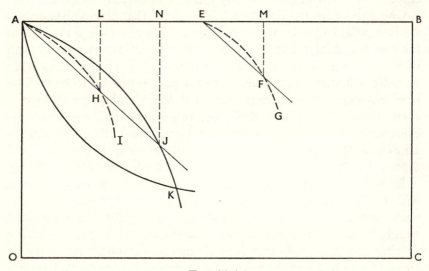

Fig. 11.1

Country 1's offer curve will be *AK* in the usual way. Country 2 has a total expenditure of *BE* (in units of importables) so that its offer curve, referred to the point *B* from which all measurements are taken, will be something like *EFG*. That is to say, if the real terms of trade between country 2 and country 1 were given by the slope of the line *EF*, country 2 would wish to trade *EM* importables for *MF* export-ables. Its pattern of consumption would then be *MB* of commodity 2 and *MF* of commodity 1, as defined by the point *F* referred to *B* as origin. The locus of the point *F* as the real terms of trade change constitutes the offer curve *EFG*.

For country 3 we take *E* as the point of origin. Total consumption is *EA* so that *AHI* could be an offer curve. With real terms of trade between country 3 and country 1 given by the slope of *AH*, consumption in country 3 would be *EL* of commodity 2 and *LH* of commodity 1.

We now recognise that the real terms of trade, assuming zero transport costs, can never be any different between country 1 and country 2 than they are between country 1 and country 3, for if country 2 could buy exportables from country 1 at a cheaper rate in terms of importables than country 3, then businessmen in country 2 could make a profit by buying from country 1 and reselling to country 3. This will compete down the price of exportables in country 3 until it is the same as in country 2.

Using the fact that the real terms of trade must be the same in equilibrium, i.e. that all countries face a common world price ratio, it is a simple matter to construct a joint offer curve for countries 2 and 3 together.

Suppose that the slope of *AJ* represents the common world ratio of prices and let *EF* have the same slope. Mark off *HJ* from *H* on *AJ* equal to *EF*. *J* is now a point on a joint offer curve for countries 1 and 2 together, representing the rest of the world's demand for exportables given the real terms of trade *AJ*. *NJ* is obviously equal to *LH* plus *MF* and, since *LN* equals *EM*, *BN* equals *BM* plus *EL*. In a similar way all other points on the joint offer curve can be built up given the separate curves *AHI* and *EFG*.

It is also clear from inspection of the diagram that if *AHI* and *EFG* take the ordinary expected shape, so will *AJK*. Furthermore, it is not difficult to see that world equilibrium will be attained when the real terms of trade stand at *AK*, *K* being the point of intersection of country 1's offer curve with the joint offer curve. By construction of the joint offer curve, demands in countries 2 and 3 together with that of country 1 will just exhaust world production at these terms of trade.

In short we do not seem to have added very much by this particular step towards reality. The offer curve *AJK* behaves in a way very similar to that for a single country. We could proceed with most of our earlier analysis just as if there were two countries only, leaving out everything in Fig. 11.1 except the two unbroken offer curves. The effect of a tariff in country 1 could be demonstrated for example exactly as in Fig. 7.1. Similarly the possibility of instability could be discussed as in Chapter 3. Many economists would feel in fact that the present argument gives grounds for supposing that we should learn very little that is new by multiplying the number of countries.

It might even be held that in this case there is a positive *disadvantage* in the more realistic model since the increased difficulty in understanding it is not justified by any real addition to knowledge.

Up to a point this is an acceptable view, but only up to a point. There exist questions which cannot even be put until a many-country model is developed. What happens for example if country 1 imposes a tariff and country 2 retaliates but country 3 does not? Again, is it really necessary for world equilibrium that country 1's balance of payments should be zero both with country 2 *and* with country 3? Might it not be sufficient if any positive balance of country 1 with country 2 is offset by a negative balance with country 3 provided only that country 2's deficit with country 1 is offset by a surplus with country 3. This implies of course that country 3's surplus with country 1 is offset by a deficit with country 2.

We see at once from Fig. 11.1 that such a situation is perfectly possible and is indeed one which commonly arises in practice. World trade would be in equilibrium if either

(i) 1 exported *MF* to 2 and *LH* to 3 in exchange for *EM* from 2 and *AL* from 3; or

(ii) 1 exported *LH* to 3 and *MF* to 2, importing *AN* from country 3 and nothing from country 2. Country 2 could now pay for its imports, *MF*, by exporting *EM* (equals *LN*) of importables to country 3.

In case (i) all countries' payments are in balance with one another. In case (ii) surpluses and deficits between countries are offsetting.

The fact that the real world is more like case (ii) than case (i) leads to the problem of international liquidity (section 4.6). Just as buying and selling within a country gives rise to a demand for a stock of money to facilitate payment of debt, so in the world economy the process of settling debts between countries generates a demand for a stock of an international currency. And in the same way that shortage of money can inhibit economic activity within a single country (see Chapter 2), so can shortage of international currency (i.e. lack of international liquidity) inhibit world trade. Obviously the pattern of international settlements, that is, whether case (i) or case (ii) applies above, has a great deal to do with the demand for international currency, a matter which claimed our attention in section 4.6. Clearly also it would be impossible to inquire fully into factors affecting the demand for international currency outside the framework of a many-country model. The student who fully understands the work of Book I should not be misled into supposing that, on that account, he now has a complete grasp of all problems of international trade.

The lesson we learn is that on some questions the naïve model may tell us a good part of what we need to know, and that relatively simple developments can suggest whether or not more can be got from further complication. On other questions more complicated models are essential even to demonstrate that a problem exists. The reader is warned also against subscribing to the view mentioned above that simplicity is desirable for its own sake. We live in a complicated world and knowledge is not to be got without effort. Naïve models are very much a second-best, and whilst it may sometimes be true that the returns from greater complexity seem scarcely worth the effort, it is always true that the most realistic model tells us most. It is also true that if *quantitative* results are required then there is no escape from the complications.

As another example, suppose that we wished to know the precise conditions for stability in the 3-country case corresponding to the result (3.3.9). There we learned that in certain circumstances economic pressures will tend to move two trading countries *away* from their equilibrium position if

$$E'_{11} + E_{22} + 1 > 0 \tag{11.2.1}$$

where the Es mean elasticity of demand for commodities 1 and 2, abroad and at home respectively. This result is of no use to us whatever in the 3-country case even though we may have drawn Fig. 11.1 and satisfied ourselves that instability occurs when the unbroken curves in the figure bend back upon themselves as in Fig. 3.2. We are no further forward until we can interpret the bending-back of the offer curve AJK in terms of the elasticity of demand for exportables in countries 2 and 3. When we find ourselves in a world of three countries rather than two, the result (11.2.1) above for two countries is of no use even though we may know the numerical values of elasticities of demand in each of the three countries. We cannot escape working the three-country case.

In fact the total foreign demand X_{w1} for exportables is the sum

$$X_{w1} = X'_1 + X''_1$$

where the single prime refers to country 2 and the double prime to country 3. If p_1 only changes, with total expenditure in both countries and all other prices constant, then we can write

$$\frac{\partial X_{w1}}{\partial p_1} = \frac{\partial X_1'}{\partial p_1} + \frac{\partial X_1''}{\partial p_1}$$

from which we deduce that

$$\frac{p_1}{X_{w1}}\frac{\partial X_{w1}}{\partial p_1} = \frac{X_1'}{X_{w1}}\frac{p_1}{X_1'}\frac{\partial X_1'}{\partial p_1} + \frac{X_1''}{X_{w1}}\frac{p_1}{X_1''}\frac{\partial X_1''}{\partial p_1}$$

or
$$E_{w1} = \frac{X_1'}{X_1' + X_1''}E_{11}' + \frac{X_1''}{X_1' + X_1''}E_{11}''$$

Now, having drawn Fig. 11.1, we might guess with some confidence that E_{w1} will take the place of E_{11}'' in the result (11.2.1) when the third country is introduced. Thus the three-country condition for stability is likely to be

$$\frac{X_1'}{X_1' + X_1''}E_{11}' + \frac{X_1''}{X_1' + X_1''}E_1'' + E_{22} + 1 < 0 \qquad (11.2.2)$$

This result may easily be confirmed by working the algebra from first principles.

From some points of view (11.2.2) is not a surprising condition to find since the E_{11}'' of (11.2.1) is simply replaced in (11.2.2) by a weighted average of the elasticities of individual foreign countries. But the economist who knows the familiar result (11.2.1) without knowing (11.2.2) might very well be tempted to wonder if an elasticity of demand numerically equal to one in any of the three countries is not sufficient to ensure stability. This is certainly true in the two-country case. On the other hand it is not true where there are three countries, for the weight multiplying the high elasticity could be small enough to nullify its effect.

In passing it is worth noting that, in international trade theory, the elasticity notation is particularly valuable since, in assessing probable magnitudes of elasticities, there is in general no need to take into account the size of the country. The unmodified response in consumption $\partial X/\partial p$ is, however, likely to be dependent upon the size of the population, for the greater the number of consumers the greater their total response to a price change. The effect of turning a response $\partial X/\partial p$ into an elasticity

$$\frac{p}{X}\frac{\partial X}{\partial p}$$

is to eliminate the size effect by dividing by X, which will equally be large for a large country. In the result (11.2.2) the effect of country size is thrown out of the response term into the weights where it can be seen more clearly. This is a feature (common to all of the algebraic formulae of Book I) which should be borne in mind when interpreting results.

We conclude this section by referring the reader to the exercises at the end of this chapter which fully illustrate the extension of the algebra to many countries.

11.3 TRANSPORT COSTS

So far we have at all times assumed that, quite impossibly, commodities can be shipped from one country to another at no cost and that the commodity 'shipping' does not exist. We now continue our review of assumptions with an attempt to test the effect of the inclusion of transport costs into the system.

As we now have some understanding of the implications of the two-country restriction we may, for present purposes, revert to this. Indeed, this is the essence of the method of 'assumption review'. Complications can be treated in turn rather than simultaneously in one single 'ideal' model.

Of course there is always the risk that transport costs create difficulties in a many-country world which do not show themselves in a two-country system. But this is a risk which we have to take given that an 'ideal' model cannot for the moment be developed. It is, moreover, a risk which is the smaller the more we condition ourselves not to forget that a model is a model and nothing else, that is, the more we engage in 'assumption reviews'.

Up to this point it has been supposed that, where there is no tariff, prices are the same at home and abroad on conversion by the exchange rate. We have in fact chosen the unit of measure in each country so that $p_1 = q_1$, i.e. the exchange rate, e, $= 1$ and hence $p_2 = q_2$. In practice, however, even where there is no tariff and the exchange rate is unity, prices will not be competed to complete equality, for a commodity bought in country 1 at price p_1 must attract additional transport costs before it can be resold in country 2. The price q_1 in country 2, therefore, must be higher than p_1/e if importers are to avoid a trading loss. The really important point about these 'transport costs' is that they may inhibit international specialisation in a manner which will become clear by the time we reach section 11.5.

We begin by representing, in Fig. 11.2, the usual two-country box with offer curves *AHI* and *AGI* intersecting at *I*. The offer curves are

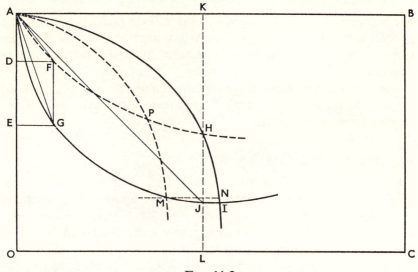

Fig. 11.2

those which would be operative *if there were no transport costs. OA* is the total amount of commodity 1 which could be produced in country 1 if total resources were put to that use. Similarly, *AB* is the foreign country's maximum possible output of importables with the resources available. But the service 'transport' also requires labour and capital. Some inputs (factors of production) must be switched from one or other of the final commodities to the provision of ships and shipping services. A third commodity exists, the demand for which is dependent upon the level of trade.

World shipping services will of course be bought in that country where their cost is least. Part of our problem therefore is to determine the area of least cost. On the other hand it is convenient for the moment to assume that country 1 has the advantage and to leave until later the discussion of why this might be so.

Suppose that, in country 1, the slope of the line *AG* measures the relative prices in the market of commodities 1 and 2. By definition of the curve *AGI* consumers would demand *OE* of exportables and *EG* of importables, leaving *AE* (or resources capable of producing *AE*) free for trading purposes. But it is not now possible to offer the whole of *AE* in exchange for *EG* since some resources must be used for shipping. Not all of *AE* can be produced. For convenience of exposition let us choose our units of resources, say labour, so that one unit of input into commodity 1 produces one unit of output. Now let a units of resources be that required to produce enough shipping to transport one unit of exportables and let b units of resources be enough to ship one unit of importables. This is simply another way of saying that, if p_1 is the cost of exportables, then ap_1 is the cost of shipping one unit of exportables and bp_1 the cost of shipping one unit of importables; or even more conveniently, a per unit is the cost of shipping exportables measured in units of exportables, etc.

If X_1' is exported and X_2 is imported, then $aX_1' + bX_2$ is the total cost of shipping in units of exportables; and if X_2 is EG at relative prices AG, then

$$X_1' + aX_1' + b(EG)$$

is the total cost of exportables plus shipping which must be AE in the diagram. Hence

$$X_1' + aX_1' + b(EG) = AE$$

or
$$X_1' = \frac{1}{1 + a} [AE - b(EG)].$$

From EG and AE (determined by offer curve AGI) and a knowledge of shipping costs a and b in terms of exportables, we deduce the quantity X_1' available for export, shown in the diagram as AD. With home relative prices p_1/p_2 given by AG, country 1 will demand EG of importables and OE of exportables. It will offer AD of exportables in exchange for its imports, leaving resources capable of producing DE free to provide all of the necessary world shipping. It follows that foreign relative prices must be AF instead of AG if AD is to exchange for EG. Exportables are relatively dearer abroad since they bear a transport cost, whilst importables are relatively cheaper since they do not. AG must be steeper than AF. We note also in passing the ambiguity which now enters into the notion of the real terms of trade. For country 1 AE/EG can be said to measure the terms of trade since there is a real sense in which the whole of AE is given up for EG. On the other hand, for country 2, AD only is received for EG so that the slope of AF and not AG is the proper measure of the terms of trade. Moreover, taking the exchange rate as unity by choice of units, the ratio of prices p_1/q_2 (which measures the real terms of trade in the model without transport costs) lies somewhere in between AG and AF according to the values of a and b.

It will now be understood that the curve AGI is no longer truly an offer curve even though it defines the quantities which will be consumed by country 1 for various ratios of home prices like *AG*. The true offer curve is constructed from points like *F* appropriate to each possible home price ratio. At *AG*, only *AD* is offered to the foreign country and not *AE*. The broken line *AFH* is the true offer curve intersecting the foreign offer curve at *H*. Obviously as *G* moves towards *J* total world trade and hence world shipping increases. *HJ* will be greater than *FG*. The shape of *AFH* will be related to *AGI* in the diagram.

For country 2 *AHI* is a true offer curve since no resources are put into shipping. Thus, at terms of trade *AH*, *AK* of importables is actually offered for *KH* of exportables. World equilibrium is attained at *H* where the two 'true' offer curves intersect. The point *J* on the curve *AGI* directly below *H* determines the home relative price ratio *AJ* where country 1 will wish to consume the pattern *J*. Country 2's relative prices are *AH* and the consumption pattern is *H*. Country 1 demands *OL* = *AK* of importables whilst country 2 consumes *KB*, just exhausting world supply. On the other hand country 1 consumes only *JL* of exportables and country 2 *HK*, which will just exhaust world supply provided that resources capable of producing *HJ* of exportables are diverted to shipping. And by the definition of the offer curve *AFH* these are precisely the resources which would be needed to sustain the necessary trade.

The reader should note particularly that the provision of shipping by country 1 creates incomes which are spent, in the same way as the production of exportables (see Chapter 1). It is quite proper therefore to begin the curve *AGJ* from the point *A*. *OA* is total expenditure measured in terms of commodity 1.

11.4 WHO PROVIDES SHIPPING?

One point remains to be cleared up. How do we justify the assumption that country 1 provides all shipping, and what are the consequences of this not being true? Consider first of all the possibility that all of the shipping might be provided by country 2. In such a case, by an argument precisely analogous to that of section 11.3, there would exist a 'true' offer curve for country 2 lying to the left of *AHI* in Fig. 11.2 and intersecting *AGI* at *M*. Since shipping is now provided by country 2, *AGI* is a true offer curve for country 1 and world equilibrium would be attained at *M*. If the point *N* on *AHI* lies due east of *M* in the diagram, then *MN* is the cost of world shipping in terms of commodity 2. Country 1's internal price ratio would be given by the slope of the line joining *AM* (not drawn in Fig. 11.2) and country

2's internal price level would be given by AN (also not drawn).

It should be noted now that it is impossible that the home and foreign internal price ratios AJ and AH appropriate to the equilibrium H (country 1 providing shipping) should *both* be the same as AM and AN appropriate to equilibrium M (country 2 shipping) *unless* one or other of the curves AHI or AMJ is a straight line. For suppose the point M coincided with J so that slope AJ equals AM. Then since N must be due east of $M = J$ and H must be due north of $J = M$, N and H cannot be coincident. The offer curve AHI must therefore be a straight line through the origin if AH is to have the same slope as AN. By a similar argument, if the true offer curve AFH cuts AHI at N (as it might) so that $H = N$, then slope AJ must be different from slope AM unless the curve AMJ is a straight line.

The result just given demonstrates that, in general, who provides the shipping makes a difference to welfare and to the real terms of trade for each country. Two distinct positions of apparent world equilibrium exist and we have to ask which will be arrived at.

Obviously M cannot be an equilibrium unless country 2 has the shipping advantage, and H cannot be an equilibrium unless country 1 has the shipping advantage, for offer curves were constructed on these assumptions.

In country 1 the price of shipping one unit of exportables cannot be different from ap_1. This follows from the assumption made above that one unit of resources produces one unit of exportables of price p_1 and a units of resources produce the shipping for one unit of exportables. The ratio of costs of exportables and shipping must be a. Let a' now be the ratio of costs in the foreign country of producing one unit of importables (price q_2) and of producing the shipping for one unit of commodity 1. Hence the price of shipping commodity 1, bought in the foreign country, must be $a'q_2$. To convert this to home currency we multiply by e, the rate of exchange. (Note especially that the ratios a/b and a'/b' will ordinarily be the same since they depend only upon technical facts and not on prices.)

The exporter in country 1 will ship in country 1 bottoms or country 2 bottoms according to which is the cheaper, that is, according as ap_1 is less than or greater than $ea'q_2$. Or to put this another way, he will look to see whether the ratio

$$\frac{bp_1}{eb'q_2} = \frac{ap_1}{ea'q_2} \gtrless 1 \qquad (11.4.1)$$

where the symbol $\gtrless$ is read 'greater than or less than'.

The interesting thing about the condition (11.4.1) is that the numerical value of the left-hand side depends only upon a ratio p_1/eq_2 which is closely related to the real terms of trade, for a and a' are both constants. In fact, as eq_2 is less than p_2, which contains the shipping cost, and as p_1/e is less than q_1, which again contains the shipping cost, the ratio p_1/eq_2 lies between p_1/p_2 and q_1/q_2, the home and foreign price ratios. p_1/eq_2 must be represented in Fig. 11.2 by a line, the slope of which is intermediate between AH and AJ (assuming the equilibrium H). In equilibrium M where p_1/p_2 is represented by the slope of AM and q_1/q_2 by the slope of AN, the ratio p_1/eq_2 will be *smaller* than in equilibrium H. (It should be remembered that the steeper the line through A representing the price ratio, the cheaper is commodity 1 relative to commodity 2. More of 1 must be given up in exchange for a unit of 2.)

It follows from this that the shipping advantage is dependent upon the terms of trade. If the terms of trade move *against* country 1, the shipping advantage could pass from country 1 to country 2 and vice versa. Thus it could happen that if the foreign price ratio q_1/q_2 lay between slopes AH and AJ with the shipping advantage in favour of country 1, and if any one of the adjusting mechanisms described in Chapter 2 were actually operating to move the economy towards the equilibrium H, the relative rise in the price of p_1 could serve to switch the ratio $ap_1/ea'q_2$ from less than unity to greater than unity. Country 1 then loses the shipping advantage and the world equilibrium position changes from H to M. But in turn world equilibrium M could not be reached, since it implies a foreign price ratio q_1/q_2 low enough to turn the shipping advantage back again to country 1 and restore the *status quo*.

In a situation of this kind a world equilibrium will be found neither at H nor at M, but in an intermediate position where the provision of shipping is shared between both countries. The actual division is determined by the condition that $ap_1/ea'q_2$ must be unity, that is, that the cost of shipping should be the same in both countries. Neither has any advantage. (To understand this fully, the reader should work especially exercise 5 at the end of this chapter.)

In the diagram (Fig. 11.2) this new intermediate world equilibrium can be thought of as a point like P, the intersection of two 'true' offer curves constructed by adding to each of the curves AHI and AGI the appropriate cost in terms of the home product of each country's *share* of shipping. The curves APM and APH in Fig. 11.2 were of course constructed on the assumption that each country provided the *whole* of the shipping, so that offer curves appropriate to a share only will lie to the right of *APM* and below *AFH* respectively. They will not therefore intersect at *P* but at some point like *P* which, to avoid complicated drafting, has not been incorporated into the figure. In fact we now see our original equilibrium *H* as a limiting case (an extreme), where the share of the home country in shipping is one and the foreign share is zero. The true offer curve for the foreign country coincides with *AHI*, and *H* is its intersection with *APH*.

If *P* is taken as illustrative of the intermediate equilibrium situation where both countries provide some shipping, then home and foreign price ratios are given by the slopes of lines joining *A* with a point on *AGI* due south of *P* for the home country and with a point on *AHI* due east of *P* for the foreign country. The reader should construct a diagram to illustrate this and to satisfy himself that it is consistent with full employment of all resources and a position where world supply equals world demand for both commodities.

Of course, if the extreme world equilibrium positions *H* and *M* are sufficiently close to one another, it may well be that the range of values of the ratio p_1/eq_2 between the two is so small that $ap_1/ea'q_2$ is either always greater than or always less than unity. In this case one or other country will always have the shipping advantage and either *H* or *M* will be approached accordingly.

One objective of our review of the effect of transport costs has now been attained. Inspection of Fig. 11.2 will convince the reader that, in general, only a slight modification of the position of offer curves results. If Fig. 11.2 were cleared of what is essentially no more than an explanation of the direction of distortion of offer curves due to transport costs, we should be left as before with a single equilibrium position. Furthermore, as soon as the share in shipping is determined, the resulting world equilibrium can be defined by the intersection of a pair of 'true' offer curves with general shapes no different from those used throughout the work of previous chapters. The effect of tariffs on the balance of payments can be analysed as before. All that is necessary is to include the possibility of a (probably negligible) shift in offer curves due to changing shipping shares following changes in the real terms of trade. With this proviso nothing seems to have changed very much.

Against this, however, a word of warning is necessary. Indeed, use of the word 'warning' is a massive understatement, for transport costs do in fact give rise to the existence of a class of non-traded commodities and hence indirectly to all of the problems already met with in this connection. It is true, as we have shown above, that as long as all commodities continue to be traded no significant change in the model is needed to reflect the conditions of the real world. Unfortunately, for a very large class of items, the additional costs involved in bringing together product and consumer physically into the same location exclude the possibility of trade completely. This is the inhibition of specialisation characterised in section 11.3 as the 'really important' consequence of the existence of transport costs. As promised, we now turn to a more detailed discussion of this point.

11.5 THE THIRD COMMODITY

In Chapter 1, in the text relating to Fig. 1.3, attention was drawn to the possibility that either or both countries in our model may be *capable* of producing both commodities traded even though, under conditions of trade, they actually do not do so. This is of course the realistic assumption, so that in Fig. 11.3 it is reintroduced.

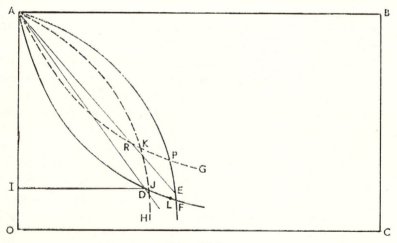

FIG. 11.3

Suppose first of all that *ADF* and *AEF* are curves representing, in the usual way, the patterns of demand for country 1 and country 2 respectively at all possible internal price ratios. But suppose also that country 1 could, by transferring resources from the production of exportables to the production of importables, manufacture any combination of both commodities defined by points along the straight line *AD*. This would imply that the slope of the line *AD* measures, in units of exportables, what would be the cost of producing importables in country 1 if they were in fact made. Technological conditions are such that the resources which would be needed to manufacture *ID* of importables do in fact produce *AI* of exportables.

In these circumstances the portion *AD* of country 1's offer curve is inoperative (cf. Fig. 11.3). If trade led to internal prices less favourable than slope *AD*, country 1 would give up foreign trade completely and go into home manufacture, for the cost of producing at home would be less than the cost of importing and hence home production would be the more profitable activity. Similarly, when country 2 can produce at home at relative costs equal to slope *AE*, then the segment *APE* of country 2's offer curve is also inoperative.

Were it not for transport costs, however, nothing would be changed by the power to produce at home. The real terms of trade would settle at slope *AF* (not drawn in Fig. 11.3) and both countries would specialise. The reader should note moreover that trade would take place even if slope *AE* were greater than slope *AD*, that is, if country 2 could produce exportables relatively more cheaply than country 1, which must of course imply that country 1 can produce importables relatively more cheaply than country 2. All that would then happen is that country 1 would specialise in importables and country 2 in exportables. *OA* would represent country 2's output and *AB* country 1's output. In all other respects the diagram would remain as before. An equilibrium trading position could be found. Only in the extreme and unlikely case where relative prices are the *same* in both countries will there be no advantage in trade and no obvious position of equilibrium.

But when transport costs are introduced the situation is very different, as may be demonstrated by the construction of 'true' offer curves in the manner of the previous section. Let the broken line *AKPG* be the true offer curve for country 1 on the assumption that it has the shipping advantage. If there were no possibility of home production of imports in either country, a world equilibrium at *P* would be implied with foreign internal relative prices given by slope *AP* (not drawn in Fig. 11.3) and home relative prices by slope *AL* (again not drawn – *L* is due south of *P*). But at relative prices slope *AP* the foreign country would find it cheaper to produce exportables for itself, for slope *AE* greater than slope *AP* implies that fewer importables are given up for each unit of exportables when productive resources are shifted into the local manufacture of exportables than when importables are simply traded for exportables produced abroad. P cannot therefore be a world equilibrium. Country 1 on the other hand *would* wish to trade, since slope AL (the trading price ratio inclusive of shipping) is less than slope AD, the cost ratio which would emerge from home production.

In practice, if both countries found themselves in the (disequilibrium) situation P just described, with complete specialisation in production and internal price ratios defined by AP abroad and by AL at home, manufacturers in the foreign country would seize the opportunity to make profits by shifting resources away from importables to a newly established exportables industry where costs are low enough to enable them to undercut home country producers. World supply of exportables will now exceed demand and price will fall relatively both at home and abroad. This process will cease only when the price of exportables abroad has fallen from AP to AR, which is the same as the foreign cost ratio AE. In other words the effective foreign offer curve is now AEF, the home offer curve being AKP as before. R is the point of intersection.

If, however, the point on ADF due south of R lies to the left of D as drawn, the home country will no longer wish to trade, for the new home price is less favourable than the cost ratio AD. Profits may be made by shifting resources out of exportables and shipping, into the home production of importables. This will encourage still greater production of exportables abroad until the point is reached where trade ceases entirely. The foreign country produces what it consumes (defined by E in Fig. 11.3) and the home country the same (D in Fig. 11.3). Both of these production patterns are feasible since both E and D lie on the cost ratio lines AE and AD. Price ratios differ in the two countries but not sufficiently to outweigh the shipping costs.

To put the matter another way, the foreign country's effective offer curve is $AREF$ whilst the home country's offer curve is a straight line from A to the point on $ARPG$ due north of D and is thereafter $ARPG$ itself. *These two offer curves do not intersect.* No trade is possible in the long run.

On the other hand if the point on ADF due south of R lies to the right of D then some trade is possible, for in this case the foreign country's offer curve will be cut by the home country's effective offer curve. Part of the foreign country's demand for exportables will be met by trade and part by its own manufacture. Thus shipping costs may either reduce trade or eliminate it completely.

A precisely analogous situation exists where the shipping advantage lies with the foreign country. In this case *AKJH* is the true foreign offer curve and *J* its intersection with *ADF*. But as slope *AJ* (not drawn in Fig. 11.3) is less steep than *AD*, it would not be profitable for manufacturers at internal prices measured by slope *AJ* to set up an importables industry at home. Complete specialisation would result.

Finally, let us suppose that the broken curves *AKJH* and *AKPG* represent the 'true' offer curves where shipping is shared in that proportion which would, in the absence of possible home production of importables, give rise to a world equilibrium at *K*. In this case relative internal prices in the home country will be measured by the slope of a line joining *A* and a point on *ADF* (not marked) due south of *K*. Such a line would be steeper than *AD*, making it more profitable for the home country to produce importables itself rather than to trade. Similarly the internal price ratio abroad would be represented by the slope of a line joining *A* and a point (not marked) on *APE* due east of *K*. This line must be less steep than *AE*, again indicating no trade.

This last example emphasises that the existence of transport costs may reduce or eliminate trade even in the most ordinary cases. Indeed, common observation confirms that complete elimination of trade always occurs for some commodities. For example, no American citizen would fly to Italy to have his hair trimmed even though this service is provided in that country a great deal more cheaply. On the other hand it is also a fact that some commodities continue to be traded despite the existence of transport costs for reasons which should be apparent from the analysis above.

At this point it may be desirable to reassure the reader that the new ideas here introduced are not in contradiction with the argument of Chapter 1 where we were at pains to point out the fallacy involved in the suggestion that only technologically efficient countries can export (i.e. compete in world markets). In Chapter 1 it was shown that as long as *relative* prices differ between countries trade *must* take place. And of course if relative prices were the same between countries there would be no advantage in trade. On the other hand we now have to concede the possibility of no trade even where relative prices differ, provided they differ by less than the transport costs involved.

But the essential principle of Chapter 1 remains untouched. The absolute level of technological efficiency in any country is irrelevant to its competitive power. What is important is simply how different are the price *ratios* between countries before trade. All that we are now saying is that, because of transport costs, these differences in price ratios must be sufficient to allow compensation for shipping. As before, if the differences in price ratios before trade are not great, then there will be no advantage from trade and no purpose would be served in attempting to promote it. The very similarities in price ratios which prevent the technologically backward home country from exporting, equally prevent the technologically advanced country from exporting to it. There can be no balance of payments problem on this account.

On the other hand the analysis above of the effect of transport costs does show up the crucial weakness of the most naïve two-commodity model. If we desire to introduce anything remotely like reality into our work, it is clearly essential to have a class of non-traded goods. Indeed, it will ordinarily be the case that non-traded items make up the greater part of the national consumption. It is for this reason that we have from time to time introduced the third commodity into the various problems and taken some trouble, especially in exercises, to show how far conclusions must be modified because of its presence.

In practice it is a simple matter to observe the magnitude of the class of non-traded goods, relevant statistics being regularly published by the governments concerned. In the United Kingdom, for example, something of the order of one-half by value of all items entering into the national income cannot be classed either as importables or exportables, and in other countries the proportion is higher. In very few countries is the proportion low enough to suggest that the problem can be neglected without danger of the gravest error. This may, therefore, be a good point to review some of the far-reaching consequences.

First, we remind the reader that, by excluding all but importables and exportables, it is possible to manage with just one relative commodity price p_1/p_2. Furthermore, this same commodity price ratio is, or is closely related to, the real terms of trade. Attention tends therefore to be concentrated upon the real terms of trade alone as the adjusting mechanism wherever an out-of-equilibrium system exists. But when a non-traded commodity is present, a new relative price ratio p_1/p_3 appears. By now the reader who has faithfully worked the exercises of earlier chapters will well understand that the new price ratio p_1/p_3 may exert an effect upon the balance of payments which is just as great and, in some cases even much greater than, the real terms of trade. It cannot be too much emphasised that many popular expositions of the causes and cures of trade imbalance are seriously misleading in their over-concentration of attention upon the real terms of trade alone. The importance of this point combined with the extreme plausibility of the superficial argument suggests that the reader would be well advised to look again at, and think deeply about, sections 3.4, 4.3 and 4.5, however well he may feel the matter to be understood.

The working of the equilibrating mechanism and associated problems of stability are vastly more complex in a two-price world. And equally difficult complications arise from the fact that governments in such a world have a new freedom of manoeuvre. For example, it is seldom realised and never stated explicitly that taxation of the non-traded commodity will alter the real terms of trade, and this will in turn have a welfare effect. Indeed, it may be that a widespread failure to understand this last point is reflected in the fact that international agreements prohibiting the indiscriminate use of tariffs precisely because of the real terms of trade effect at the same time fail to mention taxes on non-traded commodities which could have a similar, although not so powerful, effect.

To study problems of this kind algebra is essential. Diagrams must be abandoned and the work becomes exceedingly tedious, as the reader will find on coming to Book II. A whole new range of problems is opened up. On the other hand assurances are given that nothing which has so far been learned will have to be unlearned. Great care has been taken to select problems where the main features carry over to the more complicated case. And where modifications due to non-traded commodities are important, these have been mentioned as required.

11.6 THE PRODUCTION SECTOR – ELASTICITIES OF SUPPLY

Before turning to Book II, one other assumption of the naïve model should be re-examined, not because any great amendment to conclusions so far is demanded but because a most important principle is involved. On more than one occasion (e.g. Chapter 1 and Chapter 2 and in exercises) we have referred to the obvious possibility that the home country might produce some of its own importables and that the foreign country might produce some exportables. In most cases the assumption has been made that a given quantity of resources, say

labour, will always produce the same quantity of each of the commodities exportables and importables whatever the level of output of
each (see for example the text relating to Fig. 1.3). Diagrammatically
this means that the rate at which the two commodities can be
exchanged in production (relative costs) is constant, that is, *MH* and
MU (Fig. 1.3) are straight lines.

In terms of responses of supply to price changes it is easy to see that
the straight-line assumption is a very powerful one, for if competition
among producers ensures equal profits in every industry, prices must
be equal to costs, and the straight-line assumption means that costs
per unit of output are the same whatever the level of output. This
must be so if the same quantity of labour produces the same quantity
of each commodity whatever the level of output. Accordingly, there
exists only one price ratio at which both importables and exportables
can be produced simultaneously in any one country. If the price ratio
changes, then production of one or other commodity must cease
completely.

It is for this reason that we have been able to do so much without
so far making much of the concept of the response in the *supply* of
each commodity to changes in price. It will be noted that all the
formulae of earlier chapters contain elasticities of demand but no
corresponding elasticities of supply. On the other hand it is intuitively
obvious that in the real world the quantity of imports and the quantity of exports must depend in an important way on the quantities
of each commodity actually produced in each trading area. By the
same token, changes in the balance of payments due to price changes,
or changes in the real terms of trade due to tariffs or any other cause,
must equally depend upon changes in supply, that is, upon supply
elasticities. Supply elasticities should appear in our formulae as equal
partners with demand elasticities. That they do not so appear is
simply due to our assumption of complete specialisation which will
ordinarily exist on the 'straight line' supply hypothesis previously
referred to. Obviously it would be interesting to know in a more
general way how supply elasticities would appear in the model if the
straight-line assumption were relaxed and to check whether values of
zero will in every case reduce the new results to those of the simpler
case.

Unfortunately any attempt to deal with this problem diagrammatically is doomed to failure, for even in two dimensions a suitable
generalisation of the figure so far used becomes impossibly complex.
Nor is it worth while to develop in detail an algebraic model which

does no more than re-examine the ground already covered with the single addition of elasticities of supply. The reason for this is that the step from the work of this book to the much more general model, with a non-traded sector, is precisely the step from geometry with a little algebra to algebra alone which the reader must soon take. This should not be difficult if the symbolic treatment in earlier chapters has been properly studied. Moreover, the mere introduction of home production of importables turns out not to make any real difference to the problems so far treated. The main differences, and the reason for them, are easy to see intuitively from any simple example. An added inducement to leave out a more complete formal working is created also by the fact that we are thereby left with a series of useful exercises for the student to put at the end of each chapter.

On the other hand, to give a hint as to the nature of the development required and to create a basis for some further general discussion, we shall proceed to reconsider the problem of stability treated in section 3.3 on the assumption that both the home country and the foreign country each produce exportables as well as importables. For convenience we follow the working-out of the case in 3.3 and show step by step how this must now be modified.

First we have a balance of payments equation

$$p_1 x_1 - e q_2 x_2 = B = 0 \qquad (11.6.1)$$

where e is the exchange rate. This corresponds exactly to equation (3.3.1), except that a new notation is introduced where we use x_1 rather than X_1 for the quantity of exports sent abroad by the home country. This is made necessary by the fact that we have now to distinguish between the total consumption X_1' of commodity 1 by the foreign country and the amount exported to it. Since the foreign country produces some of commodity 1 for itself, the two are not the same. A similar problem arises with importables. In this connection the reader is reminded also that in identifying x_1 as exports and hence (11.6.1) as the balance of payments equation, we may be implicitly introducing the assumption that world supply equals world demand. In particular it should be noted that if we suppose that, because it is merely a definition of the balance of payments, (11.6.1) must hold for all possible prices and export/import quantities – that is, if we claim that changes in the left-hand side measure changes in B – then we immediately imply something about amounts supplied. As long as (11.6.1) is an identity, then x_1 must be the amount *actually* exported

whether world supply equals world demand or not. In such circumstances we might *not* be able to identify x_1 with the difference
between home demand and home supply. If we define S_1 as the
amount of commodity 1 which the home country is willing to produce
at a given set of prices p_1 and p_2, then it may *not* be true that

$$x_1 = S_1 - X_1 \tag{11.6.2}$$

We may have to distinguish what is *produced* from what is *consumed*
just as we did in Chapter 3 when we let stocks accumulate or
diminish. Normally we reserve the symbol S_1 and the word 'supply'
for the quantity which would be produced under competition at a
given price pattern. In other words we say that S_1 is a function of
prices ($S_1 = S_1(p_1, p_2)$), in the same way as we used the expression
'demand is a function of prices and expenditure' in Chapter 4.
(11.6.2) cannot hold identically on this definition of S_1 unless world
supply is identically equal to world demand. That is, (11.6.1) and
(11.6.2) cannot be simultaneously satisfied both *before* and *after* some
change unless world supply and world demand are equal both *before*
and *after* the change. In most cases so far this requirement has been
satisfied, but it does not make sense to assume that it holds when the
problem under review is the problem of stability as in the present case
and in Chapter 3. What we shall do in fact is to suppose that world
demand is always met by changes in stocks where it cannot be met by
changes in supply in the narrow sense, and it will turn out to be of
crucial importance to know whether such stock changes occur at
home or abroad.

   One further departure from the work of Chapter 3 is of central
importance. In that chapter we failed to distinguish between stability
of a *variable exchange-rate system* of adjustment and stability of the
world price mechanism in an 'open' world economy, that is, in a
world economy with international trade. The reason for this is that,
by coincidence, with such a simple model the two problems amount to
the same thing. Part of our present purpose is to show how a slightly
more complex model forces us to make necessary and important
distinctions between a variety of alternative stability problems,
seldom explicitly treated in economic literature even by the most
expert writers.

   We begin by asking the following question. Suppose that prices p_1
and q_2 are held constant by the authorities at home and abroad but
that the rate of exchange e is allowed to fluctuate freely, moving

against that country whose actual imports exceed actual exports. Such a system will be stable if a fall in the exchange rate (depreciation) causes a positive movement in the balance of payments B, that is, the system is stable if dB/de is positive in sign. It should be noted that this is a different question from that posed in Chapter 3 where we supposed a constant exchange rate and a constant p_1 with fluctuating p_2. Here p_2 was expected to fall when stocks of commodity 2 were building up and vice versa. Since changes in e and changes in p_2 both imply changes in the real terms of trade, the two problems may seem equivalent. We shall, however, show that although this is so for the naïve model it is not the case in general.

We begin by taking changes in equation (11.6.1) as in Chapter 3. Thus

$$x_1 dp_1 + p_1 dx_1 - eq_2 dx_2 - ex_2 dq_2 - q_2 x_2 de = dB \qquad (11.6.3)$$

or, since $dp_1 = dq_2 = 0$,

$$p_1 dx_1 - eq_2 dx_2 - q_2 x_2 de = dB \qquad (11.6.4)$$

But from (11.6.1) we have

$$x_1 = e \frac{q_2}{p_1} x_2$$

so that we may write (11.6.4)

$$\frac{dB}{de} = q_2 x_2 \left(\frac{dx_1}{de} \frac{e}{x_1} - \frac{e dx_2}{x_2 de} - 1 \right) \qquad (11.6.5)$$

The result (11.6.5) should be compared with the expression leading to (3.3.7) and with the final condition (3.3.9). Bearing in mind the fact that $dp_2/p_2 = -dq_1/q_1 = de/e$, we might be tempted to say that there is nothing to add to the conclusions of Chapter 3.

But obviously (11.6.5) is not really an answer to our problem at all, for dx_1/de has no meaning other than the ratio of changes in exports and changes in the exchange rate. We have no information about its sign or magnitude. The right-hand side of (11.6.5) is simply another way of writing dB/de and, as we shall see, its magnitude in terms of elasticities of supply and demand cannot be determined until the model is more completely specified.

In fact, as already hinted, we have to know what part of world stock changes is located in country 1 and what part in country 2. A convenient assumption is that country 2 will supply its needs of commodity 1 first out of its own production, that is, all stock changes are located in country 1. Thus we have the *identity*

$$x_1 \equiv X_1' - S_1' \tag{11.6.6}$$

It should be noted that this excludes the possibility that (11.6.2) can be satisfied also unless world supply and demand are identically equal. For importables we make the assumption

$$x_2 \equiv X_2 - S_2 \tag{11.6.7}$$

that is, stock changes are located abroad.

Given (11.6.6) and (11.6.7) we now have x_1 and x_2 as functions of prices and expenditure. But it should be especially noted that we should get a *different* function with a *different* model. With different stock change locations the functions (11.6.6) and (11.6.7) would be different. The *forms* of our functions depend upon the occurrence of events, a feature which makes it impossible to speak of any parameter, say $\partial x_2 / \partial p_2$ which we can identify as the 'response' of imports to a price change, a known entity whose magnitude could be computed independently of the problem under review.

On the other hand, given (11.6.6) and (11.6.7), we may break these down as follows:

$$x_1 \equiv X_1'(q_1, q_2 Y') - S_1'(q_1, q_2) \tag{11.6.8}$$

where X_1' is the basic demand function expressing the community's preferences and S_1' indicates the quantity of production of commodity 1 which would in the long run emerge at prices q_1 and q_2. Hence from (11.6.8) we have, remembering $dq_2 = 0$,

$$\frac{dx_1}{de} = \frac{\partial X_1'}{\partial q_1}\frac{dq_1}{de} + \frac{\partial X_1'}{\partial Y}\frac{dY'}{de} - \frac{\partial S_1'}{\partial q_1}\frac{dq_1}{de} \tag{11.6.9}$$

The next step is to compute dY/de. Once again we have to specify the course of events, further emphasising the fact that no invariant dx_1/de exists apart from the model. We are supposing in fact that failure of demand does not create unemployment and that total spending is always equal to the value of production. Hence

$$Y' \equiv q_1 S_1' + q_2 S_2' \tag{11.6.10}$$

and

$$dY' = q_1 dS_1' + q_2 dS_2' + S_1' dq_1 \tag{11.6.11}$$

again remembering $dq_2 = 0$.

It is also a characteristic of a competitive economy that price is equal to the cost of production. Suppose now that the changes dS_1' and dS_2' in supply are brought about by a shift of, say, £10 worth of productive resources (e.g. labour) from commodity 2 to commodity 1. Evidently the *cost* of producing commodity 1 is $10/dS_1'$ and of commodity 2, $-10/dS_2'$. But these costs are equal to q_1 and q_2 respectively; hence

$$-\frac{dS_1'}{dS_2'} = \frac{q_2}{q_1}$$

or

$$q_1 dS_1' + q_2 dS_2' = 0$$

Thus from (11.6.11)

$$dY' = S_1' dq_1$$

and from (11.6.9), using the new result,

$$\frac{dx_1}{de} = \frac{\partial X_1'}{\partial q_1}\frac{dq_1}{de} + \frac{\partial X_1'}{\partial Y}S_1'\frac{dq_1}{de} - \frac{\partial S_1'}{\partial q_1}\frac{dq_1}{de}$$

and, remembering that

$$-\frac{dq_1}{q_1} = \frac{de}{e}$$

$$\frac{dx_1}{de} = -\left(\frac{\partial X_1'}{\partial q_1}q_1 + S_1' q_1 \frac{\partial X_1'}{\partial Y} - q_1 \frac{\partial S_1'}{\partial q_1}\right)\frac{1}{e}$$

Or

$$\frac{dx_1}{de}\frac{e}{x_1} = -\left(E_{11}'\frac{X_1'}{x_1} - S_{11}'\frac{S_1'}{x_1} + \frac{S_1'}{x_1}C_1'\right) \qquad (11.6.12)$$

where S_{11}' is an elasticity of supply exactly analogous to elasticity of demand. In a precisely similar way, using (11.6.7) we can show that

$$\frac{dx_2}{de}\frac{e}{x_2} = \left(E_{22}\frac{X_2}{x_2} - S_{22}\frac{S_2}{x_2} + \frac{S_2}{x_2}C_2\right)$$

Substituting these in (11.6.5) gives the answer we seek, namely,

$$\frac{dB}{de} = -q_2 x_2 \left[E_{11}'\frac{X_1'}{x_1} - S_{11}'\frac{S_1'}{x_1} + \frac{S_1'}{x_1}C_1' \right.$$

$$\left. + E_{22}\frac{X_2}{x_2} - S_{22}\frac{S_2}{x_2} + \frac{S_2}{x_2}C_2 + 1 \right] \qquad (11.6.13)$$

This final result (11.6.13) may be compared with (3.3.9) which is the equivalent formula for the most simple model. We note first that if S_1' and S_2 are both zero as we assumed in Chapter 3, and if in consequence $X_1' = x_1$ and $X_2 = x_2$, then (11.6.13) above and (3.3.9) amount to the same thing. As previously asserted, in the simple case and upon the usual assumptions, a floating exchange rate will be stable if and only if an open-economy market-price is stable. In the case now before us, however, the situation could be very different. Further inspection of the work leading to (11.6.13) above will show why.

In writing equation (11.6.6) above we chose to *define* exports, x_1, as foreign demand less foreign supply $(X_1' - S_1')$. What this means is that any failure of *world* demand for commodity 1 (i.e. excess supply) shows itself as a rise in stocks in country 1 but not in country 2. This is a reasonable and obvious assumption to make if there is no production of commodity 1 in country 2, as with the simple model. In the present case, however, where country 2 also produces commodity 1, why should the failure of world demand not show itself in part by a rise in stocks in country 2? It would be reasonable and proper to allow a build-up of stocks in both countries, the amounts being dependent upon the success of salesmen in the face of falling demand.

To illustrate the consequences of this upon the problem of stability, suppose for the moment that salesmen for country 1 are completely successful and those for country 2 unsuccessful, so that all stock increases take place in country 2. We could not then write

$$x_1 \equiv X_1' - S_1'$$

The facts would require us to put

$$x_1 \equiv S_1 - X_1$$

as in equation (11.6.2). In these circumstances (11.6.6) cannot possibly hold, as previously explained. On this basis we should obtain quite a different condition for stability from that given by (11.6.13). Intermediate assumptions would give even more complex results.

The reason for all this is easy to see intuitively if we think for a moment again of the model of Chapter 3. Since there was no supply of commodity 1 abroad, it was natural to put

$$x_1 \equiv X_1'$$

Exports were determined solely by foreign demand. But imagine now that foreign importers were willing to build up stocks whenever actual consumer demand diminished. Let us suppose in fact that they are willing to buy all that is available in the home country. It would then be the case that

$$x_1 = S_1 - X_1$$

as above. And since supply is fixed, being limited by available resources, any change in exports is precisely minus the change in home demand. Now let the same conditions prevail abroad, that is, let imports be given by

$$x_2 = S_2' - X_2'$$

Home importers buy all that is available, building up or running down stocks according to the state of home demand.

A simple reworking of the problem of section 3.3 now reveals that precisely the opposite condition for stability holds from that given by equation (3.3.9). Numerically low demand elasticities give stability of a fluctuating exchange rate, whereas numerically high elasticities lead to instability. The common sense of this is as follows.

Suppose the balance of payments is balanced at a given exchange rate e^0 with prices p_1 and q_2 held constant at p_1^0 and q_2^0. Now let the exchange rate move slightly against the home country. The price of commodity 2 rises in country 1 with income constant. When elasticity of demand is high, this must be because consumers substitute commodity 1 for commodity 2 in considerable quantities. Less is available for export. Abroad the reverse situation prevails. A fall in the price of commodity 1 reduces demand for commodity 2 and more is available for import into the home country. Moreover, the price of imports p_2 will have risen whilst the price p_1 of exports remains constant. High elasticities create a balance of payments deficit which, under the conditions of the problem, induces a further movement of the exchange rate against the home country. The situation is unstable.

Where elasticities are low, however, little substitution into commodity 1 occurs following the price rise in commodity 2. The reduction in real income causes a fall in consumption of commodity 1 leaving more available for export. And abroad, the fall in price of commodity 1 leads to a greater consumption of commodity 2 and hence less is available for import. If elasticities are sufficiently low, this reduction in imports and increase in exports will outweigh the adverse effect on the balance of payments of the rise in price of imports and the balance will improve.

Of course, the assumption that importers always buy whatever is available does not appear very realistic in the simple case where there is no home production of importables. On the other hand, when there is no specialisation in production we are bound to ask 'Whose stocks build up?' and the problem of stability is much more complex. Indeed, the astute reader will notice at once that to distinguish, as we have done, between stability of exchange rates and stability of world market equilibrium is to make a highly artificial separation of two problems which in practice would be intimately bound up with one another.

If governments were to introduce a policy of freely fluctuating exchanges into a world economy, with home production of importables, it would not be reasonable to suppose that prices p_2 and q_1 change only in proportion to the change in the exchange rate e as we have assumed in the working-out above. We have in fact been imagining that home producers of importables will change their prices to match those of the imported article, at the same time adjusting the quantity supplied so that costs and prices are equated even though they may be operating under conditions of deficit or surplus demand for their product. In practice it is more likely that producers everywhere will reduce their prices and output whenever they encounter deficit demand and increase them whenever they meet excess demand whatever the state of the balance of payments. The reason we do not meet this problem with the most simple model is that only the price p_2 changes in country 1, where commodity 2 is not produced, and only the price q_1 changes in country 2, where commodity 1 is not produced. Wherever a commodity is produced, both its price and output remain fixed.

Indeed, once we leave the naïve model the true problem of stability becomes far too complicated technically to handle at the present stage. A correct treatment would require exact specification of the timing of the various changes as well as their magnitude, and the results obtained would depend in an important way on that specification. The reader is warned that even the simplest development which, for example, supposes that the rate of change of prices and e are strictly proportional to excess demand and the balance of payments deficit respectively, leads to conditions for stability far different from any we are able to derive with the present elementary algebraic methods.

These somewhat negative conclusions have been introduced at this point for three main reasons. First, students of economics will encounter elsewhere in the literature a great deal of misuse of the word 'stability' and meet allegations concerning the problem which are, to say the least, misleading. Second, as previously indicated, the work enables us to comment in a general way upon the probable modification of earlier results caused by the introduction of supply elasticities. Third, attention may now conveniently be drawn to the concept of the 'excess demand function', which commonly appears in the literature of economics and which has led to a great deal of unnecessary confusion. The last two points will be taken in turn.

11.7 GENERAL COMMENTS ON MODIFICATIONS DUE TO SUPPLY ELASTICITIES

Inspection of equation (11.6.13) above and comparison with (3.3.9) suggests that supply elasticities enter into most problems in an additive way. In general we should expect a rise in price to lead to an increase in supply under competitive conditions so that S_{11} and S_{22} will be positive in sign. Supply elasticities ordinarily occur together with a demand elasticity in the form $(E_{11} - S_{11})$. This will be a negative number which will replace the simple demand elasticity wherever it occurs. The reader will note also that in (11.6.13) demand elasticities and supply elasticities are multiplied by a 'weight' X_1/x_1 or S_1/x_1 wherever they occur. This is a feature of particular interest which again will be found to be present quite generally in models with home production of importables.

The weights which appear reflect the importance or otherwise of a country in the world economy. Let us suppose, for example, that country 1 is very small and country 2 is the rest of the world. Evidently world consumption of commodity 1, X_1', will be very large compared to exports x_1 so that the number X_1'/x_1 will be large – possibly even of the order of magnitude of 100. This will ensure that dB/de in (11.6.13) is large and positive even when elasticities of demand and supply are quite small. The presence of weights usually magnifies elasticities and hence adds to the sensitivity of the economy to price changes.

The positive terms (S/x) (C) which appear in (11.6.13) may, if desired, be incorporated into the elasticity terms as follows. We recall that E is made up of two parts, a negative income effect C and a negative substitution part earlier written as σ. Contained in term one of (11.6.13) we have therefore an expression $-C_1'X_1'/x_1$ to offset term three. Indeed,

$$x_1 = X_1' - S_1'$$

so that

$$-C_1'\frac{X_1'}{x_1} + \frac{S_1'}{x_1}C_1' = -C_1'$$

which is equal to the 'income' part of the unweighted elasticity. Terms one and three therefore must be negative and numerically greater than, or at least equal to, the unweighted demand elasticity of (3.3.9). The same applies to terms four and six.

We conclude this section by remarking that the modifications due to non-specialisation are not surprising intuitively, for essentially the formulae we are producing indicate in a general way the magnitude of adjustment of the economy in response to price or policy changes of various kinds. And the economy responds more readily, that is, it is more flexible, when changes in supply are admitted as well as changes in demand. The weights we would expect to occur, since it is reasonable to suppose that the activities of a small country are unlikely to have any great effect upon world prices in general. The reader should pay special attention also to exercise 10 at the conclusion of this chapter and note how supply elasticities appear when non-traded goods are present.

In this connection the reader is reminded of the advantages of expressing results in terms of elasticities (proportional responses) rather than absolute responses. The Es, Ss and Cs of (11.6.13) will not depend in any way on the size of the country but only on the type of commodity and the tastes, etc., of the average consumer or producer. The effect of relative size is brought out by the weights, which should appear explicitly.

This might also be a suitable point to emphasise that the effect of relative size is not always intuitively obvious and should always be carefully checked by means of a model. Mistakes are often made. It is for example commonplace to meet the argument that, because Britain is small relative to the United States, developments in the British economy will have a negligible percentage effect upon activity in North America. This may be true but it does not follow that we are free to analyse the effect of British policy as if the United States did not exist. For if it is true that British policy has only small effects in the U.S.A., it must equally be true that small changes in the U.S.A.

have large repercussions in Britain. The effect of British policy 'reflected back' from the U.S.A. is not necessarily negligible. Only a model will reveal whether it is or not.

We now come to the concept of the 'excess demand function'.

11.8 REASONS FOR AVOIDING THE USE OF 'EXCESS DEMAND FUNCTIONS'

At this point the reader should look again at equation (11.6.5) above and the remarks which follow it. Most of what we have learned so far we have discovered by expressing the consequence of policy in terms of 'parameters' called elasticity of demand or supply, about which we know something *a priori*. We believe for example that consumption is dependent only upon prices and total expenditure and that price rises, with expenditure constant, will lead to a reduction in demand for the commodity whose price has risen. We believe, moreover, that the magnitude of elasticity of demand can be computed or guessed at within limits and that it remains the same in whatever context the price change occurs.

In view of the fact that we continually encounter the entity $x_1 \equiv X_1 - S_1$ in the theory of international trade, it is tempting to try to simplify notation by defining $X_1 - S_1$ as 'excess' or 'import' demand, supposing that, because X_1 is a function of prices and expenditure and S_1 is a function of prices, then import demand is a function of prices and expenditure whose parameters (elasticities) have meaning and can be computed in the usual way. Indeed, a great deal of the literature of international trade theory is implicitly or explicitly based upon this sort of idea.

In particular the expressions

$$\left(\frac{dx_1}{de} \frac{e}{x_1} \right)$$

inside the brackets on the right-hand side of (11.6.5) are sometimes interpreted as parameters which we might call import elasticities. This would seem to be in contradiction with the argument which follows (11.6.5).

The error, as error there must be, is due to the identification of import *demand* with *actual* imports. The moment we read 'imports' for 'import demand' there is an implicit assumption that a model exists and that the system is always in some kind of equilibrium so that the demand for imports is identically equal to supply of imports at all prices.

A function x_i of prices and aggregate expenditure is not an import function, it is an import demand function. Even if we begin from a position where import demand is met so that imports and import demand are identical, a change in one price holding all other prices constant must mean in general that import demand will not be met. The elasticity of import demand is therefore not an import elasticity.

Notice that the elasticity of demand for importables is unambiguous and quite distinct from elasticity of supply. Indeed, each is derived from a different function. At no time is there any temptation to suppose that supply and demand must always be the same. Our very reason for writing x_1, however, is that we have an interest in the behaviour of actual imports. At once there is a danger of slipping into the error described at length in section 4 of the Introduction. An import elasticity with respect to price presupposes that complicated changes (involving either the balance of trade itself or stocks) are automatically associated with any price change. Import elasticity has no meaning until the complete model is specified. And when the complete model is specified we find we have no need of the concept.

The reader may be still more impressed by the dangers of the excess demand function approach when he recalls that in at least one context above x_i appeared as excess home supply instead of excess foreign demand. Finally, it should be noted that even in cases where we may not be led into actual error, a great deal is often lost by failure to set out supply and demand functions separately and explicitly. In such a case the weights which were the subject of our earlier discussion disappear with consequent loss of information. The student is strongly advised to be on the look-out for misleading uses of the concept of excess demand and always to avoid it in his own work.

This commentary and review of assumptions concludes Book I. We have, with relatively simple tools, succeeded, particularly in exercises, in surveying at some depth a great many of the problems which make news in the world of international economics. In Book II we shall dig deeper still, looking especially at underlying causes as well as symptoms. Book II includes also a commentary upon a dynamic model, which alone can illuminate and justify what often appears to the beginner to be a set of disjoint conclusions resting upon assumptions of doubtful validity.

EXERCISES

1. Consider the following three-country system of equations:

$$B = p_1 X_1' + p_1 X_1'' - e p_2' X_2$$

$$Y = p_1 O_1 \qquad p_1 = \text{constant} \qquad p_1' = p_1'' = p_1/e$$

$$Y' = p_2' O_2' \qquad p_2' = p_2'' = \text{constant} \qquad p_2 = e p_2'$$

$$Y'' = p_2'' O_2''$$

where B is the balance of payments of country 1, e is the exchange rate of country 1 into the currency of countries 2 and 3, primes being used to identify countries. For convenience the money units in countries 2 and 3 are chosen so that prices are always the same in countries 2 and 3. If Xs are functions of prices p and expenditures Y in the usual way and a 'numeraire' commodity is chosen in each country, note that the system, which presupposes that all demands are met out of stocks, is determined by a given exchange rate e.

Show algebraically that the balance B is changed unfavourably or favourably by currency depreciation according as condition (11.2.2) is or is not met.

2. Show that, under the conditions of exercise 1, it is impossible to determine the effect of country 1's depreciation upon the balance of payments of country 2 until some rule is given specifying how much of X_2 comes from country 2 and how much from country 3. Suppose that $\frac{1}{2} X_2$ is purchased from country 2. Find the effect on country 2's balance of trade of currency depreciation in country 1 and hence show that both country 1 *and* country 2's balance may be improved for certain values of demand elasticities.

3. Consider the following model of three countries in a trading relationship using the notation x_k^{ij} for exports of the kth commodity from country i to country j.

$$\left.\begin{array}{l} B = p_1(x_1^{12} + x_1^{13}) - p_2' x_2^{21} - p_2'' x_2^{31} \\ B' = p_2' x_2^{21} - p_1 x_1^{12} \end{array}\right\} \quad \begin{array}{l}\text{Balance of payments} \\ \text{(countries 1 and 2)}\end{array}$$

$$\left.\begin{array}{l} x_1^{12} = X_1' - S_1' \\ x_1^{13} = X_1'' - S_1'' \\ x_2^{21} + x_2^{31} = X_2 - S_2 \end{array}\right\} \quad \begin{array}{l}\text{If } S\text{s are amounts supplied, these} \\ \text{equations indicate that world supply} \\ \text{and demand are equated at all times}\end{array}$$

$$Y = p_1 S_1 + p_2 S_2 + p_2' x_2^{21} t_2 + p_2'' x_2^{31} t_2$$
$$Y' = p_1' S_1' + p_2 S_2' + p_1 x_1^{12} t_1'$$
$$Y'' = p_1'' S_1'' + p_2'' S_2'' + p_1 x_1^{13} t_1''$$

Expenditure equations (t = percentage import duty)

$p_1 = $ constant (numeraire) $p_1' = p_1(1 + t_1')$ $p_1'' = p_1(1 + t'')$

$p_2 = p_2'(1 + t_2) = p_2''(1 + t_2)$

Show that this system is determined given the balance of payments B and B' together with import duties. Why is it not necessary to specify the third country's balance of payments B''?

Examine the special case where $S_2 = S_1' = S_1'' = $ zero and where $t_1' = t_1'' = t_2 = $ zero and where the balance of payments in all countries is to be kept balanced. Show that if a tariff dt_1' is now imposed by country 2, we should have

$$\frac{dp_2}{p_2} = \frac{\dfrac{X_1'}{(X_1' + X_1'')} \sigma_{11}'}{\left(E_{22} + \dfrac{X_1'}{X_1' + X_1''} E_{11}' + \dfrac{X_1''}{X_1' + X_1''} E_{11}'' + 1 \right)}$$

Hence argue that the real terms of trade for country 1 will ordinarily move unfavourably.

4. Attempt to construct a diagram on the lines of Fig. 11.1 to illustrate the results of exercise 3.
5. Note that the introduction of transport costs into the model presents no problems as long as transportation is regarded as a separate commodity the demand for which is complementary to the demand for imports and exports. Thus if T_i is the quantity transported of the ith commodity by the home country and t_i is the cost of carrying one unit of i, and if primes indicate 'of the foreign country', we have the following system of equations:

$$B = p_1 X_1' + t_1 T_1 + t_2 T_2 - q_2 X_2 - t_1 T_1' - t_2 T_2' \quad \text{Balance of}$$
$$\text{payments} \quad \text{(i)}$$

$$\left. \begin{array}{l} Y = p_1 S_1 + t_1 T_1 + t_2 T_2 \\ Y' = q_2 S_2' + t_1 T_1' + t_2 T_2' \end{array} \right\} \quad \text{Expenditure equations} \quad \text{(ii)}$$

$$\left. \begin{array}{l} X_1' = T_1 + T_1' \\ X_2 = T_2 + T_2' \end{array} \right\} \quad \text{Demand for transportation} \quad \text{(iii)}$$

$$\left. \begin{array}{l} X_1' = X_1'(q_1, q_2, Y') \\ X_2 = X_2(p_1, p_2, Y) \end{array} \right\} \quad \text{Consumer demand} \quad \text{(iv)}$$

$$S_1 = S_1(t_1, t_2, p_1) \qquad S_2' = S_2'(t_1, t_2, q_2)$$
$$T_1 = T_1(t_1, t_2, p_1) \qquad T_1' = T_1'(t_1, t_2, q_2) \quad \Big\} \text{Supply equations} \quad \text{(v)}$$
$$T_2 = T_2(t_1, t_2, p_1) \qquad T_2' = T_2'(t_1, t_2, q_2)$$

$p_2 = q_2 + t_2$ and $q_1 = p_1 + t_1$ $\qquad$ Price equals cost plus transport
$$\text{cost} \qquad \text{(vi)}$$

N.B. Transport costs must be the same in both countries.

Show by counting equations and unknowns that if B is zero and p_1 is given as the numeraire price, the amounts T_i and T_i' of transport provided for each commodity by each country are precisely determined.

Show further that, in the argument of section 11.4, we have presented a special case of this system where

$$t_1 = ap_1 = a'q_2$$

$$t_2 = bp_1 = b'q_2$$

and where the supply equations (v) are replaced by

$$S_1 + aT_1 + bT_2 = \text{constant}$$

and $\qquad\qquad S_2' + a'T_1' + b'T_2' = \text{constant}$

so that Y/p_1 and Y'/q_2 are both constant (AB and AO in Fig. 11.2).

Hence show that the *shares* of world shipping ($aT_1 + bT_2$) and ($a'T_1' + b'T_2'$) are precisely determined although the actual quantities T_i and T_i' are not. Why should this be? If P in Fig. 11.2 identifies equilibrium, indicate the measure of ($aT_1 + bT_2$) and ($a'T_1' + b'T_2'$) on the diagram.

6. Compare the published figures for national income and the value of imports and exports together for the U.S.A. and each of the larger European countries. Examine the relation between the proportions of traded to non-traded goods and the physical distance between the countries concerned and their main trading partners.

7. Show that the assumptions

$$x_1 = S_1 - X_1$$

and $\qquad\qquad x_2 = S_2' - X_2'$

made in section 11.6 together imply that, in the usual diagram, imports must be read off the foreign offer curve and exports off the home offer curve. Use this fact to prove diagrammatically that the usual stability conditions of Chapter 3 are thereby reversed.

8. Replace (11.6.6) and (11.6.7) by the assumptions of exercise 7 and rework the algebra of section 11.6. Prove that in this case

$$\frac{dB}{de} = q_2 x_2 \left[\frac{X_1}{x_1} E_{11} - \frac{S_1}{x_1} S_{11} + \frac{S_1}{x_1} C_1 \right.$$
$$\left. + \frac{X_2'}{x_2} E_{22}' - \frac{S_2'}{x_2} S_{22}' + \frac{S_2'}{x_2} C_2' + 1 \right]$$

and hence show that a freely fluctuating exchange rate would, on these assumptions, almost certainly be unstable.

9. Select at random from any chapter any exercise based upon a two-commodity model with fixed supplies and extend the problem to one where there is both home and foreign production of all commodities and supplies are dependent upon prices. Show that the only effect of this generalisation will be to replace each elasticity E_{ii} or weighted elasticity $(X_i/x_i)E_{ii}$, wherever they occur in any formula, with the expression

$$(X_i/x_i)\sigma_{ii} - (S_i/x_i)S_{ii} - C_i$$

where σ_{ii} is the substitution part of the elasticity E_{ii} and S_{ii} is supply elasticity.

10. Select at random from any chapter any exercise whatever based upon a two-commodity model with fixed supplies and extend the problem to one where there is production both at home and abroad of all commodities *including a class of non-traded commodities* and supplies are dependent upon prices. Show that the only effect of this generalisation will be to replace each substitution part σ_{ii} or weighted substitution part $(X_i/x_i)\sigma_{ii}$, and each marginal propensity to consume C_i, wherever they occur in any formula, with the expressions

$$\frac{X_i}{x_i} \left[\left(\sigma_{ii} - \frac{S_i}{X_i} S_{ii} \right) - \left(\sigma_{i3} - \frac{S_i}{X_i} S_{i3} \right)(\sigma_{3i} - S_{3i})/(\sigma_{33} - S_{33}) \right]$$

and $C_i - C_3(\sigma_{3i} - S_{3i})/(\sigma_{33} - S_{33})$

respectively.

Hence justify use of the notation ψ_{i3} and ϕ_{i3} (see exercise 5, Chapter 4).

Book II

'He who knows not and knows not that he knows not is a fool.
Shun him.'
CHINESE PROVERB

12 The Genesis of International and Inter-regional Trade

12.1 FACTORS OF PRODUCTION

WE now come to a series of problems which from time to time assume importance in world affairs but which cannot be discussed except in terms of a model more general than even the least aggregative of Book I. The work so far is inadequate, basically because we have always thought of the manufacturing process as calling only for a single composite input up to now called 'natural resources'. At no stage have we introduced different kinds of inputs, for example labour, capital or land, each with their own separate prices. On the other hand a whole series of intensely practical questions arise which at bottom amount to asking, how will government policy or international trade affect the very prices of the factors of production, land, labour and capital, the existence of which we have not yet acknowledged? Or alternatively, how do prices of factors of production affect the level of trade or the balance of payments?

Unfortunately, for those who prefer simple models, problems connected with factor prices cannot be recognised until we allow varying quantities of different commodities, with more than one technique of production, to be manufactured under varying conditions of world trade. With one commodity and all resources fully employed there can be no change in national output or ratio of capital to labour used in production, whatever changes in the trade pattern occur or whatever new government policy is introduced. Hence there can be no change in the demand for, say, labour, relative to capital and accordingly no change can be expected in relative input prices.

With two or more commodities produced, however, provided they require different ratios of inputs of capital to labour, any change in supplies due to changes in demand necessarily generates a change in the relative demands for capital and labour and hence factor prices. If there is an increase in output of that commodity which uses relatively more capital and a fall in output of that which uses relatively less, there will be an increased demand for capital. Nor is the problem usually as simple as this. For with three or more commodities it is possible to increase the output of the product using most capital and decrease the output of that using least capital at the same time *reducing* the overall demand for capital, provided only that the output of the third commodity is sufficiently reduced. Similar problems arise *a fortiori* when there are three or more factors of production.

Evidently it is not possible even to begin to consider questions directly or indirectly involving factor prices until we have a model with each country using at least two factors and producing at least two commodities. What is more, we shall again and again argue that it is in fact not possible to study problems involving factor prices *in anything like a realistic way* until at least three commodities and three factors are introduced.

It may indeed be appropriate to warn the reader at once that many textbooks of international trade theory (even the most advanced) lay a great deal too much emphasis upon propositions which are true only for models with two commodities and two factors of production. In a general way it is not possible to deduce qualitative results which show the direction of movements of factor prices as a consequence of this or that policy except where only two factors exist, that is, except in a very unrealistic case. To develop more general results we must have numerical estimates of elasticities of demand and supply. It is of the utmost importance to know when we do not know, as the aphorism quoted at the beginning of this Book reminds us.

Furthermore, we have already in Book I illustrated the importance of elasticity of supply, and we shall show that the numerical value of supply elasticities sometimes depends in a crucial way upon the relative numbers of commodities and factors. Thus even a model with three commodities produced in each country is hardly enough to draw proper attention to all the important questions which arise in the real world. With these provisos in the forefront of our minds, we shall proceed in this and the next chapter to a discussion of two matters which have in the past formed the subject of considerable debate. The first concerns the basic reasons for trade rather than home production; the second asks the fundamental question 'Is trade *always* a good thing?' Both problems indirectly involve consideration of the role of factors of production in the manufacturing process and will serve as a useful introduction to the new range of problems now facing us.

12.2 On the Distinction Between International and Inter-regional Trade

From one point of view there is always a very simple answer to the question 'What causes trade?' Indeed, the work of Book I demonstrates that trade will occur if and only if relative prices *before* trade are different between countries, that is, if the ratio p_1/p_2 is different from the ratio q_1/q_2. It is of course obvious, and we have already seen, that in such circumstances some rate of currency exchange, e, will exist so that either p_1 is greater than eq_1 and p_2 is less than eq_2 or alternatively p_1 is less than eq_1 whilst p_2 is greater than ep_2, for if we had both p_1 and p_2 greater than eq_1 and eq_2, e could and obviously would be increased until one or the other changed from being greater to being less. And the two could not change simultaneously since we should then have some e at which both $p_1 = eq_1$ and $p_2 = eq_2$ or

$$\frac{p_1}{p_2} = \frac{q_1}{q_2}$$

contrary to assumption.

All of our argument so far has gone to show that where price ratios are different, competitive forces will generate an exchange rate, e, or a general level of prices such that it is cheaper for each country to buy at least one product abroad. Furthermore, there is always pressure either automatic or government-sponsored, to adjust one or other of the variables so that the value of imports and the value of exports are equated. Similar considerations obviously apply when there are many commodities produced and traded, and in an earlier chapter we have demonstrated that these conclusions are not materially affected by the existence of transportation costs. All that is necessary in the most general case is to stipulate that trade will occur if the difference in relative prices is sufficiently great to outweigh the cost of transportation at some suitable currency exchange rate.

But this answer to the question posed only shifts the real problem one stage further back. Why should relative prices be different in different countries, since the same commodities are being produced? The laws of physics are the same the world over and prices and costs are but a reflection of the laws of physics. Evidently we have no alternative but to investigate techniques of production or, what amounts to the same thing, conditions of supply.

It is useful to begin by asking why we find it natural to distinguish between the trading relations of countries like America and Britain and those of towns in the same country – say Birmingham and Brighton. Although there are many minor differences which may at first sight look important – for example, international trade involves the reconciliation of different currencies – there is in fact one and only one *basic* distinction between regional and international trade. This depends upon the following idea which we shall pursue at considerable length. If the rate of wages for comparable labour, or the price of land of the same quality, is different in Birmingham and Brighton, then it is not unreasonable to suppose that a sufficient number of individuals who are labourers or businessmen who rent or buy land will move from Birmingham to Brighton in search of higher wages or lower rents and so by competition adjust factor prices until they are the same in both places. The increased supply of labour will reduce wage rates where they are high whilst greater demand for land will raise rents where they are low. On the other hand, because the practical difficulties are so much greater, it is much less likely that the same thing will occur between countries. Within a country there is a mechanism which equates everywhere the prices of all inputs into the productive process. Internationally there is not. At bottom this is the reason why a separate theory of international trade is necessary.

Of course the kind of economist or 'practical' man who objects to models on the ground that they are unrealistic will immediately protest that immigration and emigration does take place and that some British industrialists have and ordinarily do set up in business in the United States. Even so, a separate international trade model based upon input (i.e. factor) immobility is completely justified, for no one would argue that population and capital movements between countries are sufficient to equalise wage rates and land rents throughout the world. A simple observation of the facts would immediately and resoundingly refute such a suggestion. Moreover, the type of model we shall develop will in any case immediately answer questions about the effect of any 'partial' migration of labour and capital upon all other variables. In a later chapter we shall specifically study this problem.

On the other hand we can observe that wage rates and land rents do not differ very much between Birmingham and Brighton; and although, as with all empirical hypotheses, it is impossible to prove that this is due to the competition of migrating labour and 'entrepreneurship', no alternative explanation immediately suggests itself.

The obvious implication of equal input prices everywhere is that, given the possibility of production by the same techniques in both

Birmingham and Brighton, there can be no difference in relative commodity prices, even before trade, for if input prices are the same before trade and if local competition ensures that commodity prices are equal to cost, then commodity prices must be equal before trade. The same considerations do not apply where factor prices are not equal, so that trade in commodities will ordinarily be generated.

Before the reader protests that we do in fact observe trade between towns despite equal factor prices, we hasten to add that the same commodity prices in Birmingham and Brighton before trade for those items actually produced in both places does not mean that there can be no trade of any kind between them. What it does mean, however, is that trade will tend to be confined to those items which are not produced locally. We shall find it interesting and instructive to consider this point in more detail, but as a preliminary it is necessary first to develop more precise ways of talking about the nature of the productive process.

12.3 A DIGRESSION ON PRODUCTION FUNCTIONS AND PRODUCTIVE FACTORS

The act of production consists in acquiring and using certain 'inputs' or 'factors' to create an output or product. In a general way there are a great many different techniques which can be used to manufacture a given amount of any one product. The same 'output' can often be achieved either with a little machinery and much labour or with much machinery and little labour. The set of all possible techniques for manufacturing all possible quantities of any given commodity is usually referred to by economists as the 'production function' for that commodity. Often this set is written in the form of a functional identity in every way analogous to the demand functions now familiar to the reader. That is, we put

$$S_1 = S_1(A_{11}, A_{12} \ldots A_{1n}) \qquad (12.3.1)$$

which simply says that a given set of quantities A_{11}, A_{12}, etc., of inputs of factors 1 and 2, etc., into the production of commodity 1 will yield an output of S_1 units. The form of the function S_1 will determine the set of possible techniques. For example, in the two-factor case we might have the production function

$$S_1 = 2A_{11}^2 + 2A_{12}^2 \qquad (12.3.2)$$

which indicates at once precisely how much of S_1 will emerge given inputs A_{11} and A_{12} of factors 1 and 2. (12.3.2) tells us in fact that 2 units of each input will yield 16 units of output. It tells us further that the same 16 units of output can be produced by $\sqrt{8}$ units of input 1 and zero units of input 2 and indeed by an infinite number of other combinations (i.e. techniques). Evidently the form of the production function summarises the nature of the set of techniques. Something must now be said about the definition and measurement of the productive factors A_{ij}.

It should be noted particularly that as soon as we choose to speak of a set of techniques or a production function we imply at once that inputs must be *measurable* entities. No meaning can be attributed to a functional identity such as (12.3.1) unless A_{11}, A_{12}, etc., are numbers defining *how much* of factors 1 and 2 yield the *quantity* S_1. Thus 'risk' or 'management' *per se* should never be thought of as inputs. 'Risk' is simply a reason why money or some other input might not be forthcoming for a certain project, whilst 'management' is a kind of labour with a certain skill. Nor is there any point in including in the list of inputs those which in practice do not command a price. From a technical point of view production often requires air, but as this is free we may ignore it.

A further point which has caused some confusion of thought stems from the need to specify the *quality* of certain inputs. Obviously an acre of land on the seafront at Brighton is not the same thing as an acre of land in Birmingham. The two must be treated as different factors of production. The same may be said about land with sunshine and land without sunshine. So much is obvious. On the other hand some economists have felt that there might be no limit to this qualifying process. Evidently in the last analysis any acre of land is different from any other at least in respect of the fact that it occupies a different position on the surface of the earth and probably in many other respects as well. Does it follow that there are as many factors of production as there are acres of land?

Actually, what is troubling economists who argue this way is not some peculiarity of economics as a science but the apparent absence of a general working rule. We now give such a rule. Any characteristics of the factor whose presence or absence affects that factor's power to produce any one commodity in the set of those to be considered must be specified. Other characteristics may be neglected. For example, a blue-eyed plumber may be regarded as equivalent to a brown-eyed plumber, but a plumber who has not served a period of apprenticeship might possibly have to be distinguished from one who has.

Of course we must avoid the ultimate absurdity (not unknown in the literature of economics) where a unit of input is defined as 'that which produces a unit of output'. This would reduce the notion of a production function to a useless tautology. In the usual case quality relevant to productivity will be identifiable in some way other than by linking it to the quantity of output generated. If it were not so, our theory could have no content.

It is of crucial importance to understand and accept this way of talking about factors of production, since it does imply that production functions must be the same for all countries. And the fact that production functions are the same the world over plays a big part in the theory we are to develop. In view of this it may be as well to draw attention to the fact that there is no question of principle here in any way different from that faced by the natural scientist in any field.

The chemist does not hesitate to say that the input of 2 c.c.s of hydrogen and 1 c.c. of oxygen readily yields an output of a certain quantity of water – and this despite the fact that any two different c.c.s of hydrogen must at least occupy a different position in space. The chemist is also well aware that traces of other substances in his ingredients will leave impurities in the resulting water. How far these impurities should be named and discussed is largely determined by the degree of accuracy required in the statements made. Everything depends upon what is meant by the words 'hydrogen', 'oxygen' and 'water'. The fact that greater precision implies closer specification does not mean that the laws of chemistry are invalid unless they are reduced to statements like '1 c.c. of water is produced by those chemicals which produce 1 c.c. of water in combination'. In the same way production functions may, in principle, be specified up to the degree of precision required, by choice of some quantity unit of input appropriately qualified.

We now repeat that it follows logically from our chosen definition of a productive factor that production functions must be the same everywhere. They must be the same in Birmingham and Brighton as they are in Bombay and Bahrain. We especially emphasise this because it is alternatively suggested in the literature that the claim that production functions are identical throughout the world is an empirical assumption and not a matter of logic. That is, it is an assumption of fact which could conceivably be false. In truth of course the identity of production functions follows at once from the known fact that the laws of physics are everywhere the same. This is the only sense in which the proposition is empirical.

The reader should understand also that a production function is the set of *all* known techniques that *might* be used and not the set of techniques that actually are used. That is, it is the set of all techniques which could be used *if factors were available* and has nothing to do with the empirical question whether or not factors of production *are* available in any given area. Identical production functions do not imply that different countries will use the same techniques of production.

Of course it is true that the set of known techniques of production is constantly growing in consequence of new discoveries. Economists give expression to this idea by saying that production functions are subject to technical change over time. It is also true that at any given moment of time a new and profitable technique discovered in country A may not be in use in country B only because the spread and implementation of new knowledge takes time. But this is a matter of dynamics. As long as we confine our interest to a study of the final stationary equilibrium of the dynamic system in operation at each moment of time, that is, as long as we are concerned with 'comparative statics', the only proper assumption to make is that knowledge available to one country is available also to another. Indeed, in so far as our economic model is concerned only with countries in close trading relationships, this is in any case not a bad first approximation to the truth.

To be quite fair to those who take a different point of view, however, it should be made very clear that what we are here discussing is a way of talking and not a question of fact. We do not suggest that it is illogical to make words mean something different but only that it is confusing. To illustrate just how confusing, consider an argument put up by the author of a recent survey of international economic theory.

First, it was rightly pointed out that the question whether production functions are (logically) everywhere identical depends upon the set of definitions chosen. It would not, for example, be self-contradictory to define land with sunshine as the same factor as land without sunshine and thence to argue that sunshine is an environmental or 'atmosphere' condition which affects the form of the production function. That is, we might say that the output of bananas produced by a given quantity of labour on one acre of land in the

Highlands of Scotland is different from that produced by the same amount of labour applied to one acre of the Queensland coast because background conditions make the production functions different. Conversely, it would not be self-contradictory to say that production functions are the same because *if* we had some land with sunshine in Scotland bananas would grow but they do not because in fact there is no land with sunshine. But then the author of the survey went on to claim that there would be a logical difficulty in the following case. Let country *A* be producing steel using a different technique from country *B* simply because a research team in *A* has recently made a technical advance. It is then argued that it would be ridiculous to define production functions as the same in *A* and *B* and to attribute the difference to a different endowment of a factor of production called 'research'.

Of course it would. But this is due to the doubtful nature of the second part of the proposition, not the first. Physics is the same, fortunately, in both country *A* and country *B*. There is nothing absurd about recognising that production functions are the same. What is absurd is the implied introduction into the production function of an input called 'research'. Of course there is always an input of management labour whose function is knowledge finding and knowledge disseminating. In course of time (usually a very short time) management labour will find and apply in country *B* the knowledge originally discovered in country *A*. In such circumstances the absurdity would be in *not* recognising that production possibilities are the same in both countries rather than the contrary. We agree of course that a lack of skilled labour, perhaps skilled management labour, in country *B* might make *A*'s technique impossible or unprofitable to use in country *B*. But to suppose there is some aura or background difficulty in country *B* called 'lack of research' which prevents even in the long run the application of techniques developed in *A* is to invite muddled thinking.

To illustrate still further not only that it is not true that there is any logical difficulty connected with identical production functions, but also that any other convention leads to confusion, let us pursue the alternative to its logical limit. We will allow ourselves to be persuaded to call land homogeneous everywhere and measure it in acres, subsuming differences in soil and climate into differences in production functions according to the quality and environment of the land in different regions. This will imply at once that an acre of the Rub al Khali in Saudi Arabia is a unit of land input equivalent to an acre of the Thames Valley whether it be used for the production of oil or the production of milk. It does not seem likely that anyone would wish to press the convention this far. Some quality specification is desirable.

But this leads to the problem of drawing a line between those qualities which are treated as identifying the factor and those which are presumed to lead to differences in production functions for the same commodity in different countries. Clearly no general rule exists for drawing such a line. To develop a theory we should have to name and classify every object which might be used as an input and list those characteristics which (arbitrarily) we decide should on the one hand identify the input as, say, 'land type one', or on the other determine whether or not production functions should be considered different. It is clearly much more convenient to recognise that the laws of nature are the same throughout the universe and that identical consequences follow identical activities, provided only that the objects used are the same. All that is now needed is a general rule which states that, for any number of activities *n*, a unit of any input is identical with any other unit provided only that those respects in which it may differ do not in any way affect the outputs derived from the use of that unit in each of the *n* activities. This is precisely the convention proposed in the opening paragraphs of this discussion.

To put the matter in its true perspective, consider the position, say, of a natural scientist faced with the same sort of choice of conventions. It is a fact that if water is taken from the river Test and boiled, steam and only a negligible residue results. If on the other hand the same quantity of water taken from the Test estuary near the Isle of Wight is boiled, a different quantity of steam and a considerable residue of salt is obtained. We now have a choice. Either we can say that the laws of physics differ according to whether water is boiled in Longstock in Hampshire or in the liner QE2 off the Isle of Wight; or we can say that the laws of physics remain the same but that sea water is a different substance from water taken from the river Test. This is precisely analogous to the choice facing the economist, and there can be little doubt which is the more sensible approach.

12.4 INTER-REGIONAL TRADE AGAIN

The reader is now reminded that the purpose of the somewhat tedious discussion of section 12.3 was to provide a background for our thinking about the reasons for and the nature of trade between

Birmingham and Brighton. We have shown that as a consequence of our definitions production functions are the same in both places. We have argued also that, as a matter of fact, competition and factor mobility will ensure that the prices of factors are the same wherever factor mobility exists. Provided therefore that the necessary factors are available in both towns, the same most profitable technique of production will be chosen equally in Birmingham and Brighton and accordingly commodity production costs will be the same without trade. No trade will take place in those goods actually manufactured in both places, for, as indicated in Chapter 11, transport costs will eliminate any possibility of this.

On the other hand the most superficial consideration of the facts of the real world suggests that there will be many cases where the right kind of factor will not be present in certain locations. For example, Birmingham cannot provide holidays by the sea since no land on a seafront is available on which to build a hotel. If the commodity 'holidays' is to be consumed by the citizens of Birmingham it can only be secured by the export from Birmingham of, say, bicycles in exchange. This end is automatically attained when the residents of Birmingham spend money in Brighton which they have earned in the production of bicycles in their home town.

Of course the picture we have so far drawn is still very much over-simplified, for in practice we do sometimes see in the shops goods 'imported' from another city, competing with a local product. There could conceivably be two reasons for this. First, there must always be an element of transport cost in any price, however near the factory to the point of sale, and a great part of any such cost is that arising out of loading and unloading, an element which does not depend upon the distance travelled. Hence differences in transport cost may in some cases be a negligible proportion of price. This is particularly true where differences in distance from factory to market are not great. We shall come back to this point later.

Secondly, it may be that the 'foreign' commodity on sale locally is not in fact quite the same as the local product even though at first sight it may appear to be. Like different brands of detergent, the two might satisfy the same general need but as a consequence of advertising or for some other reason the consumer may believe them to be different. In this case we have not actually violated the rule that trade between regions is impossible in commodities produced in both regions. The exception is more apparent than real.

The view of inter-regional trade presented above is over-simplified

also on another account, for even between towns within a country
not all factors are mobile. Businessmen who wish to rent cheap land
have to move in search of it. The land cannot move to the businessmen who wish to rent it.

What we have to show in fact is that within a country a sufficient
number of factors are mobile to compensate for those which are not.
Reasons must be found why the greater degree of mobility between
regions is able to explain an important discrete qualitative difference
between the kind of trade which takes place internationally and the
kind which takes place nationally. To pursue this point we need more
technical equipment.

12.5 COST FUNCTIONS

From this point on we introduce the notation q_i for the price of the
*i*th *commodity* and p_i for the price of the *i*th *factor*. In Book I and
earlier in this chapter p and q represented commodity prices at home
and abroad respectively. It is now convenient to abandon this
convention and use primes to denote foreign prices in the manner
familiar from Book I. Earlier, in discussing production functions, we
wrote A_{ij} for the input of the *j*th factor into the manufacture of the
*i*th commodity. It follows that A_{ij}/S_i is the input of the *j*th factor
required to produce one unit of the *i*th commodity. It will be found
simpler to use the symbol a_{ij} for A_{ij}/S_i since it is to be met frequently.
From these definitions it follows that

$$q_i = p_1 a_{i1} + p_2 a_{i2}, \ldots, p_n a_{in}$$

which simply says that price is equal to the total cost of producing
one unit. That is, it is the value of all the inputs required to produce
one unit. We shall follow also the common practice of using a
summation sign $\sum$ when setting out cost functions of this kind, so that
more concisely we can write

$$q_i = \sum_{j=1}^{n} p_j a_{ij} \tag{12.5.1}$$

to mean the sum of all $p_j a_{ij}$ where j takes the values 1 to n.

The reader who, in another context, may have become used to
distinguishing between 'cost' and 'profit', is reminded that one of the
inputs a_{ij} will be 'capital' and one of the prices p_j will be the rate of
profit on capital. Attention is drawn also to the fact that the inputs

a_{ij} are not to be thought of as constants whatever the values of p_j. On the contrary, each a_{ij} will be different according to the prevailing set of factor prices. This is because, given factor prices, each producer will choose the *lowest-cost* technique out of the whole set of possible techniques defined by the production function. When factor prices change, the lowest-cost technique must be presumed to change accordingly. The cost function (12.5.1), therefore, is a function showing q_i to be dependent upon the set of factor prices in what may be a complicated fashion. Factor prices determine the a_{ij}, and (12.5.1) then determines q_i.

Now consider a region R *producing in common* with another region F, say, m commodities with n factors of production. Let r factors of production be immobile; then $n–r$ factors must be mobile. Ignoring for the moment the cost of transport, trade and competition will ensure that m commodity prices $q_1, q_2, \ldots, q_m$ and $n–r$ *mobile* factor prices $p_{r+1}, \ldots, p_n$ are common to both regions. Or, to put it another way, the $m + (n–r)$ commodity and factor prices observed in F must hold also in the region R otherwise it would not be profitable to manufacture all commodities in both regions and/or mobile factors would move. Hence, using the cost functions, we have m equations

$$q_i = \sum_{j=1}^{r} p_j a_{ij} + \sum_{k=(r+1)}^{n} p_k a_{ik} \ (i = 1, \ldots, m) \qquad (12.5.2)$$

that is, in R, for each of the m commodities whose prices q_i are known from F, we have a cost function showing that the known price is equal to the total value of n factor inputs. $n–r$ of the factors have given input prices p_k determined by the prices in region F. The remaining factor prices have to be found from the equations (12.5.2).

Obviously if the great majority of factors are mobile we shall have more commodities than immobile factors. Let us suppose for the moment therefore that more commodities are actually traded than there exist immobile factors. That is, we suppose that m is greater than r.

Now it is a well-known mathematical principle that, in general, we need only r equations to determine the r unknown factor prices p_j. Consider any r of the equations (12.5.2). Since the r qs are given, we can solve for all unknown ps. The question now arises, having determined the r unknown p_js using only r of the equations (12.5.2), what will happen if we insert these newly discovered values into the remaining $m-r$ equations, together with the given factor prices p_k for the mobile factors, in order to compute the corresponding *commodity* prices (say q_t)? Will the values so determined correspond to the known commodity prices q_t for the $m-r$ commodities not needed to compute the unknown p_j? In other words, will the m equations (12.5.2) turn out to be consistent with one another, given that all commodity prices q_i and all mobile factor prices p_k are externally given?

The answer to this question is very simple. If the immobile factor prices p_j for region R, obtained by solving r of the equations (12.5.2), turn out to be the *same* as the corresponding factor prices in region F, then the equations will be consistent. The reason for this is that the identity of production functions between regions implies the identity of cost functions, for if the set of all possible techniques is everywhere the same, then for any given set of factor prices the lowest-cost technique must be the same. Hence all commodity prices will be the same. The equations (12.5.2) will be consistent when factor prices are the same in both regions R and F simply because the commodity prices q_i which are given are themselves generated by the very same cost equations and factor prices in region F.

Unfortunately it is far from certain that any or every set of r equations which can be selected from the m equations (12.5.2) has a *unique* solution. This leads to difficulties of immense proportions when all or most factors are immobile, as is the case when the 'regions' are in fact separate countries. But with the large number of mobile factors to be expected when the trading regions are within the same country, these difficulties are unlikely to arise. It is of great importance to understand fully this rather tedious logical point. We begin therefore with a numerical example.

First, note that if we have a simple equation

$$y = (x - 6)^2$$

and we are given $y = 9$ (analogous to the given commodity prices), we find that two values of x satisfy the condition

$$9 = (x - 6)^2$$

namely $x = 3$ and $x = 9$. In other words both factor prices 3 and 9 give rise equally to the commodity price 9. This fact leads to the possibility that in two trading regions, r of the traded commodity prices may be the same but immobile factor prices could conceivably be different. Indeed, in a general way we are very likely to find a good many more than two solutions to r equations in r unknowns when the form of these equations is as complex as we expect cost functions to be in practice.

If this is the case, the problem of consistency with the remaining $m-r$ equations becomes important. In fact, if there are r immobile factors whose prices are *different* in regions R and F it will usually be impossible for both regions to produce and trade more than r commodities each. The reason is that already noted. If m commodities enter into trade, then m prices must be common in all regions. Any r of these commodity prices determine the r immobile factor prices through cost equations. If these factor prices are different between regions, the remaining equations are inconsistent, that is, the remaining commodity prices must be different between regions, contradicting the assumption that the commodities concerned are traded.

This point is important enough to demand illustration by a further example. Suppose two regions R and F, each having three factors, trade three commodities. Suppose further that the three cost functions determined by production functions are:

$$q_1 = (p_1 - 6)^2 + p_2 + p_3 = £8$$

$$q_2 = p_1 + p_2 + p_3 \qquad = £14$$

$$q_3 = p_3 + 2p_1 p_2 \qquad = £30$$

for the three commodities respectively. Let the common commodity prices be £8, £14 and £30 as shown and let factor 3 be the *only* mobile factor of production, its price being £6. Suppose that in region F the factor prices p_1 and p_2 of the immobile factors are £6 and £2 respectively, which is one possible value consistent with the commodity prices quoted.

The question now is, can we be sure that factor prices in region R will be the same? We know that commodity prices must be the same because of trade and that the mobile factor 3 must be priced at £6 simply because it is mobile. Any other value for p_3 would induce a movement of factor 3 from the cheaper to the dearer region. Prices p_2 and p_3 may now be obtained by solving the first and second cost equations after substituting known prices. That is, we solve the equations

$$8 = (p_1 - 6)^2 + p_2 + 6$$

$$14 = p_1 + p_2 + 6$$

only to find that the prices $p_1 = £7$ and $p_2 = £1$ yield the required commodity prices as well as the known $p_1 = £6$ and $p_2 = £2$.

But we notice that with factor prices £7, £1 and £6 commodity price 3 as determined by the third equation would be £20 only and not £30 as assumed for region F. Or to put it another way, if q_3 is £30 in region R, as it must be if commodity 3 is traded, the third equation is consistent only if all factor prices are equalised. Evidently trade in all three commodities is possible if and only if factor prices are equalised.

Against this the reader should note that the double solution to the first and second equations opens an important alternative. Might it not be that region F, owing to the cheaper price of commodity 3 in region R, could come to specialise in the production of commodities 1 and 2 only? Commodity 3 may be manufactured *only* in region R, region F obtaining its supplies by purchase from R. In such a case different factor prices could apparently persist between regions even though commodity prices are the same, for the third equation would be inoperative in region F where commodity 3 is not produced.

12.6 THE ROLE OF FACTOR ENDOWMENTS

In order to show that, despite the possibility revealed in section 12.5, equal factor prices will ordinarily be expected *within* a country, it is necessary to give attention to the quantity aspect of production as well as the cost. This leads to some difficult but, when properly understood, very instructive argument.

We begin by reminding ourselves that a_{ij} is the amount of input of factor j required, in combination with other inputs, to manufacture one unit of the ith commodity. The total amount of the jth factor used in i is therefore $S_i a_{ij}$. Let A_j^r be the total of all factor j located in region R. We then have the following equations:

$$A_j^r = \sum_i S_i a_{ij} \text{ (for the } n \text{ factors } j = 1, 2, \ldots, n) \quad (12.6.1)$$

which state simply that the sum of all amounts of factor j used in the production of each commodity is equal to the overall total of factor j in the region. A similar set of equations exist for each region.

Consider the situation in R. Suppose first of all that the number of commodities produced, m, is greater than the number of factors employed, n. Let factor prices be given; then factor prices determine the minimum cost technique, that is, all a_{ij} of equations (12.6.1) and hence commodity prices. For the moment we take the overall factor 'endowment' of the region to be given, i.e. all A_j^r are known. This leaves the m commodity supplies S_i to be determined. Obviously none of these S_is can be negative, for negative production does not make sense. This restriction must therefore be borne in mind.

Equally obviously we cannot determine the S_is from the equations (12.6.1), for m is greater than n. To be specific, suppose there are five commodities and only three factors. We then have three equations of the type (12.6.1) to determine five unknown S_is, which is insufficient. Nevertheless the three equations which we have, plus the non-negative condition, impose severe restrictions upon the values for S_i which are admissible. Indeed, given any two Ss, say S_j and S_k, the remaining three are immediately determined completely by the three equations (12.6.1). And the value of the three S_is thus obtained may or may not turn out to be positive depending on the assigned factor prices and hence a_{ij}s.

To put the matter the other way round, for any given factor endowment not *every* factor/commodity price set is admissible. Some factor/commodity price sets may imply negative supplies, which are impossible. If region R is restricted, by the existence of a set of region F commodity prices, to production at costs equal to those in region F, there may be cases where positive production is impossible. It might be necessary to specialise in certain commodities until the number of goods actually manufactured in the region R is reduced to a figure less than the number of factors. In these circumstances factor prices are not determined fully even though commodity prices are, a fact which may be confirmed by reference to the cost equation system (12.5.1). Although restrictions on possible factor prices remain, analogous to those imposed on supply by equations (12.6.1), some degrees of freedom are left and *a range* of different sets of factor prices yield the *same* commodity prices. Accordingly the inputs a_{ij} are able to accommodate themselves to the given factor endowment in such a way as to make possible positive outputs of the reduced number of commodities.

To clarify this far from simple argument it is helpful to express diagrammatically the conclusions we have so far reached from the inspection and enumeration of equations. The reader of Book I must of course be familiar with the idea of a graph in two dimensions where the position of a point is determined by the value of two variables y and x measuring its perpendicular distance from a pair of co-ordinates. It is now necessary to imagine a three-dimensional graph with three co-ordinates placed at right-angles. A point in space thus defines three variables, one along each of the three co-ordinates. If necessary, the student may visualise two adjacent walls and the floor of a room, the point where these three surfaces meet being taken as the point of origin. Any other point in the room can then be identified by three numbers, namely, height above the floor and perpendicular distance from each of the walls.

Evidently a point on a three-dimensional graph can represent the three quantities, $S_i a_{i1}$, $S_i a_{i2}$ and $S_i a_{i3}$ of inputs 1, 2 and 3 required to produce S_i units of the ith commodity. We can accordingly show five points on the graph, one for each of five commodities produced. One

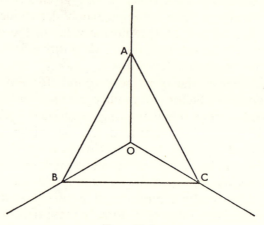

FIG. 12.1

more point also can be entered, namely, that representing the total factor endowment of the region of each of the three factors in use.

It is now convenient to imagine a flat plane placed so as to cut each of the axes of the graph at the value 1. As an aid to visualisation, we sketch this in Fig. 12.1, where ABC is the plane and O is the point of origin, that is, the corner of the imaginary room.

If a series of straight lines are now drawn, each joining the origin, O, with one of the six points of the graph, we shall have six points of intersection of these lines with the plane ABC. This is simply a procedure for transferring our six points on to the plane ABC (see Fig. 12.2).

Now consider the ratios of the amounts of any two factors, say j and k, used in any one product, say i, that is, a_{ij}/a_{ik}, and compare this with the factor endowment ratio A_j^r/A_k^r. As all S_i are positive, and as by equations (12.6.1) the factor endowments are simply the sums of factor inputs, it follows that the factor endowment ratio A_j^r/A_k^r must be smaller than the largest a_{ij}/a_{ik} for any commodity and greater than the smallest, for a fraction cannot be made greater, by adding to the top and bottom, the top and bottom numbers of another fraction which is less. In terms of the three-dimensional graph, the factor endowment point lies between the commodity point with the highest ratio of factor j to k and the commodity point with the lowest. The same must apply to the ratio of every pair of factor endowments. Furthermore, this property will be retained also by the 'shadows' of

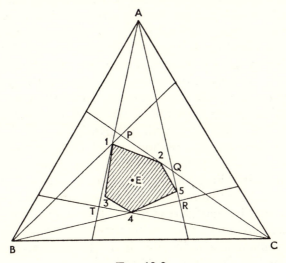

Fig. 12.2

the points graphed which appear on the plane *ABC*, for the method of transferring points on to the plane preserves ratios.

The restriction we have just noticed may be illustrated geometrically as follows. Once its meaning is understood, it is necessary only to look at the plane triangle *ABC* of Fig. 12.1, now redrawn in Fig. 12.2. The minimum-cost techniques appropriate to the given factor price configuration for each of the five commodities are entered as points 1, 2, 3, 4, 5 in Fig. 12.2. To avoid confusion with commodities, let us for the moment call the three factors *A*, *B* and *C*. Quantities of *A*, *B* and *C* are measured along axes as shown in Fig. 12.1 Thus, on Fig. 12.2, 2 is the commodity with the highest ratio of *A* to *B* and 4 is the commodity with the lowest. From the argument of the preceding paragraph it follows that the factor endowment point E must lie between straight lines joining C and 2 and C and 4 as illustrated. Similarly commodity 1 has the highest ratio A to C and 4 the lowest. E must lie between $B1$ produced and $B4$ produced. Commodity 1 has the highest ratio of B to C whilst commodity 5 has the lowest. Again E must lie between $A1$ produced and $A5$ produced. All of this means that E must lie within the polygon $1PQR4T$ if supplies are to be positive.

In fact positive supplies imply an even further restriction on the position of the factor endowment point E, for the following reason. Suppose that E were located at the point T (Fig. 12.2). In order to use up all of factors B and C, it would be necessary to use them all in commodity 1, for all other products use B and C in a lower ratio than the endowment ratio, so that if any of commodities 2 to 5 are manufactured, total usage must fall short of the total endowment. But in order to use up factors A and B in the endowment ratio defined by T, it is necessary by the same argument to produce only commodity 4, which is a contradiction. Evidently there are points even within the polygon $1PQR4T$ which, if they represent factor endowment, are inconsistent with positive S_i.

At this point we assert without proof that the positive supply condition requires that E should be within the shaded area (Fig. 12.2) bounded by straight lines joining the points 1, 2, 5, 4, 3. No proof of this is attempted for two reasons. First, we have already said enough to convince the thoughtful reader that the proposition is probably true and a lengthy, more rigorous treatment would hold up the more relevant argument. Secondly, this is a standard result which may easily be found in any book on vector analysis.

We can now see why, as previously argued, a fixed factor endowment such as E imposes a restriction upon the set of possible commodity prices, for as we change commodity prices, and hence factor prices, the position of the points 1 to 5 (Fig. 12.2) will change whilst point E remains fixed. The set of feasible commodity prices is the set for which the shaded area 'covers' the point E. By the word 'cover' we mean that E must lie inside the shaded area wherever the shaded area falls for each set of factor prices.

If E is on the boundary, say on the straight line joining 1 and 2, then the production of all commodities except 1 and 2 must be zero. Precisely at the point where the shaded area moves off of E the number of commodities which can be produced drops to two, the two commodities being determined by the numbers at either end of the boundary upon which E lies.

Now look at the problem the other way. Suppose that E lies outside the shaded area for any given commodity price configuration, and suppose further that the given commodity prices are determined by the fact that goods are available at these prices through trade. Obviously a region R cannot produce all five commodities nor indeed any at all by the given techniques if full employment of all resources is a requirement. What can happen, however, is that region R will come to specialise in two commodities or less. At this point different techniques of production are admissible even though commodity prices remain the same.

Suppose, for example, E lay at $E°$ as in Fig. 12.3. It might be possible to find two techniques, say 1° and 5° (Fig. 12.3), for commodities 1 and 5 such that $E°$ lies on a straight line joining points 1°

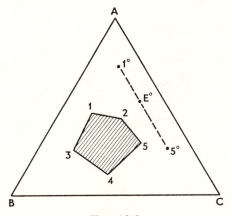

FIG. 12.3

and 5°, which is the 'shaded area' for region R, thus admitting positive supplies and at the same time satisfying cost equations at the given commodity prices. The reason why this is now possible is simply that production of fewer commodities than there exist factors enables us to determine arbitrarily as many factor prices as there are in excess of commodities and still choose the remainder so that total costs equal the given prices. Hence given commodity prices no longer imply given factor prices, and points 1 and 5 are free to move perhaps to 1° and 5° where the fixed point $E°$ lies on a straight line connecting their new positions.† It does not follow, however, that

---

† The reader with some training in mathematics may look at it this way. If two commodities are produced, we have three production equations

such an 'equilibrium' position is *bound* to exist.† It may be necessary to specialise still further to one commodity only.

One other important possibility must now be illustrated. We have already drawn attention to the fact that cost equations may have more than one solution for given commodity prices and set out a numerical example. Indeed, we should ordinarily expect multiple solutions to cost equations. The consequences of this will be that the shaded area of, say, Fig. 12.2 for any given commodity price must be expected to break up into many parts. In Fig. 12.4 we illustrate the case where two solutions can be found.

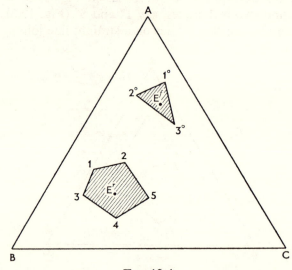

FIG. 12.4

$A_j^r = S_1 a_{1j} + S_5 a_{5j}$ for $j = 1, 2, 3$. For a solution for S_1 and S_5 to exist at all, the determinant

$$\begin{vmatrix} A_1^r & a_{11} & a_{51} \\ A_2^r & a_{12} & a_{52} \\ A_3^r & a_{13} & a_{53} \end{vmatrix}$$

must be zero which, since A_j^r is given and each a_{ji} is a function of factor prices, implies some $\phi(p_1, p_2, p_3) = 0$. In addition we have two cost equations also relating factor prices with given commodity prices. These three equations may now be solved for factor prices; hence the points $1°$ and $5°$ are identified.

† Note that the zero determinant (above note) does *not* necessarily imply positive supplies. But if the number of commodities produced is ultimately reduced to one, there exists always a positive supply which will make use of all of the factor endowment provided such factors are actually productive.

As before we have five commodities with three factors of production. Let all five commodities be produced in region R with factor endowment E^r and let commodity prices and hence factor prices in R be such that points 1 to 5 represent minimum-cost techniques for each of the five commodities. Suppose trade takes place in three commodities between regions R and F. Then these three commodity prices must be the same in both areas. Consider any three cost equations of the usual form (12.5.1) above, say for commodities 1, 2 and 3; then, given commodity prices, the set of admissible factor prices are determined for region F. One solution of the cost equations will of course yield the factor price set already operative in region R; but if the factor endowment of region F is E^f, lying outside the shaded region covering E^r, positive supplies in region F are impossible so that further specialisation would seem necessary. On the other hand if some other solution of the cost equations exists with different factor prices from those in operation in R, three new minimum-cost techniques will be determined (say $1°$, $2°$ and $3°$ as illustrated) which, with their appropriate factor prices, yield the required commodity prices and which, accordingly, could represent a trading equilibrium position provided E^f lies in the shaded region $1°$, $2°$, $3°$ (Fig. 12.4). We have in fact developed a case in which specialisation need not go quite as far as would be necessary in the absence of multiple solutions to cost equations.

Against this widening of the possibilities it should be noted, first, that not more than three commodities can ordinarily be produced in common between the two regions, for as previously explained it would be extreme coincidence if the *different* factor prices in region F, when applied to cost equations for commodities 4 and 5, generated commodity prices the same as in region R. We have again the problem of consistency of equations. Finally, we note that region R need not be producing all five commodities; it too might be led to specialise. This would occur for example if it should turn out that factor prices in F generate a cheaper commodity price 5, say, than factor prices in R. In such a case 5 would be produced in F and not in R. The shaded area in R would be reduced by the omission of 5 and that in F increased by its inclusion. Provided E^r and E^f are each covered by their respective shaded areas, a trading equilibrium is possible. The important point, we repeat, is that not more than three commodities (equal to the number of factors) can be produced simultaneously in both areas if inconsistency of equations is to be avoided.

Before attempting to re-examine the problem of factor mobility in the light of our new knowledge, it may be as well first to sum up the results for the fixed factor endowment case.

12.7 SUMMARY OF CONDITIONS FOR TRADING EQUILIBRIUM

If two regions are in a trading relation, their joint community demand and supply will determine a set of commodity prices and hence factor prices. One of the following must then hold.

1. Factor prices could be the same in both regions. In this case there is no restriction upon the number of commodities produced in common. Everything is consistent. A configuration of factor endowments in some degree coincidental is, however, implied. Factor endowment must lie in the *same* single shaded region, e.g. the polygon 12345 in Fig. 12.2.

2. Multiple solutions to cost equations are ordinarily to be expected. We may therefore have specialisation in manufacture up to the point where the *same* number of commodities are produced in common as the existing factors of production. Whether this case or case (1) will emerge depends jointly on the pattern of factor endowments and the properties of the common cost functions. Factor endowment ratios must lie in the shaded areas appropriate to the factor prices of the region (Fig. 12.4). Factor prices will *not* be equalised.

3. Specialisation in production may occur so that at most one commodity fewer can be produced simultaneously in both regions than the number of factors in use. Again, factor prices will not be equal between regions. This type of equilibrium position is a possibility whatever the factor endowment of the two regions and whether or not multiple solutions exist to cost equations (Fig. 12.3).

It is an exaggeration, but perhaps not too much of an exaggeration, to say that the greater part of our international difficulties stems directly from the fact that equilibrium in trade between countries is rarely that of case (1) above. These difficulties are not present within countries simply because case (1) ordinarily obtains.

If factor prices were everywhere equal there could be no such thing as a relatively underdeveloped territory. All would be equally 'developed'. Standards of living throughout the world would have been brought precisely into line long before 'colonialism' could have had time to become an ugly word. In no case would it be possible for 'protectionists' to argue that their industry should be shielded by tariffs from the 'unfair' competition of 'sweated labour', for all labour would be equally sweated. One suspects that in such a world even the balance of payments problem would be more tractable when one reflects upon the complete absence of such a problem between Birmingham and Brighton. This happy state of affairs is not entirely due to the non-existence of a government in Brighton willing and able to encourage Brightonians to spend more than the value of their product.

In view of the obvious lack of correspondence between the facts we actually observe and the equal factor price world described in the previous paragraph, it is disturbing that more than a few economists have allowed themselves to be persuaded (by arguments which, for this very reason, must be carefully considered in a later chapter) that trade in commodities is at least in part a substitute for factor mobility. Although statements to this effect may be found in the majority of modern texts on the subject, we shall argue the opposite. Indeed, what seems superficially remarkable to the present writer is the fact that within countries, despite the obvious immobility of some factors, factor prices do seem to be so much in line with one another in different regions. This is the phenomenon we hope to be able to explain with the aid of the techniques so laboriously introduced above and a theorem which must now be developed.

12.8 A Basic Theorem

First, let us suppose that the axes of Fig. 12.1 refer only to the *immobile* factors. We need not be concerned in the diagram with factors which are mobile. Now consider all commodities which enter into trade. Let q_j be the price of an export, j, from region R and let q_j' be the price (cost) of j in region F if it were produced with the going factor prices in F. One thing we can be sure of is that q_j is less than or equal to q_j' which we write:

$$q_j \leqq q_j'$$

for if we had

$$q_j > q_j'$$

it would not be profitable to import j into F. For commodities, say k, which are produced *in common* in both countries we have

$$q_k = q_k'$$

whilst for imports into R we have

$$q_i' \leqq q_i$$

Note especially that although the statement that prices of commodities produced in common are equal implies that transport costs are negligible, we do not really need this for the argument which follows. The statements about exports and imports still hold. The point we are about to make, however, comes out more clearly if we begin by supposing transport costs to be negligible for the moment.

Now consider Fig. 12.4. We are about to show that if we include as points of the type 1, 2, 3, 4, etc., all commodities which enter into trade and are *produced* in R, and as points of type 1°, 2°, 3°, etc., all commodities traded which are *produced* in F *whether commodity prices are equal or not, i.e. whether produced in common or not, then it is impossible that the two shaded areas should overlap unless factor prices are equal.*

We prove this proposition by assuming the contrary and by showing that such an assumption immediately leads to a contradiction. Suppose, therefore, that the two shaded regions of Fig. 12.4 do in fact overlap but that factor prices are different although commodity prices satisfy the conditions for a trading relation. Clearly, when there is overlap we can choose a single factor endowment of immobile factors, say E (Fig. 12.5), such that when the point E is transferred to the plane ABC (see section 12.6) it lies simultaneously in *both* shaded areas. The endowment of mobile factors can be chosen at will and need not be the same in R and F. This means that there can exist two imaginary regions R and F with the *same* endowment of immobile factors, being in a trading relationship with one another but with different factor prices.

Being in a trading relationship implies, as stated above,

$$q_j \leqq q_j' \quad \text{for exports from } R$$

$$q_i' \leqq q_i \quad \text{for imports into } R$$

$$q_k = q_k' \quad \text{for commodities produced in common.}$$

Furthermore we need not worry about k, for commodities produced in common are either imports or exports and may be thus subsumed in j or i.

From the ordinary cost equation for goods produced in R we have, including mobile factors,

$$\sum_s p_s A_{rs} = q_r S_r \qquad (12.8.1)$$

where S_r is total output of commodity r and A_{rs} as before is the total input of factor s required for the output of S_r units of r. Adding together all the equations of this kind for each of the r commodities, we have

$$\sum_r \sum_s p_s A_{rs} = \sum_r q_r S_r \qquad (12.8.2)$$

which says simply that the total value of all inputs, *this time including mobile factors*, is equal to the total value of output. Similarly in region F we have

$$\sum_r \sum_s p'_s A'_{rs} = \sum_r q'_r S'_r \qquad (12.8.3)$$

Now suppose that factor prices p'_s in region F actually applied in region R, where S_r is produced with inputs A_{rs}. One thing is certain: since q'_r, the product price in F, is the lowest possible cost when factor prices are p'_s, then commodity prices in R which would exist with factor prices p'_s and techniques A_{rs} cannot be less than those which exist in F or would exist in F if the commodity were produced there with a minimum-cost technique. Hence we may write:

$$\sum_r \sum_s p'_s A_{rs} \geqq \sum_r q'_r S_r \qquad (12.8.4)$$

All that (12.8.4) says in effect is that total cost of all production, if one uses techniques which may not be minimum-cost, may be more and certainly cannot be less than output valued at the lowest possible commodity prices given factor prices. Moreover, we know from the price conditions to be satisfied by two countries in a trading relationship that

$$q'_r \geqq q_r$$

if r is a commodity produced in region R. Note that it is not necessary that the commodity should actually be produced in region F. q'_r is simply the minimum possible cost if it were produced. Thus we have, from (12.8.4),

$$\sum_r \sum_s p'_s A_{rs} \geqq \sum_r q'_r S_r \geqq \sum_r q_r S_r \qquad (12.8.5)$$

By a similar argument it follows also that

$$\sum_r \sum_s p_s A'_{rs} \geqq \sum_r q'_r S'_r \qquad (12.8.6)$$

Subtracting the inequality (12.8.5) from (12.8.2) and the equality (12.8.3) from (12.8.6) yields

$$\sum_r \sum_s (p_s - p'_s) A_{rs} \leqq 0 \qquad (12.8.7)$$

and $$\sum_r \sum_s (p_s - p'_s)A'_{rs} \geqq 0 \qquad (12.8.8)$$

We may now sum the left-hand sides of (12.8.7) and (12.8.8) as follows. In each case the left-hand side in words is the difference in total value of all factors of production in the region valued first at region R factor prices and second at those of region F. Let the total endowment of the sth factor in R, whether mobile or immobile, be T_s; then

$$\sum_r \sum_s (p_s - p'_s)A_{rs} = \sum_s T_s(p_s - p'_s) \leqq 0$$

Similarly for region F we have

$$\sum_r \sum_s (p_s - p'_s)A'_{rs} = \sum_s T'_s(p_s - p'_s) \geqq 0$$

But another condition for equilibrium between two countries is that the prices of mobile factors of production should be the same. For mobile factors $(p_s - p'_s)$ must be zero, so that mobile factors may be dropped from the condition above leaving

$$\sum_s E_s(p_s - p'_s) \leqq 0$$

and $$\sum_s E_s(p_s - p'_s) \geqq 0$$

where E_s is the endowment of the sth immobile factor of production which, by assumption, is the same in both regions. Thus it must be true that

$$\sum_s E_s(p_s - p'_s) = 0 \qquad (12.8.9)$$

We now recall that the factor endowment point E was chosen quite arbitrarily subject only to the restriction that it must be a point within the region of overlap of the two shaded areas (Fig. 12.5) if such an area of overlap exists. Provided only that we exclude the irrelevant and exceptional case where the area of overlap is no more than a single point, it is always possible to vary E within limits for any given set of factor prices p and p' subject still to the requirement that (12.8.9) should be satisfied. That is, (12.8.9) must be satisfied for any E within limits. This is possible only if each $p_s = p'_s$ so that $p_s - p'_s = 0$. Thus if there is overlap, and if the conditions for a trading equilibrium are to be met, factor prices must be identical in both regions both for mobile and immobile factors. We must be in case (1) of section 12.7.

It is important to note carefully what we have now proved. Our proposition is one about the possible configuration of prices and corresponding techniques of production which in no way depends upon all commodities being traded or absence of transport costs, or even upon factor endowments. What we have is a theorem quite beyond any conclusion intuitively obvious, which says:

Theorem

Let the factor prices p_m and p'_m of each mobile factor be the same in two regions R and F. Let type j commodities be those produced in region R, so that

$$\text{minimum } q_j \leqq q'_j$$

where q'_j is the lowest possible cost at which j could be or is produced in F with factor prices p'. Similarly, let type i commodities be those produced in F satisfying the condition

$$\text{minimum } q'_i \leqq q_i$$

where q_i is the lowest possible cost at which i could be or is produced in R with factor prices p.

If now there exists a single factor endowment which *could* be assigned to regions R and F instead of those already existing in R and F which would permit positive quantities of commodities of type j to be produced in R and positive quantities of i to be produced in F without change of technique, then *all* factor prices must be the same in R as in F whatever the *actual* factor endowments in R and F.

Note especially that equal factor prices is a necessary condition even if there is complete specialisation. There is no assumption in the above argument that any commodity is produced simultaneously in both regions. What this means in effect is that if there is specialisation in production, shaded regions *cannot* overlap. For example, in Fig. 12.3 the line 1°,5° cannot overlap the shaded polygon.

The theorem set out gives us in fact an important clue as to the actual consequences of two regions entering into trade. Let A, B and C in Fig. 12.5 represent immobile factors as in Fig. 12.4, and let the points 1, 2, 3 and 1°, 2°, 3° indicate the techniques of production for commodities at the going factor prices *before* trade, whatever these may be, in regions R and F respectively. We assume that all mobile factor prices have been equalised before trade by factor movements. If the triangles overlap, there must be at least a tendency towards factor price equalisation on the opening-up of trade. It is easy to see this, as follows. Commodity prices are determined by factor prices (given production functions) and commodity prices alone determine which commodities are traded and in which direction. Hence no matter what the factor endowment, the immediate change in commodity prices will be the same. The overlap permits us to assign a factor endowment E for both regions R and F lying in the interior of both triangles. In such a case we know from the theorem above that

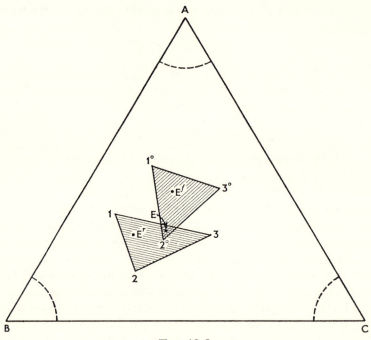

FIG. 12.5

in the final equilibrium factor prices must be the same in both regions.

This follows from the fact that however the triangles 1, 2, 3 and 1°, 2°, 3° change their position with changing factor prices, E must always lie in their interior, for E must always be a weighted average of techniques in use. Hence the two triangles must always have a region of overlap whatever the going factor prices so that they must overlap also in the final equilibrium. But by our central theorem this implies full and complete factor price equalisation.

As a matter of fact this conclusion is by itself intuitively obvious, for if the regions R and F have identical factor endowments they are economically speaking identical regions from the point of view of cost. Their price patterns can differ only if their respective populations demand different things, i.e. if tastes differ. The opening-up of trade is equivalent to replacing the pattern of private regional demand with a common world demand. In such circumstances similar price patterns will naturally emerge.

The really important point, however, is not that in the special case of identical factor endowments full factor price equalisation is implied, but rather that, if it is implied, the first step towards equilibrium must be towards factor price equalisation whatever the factor endowments of the regions R and F. In any particular case R and F will not have a common factor endowment E. Rather we should expect two distinct factor endowments, say E^r and E^f (Fig. 12.5). Even so, the fact of the overlap and hence the possible existence of E implies that the initial movement of factor prices must be towards equality. Indeed, this movement must continue until one or other or both of E^f and E^r lie in the boundary of their respective shaded areas. Suppose E^f now lies on the new position of the line 1°, 3°. In this case production of 2 in region F must be zero. The point 2° is dropped and the weighted averages of inputs into commodities *in production* would no longer overlap.

In general, of course, many more commodities than three will be in production. Any commodity can be supposed dropped from production provided it leaves the factor endowment in the interior of the figure obtained by joining all points representing production techniques for commodities remaining in production. As long as the resulting areas have an overlap, the process of factor price equalisation will continue. As soon as they cease to overlap we cease to be sure that equalisation will continue. It may do so, but we cannot show that it must.

The fundamental theorem quoted above, besides suggesting the valuable result just noted, also tells us something of the mechanism of adjustment. Consider again Fig. 12.5. Let the points 1, 2, 3 and 1°, 2°, 3°, unlike those of our earlier discussion, represent all commodities produced and not just those which can be traded. Suppose that R and F have different factor prices and are about to enter into trade for the first time. If we exclude from the region R shaded area those commodities whose price in R is higher than the corresponding price in F, at the same time excluding from the F shaded area those whose price in F is higher than the corresponding price in R, the conditions for a trading equilibrium are satisfied by the remaining commodities. Since factor prices are not equal, there can be no overlap, i.e. it must be impossible to choose a single point which is simultaneously a weighted average of the residual commodity techniques in both R and F.

From the diagram it is easy to see what this means. Either the point $2°$ must be dropped to ensure no overlap, or 3 or 1 or any combination of the three. It follows either that the price of commodity 2 is higher in F than in R, or commodities 1 or 3 or both have higher prices in R than in F. Hence when trade begins R must export 2 and import 3 or 1. R will in fact produce more of 2 and/or less of 3 or 1. In F the opposite will be the case. But E^r must remain a weighted average of the points 1, 2 and 3, the weight being proportional to the quantity produced of each commodity. To satisfy this condition, the point 2 (more produced) must move towards the factor endowment point, since it now has greater weight, whilst 1 and 3 move away. Similarly points $1°$ and $3°$ move towards E^f whilst $2°$ moves away.

Evidently the region of overlap grows greater with trade. The two triangles (Fig. 12.5) tend if anything to come together. This coming together will lead to one or other of a number of possibilities. Either of the two triangles may come to overlap the factor endowment point of the other region (factor endowment points of course remain stationary), in which case factor price equalisation will be complete. Case (1) of section 12.7 will obtain. Alternatively the line $1°, 3°$ may come up against E^f, in which case production of commodity 2 in F must be zero and the point $2°$ drops out. Or again, 1, 2 or 2, 3 may reach E^r, in which case either point 1 or 3 disappears. In either of these events we are in case (3) of section 12.7 where there is specialisation in production. More general cases with more commodities are more complex but the principle is the same.

It should be particularly noted that the converse of our fundamental theorem is not true. If areas like the triangles of Fig. 12.5 do *not* at any time overlap, we cannot be sure whether trade will draw them together or push them apart. It is just as easy in fact to construct quite ordinary examples where, before trade, the areas do not overlap and where the opening-up of trade sends them further apart, as it is to construct examples where the figures come together despite the fact that they do not overlap initially. Unfortunately we do not have in the work above any simple criterion which will enable us to make informed guesses about the movements of factor prices. A great deal depends, as we have already suggested and as we shall see in a later chapter, on whether or not more than one solution exists to certain sets of equations. It will be argued in fact that many solutions are likely and it is precisely this which gives rise to the cases (2) and (3) of section 12.7. But for case (2) a great deal might be said on the probable effects of government policy upon factor prices, on purely *a priori* grounds and without the need for numerical investigation, precisely on the lines of Book I. As it is, however, we shall have reluctantly to conclude that in a general way nothing can be said, and that a great deal of what has been said is without proper foundation in fact. A method of dealing with the problem numerically will be proposed.

12.9 BACK TO THE DISTINCTION BETWEEN INTERNATIONAL AND INTER-REGIONAL TRADE

Against the pessimistic conclusion above we do have in the foregoing analysis a bonus on top of some understanding of the operation of the adjusting mechanism. It is possible to present an argument running in terms of probability which may be thought to settle the central question of this chapter, namely, why do we get factor price equalisation between regions but not between countries?

To see this, we remind ourselves again that the factors of Fig. 12.5 are immobile factors only. Mobile factors are not included. What we are likely to have, in the case of trade within a country, is many more commodities produced than factors which are immobile. In Fig. 12.5 we have illustrated the case of three commodities and three immobile factors. As we are limited by our diagrammatic approach to three dimensions, let us consider the effect of variations in relative numbers of commodities and factors first by reducing the number of commodities, leaving the number of factors at three. Let there be one and only one commodity; then the technique of production used in its manufacture before trade will be represented by a single point in the triangle *ABC*.

Now in the ordinary way the technique in use before trade will be determined by factor endowment and, in the case of more than one commodity, upon consumers' order of preference for commodities and upon the nature of production functions (i.e. the laws of physics). And we have little or no *a priori* information about the way these basic determinants occur. If this were all, we should have to recognise that only ignorance can be inferred from ignorance and resist the temptation, common in some quarters, to assign equal probabilities to events about whose probability distribution we have no evidence.

In the present case, however, there is a cause operating which we know will influence probabilities *whatever* the probability distributions of the basic determinants, namely, the difference between numbers of commodities and immobile factors which is the subject of the present discussion. To trace the role of these differences in numbers it is convenient to assign arbitrarily a probability for the occurence of each particular input proportion (technique) and to study the 'model' so developed. We begin therefore by supposing that each point in ABC (Fig. 12.5) is equally likely to represent the technique point for a single commodity before trade in some region R. Then the probability that a region F will, before trade, use the same technique is statistically speaking zero, that is to say the probability of 'overlap' in the sense in which we have been using it is, with one commodity, minute. For two points to overlap, they must be the same point.

On the other hand if we have two commodities produced in each region, then the 'shaded areas' corresponding are the straight lines joining the two given points in each region. If two lines are drawn joining pairs of points randomly allocated to the triangle ABC, the probability that they intersect is much greater than zero. If we have three commodities, the weighted averages of techniques will ordinarily be triangles, as in Fig. 12.5, with an even greater probability of intersection. More commodities still generate polygons with a high (but decreasing) probability that the area covered by each polygon increases as another commodity is added. The probability of intersection increases as the area of the polygon increases.

Now consider the effect of decreasing the number of immobile factors to illustrate what happens when the dimension of the immobile factor 'space' changes. If there are no more than two immobile factors, the triangle ABC collapses into a single line. Technique points must now be distributed over a line instead of a triangle. Weighted averages of techniques form a line, and two lines lying in a line necessarily overlap if they are long enough. Direction no longer matters; the probability of overlap is much increased. Finally, if no more than one immobile factor exists, the triangle ABC reduces to a single point. All techniques lie in the point so that overlap is inevitable. All factor prices must be equalised.

The general conclusion is of course that the greater the excess of commodities produced over immobile factors, the greater the probability of factor price equalisation. It may well be, therefore, that we note equal factor prices within countries, but not between countries, simply because many more factors are mobile within countries than are mobile between countries. This has two effects. First, mobile factor prices are equalised before trade in any case, and second, when a high proportion of factors are mobile, then there must be *ipso facto* a higher ratio of commodities produced to immobile factors and hence the probability of factor price equalisation by trade is much enhanced.

The extreme case where one factor only is immobile is of particular interest. Of course the result in this case is obvious without the elaborate argument foregoing. Indeed, it was pointed out at the outset that with no more than one immobile factor any commodity produced must be cheaper where the immobile factor is cheap and dearer where it is dear. Demand for the product from the cheap source will raise the commodity price there and the ensuing 'profit' will accrue to the immobile factor so that its price will rise to equality with that in the dear source. Note that the 'excess profit' cannot be absorbed by a mobile factor since the reward of mobile factors must always be the same between regions.

The special interest of the single immobile factor case lies in the fact that it is tempting to conjecture that, for each region within a country, not more than one immobile factor is ordinarily to be expected. Everything depends upon what is meant by the word 'region', for it seems likely that (again within a country) the greater part of the class of immobile factors is made up of land of various qualities so that, if the region is taken small enough, almost by definition of a 'region' only one immobile factor can exist. A country could in fact be divided into areas where land is of a given quality in a given environment. We should then conclude at once that factor-prices would, in the absence of transport costs, be completely equalised throughout the country.

On the other hand we should not, from this argument, suppose that all the work of this chapter has been a waste of time, for at least two reasons. First, it is easy to construct a plausible case where two or more immobile factors exist which cannot be eliminated by reduction of the size of the region. Furthermore, the more we reduce the size of the region and hence the number of immobile factors, the more we reduce the number of commodities produced. Second, we have gained valuable insight into the working of the international trade mechanism between countries where many factors are immobile and where by definition of a country we cannot reduce the size of the region. We shall expand briefly on both these points.

Consider two regions *R* and *F* each consisting of meadow land suitable for grazing cattle, but also with a hill with grass which will feed only sheep. Suppose also that there are coal deposits in both regions which underlie both the grazing land and the hill, but it is impossible, or at least inconvenient, to sink the mine shaft on the hill. Here we have three distinct *immobile* factors of production in both regions in a case where it is impossible to subdivide the regions any further. The pit-head must be either in the meadow or on the hill, and wherever it is sited coal would be drawn from a region different from that in which the pit is located if meadow and hill land were separately considered. We assume also that labour and capital are present as mobile factors. It is instructive to develop a diagram as Fig. 12.5 for this case.

Let *A* be hill land, *B* meadow land and *C* coal deposits. E^r and E^f may take the positions shown in Fig. 12.5, since both regions are endowed with some of each factor. On the other hand, if commodity 1 represents sheep then both points 1 and 1° must lie on the line *AB*, for coal deposits are not used in the production of sheep whatever the factor prices. Similarly, if commodity 2 represents cattle the points 2 and 2° also must lie on *AB*. Furthermore, hill land is of little use for cattle so that however cheap hill land may become neither 2 nor 2° on *AB* will ever move outside of, say, the area around *B* bounded by the dotted line (Fig. 12.5). The same may be said of sheep on meadow land owing to the risk of disease, although perhaps with less force. 1 and 1° will probably lie on *AB* within, say, the dotted line around *A* (Fig. 12.5). Again the production of coal uses little land, however cheap it may be. 3 and 3° will lie near *C* within the dotted line although this time not confined to the boundary of *ABC*, since either or all three factors may conceivably be used to mine coal.

The interesting conclusion which can be inferred at once from our central theorem is that factor prices in this case must be completely equalised between regions *R* and *F*. Clearly it is impossible that all factors should be in use without some coal at least being produced in both regions together with some sheep and/or some cattle. As the figure is now drawn it is impossible that weighted averages of techniques should not intersect whatever the factor prices and hence techniques chosen. No equilibrium is possible except full factor price equalisation.

It is worth noting especially that if in any one region there is associated with each immobile factor a commodity *in production* which uses some of its own immobile factor and little or nothing of any other, there is a strong presumption of factor price equalisation whatever the situation in its trading partner. This is because weighted averages of techniques used in the region concerned must cover all possible techniques, at all factor prices. The 'shaded area' for the given region must cover the greater part of ABC so that there must always be overlap.

Again, if two regions continue to produce at the same time, whatever the pattern of prices, any one commodity which uses any one immobile factor and nothing at all of any other immobile factor, then factor price equalisation is inevitable. For in this case some vertex like C in Fig. 12.5 is always included in the shaded areas of both regions whatever the factor prices, so that the vertex itself constitutes a point of overlap.

All or any of these ideas are applicable to trade between countries as well as trade between regions, and it is this which justifies the claim made above that the work of this chapter gives insight into the basic causes of trade. Too much, however, should not be read into the results quoted. It is one thing to carry out this kind of exercise when the number of immobile factors is small and the number of commodities large. It is quite another to attempt to infer anything at all on *a priori* grounds when there are many immobile factors, as is the case between countries. All the actual empirical evidence we have suggests that for many countries factor endowment and hence factor price patterns are so different that intersection is unlikely. With many mmobile factors we have many vertices like AB and C (Fig. 12.5) and many dimensions. Weighted averages of techniques in use for each country are likely to 'cover' only a relatively small area of the available many-dimensional 'space'. Overlap is much less likely, in which case nothing can be said as to the probable effects of trade on factor prices without numerical inquiry, as explained in later chapters. Furthermore, in the case of trade between countries transport costs become much more important, with consequences we must now briefly comment upon.

12.10 TRANSPORT COSTS

Necessary conditions for the existence of a trading relationship as given above (section 12.8) are:

$$q_j \leqq q_j' \qquad \text{for exports from the home country}$$
$$q_i' \leqq q_i \qquad \text{for imports from abroad}$$
$$q_k = q_k' \qquad \text{for commodities produced in common.}$$

The corresponding conditions when we recognise the existence of transportation costs are:

$$(a)\ q_j + t_j \leqq q_j' \qquad \text{for exports from the home country}$$

$$(b)\ q_i' + t_i \leqq q_i \qquad \text{for imports from abroad}$$

and $\quad (c)\ q_k + t_k = q_k' \big]$ for commodities produced in common

or $\qquad\qquad q_s' + t_s = q_s \big]$ and traded

where t_i is the cost of transport of one unit of the ith commodity. (In the interpretation of these conditions the reader is reminded that the qs here are costs of production. Where the item concerned is not actually produced, the market price will be different from cost.)

If this were all, the situation with transport costs would be no different from that of section 12.8, for the 'with transport costs' conditions imply the 'without transport cost' conditions. Unfortunately, where transport is not costless a fourth class of commodities may be produced in common, namely those where

$$(d)\ q_r + t_r > q_r' \text{ and } q_r' + t_r > q_r$$

These are the non-traded commodities. As explained in Chapter 11 (Book I) transport costs eliminate trade in items satisfying (d). We have to ask how far this possibility modifies the argument so far presented.

Notice first that, if we eliminate from consideration all those commodities for which (d) holds, the theorem of section 12.8 may be applied to those which remain, for the conditions (a)–(c) imply those of section 12.8. Since factor prices can never be equal where transport costs exist,† it follows that, if the set of all weighted averages of techniques in use abroad in the production of all commodities except those satisfying (d) overlaps the set of all weighted averages of techniques used in the home country excluding those satisfying (d), then there must exist at least one commodity in production abroad satisfying (a) and/or one commodity in production at home satisfying (b). The situation cannot be one of equilibrium. Production of the 'maverick' commodities must be falling and the 'shaded areas' coming together. Hence factor prices will become more equal.

Notice that this pressure to equalise factor prices must tend to equalise q_j and q_j' in category (a) and q_i' and q_i in category (b). That is, it will tend to eliminate items from (a) and (b) and switch them to (c) or (d). In the same way more equal factor prices will tend to switch

† Because commodity prices cannot be equal.

items from category (c) to category (d). As long as 'overlap' persists, more and more items will appear in (d) and fewer in (a) and (b). In the end we shall have all items in (c) and (d). This corresponds to case (1) in section 12.7.

Attention is drawn, however, to an important difference from case (1). If there are no more than m immobile factors there cannot, except by extreme coincidence, be more than m items in category (c). For if we have m equations of the type

$$q_i = q_i' + t_i$$

or

$$q_j' = q_j + t_j$$

and if we take all world prices q_i' and q_j' and all mobile factor prices as given, then the remaining m immobile factor prices are determined by the m conditions (c). Since these factor prices *must* be different from the corresponding prices abroad (because of the existence of t), it would be highly coincidental if any more equations of category (c) could be satisfied. Since nothing can be in (a) or (b), the remaining commodities fall into category (d). Far from making all commodities 'tradeable' as in case (1) of section 12.7, we have all commodities excluded from trade except a certain number equal to the number of immobile factors.

Again, it should be observed that those commodities which hang on longest in category (c) will be those with the lowest transport costs. Hence it will tend to be the m commodities with the lowest transport costs per unit which determine ultimately the difference between factor prices in two regions, given that the analogue of case (1) of section 12.7 holds.

On the other hand cases (2) and (3) of section 12.7 are still very much with us. At any time factor endowments may be such that specialisation is induced as explained in section 12.7. Items may remain in categories (a) and (b) provided there is specialisation, and for this reason many more commodities may continue to be traded than there exist immobile factors, provided only that 'shaded areas' do not intersect. Furthermore, if 'shaded areas' do not intersect before the opening-up of trade, there is no reason whatever to expect that there will be any movement towards the equalisation of factor prices. Factor prices may become less equal. In this case we no longer have any reason to believe that those commodities with the lowest transport costs are necessarily traded or even that they play any special part in the determination of factor prices. It is easy to construct cases where items in category (*c*) have much higher transport costs than those in either (*a*), (*b*) or (*d*).

12.11 CONCLUSIONS

We may now summarise the conclusions of this chapter. First, we noted that, although it was established in Book I that trade will take place whenever *relative* costs are different between countries and that overall 'inefficiency' or 'lack of productivity', for whatever reason, does not of itself inhibit trade, nothing had, up to this point, been said about the reasons for difference in *relative* prices before trade. The work of the present chapter now makes it clear that there are two main causes of differences in relative prices. These are:

(i) Differences in factor endowment ratios.
(ii) Differences in consumer preferences in different regions.

The analysis of the effect of (i) above is particularly informative provided care is taken to interpret differences in skill and education and perhaps even differences in effort per hour of the labour force in various countries as differences in factor endowment. That is, skilled labour is different from unskilled labour, and similarly land with one kind of climate is different from land with another. This particular approach was defended against alternatives.

Many of the world's problems arise because factors of production are not, or are only imperfectly, mobile across the boundaries of countries. The more mobile are factors of production, the more alike in their production activity countries become.

We should look for two kinds of situations in international trade. First, there are countries whose relative factor endowments are similar. Here we should expect the same sorts of commodities to be produced. Trade will tend to take place in the same number of commodities as there exist immobile factors of production. With moderate transport costs many goods will be non-traded. Factor prices will be much about the same in both areas. Advanced industrialised countries with a well-educated labour force and similar climatic conditions would settle into an equilibrium of this kind.

Second, we have the case where factor endowments are very different between trading regions. Here almost anything can happen. If the number of immobile factors of production is small relative to the total number of different kinds of factor, and if at the same time transport costs are generally very low, we should look for a high degree of specialisation in production with factor prices the same between regions. The typical case would be local trade within a country, say that between Birmingham and Brighton. If transport costs are high and a high proportion of factors are immobile, we must expect a moderate degree of specialisation with very different factor prices between countries. Commodities traded and produced in common cannot exceed the number of immobile factors.

It is of course a great pity that there is more than one possibility. If we could be sure that trade equalised factor prices, we could at once be confident of the probable outcome of various kinds of government policy. As it is, nothing can be said without a great deal more knowledge. The problem is not difficult, however, once we have numerical estimates of certain important parameters. We shall show in later chapters how factor price changes may be computed.

EXERCISES

1. Study the diagram for the two-factor/two-commodity model presented in the article 'The Factor Price Equalisation Myth' (Pearce, *Review of Economic Studies* [9]). Show by means of this diagram that it is impossible to satisfy the conditions for an international trade equilibrium with one country producing two commodities and a second country specialising in one commodity only, if the factor endowment ratio capital/labour for country 2 is greater than the ratio of capital/labour used in the production of commodity 1 in country 1 and less than the ratio capital/labour used in the production of commodity 2. Hence confirm the basic theorem of section 12.8 for this special case.

2. Note that with a two-factor/two-commodity model the triangle *ABC* of Fig. 12.5 reduces to a single line *BC* and the 'shaded areas' become segments of that line. Using the diagram referred to in exercise 1, construct a case where factor prices become less equal on the opening-up of trade between two countries and show that in the case you have constructed 'shaded areas' do not overlap. Construct also a case where 'shaded areas' do not overlap at the moment of opening up trade but where, nevertheless, factor prices do tend to be equalised by trade.

3. Referring again to the diagram and article of exercise 1, show that in every case (two factors/two commodities) where trade can

cause factor prices to diverge instead of moving towards equality there must exist at least one factor price ratio for which the line segment (analogous to the shaded areas of Fig. 12.5) reduces to a single point only even though two commodities may continue to be produced.

4. Reconsider section 12.10. Retrace the proof of the basic theorem of section 12.8, this time including transport costs explicitly. Assume that transport is itself a commodity with zero transport cost. Show that the theorem of section 12.8 still holds provided we exclude from consideration all commodities in category (d) of section 12.10.

5. Using again the basic geometry of exercise 1, construct a three-commodity/two-factor model. Show diagrammatically that, in the absence of transport costs, at least one commodity must be dropped from production by one country. Now introduce transport costs appropriately and construct a case where trade takes place in commodities with high transport costs but is obstructed for one commodity with low transport costs.

6. Examine, in the light of the remarks in section 12.11, the nature of trade
    (a) between the U.K. and Western Europe, and
    (b) between the U.K. and India.
Suitable figures are published by the U.K. Board of Trade in the Overseas Trade Accounts.

13 On Measuring Policy Gains or Losses

13.1 An Historical Note

IT is of course impossible for any government not to have an economic policy, for to do nothing is to have a policy. It is alarming to reflect therefore that there exists only a narrow class of policy changes which we can confidently expect to meet with universal approval. This is the class of changes which makes *everybody* better off. If a policy change makes one group of persons better off and one group worse off, we can be fairly sure that it will be opposed by some. Furthermore, when some may gain and some may lose it is quite impossible to find any objective principle upon which to decide whether we ought to favour the pros or the cons.

One distinguished writer has said that only an 'excess of philosophy' could lead anyone to doubt that it is a 'good' thing to take a crust of bread from a city alderman at a public banquet and give it to a starving beggar; and perhaps this is so. But we can never be quite sure how deserving the alderman is and how much he may be enjoying his crust, nor can we know to what extent the condition of the starving beggar reflects 'just' punishment for his obstinate refusal to conform to the accepted standards of society.

Of course we could find out some of these things and perhaps make a judgement. Society in fact continually does precisely this to a greater or less degree. Everyone has some idea about what is 'fair', and these ideas play a great part in, say, the fixing of taxes. The same applies to certain kinds of wage negotiations. No economist will dispute that policy can affect the distribution of real wealth between individuals, and indeed this is usually one of the objects of policy. The important thing to remember about activity of this kind, however, is that it is purely a matter of deciding what is justice. No economic principles are involved. On the other hand economists should play and have played an important part in explaining the probable consequences of attempts to achieve justice or in explaining why this or that policy may have unforeseen consequences relevant to problems of right and wrong. It is also true of course that economists are led by their training not to overlook points which might otherwise be missed. All of this can be well illustrated by reference to controversy in the field of international trade, and it is the purpose of this chapter to review related arguments which are far from easy to understand. Common sense is not always a sufficient qualification for a choice of 'right' action.

Let us begin by asking the obvious. Is international trade desirable? In particular, is it desirable in the only sense in which an economist can say for certain it is desirable – that is, does it make *everyone* better off? Looking back on the course of history many curious and differing views on this question have from time to time prevailed, most of them based on something much less than half of the truth.

In the days, for example, when gold and wealth seemed to be synonymous terms and when gold and silver were the most important forms of money, it appeared obvious to some writers that foreign trade must be unambiguously a good thing, for foreign trade was then the only source of 'wealth'. A surplus on the balance of payments created an inflow of gold, i.e. wealth. In these circumstances and on this narrow definition of gain, trade could not benefit both parties. The country with a surplus could earn gold only at the expense of some other country with a trading deficit.

Later this 'Mercantilist' view came to be replaced by argument which shifted the emphasis away from the gold acquired towards the enjoyment of the commodities traded. The exchange of commodities must lead to some kind of gain for both parties, otherwise there would be no agreement to exchange. A more sophisticated version of this approach traced the source of mutual gain to the fact that commodities could, if there is trade, be wholly produced in the region with the lowest manufacturing cost.

One is tempted to seize upon this fairly obvious truth as an example of the exceptional case where everybody gains. Trade is then seen as unambiguously good and should not be interfered with. But other commentators noted that growth and development of trading partners induces change at home. Some industries advance and others decline. An industry experiencing difficult times looks for a scapegoat and finds it in 'unfair' foreign competition. We hear the suggestion that countries whose wages are low have a competitive advantage over countries whose wages are high and that the importation of commodities produced by cheap labour will have the effect either of creating unemployment or of reducing the standard of living of industrial labour at home.

The reader who has come this far will realise at once that many of the arguments above are based upon a less than perfect understanding of the working of the competitive system or at best upon rather doubtful assumptions. The work of preceding chapters does, however, suggest that there is usually some underlying element of truth in almost every argument. For example, we have noted the possibility that trade in commodities equalises factor prices so that wages must fall relatively in one country and rise relatively in another. On the other hand it is far from obvious even where wages fall that a real loss for any section of the community is implied, for the gains from trade may outweigh the loss wherever it is experienced. How in fact does one decide where the whole truth lies? Whatever we may say about the advantages of buying cheap through trade, if one section of the community is bound to lose in real terms we must hesitate before we say that trade is unambiguously good. But hesitation is not necessarily rejection.

Again, in an earlier chapter we have shown that a tariff on imports improves welfare in the tariff-imposing country. Some interference with trade therefore seems *per se* to be an advantage to the country raising the tariff. The fact that this advantage is bought at the expense of the foreign country may or may not be an argument against it. Much depends upon whether policy is to be directed solely to the advantage of the policy-maker or whether it is designed to be to the advantage of all.

Finally, we note in modern times a resurgence of Mercantilism in a different guise. Every country aims at a surplus on its balance of payments, and hence at the accumulation of large reserves of gold and foreign currency, not because it is any longer thought that gold is the only form of wealth, but because large reserves are seen as a source of strength. When foreign currency and gold holdings are limited, some government policy, which may otherwise be considered desirable, e.g. encouragement of consumer spending to stimulate growth, may be inhibited by fear of creating a balance of payments problem due to excess spending (see Chapter 4). Large reserves therefore permit a more flexible policy at home. No trade at all might allow this flexibility but at an obvious cost in welfare.

Three pages of writing cannot of course outline a history of the development of economic thought. The reader is warned therefore against any neat association of doctrine and date. Among each generation of writers an advocate can usually be found for almost any point of view. All that happens is that circumstances determine which is currently the most acceptable. The trained economist should therefore be armed with some kind of technique to enable him to pick his way between conflicting claims. Our object now is to develop such a technique.

Choice of a policy, or rather a policy change, involves two things. First, we need to work out the consequences of the policy change; only then are we in a position to decide whether these consequences are good or bad. Although much of Book I was concerned with consequences, the reader will recall that we have from time to time used as a measure of 'welfare' the change in the total value of all goods consumed determined by initial prices (Chapter 6). We have assumed throughout that any policy which increases the value of total consumption is good, and indeed that the increased value is a rough measure of that good. The time has come to defend this approach in a rather more sophisticated way.

13.2 IDENTIFYING A 'GOOD' POLICY FOR THE SINGLE CONSUMER

The reader should note at once the ambiguity of any claim that the value of all goods consumed has increased, even for a single individual. We have in fact to compare two situations, that existing before the policy change and that existing after. Before the change we represent the set of commodity prices existing as q^0 and after as q^1. The two consumption patterns for any individual may be similarly written x^0 and x^1. Thus q^0x^0 means the total value of consumption in situation zero and q^1x^1 the total value of consumption in situation one.

One measure of the change in the value of goods consumed is of course $q^1x^1 - q^0x^0$; but this is not very helpful, for the following reason. Suppose that, in situation one, the actual commodities consumed are precisely the same as in situation zero, but that prices have doubled. By the measure suggested we have a large change in the value of goods consumed but the community is clearly no better and no worse off. Change in value does not give us the result we need. To eliminate what is obviously the effect of changes in the purchasing power of money we must evaluate the welfare change either in terms of prices q^1 or in terms of prices q^0. In other words we must choose either

$$q^0x^1 - q^0x^0 = q^0(x^1 - x^0)$$

or

$$q^1x^1 - q^1x^0 = q^1(x^1 - x^0)$$

as the real change in the 'value' of total consumption. The question now is, can we justify either of these measures and, if so, which is the better to use?

Common sense cries out that either will do; for given that q^0 is not so very different from q^1, it seems likely that if either of the two measures are greater than zero then both will be. What we are in fact doing is valuing the change in our collection of goods, that is, valuing $(x^1 - x^0)$, which we may for convenience write dx^0. Intuition suggests that the use of different price sets for valuing purposes is unlikely to make so much difference that losses come to look like gains and vice versa. One can agree at once that the measures will be different, but it seems less likely that they will be so different as to turn negative into positive. On the other hand intuition is notoriously unreliable, so that some rigorous argument must be introduced. The dangers of the technique will also be demonstrated.

First, assume that the collection of goods x^1 is preferred to the collection x^0. For the moment we leave aside the question of what we mean by the word 'preferred', noting only that whilst it is easy to see how an individual will ordinarily be able to say that he would rather have x^1 than x^0, this is not true of the community as a whole. Indeed, what we are looking for is precisely some criterion to enable us to say that for the whole community x^1 is preferred to x^0. It would be convenient to be able to identify this situation by observing that the value of

$$(x^1 - x^0) = dx^0$$

is positive, i.e. that

$$q^0 dx^0 > 0$$

Notice that if we were talking of a *single individual* consuming either x^1 or x^0, there is one thing we would know at once, namely,

$$q^0 x^0 < q^0 x^1 \tag{13.2.1}$$

that is, we know that the value of consumption x^0 at prices q^0 must be less than the value of x^1 at the same prices, for if it were otherwise x^1 could have been purchased when x^0 was in fact chosen, which contradicts the notion that x^1 is preferred. But (13.2.1) may be rewritten

$$q^0(x^1 - x^0) > 0$$

that is, the change in consumption valued at original prices must be greater than zero. In other words x^1 can be preferred to x^0 *only* if

$$q^0 dx^0 > 0 \tag{13.2.2}$$

which is the criterion we have been using.

Unfortunately the fact that

$$q^0 dx^0 > 0$$

does not allow us to assume that x^1 *must* be preferred to x^0. All that we know is that if there is to be a gain (13.2.2) must be satisfied, which is not the same thing. A simple counter-example will be enough to satisfy the reader of this.

Suppose an individual consumer is quite indifferent whether he has 1 lb. of coffee or 1 lb. of tea. Both please him equally well, so that he would naturally choose whichever is the cheaper in price. In both situations zero and one he has sixpence to spend, but in situation zero, tea is 1s 6d and coffee is 6d a lb., whilst in situation two coffee is 1s 9d and tea 1s. We then have $x^0 = 1$ lb. coffee and $x^1 = \frac{1}{2}$ lb. tea, so that

$$q^0(x^1 - x^0) = q^0 dx^0 = 9d - 6d = 3d > 0$$

Condition (13.2.2) above is met even though x^0 must be preferred to x^1 since it is greater in quantity and the consumer is indifferent between coffee and tea.

Note that if we were considering a change of policy which would take the consumer from situation one to situation zero instead of from situation zero to one, the test (13.2.2) would yield

$$q^1(x^0 - x^1) = q^1 dx^1 = 1s\ 9d - 6d = 1s\ 3d > 0$$

which is what we must expect from (13.2.2) when we know that x^0 is preferred to x^1.

This last observation immediately suggests how we might find a sufficient condition for x^1 preferred to x^0, for if x^0 is preferred to x^1, then by (13.2.2)

$$q^1(x^0 - x^1) = q^1 dx^1 > 0$$

which implies $\qquad q^1(x^1 - x^0) = q^1 dx^0 < 0$

If, therefore, it is observed that

$$q^1 dx^0 > 0 \qquad\qquad (13.2.3)$$

we can be sure that it is desirable or at least can do no harm to adopt a policy which takes the consumer from x^0 to x^1; for if x^0 is preferred to x^1, the opposite of (13.2.3) must hold so that (13.2.3) implies that x^0 is not preferred to x^1. Therefore a probable gain and certainly no loss is involved in moving to x^1.

We may now sum up as follows. If *both*

$$q^0 dx^0 > 0$$
and
$$q^1 dx^0 > 0$$

(13.2.4)

we can be sure that a policy which changes a single individual's consumption from x^0 to x^1 is desirable. If on the other hand we have

$$q^0 dx^0 > 0$$
but
$$q^1 dx^0 < 0$$

we are unable to tell whether the policy is desirable or not. It should be noted that

$$q^0 dx^0 > 0$$
$$q^1 dx^0 < 0$$

imply

$$q^0 dx^1 < 0$$
$$q^1 dx^1 > 0$$

since

$$dx^0 = - dx^1$$

so that we learn no more by testing whether it is desirable to move in the reverse direction from x^1 to x^0. This is of course exactly what we should expect.

It follows from all this that when we test for the desirability of a policy we may get a clear answer as in (13.2.4) but we may not. And this is not all. We emphasise again that although everything we have said so far holds true for an individual who is spending his income as he chooses when faced by money prices, it is *not* obviously true of the community as a whole. In every case the measures $q^0 dx^0$ of Book I referred to the community as a whole. No reference was made at all to the way in which dx^0 is *shared out* among individuals. The dx^0 is an aggregate of all dx_r^0 where dx_r^0 is the change in the consumption pattern of the rth individual. Note that the dx_r^0 is in no sense a share of dx^0, i.e. the fact that dx^0 might be positive does not by any means imply that dx_r^0 is positive. The reason for this is that a change in policy not only brings about changes in commodity prices but, as we have seen in the previous chapter, it ordinarily leads also to changes in factor rewards. A tariff may make more 'real income' available to the community as a whole by improving the real terms of trade, but it may at the same time reduce wage rates in such a way that some *individuals* are worse off than before. We may have in effect

$$q^0 dx_r^0 < 0 \quad \text{for, say, the } r\text{th individual}$$
and
$$q^0 dx_s^0 > 0 \quad \text{for, say, the } s\text{th individual}$$

even though in the aggregate the conditions (13.2.4) for a 'good' policy could be met.

No matter how large a gain we seem to be making in terms of the conditions (13.2.4), as long as there exists the possibility that a single individual may be the loser it is impossible to say that a policy is desirable. Or more strictly, we have no objective principle upon which we can say the policy is desirable. There can be no unanimous agreement. The point about this is not that it is impossible to act without unanimous agreement but rather that we cannot act without unanimous agreement unless we call into operation some organised method of imposing the 'general will'; for example, a democratically elected government must decide whether on the whole a few should suffer for the general good and if so whether or not compensation might be offered.

All of these difficulties have given rise to a great deal of discussion among economists and many ingenious arguments have been devised in attempts to solve this 'welfare' problem. We venture to assert, however, that nothing of value has been said and nothing can be said which goes beyond the following rather simple principles.

First of all, let us try to deal with the problem of the region of ignorance in the case of the individual. Suppose that we have

$$q^0 dx^0 > 0$$

but that we do not know the sign of $q^1 dx^0$. We cannot make up our minds whether the policy under review is desirable or not, but we do at least know that

$$q^1 dx^0 = (q^0 + dq^0)dx^0 = q^0 dx^0 + dq^0 dx^0 \qquad (13.2.5)$$

where dq^0 is the change in q^0; and we know also that the first term on the right-hand side of (13.2.5) is positive by hypothesis. If the whole expression is negative, this can only be because $dq^0 dx^0$ is negative and numerically greater than $q^0 dx^0$.

Now consider the meaning of dx^0 and dq^0. These are changes which are consequent upon some change in policy, for example the imposition of a tariff or the depreciation of the exchange rate. But a policy can be imposed with as great or as little severity as we like, and the smaller the tariff rate, say, the smaller will be dq^0 and dx^0. By reducing the tariff to as low a rate as we like we can make dq^0 and dx^0 as small as we like. Intuitively it is easy to see that as the tariff rate is reduced, the second term on the right-hand side of (13.2.5) will become numerically smaller at a faster rate than the first term, for the second term is the product of two diminishing terms whilst q^0 remains constant. For example, we may have $q^0 = 1$, with $dx^0 = 2$ and $dq^0 = -2$. In this case $q^1 dx^0$ is negative. But as we diminish the tariff rate so that dx^0 and dq^0 reduce to, say, $\frac{1}{2}$ and $-\frac{1}{2}$, term two becomes $-\frac{1}{4}$ whilst term one falls only to $\frac{1}{2}$. $q^1 dx^0$ turns positive.

This change of sign must always occur as the policy is applied less and less severely provided only that the rate of change of q^0 due to the policy change is not infinite. To see this more formally let us write the right-hand side of (13.2.5) in the form

$$q^0 \frac{dx^0}{dt} dt + \left(\frac{dq^0}{dt} dt\right)\left(\frac{dx^0}{dt} dt\right)$$

$$= q^0 \frac{dx^0}{dt} dt + \frac{dq^0}{dt}\frac{dx^0}{dt} dt^2 \qquad (13.2.6)$$

where dt is the measure of the policy change (say a change in import duty) and dx^0/dt, dq^0/dt are the rates of total response of the variables to the policy change. Provided the total response rates are finite whatever the value of the tariff t, it is always possible to choose dt sufficiently small to make it reasonable to neglect the second term.

From this we conclude that whenever

$$q^0 dx^0 > 0$$

it is always possible to apply the policy *in some degree* such that both

$$q^0 dx^0 > 0$$

and $$q^1 dx^0 > 0$$

that is, so that the individual gains unambiguously. If (13.2.2) holds, therefore, we are observing a signal which says that there exists at least some degree of severity at which the policy can be applied so as to be sure there will be a gain. If we could be sure that, when we obtain the result $q^0 dx^0 > 0$ *for the community as a whole*, as in Book I, the same holds true for each individual within the community, then equation (13.2.6) above would admit of immediate practical application.

From Book I we found that, for any policy, it is always possible to express the value of $q^0 dx^0$ in terms of elasticities of supply and demand and other observable variables. Given elasticities, which are computable in principle, we know therefore the sign of $q^0 dx^0$. In other words we know whether an increase or reduction in the value of the policy variable (tariff or exchange rate, etc.) will lead to a gain provided the change is small enough. What we do not know, however, for large changes are the prices q^1. Indeed, for large changes in the policy variable we do not really know dx^0 and hence we are not sure of $q^0 dx^0$.

For the benefit of less mathematically orientated readers this last apparent contradiction ought perhaps to be further explained. In Book I, where the rules for taking changes on both sides of an identity were developed (section 3.3), results were obtained by neglecting terms like dx or Δx where these can be taken to be arbitrarily small. This in fact is the principle which we have applied in reference to (13.2.6). Again in Book I, beginning with any function of three variables p_1, p_2 and Y,

$$X(p_1, p_2, Y)$$

we habitually wrote

$$dX = \frac{\partial X}{\partial p_1} dp_1 + \frac{\partial X}{\partial p_2} dp_2 + \frac{\partial X}{\partial Y} dY$$

for the total change in the function due to changes dp_1, dp_2 and dY where $\partial X / \partial p$, etc., are response rates.

It should now be understood that this is an approximation only, the accuracy of the approximation being dependent on the extent to which the response rates $\partial X / \partial p$ change as a result of changes in any p or Y. In Chapter 4 the method was justified by the analogy of moving up a hill. The change in height is given by the steepness of the hill at a point multiplied by the horizontal distance travelled. But clearly if the steepness varies from point to point over the horizontal distance travelled our result can be no better than a first approximation. On the other hand it is easy to see that, in a general way, the less the horizontal distance travelled, the closer the approximation to the change in height.† We may make our estimate as close as we like to the true change by reducing the distance over which the estimate is made.

It is for these reasons that we cannot say, from the work of Book I, that we know either q^1 or even dx^0 when the change in the policy variable is large. We do, however, have a first approximation and we may proceed as follows. Evidently the sign of our approximation to $q^0 dx^0$ does not depend on the magnitude of the policy change

† Better approximations may be made if we have some knowledge of the rates of change of slopes at a point. These again are computable parameters. But it is beyond the scope of this book to go into this.

contemplated, even though the true $q^0 dx^0$ might so depend, for our estimate is uniquely determined by the values of elasticities at the point of take-off. For example, it was shown in Chapter 10 that the welfare effect of growth in output at home is (under the conditions of the model) given by the formula

$$dw = q^0 dx^0 = \left[1 + \frac{C_2}{E_{11}' + E_{22} + 1} \right] dv$$

where dv is the growth in the value of output, C_2 is the marginal propensity to consume good 2 and the Es are elasticities. Evidently the sign of this expression is determined by the magnitude of the parameters C_2, E_{11} and E_{22} and *not* by the magnitude of dv. But this is only because the formula is an approximation to $q^0 dx^0$. If the change dv were large it could be that the values for E at the take-off point give a positive result but that the values of E in the after-growth position have fallen low enough to give a negative result if applied in the formula. This does not mean that the formula gives the wrong result. What it does mean, however, is that the country might be allowed to grow too much. We have a case in fact where $q^0 dx^0 > 0$ but $q^1 dx^0$ could be less than zero.

The difficulty really is that although the criterion $q^0 dx^0 > 0$ tells us correctly that it helps to grow, it does not warn us that the policy can be overdone. This need not worry us, however, for the best position can always be found step by step. If the criterion $q^0 dx^0 > 0$ shows a policy to be desirable, it is always possible to apply it in moderation. New elasticities may then be computed from the experience gained and the policy can be reinforced or weakened according as the new $q^0 dx^0$ is greater than or less than zero. In this way the best position is attained by an iterative process. We have in fact a practical method for finding by a series of operations, say the optimal tariff. When we reach the point where $q^0 dx^0$ is zero no more change can be beneficial.

Indeed, we may go much further than this by making use of the idea embodied in (13.2.6). By the methods already developed it is possible to make an estimate of

$$q^1 dx^0$$

itself, for we know that

$$q^1 = q^0 + dq^0$$

and the techniques of Book I give us a first approximation for dq^0, subject of course to the same limitations as our estimate of dx^0. To illustrate the use to be made of this fact we carry out the operation for the problem of Chapter 10.

Care must be taken to use the formula for $q^1 dx^0$ in the form (13.2.6) above. This is because the product $dq^0 dx^0$ as it occurs in (13.2.5) is ambiguous until we associate with it a given level of the policy change (e.g. dt in (13.2.6). Note that throughout Chapter 10 prices are the same at home and abroad so that we may keep the notation q for commodity prices adopted for Book II. Only one price changes, namely q_2, so that we have simply to compute dX_2/dv; that is, we need not concern ourselves with the value of dX_1/dv since dq_1/dv is zero, 1 being the numeraire commodity. Thus

$$\frac{dX_1}{dv}\frac{dq_1}{dv} = 0$$

so that we have

$$\frac{dq^0}{dv}\frac{dx^0}{dv} = \frac{dq_2}{dv}\frac{dX_2}{dv} = \left(\frac{\partial X_2}{\partial q_2}\frac{dq_2}{dv} + \frac{\partial X_2}{\partial Y}\frac{dY}{dv}\right)\frac{dq_2}{dv}$$

But dY/dv is unity by equation (10.3.5), so that using (13.2.6) we may write down at once the answer we need in terms of dq_2/dv. In fact,

$$q^1 dx^0 = q^0 dx^0 + \frac{dq_2}{dv}\left(\frac{\partial X_2}{\partial q_2}\frac{dq_2}{dv} + \frac{C_2}{q_2}\right)dv^2$$

With (10.3.14) and (10.3.8) this yields

$$q^1 dx^0 = \left(1 + \frac{C_2}{E'_{11} + E_{22} + 1}\right)dv - \left(\frac{C_2^2(E'_{11} + 1)}{q_2 X_2(E'_{11} + E_{22} + 1)^2}\right)dv^2 \quad (13.2.7)$$

The sign of $q^1 dx^0$ (or rather our estimate of this) now clearly depends upon the magnitude of dv. If we choose dv small enough the sign of (13.2.7) must be the same as its first term, that is, the same as $q^0 dx^0$. But if dv is large, say unity, this need not be the case. Suppose for example C_2 is $\frac{1}{2}$ and E'_{11} and E_{22} are equal at something very slightly less than $-\frac{3}{4}$. Then the value of term one will be positive but small whilst term two will be negative and will outweigh it.

By the computation (13.2.7) we have an immediate aid to the previously outlined procedure for finding an optimum policy. We may in fact make estimates both of $q^0 dx^0$ and of $q^1 dx^0$ in the manner explained. If then $q^0 dx^0$ is positive but there exists some level of policy at which the estimate of $q^1 dx^0$ turns negative, a good first step might well be to choose that level of application of the policy which puts $q^1 dx^0$ at zero (for example, in the problem above we might choose the value of dv which makes (13.2.7) equal to zero). Although it is not certain that there can be no loss as a result, since Es may change over the range dv, at least we have a good first approximation. The method may then be reapplied with newly computed elasticities until, as before, we find the point where $q^0 dx^0$ also is zero for small dx^0. The purpose of the amended procedure is simply to attain the desired objectives with fewer steps in the iterative process.

13.3 Identifying a 'Good' Policy for the Community as a Whole

The argument above deals satisfactorily with the 'region of ignorance' due to the ambiguity in the valuation of the change in consumption present even in the single-consumer case. It is necessary now to face the community problem already noted, which arises out of the impossibility of making 'interpersonal comparison of utilities'. We have set out a numerical test which, if the data is available, permits us to decide whether or not a policy is good from the point of view of each individual consumer. But to make practical use of this test it would be necessary, strictly speaking, to apply it to each and every individual in the community. It is not possible to say with certainty that a given policy is desirable unless we are sure that for each individual, r,

$$q^0 dx_r^0 > 0$$

But we have already drawn attention to the fact that, in the general case, we must expect any change of policy to be good for some people and bad for others.

To overcome this difficulty a 'principle of compensation' has been proposed which operates as follows. Suppose the community finds itself in situation A with a certain distribution of commodities among individuals and we are required to judge whether some other attainable quantity and distribution, say A^*, is better. Applying the principle of compensation, we say that A^* is better if those individuals who gain in situation A^* could compensate the losers; that is, if they could bribe the losers (with some of their gain) to accept the new situation and still leave themselves better off. If compensation were actually paid, everyone would then be better off in situation A^*

It was of course soon noted that a case can be very easily constructed where, in situation A, A^* appears better by the compensation principle, but in situation A^*, A looks better by the same test. A trivial example will be sufficient to establish this. Let William like butter but have little use for cheese and let Charles have completely opposite tastes. In situation A let the total of all commodities available be 5 lb. butter and 2 lb. cheese and let William have *all* the purchasing power. Charles has nothing. In situation A^* all the purchasing power may be assumed to be in Charles's hands. This time William has nothing. The total of all commodities available could be 7 lb. butter and 1 lb. cheese.

If situation A applies, Charles will evidently gain by moving to A^*. Furthermore, Charles could bribe William to accept the change by offering him, say, 6 lb. butter which he prefers to 5 lb. butter and 2 lb. cheese. The compensation test is met. A^* is preferred to A. But if situation A^* prevailed it is clear that William would gain by moving to A. He could moreover bribe Charles to accept the change with an offer of 2 lb. cheese, which Charles prefers, to 7 lb. butter and 1 lb. cheese. By the principle of compensation A is better than A^*. We are unable to rank situations A and A^* in order of merit even when the principle of compensation is invoked.

The impossibility of ranking social states revealed by the example above has led some economists to suggest a double compensation check analogous to the two parts of the requirement (13.2.4) above. It has been argued that, before it is possible to be absolutely sure that a change of policy which carries the economy from situation A to, say, A^* is a good thing, it must

(i) be possible, in a move from A to A^*, for those who gain to compensate those who lose, and

(ii) be impossible for those who would gain by the reverse move from A^* to A to compensate those who lose.

An elaborate diagrammatic treatment of this problem in terms of a concept called a 'utility possibility curve' is to be found in the literature. We shall not, however, introduce this here since it adds nothing to what we already know. The technique, based on the assumption that welfare is measurable, is useful to illustrate the possibility of the case of William and Charles and the need for the double compensation criterion, but it in no way contributes to a practical solution. 'Utility' or 'satisfaction' is not measurable. To pretend that it is may be a help in developing ways of thinking about the problem, but such a pretence can only act as a scaffolding which must be discarded when the final structure is complete. And as it happens we are able to do without even the scaffolding.

Suppose that we have two situations A and A^* where aggregate consumption of the whole community is x^0 and x^1 respectively. Suppose further that

$$q^0 dx^0 < 0 \tag{13.3.1}$$

if a change is made from A to A^*. We can be sure that it is impossible for *everyone* to be better, or at least as well, off as a consequence of such a change however wealth is redistributed. This follows from the fact that for the rth individual not to lose it is necessary to have

$$q^0 dx_r^0 \geqq 0 \tag{13.3.2}$$

where dx_r^0 is the change in the rth individual's consumption pattern. And if (13.3.2) is satisfied for every individual, (13.3.1) cannot be satisfied for the community as a whole by simple addition.

It follows that, as for the individual,

$$q^0 dx^0 > 0 \tag{13.3.3}$$

for the community as a whole is a *necessary* condition for compensation to be possible, i.e. for everyone to be better off.

We must not of course expect the condition (13.3.3) always to be *sufficient* for a welfare gain, for we have already seen that it is not even sufficient in the case of the individual. We may hope, however, that it may be so if the policy leading to the change is applied with sufficient restraint in the sense already discussed and if the gain is suitably shared.

In order to demonstrate this, it is necessary first to show that, as long as (13.3.3) is satisfied it is possible to find some distribution of the available dx^0 between individuals so that, for each person r, (13.3.2) is satisfied. This is achieved by assigning changed amounts of each commodity to every individual in proportion to the changes in the total of each commodity available as defined by the numbers dx^0. For example, if there were, say, three commodities, the inequality (13.3.3) written in full would read

$$q_1^0 dX_1^0 + q_2^0 dX_2^0 + q_3^0 dX_3^0 > 0$$

Let λ_r be a positive number less than 1 representing the share of the change to be assigned to the rth individual. Then the rth individual would receive

$$\lambda_r dX_1^0 + \lambda_r dX_2^0 + \lambda_r dX_3^0$$

plus his original consumption, so that the condition

$$q^0 dx_r^0 = \sum \lambda_r q_i^0 dX_i^0 > 0 \tag{13.3.4}$$

would be satisfied for each individual. Since λ_r is a positive fraction, we have chosen a satisfactory distribution, for (13.3.3) implies (13.3.2) even though some elements of dx^0 will ordinarily be negative, that is, even though each individual will receive less of some commodities and more of others.

Next we note that, if λ_r is chosen sufficiently small and/or dx^0 is made sufficiently small by a moderate application of policy, then the fact that (13.3.2) is satisfied for each individual can be made to imply that every individual experiences a welfare gain by the argument of section 13.2. Our conjecture turns out to have been correct.

It is natural now to wonder whether, given (13.3.3), that, as with the individual,

$$q^1 dx^0 > 0 \tag{13.3.5}$$

implies that the community *must* gain from the change when q^1 is the new valuation of the set of commodity changes. This raises a difficulty. If a change in the pattern of consumption $\lambda_r dx_r^0$ is assigned arbitrarily to the rth individual for any given total money expenditure, there is one and only one set of prices q_r^1 which will induce him to purchase, on a free market, just the pattern of consumption so assigned. There is no reason at all why the prices q_r^1 so determined for the rth individual should be the same as the prices q_s^1 which would induce the sth individual to demand his assigned 'ration' of commodities. Particular attention should be paid to the fact that the tests developed for the individual rest upon the implicit assumption that q^0 and x^0 and q^1 and x^1 are the prices and consumption patterns respectively which would emerge *in a free market*. To overcome the difficulty here described, we imagine a further redistribution as follows.

Suppose, given (13.3.3), that we have shared the aggregate dx^0 proportionately between individuals as described above. Since the distribution of commodities is not one which would be freely chosen by consumers, we have a situation rather like war-time rationing where there is an obvious advantage in some further exchange of commodities between individuals. A barter market would appear and exchange would continue until every individual is satisfied with a new pattern of consumption, say x_r^{1*} for the rth person. As each individual was by our construct better off with consumption x_r^1 than x_r^0, and as no person will exchange unless to do so makes him better off, it follows that for the rth individual x_r^{1*} is preferred to x_r^1. Therefore x_r^{1*} is preferred to x_r^0. Furthermore, as the process of barter cannot change the aggregate of all commodities, we have

$$q^0(x^{1*} - x^0) = q^0 dx^{0*} = q^0 dx^0$$

Finally, we note that the bartering process would carry each person to the point where the rate at which he is willing to exchange one commodity for another is the same as for every other person. If it were not so a gain could be made by further barter. This common exchange rate is equivalent to a relative price. Hence a set of commodity prices, the same for all individuals, exists together with a distribution of money income which would induce the rth consumer to buy the pattern of commodities x_r^{1*}.

We have now shown that if some policy can make available a new pattern of consumption x^1 at a time when current prices are q^0 and current consumption x^0, and if

$$q^0 dx^0 > 0$$

then it is possible to find a set of prices q^1 and a distribution of money income such that the market is just cleared of x^1 and such that every individual in the community is better off, provided once again that the policy is applied with the required degree of moderation. Naturally also the new distribution must satisfy

$$q^0 dx_r^{0*} > 0$$

for every individual r, for this is a necessary condition for being better off.

In the light of all this, consider again whether we might find the sufficient condition for all to be better off in situation A^* than A analogous to the condition

$$q^1 dx_r^0 > 0 \qquad\qquad (13.3.6)$$

for the individual. As we have already found it necessary to consider two alternative distributions, the ambiguity of the question put is clear. A^* means a new consumption pattern x^1. But it must also mean some distribution of that consumption pattern between individuals. It is useless to try to order social states unless our definition of a social state includes some specification of the share-out; it is most unlikely that there could be agreement that two distinct patterns of total consumption always rank the same whatever the share-out.

It is important to understand that the absurd contradiction developed in the Charles/William situation outlined above (p. 374) arises precisely because the impossible is attempted. We showed that in situation A Charles could gain by moving to A^* and could compensate William. If we suppose the compensation actually to be made, we move to a social state A^{**} different from A^* in that the *share-out* is different from A^* although the total product available is the same. Similarly it was shown that in situation A^* William would gain by moving to A and could compensate Charles, but the after-compensation situation is again a new social state A^{***} different from A. It makes sense to say that A^{**} is unambiguously better than A and that A is unambiguously worse than A^{**}. Both gain by moving to A^{**} and both would lose by moving back to A. Similarly A^{***} is unambiguously better than A^*. The fact that we cannot rank A and A^* or for that matter A and A^{***} simply reflects the fact that we cannot rank situations where some gain and some lose. But the important point is that *we do not need to be able to rank every situation*. If we can find objective rules for showing that a move from A to A^{**} is unambiguously good, we should make the change even though we may feel that a still better situation might exist if only we knew how to find it. All of this implies that right policy involves *making the compensation*, that is, we must move to A^{**} and not to A^*.

This does not mean that value judgements should not be made by proper persons at the proper time regarding the right ranking of A and A^*. As earlier indicated, this cannot be avoided whether we like it or not, for to do nothing is to do something. The point made in the early paragraphs of this chapter and now made again, is simply that it is no use pretending that we have an *objective* principle enabling us to choose between A and A^* when we have not, and never can have. The compensation principle is one which can be applied only if the compensation is made, i.e. it ranks only A and A^{**}. To pretend that it ranks A and A^* is to pretend what can never be true.

All of this emphasises that, when we set down the criterion

$$q^1 dx^0 > 0 \qquad\qquad (13.3.7)$$

for the community as a whole, the q^1 must refer to that set of prices which will clear the market *after* any necessary compensation. Different patterns of compensation will ordinarily lead to different sets of prices q^1 and we do not wish, for reasons given above, to consider the *before*-compensation state. With this in mind we now show finally the kind of meaning which can be attributed to a test (13.3.7) for the community as a whole.

The first thing we know from (13.3.7) is that

$$q^1 dx^1 < 0$$

where as before

$$dx^1 = x^0 - x^1 = - dx^0$$

From this it follows, by the inferences from (13.3.1), that if a change is made from x^0 to x^1, it is impossible to reverse the policy, however moderately, and compensate so as to make everyone better off. What (13.3.1) tells us therefore is that the second part of the compensation test is satisfied. In any move from x^1 to x^0, provided q^1 clears the market of x^1, those who gain cannot compensate those who lose. The test (13.3.7) therefore, together with (13.3.3), indicates that a move from A to A^* could make everyone better off whilst it is impossible to make everyone still better off with a move back to A however wealth is redistributed.

Next, it is easy to see that if (13.3.7) is satisfied, it is surely possible to choose an income distribution which would enable each consumer to buy at least what he bought in the old situation. In fact

$$q^1 dx^0 = q^1(x^1 - x^0) > 0$$

implies

$$q^1 x^1 > q^1 x^0$$

which means that total expenditure at the new prices is greater than the cost of the old pattern of consumption at the new prices. There is enough aggregate expenditure to ensure that, for each individual,

$$q^1 dx_r^0 > 0$$

as required. There is a sense therefore in which we might say that (13.3.7), provided it is attained after the 'right' sort of income redistribution, is a sufficient condition for every individual to be better off. But note especially the proviso 'after the right sort of income redistribution'. Since the price q^1 depends on the income distribution, it does not follow that in any case where we observe (13.3.7) the policy must have been 'good' (see exercise 3 at the end of this chapter). Evidently in any practical case it is better to follow the procedure established in the case of the individual consumer. Given (13.3.3), the policy, with a suitable distribution, is good, but as soon as we observe that

$$q^1 dx^0 < 0 \qquad (13.3.8)$$

or

$$q^1 dx^1 > 0 \qquad (13.3.9)$$

then we may infer, as with the individual, that the policy under review has *overshot the mark*. It is being applied too fiercely, for (13.3.9) satisfies a condition like (13.3.3) which we have already shown means that, if we begin from a social state x^1 with prices q^1 and apply the reverse policy leading back to x^0 with a *sufficient degree of moderation*, everyone can be made better off than in social state x^1. A sufficient degree of moderation means that we must not go right back to x^0 as long as

$$q^0 dx^0 > 0$$

for this in turn means that the policy of moving back again towards x^1 can increase the welfare of all.

It may be as well at this point to summarise what has now been proved and what *cannot* be proved:

(i) It *cannot* be proved that

$$q^1 dx^0 > 0$$

by itself implies that everyone must be better off for every redistribution, for obviously we could choose a redistribution which gives zero to some one individual.

(ii) It *cannot* be proved that if

$$q^1 dx^0 < 0$$

then at least some individual must be worse off in consequence of a move from x^0 to x^1, for the individual may be better off even though he cannot buy what he bought originally. In the aggregate a region of ignorance exists as before.

(iii) It *cannot* be proved that if, for some redistribution of money expenditure

$$q^1 dx^0 > 0$$

then there exists at least one distribution which will make everyone better off (see exercise 3 to this chapter).

What we have proved, however, is:

(iv) That if for *every* redistribution of money expenditure

$$q^1 dx^0 > 0$$

then there exists at least one redistribution which will make everyone better off. In particular the distribution of money expenditure which allows each person to buy at least what he bought before the change will achieve the required result; and

(v) That if $q^1 dx^0 < 0$ the proposed policy will overshoot. Some less vigorous application of the policy is desirable if only because this is bound to yield an improvement over the situation x^1 by the result (13.3.3).

In sum we can say that, in the case of the community as a whole, there is a slight extension of the region of ignorance. Even if the condition (13.3.7) is satisfied, we cannot be sure that the change is desirable unless it is satisfied for every conceivable distribution of money expenditure.

This should not worry us, however, for we have the really important results. We know that (13.3.3) implies that some measure of the policy under review is desirable. The test (13.3.7) will warn that the policy is being over-applied if it is not met just as it does in the case of the individual. If it is met, we must mean that it is met for some tentative redistribution of money expenditure thought to be just. It would then be reasonable to adopt the policy and afterwards reconsider both the distribution of expenditure and the possibility of a further policy change beginning from the new position.

The rules above are simple even though their precise application would require some detailed knowledge of expenditure distribution between individuals both before and after policy changes. Furthermore, it may be the case that a rule of thumb calling for the moderate application of any policy satisfying (13.3.3) followed by some reappraisal of income distribution would quite quickly carry any economy to a 'best' position where

$$q^0 dx^0 = 0$$

for any further change. *Indeed, this is precisely why in Book I the reader was allowed to understand that any policy satisfying (13.3.3) could be said to improve welfare.* On the other hand a fuller understanding of the welfare problem is sometimes helpful, as we shall show in a later chapter.

Two caveats should now be entered. In computing the dx^0 for the test (13.3.3) we are, or should be, comparing social states after redistribution. It may well be that some aggregate consumption x^1 is attainable from a position x^0 if there is no redistribution of purchasing power between individuals, but is not attainable if the redistribution actually takes place. In other words x^1 and hence dx^0 is as much dependent on the redistribution as the q^1 which has been the subject of so much discussion.

For example, if the policy under review is the imposition of a tariff, it could be that redistribution of expenditure between individuals consequent upon an increase in welfare will shift the offer curve to a new position leading to a further change in the real terms of trade. What this means in effect is that in computing the value of $q^0\,dx^0$ care must be taken to include the effect of any proposed redistribution policy.

In the work of Book I it has been explicitly assumed that all redistributions of purchasing power are uncorrelated with tastes, and it may well be that this is a reasonable first approximation. If this conjecture is correct we need not be concerned with redistribution and the various results of Book I can be used as they stand. Furthermore, it will be true in this case that if (13.3.7) is satisfied, it will be satisfied for *all* redistributions as required in proposition (iv) (p. 380). All our difficulties disappear and all tests hold as for the individual. We need only ensure that 'proper' redistribution of purchasing power does in fact take place after any policy change. It may not perhaps be too far wrong to assume that this is automatically effected by day-to-day operations of the taxation authorities, according to the 'general will'.

If tastes and redistribution, on the other hand, are correlated, we need not despair. Given that we know something about consumer behaviour in the various social groups affected, it is not impossible to amend the work of Book I to take account of this new complication. All that is necessary is to introduce separate demand functions for the various social groups and complicate the results of Book I accordingly. No new principle is involved.

The second caveat concerns a well-known argument which has been much canvassed. If any required redistribution of income is effected through taxation, this is itself a policy which may help to determine the quantity of the various commodities to be redistributed on the production side as distinct from demand. One hears a great deal for example about the disincentive effect of taxation. To put the matter in its worst possible light, what should be done if it became clear that a redistribution of income in favour of individual 1 would raise the total of all commodities to be divided between both individuals 1 and 2?

Three things may be said about this. First, there really is no difficulty in principle, for all that we have to do is to take into account, as before, the effect of any proposed income redistribution in computing the consumption change dx^0 between the two social states. In particular, if any increase in reward would induce individual 1 to put out more effort, there is no reason why some of individual 2's income should not be transferred to him provided the increase in output is sufficient to allow individual 1 to be reimbursed. If it is not sufficient, individual 1 is demanding at least £1 of extra income for each £1's worth of extra output, which implies that he is indifferent between leisure and commodities. The policy implies no gain to anyone, as application of the techniques outlined above should reveal.

Second, in most of the applications with which we have been concerned, the disincentive effect of taxation is likely to be unimportant, the more so because there is unlikely to be any great disincentive effect in a properly applied policy which by definition could make everybody better off without extra effort, i.e. assuming constant labour input.

Third, it is known that methods of income redistribution can be devised which have little or no disincentive effect. A poll tax is precisely such a tax. It may well be that redistributive measures could be introduced which would avoid the whole difficulty we are now facing.

One more important point remains to be made on the subject of policy. If a series of iterative steps take us to a position where any further policy change whatever, however moderately applied, shows

$$p^0 dx^0 = 0 \qquad (13.3.10)$$

this does not necessarily mean that Utopia is attained. All that it does mean is that, given the distribution of commodities with which the iterative process began, there is no further change that can make *everyone* better off. There is no implication whatever that the final distribution of real income is optimal. In the last analysis a value judgement must be made as to what is a 'fair' distribution of real income.

If the distribution of income were judged to be 'unfair' and a redistribution was effected, it might then be noted that the condition (13.3.10) was no longer met so that further changes of policy would be desirable. The condition (13.3.10) is necessary to an optimum but it is not sufficient. To find a sufficient condition, a value judgement is necessary and it is at this point that the economist has nothing to say. All our work has been designed to show how, if (13.3.10) is not satisfied, we may proceed towards a position where it is met by a series of steps which all can agree are good. The problem of choosing an ultimate 'share-out' of welfare is avoided. This is desirable since, the world being what it is, it is *changes* in the *status quo* which are most resisted. Our rules offer us some help in isolating those sets of changes from the *status quo* on which we can all agree from those where we are unlikely to agree. (13.3.10) is economically efficient but it need not necessarily be 'just'.

It should be noted also that this last comment is all that we need in effect to justify the welfare conclusions of Book I. If a policy indicates

$$q^0 dx^0 > 0$$

unambiguous gains can be made by moving in this direction. Every problem in welfare economics yields to this test, a fact which we shall illustrate in the two following chapters by reference to certain well-known problems. Before trying to do this, however, we append a short note on the problem of actual numerical measurement of gains.

13.4 Numerical Measurement of Gains

A gain in economics means, in the last analysis, a gain in welfare, that is, in satisfaction derived from the enjoyment of commodities which enter into exchange. But satisfaction is a subjective phenomenon which is not measurable. All that we can really do in economics is to identify situations which would be selected by the community rather than any other if free choice were available, and to attempt to guide the economy into such situations. This in fact is all that is attempted in the work above, although the form of words used in the interests of clarity may at times have seemed to suggest more than this.

On the other hand it has currently become fashionable to talk of 'measuring' the gains from, say, trade in terms of money or some other unit. The motive for this is sensible at first sight but less so on mature reflection. It may be that authority wishes to choose between some intangible advantage – say political alignment or international goodwill – and an alternative advantage in terms of an increase in national income. The imposition of a tariff, for example, may yield a gain in the sense that it leads to a preferred position to one of no tariff. But how does one decide whether the gain so attained is desirable in the face of objections from trading partners which may lead to political differences? This is, in the end, a matter on which responsible government must make up its mind in the absence of objective principles. It is not unreasonable, however, for governments to ask in such circumstances for some measure of what the country will lose if the tariff is not imposed.

The correct short answer is that there is no measure, at least until we are precisely informed what it is to be a measure of. If what is required is a figure representing the change in the value of consumption, then we must ask whether prices before or after are to be used as the basis of valuation, that is do we want

$$q^0 dx^0$$

or $$q^1 dx^0$$

Either may be thought suitable. If on the other hand what is required is a number expressing the degree of human happiness, the question is no longer one for an economist.

One would suspect in fact that what the politician is really asking for is some figure in money terms which, given his own subjective feelings about the value of money, will enable him to compare an economic loss with some other real or imagined non-pecuniary advantage. In such a case it would not be unreasonable to present both valuations of the expected change in consumption patterns with a statement that there really is no more precise answer to the question put, even in principle. The essential difficulty is that the only measure of the 'worth' of anything (and this applies also to money) is something else which is commonly exchanged for it, that is, we can do no more than compare the relative utilities or disutilities of different objects or activities. And to make matters worse, relative utilities clearly depend upon how much of the various items we possess. The length of the measuring rod depends upon what is being measured. The economist lives in a nightmare world where only the general relativity theory applies.

What we are really saying when we present the policy-maker with two figures

$$q^0 dx^0$$

and $$q^1 dx^0$$

is something like this. Both are money measures of the change in welfare between situation A and A^*. They are different even though they are intended to measure the same thing simply because the 'value' of money changes as a consequence of the very change in welfare we are trying to measure. If one number is demanded we cannot give it, for a number must be a number of something, whether cabbages or doormats. And we know of nothing intrinsic whose 'value' does not change as a consequence of a change in policy.

Those responsible for the making of value judgements should be invited to make the best use of this information they may. Their task is already difficult. Any economist who presents just one figure or who implies even that the presentation of a single figure makes sense can only be adding to a confusion which is already mighty. There can be no escape from the making of value judgements, but we can at least try to prevent their being made under false pretences.

The remarks above should not be taken to mean that money measures of gains from policy changes should never be made. On the contrary the whole emphasis of this work has been on the desperate need for more measurement in economics and not less. All that we wish to say here is that we have at hand two measures (both applying to any economic problem whatever, however complex the changes envisaged), one at least of which is readily computable, namely $q^0 dx^0$, which together give us the greatest help we are likely to find in the making of value judgements. It is unlikely that any further argument on the subject of what does or does not measure economic gain will yield useful results.

EXERCISES

1. Turn up in the textbook *Economics* by P. A. Samuelson (6th ed., pp. 438–43), the explanation of the concept of 'indifference curves'. Show that if x^0 is on the consumption-possibility line, then

$$q^0 dx^0 > 0$$

if x^1 lies to the north-east of the consumption-possibility line and

$$q^0 dx^0 < 0$$

if x^1 lies to the south-west of the consumption-possibility line. (q, x and dx here have the meaning of the text of Chapter 13 of the present book.)

Hence show diagrammatically that

$$q^0 dx^0 > 0$$

does not necessarily imply that x^1 gives greater welfare than x^0 unless

$$q^1 dx^0 > 0$$

2. Suppose that in moving from social state A to social state $A*$ we find
$$q^0 dx^0 > 0$$
and
$$q^1 dx^0 < 0$$

Show why it is, in spite of the argument of section 13.3 – which, if not carefully read, may seem to imply that with suitable redistribution of income everybody may be better off in $A*$ than A, but may be made better off still by moving back to A – that it is not after all true that there exists a redistribution of all commodities available in social state A which could make everyone better off than they were to begin with.

3. Let there be, in social state A, 10 units of commodity 1 available and 5 units of commodity 2. In social state $A*$ there are 5 units of 1 and 10 units of 2. Let two individuals X and Y take commodities 1 and 2 in fixed (but different for X and Y) proportions whatever the pattern of prices. Prices which will clear the market now depend upon money income distribution (i.e. expenditure). Show that there exists a money distribution such that
$$q^1 dx^0 > 0$$

for a move from A to $A*$ but that it is impossible none the less to find any distribution such that both X and Y are better off in $A*$. Hence justify the argument in the text (section 13.3).

Hint: Prove that, whatever the income distribution, prices form so that the actual amounts consumed depend only on the social state and not at all upon expenditure and prices.

4. For the problem leading to the result (7.5.22), re-estimate the gain or loss this time using
$$dw* = q^1 dx^0$$
instead of
$$dw = q^0 dx^0$$

as in (7.5.22). Prove that the best estimate of $dw*$ is given by

$$q_2 X_2 \left[\frac{E_{22} + C_2}{1 + E'_{11} + E_{22}} \right] dt + q_2 X_2 \left[\frac{(1 + E'_{11} - C_2)(E_{22} + C_2)(1 + E'_{11})}{(1 + E'_{11} + E_{22})} \right] dt^2$$

5. Using the result of exercise 4, find the tariff which would be imposed if we aim at
$$q^1 dx^0 = 0$$

that is, if we take the first step in the iterative procedure for finding an optimal tariff explained in section 13.2. Show that, if an optimal tariff exists at all, this first step must set the tariff too high provided

$$\sigma_{22} \neq 0$$

where σ_{22} is the substitution part of the elasticity (see Introduction, section 5). Prove that the next step in the iterative process must be to reduce the tariff, given constant elasticities. Prove also that if σ_{22} is very small, the optimal tariff will be determined at once even though the level of tariff imposed may be quite high.

6. Using Figs. (7.1) and (7.4), show that the too high estimate of the optimal tariff referred to in exercise 5 above manifests itself diagrammatically in the impossibility of drawing a tangent to the offer curve AGE (Fig. 7.1)) at any point other than E such that the tangent cuts AGE also at E. Consider the connection between the shape of the offer curve AGE and the implicit assumption of constant elasticity over the range of tariff zero to dt.

7. Consider the meaning of the result (13.2.7) in the light of Fig. 10.1.

14 On Identifying Gains or Losses for a Particular Factor

14.1 INTRODUCTORY REMARKS

By way of illustration and for the sake of completeness we shall, in this and the next chapter, review at greater length two of the controversies mentioned in section 13.1. Both may be settled in consequence of the technique we now have at our disposal. We begin with the popular argument that in appropriate cases it is desirable to protect the worker against the 'ruinous competition of cheap foreign labour'.

For the most part economists have rejected this suggestion, at least in its superficial form. On the other hand, although the proposition is neither obvious nor in fact necessarily true, few have ever sought to deny that the opening-up of trade might bring about a fall in the wage rate for, say, unskilled labour, if unskilled labour is a factor of production abundant in the trading partner. It was soon noted, however, that to say that wages will fall is a very different thing from saying that unskilled labour will thereby lose in *real terms*. Trade not only changes factor prices but changes *commodity* prices as well. Who is to say that lower wage rates with lower commodity prices will not in fact improve the welfare of even the unskilled workers? It is important to distinguish very carefully between a fall in the *share* of national income accruing to unskilled workers and a fall in their *real* well-being in the sense of Chapter 13. The technique of Chapter 13 will allow this.

Economists first argued that, since trade brought a gain by ensuring that each commodity is produced by that country having a comparative advantage, it is unlikely that any productive factor will lose in absolute terms, for the share of the gain accruing to the group with a smaller relative reward will in all probability outweigh any loss.

The situation is still further complicated by a failure on the part of some disputants to distinguish properly between the situations actually being compared. It is sometimes not made clear precisely what the complaint is. The argument that one section of the community suffers by the existence of trade may imply that it is desirable that trade should be cut off altogether or it may imply that trade should be limited by the imposition of a quota or tariff. These two questions could be very different. The work of Book I shows that a tariff can improve welfare. The imposition of a tariff therefore might not only achieve a more desirable distribution of national income in the sense of the protection argument, but it could also increase the total to be shared. On the other hand a barrier large enough altogether to cut out trade which might otherwise take place would almost certainly reduce welfare overall. The removal of such a barrier may reduce the share of national income accruing to unskilled labour or some other factor, but it would inevitably provide something in compensation.

Curiously enough, on the basis of a proposition known as the Stolper–Samuelson theorem [14], this last argument has recently come to be questioned, although, it should be added, not by Stopler or Samuelson. It is well worth spending a little time investigating the Stolper–Samuelson theorem since some of the controversy surrounding it represents a good example of a somewhat disturbing trend in modern economic theory. Recent years have seen a welcome move away from intuitively based argument towards the creation of exact models giving precise answers, that is, exact measures in terms of elasticities of demand and supply of the consequences of policy, all of course being subject to the limitations of the model. In the early stages of such a transition, however, the trend towards exactness inevitably leads to some degree of over-simplification. Even the most trivial model seems to be quite complex when intuition gives way to exact argument. What then sometimes happens is that an apparently exciting result emerges which is, but is not immediately seen to be, a consequence of the simplification, having little to do with the real world.

All of this might not matter were it not for the fact that there is a natural human reluctance to abandon an exciting result once it is obtained. A great deal of intellectual effort comes to be poured into the, usually fascinating, but nevertheless unrewarding, task of finding conditions in which properties of the trivial model carry over into something more realistic. By the time these conditions are identified and found to be impossibly restrictive, so much interest has been aroused in the logic that many of the participants in the debate have lost sight of the real problem from which the argument began. The reader may judge for himself from what follows whether the not entirely abated storm in a teacup created by the publication of the Stolper–Samuelson paper is not a case in point.

14.2 A Misleading Short Cut

The Stolper–Samuelson proposition begins from the observation that if any factor price rises relative to *all* commodity prices then the supplier of that factor is unambiguously better off. It is of course not really necessary to prove this obvious proposition, but we shall do so simply as an exercise in the use of the work of Chapter 13.

Let L represent the total quantity of the factor whose price is p_1, let q_i be the ith commodity price and let X_i be consumption of it by factor 1. We then have

$$\sum_i q_i^0 X_i^0 = Lp_1^0$$

and

$$\sum_i q_i^1 X_i^1 = Lp_1^1$$

which says simply that total expenditure of L units of the factor equals total receipts in each of situations zero and one. We now measure both expenditure and income in factor units and write

$$\sum_i (q_i/p_1)^0 X_i^0 = L$$

and

$$\sum_i (q_i/p_1)^1 X_i^1 = L$$

that is, we divide each equation by p_1^0 and p_1^1 respectively. But by assumption

$$(q_i/p_1)^1 < (q_i/p^1)^0$$

for each i, since p_1 rises relatively to each q_i. It follows that

$$\sum (q_i/p_1)^0 X_i^1 > L = \sum (q_i/p_1)^0 X_i^0$$

or, multiplying throughout by p_1 and subtracting the right-hand side from the left-hand side,

$$\sum q_i^0 dX_i^0 = q^0 dx^0 > 0$$

which is the first of the required conditions for a welfare gain.

The second condition, namely,

$$q^1 dx^0 > 0$$

may be obtained in an exactly similar way by observing that

$$\sum_i (q_i/p_1)^1 X_i^0 < L = \sum_i (q_i/p_1)^1 X_i^1$$

It follows that any class of labour whose wage rate rises relative to all commodity prices is unambiguously better off however many factors exist or commodities are produced and consumed. This step is of course not open to question. The difficulty arises out of the second stage of the argument.

The Stolper–Samuelson model as originally presented ran in terms of two commodities and two factors, both commodities being produced in the country under review. We now look for a relationship between commodity and factor prices based upon this assumption.

At this point it is convenient to ask the reader to acquire a simple piece of mathematical knowledge over and above that normally taught in school. It must already be clear that a great many of the algebraic operations in this book amount in effect to the simultaneous solution of a number of independent linear equations. It will be of considerable assistance in organising the work that follows if it can be supposed that the reader now understands how to solve such an equation system by the method of determinants and how to evaluate determinants when set out. Although not more than two or three pages of writing would be needed to explain what is required, this will not be attempted here, for there are now available a superfluity of texts setting out the technique in the simplest language (R. G. D. Allen, *Mathematical Analysis for Economists*, pp. 472–80, and A. Kooros, *The Elements of Mathematical Economics*, pp. 287–91, are recommended [1] and [5]).

In a two-commodity/two-factor world the cost identities of Chapter 12 may be set out as follows

$$q_1 = a_{11}p_1 + a_{12}p_2$$

$$q_2 = a_{21}p_1 + a_{22}p_2$$

where a_{ij} is the input of the jth factor required, in combination with other factors, to produce one unit of the ith commodity.

We now take changes on both sides in the manner of Book I to yield

$$dq_1 = a_{11}dp_1 + a_{12}dp_2 + p_1 da_{11} + p_2 da_{12}$$

and $\qquad dq_2 = a_{12}dp_1 + a_{22}dp_2 + p_1 da_{21} + p_2 da_{22}$

Recalling that the techniques of production chosen at the going factor prices are minimum-cost techniques, it must follow that

$$\left. \begin{array}{l} p_1 da_{11} + p_2 da_{12} = 0 \\ p_1 da_{21} + p_2 da_{22} = 0 \end{array} \right\} \qquad (14.2.1)$$

and

for if either left-hand side was different from zero it would have been possible to reduce cost. In fact the left-hand sides of (14.2.1) are the changes in cost which would occur if inputs were changed (still producing one unit of output) whilst prices are held constant. If these cost changes were not zero, it would be possible to reduce cost by making them (or their opposites), which contradicts the assumption that cost is minimised.†

Hence we have

$$dq_1 = a_{11}dp_1 + a_{12}dp_2 \atop dq_2 = a_{21}dp_1 + a_{22}dp_2 \Bigg\}$$

(14.2.2)

(14.2.2) is a very convenient result and indeed lies at the heart of all factor price problems. The reader should make a point of understanding here and now that the changes in factor prices for every single problem of Book I may be immediately derived from (14.2.2) simply and without difficulty, for we have now before us a relation which enables us to solve for dp_1 and dp_2 in terms of dq_1 and dq_2 and the coefficients a_{ij}. By substitution of the results in Book I for dq_1 and dq_2 we may obtain factor price changes in terms of elasticities of demand and supply and the inputs a_{ij}. Note that the inputs a_{ij} are crucial parameters of the same key importance as elasticities and may be, as it happens, much more readily observed than elasticities since they are quantities actually in use.

For the moment, take q_2 as the numeraire price so that dq_2 is zero. By the method of determinants we write down

$$dp_1 = \frac{\begin{vmatrix} dq_1 & a_{12} \\ 0 & a_{22} \end{vmatrix}}{\begin{vmatrix} a_{11} & a_{12} \\ a_{21} & a_{22} \end{vmatrix}}$$

† A particularly vigilant reader might agree that if certain changes in technique $+da_{ij}$ actually increase cost, then it must be true that changes $-da_{ij}$ would decrease q_i, but he might be tempted to argue that it is not obvious that changes $-da_{ij}$ would leave output unchanged at one unit just because changes $+da_{ij}$ are assumed to do so. The answer to this is that if

$$S_i = S_i(A_{i1}, A_{i2}) = 1$$

is the production function and if

$$dS_i = (\partial S_i / \partial A_{i1})(dA_{i1}) + (\partial S_i / \partial A_{i2})(dA_{i2}) = 0$$

then it follows that $dS_i^* = \left(\dfrac{\partial S_i}{\partial A_{i1}}\right)(-dA_{i1}) + \left(\dfrac{\partial S_i}{\partial A_{i2}}\right)(-dA_{i2}) = 0$ as required.

or, dividing both sides of this equation by p_1 and inserting p_2, q_1 and q_2 in the top and bottom of the right-hand side,

$$\frac{dp_1}{p_1} = \frac{\begin{vmatrix} \dfrac{dq_1}{q_1} & \dfrac{p_2 a_{12}}{q_1} \\[2ex] 0 & \dfrac{p_2 a_{22}}{q_2} \end{vmatrix}}{\begin{vmatrix} \dfrac{p_1 a_{11}}{q_1} & \dfrac{p_2 a_{12}}{q_1} \\[2ex] \dfrac{p_1 a_{21}}{q_2} & \dfrac{p_2 a_{22}}{q_2} \end{vmatrix}} \tag{14.2.3}$$

or again

$$\frac{dp_1}{p_1} \Big/ \frac{dq_1}{q_1} = \frac{\dfrac{p_2 a_{22}}{q_2}}{J} \tag{14.2.4}$$

where J is the determinant forming the denominator of the right-hand side of (14.2.3).

The interest of (14.2.4) lies in the fact that the left-hand side is the ratio of the percentage changes of the factor price p_1 and the commodity price q_1. Thus if the right-hand side is positive and greater than unity, the percentage change in p_1 is greater than the percentage change in q_1 whether both rise or fall. If the change is in a positive direction p_1 rises, which implies, since q_2 does not change, that it rises also relative to q_2. Accordingly, the case where the right-hand side of (14.2.4) is positive and greater than unity is precisely the case already identified where the factor whose price is p_1 must be better off in real terms.

We see also that

$$\left(\frac{p_2 a_{22}}{q_2}\right) > \left(\frac{p_1 a_{11}}{q_1}\right)\left(\frac{p_2 a_{22}}{q_2}\right) - \left(\frac{p_2 a_{12}}{q_1}\right)\left(\frac{p_1 a_{21}}{q_2}\right) \tag{14.2.5}$$

for each of the bracketed elements is positive and less than unity since each represents part of the cost divided by total cost. Thus the first term of the right-hand side of (14.2.5) is less than the whole left-hand side and the remaining term on the right-hand side is negative.

Suppose, in case (i), the whole of the right-hand side of (14.2.5) is a positive number. Then, dividing both sides by the right-hand side, we learn that the right-hand side of (14.2.4) is greater than unity. Accordingly, whenever both dp_1 and dq_1 are positive we must have the owners of factor 1 unambiguously better off.

In order to show that q_1 and hence p_1 will rise if trade is inhibited, Stolper and Samuelson took over and systematised an earlier intuitive argument. Economists seeking to explain the basic causes of differing comparative advantage in terms of factor endowment had already suggested that 'each country would be able to produce most cheaply those commodities which use a relatively high proportion of its most abundant factor', and this is the final step required.

In fact there are a dozen reasons why we might expect this last proposition to be meaningless or not empirically justified. Nevertheless, for the moment it is convenient to accept it. Thus, in the two-factor/two-commodity case under discussion, we could suppose, without any loss of generality, that commodity 1 is an import, and that factor 1 is the factor most abundant abroad. From this, to be consistent with the comparative advantage argument, we should have to conclude that

$$\frac{a_{11}}{a_{12}} > \frac{a_{21}}{a_{22}}$$

which simply says that commodity 1 uses factor 1 in a higher ratio than commodity 2. Hence

$$\left(\frac{p_1 a_{11}}{q_1}\right) \bigg/ \left(\frac{p_2 a_{12}}{q_1}\right) > \left(\frac{p_1 a_{21}}{q_2}\right) \bigg/ \left(\frac{p_2 a_{22}}{q_2}\right)$$

which implies J of (14.2.4) positive as required.

If now we suppose that the importation of commodity 1 is restricted, its price will presumably rise, i.e. dq_1 is positive; hence dp_1 is positive and the conditions of the theorem are satisfied. Factor 1 will be unambiguously better off in real terms. On the basis of this result it has been widely held that protectionists might after all be justified in their complaint that unskilled workers should not be exposed to the competition of cheap foreign labour despite the contrary arguments of the classical economists. If labour (factor 1) is abundant abroad, that is, if it is cheap, then to keep out the product of foreign labour will be to raise real wages at home.

As a piece of logic the argument we have just concluded is impeccable. As a general proposition intended to be an aid to policy-makers, however, it has very little to commend it, as its originators well understood. In particular the simplicity and certainty of the result is more a consequence of the limitations of the model than it is a manifestation of some underlying harmony of economic behaviour universally present. Before commenting further upon this we proceed to identify the main points at which the proof breaks down on generalisation.

First and foremost, the whole proposition rests crucially upon the fact that the model has only two products and two factors of production. Indeed, the alert reader will already be wondering why we have been able to prove so much by looking only at cost equations and without any reference to the pattern of consumer demand. The answer in brief to this is that, with two commodities only, if the output of one commodity increases the other must diminish. Such a unidirectional change at once identifies which commodity price goes up and which goes down from the cost side alone. Demand serves only to determine the amount of the change and not the direction. On the other hand the direction of change when three or more commodities are present, that is, the determination of those commodities which increase and those which diminish in output, and the proportions in which their output changes, depends upon a complex interaction of *both* cost *and* demand. What this means is that we should not expect to be able to solve any realistic economic problem concerning factor prices without reference both to demand elasticities *and* supply elasticities.

To be more specific, consider the intuitive argument which Stolper and Samuelson set out to systematise. If country *A* has an abundant supply of cheap labour it will accordingly produce most cheaply commodities using a high proportion of labour in their manufacture. Country *B*, being endowed with less unskilled labour, will begin to import labour-intensively-produced commodities. This will reduce the manufacture of labour-intensive commodities in country *B*, demand now being met by imports, and hence reduce the demand for labour. The price of unskilled labour will fall in country *B*.

But note that this plausible argument turns on the implicit aggregation of commodities into two groups, those which are labour-intensive and those which are not. Consider the consequences of the alternative. Suppose that country *B* produces three commodities, 1 with the highest ratio of labour to capital, 2 with the next-highest ratio and 3 with the lowest. Suppose that it begins to export 2 and 3 and to import 1 from *A*. As the price of 1 falls output will fall, with a corresponding rise in the output of 2 and 3. It is of course true that the fall in production of 1 will reduce the overall demand for labour, but if the increase in the output of 2 is proportionately greater than the increase in the output of 3, then a more than proportionate increase in demand for labour will result. Why should this not increase the overall demand for labour and raise its price instead of reducing it? This question cannot be answered without consideration of the pattern of demand as well as supply.

Of course, if the price of labour does rise in B where labour is already scarce, and if it is true (we shall see that it might not be) that the high relative cost of labour at home is the fundamental reason for the relative cheapness of commodity 1 abroad, then 1 may become still dearer relatively at home, thus encouraging still more trade until production in B of commodity 1 ceases entirely. This is a simple reflection of the fact already noted in Chapter 12 that, unless there is full factor price equalisation, it is impossible to have more commodities produced in common than there exist factors of production. This leads to the following observation.

If we simply *assume* as some writers have that all three commodities can remain in production in B after trade, it is easy to prove that with not more than two factors of production the Stolper–Samuelson result persists. Indeed, we now have a third equation

$$dq_3 = a_{31} dp_1 + a_{32} dp_2$$

to add to the equations (14.2.2) above, and we know that by assumption all three must be consistent; that is, it does not matter when we solve for dp_1 whether we use equations one and two or equations two and three; the result must be the same. Thus

$$dp_1 = \frac{\begin{vmatrix} dq_1 & a_{12} \\ 0 & a_{22} \end{vmatrix}}{\begin{vmatrix} a_{11} & a_{12} \\ a_{21} & a_{22} \end{vmatrix}} = \frac{\begin{vmatrix} 0 & a_{22} \\ dq_3 & a_{32} \end{vmatrix}}{\begin{vmatrix} a_{21} & a_{22} \\ a_{31} & a_{32} \end{vmatrix}} = \frac{\begin{vmatrix} a_{12} & 0 \\ a_{32} & dq_3 \end{vmatrix}}{\begin{vmatrix} a_{12} & a_{11} \\ a_{32} & a_{31} \end{vmatrix}} \qquad (14.2.6)$$

from which we deduce that the sign of dq_3 is determined by the sign of the denominator of the extreme right-hand side. On our assumption above, that commodity 3 uses the lowest proportion of labour to factor 2, say capital, the denominator of the right-hand side will be negative so that dp_1 and dq_3 must be of opposite sign. If we suppose that the introduction of trade forces a reduction in the home cost of producing imports, then the price of labour, p_1, falls more than proportionately to q_1; q_2 remains unchanged and q_3 rises. Hence labour is unambiguously worse off and the Stolper–Samuelson case seems to be proved. But this is simply assuming what we want to prove, i.e. the existence of an equilibrium with equal factor prices.

What is wrong is the assumption that the cheap importation of

commodity 1 causes the *home cost of producing* q_1 to fall. This does
not necessarily follow just because output of commodity 1 falls. If
the demand for, and output of, commodity 2 rises very sharply
owing to the fall in production of commodity 1, its cheapened price,
and/or the real income effects of new trading opportunities, the
overall demand for labour in country B could rise and the home cost
of producing both commodities 1 and 2 might rise relative to
commodity 3. Clearly, however, this process could not lead to an
overall equilibrium *with all three commodities* in production in
country B, for the production cost in country B of commodity 1
begins by being higher than the world price and then rises. What will
happen is that commodity 1 will go out of production in B,
which will specialise in commodities 2 and 3 only, as previously
indicated.

Of course we do not *know* that this will happen. Everything
depends on the interaction of demand and supply conditions. An
equilibrium with equal factor prices in both countries might emerge
in which case specialisation may not result. The point we wish to
make here is that with three commodities, to look at equation
(14.2.6) above and to assume that the cheap importation of commodity 1 implies $dq_1 < 0$ is simply to beg the question at issue. We can
only be certain that the price q_1 (cost in B) will fall if not more than
two commodities are produced. In such a case the overall demand for
labour must fall since the output of the capital-intensive commodity
rises and that of the labour-intensive commodity falls.

The lesson we learn from this simple development of the model is
that no theorem purporting to explain factor price movements or
factor welfare is possible without some consideration of the conditions of supply *and* demand. Nor is this all. Further extensions of
the model illustrate even more powerfully the main theme of this
chapter.

14.3 THREE COMMODITIES, THREE FACTORS

Suppose for example that we have three commodities and three
factors of production. In this case it is not possible to show that the
price of labour falls even when it is *assumed* that the home cost of
producing importables falls. Furthermore, if it is assumed that the
price of labour does fall it need not fall more than proportionately
to the cost of producing importables. We have in fact three equations,
this time in three changes of factor prices, namely,

$$dq_1 = a_{11}dp_1 + a_{12}dp_2 + a_{13}dp_3$$
$$dq_2 = a_{21}dp_1 + a_{22}dp_2 + a_{23}dp_3$$
$$dq_3 = a_{31}dp_1 + a_{32}dp_2 + a_{33}dp_3$$

from which we deduce

$$dp_1 = \frac{\begin{vmatrix} dq_1 & a_{12} & a_{13} \\ 0 & a_{22} & a_{23} \\ dq_3 & a_{32} & a_{33} \end{vmatrix}}{|a_{ij}|} \tag{14.3.1}$$

where $|a_{ij}|$ is the determinant of coefficients, a_{ij}.

Note that only one commodity can be chosen as numeraire, so that only dq_2 can be set at zero. Hence choice of sign for dq_1 no longer determines the sign of dp_1 on at least three counts. First, we do not know the sign of dq_3. Second, the fact that all inputs a_{ij} are necessarily positive does not determine the sign of the numerator of (14.3.1), even if we assume that both dq_1 and dq_3 are positive when trade is restricted. Third, even if the sign of the numerator were known, the arguments about factor intensity used in the case of two factors are insufficient to determine the sign of the denominator of (14.3.1). Anything can happen.

Finally, we note that if we had been able, on reasonable assumptions, to determine the sign of the right-hand side of (14.3.1) so that we could say that p_1 rises when q_1 rises, we should still be unable to settle the welfare question, for all the arguments used above to show that p_1 rises *relative* to q_1 and q_2 break down in their turn. The Stolper–Samuelson theorem on these counts alone is simply a proposition about two-dimensional models of no significance to the real world of many factors.

At this point it may be desirable to repeat a warning carefully emphasised by Stolper and Samuelson in their original paper but perhaps overlooked by some of their readers. There may be a temptation to feel that, since the meaning of a 'commodity' is to some extent arbitrary (for example, are shoes size 7 a different commodity from shoes size 8?), there is no objection to lumping all commodities into two groups, say importables and exportables. The truth is, however, that for some problems this process of aggregation obscures the very problem we are trying to study. If two objects exist whose prices need not move in proportion to one another and/or the outputs of which need not move in proportion, then they must, for the purpose of the present argument, be treated as *different* commodities. Otherwise we have a composite commodity whose price or cost may change even though factor prices do not change, solely because of changes in the composition of the elements making it up. Whether or not the real world contains two or more than two commodities on this definition is a question of fact about which it should not be hard to make up our minds.

14.4 Another Misleading Short Cut

So far we have been concerned with one particular simplification of the Stolper–Samuelson theorem, namely, that which restricts the number of commodities and factors to two. But at least one other simplification is crucial. The classical argument suggesting that a country produces relatively cheaply that commodity using the higher proportion of its most abundant factor of production itself rests upon a particularly restrictive simplification. A reading of the work of early writers putting forward this proposition suggests that what they must have had in mind was a model which permits production by one technique only. That is, if the output of one unit of, say, wheat demands an input of two units of land and one unit of labour in the United Kingdom, then it demands the same inputs *anywhere else in the world*. To satisfy this requirement the laws of plant biology and physics must be assumed to be such that only those inputs can produce at all. The less intensive cultivation of a wider acreage must be assumed to produce nothing at all, as must the more intensive cultivation of a smaller acreage.

We have seen in an earlier chapter that it is most convenient to use a form of words implying that production functions are identical everywhere in the world. To this, for the proposition under review to be true, the classical writers seem to have added implicitly the assumption that there is only one kind of land and only one way to produce wheat. The inputs a_{ij} of our model are assumed to be constants.

Given this assumption, we may at once write our two cost functions in ratio form

$$\frac{q_1}{q_2} \equiv \frac{a_{11}p_1 + a_{12}p_2}{a_{21}p_1 + a_{22}p_2} \equiv \frac{a_{11}}{a_{21}} \frac{1 + \dfrac{a_{12}p_2}{a_{11}p_1}}{1 + \dfrac{a_{22}p_2}{a_{21}p_1}} \tag{14.4.1}$$

thus demonstrating that if

$$\frac{a_{12}}{a_{11}} > \frac{a_{22}}{a_{21}} \tag{14.4.2}$$

then q_1/q_2 rises continuously as p_2/p_1 rises. Thus in a country where factor 1 is relatively cheap, i.e. where p_2/p_1 is higher than abroad, we have q_1/q_2 higher than abroad, i.e. commodity 2 is relatively cheap. And by (14.4.2) commodity 2 uses the higher proportion of the relatively cheap factor. The above is a formal proof of what is of course intuitively obvious. But we have learned to mistrust our intuition, and we need the proof to see why the proposition may be false in a world where many techniques of production are possible.

It should be noted in passing that we have been using the word 'abundant' synonymously with 'cheap'. The formal working-out now reveals that what we must mean is 'cheap'. Commodity 2 is relatively cheap only in countries whose p_1 is relatively low. Factor 1 may be as abundant as we like in the sense of there being relatively more of it in a country. But if it also happens that demand before trade is relatively high for the commodity using the higher proportion of the abundant factor, it may still happen that the abundant factor is relatively dear. Even in a two-factor/two-commodity world, therefore, demand conditions cannot be ignored entirely.

It is now established that, on the classical assumption that one and only one technique of production exists, it will be true that a country will export that commodity which uses the higher proportion of its relatively *cheap* factor of production. This is, of course, a proposition which makes sense only if there are two factors of production, so that we find yet another reason why the Stolper–Samuelson theorem holds only for the impossibly unrealistic two-factor model. But we are not just now interested in this. Our present concern is with the significance of the single-technique postulate.

Obviously in the real world many different techniques of production are used to grow or manufacture the same commodity. The very words 'intensive' and 'extensive' cultivation of land give expression to this. And it is irrelevant to the present problem *whether* different techniques are in fact used. The production function is the set of all techniques which *could* be used if they were cheapest and not the much narrower set of techniques which is observed to be used in practice. It is hardly a matter for dispute that there must be very many different ways of making anything. If the world used the same technique everywhere we should suspect this to be because factor prices were the same everywhere, and not because the laws of physics demanded it.

Accordingly, in any realistic model designed to study the relation between factor and commodity prices we must let the chosen techniques a_{ij} be dependent on factor prices. In this case the argument from equation (14.4.1) breaks down. As long as (14.4.2) is satisfied, it is of course true that q_1/q_2 rises as p_2/p_1 rises. But as p_2/p_1 rises, producers attempting to minimise cost will try to substitute factor 1 which is becoming cheaper for factor 2 which now costs more. In quite ordinary circumstances this could happen faster in commodity 1 than 2. A point might be reached where, for some level of p_2/p_1,

$$\frac{a_{12}}{a_{11}} < \frac{a_{22}}{a_{21}}$$

in which case a further increase in p_2/p_1 will lead to a fall in q_1/q_2 rather than a rise. This fall could continue until the value of q_1/q_2 reaches a point lower than the value, say $(q_1/q_2)^0$, from which the original rise began. If country A has a low p_2/p_1, say $(p_2/p_1)^0$, yielding $(q_1/q_2)^0$, country B may have a high p_2/p_1 but q_1/q_2 lower than $(q_1/q_2)^0$. Country A would import q_1 even though *in country A* the manufacturing technique used for commodity 1 calls for a higher proportion of factor 2 than that for commodity 2 and even though, in country A, it is factor 2 which is relatively cheap. This is in contradiction with the classical proposition and in contradiction with the Stolper–Samuelson assumption.

We could indeed take the matter further. There is nothing known about production functions to rule out the possibility that as the price ratio p_2/p_1 rises still more, a further change in relative 'factor intensities' occurs. So that once again we have

$$\frac{a_{12}}{a_{11}} > \frac{a_{22}}{a_{11}}$$

q_1/q_2 will now begin to rise again, but at factor price, ratio $(p_2/p_1)^1$ may not be as high as $(q_1/q_2)^0$. With country B in this position, A would still import commodity 1 and export commodity 2 even though it is now true that production of commodity 1 calls for a higher proportion of A's relatively cheap factor in *both* countries.

Obviously on purely logical grounds we cannot establish the classical proposition when there are many possible production techniques, that is, for the real world. Nor can we establish the proposition empirically, for the real world contains many factors and commodities and hence the classical argument cannot apply. To those with a lingering penchant for aggregation it may be added that an attempt to test empirically the classical belief, using the most sophisticated aggregation technique, led to the conclusion that the United States exports labour-intensively produced commodities even though that country is obviously capital-rich. The United States, as someone has put it, has been shown to be an underdeveloped territory.

We shall have a great deal more to say in Chapter 16, below, on the problem of factor intensities in a more general context. In the meantime another important point remains to be cleared up which is more directly concerned with the welfare problem before us. The proof given in the early part of this chapter, that labour will be worse off in real terms if the price of labour falls relative to all commodity prices, rests upon the assumption that the total reward of labour is the price paid multiplied by the quantity of labour supplied. Total spending of labour is supposed to equal total wages received. This is all right provided we neglect taxation entirely, including tariffs and subsidies. It is all right, for example, if we were concerned to compare trade and non-trade positions. But it is not all right if we are asking about the effect of some practical policy. If a tariff is imposed, we have already seen (Chapter 7) that the total expenditure of the community as a whole is greater than the total paid to all factors of production by an amount equal to the tariff revenue. In such a case, the welfare of labour as a whole must not be measured by what wages can buy but by the real purchasing power of wages *plus* labour's share of the tariff revenue.

The reader should not make the mistake of supposing that, because tariff revenue is given, in the first instance, into the hands of government, it should not be counted as adding to the welfare of the workers. There are many ways of seeing that such a view would be wrong. We might suppose that there is no government expenditure, in which case the tariff proceeds would have to be given direct to individuals in the form of cash in addition to wages; or we might assume that the services provided by government are given and fixed, however the revenue is raised, in which case general taxation must be reduced *pari passu* when a tariff is imposed. Either way, labour's share of the tariff revenue must be added to the wage rate, or the wage rate less tax, to compute welfare.

All of this underlines a point made at the beginning of this chapter. Even if it had been possible to show that the inhibition of trade raises the real purchasing power of the wage rate, this certainly does not show that it is always in the interest of labour to protect itself by adding to a tariff already in existence. We do not know that an increase in the tariff rate will always increase tariff revenue even though we know that in ordinary circumstances it will improve the real terms of trade. Indeed, we can be sure that at some level of tariff an increase in the rate must diminish total revenue, for if the tariff is so high that there is no trade at all there can be no tariff revenue. At some point revenue is bound to begin to fall. Suppose the tariff revenue is in fact falling. To increase the tariff rate might raise the wage rate but it might equally well diminish the money spending of labour, since it diminishes labour's share of the tariff revenue. In such a case, to establish that labour gains in real terms, we have to show not that the wage rate rises relative to every commodity price, but that the wage rate plus tariff revenue rises relative to every commodity price. This is a very much more complex problem than that tackled by Stolper and Samuelson.

If the Stolper–Samuelson theorem faced no other difficulty, all that it could be said to have shown is that labour, say, would be worse off under free trade with a labour-abundant trading partner, than it would have been if a tariff were imposed large enough to prevent trade altogether. It would prove this only because in both situations the tariff revenue is zero. What it would not tell us is whether or not labour might be better off still at some level of tariff which merely reduces trade rather than extinguishes it. Nor does it enable us to discover whether or not in the intermediate situation any other factor is better or worse off, a question which is of at least equivalent interest.

What was exciting about the Stolper–Samuelson theorem when it first appeared was that it seemed to give an exact qualitative answer, in no way resting upon measures of elasticity which might have been thought hard to compute, to the question 'Who receives the gain from trade?' In the event, however, it turns out that the behaviour of the Stolper–Samuelson model is a characteristic of its extreme simplicity in no way reflecting economic behaviour in the real world. Nothing is really left which could be said to be of immediate value to the policy-maker.

We hasten to emphasise, however, that none of this necessarily implies that the original inquiry was useless or a waste of time. Knowledge is knowledge whether it is applicable or not. What is slightly disturbing on the other hand is the extent to which the theorem continues to occupy such a large place in our textbooks. Rather than look for an alternative approach to the original problem, the academic world has tended to concentrate upon detailing the precise assumptions upon which the theorem (or parts of it) are true, even in many dimensions. Quite recently, for example, considerable intellectual effort has gone into an attempt to find what restrictions might be imposed upon the elements a_{ij} which enter into the determinants (14.3.1) so as to be sure that, if all commodity price changes other than q_1 are zero, then dp_1 is of the same sign as dq_1 and p_1 rises relative to q_1. There is a sense of course in which this represents a generalisation of the results developed from (14.2.3), but it is difficult to see how the information gained could be used even if sufficient conditions were found. It should be noted that, however fascinating and difficult such problems may be, they have very little to do with the original welfare inquiry from which we began.

It would be wrong of course to object to continued investigation of the mathematical properties of arrays of factor inputs when certain constraints are imposed even if one suspected that such inquiries were provoked more by the elegance of the problem than by the urgent need for practical results. On the other hand it would be still more wrong to ignore the fact that it has already been shown that no answer is possible to the important practical question originally posed by the classical economists, except one which depends upon numerical values of elasticities of supply and demand, particularly when we have at our disposal a technique permitting us to develop exact answers.

It may be possible to discover elegant restrictions upon production functions which are *sufficient* to ensure that qualitative answers can be given whatever the patterns of demand, but we already know fairly well from our counter-examples that such conditions are unlikely to be met in the real world. And at the same time we already know enough to give both necessary and sufficient conditions, in terms of elasticities which we might hope to compute, precisely identifying the welfare consequences of any policy whatever. There is a case for making these results, however clumsy they may be, the principal content of our textbooks. Since the conditions we have are both necessary and sufficient, there is little scope for further mathematical enquiry other than to seek improved methods of inferring something about likely values of elasticities of demand or supply.

14.5 A More Correct Approach

In support of the arguments above, we proceed now to investigate the circumstances in which the imposition of a tariff will raise the real income of *both* of the two factors of production in a two-product/two factor model. The purpose of this exercise is of course simply to demonstrate the technique. The method used may be applied without modification to more realistic models. We do not do so at the present time only because the introduction of more commodities and factors increases to an enormous extent the tedious nature of the computations, at the same time involving no new principle.

Clearly, no conclusion is possible until the division of tariff revenue between the two factors of production is determined. As an example we suppose that benefits are distributed in proportion to factor prices. Let the value of total consumption in country A be

$$\sum_i q_i X_i$$

where X_i is quantity consumed of the ith commodity and q_i is price. Let p_j be the price of the jth factor and let A_j be the total endowment of the jth factor. Then the total value of consumption of the owners of the jth factor will be

$$Y^* = \frac{p_j A_j}{\sum_j p_j A_j} \sum_i q_i X_i \tag{14.5.1}$$

Let X_i^* the consumption of the ith commodity by the owners of the jth factor in which we are interested. The welfare change for the owners of the jth factor will then be

$$dw_j = \sum q_i dX_i^* = dY^* - \sum_i X_i^* dq_i \tag{14.5.2}$$

Put
$$\lambda_j = \frac{p_j A_j}{\sum_j p_j A_j} \tag{14.5.3}$$

Then from (14.5.1) we have

$$dY^* = \lambda_j(\sum_i q_i dX_i + \sum_i X_i dq_i) + (\sum_i q_i X_i)d\lambda_j \tag{14.5.4}$$

Hence from (14.5.2)

$$dw_j = \lambda_j \sum q_i dX_i + \lambda_j \sum X_i dq_i + (\sum q_i X_i)d\lambda_j - \sum X_i^* dq_i \tag{14.5.5}$$

In the ordinary way it would be necessary now to introduce distinct and separate demand functions for the two classes of consumers, the owners of the jth factor of production and the rest of the population. We should have to write

$$X_i = X_i^* + X_i^{**} = X_i^*(q_1, q_2, Y^*) + X_i^{**}(q_1, q_2, Y^{**})$$

where ** indicates 'belonging to the rest of the population'. Our results would then depend upon the numerical values of elasticities of demand for each of the two groups. Throughout this book, however, we have been making the assumption that the average or 'representative' consumer in each group has roughly the same preferences, so that redistribution of money expenditure makes only a negligible difference to the aggregate consumption of each commodity. This implies that

$$X_i^* = \lambda_j X_i$$

so that terms two and four in (14.5.5) cancel each other out.

For present purposes it is enough to accept this assumption. Thus we have

$$dw_j = \lambda_j \sum q_i dX_i + (\sum q_i X_i) d\lambda_j \qquad (14.5.6)$$

It is now necessary to find the value of $d\lambda_j$ from (14.5.3). The simplest way to proceed with this, recalling that we are interested only in the two-factor/two-commodity case, is to rewrite (14.5.3) in the form

$$\lambda_1 (p_1 A_1 + p_2 A_2) = p_1 A_1$$

Taking changes, remembering that As are constant, gives

$$(p_1 A_1 + p_2 A_2) d\lambda_1 + \lambda_1 A_1 dp_1 + \lambda_1 A_2 dp_2 = A_1 dp_1 \qquad (14.5.7)$$

But if the tariff rate is initially zero, so that tariff revenue is zero, then

$$p_1 A_1 + p_2 A_2 = \sum_i q_i X_i$$

which simply says that the sum of all incomes equals the value of output equals aggregate expenditure. Thus from (14.5.7)

$$(\sum_i q_i X_i) d\lambda_1 = (1 - \lambda_1) A_1 dp_1 - \lambda_1 A_2 dp_2 \qquad (14.5.8)$$

Assuming that q_1 is kept constant as the price of the numeraire commodity, values for dp_1 and dp_2 may now be written in terms of dq_2 as explained in section 14.2 (see (14.2.3)). Thus

$$dp_1 = -\frac{a_{12}}{|a_{ij}|} dq_2 \left.\right]$$

and $\qquad dp_2 = \frac{a_{11}}{|a_{ij}|} dq_2 \left.\right\}$ $\qquad (14.5.9)$

where $|a_{ij}|$ is the usual determinant of factor inputs required to produce one unit of output.

Putting (14.5.9) in (14.5.8), we have

$$(\sum_i q_i X_i)d\lambda_1 = - \left[\frac{(1 - \lambda_1)A_1a_{12} + \lambda_1 A_2 a_{11}}{|a_{ij}|}\right]dq_2 \quad (14.5.10)$$

In turn (14.5.10) may be put in (14.5.6) to give

$$dw_1 = \lambda_1 \sum_i q_i dX_i - \left[\frac{(1 - \lambda_1)A_1a_{12} + \lambda_1 A_2 a_{11}}{|a_{ij}|}\right]dq_2 \quad (14.5.11)$$

which is the measure of welfare change we seek.

It is now a simple matter to set up a model as in Chapter 7 to solve for the changes dX_i and dq_2 in terms of elasticities of demand and supply, but as it happens there is no need to carry out this work in full at the present time. The point we wish to make can be made without going to this trouble.

It does not of course make sense for the present problem to use the model of section 7.5 exactly as it stands, since only one commodity is assumed to be produced. But a suitable result is quickly established for the two-commodity case.

As usual, total national expenditure Y is the total value of output plus tax revenue, so that

$$Y = \sum q_i S_i + tq_2' x_2 = \sum q_i X_i \quad (14.5.12)$$

where imports are

$$x_2 = X_2 - S_2$$

and q_2' is the foreign price of importables. t is the tariff rate.

Taking changes in (14.5.12) yields

$$\sum q_i dX_i + \sum X_i dq_i = \sum q_i dS_i + \sum S_i dq_i + q_2' x_2 dt \quad (14.5.13)$$

if t is initially zero. We know also, from section 11.6, that

$$\sum q_i dS_i = 0$$

so that

$$\sum q_i dX_i = \sum (S_i - X_i)dq_i + q_2' x_2 dt \quad (14.5.14)$$

In a two-commodity world with commodity 1 as numeraire, this becomes

$$\sum q_i dX_i = - x_2 dq_2 + q_2' x_2 dt$$

But

$$q_2 = q_2'(1 + t)$$

or

$$dq_2 = q_2' dt + dq_2'$$

Hence

$$\sum q_i dX_i = - x_2 dq_2' \quad (14.5.15)$$

Thus, finally, we may put (14.5.15) into (14.5.11) to obtain

$$dw_1 = -\lambda_1 x_2 dq_2' - \left[\frac{(1-\lambda_1)A_1 a_{12} + \lambda_1 A_2 a_{11}}{|a_{ij}|}\right] dq_2 \quad (14.5.16)$$

In the ordinary way we should now have to solve for dq_2' and dq_2, but the form (14.5.16) permits us to comment at once. It is known of course that when a tariff is imposed the real terms of trade improve, i.e. dq_2' is negative. The first term of (14.5.16) is factor 1's share of the real terms of trade improvement. Term two is the change in factor 1's share of money expenditure.

If the Stolper–Samuelson assumptions were justified, we should know also that $|a_{ij}|$ is negative, for country 1 exports commodity 1 which must therefore, according to the discredited classical theory, use a relatively high proportion of factor 2 which is country 1's abundant factor. Thus

$$\frac{a_{11}}{a_{12}} < \frac{a_{21}}{a_{22}}$$

which is the same thing as saying that $|a_{ij}|$ is negative.

It is also fundamental to the Stolper–Samuelson approach that 'protection' of commodity 2 by a tariff must increase production of commodity 2. Hence the price q_2 must rise. dq_2 is positive. And since all other elements of terms two in (14.5.3) are positive, term two itself adds to welfare. Factor 1 gains on two counts, first from the real terms of trade improvement and second from its increased share of total money expenditure. But of course $|a_{ij}|$ may not be negative, nor may the tariff protect as we saw in section 8.2. It is not at all certain therefore, indeed there is not even a probability, that a tariff will 'protect' the home labour force from the 'competition' of cheap foreign labour. Everything, as usual, depends upon the facts of the case.

More interesting still is the effect of the tariff upon the welfare of the abundant factor 2. Suppose $|a_{ij}|$ is negative and dq_2 is positive as required by Stolper–Samuelson. As sometimes presented, the Stolper–Samuelson theory would seem to suggest that factor 2 must lose. But this is not so. Clearly, if $d\lambda_1$ is positive $d\lambda_2$ must be negative, since the λs are proportions. Hence, for factor 2, the welfare terms corresponding to those in (14.5.11) will be of different sign.

The question whether factor 2 gains or loses by the tariff is settled by the numerical values of the two terms, that is, by whether the share of the tariff gain outweighs the loss due to changing factor

prices. Moreover, it is clear that there is no *a priori* reason for sup-
posing that one term is necessarily larger than another, for $|a_{ij}|$ may
be numerically very small indeed, making dw large, or it may be large
enough to allow the left-hand term to be dominant.

More important still, if we had not begun by assuming that no
tariff existed initially, in particular if the existing tariff had been
greater than the optimal tariff, quite a different result would appear.
Since there would then be an overall loss of welfare from raising the
tariff, the scarce factor could lose by protection. Having in mind also
the fact that our model is still subject to all the Stolper-Samuelson
simplifications, it is obvious that the problem as it occurs in the
real world is very complex. It is clear that no qualitative answer
independent of numerical elasticities can ever be found, for what we
have developed above is an obvious counter-example to any such
suggestion.

EXERCISES

1. For the problem of section 14.5 compute the dw_1^*, dw_2^* measure of
   Chapter 13 for factors 1 and 2 respectively. That is, value the
   change in consumption for each factor at post-policy prices.
   Hence show that even if both factors gain as a consequence of the
   tariff there must of necessity be a conflict of interests over the
   level of tariff to be charged unless there is some further redistribution of income between the two factors, introduced as a
   supplementary policy.
2. Let

$$\lambda = \frac{p_1 A_1}{p_1 A_1 + p_2 A_2}$$

be the share of the owners of factor 1 in national expenditure, and
let

$$(1 - \lambda) = \frac{p_2 A_2}{p_1 A_1 + p_2 A_2}$$

be the share of the owners of factor 2.

Note that λ and $(1 - \lambda)$ as written are functions of p_1 and p_2.
But as ps are dependent on qs, we might as well think of λ as
dependent on qs. Thus

$$\lambda = \lambda(q_1, q_2)$$

By taking changes in the expression for λ as a function of ps and solving for the change in ps due to change in q_1 ($q_2 =$ constant see (14.2.2)), prove that

$$\frac{1}{\lambda}\frac{\partial \lambda}{\partial q_1} = \frac{q_2(1 - \lambda)}{p_1 p_2 |a_{ij}|}$$

Find the equivalent expression for

$$\frac{1}{\lambda}\frac{\partial \lambda}{\partial q_2}$$

and hence prove that

$$q_1 \frac{\partial \lambda}{\partial q_1} + q_2 \frac{\partial \lambda}{\partial q_2} = 0$$

Show also that

$$\frac{\partial \lambda}{\partial q_1} = -\frac{\partial (1 - \lambda)}{\partial q_1}$$

3. Consider the following equation system:

$X_i^* = X_i^*(q_1, q_2, Y^*)$ Demand equations for owners of factor 1

$X_i^{**} = X_i^{**}(q_1, q_2, Y^{**})$ Demand equations for owners of factor 2

$S_i = S_i(q_1, q_2)$ Supply equations

$q_1(X_1' - S_1') - q_2'(X_2 - S_2) \equiv 0$ Balance of trade zero

$Y = q_1 S_1 + q_2 S_2 + t q_2'(X_2 - S_2)$ Expenditure

$Y^* = \lambda Y$ (λ as defined in exercise 2)

$q_1 = q_1' =$ constant

$q_2 = q_2'(1 + t)$ (where t is the tariff rate)

together with a similar set of equations for the foreign country.

Assume that t is zero at home and abroad and find the effect upon the real terms of trade of the imposition of a home import duty dt. Show that the result (corresponding to (7.5.19)) is given by

$$\frac{dq_2'}{q_2'} = -\left[\frac{e_{22} + Y\left(\dfrac{C_2^* - C_2^{**}}{X_2 - S_2}\right)\dfrac{\partial \lambda}{\partial q_2} + \lambda C_2^* + (1 - \lambda)C_2^{**}}{1 + e_{11}' + Y'\left(\dfrac{(C_1^* - C_1^{**})'}{X_1' - S_1'}\dfrac{\partial \lambda'}{\partial q_2}\right) + e_{22} + Y\left(\dfrac{(C_2^* - C_2^{**})}{X_2 - S_2}\dfrac{\partial \lambda}{\partial q_2}\right)}\right] dt$$

where
$$e_{ii} = \frac{X_i^*}{X_i - S_i} E_{ii}^* + \frac{X_i^{**}}{X_i - S_i} E_{ii}^{**} - \frac{S_i}{X_i - S_i} S_{ii}$$

$$+ \frac{S_i}{X_i - S_i} (\lambda C_i^* + (1 - \lambda) C_i^{**})$$

where $\partial\lambda/\partial q_2$ has the meaning of exercise 2 and where all other symbols have the usual meaning, * and ** indicating 'belonging to the owners of factor 1 and factor 2 respectively'.

Show that the result above reduces to the usual one (see exercise 9, Chapter 11) if preferences (i.e. demand equations) for the owners of factors 1 and 2 are identical.

Hence show that when explicit allowance is made for income redistribution the effect will be to replace elasticities of demand with weighted average elasticities of the groups, and prop-ensities to consume, C_i, by weighted averages, at the same time adding a (usually small) income redistribution term

$$Y \left(\frac{C_2^* - C_2^{**}}{X_2 - S_2} \right) \frac{\partial\lambda}{\partial q_2}$$

Justify therefore the insistence throughout this book that the assumption of zero redistribution effect is likely to give a good first approximation.

4. Rewrite the result (14.5.16) for dw_1, making proper allowance for income redistribution. Recall that in general

$$\lambda X_i \neq X_i^*$$

Use the fact that $dq_2 = q_2' dt + dq_2'$ together with the result from exercise 3 to express dw_1 solely in terms of known parameters and observable variables in the usual way. Show that there is no reason to amend anything argued in section 14.5 in the light of this new information.

5. Consider the identities

$$A_i \equiv \sum_j S_j A_{ji}$$

which say that factor usage equals factor endowment. Suppose that q_k changes with all other qs constant. Deduce that

$$\sum_j a_{ji} \frac{\partial S_j}{\partial q_k} = -\sum_j S_j \frac{\partial a_{ji}}{\partial q_k}$$

Hence show that in general $\partial S_j/\partial q_k$ becomes very large if $|a_{ij}|$ approaches zero. Hence indicate that, even when $|a_{ij}|$ approaches zero, the income redistribution term in the result of exercise 3 is unlikely to be greater in magnitude than the elasticity term e_{22}. Remember that S_{jk} is an alternative way of writing $\partial S_j/\partial q_k$.

To be attempted after reading Books I and II

6. Prove that

$$\frac{q_k}{\lambda_r}\frac{\partial \lambda_r}{\partial q_k} = \frac{q_k}{p_r}\frac{\partial p_r}{\partial q_k} - \frac{q_k S_k}{\sum_i p_i A_i}$$

that is, that the elasticity of the rth factor share with respect to the kth commodity price is equal to the elasticity of the rth factor price with respect to the kth commodity price, less the ratio of the value of the kth output to total factor cost.

15 More Supply Theory and a General Proposition on Gains from Trade

15.1 INTRODUCTION

AT the beginning of Chapter 13 reference was made to the classical question 'Is international trade a good thing?', and by now the reader will be aware that this is a many-sided problem. On the one hand we have shown that the restriction of trade unaccompanied by a re-adjustment of the tax structure can lead to a gain by one section of the community with a real loss to another. On the other hand it has also been proved that, with or without changes in the tax structure, all parties could gain or all could lose according to circumstances. It has become clear that we cannot infer that trade is universally beneficial simply because individuals can be observed to engage in trade even though they are not obliged to. We should already be well conditioned to mistrusting our intuition and be surprised by nothing.

Furthermore, we do have a technique at our disposal, described in Chapter 13, which tells us at once whether or not it is a good thing to open up trade from a position of no trade or restrict it from a position of free trade, so that in a sense we do not need the work we are about to do. On the other hand, as it happens, it is possible to show quite generally that, *whenever the home cost of production of each com-modity is equal to its home market price* (i.e. in the absence of taxes or subsidies on production) *and in the absence of subsidies on exports*, then trade is unambiguously good in the sense of Chapter 13. It does not matter whether trade is free or restricted; its *complete* abolition is undesirable given the italicised conditions. For what it is worth we shall prove this point in what follows.

Before we proceed, however, it is desirable to try to set the whole proposition in perspective. There are in fact two good reasons why we ought not to waste time upon it, but two equally good reasons why we should. In the first place there are very few circumstances in which the theorem to be proved is more immediately applicable to practical problems than the results of Chapters 13 and 14. Indeed, we are simply working a special case of a theorem of Chapter 13. Secondly, the italicised provisos are much more powerful than they may seem to be at first sight. Too much emphasis on the result and too little on the qualifications might well serve to extend the already too prevalent belief that trade should be encouraged at any price. Proposals to subsidise exports are commonplace, although it is hard to imagine circumstances where a subsidy will benefit anyone except the lucky foreign recipient.

The two reasons why we have after all chosen to treat the problem are, first, that it already occupies an important place in the literature (certainly much too important) and there is some need to cut the argument down to size. Second, the approach we have chosen affords an excellent excuse for the development of certain results in the theory of supply which are of the utmost importance generally, although a full treatment lies outside the scope of this book. We begin therefore with some theory of supply.

15.2 Intermediate Products

As we are later to emphasise once again the importance of the relative numbers of factors and commodities, it is instructive and perhaps necessary to develop a more realistic view of the productive process than that introduced in Chapter 12. At first sight the idea of a set of inputs (factors of production) yielding a given output (commodity) seems quite straightforward. On the other hand the simplest attempt to apply such a notion to the real world leads quickly to a morass of practical difficulties. The empirical worker will point out at once that it is not at all easy to classify the ordinary objects of everyday life into one or other of the classes 'factor' or 'product'.

For example, coal is the product of labour and mineral resources and is at the same time a commodity supplied to the final consumer as fuel. But it is also a raw material used in the production of, say, steel, which incidentally is itself an input used in the mining of coal. Many objects are both products and factors in a bewildering complex of interacting processes.

The reason why some economists have found in these facts more difficulty than exists in reality is perhaps that it is natural to identify a productive process with the activities of a single factory or firm. For reasons connected with the actual social organisation of productive activity it is commonplace to identify groups of individuals engaged in manufacture by some firm's name, for example, Imperial Chemical Industries, or Lever Bros. Sometimes such a firm's name is associated with one 'commodity' like soap, sometimes with a group of allied commodities, e.g. chemicals, and sometimes with widely different products. A firm may consist of many factories or plants manufacturing the same or different objects.

It is true of course that, for some purposes, it is both necessary and helpful to study factories or firms as separate entities; for example, so as to inquire whether we are correct in assuming that competition leads to production at minimum cost. Or we may be interested in studying how firms grow and are financed or where factories will be located. In the present context, however, it is of the utmost import-ance to disassociate any idea of a firm or factory from the notion of a productive process. It is precisely the purchases between factories which look like both inputs and outputs simultaneously and hence give rise to a confusion of thought. On the other hand, let us begin by distinguishing between inputs in the chain of a manufacturing process, which are themselves objects of manufacture, and inputs which are 'gifts of nature'.

To this end we introduce the notion of a *basic* (non-produced) factor as distinct from an *intermediate* input or factor. Basic factors are the true inputs and commodities are the true outputs. Inter-mediate factors, although they play an important role in our scheme of thought, are neither inputs nor outputs in the strict sense. They disappear as soon as we consider each productive process as a so-called 'vertically integrated' activity, as explained below, rather than the operation of a single firm. For example, the operations ending in, say, the appearance of a motor-car are not only those carried on by the Ford Motor Company. On the contrary, they comprise the whole process, beginning with the planting of rubber trees and the mining of iron ore, including the creation and using-up of the necessary capital equipment and ending with the final assembly of the vehicle. The basic factors of production are the labourers, miners and engineers together with the various kinds and qualities of land. Intermediate factors include the rubber, steel, machinery, and buildings, etc., whilst the motor-car itself is the final 'commodity'. The same physical object can in some cases be either a commodity or an inter-mediate factor, as we have already noted. Which it is depends upon the purpose for which it is used. In case it should already be felt at this stage that this is too complex a view, we remark that a method of computation of inputs making use only of information derived from firms is given below. And the reader who reflects upon possible alternative ways of treating the data will quickly discover that this apparently bold step leads to greater conceptual simplicity in the end.

To sharpen our definitions still further, we draw attention to yet another possible ambiguity. It is sometimes suggested that it is not always clear whether an object is really an input into a given process or not. For example, are the canteen facilities provided by a steel mill part of the input required to produce rolled steel, or is this a commodity purchased by the firm on behalf of its workers? The answer must be that it is a true intermediate factor since it enters into the *cost* of production. Any expense which in fact forms part of the price of the product must necessarily be payment for a factor, either basic or intermediate. This is the final test.

One more point must be made in regard to definitions. *Imported* factors of production, whether basic or intermediate, must be separately distinguished, since we shall find that intermediate factor imports have more in common with basic factors than with home-produced intermediate factors. The reason for this is obvious. We are concerned to analyse the underlying causes of trade and we have found that a great part of the explanation lies in differing factor endowments between countries. We have also found that the prices commanded by the true 'basic' factors of production need not be the same in all countries. If imported intermediate products are treated as 'intermediates', the process of 'vertical integration' will carry us back to factors such as land and labour which are located abroad as well as at home. For example, if rubber-producing activity abroad is treated as an integral part of the whole process leading to the output in the United Kingdom of a motor-car, then we find that inputs of land and labour in, say, Malaya become inputs (factors) in that process. Such a convention dulls the edge of our analysis.

In accepting the word meanings above, however, the reader should not be misled into supposing that they are any more than conventions adopted for clarity of exposition or for their suitability as a framework for measurement and prediction. Whether an object is manufactured or is a gift of nature is a question of fact not open to dispute, but whether it should be called a factor or a commodity is a matter of definition whose only justification is convenience. The reader must learn to judge by experience the value in explanation of one or other sets of definitions. What is really important is where our definitions lead us. What in fact does all this mean in terms of the cost equations which played such a prominent part in Chapter 12?

This question is best answered by an example. Consider a country in which two commodities are produced, namely, coal and steel. First, we set down inputs and outputs in the manner of Chapter 12. We have:

Coal: is produced by labour, capital and steel.

Steel: is produced by labour, coal, capital and *imported* iron ore.

For convenience we number the products and/or intermediate factors, coal, steel and iron ore, 1, 2 and 3 respectively. The basic (non-produced factors) labour and capital are numbered 1 and 2. Prices q_i are used for commodities and/or intermediate factors, a prime (q_3') being used to indicate a foreign price. p_1 and p_2 are the prices of the basic factors. With these conventions, the non-vertically integrated cost equations may be written:

$$q_1 = a_{11}p_1 + a_{12}p_2 + b_{12}q_2 \qquad (15.2.1)$$

$$q_2 = a_{21}p_1 + b_{21}q_1 + a_{22}p_2 + b_{23}q_3' \qquad (15.2.2)$$

to express the facts given in words above. a_{ij} is the input of the jth basic factor required, in combination with other inputs, to produce one unit of the ith output; b_{ij} is the quantity of the jth intermediate factor (or imported factor) required for the same purpose. Note especially that information for the construction of non-vertically integrated cost equations can be obtained from firms in the ordinary sense. Cost equations for the vertically integrated process are then easily deduced from (15.2.1) and (15.2.2) as follows.

All that is necessary is to substitute the right-hand side of (15.2.2) for q_2 in (15.2.1) to obtain

$$q_1 = (a_{11} + b_{12}a_{21})p_1 + (a_{12} + b_{12}a_{22})p_2 + b_{12}b_{21}q_1 + b_{12}b_{23}q_3' \quad (15.2.3)$$

or $\quad q_1 = \left[\dfrac{a_{11} + b_{12}a_{21}}{1 - b_{12}b_{21}}\right]p_1 + \left[\dfrac{a_{12} + b_{12}a_{22}}{1 - b_{12}b_{21}}\right]p_2 + \left[\dfrac{b_{12}b_{23}}{1 - b_{12}b_{21}}\right]q_3'$

$$(15.2.4)$$

which is an equation of the form

$$q_1 = \alpha_{11}p_1 + \alpha_{12}p_2 + \alpha_{13}q_3' \qquad (15.2.5)$$

(15.2.5) is now a cost equation for commodity 1 written in terms of basic inputs 1 and 2 and the imported factor 3. The coefficients α_{11}, α_{12} and α_{13} are simply the quantities of the basic inputs required in combination to produce one unit of output, similar in every way to the inputs a_{ij} and b_{ij}. Notice that choosing a_{ij} and b_{ij} so as to minimise cost q_i implies that α_{ij} are chosen so as to minimise cost. It is a fundamental assumption of all our work that competition ensures that all producers minimise cost.

Substituting equation (15.2.5) in (15.2.2) will now give a vertically integrated cost equation for commodity 2, again of the form

$$q_2 = \alpha_{21}p_1 + \alpha_{22}p_2 + \alpha_{23}q_3'$$ (15.2.6)

Clearly, all the argument of Chapter 12 may be at once applied to the equations (15.2.5) and (15.2.6) without modification, provided only that we treat the input 3 as if it were a *mobile* factor of production. Note that 3 satisfies the condition of a mobile factor in that its price must always be the same as the world price, and just that amount will be imported which will make it possible to choose minimum-cost technique at the given prices. We shall come back to the problem of imported factors later. In the meantime some mention should be made of the role of 'capital' in the process of production.

15.3 A DIGRESSION ON THE MEANING OF THE FACTOR 'CAPITAL'

In setting out cost functions in the vertically integrated form (15.2.6), we have reduced every input to a basic non-produced item such as labour. All intermediate products like machines or buildings have disappeared. Moreover, the price p_2 of each class of labour or land is its going market price or rental. The total input of labour, it must be recalled, is the input which is engaged not only in putting together the motor-cars but also in producing the iron ore and the steel, not to mention sustaining the flow of new blast furnaces required to produce the steel.

Now consider the following mental experiment. Let us take all the various classes of workers engaged in productive activity in some complex industrialised society and set them down in a newly discovered and uninhabited country having at its disposal just the quantity of basic inputs, land, and mineral resources which were available at home. Let each person be instructed to do exactly what he was doing before. Shall we then have a production complex precisely as before? The answer is obviously 'No'. The welder would be demanding the parts which he is required to weld, the blast furnaceman his blast furnace, and the car assembly man his parts. None of these would be immediately available.

The reason for this is, basically, that we have left the *timing* of our operations out of account. All of the *produced* inputs required by each worker, that is, the so-called 'work in progress', is missing. To create work in progress it is necessary to begin each worker at his job in the new country at a different moment of time, the earliest being the mineworker, who digs the iron ore from the earth, the latest being the operator on the final motor-car assembly line. Nor is this all. It would almost certainly be quite impossible to create directly a modern industrial complex even by starting each worker at some appropriate moment in time, for the mineworker demands some mining equipment which is itself manufactured from the ore produced in the mines. Neither the chicken nor the egg can be shown to come first, as those whose duty it is to create capital in underdeveloped countries well understand.

Fortunately none of this matters from the point of view of the cost equation (15.2.6), for this simply enumerates the basic factors actually at work in the process to sustain a flow of output of one unit per unit of time *with one exception*. The exception is the *quantity of money capital* tied up in the process. One of the inputs α_{ij} must be thought of as money, and its corresponding price is the rate of interest, i.e. the rental price of money. The quantity of money capital acts as a proxy factor for the work in progress.

There are two possible ways in which this may be explained. Much the most accurate and sensible way of explaining it is to analyse each productive process, noting the time which would have to elapse between the first input of a basic factor and the moment of appearance of the first unit of the final product. A slightly more extended account of this problem is given in an appendix to this chapter. In the meantime we assert that it can be shown that it is possible in principle to compute a 'maturity time', even in the most complex economy, for each basic factor engaged in the process. Basic factors with different maturity times must be thought of as different factors.

What is revealed by this approach is the fact that the true 'cost' of employing a factor is different according to the maturity time, even though the same homogeneous unit of labour with the same wage rate is engaged in each case. The cost is different simply because, by custom, labour will not wait for its maturity time to elapse before claiming the reward due for work completed. Money capital is necessary to bridge the gap between the payment of labour and the sale of the product of that labour, and the owners of money capital in turn demand payment. If the going wage rate per unit of time is p_i and the rate of profit on money capital is r, then the true cost of employing a unit of labour *and* of waiting t_i periods of time for that product to 'mature' is

$$p_i(1+r)^{t_i} \qquad\qquad (15.3.1)$$

by the ordinary formula for compound interest. This 'true price' is clearly different for each t_i even though p_i may be the same. If the prices of equation (15.2.6) are taken to be the going wage rates or rentals, a further factor 'capital' is needed in order to make up the difference between going wage rates and the true cost (15.3.1) (see appendix to this chapter).

The other more intuitively obvious but less accurate way to see the role of the factor 'capital' is simply to regard the collection of inputs, which above we have called work in progress, as itself an input necessary to establish *immediate* production. This is justified by an earlier observation that it is precisely the lack of work in progress which made it impossible for the imaginary community newly transplanted to take up work exactly where it left off. Money capital is the money required to rent work in progress from some other community already established. Note that work in progress is continuously in existence and will always be owned by someone, and the owner of such assets will exact a 'rent' for their use, namely, the rate of interest.

What all this means in terms of the cost equation (15.2.6) is that we could, if we liked, choose the convention which assigns a time subscript to each class of labour, at the same time assuming that the price p_1 includes the element of capital tied up as in the formula (15.3.1). In this case we need not include 'money' as a factor of production. But such a convention has two disadvantages. First, it obscures the fact that we should then have a complex relation between the 'prices' of 'factors' arising from the fact that the price of labour with maturity time t_j could be computed from the price of labour with maturity time t_i once we know the rate of interest. Factor prices would not be independent of one another. The system would contain a great many more equations than those so far set out. It should be noted particularly that this would make nonsense of the counting of equations and unknown prices which is so important in Chapter 12.

Second, the proposed convention apparently eliminates 'capital' as a factor of production even though the stock of capital with which a country is endowed is a vital determinant of the pattern of trade. We obscure both the quantity and price of a crucial input which plays a major role in the analysis. It is natural then to drop time subscripts and to introduce a factor capital which can be thought of, in most contexts in this book, alternatively as the money required to sustain the productive process with rental price r, or as an index of maturity times with a 'price' dependent upon r (see appendix).

The reader should understand, however, that there are some economists at the present time who take the view that the whole idea of 'capital' as a factor of production is a gigantic confidence trick designed to avoid the unpleasant necessity of inquiring into certain very complex dynamical problems. The reason for this is quite clear whether we look upon capital either as money requirement or as work in progress. The money capital requirement evidently depends upon the prices p_i of the basic factors purchased. Alternatively it is impossible to aggregate the multitude of objects which make up work in progress into a single factor, capital, without attaching some kind of weight to each. The natural weight to attach is 'value'. But value once again depends upon the price of basic factors, or appears to. Either way we have no separate *measure* of capital independent of other factor prices, so that in this respect capital is unlike any other factor. If the jth factor is capital, the measure a_{ij} seems to have to depend upon factor prices p_k.

Against this, everyday experience, as well as our earlier argument, cries out that work in progress ought to be a real and meaningful quantity. Few would wish to deny that there is a proper sense in which one process demands more work in progress than another. It is also a matter of common observation that, between countries, there is an obvious difference in the character and quantity of the objects which make up work in progress, which the ordinary person would wish to characterise as more or less 'capital'. All that can be in dispute is the appropriate measure.

To the present writer two things seem to be causing the current confusion of thought. The first is an understandable human propensity to call different but related things by the same name. Thus, in various contexts, the word 'capital' is used to describe:

(a) money originally subscribed by shareholders;

(b) current 'value' of work in progress and part-worn equipment; and

(c) some proper aggregate of the maturity time of basic factors in all currently operating processes.

Obviously the passage of time and changing prices, together with the fact that part-worn objects such as machines and buildings have no obvious price even when their original cost is known, make (a), (b) and (c) very different entities.

The second cause of confusion of thought probably finds its origin in the attempts of scholars untrained in mathematics to solve what is an essentially many-dimensional mathematical problem using diagrammatic techniques on a two-dimensional blackboard. It may not be possible to adapt traditional geometric demonstrations of the existence of minimum-cost production techniques to cases where one of the inputs is dependent upon the price of other factors. But this does not mean that a minimum-cost technique does not exist or even that there is any special problem connected with it.

Happily, the capital with which we are concerned is item (c) above. This is unambiguous and can be computed (see appendix to this chapter). It has nothing to do with dynamic processes or past history but only with productive processes currently in operation or planned.

We need to establish a cost equation (15.2.6) for each process with the usual properties, but with some α_{ij} representing capital, and some r or function of r representing the price of capital. The way this is done is set out more fully in an appendix to this chapter which need not detain the reader who is prepared to accept the following argument.

Given current basic factor prices p_i and interest rate r, there must exist, among all the technical possibilities, some lowest-cost technique of production when the price of each basic input is expressed in the form (15.3.1). Note that the problem of choosing a minimum-cost maturity time is no more difficult in principle than that of choosing the minimum-cost ratio of inputs of basic factors. We may in fact write our cost function in the form

$$q_i = \sum_j p_j (1 + r)^{t_j} a_{ij} \qquad (15.3.2)$$

Once we have a cost function in any form, it is easy enough to write it in any other. Thus, by adding a term and subtracting again, we have

$$q_i = \sum_j p_j a_{ij} + \left[\sum_j p_j (1 + r)^{t_j} a_{ij} - \sum_j p_j a_{ij} \right] \qquad (15.3.3)$$

so that the expression in square brackets must be the cost of capital. It is left to the appendix to this chapter to show how the formula so obtained turns out to be consistent both with the product of r and money capital tied up and with the product of an index of timing or, as it is sometimes called, 'roundaboutness', and a price of roundaboutness. Cost equations expressed in terms of the roundaboutness index have the usual properties.

The only other element in our problem which we have need to quantify is the capital endowment of a given country. This is easy in principle and need have nothing to do with the form that its existing work in progress may take. It may be a difficult task in practice, but no conceptual problem is involved in computing the maturity times of basic factors tied up in actual processes whether optimal or not. This is the real capital. To convert maturity times to units comparable with those for capital in the cost equation we simply work out at current prices and interest rate how much money capital would be required to re-create existing processes exactly as they are. It is shown in the appendix to this chapter that this measure of capital, for the small changes we are interested in, remains constant if and only if there is no saving by the community, that is, there is no investment.

The reason why we escape so lightly from conceptual problems is because we are here concerned only with the question of how any given stock of 'roundaboutness' might be used if the quality of the objects reflecting it were changed. We say nothing about the time it would take to change the nature of the objects or how we get from a set of objects which is not appropriate for minimum-cost techniques (given current prices) to one which is. To examine this much more difficult question we should need a truly dynamic model with a great deal more technical information than the straightforward details of the set of techniques currently in use. On the other hand we emphasise again that, for the kind of problem studied in this book, the meaning of capital is unambiguous and no contradiction or undefined concept is involved. Cost equations may be used in the form above, including capital as a factor, without any fear that we might be engaged on an exercise which has no relevance to the real world.

15.4 THE THEORY OF SUPPLY

We now introduce the notion of a production possibility set for any given country. For the moment we exclude all consideration of imported raw materials and define the production possibility set in the form in which it is most familiar to economists. With any given fixed endowment of basic factors of production, and provided no import of raw materials is possible, there is an obvious limit to what can be manufactured whatever the chosen technique. On the other hand there is evidently a wide area of choice. For example, a region endowed with, say, 10 labourers and 5 acres of land could produce perhaps 10 tons of potatoes and 50 bushels of wheat. Alternatively with the same aggregate input of 10 labourers and 5 acres of land it may equally be possible to produce 10 bushels of wheat and 50 tons of potatoes, or one of many other possible combinations of quantities.

An element, *s*, of the set *S* of all production possibilities is simply a collection (or *vector*) of commodity quantities like 10 tons of potatoes and 50 bushels of wheat, i.e. any element *s* of *S* is a pattern of supplies $S_1, S_2, \ldots, S_n$. The whole set *S* is the collection of all possible supply patterns, *s*, feasible with the given factor endowment. Fig. 15.1 represents the set *S* diagrammatically and reveals the logic of our choice of symbols.

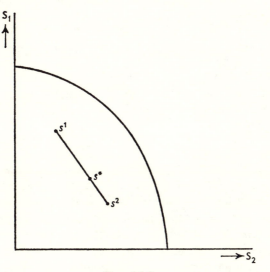

FIG. 15.1

Supplies of commodities 1 and 2 are measured along the axes. As with any ordinary graph, a point such as s^1 defines, by its position, two quantities S_1^1 and S_2^1. S_1^1 is the distance of s^1 from the S_2 axis and S_2^1 is the distance of s^1 from the S_1 axis. The production possibility set *S* is the set of all points lying within the region bounded by the curve in Fig. 15.1 and the two axes, and all points in the boundary itself.

We shall discover that the shape of the production possibility set is of very great importance. Indeed, most of our results will depend upon the fact that it must be convex in the ordinary meaning of that word. Unfortunately it is impossible to visualise a convex set in more than three dimensions, so that we must give a precise algebraic definition of convexity which does not depend upon visual imagination.

Consider any two points like s^1 and s^2 (Fig. 15.1) lying in *S*. No matter where s^1 and s^2 are located, it is obvious that every point on the straight line drawn between s^1 and s^2 must also be a point in the set S if S is convex in the ordinary sense. In other words it is impossible that a point like s^* should lie outside the boundary of S unless the boundary curves inwards. We note also that there is a very simple way of characterising the set of all points on the straight line connecting s^1 and s^2. It is easy to see, for example, by elementary geometry, that if s^* lies at a distance from s^1 equal to a fraction θ of the whole distance s^1s^2, then the co-ordinates of the point s^* will be

$$S_1^* = S_1^1 - \theta(S_1^1 - S_1^2) = (1 - \theta)S_1^1 + \theta(S_1^2)$$

and
$$S_2^* = S_2^1 + \theta(S_2^2 - S_2^1) = (1 - \theta)S_2^1 + \theta(S_2^2)$$

That is, the elements of the vector s^* are weighted averages of the elements of the vectors s^1 and s^2, the weights being θ and $(1 - \theta)$ where θ is a number lying between 0 and 1. It is usual to express this fact by writing

$$s^* = \theta s^2 + (1 - \theta)s^1 \qquad\qquad (15.4.1)$$

A straight line joining the points s^1 and s^2 is therefore the set of all points satisfying (15.4.1) for all values of θ between 0 and 1. Obviously, if θ is 0 s^* is s^1, and if θ is 1 s^* is s^2.

The reader may now easily satisfy himself that the same approach may be used in three dimensions, that is, with three commodities, by reflecting on the fact that the S_1 co-ordinate of any point lying on a straight line connecting two points s^1 and s^2 in three-dimensional space cannot be less than the smaller, or greater than the larger, of the S_1 co-ordinates of s^1 and s^2. It must in fact always be a weighted average of the S_1 co-ordinates of s^1 and s^2. And the same is true of other co-ordinates as in the two-dimensional case.

Following this lead, we say that a set S of n dimensional vectors is convex if for all pairs of vectors s^1 and s^2 contained in S each point s^* defined by the equation (15.4.1) for values of θ between 0 and 1 is also in S. This is a straightforward generalisation of the simple idea with which we began.

We now draw very special attention to a fundamental assumption of all of the work so far. Although we have written down a cost function supposing it at the same time to be *minimum* cost, we have not yet considered whether the *level* of output as opposed to technique (ratio of inputs) has any influence upon cost. On the other hand it is a commonplace notion that there exist in the real world economies of scale; that is, the larger the output of a product, the lower is the cost of production. (Discussion of this idea can be found in any textbook of micro-economic theory.) What we have all the time been supposing is that at a certain level of output for each individual manufacturing plant, economies of scale will cease and no more gains from size can be won. When we let techniques of production change because of changed prices, or when the aggregate supply for the country as a whole of any given product changes, we must imagine that the number of separate plants in the industry changes also so that each individual factory can be large enough to earn all possible economies of scale at the new factor prices. For example, if aggregate output of a product jumps from 10 million tons to 15 million tons, and if an individual plant must produce 1 million tons or more before minimum possible cost is attained, then not more than five new plants must be set up. Similarly, if output is to fall to 5 million tons then at least five plants must close down. In this way the scale of *national* output makes no difference to the minimum-cost price, although the scale of output of each individual plant does. At the national level cost depends only on factor prices as implied by cost equations. Note especially that competition will secure the result we need, for no factory can survive if its cost is greater than selling price.

On these assumptions we are able quite simply to prove:

Theorem: The production possibility set is convex.

Proof: The proof is in fact trivial. Suppose that it is possible with a given factor endowment to produce patterns of supply s^1 and s^2. Then simply by scaling down the number of factories appropriately we can produce the fraction θ of each element of the pattern s^1 using the fraction θ of total factor endowment. This clearly leaves $(1 - \theta)$ of the given factor endowment, which is sufficient by the same argument to produce $(1 - \theta)$ of each element of the production pattern s^2. Thus, with the given factor endowment, the production pattern

$$s^* = \theta s^1 + (1 - \theta)s^2$$

may be produced so that s^* is in the set S. Hence the set S is convex.

Armed with this knowledge we proceed now to investigate precisely how the supply of each commodity depends upon commodity prices.

We shall begin by showing that, given commodity prices, the forces of competition will choose supplies of the various goods so as to maximise the value of the national product; that is,

$$Y \equiv \sum q_i S_i \tag{15.4.2}$$

is maximised. It will then be necessary to inquire in what circumstances the maximising pattern of supplies, given prices, is unique. If the pattern is not unique it cannot be said to depend upon prices alone.

In order first to be quite sure of the meaning of the various symbols used, consider the ordinary cost equations:

$$q_i = \sum_j p_j a_{ij} \qquad (15.4.3)$$

together with the equations

$$A_i = \sum_k S_k a_{ki} \qquad (15.4.4)$$

familiar from Chapter 12, expressing the fact that the overall usage A_i of the ith factor is the sum of the inputs $S_k a_{ki}$ ($k = 1, 2, \ldots, n$) required to produce the sum of all outputs S_k.

In view of what has been said above about the use of intermediate products as inputs for the manufacture of final products, there are evidently two ways of interpreting (15.4.3) and (15.4.4). Either the equations (15.4.3) are 'reduced' equations, like (15.2.5) above, in which case the a_{ij} are basic (non-produced) inputs; or they are unreduced like (15.2.1) and (15.2.2) above with some a_{ij} being intermediate inputs. If we interpret (15.4.3) as reduced equations, then A_i cannot be the endowment of the ith basic factor unless the S_k are supplies of commodities *excluding* that part of output used later as inputs. The S_k cannot be the total output of k, that is, it cannot measure both that part which is final output and that part which is used elsewhere as an input, for this would involve double counting. If the a_{ki} are defined as strictly non-produced inputs, and if at the same time some part of the jth output S_j is used in fact as an input into commodity k, then S_j will appear in the summation (15.4.4) and part of the ith input into j will be double counted, once in S_j and once in S_k. The usage A_i would therefore be greater than the factor endowment.

With equations still in the reduced form, however, it should be noted that there is no inconsistency if the S_j are interpreted as net output. Provided the symbol for supply is taken to mean only that part of the total product of the industry sold to consumers, no double counting is involved and the equations (15.4.4) will be satisfied with A_i truly the endowment of the ith basic factor.

If on the other hand equations (15.4.3) and (15.4.4) are supposed to be in the unreduced form, then there is no double counting in

(15.4.4). The a_{ki} represents only that quantity of the ith input used *directly* in the production of k. Quantities of i which are used indirectly through intermediate inputs are not included. In this case we need additional equations to go with (15.4.4).

Denoting the amount of the jth output used in the production of other commodities by S_j^*, keeping S_j as the symbol for total output of the jth product, we have equations

$$S_j^* = \sum_k S_k a_{kj} \qquad (15.4.5)$$

as supplementary equations to (15.4.4) where a_{kj} is the input of the jth output needed to produce (in conjunction with other factors) one unit of k. (15.4.5) simply expresses the fact that for all intermediate factors j the sum of the usage of j is equal to the total sold to firms. When this second interpretation of (15.4.3) and (15.4.4) is adopted, the S_k measure the *total* output of k, whether sold to firms or to consumers.

In fact, throughout the present work, except where otherwise specified, the a_{ki} and the S_k should be taken in the first sense. Supplies are supplies sold to consumers only and the a_{ki} are the inputs of basic factors whether applied directly or indirectly through intermediate inputs. In particular, the work of Chapter 12 would be nonsense if the words 'product' and 'factor' were interpreted in any other way. It should be clear also that all that has been said about welfare requires that X_i should measure sales to consumers only. No improvement in welfare can be effected by selling more intermediate factors to firms, and to include such sales in consumption would be to double count. It is emphasised also that nothing of the work so far completed is either lost or in need of modification as a result of our now widened view. When, in Book I, expenditure was computed by measuring the value of output suitably adjusted for tariffs or balance of payment gaps, the 'value of output' meant precisely the net value of sales to consumers as above. All that we need to realise is that implicit in the system of equations of Book I is the subsidiary system (15.4.3), (15.4.4) and (15.4.5). But since we have not felt the need (other than in Chapter 14) to inquire into changes in factor prices or into activity in the market for intermediate factors, we have been able to ignore this important sector of the economy. Part of the purpose of this chapter is to draw aside the veil which has so far obscured the working of one section of the model. Note finally that the s of the production possibility set must be supplies for consumption only and not gross supply, for it is always possible to increase gross supply by reducing consumption. If any product can be used to produce itself, then gross output is maximised only when there is no consumption except in production. The concept of the production possibility set is reduced to nonsense, We now turn to the proof that competition maximises the value of output.

Consider the following. If the A_i are the fixed endowments of basic factors, then (15.4.4) says that factor endowments will be just fully employed. On the other hand this is not trivially true but is a consequence of competition. The only fact of nature which we know is that

$$A_i \geq \sum_k S_k a_{ki} \text{ for all } i \qquad (15.4.6)$$

which expresses the truth that it is impossible to use *more* than the factor endowment. Competition, given sufficient aggregate demand, ensures full employment of all factors having a price simply because any unused factors will tend to offer their services more cheaply, making it profitable for firms to use more. But for the moment we have to consider *all* choices open to the community whether consistent with competition or not. Thus we retain the form (15.4.6).

We may now multiply the inequalities (15.4.6) by p_i the ith factor price, and sum to obtain

$$\sum_i p_i A_i \geq \sum_i \sum_k S_k p_i a_{ki} \qquad (15.4.7)$$

In the same way, if q_k is by definition the lowest possible cost when factor prices are p, we must have

$$q_k \leq \sum_i p_i a_{ki} \qquad (15.4.8)$$

where the a_{ki} are now interpreted as all conceivable inputs which will produce one unit of output. (15.4.8) then says it is impossible to choose a production technique cheaper than the cheapest. Competition ensures that the equality will hold in (15.4.8), that is, that the cheapest technique will be chosen. (15.4.7) and (15.4.8) together imply

$$\sum_i p_i A_i \geq \sum_k q_k S_k \qquad (15.4.9)$$

where S_k is any feasible output whatever. But for given factor prices p_i the left-hand side of (15.4.9) is the *constant* value of the factor endowment, the same whatever choice of technique a_{ki} and/or outputs S_k is made by the community. Thus $\sum_k q_k S_k$ is at a maximum when the equality prevails in (15.4.9), that is, under competition.

The reader should now note most carefully what we have and have not proved. We began with a given pattern of *factor* prices p and we have shown that competition will ensure the production of those commodities which will give the greatest value of the national product when the price at which commodities are valued is the lowest possible cost of production, given p. We suppose for the moment that one and only one production pattern, s, yields the maximum although this is not always the case as we shall later demonstrate. It follows that the production pattern s is given uniquely when p is given. It does not follow at once that s is given uniquely when q is given unless we know beforehand that one and only one factor price pattern p is associated with each commodity price pattern q. In other words we have proved that s is a function of p but we have not yet proved that s is a function of q.

Suppose in fact that there are two patterns of factor prices, p and p^*, both of which permit minimum-cost production at the same cost q. It is not of course obvious that this is impossible, for a higher price for one factor could easily offset a lower price for another. In such a case we might have

$$\sum_i p_i A_i = \sum_k q_k S_k \qquad (15.4.10)$$

and

$$\sum_i p_i^* A_i = \sum_k q_k S_k^* \qquad (15.4.11)$$

We should arrive at the results (15.4.10) and (15.4.11) first by taking factor prices p and following the argument through (15.4.6), (15.4.7), (15.4.8) and (15.4.9) and then similarly for p^*.

But (15.4.10) and (15.4.11) represent an obvious contradiction, at least on the assumption that one and only one pattern of supply yields maximum value of output; for either

$$\sum_k q_k S_k > \sum_k q_k S_k^*$$

in which case

$$\sum_i p_i^* A_i < \sum_k q_k S_k$$

contrary to (15.4.9), or

$$\sum_k q_k S_k < \sum_k q_k S_k^*$$

in which case

$$\sum_i p_i A_i < \sum_k q_k S_k^*$$

contrary to (15.4.9), or

$$\sum q_k S_k = \sum q_k S_k^*$$

which contradicts the assumption that only one pattern of supply yields a maximum.

What this proves of course is that one and only one p is associated with each q as long as production is confined to the 'possibility set' defined by a given factor endowment. And this is precisely the conclusion we should expect from the basic theorem of Chapter 12, which implies that two regions must have the same factor prices if they have the same commodity prices and the same factor endowment. Our final conclusion therefore is that, given a factor endowment, the supply pattern is uniquely determined by commodity prices. Supply is a function of commodity prices as we set out to show.

The reader may now be forgiven for wondering how it is we have been able to prove so much without appealing to the convexity property of the production possibility set, particularly when, at the outset, it was asserted that everything depends upon this convexity. The reason is very simple. In the argument above we implicitly made use of the assumption that cost is independent of scale. In using (15.4.8) whatever the supply pattern s, we supposed the absence of *external* economies, that is, economies due to an increase in the number of firms rather than the size of each firm. This of course is precisely the assumption we need to prove convexity of the production possibility set as explained above.

The fact that competition maximises the value, Y, say, of the national product, given q, is a conclusion of the utmost importance quite apart from its value in establishing the existence of supply functions. It will, in particular, be used at a later stage to prove the main proposition of this chapter, namely that in the usual circumstances some trade is better than no trade. In the meantime it is useful to note a number of further implications.

Consider first Fig. 15.2(a). This illustrates a production possibility set satisfying the condition of convexity. Suppose that Y is the total money value of the national product. Let OA be the amount of commodity 1 which could be purchased for Y at price q_1 and OB be the amount of commodity 2 which could be purchased for Y at price q_2. Then

$$Y = (OA)q_1 = (OB)q_2$$

or $\qquad\qquad OA/OB = q_2/q_1$

Clearly, at prices q_1 and q_2, Y is maximised when OA is maximised. Evidently also OA is maximised when OB is maximised. If the community is free to choose any point in the production possibility set but will always choose that point which maximises Y, OB and OA, it must choose a point like C which is on the boundary of the production possibility set. If a production pattern in the interior of the set is chosen, then some point in the set will lie to the north-east of AB which, if chosen, would lead to a higher OA, OB and hence Y, given

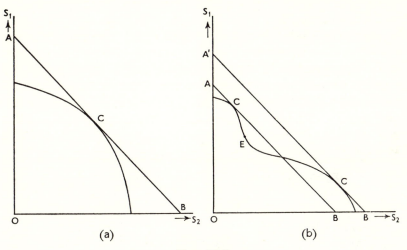

FIG. 15.2

prices. We have the important conclusion therefore that under competition the chosen production pattern must be the point where the price ratio line AB is tangent to the production possibility set.

Notice that the convexity property of the production possibility set implies that the slope of the boundary increases numerically as more of commodity 2 is produced. But the slope of the boundary must be tangential to

$$OA/OB = q_2/q_1$$

Hence an increased supply of commodity 2 implies a higher q_2 relative to q_1. That is, if q_1 is constant, a high q_2 calls forth a high supply. Thus we have

$$S_2 = S_2(q_1, q_2)$$

such that

$$\frac{\partial S_2}{\partial q_2} > 0 \qquad (15.4.12)$$

and by a similar argument

$$\frac{\partial S_1}{\partial q_1} > 0 \qquad (15.4.13)$$

Furthermore, since

$$\sum q_i S_i$$

is maximised, given q, small changes in S_i can have no effect upon the total. Thus

$$\sum_i q_i dS_i = 0 \qquad (15.4.14)$$

The result (15.4.14) is of course obvious in two dimensions from the Fig. 15.2(a), for the slope of the boundary of the production possibility set is the ratio of the changes dS_1 and dS_2 in the quantities produced defined by a small movement around the boundary. In the neighbourhood of the tangency point, C (Fig. 15.2(a)), therefore, we have

$$\frac{dS_1}{dS_2} = \frac{OA}{OB} = \frac{q_2}{q_1}$$

Remembering that dS_1 is negative if dS_2 is positive, we have

$$q_1 dS_1 + q_2 dS_2 = 0$$

which is (15.4.14). This is a fundamental result which we made use of in section 11.6 and which plays a crucial part in the development of the more complex models introduced in Chapters 17 and 18.

A special case of (15.4.14) is of interest. If the changes dS_1 are those due to a change in some one price q_j, all other prices constant, we may write

$$\sum_i q_i \frac{\partial S_i}{\partial q_j} = 0 \qquad (15.4.15)$$

which when applied to the two-commodity case taken with (15.4.13) tells us that

$$\frac{\partial S_1}{\partial q_2} < 0 \qquad (15.4.16)$$

Again the reader will note from Fig. 15.2(a) that the quantity of each commodity supplied is dependent only upon the slope OA/OB, that is, upon the price *ratio* q_2/q_1. Raising prices proportionately will make no difference to the quantity supplied. Accordingly

$$\frac{\partial S_1}{\partial q_1} dq_1 + \frac{\partial S_1}{\partial q_2} dq_2 = 0 \qquad (15.4.17)$$

if $$dq_1 = \lambda q_1$$

and $$dq_2 = \lambda q_2$$

where λ is a constant of proportionality. Thus

$$\frac{\partial S_1}{\partial q_1} q_1 + \frac{\partial S_1}{\partial q_2} q_2 = 0 \qquad (15.4.18)$$

which taken in conjunction with (15.4.15) implies that, in the two-commodity case,

$$\frac{\partial S_1}{\partial q_2} = \frac{\partial S_2}{\partial q_1} \qquad (15.4.19)$$

This again is a crucial result which is in fact true also where there are any number of commodities.

Equations (15.4.12)–(15.4.19), excluding (15.4.17), summarise our most important a priori *conclusions on the nature of supply functions under competition.* It should be noted that all depend very heavily on the convexity of the production possibility set. To emphasise this point, consider Fig. 15.2(b). Here the production possibility set has been drawn bounded by the curve CEC' which is not convex. If, as in the convex case, the slope of CEC' measures the price ratio, the same commodity price ratio may occur, say, at C and C'. AB is parallel to $A'B'$. C does not maximise the value of output at the given commodity prices although it is a point of tangency of the boundary of the production possibility set with AB. Even if competition ensured a production pattern on the boundary of the set, supply curves, if they existed, might be downward-sloping instead of upward-sloping at E. A reduced supply might imply higher cost.

The reader should be aware that, if we had reason to believe in the existence of external economies, Fig. 15.2(b) would be a possibility. The points C and C' could represent competitive equilibrium positions. Even though relative commodity prices are the same at C and C', the different patterns of production may induce different factor prices at C and C'. If the inputs a_{ki} of (15.4.7) are interpreted as

$$A_{ki}/S_k$$

that is, total actual input divided by actual output, and if q_k is interpreted as the lowest possible cost at outputs C and C', given factor prices, then (15.4.7)–(15.4.9) could be satisfied at C. The rest of the argument breaks down, however, because minimum cost q is now dependent upon the output pattern s, as well as upon factor prices.

We can no longer establish the contradiction as in the passage following (15.4.10) and (15.4.11) because it might not be possible to produce the quantity S_k^* at minimum-cost price q_k when factor prices are p even though it is possible to produce S_k at lowest cost q_k. The difference in the number of factories might give rise to economies or diseconomies.

Clearly, as long as individual factory managers are unaware of possible gains from increasing the number of plants making up the industry, they must be unaware of the existence of C' and believe C to be maximum value of output. C could be equilibrium at prices q. If such a situation did exist, there may be an argument in favour of some kind of interference with the competitive process, and indeed the 'infant industry' claim mentioned in section 8.1 has been linked with the concept of external economies. The reader should not allow himself to be too easily taken in by this particular sophistry, however. If the pattern of supply is C and the possibility of producing at C' exists, either this is known or it is not known. If it is not known by anyone, then there can be no argument about the need for a subsidy to encourage a move to C'. If it is known, as it must be if the desirability of some interference with the competitive process is being argued on precisely these grounds, then why does the industry continue to produce at C when C' is by definition a position of lower cost? The fact that economies are 'external' to the factory does not prevent the building of many factories, if necessary, by one firm. The concept of an external economy is almost a contradiction in terms. If the presence of external economies is known, it becomes 'internal', that is, it can be exploited by any single producer. In truth, if Fig. 15.2(b) were really a possibility, production could take place at C only if total production were concentrated in the hands of a single monopolist or monopolistically organised group and if output were deliberately restricted, so as to earn a higher price for an artificially limited output. Unexploited economies of scale can exist only when the producer is aware of the effect of his own activities upon market price. The infant industry argument therefore is logically consistent only where the manufacturer himself would not find it profitable to exploit known economies.†

Partly for reasons implicit in the argument of the previous paragraph and partly because of the present writer's belief that there is

† Or perhaps where the existence of economies is in doubt, so that management believes they exist when the suppliers of capital do not. Alternatively, the argument of Book I, section 8.1, may be valid.

little evidence to suggest that the case of Fig. 15.2(b) is of any great empirical significance, we shall continue to assume that changes in the number or scale of output of individual plants in an industry will not affect costs, given factor prices (see also Book I, section 7.15). This should not of course be taken to mean that we claim that in the real world no producer is ever conscious of the effect of the level of his sales upon prices or that no economies of scale remain to be earned. All that we would wish to suggest here is that these features of the economy are not likely to have an influence powerful enough to nullify the results obtained on the competitive assumption. It is not hard to introduce monopoly practices into our model. But to do so obscures conclusions which are almost certainly correct and only partially modified in the more general case (see, for example, section 17.5 below).

15.5 SUPPLY THEORY – MANY COMMODITIES

The purpose of this short section is to assert that all the results of the previous section hold equally however many commodities are produced *except* (15.4.16). This is replaced by the sign conditions

$$\begin{vmatrix} \dfrac{\partial S_i}{\partial q_i} & \dfrac{\partial S_i}{\partial q_j} \\[2mm] \dfrac{\partial S_j}{\partial q_i} & \dfrac{\partial S_j}{\partial q_j} \end{vmatrix} \geqq 0 \qquad (15.5.1)$$

and

$$\begin{vmatrix} \dfrac{\partial S_i}{\partial q_i} & \dfrac{\partial S_i}{\partial q_j} & \dfrac{\partial S_i}{\partial q_k} \\[2mm] \dfrac{\partial S_j}{\partial q_i} & \dfrac{\partial S_j}{\partial q_j} & \dfrac{\partial S_j}{\partial q_k} \\[2mm] \dfrac{\partial S_k}{\partial q_i} & \dfrac{\partial S_k}{\partial q_j} & \dfrac{\partial S_k}{\partial q_k} \end{vmatrix} \geqq 0 \qquad (15.5.2)$$

and so on.

These many-commodity results follow with great simplicity from the same piece of information used in the previous section, namely, that competition maximises the value of the national product subject to the constraint imposed by the limited factor endowment. The proof, however, rests upon a knowledge of the properties of convex functions which we do not expect the ordinary reader to possess. The

curious or the sceptical will find some guidance in exercise 6 at the
end of this chapter.

15.6 SUPPLY THEORY – MORE COMMODITIES THAN BASIC FACTORS

We now come to another general problem of very great importance,
much less familiar to economists than those so far treated. In writing
supply as a function of commodity prices we explicitly assumed that
one and only one pattern of supply is associated with each technique
of production. In the *usual case* this will not be so. Many patterns of
supply will yield the same value of national product, given prices.
Prices alone may be insufficient to determine supplies of the various
commodities. The building blocks we use to analyse the consequences
of policy are the basic demand and supply responses to each price
change, *everything else held constant*. In the case of supply we have
to examine very carefully just what is the 'everything else' which we
do hold constant.

Consider the simplest possible case where two commodities are
manufactured from a single input, labour. It is immediately obvious
that the production possibility set for such an economy must be as in
Fig. 15.3. The boundary of the block must be a straight line. In terms
of cost equations we must have

$$q_1 = a_{11}p_1$$

and
$$q_2 = a_{21}p_1$$

In this case the coefficients a_{11} and a_{21} are constants. They do not
depend upon factor prices because only one lowest-cost production
technique is possible. To produce one unit of commodity 1, a_{11} units
of labour is the minimum requirement and no other alternative is
available. Hence, dividing the two cost equations, we observe that
the ratio of commodity prices q_2/q_1 is always constant at a value
a_{21}/a_{11} whatever the chosen supply of each commodity. Indeed, all we
are saying is that the costs of the two commodities measured in units
of labour are always constant.

Notice that this case is not in contradiction with anything we have
said so far. The production possibility set is convex just as before;
all that is different is that the boundary of the set is a straight line.
The difficulty comes when we try to choose, for commodity prices
$(a_{11}p_1)$ and $(a_{21}p_1)$, the pattern of supply which maximises the value of

national output, for we note that the tangent to any point in AB, the boundary of the production possibility set, is AB itself. Any point in AB yields the same total value of the national product.

In terms of the supply function we note that specification of the price ratio is insufficient to determine the pattern of supply. We cannot write

$$S_1 = S_1(q_1, q_2)$$

for we do know S_1 from q_1 and q_2. On the other hand it should be

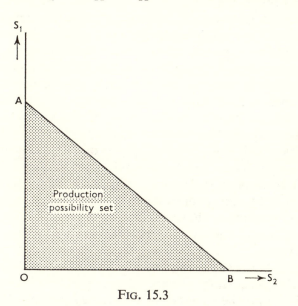

FIG. 15.3

noted that if prices are *different* from $(a_{11}p)$ and $(a_{21}p_1)$, the maximum national income *is* uniquely determined. If the market price ratio q_2/q_1 is greater than the slope of AB, suppliers will produce OB units of commodity 2 and nothing of commodity 1, that is, the point B defines the competitive equilibrium. If q_2/q_1 is less than the slope AB, only commodity 1 will be produced. In both cases the value of national output is maximised at market prices.

In short we are dealing with a very odd supply function. Over one range of prices S_1 and S_2 are fixed at, say, S_1^0 and zero respectively, the response rates to price changes being zero. At a certain critical level of prices the response rates become infinite and S_1 and S_2 are indeterminate. At all remaining price levels S_2 is fixed at S_2^0 and S_1 is zero, the response rates again being zero.

As we are for the most part dealing with small changes in our variables, it is tempting to say that there is no problem. All that we need do is to remember that response rates might be zero or might be very large indeed. It might further be suspected that the case we are dealing with arises out of the unrealistic assumption that only one factor of production, labour, exists.

Unfortunately there is every reason to believe that the 'infinite' response rate will be quite normal and that we shall ordinarily be 'stuck' at precisely the point where the difficult switchover comes. As a beginning, suppose that there existed a primitive community all of whose products were manufactured by homogeneous labour alone and where no international trade took place. All commodity prices would be determined by relative labour inputs. The community would produce precisely what was demanded by consumers at the going prices. Supply would accommodate itself to demand without any price change. No supply function exists. If prices could change, the response rate in supplies would be infinite; but in fact prices cannot change unless all but one commodity goes out of production.

On the other hand the reader should note that as soon as international trade is permitted, market prices *may* change and specialisation will occur. Suppose for example that two primitive communities of the kind mentioned above attempt to enter into trade. Evidently, since there is only one factor of production and the laws of physics are everywhere the same, relative prices before trade must be the same in both regions. The existence of any appreciable transportation costs would immediately prevent any trade at all. All commodities would enter into the category of non-traded goods. We should be left with the same situation as before trade. Supply responses would be infinite but, as prices can never change, the numerical value of responses is irrelevant.

Against this we note at once that, if the same 'infinite' elasticities of supply can be present when there are many factors of production, there is no reason at all why, before trade, factor prices and hence commodity prices should be the same. The opening-up of trade may, and ordinarily will, change market prices to something different from the limited admissible set and some commodities must go immediately out of production. The 'infinite' supply responses operate to create drastic changes in the supply pattern. But equally some commodities may become non-traded as in the two-commodity case, so that we need a rule to know where we stand.

We now draw attention to the fact that the 'infinite' supply responses must be expected, not only when we have one single factor of production but also whenever *the number of commodities in production exceeds the number of basic factors*. Note that in the two-commodity case supply responses become zero as soon as one commodity goes out of production. Infinite responses disappear as soon as the number of commodities and factors become equal.

Fortunately, it is not at all difficult both to identify the difficulty and find a way around it. Consider the familiar equation:

$$A_i = \sum_j S_j a_{ji} \qquad (15.6.1)$$

indicating that the total endowment of the ith basic factor must always be equal to the sum of the amounts used in production of each of the final commodities, both directly and indirectly through intermediate factors.

As our factors are the basic, unproduced gifts of nature, and as we are largely concerned with highly developed communities, the number of commodities will ordinarily exceed the number of factors. Let us for the moment, however, suppose that the number of goods and factors is the same. In this case we have just exactly as many equations (15.6.1) as we have supplies S_j. It is possible, therefore, to solve for each S_j in terms of inputs a_{ji} and factor endowments A_i. To fix our ideas, we set this solution out in full for the 2×2 case:

$$S_1 = \frac{\begin{vmatrix} A_1 & a_{21} \\ A_2 & a_{22} \end{vmatrix}}{\begin{vmatrix} a_{11} & a_{21} \\ a_{12} & a_{22} \end{vmatrix}} \qquad S_2 = \frac{\begin{vmatrix} a_{11} & A_1 \\ a_{12} & A_2 \end{vmatrix}}{\begin{vmatrix} a_{11} & a_{21} \\ a_{12} & a_{22} \end{vmatrix}} \qquad (15.6.2)$$

We now recall that the inputs a_{ij} are functions of factor prices, so that the expressions (15.6.2) represent supply expressed as functions of factor prices and factor endowments. But we know also that factor prices are dependent on commodity prices through the cost equations, so that by substitution of qs for ps in (15.6.2) we may deduce that supply functions exist in the form

$$S_1 = S_1(q_1, q_2, A_1, A_2)$$

These say, very reasonably, that supply is dependent upon commodity prices and factor endowments A_1 and A_2.

But now consider what happens when we have more commodities than factors. In particular, let us examine the case of three commodities and two factors. Clearly we can no longer solve the equations like (15.6.1), for we have three unknown S_j but only two equations, one for each factor of production. Nevertheless we are not entirely defeated. We can, and it is convenient to do so, shift the term in S_3 on to the left-hand side of the equations (15.6.1) and treat it as a constant as follows. We write

$$A_i - S_3 a_{3i} = S_1 a_{1i} + S_2 a_{2i} \ (i = 1, 2)$$

and solve these two equations for S_1 and S_2. Thus, for example,

$$S_1 = \frac{\begin{vmatrix} (A_1 - S_3 a_{31}) & a_{21} \\ (A_2 - S_3 a_{32}) & a_{22} \end{vmatrix}}{\begin{vmatrix} a_{11} & a_{21} \\ a_{12} & a_{22} \end{vmatrix}} \tag{15.6.3}$$

Now consider what we have. Evidently the commodity prices q_1 and q_2 are sufficient to determine factor prices, for we have the two cost equations

$$q_1 = p_1 a_{11} + p_2 a_{12}$$

$$q_2 = p_1 a_{21} + p_2 a_{22}$$

which we may solve for p_1 and p_2 in terms of q_1 and q_2. Remembering that the a_{ij} in (15.6.3) are functions of p_1 and p_2 alone, we have, by substitution in (15.6.3), supply equations of the form

$$\left.\begin{aligned} S_1 &= S_1(q_1, q_2, S_3, A_1, A_2) \\ S_2 &= S_2(q_1, q_2, S_3, A_1, A_2) \end{aligned}\right\} \tag{15.6.4}$$

and

Inspection of (15.6.3) tells us what we feared, namely, that an excess of commodities over factors destroys the belief that supply can be written as a function of commodity prices and factor endowments alone; for suppose *commodity* prices are given and fixed, it must then be true, through the cost equations, that factor prices are given and fixed. Only one pair of factor prices is consistent with any given fixed commodity price pattern as we have seen. Hence all a_{ij} are given by commodity prices. But we still have not determined all supplies. Indeed, we may choose S_3 at any quantity we like, putting the chosen number for S_3 in the equation (15.6.3) to obtain corresponding values for S_1 and S_2. Any other arbitrarily chosen value for S_3 will lead to some different S_1 and S_2 all consistent with the equations (15.6.3) and all consistent with the same commodity prices and a_{ij}.

There exists an infinity of possible supply patterns all consistent with the same set of commodity prices.

Since for all this infinity of supply patterns the conditions of competitive equilibrium are met, it is clear that all lie on the boundary of the production possibility set. As before, the set S is convex but the many-dimensional analogue to the line AB (Fig. 15.2 (a)) touches S at many points instead of one single point, just as a tangent would in Fig. 15.3. The production possibility surface contains *linear segments*. If the reader wishes to visualise in three dimensions what the production possibility set must look like with two factors only, he should think of one-half of a cone or a cylinder lying across the three axes of reference. A flat plane tangential to a cone or a cylinder touches it in a continuous line of points. Notice that if we had postulated three commodities but only one factor of production, all prices would be irrevocably fixed. The boundary of the production possibility set would reduce to a flat plane which the tangent plane would touch everywhere. In this case, following the argument above counting equations and unknowns, we should have just one supply function, as under

$$S_1 = S_1(S_2, S_3, A_1) \qquad (15.6.5)$$

The supply of commodity 1 would have to be written as a function of supplies two and three and the factor endowment only. Complete elimination of prices occurs because in equations like (15.6.4) it is the *ratio* of prices which matters. In (15.6.5) even this disappears.

What we have thus shown is that, although economists often write supply simply as a function of all commodity prices alone (with the implicit assumption that factor endowments are constant and hence need not be written explicitly in the function), this is incorrect except in the case where the number of factors is equal to the number of commodities. By 'incorrect' we mean that it is *logically inconsistent* with the fundamental assumptions of this book, and indeed with the usual assumptions which most economists make when dealing with the theory of international trade. That is, we should not simultaneously suppose that it is reasonable to believe that factor prices alone determine cost and hence prices and at the same time let supply be dependent upon commodity prices alone.

We have given above good reasons why commodity prices are probably not dependent on the scale of output. It has been argued that, given factor prices, increasing the number of plants in a given industry should not influence the cost of output, at least not to any degree. From this (15.6.4) and (15.6.5) follow logically. Only if it could be shown empirically that costs do in fact depend on the number of factories as well as on factor prices would the old supply functions be reinstated. And even then the difficulty would be thrust underground rather than solved.

15.7 A METHODOLOGICAL DIGRESSION

At this point some further methodological discussion might be fruitful. The object of all scientific inquiry is to find a set of concepts, or basic building blocks, which are consistent, and in terms of which it is possible to explain every event which happens and/or predict the consequence of any action. This result is achieved when each event can be shown to be no more than a particular configuration of the behavioural consistencies common to all events. In particular the common consistencies of economic behaviour which form the building blocks of all the work of this book are the consumers' responses to price and income changes and suppliers' responses to price changes. It will be noticed that our object throughout has been to express the consequences of policy, either applied or proposed, in terms of these responses. The greater part of the efforts of econometricians and statisticians therefore should be directed towards the measurement of basic responses and towards the testing of their up-to-dateness and accuracy. Once we have these numbers, all else follows by the methods of this book.

Even so there remain important choices to be made. It is useless to appeal to econometricians for measures of elasticities until we have quite made up our minds just what figures we need. The kind of theory we have been developing in the early chapters of this second book is most useful in this respect. Indeed, the point we have reached in the present argument is an important crossroad.

We emphasise first that the question whether or not there exists in the real world 'external' economies or diseconomies of scale, which imply that, even though each industrial plant produces at its lowest possible cost, a change in the number of plants would change minimum cost, is a question of *fact* which must be either true or false. Whether or not there exist more commodities than factors is also a fact which must be true or false. It has already been pointed out that the arbitrary classification of factors into groups with some kind of average price obscures this last problem rather than solves it. If two objects exist which are used in production and whose prices can, in principle, vary independently, then we have two factors whether we like it or not. Unfortunately these social facts of the real world are not easy to check, although one day they must be checked. Lack of this particular piece of knowledge is a most important obstacle to future progress.

The truth is that we cannot with certainty frame our model in the best way without further information which we have not got. Let us suppose for the moment that we believe in the existence of external diseconomies due to changes in the number of factories producing a given product. What this means in terms of cost equations is that the inputs a_{ij} depend not only on factor prices but also upon supplies S_i. Even when there are more commodities than factors (say three commodities and two factors), it is not now true that the price of one commodity is determined by the other two. In the case where a_{ij} do not depend on supply, two commodity prices are sufficient to determine the two factor prices by solving two of the cost equations. The third commodity price, therefore, is immediately fixed by putting the two known factor prices into the third cost equation. When, however, the a_{ij} do depend on S_i, then factor prices are not determined unless S_i is given. Hence the third commodity price is not given. The production possibility set need not now have linear segments and supplies are uniquely determined by commodity prices.

In such a case we could write

$$S_i = S_i(q_1, q_2, q_3, A_1, A_2) \qquad (15.7.1)$$

and the econometrician could be asked to compute the responses $\partial S_i / \partial q_j$ which then become our basic building blocks. The calculated numbers remain the same whatever the problem under review. But now suppose that our belief in external diseconomies is without foundation in fact. Suppose in fact that the a_{ij} do not depend upon aggregate production. Consider the method by which the econometrician would proceed.

Given (15.7.1), he might take changes and write

$$dS_i = \sum_j \frac{\partial S_i}{\partial q_j} dq_j \qquad (15.7.2)$$

assuming of course that factor endowments remain unchanged. It might then be supposed that the stable unchanging feature of economic life, that is, the consistencies we seek, are the responses $\partial S_i / \partial q_j$, which give expression to the laws of physics operating through production functions and behaviour which consistently minimises costs. On the other hand events would operate period by period to change dq_j and hence dS_i. If our observations were *exact* over three time periods (one for each commodity price), we could note the successive values of dS_i and dq_j. Put in equation (15.7.2) this would give us three equations in the three unknowns, $\partial S_i/\partial q_1$, $\partial S_i/\partial q_2$ and $\partial S_i/\partial q_3$, which we are trying to determine. These three equations we should expect to be solvable to give the information we need.

Unfortunately for the econometrician not armed with a knowledge of the theory of this chapter, the following difficulty will arise. Absence of external diseconomies and the excess of commodities over factors gives rise to a relationship between commodity prices which must always exist. As we have seen, not all commodity price patterns are possible; any two commodity prices determine the third according to a rule which we write

$$q_1 = q_1(q_2, q_3)$$

Taking changes gives

$$dq_1 = \frac{\partial q_1}{\partial q_2}dq_2 + \frac{\partial q_1}{\partial q_3}dq_3 \qquad (15.7.3)$$

Hence, whatever happens in the economy, it is impossible to observe changes which do not fit some equation like (15.7.3). But for any three sets of observations dq to fit (15.7.3) it is necessary [5, pp. 298–301] that the determinant

$$\begin{vmatrix} dq_1^1 & dq_2^1 & dq_3^1 \\ dq_1^2 & dq_2^2 & dq_3^2 \\ dq_1^3 & dq_2^3 & dq_3^3 \end{vmatrix}$$

should be zero, where dq_i^j is the jth observation of the change in the ith price.

A check now shows that this is precisely the determinant which must appear as a divisor when the econometrician attempts to solve the equations (15.7.2). All responses $\partial S_i/\partial q_3$ will appear as zero divided by zero, or some number divided by zero. We are in short asking the econometrician to perform an impossible task – to measure in fact something which does not exist.

The only proper procedure, when there are no external diseconomies and an excess of commodities over basic factors, is to write the supply equation in the form (15.6.4). The rule is that we count the number of commodities m and the number of factors n, and, for every commodity in excess, we write into the ith supply function some S_j where j must of course be different from i. We have supply functions for the first n commodities, the remaining m-n supplies appearing as variables upon which the first n supplies depend. When a supply variable is introduced as an argument, we drop its price from the function.

In this last connection we mention again that any supply pattern s which maximises national product Y at prices q must also maximise Y at prices λq (where λ is any positive number); for if $Y = Y^0$ for prices q^0, the production pattern s^0 must yield a national product λY^0 at prices λq^0. And if λY^0 is not the maximum possible but some production pattern s^* yields Y^* which is greater than λY^0, then some national product Y^*/λ which is greater than Y^0 is obtainable at prices q^0 using the supply pattern s^*. This contradicts the assumption that Y^0 is a maximum at price q^0. Hence prices must appear in supply functions as price *ratios* so that multiplying all prices by λ can have no effect on supply. This explains why, when we have only one factor of production, no price appears (see (15.6.5)). A single price cannot be a price ratio.

Having counted commodities and factors, the rule above gives us the only proper form for the supply function. If the econometrician now applies his art to supply functions in the new form, the difficulty we been discussing cannot arise. But note that we then have a quite different set of building bricks, which must be used in a very different way. Even if the form of function

$$S_i = S_i(q_1, q_2, q_3) \qquad (15.7.4)$$

had any meaning so that $\partial S_i/\partial q_j$ could be computed, these would be quite different numbers from the $\partial S_i/\partial q_j$ of an equation of the form

$$S_i = S_i(q_1, q_2, S_3) \qquad (15.7.5)$$

for in the one case we are asking what is the response of supply to, say, a change in the price of commodity 2 with both prices 1 and 3 constant, whereas in the other we ask what is the response when price 1 and *supply* 3 are held constant, with *price* 3 varying in sympathy. The two responses, if both existed, would be related in a complicated way, but they would be quite different numerically. Much more important is the fact that even when any $\partial S_i/\partial q_j$ of (15.7.4) is indeterminate or infinite, all $\partial S_i/\partial q_j$ of (15.7.5) will be sensible computable numbers which can be used in the ordinary way.

The point we wish to make is that if we believe, as the present author does, that external economies or diseconomies are unlikely to be an important feature of the real world and that the number of commodities will ordinarily exceed the number of factors, we must use the form (15.7.5). To do otherwise is to produce nonsense answers even though they may not look nonsense until we begin to examine the numerical relationships between supplies and factor inputs in detail.

15.8 PROPERTIES OF SUPPLY FUNCTION – MORE COMMODITIES THAN FACTORS

Fortunately, in this book it usually turns out, when dealing with an extended model, that no question put admits of a qualitative answer without measurement. To prove this it has ordinarily been sufficient to produce an example – the three-commodity/three-factor case being most convenient. As it happens, therefore, the present section on the properties of the supply function (15.7.5) appears as something of a digression. The section has been included, however, since the whole problem is immediately raised as soon as any attempt is made to link theory and measurement.

First, we observe that the principal properties of the responses $\partial S_i/\partial q_j$ of (15.7.5) are not in any way altered when factors are in excess of commodities. In the case where the number of commodities and factors are the same, we proved or alleged the results (15.4.12)–(15.4.19) and (15.5.1)–(15.5.2) as a direct consequence of the convexity of the production possibility set and the maximisation of the national product. Now consider the meaning of a supply response when the supply function is written in the form

$$S_i = S_i(q_1, \ldots, q_r, S_s, \ldots, S_n) \qquad (15.8.1)$$

where commodities s to n are in excess of the number of factors. $\partial S_i/\partial q_j$, where j lies between 1 and r, means the rate of change of S_i due to a change in q_j when all other prices 1 to r and all supplies s to n are held constant. If supplies s to n are held constant, any changes in the production pattern which occur are between points in a *reduced* production possibility set which we will call R. The reduced set is made up of all points in the full set S such that the supplies S_s to S_n are constant at the value given in the supply equation. All that we need to prove therefore is that the reduced set R is also a convex set. And convexity of R follows at once from convexity of S together with the fact that any weighted average of two equal numbers is the same number. Thus if s^1 and s^2 are points in R, all weighted averages lie in S by convexity of S, and hence lie in R since R consists of *all* elements of S with supplies S_s to S_n constant.

It is worth while reflecting for a moment upon what this result really means. What we are saying in effect is that we may *still* say that the supply of the ith commodity must increase when its price rises even though it is only all other prices in the group 1 to r which are remaining constant. Prices in group s to n must change in such a way that supplies s to n remain constant. In the same way all of the results (15.5.1)–(15.5.2) hold for prices 1 to r with the same meaning attached to the responses. We have to use this hybrid way of talking simply because the whole idea of the response of supply due to a price change, *all other prices constant*, is meaningless. To raise one price, keeping all others constant, is to arrive at a configuration of prices where not all commodities can be produced.

We now know something about the properties of the basic responses $\partial S_i / \partial q_j$, but to make use of (15.8.1) in the manner of Book I we need also the unfamiliar responses $\partial S_i / \partial S_s$. This is the rate of response of the ith supply to a change in the supply of commodity s with all prices 1 to r constant and all other supplies $(s+1)$ to n constant. It is important to note that prices 1 to r constant implies *all* prices constant in spite of the remarks made when we considered the meaning of $\partial S_i / \partial q_j$. The reason why all prices remain constant is that all factor prices are determined fully by the r commodity prices 1 to r. If these remain constant, so must factor prices and hence so must *all* commodity prices. That we can change supply without changing commodity prices is a reflection of the difficulty which led to the present approach, namely, that commodity prices do not determine supply uniquely. On the other hand this very properly enables us to say a great deal about the response $\partial S_i / \partial S_s$.

In the ordinary way of course we should simply ask the econometrician to estimate $\partial S_i / \partial S_s$ in the same way he estimates $\partial S_i / \partial q_j$. Against this, in the absence of reliable estimates we have consistently in this book made use of our knowledge of the sign (positive or negative) of responses in order to deduce qualitative results. Anything we can infer therefore about $\partial S_i / \partial S_s$ may be valuable not only to ourselves but also to the econometrician devising some estimating method.

Accordingly we look back at the identity (15.6.3) and take changes, remembering that if neither factor prices nor commodity prices change then all a_{ij} must also remain constant. From (15.6.3) we deduce that

$$dS_1 = \left(\frac{a_{32}a_{21} - a_{31}a_{22}}{a_{11}a_{22} - a_{12}a_{21}}\right) dS_3$$

or the ratio of changes dS_1/dS_3 all prices constant, which is of course $\partial S_1/\partial S_3$, is given by

$$\frac{\partial S_1}{\partial S_3} = \left(\frac{a_{32}a_{21} - a_{31}a_{22}}{a_{11}a_{22} - a_{12}a_{21}}\right) \tag{15.8.2}$$

The same procedure may be applied however many commodities are in excess and the result will always be given as the ratio of determinants of factor inputs. We can be satisfied therefore that we cannot in a general way put signs on $\partial S_i/\partial S_s$ without further information from econometricians. On the other hand the result (15.8.2) is bound to be of very great value in any attempt to estimate $\partial S_i/\partial S_s$, since the a_{ij} are directly observable inputs.

One further point must now be made in defence of the use of type (15.8.1) supply equations as basic building blocks. The astute reader might well suspect that the r equations of (15.8.1) can be solved for each commodity price q_i in terms of S_1 to S_r, leading to r equations of the form

$$q_i = q_i(S_1, \ldots, S_n) \tag{15.8.3}$$

And since the choice of the first r commodities was arbitrary, all n prices can be represented in this way. What now are the properties of the responses $\partial q_i/\partial S_j$ of these equations? Might not these be more convenient building blocks in view of their more satisfactory symmetry?

This approach is equivalent to asking 'At what set of prices will any given pattern of supply be that which maximises the value of output?' rather than 'What pattern of supply maximises the value of output given prices?' It should be noted that the answer to the former question is unique even when there are linear segments in the production block and that the answer to the second question is accordingly not unique. What we mean by this is that any point on the boundary of the production possibility set uniquely determines the slopes (and hence commodity prices) at that point even when many points yield the same value of output. It follows that the functions (15.8.3) exist, and the responses $\partial q_i/\partial S_j$ exist and are sensible numbers even though responses $\partial S_i/\partial q_j$ do not exist when supply equations are written in the ordinary way. But note that only price ratios would be given. To determine absolute prices some aggregate value of output must be specified.

The reason why we set our face against this apparently more beautiful and symmetric approach to the theory of supply is simply that, as we might expect, the same old difficulty now comes in by the back door. Whilst it is true that the responses $\partial q_i / \partial S_j$ exist, are sensible, and could perhaps be computed, it is also true that we should have difficulty in making use of them for the purpose of prediction. The reason may be seen as follows.

Suppose that, as a consequence of some policy, it was known that each price q_i would change by an amount dq_i, and suppose further that, armed with our knowledge of the numbers $\partial q_i / \partial S_j$, we wish to predict the changes dS_k which will occur in supplies as a consequence. Following what amounts to the procedure of Book I, we should write the n equations

$$dq_i = \sum_j \frac{\partial q_i}{\partial S_j} dS_j \qquad (15.8.4)$$

and attempt to solve these for each dS_j. But such an attempt must inevitably lead to disaster. We already know in fact that no solution for dS_j is possible where there are linear segments in the production possibility set. Provided the numbers $\partial q_i / \partial S_j$ were perfectly accurate, we should simply get the meaningless result 0/0 for each dS_j.

The reader should note especially what might be the *practical* consequences of failure to choose the right theoretical building blocks. The equations (15.8.4), in the absence of numbers, can *apparently* be solved, so that in the ordinary way each dS_j can be expressed as the ratio of two determinants made up of elements $\partial q_i / \partial S_j$. Suppose we set out the result in this form which, the reader is reminded, is the method of Book I. We then approach the econometrician for his estimates of $\partial q_i / \partial S_j$ and fill them in. If the estimates given to us are exact we should, as already explained, get the result 0/0, but it is impossible to believe that the numbers we shall be given could be accurate to this degree. We may finish up with, say, 0·005/0·001 which is 5, or 0·001/0·005 which is 0·2, according to chance errors in observations which have nothing to do with economics at all. We could be deluded by these numbers into supposing that we have a meaningful result, and even if we were not, the result 0/0 gets us no further forward.

Special attention should be paid to the fact that attempts to solve problems in the manner of Book I may be subject to precisely this difficulty if supply functions are wrongly specified. Nonsense results can easily be written down if the full consequences of the model postulated are not carefully considered. If we work with a model with more commodities than factors, and at the same time present results in terms of the parameters $\partial q_i/\partial S_j$ of (15.8.4), there is a risk that, without knowing it, we have computed a formula which says that the consequence of some policy is measured by the ratio $0/0$, and this absurdity may not be revealed even when estimates of parameters are applied to the formula.

15.9 THE PROBLEM OF IMPORTED RAW MATERIAL

The next step in the construction of supply functions must be to consider the role of imported raw materials, which play an important part in economic activity in the real world. It would be hard to defend the practical usefulness of the work so far if the presence of imported raw materials called for any serious modification of the model.

It will be recalled that our point of departure was the production possibility set which was shown to have the convexity property. We now extend the notion of the production possibility set to include importation of factors of production. At first sight this may seem like a contradiction in terms since, by definition, the production possibility set includes only those selections of output patterns attainable with a *fixed* factor endowment. If we are free to import productive inputs, how can production possibilities be limited? The answer is that an unbounded production possibility set makes perfectly good sense. We shall see later that the quantity of factor imports will be limited by the maximising process given import prices.

The production possibility set extended as required is best illus-trated diagrammatically taking the simplest case of one imported factor and one product. In Fig. 15.4 the quantity of the imported factor is measured negatively from the origin O whilst the product is measured in a positive direction. OA is the quantity of output which can be manufactured from home resources with zero import-ation of any input. The curve AB defines the limit of what can be produced with successively larger factor imports. Obviously there is no lower boundary, in principle, to the production possibility set lying to the left of AB, although it may be useful to think of some limit imposed by world endowment of the imported factor. Not more of a factor can be imported than the total quantity existing in the universe.

We have now to show that the extended production possibility set is convex. Clearly in the general case each point in the set represents n numbers, r being products measured positively and $n-r$ being imported factors measured negatively. As before, let s^1 and s^2 be any points in the set. If s^1 is a possible production programme, then θs^1 is a programme involving θ times the number of firms and θ times the raw material imports. If θ is a positive number between zero and unity, then the programme θs^1 uses only the fraction θ of national

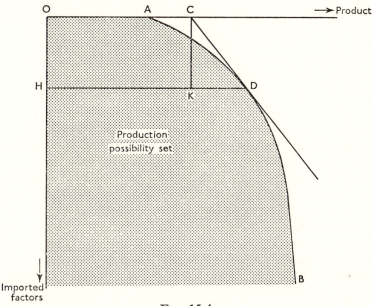

FIG. 15.4

resources. Similarly a programme $(1-\theta)s^2$ will demand the fraction $(1-\theta)$ of the national resources. At the same time a fraction $(1-\theta)$ of imported raw materials used in the programme s^2 would be required. It follows that the programme $\theta s^1 + (1-\theta)s^2$ is feasible since this uses all national resources plus exactly the weighted average of the imports under s^1 and s^2 indicated as imported by the programme $\theta s^1 + (1-\theta)s^2$. The production possibility set therefore is convex.

Now consider the argument above leading to equation (15.4.9). Evidently equations (15.4.6)–(15.4.8) hold equally whether A_i is an imported input or one which forms part of the fixed factor endowment. The point of difference comes only when we come to argue that $\sum p_i A_i$ is a fixed upper limit to the value of the national product. This is obviously no longer the case since the A_i include some variable factor import, say A_j^*. On the other hand if we shift all imported raw material to the right-hand side of the inequality (15.4.9), so that we have

$$\sum_i p_i A_i \geqq \sum_k q_k S_k - \sum_j p_j A_j^* \qquad (15.9.1)$$

the left-hand side does now become an upper limit to the right-hand side. Evidently competition maximises the value of the national product sold to consumers or exported, *less* the value of imported intermediate factors.

In Fig. 15.4 the maximised entity is obviously measured by the intercept OC along the product axis. HD is the total value of the national product whilst KD is the value of imported raw materials expressed in units of the product. The slope of the line CD is equal to the ratio of the product price and the imported raw material price. OC is HD minus KD and is clearly maximised when the price ratio CD is a tangent to AB, the boundary of the production possibility set.

Evidently nothing is changed. All the conclusions reached in the simple case, without imported raw materials, apply equally and for the same reasons when imported raw materials are present. The only point to remember is that some of our supplies S_k are raw material imports measured negatively. Thus the price of imported raw material appears in supply functions, but this is of course no more than intuition would lead us to expect. Common sense suggests that the quantity of any product which will be produced for any set of prices will ordinarily depend also upon the price at which raw materials can be imported.

In view of this, the reader may well ask how far it is possible to maintain the dichotomy between the hidden (factor market) part of the model and the commodity part which we looked at in Book I. If imported raw materials enter into the balance of payments and the balance of payments is an object of study, is it not necessary to bring the factor market explicitly into consideration?

The answer to this is that it *is* necessary only in part. The negative 'supplies' of imported raw materials are in fact demands for raw materials and are functions of prices just like any other demand functions. On the other hand they have the *properties* of supply functions with a reversed sign. In the aggregate model of Book I it is convenient as a first approximation to imagine that demand for imported raw materials is included in ordinary consumer demand. It is true of course that demand for imported raw materials depends on production rather than aggregate expenditure, and to that extent we should expect some degree of error. But a moment's reflection suggests that very little of Book I need be changed on this account. In a less aggregative model all that is necessary is to remember that in assigning properties to demand functions for imported raw materials we should make use of the theory of this chapter rather than the ordinary theory of demand. Behaviour in the remainder of the factor market may remain hidden except when we have some specific question to be put as in say, Chapter 14 above. In this case examination of the identities (15.4.3) and (15.4.4) will, as usual, tell us all we need to know (see Chapters 17 and 18).

15.10 THE GAINS FROM TRADE

This chapter began with a promise to show that, subject to certain qualifications, some trade is better than no trade in the sense of Chapter 13. We have now at last assembled the enormous amount of apparatus required to prove this point.

Let us suppose that the community consumption pattern after trade is represented by the vector x^1; that is, we are reverting to the notation of Chapter 13. Similarly s^1 is the pattern of production chosen from the production possibility set S. We shall show that the essential condition necessary to ensure that the trading position, whatever the distribution of money income between individuals, is better than no trade at all, is the inequality

$$q^1 x^1 \geqq q^1 s^1 \qquad (15.10.1)$$

that is, the value of consumption must be greater than or equal to the value of production. In the case where raw materials, a^1, are imported at prices, p^1, the required condition is

$$q^1 x^1 \geqq q^1 s^1 - p^1 a^1 \qquad (15.10.2)$$

Note that these conditions will ordinarily be satisfied, even where impediments to trade exist, such as tariffs or quotas, for $q^1 x^1$ is total expenditure and the right-hand side of (15.10.2) is the value of national product less imported raw materials, i.e. the incomes of factors of production. In the ordinary way, therefore, in conditions of equilibrium, the equality will hold in (15.10.1) and (15.10.2). But note especially that if an import tariff is in operation or if a quota has been imposed, total expenditure will exceed the value of production (see Book I, Chapters 7 and 9). The inequality will hold in (15.10.1) and (15.10.2) but in any case the required conditions are met.

Now consider the consumption possibilities open to the country under investigation if it ceases to trade entirely. It is free to choose only some pattern s^0 which must be contained in the production possibility set S. Note that, in the case where raw materials are ordinarily imported, 'no trade' imposes the further restriction that the imported raw material elements of s^0 must be zero; but s^0 is still an element of the set S. Furthermore we know that competition ensures that

$$q^1 s^1 - p^1 a^1 \geqq q^1 s^0 \qquad (15.10.3)$$

for competition maximises the left-hand entity given prices. Hence

$$q^1 x^1 \geqq q^1 s^0 = q^1 x^0 \qquad (15.10.4)$$

which may of course be written

$$q^1 dx^0 \geqq 0 \qquad (15.10.5)$$

which is the sufficient condition for a gain in welfare of Chapter 13.

We recognise also that (15.10.5) is true whatever the distribution of income before trade and whatever the distribution of income after trade. This implies that for *any* 'before trade' position x^0, the opening-up of trade must lead to a set of prices q^1 and a consumption pattern x^1 satisfying (15.10.5) whatever redistribution of money income is applied. Thus a policy of trade satisfies criterion (iv) of section 13.3. We can be quite sure that there exists a particular distribution of welfare which makes everyone better off or at least as well off. Trade therefore is ordinarily a good thing.

In the view of the present writer, however, the interest of this result lies much more in what it does not mean rather than what it does. The common-sense notion that trade must be a good thing or nations would not trade turns out to contain only a very modest kernel of truth. It would be unbelievably wrong to interpret any known result to mean that trade should be encouraged at any price.

It is not true for example that subsidised trade is better than no trade, although it might be. With a subsidy in operation the value of consumption is ordinarily less than the value of output, for a tax must be imposed on income to pay the subsidy which goes abroad. Thus neither inequality (15.10.1) nor (15.10.2) holds. It is easy in fact to construct examples of subsidised trade which make everyone worse off. Furthermore it should be remembered that even un-subsidised trade cannot be said to be good unless a satisfactory redistribution of income is applied exactly as we have assumed throughout this book.

Much more important still, it is *not* true that a reduction in trade is necessarily bad, for the imposition of a tariff can, as we have already seen, lead to a gain. By the same token the imposition of a quota can lead to a gain. The argument above does not permit comparison of varying levels of trade but only of trade and no trade.

In short, it is difficult to imagine any practical problem to which our central result might be relevant. Almost always it will be necessary to work out the consequence of any proposed policy change before an attempt can be made to pronounce upon its welfare effect. Indeed, the sum and substance of the classical 'gains from trade' proposition as it now stands would seem to be this. Trade may permit a country to extend the range of its consumption possibilities by allowing a point to be reached which lies outside its production possibility set. Obviously any activity which widens the range of choice without reducing any of the previously existing alternatives can be said to be a good thing, but such a general argument gives no clue as to how far or in what way the activity should be carried on. Answers to these questions come only after a great deal more analysis and measurement on the lines laid down earlier in this book.

APPENDIX TO CHAPTER 15

NOTES ON THE PROBLEM OF CAPITAL

The purpose of these notes is to show that it is possible to define exactly the meaning of the apparently imprecise notion 'capital', or 'work in progress', in such a way that a factor, capital, may be introduced into supply theory, at the same time maintaining with a high degree of accuracy every property of each equation set out in this book. The reader is warned however, that this section is written in a rather elliptical manner since a more profound study of capital theory lies outside the scope of the present work. The argument is developed solely because the concept of capital is currently under attack and yet it plays a central part in a great deal of what remains to be said.

First, we remark that the notion of 'price' in economics is not always as clear as it might be. Some commodities like motor-cars are durable; that is, the act of consumption covers more than one time period. Others like food are consumed in a single act. In the same way some inputs into production are used up over many time periods, e.g. machines and buildings. Others like fuel are used up at once. A special problem arises, in the case of durable commodities or factors, not present where consumption takes place entirely in one single time period.

It is a fact of the world that durable goods are sometimes rented and sometimes sold outright. On the other hand we sometimes use the word 'price' to indicate rental per unit of time even though the same word can indicate the charge for an outright sale. For example, we talk about the wage rate as the price of labour rather than the rent of labour, only, perhaps, because it is no longer the practice to sell slaves outright in a slave market. Again, a royalty on, say, oil-bearing land is really a rental for the use of that land even though the rental price may in fact be calculated on the number of units of oil extracted.

The point is raised simply because in any formal model of an economic system it is usually necessary to be consistent. We shall therefore insist that every 'price' in our model is in fact a rental per unit of time, whether the price concerned is for a commodity consumed or a commodity which is itself an input. Basic inputs also are rented. Of course we shall sometimes have an interest in the outright sale price, although much less often in theoretical discussion than some economists may suppose. Note that even in the theory of consumer demand the quantities demanded may be thought of either as quantities sold or quantities 'in use' by consumers. (See, for a more extended discussion, Pearce [10, pp. 40–3]). If the market price for outright sale is ever needed, the following relationship is known to hold:

$$q_i = \frac{rq_i^*}{1 - (1+r)^{-l_i}} \tag{15.A.1}$$

where q_i is the rental price, l_i the life of the machine or consumer durable, r the market rate of interest on money and q_i^* the market price for outright sale.

Throughout this book the reader who wishes to develop exact habits of thought must think of 'price' as q_i, not q_i^*; but the formula (15.A.1) gives an easy conversion. As a necessary corollary, quantities demanded are quantities *in use*, and by the same token quantities supplied are not the quantities currently produced but the total stock which current production will sustain.

To the reader who may feel that this is a radical departure requiring a rethinking of much that has gone before, we make the following points. First, in all our work we are comparing positions of equilibrium with new positions of equilibrium. In these circumstances we should accept a balanced age composition of equipment as a reasonable first approximation; that is, there should be in existence an equal proportion of each 'vintage' of each durable item. Thus, if the life of the ith product is l_i, an output or purchase of X_i/l_i per time period will sustain a stock of X_i. Hence

$$X_i^* \simeq X_i/l_i$$

where X_i^* is demand (or supply) in use in the time period and $\simeq$ means 'approximates to'. We further note that if the rate of interest is small we may deduce from (15.A.1) that

$$q_i \simeq q_i^*/l_i$$

Hence

$$q_i^* X_i^* \simeq (q_i l_i) X_i/l_i = q_i X_i$$

which is only another way of saying that the value of sales required to sustain a given stock of equipment is, for relatively low rates of interest, not so very far different from the cost of renting the given stock.

A moment's reflection reveals that this simple fact justifies all our work so far, provided we confine our interest to states of equilibrium. The distinction between starred and unstarred variables becomes crucial only when we wish to study the dynamics of a problem, that is, the route by which we pass from one stationary state to another.

Two more points must be made. First, we remind the reader that a high proportion of the commodities we talk about are not durable. In this case l_i is unity and, for short time periods and hence for small r, the starred and unstarred variables are identical. Second, our present definitions carry implications as to the meaning of inputs a_{ij}. These now become the inputs in use required to maintain a stock of one unit available for use. This definition is necessary to retain consistency with the familiar equations

$$A_j = \sum_i S_i a_{ij}$$

If S_i is the quantity of the ith commodity available for use and a_{ij} is the quantity in use of the jth input necessary to sustain one unit of i in use, then A_j is the total quantity of the jth input in use in the period.

Throughout the following it is convenient to pretend also that each producer or owner of durable equipment does not sell his output but lets it at hire to the user. As our concern is to describe vertically integrated processes of the type described in section 15.2, this pretence will have no effect upon our final answer. It should be noted, however, that such a convention would induce misleading results if our interest were centred on individual firms. A firm which sells its product outright ties up less capital than one which simply rents, for the one receives all of its revenue at the moment of sale whilst the other has to wait for some part until the end of the life of the rented equipment. Conversely a firm which hires its manufacturing equipment ties up less capital than one which buys. But the two firms together, if vertically integrated, require the same capital whether the second rents or buys from the first. We now proceed to introduce capital explicitly into our model.

The existence of capital arises solely because production takes time, that is, because it is necessary to hire labour and machines, etc., a number of time periods *before* the flow of output can commence and hence before any revenue from sales is to be expected. Accordingly the 'true' cost of (notionally) hiring a piece of equipment is not just the hire price at the time of hiring but the hire price plus compound interest (profit) up to the time when the flow of revenue commences. Let t_j be the number of time periods which elapse between the actual hiring of the jth factor and first appearance of the product flow.† Then with each factor of production we have associated a maturity time t_j.

Note especially that we shall quite ordinarily have two or more factors which are physically the same yet have different maturity times. Thus a machine may be used, say, in the tenth time period before commencement of the product flow, to shape, say, a piece of steel. In the ninth time period before the product appears the *same* machine could be used to perform a second operation upon the part emerging from the first operation. In such a case it is convenient to define the two inputs as different, not because the operation is different but because the maturity time is different.

† For a fuller account of this concept of 'maturity time' see Gabor and Pearce, 'The Place of Money Capital in the Theory of Production' [11].

Since p_j is the hire price per time unit and a_{ij} is the quantity hired,

$$p_j(1+r)^t{}_j\,a_{ij}$$

is the true cost of the input inclusive of the interest charge for the maturity time. Thus, on this definition of p_j, we must write for the cost functions (15.2.1)

$$q_i = \sum_j p_j(1+r)^t{}_j a_{ij} \qquad (15.A.2)$$

bearing in mind at the same time the fact that some j may be the same physical object as some input k, in which case $p_j = p_k$.

Now suppose that, as in equations (15.2.1) and (15.2.2), some of the commodities i are intermediate products and we wish to eliminate these from the equation system to describe the vertically integrated process. Since the p_j are known hire prices, we may proceed exactly as in Chapter 15 with one important proviso. In reducing the system it is essential to preserve carefully the time dimensions.

This will happen automatically as a consequence of the substitution process described above (section 15.2). If, for example, say, p_k of equation (15.A.2) refers to some intermediate commodity k, which itself has a cost equation, and if t_k is the maturity time of k in the production of i, then the interest charge for each input into k will on substitution in (15.A.2) be multiplied by

$$(1+r)^{t_k}$$

pushing maturity times of basic factors in (15.A.2) further back into the past.

As it happens it is much easier to understand the implications of the substitution if we use a slightly different method of reduction of the cost equations so as to preserve the form. This is best explained by an example. Consider the equation

$$y = 3x + \tfrac{1}{2}y.$$

The obvious way to handle this is to write

$$\tfrac{1}{2}y = 3x$$

But we could have proceeded as follows. Substitute for y in the right-hand side and put

$$y = 3x + \tfrac{1}{2}(3x + \tfrac{1}{2}y)$$

$$= 3x + \tfrac{3}{2}x + \tfrac{1}{4}y$$

Now substitute again to get

$$y = 3x + \tfrac{3}{2}x + \tfrac{1}{4}(3x + \tfrac{1}{2}y)$$

$$= 3x + \tfrac{3}{2}x + \tfrac{3}{4}x + \tfrac{1}{8}y, \qquad \text{and so on.}$$

It will be noted that the item in y on the right-hand side gets smaller and smaller until it can be neglected and the remaining terms approximate more and more closely to $6x$ at each iteration.

If this method of reduction of cost equations is used rather than that set out in section 15.2 above, the economic meaning of the terms of the reduced equation becomes much more obvious. Again an example will illustrate the point. Consider two cost equations as follows:

$$q_1 = p_1(1+r)^{t_1}a_{11} + p_2(1+r)^{t_2}a_{12} + q_2(1+r)^{tq_2}b_{12} \quad (15.\text{A}.3a)$$

$$q_2 = p_1(1+r)^{t_1}a_{21} + p_2(1+r)^{t_2}a_{22} + q_1(1+r)^{tq_1}b_{21} \quad (15.\text{A}.3b)$$

Note that we have used the notation tq_i to represent the maturity time for intermediate products.

Substituting (15.A.3b) into (15.A.3a) yields

$$q_1 = p_1(1+r)^{t_1}a_{11} + p_2(1+r)^{t_2}a_{12} + p_1(1+r)^{(t_1+tq_2)}(b_{12}a_{21})$$

$$+ p_2(1+r)^{(t_2+tq_2)}(a_{22}b_{12}) + q_1(1+r)^{(tq_1+tq_2)}(b_{12}b_{21}) \qquad (15.\text{A}.4)$$

which is an equation like

$$y = 3x + \tfrac{1}{2}y$$

treated above. We observe further that the expression multiplying q_1 in (15.A.4) must be less than unity since all terms in (15.A.4) are positive in sign and sum to q_1. The iterative method of solution described above will therefore rapidly reduce the term in q_1 to something which can be neglected. What we have left will be a cost equation like (15.A.4) with no terms in q, which is the reduction we set out to attain. Only *basic* non-produced factors appear.

It will be seen also that each term consists of a hire price p_i of a basic factor, a compound interest term, and a quantity hired of the basic factor. The number $b_{12}a_{21}$ which occurs, for example, in (15.A.4) is the quantity hired of the factor 1 required to sustain in use the b_{12} units of intermediate product 2, which is required to be in use in the production of commodity 1. Its maturity time is the tq_2 units of time which we must wait for intermediate product 2 to appear, plus the time which elapses between the use of intermediate product

2 and the appearance of product 1. Note that $(b_{12}a_{21})$ is the same physical input as a_{11} but that it has a different maturity time $(t_1 + tq_2)$ compared with t_1. Following our rule therefore that a different maturity time means a different factor, we assign a new subscript to $(b_{12}a_{21})$ and call it factor 3 and so on. Thus when the term in q_1 is negligible we can write (15.A.4) in the form

$$q_1 = p_1(1 + r)^{t_1}\alpha_{11} + p_2(1 + r)^{t_2}\alpha_{12} + p_3(1 + r)^{t_3}\alpha_{13} + p_4(1 + r)^{t_4}\alpha_{14}$$
(15.A.5)

t_3 and t_4 of (15.A.5) are the $(t_1 + tq_2)$ and $(t_2 + tq_2)$ of (15.A.4) respectively whilst α_{13} and α_{14} are $(b_{12}a_{21})$ and $(a_{22}b_{12})$.

Equation (15.A.5) is a cost equation for the vertically integrated process manufacturing commodity 1. Each input is basic and the maturity time has been computed whether the factor is applied directly in the final process or indirectly through some intermediate product. Having now reached the point where we have been able to compute the numbers α_{ij} which measure basic inputs in use exclusive of an input 'capital', the next step is to show that we may still further operate on equation (15.A.5) to develop an equation of type (15.3.3); that is, with a 'capital' input of the form $p_k\alpha_{ik}$ replacing the compound interest multipliers

$$(1 + r)^{tt}$$

Before we turn to this, however, a brief digression on the development of economic thought on the subject may add to the reader's understanding.

It has long been understood that *time* is the essence of capital. Economists writing at the turn of the century and before spoke of an increase of capital as a lengthening of the 'roundaboutness' with which the basic factors were used. The greater the degree of 'roundaboutness', the greater the quantity of capital. Objects like machines which are useful only in their power to produce and not as a final product are simply work in progress, that is, a manifestation of the degree of 'roundaboutness'.

This approach failed, if it can be said to have failed, because of the difficulty of knowing how the degree of roundaboutness could be measured and hence observed. Furthermore, the notion of a vertically integrated process such as that described by equation (15.A.5) fell into disrepute because of a difficulty known as 'the problem of Adam's spade'. In order to produce steel, steel itself is needed to make the blast furnace. Steel for the blast furnace was itself produced earlier in time and no doubt required in turn some steel to make it, manufactured at an even earlier time and so on *ad infinitum*. In the last analysis any process which we observe in the world today has as an essential input some infinitesimal part of the input with which Adam fashioned the first crude spade, or whatever other tool he may have used. It is impossible, it is argued, to describe a vertically integrated process with complete accuracy in the absence of detailed knowledge of all processes which have ever existed in the history of the world.

Both of these arguments miss the point. An historical account of how an object in modern-day use was actually evolved has little to do with the quantity of capital we seek to measure. The reader will note that we deduced equation (15.A.5) solely on the basis of information about *manufacturing processes currently in operation.* Capital, in the sense in which we use it here, is intended to sum up the information about the *timing* of basic inputs implicit in equation (15.A.5). What we have to do is to identify the basic non-produced inputs in existence and attach to each unit a time subscript appropriate to the process for which it is at the moment an input. The manipulations leading to equation (15.A.5) show precisely and exactly how this may be done, at least in principle, by collecting data from each firm now engaged in business activity. No historical inquiry is necessary.

The act of 'saving', 'waiting', or 'capital accumulation' consists in taking a basic factor out of a use where it has a given maturity time and switching it to a use with a longer maturity time. Note that this will involve a loss of product for a period equal to the difference in the two maturity times. Someone must not spend for the period; that is, someone who receives income must refrain from consuming the value of the final product lost.

Notice that a switch of a factor from one use to another with the same maturity time will change the technique of production but will not change the quantity of capital. The nature of the objects which make up work in progress will change and probably their prices, but there need be no change in the basic factors in use nor in their timing pattern.

The difficulty of aggregating all the information contained in (15.A.5) into a single measure, allied to some degree of uncertainty over the question to be put, seems to have directed the attention of some economists away from the fruitful concept of 'roundaboutness' towards the objects which make up work in progress itself. These objects can be valued so as to obtain a money measure as the desired aggregate. But as noted above, objects and their values can change without any change in roundaboutness. Computation of capital is difficult enough when we concentrate upon timing. But it is doubly difficult when we turn our attention to the objects. Time is homogeneous but objects are not.

Notice also that the time subscript to basic inputs is a property of the process in which the input is used but it does not in any way require the process to be optimal, that is, minimum-cost or 'best' practice. The capital stock expressed as a time subscript is a real entity in no way dependent upon the existence of 'equilibrium'. It is possible to pass from disequilibrium to equilibrium without in any way affecting the quantity of the capital stock. On the other hand 'prices' have little meaning in a state of disequilibrium. They will be changing at each moment of time according to some dynamic rule (see for example exercise 3, Chapter 3). There is no ambiguity about timing but there may be considerable ambiguity about the value of work in progress.

One other point needs to be made. Some of the objects in use in a manufacturing process at any moment of time may themselves have been manufactured in the past but may now be obsolete in the sense that there does not exist a process currently engaged in their production. To put this another way, we may have a process like (15.A.3a) in operation using an object b_{12} which is durable, but the process (15.A.3b) may be discontinued. In this case it is not proper to apply the manipulations leading to (15.A.5) even if we knew the details of equation (15.A.3b). If we did so, we should end up with quantities of basic factors 1 and 2 shown as employed in process 1, in excess of the quantities actually in existence. The essential condition

$$A_j = \sum_i S_i a_{ij}$$

would not be met for the jth basic factor. Logically we must treat b_{12} as a basic factor endowment bequeathed upon society by past activity. The price of b_{12} will be determined by supply and demand in the same way as the wage rate or the rental of any basic factor. We are free to move b_{12} from one use to another but not the quantities of primary inputs embodied in it.

It is misleading to call b_{12} capital even though it might have a great deal to do with what a businessman would describe as 'fixed capital'. It is in truth no different from labour except that the one is 'owned' by the business and the other is rented. From a national point of view, organisation into firms and questions of ownership are irrelevant. This can immediately be seen if we imagine all basic factors, including b_{12}, moved to Mars in an attempt to reinstate the existing technology there. What would be missing is the work in progress, that is, the timing. This is exactly equivalent to the information embodied in (15.A.5), which is purely technical. It has nothing to do with who owns what. As earlier indicated, many of our difficulties over the concept of capital arise out of the fact that the same word is currently used to describe too many different things. Before attempting to find an aggregate measure of capital, it is desirable to know what we mean by the word. It is hoped that this meaning has now been established so that we might proceed to the problem we have set ourselves.

Notice first that each α_{ij} is a quantity of a basic factor in use together with a unique maturity time. As in earlier sections of this book, we may accordingly write

$$A_j = \sum_i S_i \alpha_{ij} \qquad (15.A.6)$$

where A_j is the overall total of the jth factor in use with the same identifying maturity time j. The actual physical factor endowment is of course the sum of all A_j, which are physically the same even though maturity times are different. When we have specified the A_j we have *ipso facto* specified the capital structure so that the disaggregated capital structure may easily be computed for any given state of the economy, first from equations (15.A.5) and then from equations (15.A.6).

It is also true that we could, if we had so chosen, have used the equations (15.A.5) and (15.A.6) as they stand for most of the argument of this book. The coefficients $p_j(1 + r)^{t_j}$ of the α_{ij} in (15.A.5) could be our 'prices' instead of the pure rent p_j. That is, factor prices could be defined to be rentals and interest charge together rather than rentals alone. Equation (15.A.5) would then take the form and have the properties of equation (15.2.6). But this course would have at least two disadvantages. First, even though in the long run it could turn out that our current ways of talking about capital are not the best and that use of a language consistent with equation (15.A.5) has advantages, it is better to follow more familiar methods so long as they do not break down completely. Secondly, time-subscripted factors imply that the A_j of (15.A.6) cannot any longer be regarded as constants, even when there is no net capital accumulation, contrary to the assumptions of Chapter 12 where the concept of 'factor endowment' was first introduced. This difficulty is not insuperable but it is more convenient to proceed another way. Consider in more detail the various changes which can be made in an existing technology.

In the first place we are free (if cost-minimising demands it) to take a physical unit of, say, labour with maturity time t_i from use in the production of r to use in the production of s. This act will have no consequence on production for t_i units of time but it will, after that time, reduce the value of the product flow, r, by precisely the same amount as it increases the value of the product flow, s. The capital structure, that is all A_i, remain the same but the nature of the objects making up work in progress will change.

Next, we could take units of labour from use r where they have maturity time t_i and transfer them into a use s where maturity time is t_k. This act will diminish A_i and raise A_k by the amount transferred, with consequent effects upon the nature and value of work in progress. Note that once we are given commodity prices and technical data, we can work out and evaluate all the changes in work in progress by making use of equations (15.A.5) and (15.A.6) above. We have in any case a complete description of the capital structure in the new quantities A_i and A_k. What we have to determine is whether, and in what sense, there is capital accumulation and whether an act of saving or 'waiting' has been involved. To do this we make use of prices, although we again insist that this is merely a convenience. Capital has a perfectly clear meaning independent of prices.

In process r capital usage will of course diminish, although it will take time to work out the full effect. Assuming that equations (15.A.5) and (15.A.6) are satisfied, the work in progress before the moment of withdrawal attributable to one unit of labour withdrawn will include objects equivalent to p_i worth of embodied labour embodied in the current time period, $p_i(1+r)$ embodied in the previous time period and so on up to $p_i(1+r)^{t_i-1}$ embodied t_i-1 time units ago. In the first time period after withdrawal the first p_i worth will disappear, for no equivalent object will have been manufactured. This represents dis-saving and capital decumulation. In later time periods the remaining objects will disappear successively.

On the other hand process s will be accumulating capital. In the first period after the transfer of labour new objects will appear in the sth process equivalent to p_k and in the second $p_k(1+r)$ and so on. Furthermore, since p_i and p_k are the same, the saving implied will be exactly equal to the dis-saving in process r. Paradoxically, the transfer of labour implies no *net* saving in the community as a whole for at least t_i periods of time after the actual act of transference. When does net saving occur?

As an example, suppose that t_k is one time period on from t_i, that is

$$t_k = t_i + 1.$$

At time $t_k - 1$ after the act of transfer all the embodied labour, associated, in process r, with the labour transferred, will have disappeared and an equivalent amount will have appeared in process s. But in addition, in process s, there will be objects equivalent to embodied labour $p_k(1+r)^{t_k-1}$. This represents *additional* saving or waiting, a fact which is easily seen as follows.

At time t_i the flow of product r will be reduced in value by the amount $p_i(1+r)^{t_i}$. In the following time period the flow of s will be increased to the value $p_k(1+r)^{t_k}$. Clearly the community must *wait* for this new consumption for one period of time, in consequence of which it is rewarded with an increased flow of value of output. We ought to find that the increased flow of value is just sufficient to pay the rate of profit on the saving involved. To check this, consider the difference

$$p_k(1+r)^{t_k} - p_i(1+r)^{t_i} = p_i(1+r)^{t_i}(1+r-1)$$

$$= r[p_i(1+r)^{t_i}] \qquad (15.A.7)$$

given that p_i equals p_k and t_k differs from t_i by one time unit. This result tells us that the increased value of the national product flow will be just sufficient to pay, for ever, the interest on the increment of work in progress, which is

$$p_k(1+r)^{t_k-1} = p_i(1+r)^{t_i}$$

Finally, we could transfer units of labour from use r to use s with different maturity times in a way which demands an act of saving; but at the same time we might transfer units of, say, land from use l to use m in a way implying dis-saving. If the saving and dis-saving is of equal magnitude, no net saving need be involved at all. We have to find a suitable criterion to determine whether or not, in a general way, net saving has occurred.

Consider the transfer of an amount dA_i of the ith factor. As indicated above, its removal from or appearance in the capital structure must be equivalent to the destruction or creation of objects represented by

$$(p_i + p_i(1+r) + p_i(1+r)^2 \ldots p_i(1+r)^{t_i-1})dA_i.$$

This expression is easily summed† to give

$$p_i \left[\frac{(1+r)^{t_i} - 1}{r} \right] dA_i$$

If the sum of the quantities obliterated and created is zero, then no net saving is involved. That is, if for any set of changes in the capital structure – say dA_i, dA_j, dA_k, etc. – the condition

$$\sum_i p_i \left[\frac{(1+r)^{ti} - 1}{r} \right] dA_i = 0 \qquad (15.A.8)$$

is met, then no net saving is involved.

It should of course be understood that any net saving will ordinarily be spread over a number of time periods. The expression on the left-hand side of (15.A.8) gives aggregate net saving over all periods during which changes in the form of work in progress are taking place following the physical transfer of units of the basic factor. But none of this is in any way foreign to the fundamental method of this book, which compares equilibrium with equilibrium. On the contrary it is precisely in the same tradition of thought.

We now look again at the equations (15.A.5). The problem is to get rid of the time subscript and to introduce in its place a variable which we can call 'capital' in such a way that we explicitly recognise all the truths of these notes and at the same time justify the manipulations performed elsewhere in the book. To this end we write (15.A.5) as

$$q_i = \sum_j p_j(1+r)^{t_j}\alpha_{ij}$$

$$= \sum_j p_j\alpha_{ij} + \sum_j p_j[(1+r)^{t_j} - 1]\alpha_{ij}$$

$$= \sum_j p_j\alpha_{ij} + r\sum_j p_j \frac{[(1+r)^{t_j} - 1]}{r}\alpha_{ij} \qquad (15.A.9)$$

In view of (15.A.8), the form which now appears in term two of (15.A.9) looks interesting. Term one of (15.A.9) is of course the total

---

† Sum $= p_i + \ldots + p_i(1+r)^{t_i-1}$ (a)
$(1+r)$ sum $= p_i(1+r) + \ldots + p_i(1+r)^{t_i}$ (b)
Subtracting (a) from (b) and dividing by r gives the answer above.

rental of basic inputs α_{ij}, just as we want it to be. To correspond exactly with (15.2.6) with a capital factor, term two of (15.A.9) should be the rental of 'capital'. We are encouraged in this view by the observation that it is made up of r, the rent of money per unit/time, multiplied by an expression which could be the value of money capital. Indeed, by comparison with (15.A.8) it is clear that the expression we have is the value of work in progress tied up in the flow of output required to sustain a stock of one unit of the product.

From the point of view of this book one difficulty remains. It is tempting to let the unit of capital be money and to define the input capital precisely as in (15.A.9), treating r as the rent of money capital. Unfortunately this is out of harmony with our approach, which requires us to have a factor capital whose unit of measurement is independent of prices. What we want in effect is a proxy for the information about timing bound up in the timed quantities A_i, A_j, etc., central to these notes. Money capital is a quantity which involves both the timing and prices. We must separate the two or we shall be back precisely where we were – looking at the value of the objects instead of the timing.

The solution is simple. We rewrite the whole of term two of (15.A.9) as follows:

$$\sum_j \left\{ \frac{p_j[(1+r)^{t_j} - 1]r^0}{p_j^0[(1+r^0)^{t_j} - 1]} \right\} \left\{ \frac{p_j^0[(1+r^0)^{t_j} - 1]}{r^0} \alpha_{ij} \right\} \qquad (15.A.10)$$

where p_j^0, and r^0 represent *base period* prices and interest rate respectively; that is, p_j^0 and r^0 are initial prices if we are taking changes. Notice now that the expression in the right-hand 'curly' bracket contains no variable price. It is a quantity solely dependent upon the quantity α_{ij} and its implicit t_j, both of which are chosen so as to minimise cost. The choice of suitable α_{ij} depends upon the productive power of various inputs with different timings, and term two reflects the choice of timing of these inputs.

The term in the first bracket on the other hand is an index of the 'price' of the timed input. That is, it is a rental index for a particular timed quantity. The two terms of (15.A.10) measure a price and a quantity in an unambiguous way. Each can be varied independently of the other, exactly as any price and physical input.

Now consider the properties of the quantity measure we have chosen for capital. The total quantity of capital in use in the ith process will be

$$\sum_j S_i \frac{p_j^0[(1+r^0)^{t_j} - 1]}{r^0} \alpha_{ij}$$

so that the aggregate of *all* capital in use in the community will be

$$\sum_i \sum_j S_i \frac{p_j^0[(1+r^0)^{t_i} - 1]}{r^0} \alpha_{ij} \qquad (15.A.11)$$

But

$$\sum_i S_i \alpha_{ij} = A_j$$

by definition of α_{ij} and A_j. Hence we may write (15.A.11)

$$\sum_j \frac{p_j^0[(1+r^0)^{t_j} - 1]A_j}{r^0} \qquad (15.A.12)$$

which is then a convenient *definition* of the capital stock of the community.

Note that (15.A.12) is unambiguous and quite easily computed in principle from technical information currently available. *It is furthermore not even dependent upon any assumptions of equilibrium or optimal allocation of resources.* All that we require is that each basic physical input should have a base market price p^0 and hence a rental and that the timing of each process in existence at the moment of computation should be known.

In addition, (15.A.12) has the following 'ideal' property. For base prices and interest rate p_j^0 and r^0 which are equal to or close to existing prices and interest rate, constant capital stock corresponds with negligible error to zero saving. Indeed, changes in A_j which keep (15.A.12) constant satisfy

$$\sum_j \frac{p_j^0[(1+r^0)^{t_j} - 1]}{r^0} dA_j = 0$$

which is, or is close to, (15.A.8) according as p_j^0 and r^0 are, or are close to, p_j and r_j. If in fact we accept this definition of *real* capital, the approximation involved is no different from and no less accurate than that which we have used continuously throughout the whole book when we write

$$d(px) = xdp + pdx.$$

Two more small points remain to be made. First, when cost equations are written in the form (15.A.9), some of the α_{ij} will refer to the same physical basic input. Since we now have no interest in time subscripts for these inputs, similar physical objects may be added together to yield terms which we shall write $p_j a_{ij}$. The requirement

$$\sum_i S_i a_{ij} = A_j$$

where A_j is the fixed factor endowment is now reinstated and the A_j stands without time subscripts.

The second point concerns the capital term. If a high level of accuracy is required, this term may be left as the sum of many terms as in (15.A.10). For simplicity, we might write the price part as p_j and the quantity part as α_{ij}, so that (15.A.10) as a whole becomes

$$\sum_j p_j \alpha_{ij} \qquad\qquad (15.\text{A}.13)$$

No special difficulty is involved in having many capital terms rather than one. On the other hand it is common practice in economics when we have an aggregate such as (15.A.13) to write an index $\bar{p}_j$ of the rentals of timed capital items and an index $\bar{\alpha}_{ij}$ of capital quantities, and various ways of constructing such indices so as best to preserve the property

$$\sum_j p_j \alpha_{ij} = \bar{p}_j \bar{\alpha}_{ij} \qquad\qquad (15.\text{A}.14)$$

have been much discussed. Indeed, this is the so-called 'index number problem' in its classical form. In choosing an index number satisfying (15.A.14), it is desirable also that when we write

$$\sum_i S_i \bar{\alpha}_{ij} = A_j$$

where A_j is the aggregate capital stock, care should be taken to preserve the condition that constant A_j implies zero saving. But there seems no good reason to suppose that this cannot be done up to the usual level of approximation. Thus $\bar{\alpha}_{ij}$ is the required capital input measure and $\bar{p}_j$ its rental.

CONCLUSIONS

To some readers it may appear that we have, in these notes, worked very hard to very little purpose; for in the end what is proposed as a definition of capital is no more than the value of all equipment and work in progress, the valuation being at base-year prices and interest rate. It has seemed appropriate, therefore, to introduce a few concluding comments.

First, we remark that there is nothing wrong in not being surprised by our conclusion. It would be far more disturbing if we had come up with something different, for we are after all simply developing a precise definition of a commonplace idea. What is important is that we have achieved precision and compatibility. One of the problems which has disturbed capital theorists is the difficulty of valuing work in progress and part-worn equipment when there is no market for these objects. The method proposed above demands only technical knowledge and a base price for basic inputs. No problem of 'depreciation' rates is involved. The difficulty is solved by concentration upon timing, rather than objects. It should be noticed also that there is no circularity in the argument. All the inputs α_{ij} in equations (15.A.5) are physical entities with an unambiguous unit of measurement, and the rate of interest can ordinarily be determined from the simultaneous solution of demand equations (15.A.5) and supply equations (15.A.6), given the capital structure A_j. It is perhaps worth remarking that this system of equations cannot be solved for r unless at least one basic factor is in use with at least two different maturity times; but this will ordinarily be the case.

Finally, we reaffirm that with our chosen definition of capital, all the properties of cost equations hold for precisely the reason given in the text, and the aggregate stock of capital behaves like a factor endowment, being fixed and given in the absence of an act of saving.

EXERCISES

1. Consider the units in which the qs, ps, a_{ij}s and b_{ij}s of equations (15.2.1) and (15.2.2) are measured. Follow the manipulations leading to (15.2.5) and show that α_{ij} must be measured in units of factor j per unit of commodity i.
2. Consider the production possibility set S of all pairs of outputs (S_1, S_2) satisfying the condition

$$\alpha S_1^2 + \beta S_2^2 \leqq \gamma$$

   where α, β and γ are positive constants. Show that this set is convex on the definition of section 15.4.
3. Note that the boundary of the production possibility set in exercise 2 is defined by

$$\alpha S_1^2 + \beta S_2^2 = \gamma \tag{i}$$

Treat S_1^2 as $S_1 \times S_1$ and take changes in (i). Hence prove by the argument following (15.4.14) that the slope of the boundary of the set S is given by

$$-\frac{dS_1}{dS_2} = -\frac{\beta S_2}{\alpha S_1} = \frac{q_2}{q_1} \qquad\qquad \text{(ii)}$$

Solve the equations (i) and (ii) to show that

$$S_1 = \sqrt{\left(\frac{\gamma \beta q_1^2}{\alpha \beta q_1^2 + \alpha^2 q_2^2}\right)}$$

is the supply equation for commodity 1. Show that this and the equivalent equation for S_2 satisfy all the conditions (15.4.12)–(15.4.19).

4. Let S_1 measured negatively be imports of raw material and let S_2 be the product. If the production/factor-imports possibility set is the set S such that

$$S_1 + \alpha S_2^2 \leqq \beta$$

whre α and β are positive constants, show by the methods of exercise 3 that it will not be profitable to import raw materials if the product price at home falls below $2\sqrt{\alpha}\sqrt{\beta}$ times the price of the raw materials.

   Prove that when due allowance is made for the fact that raw material imports are measured negatively, all of the conditions (15.4.12)–(15.4.19) are satisfied by the functions S_1 and S_2 as claimed in section 15.9.

5. Construct a case where every individual in the home country is worse off under subsidised trade than they would be with no trade at all.

Exercises to be attempted after reading Books I and II

6. The fact that, given q, competition maximises

$$\phi = \sum q_i S_i = qs$$

by selecting a unique maximising vector s from a compact set S of production possibilities implies that ϕ may be regarded as a function of a vector q of commodity prices alone. Prove that ϕ so regarded satisfies the condition

$$\lambda\phi(q^1) + (1 - \lambda)\phi(q^2) \geqq \phi(\lambda q^1 + (1 - \lambda)q^2)$$

and so is a convex function.

Show also that

$$\frac{\partial\phi}{\partial q_i \partial q_j} \equiv \frac{\partial S_i}{\partial q_j} \qquad \text{(i)}$$

Hint: Use the fact that

$$\phi = qs$$

is homogeneous of order one so that

$$\sum_i q_i \frac{\partial\phi}{\partial q_i} = \phi$$

Now confirm from any suitable mathematical text that the Hessian determinant of any convex function has positive principal minors, and so prove from (i) the results (15.5.1) and (15.5.2), etc.

7. Read or re-read the appendix to Chapter 15. Turn up the article by Gabor and Pearce, 'The Place of Money Capital in the Theory of Production' [11]. Explain why, with the vertically integrated processes for the economy as a whole treated in the appendix, the term

$$(1 + r)^{-z_i}$$

which occurs in formula (xi) for capital in the article does not appear in formula (15.A.9) in the appendix. Show that the two formulae mentioned amount to the same thing when it is recalled that price in the article is selling price and that price in the appendix is rental.

16 The Factor Price Equalisation Controversy

IN our discussion in Chapter 12 of the underlying causes of international trade, much was made of the fact that within any country a powerful mechanism is at work which will ordinarily bring about the equalisation of factor prices. On the other hand it was asserted more than once that, where there exists a relatively high number of immobile factors of production, as when mobility must be across national frontiers, no such mechanism necessarily exists. Even where commodities can be traded and hence where commodity prices are equalised, there should be no *a priori* expectation that equal factor prices must follow. As this important allegation is directly contrary to what appears in many textbooks written for non-specialists, and as in Chapter 12 no 'proof' or argument was presented beyond the elementary demonstration that sets of equations can have more than one solution even when the number of equations and unknowns is the same, the most careful examination of the whole question is evidently called for. Indeed, delay in treating the matter was due only to the need to assemble the apparatus necessary for adequate discussion.

Recall first of all that we did, in Chapter 12, establish one set of conditions which, if they exist before trade, will ensure at least a tendency to factor price equalisation. We showed in fact that, if before trade there is an 'overlap' of the set of all possible weighted averages of production techniques, then factor prices must become more equal after trade (section 12.8). But this is not as important a result as may appear at first sight. One difficulty is that it is very much an over-sufficient condition; that is, if there is no overlap there could still be equalisation of factor prices. Furthermore, the question of whether there is overlap or not is a question about the properties of cost functions. Until we know what properties of cost functions are likely to secure overlap, the work of Chapter 12 is of little practical value.

Of course the theorem might be useful if we were looking at a particular case where we have observed the techniques of production in use and wish to predict the effect of trade. But in such a case we really have no need of a theorem, for the exact factor price changes which interest us can immediately be computed as explained in the conclusions at the end of this chapter (section 16.7). The difficulty is that we do not get from the overlap theorem any general result which will enable us to say in every case without further inquiry whether or not trade characteristically brings about a tendency to equalise factor prices, and this for obvious reasons is the kind of result economists have sought.

As a matter of fact we shall conclude that no such general theorem can be proved. Indeed it is to be hoped that a time will come when the greater part of the material of this chapter can be left out of textbooks on international trade theory and attention concentrated on matters of greater practical value. For the present, however, it has seemed essential to trace the history of an idea which went wrong and to explain why it did go wrong, if only because there is considerable evidence of widespread reluctance to give it up.

On the other hand, in questioning the practical value of the conclusions so far reached, care must be taken not to obscure in any way the immense importance of the very real problem which gave rise to the argument in the first place. Indeed, one of the most powerful reasons for spending so much time and effort on the matter is the unfortunate fact that general agreement upon a wrong answer could be disastrous.

Commonplace observation of the world around us leaves no doubt that the real rewards of factors of production differ widely in different parts of the world even where the countries concerned are in a close trading relationship. The general tone of Chapter 12 suggested that we ought not to be surprised at this. The underlying cause of the difference would seem to be the immobility of natural resources and perhaps the low mobility of capital stock. To put it another way, some people are poor because they do not own their 'fair' share of the world's natural resources and/or capital wealth accumulated in past periods by our predecessors, even though all are equally children of Adam. Or alternatively the share which they do possess, even if it is fair, is not well balanced in composition, that is, they may have natural resources but no capital or vice versa.

If all this is true the conclusion of Chapter 12 is in itself a powerful argument for giving outright aid to poorer countries or possibly for the exchange of capital stock for rights in natural resources. Indeed, if the maldistribution of resources is the sole cause of maldistribution of income, then the recipient of aid need feel no obligation to the giver, for in such circumstances the 'failure' to develop an economy cannot be said to be a failure in any ordinary sense of that word. Without resources development is, by definition, impossible.

If on the other hand it could be shown, as in some quarters it may be believed to have been shown, that international trade in commodities is a full substitute for factor mobility and would, in the absence of impediments, lead to the complete equalisation of real factor rewards, then the argument above is entirely rejected. Differences in wealth per head would be due, in the main, to impediments to trade and not to accidents of nature or history; and it could be argued that poor countries are poor because of a genuine failure to take proper advantage of trading opportunities. 'Trade not Aid' could be held, not only to be a just and proper policy, but also one consistent with the ordinary human desire not to be patronised by the rich. Obviously we have here an issue of first-rate importance.

16.2 SOME COMMENTS ON THE LITERATURE

The widespread belief that trade does tend to equalise factor prices found its origin in an argument already noted in Chapter 14. Thinking in terms of a simple model of two commodities and two factors, and assuming implicitly that one and only one technique of production is possible for each commodity whatever the factor prices, early writers took it for granted that 'a country will produce relatively cheaply that commodity which uses the higher proportion of its relatively cheap factor of production'. That is, lower-wage countries will produce most cheaply those commodities using the most labour. Hence high labour-using commodities will be exported, increasing the demand for labour and thereby increasing the price of labour relatively. The reverse will happen in the foreign country so that factor prices will tend to be equalised by trade. In this connection the argument of Chapter 14 is well worth repeating and expanding since it clearly illustrates the fundamental problem.

In the case of the two factors and two commodities only, it is possible to manipulate the cost functions

$$q_i = \sum_j a_{ij} p_j$$

to obtain the relationship

$$\frac{q_1}{q_2} = \left[\frac{a_{11}}{a_{21}}\right] \left[\frac{1 + \dfrac{a_{12}\,p_2}{a_{11}\,p_1}}{1 + \dfrac{a_{22}\,p_2}{a_{21}\,p_1}}\right] \qquad (16.2.1)$$

as in Chapter 14. This is simply one cost equation divided by the other with the ratio a_{11}/a_{21} taken out on the right-hand side. What we now have is a 'function' defining q_1/q_2 once p_2/p_1 is given, for the techniques a_{ij} are determined by the cost-minimising condition as soon as the factor price ratio p_2/p_1 is given. Note especially that doubling factor prices leaves each a_{ij} unchanged. This must be the case, for by inspection of cost functions we see that doubling factor prices keeping a_{ij} constant doubles commodity prices. If the unchanged a_{ij} did not give minimum-cost techniques at the new price but some a_{ij}^* yielded a cost lower than twice the original cost, then $\sum_j a_{ij}^* p_j$ must be less than the original cost q_i which contradicts the assumption that a_{ij} is minimum-cost at prices p_j. This confirms that a_{ij} changes only when the price *ratio* p_2/p_1 changes. Thus, for short, we write the equation (16.2.1)

$$\frac{q_1}{q_2} = f\left(\frac{p_2}{p_1}\right) \qquad (16.2.2)$$

to read 'q_1/q_2 is a function of p_2/p_1', meaning no more than that q_1/q_2 is uniquely determined when p_2/p_1 is given.

Now reconsider our central problem. We would like to be able to show that, if two countries enter into a trading relationship, their real factor rewards will be equalised. First, we know that the cost function (16.2.2) is equally applicable to both countries since the laws of physics are the same in both countries (see Chapter 12). Next, we have seen that trade will bring commodity price ratios q_1/q_2 into equality. As long as two countries have a trading relationship, each producing some of the two commodities traded, q_1/q_2 must be the same in both countries and the equation (16.2.2) must hold in both countries. Does it follow that p_2/p_1 must therefore be the same in both countries? The answer in general is 'no'.

Suppose for example the equation (16.2.2) took the form

$$\frac{q_1}{q_2} = \left(\frac{p_2}{p_1} - 6\right)^2 \qquad (16.2.3)$$

and suppose that after trade the world prices of commodities were equal, that is,

$$\frac{q_1}{q_2} = 1$$

Solving the equation

$$1 = \left(\frac{p_2}{p_1} - 6\right)^2$$

we find that p_2/p_1 may take *either* the value 7 or the value 5, for both $(1)^2$ and $(-1)^2$ are equal to 1.

Thus we could have two countries in a trading relation with factor price ratios $p_2/p_1 = 7$ and $p_2/p_1 = 5$ respectively but with commodity prices equal. Factor prices need not be equalised by trade.

Thus, as earlier implied in Chapter 12, the whole problem reduces to one of finding what kind of restrictions on (16.2.2) are sufficient to ensure that one and only one price ratio p_2/p_1 is associated with each q_1/q_2 and of inquiring whether such conditions are likely to be met by cost functions of the kind (16.2.2). In the terminology employed by mathematicians, we wish to know whether an inverse function f^{-1} exists to f in order that we may write

$$\frac{p_2}{p_1} = f^{-1}\left(\frac{q_2}{q_1}\right) \tag{16.2.4}$$

meaning that p_2/p_1 is *uniquely* determined by q_2/q_1.

Note that, in our example, no such inverse exists, for we have, from (16.2.3),

$$\pm\sqrt{\frac{q_1}{q_2}} = \frac{p_2}{p_1} - 6$$

or

$$\frac{p_2}{p_1} = \pm\sqrt{\frac{q_1}{q_2}} + 6 \tag{16.2.5}$$

which tells us that *two* values for p_2/p_1 are associated with each value for q_1/q_2. Note also that the existence of an inverse to a function f is the *exception* rather than the rule, and that in general many values of p_2/p_1 can generate the *same* q_1/q_2.

But consider the form of function (16.2.1) which is our cost function. Let us imagine that the techniques a_{ij} are constant numbers whatever the value of p_2/p_1. This is the assumption implicitly introduced by those economists who first developed the factor price equalisation argument. There is one and only one way of producing one unit of each commodity, namely, with inputs a_{11} and a_{12} for commodity 1 and with inputs a_{21} and a_{22} for commodity 2, and these inputs cannot be varied. Clearly if a_{12}/a_{11} is greater than a_{22}/a_{21}, then q_1/q_2 will always rise as p_2/p_1 rises. If on the other hand a_{12}/a_{11} is less than a_{22}/a_{21}, then q_1/q_2 will fall as p_2/p_1 rises.

In other words, on the given assumptions, q_1/q_2 is either a continuously increasing or a continuously decreasing function of p_2/p_1 and it is easy to see that such a function *must* possess an inverse. As the number p_2/p_1 passes through all the values it might take from zero to infinity, q_1/q_2 takes successively higher numbers. Only if q_1/q_2 first rises and then falls, or first falls and then rises, can it repeat itself for different p_2/p_1. Thus the assumption of *fixed* coefficients a_{ij} is sufficient to validate the factor price equalisation argument. In so far as they assumed the a_{ij} of (16.2.1) to be constant, and in so far as they assumed only two factors of production, the claims of our predecessors were correct. The difficulty with the fixed coefficients assumption, however, is that it is resoundingly refuted by the facts. Many observations have been made both between countries and in the same country over time and all show wide differences in techniques employed. Indeed, this question is so well settled as not to warrant further discussion even if it were ever in doubt.

On the other hand vigorous attempts have recently been made to rehabilitate the original theory on the basis of a new hypothesis despite the fact that, in some ways, the new hypothesis is much less sensible than the old. We shall justify this comment later. In the meantime consider again properties of the cost equation (16.2.1).

In section 14.2 it was established that, for small changes, variations in q_i are generated solely by changes dp_i in p_i, the effect of changes in techniques being negligible. It is reasonable therefore to suppose that the same applies to cost equations in the form (16.2.1) above. If this is the case, (16.2.1) will behave for small changes as if the a_{ij} were fixed. That is, as long as a_{12}/a_{11}, even though it is changing, remains greater than a_{22}/a_{21}, q_1/q_2 will rise as p_2/p_1 rises and so on. This is a proposition which we shall prove rigorously at a later stage.

To some economists, perhaps because of the classical habit of talking as if only two factors of production, land and capital, exist, it seemed plausible to conjecture at this point that if commodity 1, say, is produced by relatively capital-intensive methods it will always be so irrespective of factor prices. That is to say, if, for any factor price ratio, minimum-cost conditions demand

$$\frac{a_{12}}{a_{11}} > \frac{a_{22}}{a_{21}} \qquad\qquad (16.2.6)$$

where factor 2 is capital, then the inequality (16.2.6) will hold *whatever* the price ratio.

Such a proposition immediately reinstates the factor price equalisation theorem despite the admitted variability of production techniques; for only if, at some point, a reversal of factor intensities occurs, that is, if as p_2/p_1 rises a_{12}/a_{11} falls faster than a_{22}/a_{21} until eventually it becomes less than a_{22}/a_{21}, will the price q_1/q_2 begin to fall, thus repeating itself for different p_2/p_1 contrary to the requirements of the theory. As long as we believe that factor intensities do not, as a matter of fact, reverse themselves at any factor price level, then factor price equalisation is assured. Thus was born the 'factor intensity' hypothesis, the influence of which has been wholly bad, but which nevertheless continues to flourish in areas of the subject quite outside that at present under discussion, with equally misleading consequences.

We have remarked above that the factor intensity hypothesis is much less sensible than the original fixed coefficient hypothesis it replaced. The reason for this has nothing to do with the likelihood or otherwise of it being satisfied. It is less sensible because, unlike the fixed coefficient condition, on purely theoretical grounds it can be shown to have *nothing whatever to do with the problem* as soon as we have more than two factors of production. If techniques were invariant so that all a_{ij} have to be constant whatever the factor prices, factor price equalisation would be assured however many factors and commodities exist. But as soon as we allow techniques to vary, the two-commodity/two-factor world is the only world in which factor intensities have relevance. Those who continue to study factor intensities either do not understand the problem or they believe wrongly that factors can somehow be aggregated into two groups, capital and labour, without serious disturbance of the theory. Consider for a moment some aspects of the many empirical inquiries which have been undertaken.

First, one notes, with something between deep concern and wry amusement, that empirical investigators seem to divide themselves almost equally between those who conclude that a cross-over in factor intensities not only occurs but is almost inevitable, and those who conclude, by contrary, that the facts support the hypothesis and that, if factor price equalisation does not occur, it must be inhibited by some other cause than the cross-over of factor intensities.

The reason for this difference of opinion is, so far as the present writer is able to judge, that whenever the multitude of factors of the real world have to be fitted into one or other of the only two boxes, capital or labour, which the theory allows, there is more than one way of doing it. The answer which one gets depends entirely upon the method of aggregation chosen, a fact which reflects the observation above that whenever there exist more than two factors of production factor intensities are irrelevant to the problem. However we choose to aggregate, the answer we get can tell us nothing about the matter we are investigating, as we shall show later by example.

Before we turn to this, however, the reader is invited to look at another difficulty. Let us assume, impossibly, that there are only two factors of production whose prices can vary independently and that empirical investigators are after all looking at the right thing for the right reason. The problem of the number of commodities now arises. Inevitably the very large number of commodities which exist are, and must be, grouped into classes in some measure, but no one has yet had the courage to reduce the number of classes to two. Almost always twenty or so 'commodities' have been taken and their factor intensity rankings compared.

On the other hand, consider what the theory says. If we have n commodities we have n-1 equations like (16.2.1) above. Suppose that any single one of these shows the cross-over and that in two countries products 1 and 2 have the same price but factor prices are different. Obviously the remaining commodity prices *must* be different between countries. The commodities concerned *cannot* be traded.† What does all this mean for the empirical investigator?

It certainly means that if there exist only two factors (defined as the theory requires), and if the observer notes that, say, twenty commodities are traded, there *must* be equal factor prices and identical techniques of production. No cross-over in factor intensities could be observed because everyone would be using the same ratio of factor inputs. Indeed, if the investigator finds that twenty commodities produced by two factors are traded and produced in common, and hence have a common world price, and if factor prices are *not* equal,

---

† In saying this we do concede of course the remote possibility that there could be a cross-over in factor intensities in other products and that, in some incredibly coincidental case, we could have the *same* two *different* factor prices yielding the same commodity prices for three or even more commodities, in which case three commodities could be traded with factor prices different. But this is not usual, indeed it would require an unbelievable regularity of cost functions. What is implied is the consistency of many equations in two unknowns (see Chapter 12).

then he is bound to conclude that there is something wrong with his definition or measurement of a factor quantity and/or price. Even more important, the same applies if only three commodities are produced in common and traded.

This raises an important point often treated in a misleading way even in purely theoretical discussion. The usual approach when dealing with the problem of factor price equalisation is to consider separately three cases, that where the number of commodities is greater than the number of factors, that where the number of commodities is equal to the number of factors and that where the number of commodities is less than the number of factors.

From one point of view this is absurd. Much depends on what is meant by the words 'number of commodities'. Most writers must be supposed to mean *the number of commodities produced in common and traded*, for they state a theorem which says that, when the number of commodities exceeds the number of factors (two), if any one pair of commodities traded shows no factor reversal, then factor prices must be equalised, adding the words 'provided there is no specialisation'. Quite misleadingly this is given as a reason why factor price equalisation is more likely when there are many commodities, for it may then be claimed that only one pair out of many need have the special properties required. The greater the number of commodities from which a pair may be selected, the greater the probability of finding one pair which does not show factor intensity reversal. This kind of claim, if we have properly interpreted it, is in the nature of a pleonasm. If more commodities are *produced and traded* than factors, there *must* be factor price equalisation. Nothing need be said at all about cross-over of factor intensities. It is impossible to have all commodity prices equal and factor prices different since we should have in such a case fewer unknowns than we have equations (see Chapter 12). No solution can exist unless the (many) equations are consistent, and they cannot ordinarily be consistent unless factor prices are equal (but see footnote, p. 483).

In short, if one ever thought it worth while to have a factor price equalisation theorem to cover the case where more commodities are produced and traded than there exist factors, all that would be necessary would be to write:

Theorem 1: Factor prices must be equalised by trade whenever, in a trading equilibrium, more commodities are produced in both countries and traded than there exist basic factors of production.

No factor intensity condition on cost equations is required and the proof of the theorem simply consists of counting equations and unknowns.

But of course this theorem misses the point. What we really want to know is, if more commodities *exist* than basic factors, whether traded or not, under what conditions will there be factor price equalisation? In other words we want to be able to predict what will happen as a consequence of trade before the trading takes place; that is, we have to look at all commodities and say whether, in view of the properties of cost functions, trade will or will not equalise factor prices. It is nonsense to suppose that we know without inquiring how many commodities will in fact enter into trade, for to do so must prejudge the whole problem as we have seen.

The (two-factor) theorem we seek, if a two-factor theorem could be believed to have any applicability, would say:

Theorem 2: In a two-factor world with many commodities, factor prices will be equalised by trade if every pair of commodities selected from all those which exist shows no cross-over of factor intensities and if after trade at least two of the traded commodities continue to be produced by both countries.

This is a very different theorem, in fact exactly the reverse of that quoted in some textbooks. Here we have to have the restriction on *every* pair of cost functions of the type (16.2.1), not on just one of them. The reason is that we do not know beforehand which are going to be the two commodities traded. If it happens to be two without a cross-over in factor intensity, then factor prices must be equalised and more than two commodities can be produced in common. If on the other hand it happens to be two commodities exhibiting the cross-over which remain in common production, we do not know whether factor prices will be equalised or not. If they are not, then not more than two commodities can be produced in common.† Note that this might be interpreted to mean that the more commodities there are,

† The reader is assured at this point that there is nothing odd about this possibility. It is a simple matter to construct examples to show that there is no less a probability that economic competition will force specialisation than that it will equalise factor prices. If it seems a strange and unlikely notion that a country will find itself forced to specialise up to the point where it produces at home no more than two of the commodities entering world trade, this is probably the consequence of the strange and unlikely assumption that only two factors exist, rather than anything else.

the less likely we are to be sure of factor price equalisation on *a priori* grounds, for there are then more pairs of commodities to show factor reversal. This is the exact opposite of the usual argument.

Consider what all this would imply for the empirical worker if he really were in a two-factor world. The observer *cannot* look at a world where trade is absent. If he confines his attention to two countries only, and if we ignore for the moment the existence of transport costs and other impediments to trade, he is bound to observe either equal factor prices – which he doesn't – or else he must observe that not more than two traded commodities are produced in at least one of the countries. In a many-country world the same must be observed between each pair of countries. If, on the other hand, he is able to find countries with different factor prices producing more than two traded products, he must conclude that there is something wrong with his observations. Either there exist more factors than two, in which case he is looking at the wrong thing, or, as we previously indicated, measurements of prices and/or quantities must be wrong or are in contradiction with the cost-minimising assumption which underlies the whole theory.

The empirical investigator who finds that factor prices are equal has of course nothing to explain. If on the other hand he discovers factor prices to be different, he might seek to explain this by the cross-over of factor intensities – but only if the number of traded commodities produced in common is reduced to two and if the cross-over occurs in the traded commodities. As a matter of fact, however, we do not find in the real world all countries producing just two of the commodities which enter into world trade. Nor do we find factor prices equalised. The most obvious inference which emerges with complete unanimity from all the statistical inquiries studied by the present writer is one which none of their authors remark upon. Not surprisingly, all published results fail to contradict the hypothesis that more than two basic factors of production exist. They demonstrate conclusively that it is impossible to aggregate existing factors into two groups without at the same time destroying the very basis of the theory we wish to test. The conclusion we are forced to is that empirical investigators have been looking at the wrong thing with the wrong model in mind.

Before turning to something a little more realistic, one more small point should be dealt with. For the argument so far to make sense, we must be thinking of a factor as a *basic* non-produced factor. If it were otherwise, that is, if one or more of the inputs is also a manufactured product, then we should have a new equation for each such input. For example if, in equation (16.2.1), input 1 was also output 1, we should have

$$p_1 \equiv q_1$$

Thus by substitution in

$$q_1 = a_{11}p_1 + a_{12}p_2$$

we have

$$q_1 = \left[\frac{a_{12}}{1 - a_{11}}\right] p_2 \qquad (16.2.5)$$

Evidently in this simple case only one technique of production will ever be used whatever the pattern of prices, for if a cost function takes the simple form

$$q_1 = \alpha p_2$$

as (16.2.5) does, there can be only one minimum-cost value for α, namely, the smallest quantity α which will produce one unit of output; and this will be the same whatever the price p_2. To put the matter another way, when there is but one *basic* factor of production there can be but one pattern of relative prices, reflecting simply the relative quantities of the basic input required to manufacture one unit of each product, whether that product is for final consumption or intermediate input. Obviously in such a case real factor rewards must be the same throughout the world even if cost functions, expressed in terms of basic *and* intermediate factors, somewhere exhibit a changeover in relative factor intensities. In the same way, if we have many basic factors and many intermediate factors, cost functions must be reduced to their basic form as explained in section 15.2 before any part of the theory of this chapter can be applied.

We have raised this matter first because the crucial importance to the theory of looking only at the basic factors is yet another feature of the problem which seems to have received less attention than it deserves, and second because we wish it to be clearly understood that by factors we mean, in all that follows, basic factors plus capital (as defined in the appendix to Chapter 15). The fact that 'capital' is included as a factor is especially worthy of note, since the question whether the equalisation of factor prices implies the equalisation of the money rate of interest is one which has been raised recently in the literature. The reader who has studied the appendix to Chapter 15 will understand at once that if factor prices p_i are rentals of basic factors and 'capital', the equalisation of p_i implies the equalisation of r, the money rate of interest. The rental of capital is a number which is a function of all basic factor rentals and r. Moreover, for given basic factor rentals, the capital rental rises continuously as r rises. Hence r is uniquely determined by basic factor rentals and capital rental. We turn now to a more general discussion obviously more applicable to problems of the real world.

16.3 A THREE-FACTOR/THREE-COMMODITY EXAMPLE

We first remind the reader that, even in the most general context, it makes no sense to try to consider a case where the number of goods produced in common and traded exceeds the number of basic factors, for if factor prices are not equalised then the number of goods produced in common *cannot* exceed the number of basic factors on the assumptions of the model. The really interesting question is, if m factors exist in the world and n commodities with $n > m$, then for *every* selection of m commodities taken from n, in what circumstances will the m factor prices be *uniquely* determined by the selected m commodity prices? The essential problem therefore *always* has the same number of factors and commodities. At a later stage we shall consider briefly the 'partial' equalisation which may or may not occur if the specialisation extends to the point where less than m commodities are produced in common and traded; but even this turns out, not unexpectedly, to be but a facet of the ordinary $m \times m$ problem, so for the time being we confine our attention to the $m \times m$ case.

It is instructive to begin with a numerical example which has a number of interesting features. Suppose that three commodities may be produced by three factors of production: land (ld), labour (lbr) and capital (c). Suppose further that commodities 1 and 2 can be produced by one technique and one technique only, whereas commodity 3 has two possible techniques. We set out this information below in the form of two tables showing the inputs of land, labour and capital required to produce one unit of output of each of commodities 1, 2 and 3. It will be noticed that rows one and two, giving the inputs for commodities 1 and 2, are the same in both tables. This is because, for these commodities, one production technique only is possible. In the case of commodity 3 more labour and land is used, but less capital, in country A than in country B.

From these tables it can be seen that, on one possible interpretation at least, the factor intensity condition (16.2.6) is everywhere met. Wherever the A technique is labour-intensive or land-intensive with

TABLE I (a)

Technique for country A

	ld	lbr	c
Commodity 1	9	36	27
Commodity 2	18	27	27
Commodity 3	30	20	24

TABLE I (b)

Technique for country B

	ld	lbr	c
Commodity 1	9	36	27
Commodity 2	18	27	27
Commodity 3	24	16	30

respect to capital, it is so also in case *B*. Similarly if any commodity is labour-intensive with respect to land with one technique, it is so with the other. There is no cross-over in any pair of factor intensities, or, to use mathematical language, no minor of order two of the determinants of the arrays of numbers in the tables changes sign between *A* and *B*. But what of the intuitive notion that somehow the three-factor case can be reduced to the two-factor case by an aggregation process?

First of all we remark that it is hard to see how any meaningful average can show aggregate factor intensities crossing over, whatever that might mean, when no single individual factor intensity itself crosses over. Even so, in order to explore every possibility, the figures in the table have been chosen (although they need not have been) so that if land and labour are combined into one factor giving equal weight to each, then there will be a factor intensity switch in the ordinary sense. That is to say, if column one of each table is added to column two, and the resulting figures are taken to define quantities of a composite factor input land/labour, then commodity 3 will be seen to be relatively capital-intensive in the case of technique *B*, but relatively land/labour-intensive with technique *A*.

On the other hand it is immediately clear that this result is entirely dependent upon the choice of units; for suppose that we chose to measure land in square miles instead of square yards. Then column one would be reduced to negligible figures and the simple addition of columns one and two would no longer yield the cross-over in factor intensities even though the real situation is not in any way affected by choice of units.

To this argument it will immediately be objected that a change of unit implies that some change in weighting would be appropriate in forming the composite factor land/labour. Furthermore it is obvious that, however units of measurement are chosen, there must, with the figures of the tables, be some weighted average of columns one and two which will exhibit the factor intensity change-over in the reduced case.

But by the same token there always exist weights such that the change-over does not appear, and who is to say that one set of weights is more appropriate than another? In short, if the tables quoted give expression to the facts of life there is no way of deducing, from that information alone, any meaningful property in terms of factor intensities the consequences of which parallel those of the two-dimensional case.

The intuitive reaction to this of the empirically minded economist would probably be to try to import more information in order to define proper weights, using, say, base-year factor prices. But the very nature of the problem under examination implies that every conceivable set of factor prices must be considered. And we have already shown that choice of one set of prices as base will show a factor intensity change-over whilst choice of another will not. Nor is it possible to use factor prices appropriate to each technique as a set of variable weights, for this is equivalent to the abandonment of all attempt to separate the values of inputs into their two components, price and quantity, when these two components are in fact the object of the study.

In short, there is no alternative but to consider explicitly the three (or more) factor case and ask whether there is any property of the arrays of figures, exactly as they are set out, sufficient to ensure factor price equalisation.

What we have shown so far is that the crossing-over of factor intensities in any sense is *not* such a condition, for in our example there is no such cross-over. On the other hand factor prices of 1, 1 and 2 for land, labour and capital respectively, when applied to technique *A* yield commodity prices 99, 99 and 98. And the same commodity prices occur if technique *B* is used with factor prices (approximately) 1·2, 1·23 and 1·65. A check confirms that in both cases commodity prices are minimum-cost prices. Evidently factor price equalisation is not implied, for the figures show that two countries could be in trading equilibrium with identical commodity prices even though different techniques of production are employed with consequent different factor prices.

Furthermore it is easy to see that factor endowments and demand conditions in each of two countries before trade could be such that in *A*, factor and commodity prices are 0·9, 0·9 and 2·1 and 97·2, 97·2 and 95·4 respectively, and in *B*, 1·1, 1·1 and 1·75, and 96·75, 96·75 and 96·5. In both of these cases commodity prices are again generated by minimum-cost techniques at the going factor prices so that the quoted price patterns are admissible. If they existed, country *A* would export commodity 3 and import commodities 1 and 2, and equilibrium prices could well be those of the preceding paragraph given appropriate demand functions.

In such a case there is not even a tendency for trade to equalise factor prices, for the final equilibrium price pattern is, if anything, even more disparate than that which existed before trade. Nor would it be difficult to construct examples showing much greater diversification of factor prices, particularly if we were not constrained by the need for simplicity.

Before we leave this example it may be worth while to use it once more to test the validity of yet another contemporary idea characteristic of those which seem to have been precipitated by current, rather difficult, theoretical controversy. Imagine that an inquiry has been initiated, the object of which is to offer advice to certain less developed countries which suffer chronic balance of payment difficulties and which are accordingly seeking to expand exports. It might be felt that one possible solution could be to encourage investment in those industries where the territories concerned have a 'comparative advantage'.

One wonders of course why, having come thus far, we should not simply look to see which products are cheapest relative to world prices and thus, like any ordinary businessman, advise investment in whatever is most profitable. But it might be thought that a short cut is available. Influenced perhaps by the theory under discussion in this chapter, it might be argued that, since the countries in difficulty are clearly those endowed with large quantities of cheap labour, all that would be necessary would be to encourage investment in labour-intensive manufactures.

On the other hand we already well understand that this might not be good advice. As we have already seen, if factor intensities reverse themselves anywhere, commodities using relatively more capital, say, than labour might be relatively cheaper (i.e. possess the comparative advantage). The present author has encountered investigators who accordingly set out to test empirically whether factor intensities did indeed cross over. Faced with the inevitable problem of aggregating many factors into just two, it was decided, for what might well be thought to be good reasons, to compare the ratio of what economists call 'value added' to labour. Value added is simply the value created by the productive process and would ordinarily be sales less raw materials.

The conclusions reached seemed to be:

(i) that factor intensities so defined did not exhibit reversal;
(ii) that therefore factor prices would be equalised by trade; and
(iii) that the distressed territories would be best advised to invest in labour-intensive products.

We leave it to the reader to expose all the fallacies in the argument and content ourselves solely with a single further reference to the example of this section. Assume that we are looking at factor and commodity prices *before* trade opens, as indicated above. In Table II we set out the ratios (*a*) of product price to labour input, and (*b*) of value, less wages, to labour input, using the data from Table I and associated text.

TABLE II (a)

Ratio of product price to labour input

	Technique A	Technique B
Commodity 1	97·2/36	96·75/36
Commodity 2	97·2/27	96·75/27
Commodity 3	95·4/20	96·5/16

TABLE II (b)

Ratio of product price net of labour cost to labour

	Technique A	Technique B
Commodity 1	64·8/36	57·15/36
Commodity 2	72·9/27	67·05/27
Commodity 3	77·4/20	78·9/16

Clearly there is no cross-over in 'factor intensities' on either definition in any commodity. Nor would there be if after-trade prices were taken as in our example. Notice also that before trade labour is relatively cheap in country *A* using technique *A*. But country *A* will obviously find it most profitable to export commodity 3, which uses relatively *little* labour by any reasonable measurement. Indeed, at the going prices this is the *only* commodity which the labour-rich country can export.

If the technical facts of the real world had been like those of Table I, an investigator working on the lines indicated would have toiled much harder than he need have done only to give the wrong advice after all. And how do we know that the facts *are* not as in Table I, or at least that the true facts, whatever they are, do not generate similar results?

The moral of this cautionary tale is once again that factor intensities have very little to do with our problem. The world is unfortunately not so simple a place. The time has come therefore to engage in some more, far from easy, theoretical inquiry.

16.4 THE MOST GENERAL THEOREM

Fortunately the general approach and the essential question to be solved remains precisely the same in many dimensions as it was in two. What differs is the solution. We can only be sure that trade will bring about at least a tendency to equalise factor prices in a world with *n* commodities and *m* factors if *any* selection of *m* commodity prices *uniquely* determines factor prices. To be quite sure that this statement is not misunderstood, we emphasise once more that 'any' means 'every'. The process of competition will ordinarily induce specialisation (if it does not equalise factor prices) in such a way that the number of commodities produced in common and traded is equal to *m*. But we do *not* know which *m* out of the *n* will be selected for specialisation. Thus we cannot be sure that, despite specialisation, factor prices must be equalised unless we specify that any selection of *m* cost functions will have the required property whatever it turns out to be.†

This being said, we may now turn to the purely mathematical problem of finding the conditions under which *m* equations of the form

$$q_i = \sum_{j=1}^{m} a_{ij} p_j$$

possess an inverse. That is, in what circumstances, given *m* numbers

† We are of course assuming $n > m$. If $n < m$, many more possibilities would be opened up, depending on conditions of demand in each country. We have not treated this case since it seems highly unrealistic. In view of the fact that by factors we mean the basic non-produced endowments of nature, it seems highly improbable even to the point of impossibility that the number of commodities in the world should be less than the number of factors.

q_i, would it be possible to solve these m cost equations to obtain a *unique* set of m numbers p_j. If, having found the required properties of the cost equations, we discover that every selection of m cost equations of the real world actually does have these properties, we could be sure that wherever any m commodities are both produced in common and traded by any two countries these countries must have

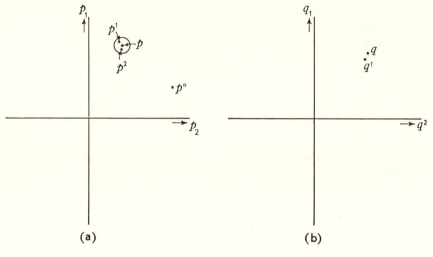

(a)   (b)

Fig. 16.1

the same factor prices. This is no more than a generalised version of the argument with which this chapter began.

In order to simplify enormously the discussion which follows, we now invite the reader to develop a new way of talking, familiar to mathematicians but not so far employed in this book. As we did occasionally in Chapter 13 and elsewhere, we shall represent the m numbers q_i by just one single symbol q and the m numbers p_j by a single symbol p. We then notice that on any ordinary graph p and q may be represented as points. For example, on Fig. 16.1 (b) we have a point, q, representing the two numbers q_1 and q_2 which measure the perpendicular distance of q from the q_2 and q_1 axes respectively. Similarly, in three dimensions we should have three axis planes of reference as in section 12.6. The reader is reminded that in section 12.6 he was invited to visualise a point in a room which has three numbers associated with it measuring its distance from any two adjacent walls and the floor. We shall in practice carry on the argument in two dimensions, but by extending the idea of a line on a page to a line of points in a room the reader will be able to visualise the same geometric reasoning in three dimensions, and this will be sufficient to illustrate all the difficulties and to demonstrate the full implications of the various questions raised.†

The set of all points p is called P space and the set of all points q is called Q space. We represent the m cost functions by writing

$$f : P \rightarrow Q$$

to be read f is a mapping of P onto Q. This simply means that given any point p in P a point q in Q is uniquely determined by the m cost equations. Thus we are inquiring into the circumstances in which an inverse mapping

$$f^{-1} : Q \rightarrow P$$

exists so that each point q in Q determines uniquely a point p in P. If in fact two points, say p and p^0, *both* map onto q (Fig. 16.1), then no such inverse exists.

At first we look at a much narrower problem. Consider a point p in P. Now imagine a very small loop or circle drawn around p (Fig. 16.1 (a)) with centre p. Can there exist *within the small circle* two distinct points, say p^1 and p^2, *both* of which map into the *same* point q^1 in Q? Suppose two such points do exist. From cost equations we know (see Chapter 14) that

$$dq_1 = a_{11} dp_1 + a_{12} dp_2$$
$$dq_2 = a_{21} dp_1 + a_{22} dp_2 \tag{16.4.1}$$

holds for any small changes whatever. Let the a_{ij} be evaluated at the point p at the centre of the circle and consider first the change dp^1 from p to p^1 and second the change dp^2 from p to p^2. Since by definition *both* p^1 and p^2 map onto q^1, the corresponding changes dq must be the same. By subtracting the two sets of equations like (16.4.1), therefore, we obtain

$$a_{11}(dp_1^1 - dp_1^2) + a_{12}(dp_2^1 - dp_2^2) = 0$$
$$a_{21}(dp_1^1 - dp_1^2) + a_{22}(dp_2^1 - dp_2^2) = 0 \tag{16.4.2}$$

We note especially that the variables $(dp^1 - dp^2)$ of the equations (16.4.2) cannot both be zero, for by assumption the points p^1 and p^2 are different.

---

† A rigorous many-dimensional treatment requires a considerable knowledge of mathematics. Such a proof can be found in an article by the present author in the *International Economic Review*, October, 1967 [12].

But consider what happens if we try to solve the equations (16.4.2) in the usual way by the method of determinants. In each case the numerator of the solution for $(dp_i^1 - dp_i^2)$ will be zero because of the two zeros on the right-hand side. In order for this to be consistent with a non-zero solution, the denominator must also be zero. In other words the *existence* of the two points p^1 and p^2 implies

$$\begin{vmatrix} a_{11} & a_{12} \\ a_{21} & a_{22} \end{vmatrix} = 0 \qquad (16.4.3)$$

or

$$\frac{a_{11}}{a_{12}} = \frac{a_{21}}{a_{22}}$$

when a_{ij} is evaluated at the point p, being the centre of the small circle (Fig. 16.1). Note that (16.4.3) identifies the factor intensity cross-over point which we noted in earlier sections. If we say that factor intensities cannot reverse themselves, we are saying that (16.4.3) cannot be satisfied and hence that p^1 and p^2 cannot exist.

On the other hand consider the consequences of passing to three dimensions. In this case we have three equations of the type (16.4.2) but the argument follows the same lines. To rule out the two points p^1 and p^2 we should have to have the determinant $|a_{ij}|$ of factor inputs different from zero as before. The important new feature is that $|a_{ij}|$ is now a 3×3 determinant which certainly requires more than a factor intensity condition to keep it non-zero. A 3×3 determinant can easily be zero for a great many reasons totally unconnected with factor intensities, as one would suspect from the numerical example with which we began.

Our result does, however, suggest that the general condition on production functions (sets of techniques a_{ij}) which we are looking for might be that for *every* p in P the corresponding determinant $|a_{ij}|$ should be different from zero. As long as this condition is met we might hope there could never be two points anywhere like p^1 and p^2 mapping into the same q. Unfortunately we are a long way from proving this as yet.

The reader is reminded that we have so far considered only points p^1 and p^2 which lie in a very small circle or 'neighbourhood' around p. The reason for this is that when we take changes in cost equations to arrive at (16.4.1) some approximation is involved, for if two numbers x and y change by amounts dx and dy, their product changes by

$$xdy + ydx + dydx$$

This may easily be confirmed by evaluating $(x+dx)(y+dy)$ and subtracting xy. It follows that even when we allow the sum of all pda to be zero, because of the minimum-cost property of cost functions (see section 14.2) we ought still to write

$$a_{i1}dp_1 + a_{i2}dp_2 = da_{i1}dp_1 + da_{i2}dp_2 \qquad (16.4.4)$$

instead of (16.4.1). Note that in (16.4.4) we assume dq to be zero since we wish to discuss the validity of the principle used leading to (16.4.3). We shall apply what we have to say about (16.4.4) more directly in a moment to (16.4.2). Dividing (16.4.4) by some non-zero dp, say dp_1, yields

$$a_{i1} + a_{i2}\frac{dp_2}{dp_1} = da_{i1} + da_{i2}\frac{dp_2}{dp_1} \qquad (16.4.5)$$

Notice now that the smaller we make the circle surrounding p (Fig. 16.1), the closer the right-hand side of (16.4.5) approaches zero, for the smaller the changes in price dp the smaller the change in techniques da. On the other hand if we think of (16.4.5) as two equations to be solved like (16.4.2), the 'unknowns' are 1 and dp_2/dp_1, neither of which approach zero as dp approaches zero. If we write δ_i for the right-hand side of (16.4.5) and solve, we have

$$1 = \frac{\begin{vmatrix} \delta_1 & a_{12} \\ \delta_2 & a_{22} \end{vmatrix}}{|a_{ij}|} \qquad (16.4.6)$$

which implies that $|a_{ij}|$ approaches zero as δ_i approaches zero.

What we have really proved is that $|a_{ij}|$ must be zero when evaluated at the point p if, for every circle around p *no matter how small the diameter* of the circle, two points p^1 and p^2 can be found generating the same q. To put the matter the other way around, we have proved that if $|a_{ij}|$ is *not* zero at p then p^1 and p^2 cannot exist within a circle around p *provided the circle is small enough*. We have *not* proved the same for *any* circle around p, for if δ is not close to zero, then $|a_{ij}|$ can be a number not close to zero whilst still satisfying (16.4.6).

This difficult point can perhaps be clarified by a simple example in one dimension only. Let

$$q_1 = a_{11}p_1$$

represent the cost function in a model with just one commodity and one factor of production. Suppose quite impossibly that a_{11} is always equal to p_1. The reader is asked to accept for the moment the economic nonsense implied by this since we are concerned only with a mathematical point and we wish to keep the example as simple as possible. We now have

$$q_1 = p_1^2$$

as our cost function. Consider any number for p_1, say 2, and a one-dimensional 'neighbourhood' of it. In two dimensions the 'neighbourhood' of a point is the small circle around it which figured in the discussion above. In one dimension the neighbourhood becomes a line segment, that is, a neighbourhood of the number 2 is the set of all numbers from $2 - \delta$ to $2 + \delta$, where δ is a small positive number.† Notice that if δ is $\frac{1}{2}$ then a neighbourhood is defined of the number 2 which is small enough to ensure that no two points within it yield the same q. As p_1 ranges from $1\frac{1}{2}$ to $2\frac{1}{2}$, q_1 rises continuously from $2\frac{1}{4}$ to $6\frac{1}{4}$ and does not repeat itself. On the other hand if we take $\delta = 3$ and extend the neighbourhood from -1 to $+5$, then different numbers *can* be found within the neighbourhood which yield the same q_1, e.g. $-\frac{1}{2}$ and $+\frac{1}{2}$ which both generate $q_1 = \frac{1}{4}$.

What our theorem proves is that as long as $|a_{ij}|$ is not zero (in the present case $|a_{ij}| = p_1 = 2$), then we can always choose δ small enough to ensure the existence of an inverse *over the neighbourhood* defined by δ. But what happens in our example at the point $p_1 = 0$ where $|a_{ij}|$ is zero? A neighbourhood of zero is the set of numbers from $-\delta$ to $+\delta$. Notice that no matter how small we make δ, two ps generating the same q remain within the interval. For the numbers $-\frac{1}{2}\delta$ and $+\frac{1}{2}\delta$ both lie in the neighbourhood and both yield the same q_1, namely $\frac{1}{4}\delta^2$. This example illustrates the significance of a non-zero $|a_{ij}|$.

We should now like to be able to prove that if the point $p_1 = 0$ were not there, that is, if at *all* points $|a_{ij}|$ is different from zero, then two ps generating the same qs cannot exist, whether they are very close together like

$$+ \frac{1}{10^{10}} \quad \text{and} \quad - \frac{1}{10^{10}}$$

both yielding $\qquad q_1 = \dfrac{1}{10^{20}}$

or far apart like -6 and $+6$ both yielding $q_1 = 36$.

† By analogy, in three dimensions the neighbourhood is a solid sphere of radius δ.

In terms of the diagram Fig. 16.1 we have shown that if $|a_{ij}|$ is different from zero at each point p in P, then, for any point p generating q, no other point p^0 generating the same q can exist within a small circle surrounding p. We have not proved that such a point p^0 cannot exist outside the circle as in the diagram. The condition $|a_{ij}|$ everywhere different from zero implies that the mapping

$$f: P \to Q$$

is everywhere locally one to one but not necessarily globally one to one. The meaning of the terms locally one to one and globally one

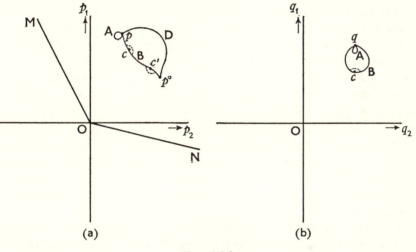

(a)   (b)

FIG. 16.2

to one are fully illustrated by the example $q_1 = p_1^2$, which is not globally one to one but is locally one to one everywhere except at the point where p_1 is zero. What we have to prove is that in the special case of cost functions the existence of a local inverse everywhere implies the existence of a global inverse.

Suppose that two points p and p^0 situated far apart as in Fig. 16.2 (a) did in fact map onto the same q. Join p and p^0 by a continuous arc B and consider the image of B in Q space, that is, consider the set of points in Q generated by the set of points in the arc B. Since both p and p^0 map onto q, the image of B in Q must be a 'closed' loop (say B in Fig. 16.2 (b)) beginning and ending at q. Construct also an arc A in P beginning and ending at p. The image of A in Q must again be a loop beginning and ending at q similar to the image of B.

Suppose that we now distort the arc B in Q very slightly at c (Fig. 16.2(b)) and consider the inverse image in P of the new arc. The inverse image is the set of points in P generating the distorted arc in Q. We must of course assume that there may be more than one point in the arc pp^0 generating the same point c in Q, since we have not yet proved the contrary. So we illustrate two such points marked c and c'. From the previous work we know that c and c', if it exists, must be separate distinct points; for $|a_{ij}|$ is different from zero at each of them. The distortion of B in Q at c will therefore imply two distortions of pp^0 at c and c'. Indeed, many more distortions of pp^0 may be implied if there are many more inverse images of c in the line pp^0.†

But however many distortions there are in pp^0, all must have the same two crucial properties. First, the distortion must be a unique curve provided the distortion itself is small enough, for if there were two distinct curves near c', say, both generating the same small distortion of B in Q, we must have two points near c' generating the same point q, impossible by our earlier work if $|a_{ij}|$ is different from zero at c'. Next, the distortion cannot *break* the arc pp^0 as long as there is no corresponding break in the image in Q, for if there were such a break the two 'ends' must generate overlapping images in Q so as to create a join in Q. If there were a break, therefore, at the moment of the break there would again be two points arbitrarily close together in P generating the same q, which is impossible if $|a_{ij}|$ is everywhere different from zero.

Thus small distortions of B in Q imply small distortions of pp^0 but no breaks, and, as long as q is fixed, no movement of the end points p and p^0. The inverse image of the distorted loop B in Q must always consist of a continuous unbroken arc joining p and p^0 (plus perhaps other points separate and distinct from the arc which do not interest us).

But the new distorted arc pp^0 and its image constitute a new arc and its image no different from that from which we began. A still further small distortion can be introduced and the same arguments applied. Thus by successive small displacements we can reduce the arc B in Q to the arc A in Q. Consider now the inverse image of A in Q. In the first place this contains the arc A in P from which A in Q was constructed. But by the argument above it contains also some distortion of the arc pp^0 linking p and p^0, say the arc D (Fig. 16.2(a)).

The arc D may of course follow (be coincident with) the loop A

† There may even be points in Q generating c quite distinct and separate from the line pp^0, but we need not be concerned with these.

over part of its length, but it must sooner or later break away from *A* since it must by definition reach p^0. Wherever the breakaway occurs (in Fig. 16.2(a) it is at p), there must evidently exist, in an arbitrarily small neighbourhood of the breakaway point, two points in *P* generating the same q in *Q*, for we then have two arcs generating the same segment of the loop *A* in *Q*. But this contradicts the assumption that $|a_{ij}|$ is different from zero at the breakaway point. Hence the two points p and p^0 generating q cannot exist. Notice also that the arcs and loops of Fig. 16.2 can just as easily be visualised in three dimensions as in two and the argument goes the same way. Clearly our new result holds for the three-factor/three-commodity case and the reader is assured that everything proceeds analogously however many dimensions are introduced (see note 1, p. 495).

Another way of stating what we have just proved is that whenever there are two solutions, say p and p^0, to a set of cost equations given a vector of commodity prices q, even if p and p^0 are far apart there must exist some other vector q^1 of commodity prices yielding two solutions p^1 and p^2 which are arbitrarily close to one another. Hence somewhere $|a_{ij}|$ must vanish. Thus, to rule out multiple solutions to cost equations it is sufficient to have $|a_{ij}|$ different from zero everywhere, as we originally conjectured.

Unfortunately we are not quite out of the wood yet. The argument we have used contains hidden assumptions which have been the subject of some critical comment. It is easy in fact to set down examples of general mathematical functions which have a local inverse everywhere but no global inverse in apparent contradiction to everything said above. It is important therefore to consider how these exceptions might arise.

Purely mathematical exceptions (as opposed to those with any economic significance) readily occur when the distortions in *B* in the space *Q* (Fig. 16.2) required to contract *B* until it is coincident with *A* have the effect of distorting the arc pp^0 to infinity. In case this is hard to imagine, readers who understand the meaning of the simple trigonometrical functions sine and cosine may care to consider the equations

$$q_1 = e^{p_1} \cos p_2$$
$$q_2 = e^{p_1} \sin p_2 \tag{16.4.7}$$

where e is the base of the natural logarithms, that is, a pure number (approx. 2.72).

This mapping is locally one to one but not globally one to one.

Indeed, if we choose q_1 and q_2 equal, and equal to some given number, it is possible to select some p_1 so that the equations (16.4.7) are satisfied whenever $\sin p_2$ equals $\cos p_2$, which it does at an infinite number of distinct and separate values of p_2.

The explanation is simple. If we construct an arc as in Fig. 16.2 joining two points in P space yielding the same q, we shall find that its image in Q space loops around the point $(0, 0)$; that is, the origin O (Fig. 16.2(b)) will always be in the *interior* of the loop. In order to contract the loop as desired, it will be necessary to pass the point $(0, 0)$, which turns out to be impossible. Inspection of equations (16.4.7) makes it clear that the inverse image of the point $q_1 = 0$, $q_2 = 0$ does not exist. The values of the functions (16.4.7) approach zero as p_1 approaches minus infinity, but they never attain the value. Thus the loop D (Fig. 16.2(a)) is drawn off towards infinity where our argument breaks down.

Consider now why this difficulty is not relevant to any economic discussion. The peculiarity of the equations (16.4.7) lies in the fact that certain very large values of p, approaching infinity, generate perfectly ordinary values of q. There would be no difficulty if in each case some q_i approached infinity whenever any p_j approached infinity, and no q_i ever approached infinity *unless* some p_j approached infinity.

By a stroke of good fortune this must always be the case with cost functions, for they take the form

$$q_i = \sum_j a_{ij} p_j$$

where in the nature of things it must be a fact that a_{ij} are all ordinary positive finite numbers. It is nonsense of course to try to imagine an infinite input of a factor being required to produce one unit of output, for we know that there exists only a finite number of elementary physical particles in the universe. Hence whenever all p_j are finite, all q_j must be finite. Conversely whenever p_j tends to infinity some q_i tends to infinity unless *all* a_{ij} become zero. This last possibility is of course ruled out by the assumption that at least some quantity of all factors must be in use, or, what amounts to the same thing, $|a_{ij}|$ is different from zero.

It should now be noted that we implicitly introduced these very reasonable assumptions at a crucial point in our proof. In equations (16.4.5) and (16.4.6) above, if any a_{ij} is near to infinity the argument following (16.4.6) does not hold. However close δ may be to zero, equation (16.4.6) can be satisfied, if some a_{ij} approaches infinity, without any implication of zero $|a_{ij}|$. But as it is absurd to imagine that a_{ij} could approach infinity, we have no need to concern ourselves with imaginary possibilities. *For cost functions it must be true that $|a_{ij}|$ different from zero everywhere implies that one and only one set of factor prices is associated with each set of commodity prices. If this condition was universally met for all groups of commodities, factor price equalisation, or at least partial factor price equalisation, would be assured.*

One more objection must now be dealt with. It has been argued by some economists that the theory developed above does not tell us what we want to know since it may depend upon the evaluation of

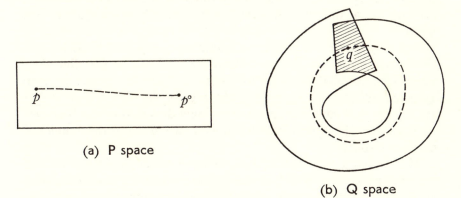

(a) P space

(b) Q space

Fig. 16.3

the determinant $|a_{ij}|$ when factor prices are negative. This is an important point, even though, as we shall show, the criticism is based upon a misunderstanding.

First of all, suppose it were true that no value could be put on $|a_{ij}|$ whenever any factor price is negative. The set of points making up the space P in Fig. 16.1(a) would then be confined to the north-east quarter of the diagram. The space would have a *boundary*. The attempt to contract the loop B in Q (Fig. 16.2(b)) until it coincides with A may be frustrated because the inverse image D in P of the distorted arc pp^0 reaches the boundary and can go no further. This possibility will manifest itself in the space Q by a 'hole' within the loop B in Q just like the missing point $(0, 0)$ in the previous example. The above pictorial explanation may help in understanding this. Any mapping $f: P \rightarrow Q$ of the kind with which we are at present concerned may be thought of as a distortion of a 'shape' P into a new 'shape' Q. Suppose that P space has a boundary as illustrated in Fig. 16.3. Provided we simply stretch and/or bend the space P, the local inverse property is not violated. Accordingly we imagine the rectangle P stretched and bent in a circular way so that the two ends overlap as in Fig. 16.3(b). The points p and p^0 can be made to coincide so that both map onto the point q in Q as shown.

We have here another example of a mapping where two points p and p^0 map into the same q but no points can be found arbitrarily close together which map into the same q. Indeed, the only points in Q which have *more* than one point in their inverse $f^{-1}(q)$ are those contained in the shaded area of overlap. Each of these points has two points in its inverse, one each at different ends of the rectangle P. As they are at different ends they cannot be arbitrarily close to one another.

It is easy to see now where the argument of Fig. 16.2 breaks down. The image of the arc pp^0 is shown in Fig. 16.3 as a broken line. Any attempt to contract this loop towards q is frustrated by the 'hole' in Q space. When the loop reaches the edge of the hole it is clear that the arc pp^0 will have been correspondingly distorted to the *boundary* of P space. The hole can exist in Q space because the boundary exists in P space.

This example shows that our principal result *might* not hold if there is any boundary to P space. Before proceeding to a further discussion of this point, however, it is desirable to refer at once to a useful proposition which we shall need at a later stage. Suppose there is a boundary to P space. Suppose indeed that P space is a rectangle as in Fig. 16.3. In order to get an overlap when constructing Q space, it is clearly necessary to push a boundary point of P into the interior of Q; that is, most of the boundary of the shaded area in Fig. 16.3(b) no longer forms part of the boundary of Q. Conversely, if part of the boundary of P does lie in the interior of Q, there must exist two points in P yielding the same Q. We might be led therefore to conjecture the following:

Theorem 3: If f:P→Q *is a mapping of a convex bounded region* P *onto* Q *such that no two points in* P *arbitrarily close generate the same point* q, *then an inverse function exists if and only if no boundary point of* P *maps into the interior of* Q.

No attempt will be made to prove this theorem here,† since it is

† A proof is given by the present writer in a note entitled 'Rejoinder to Professor McKenzie', *International Economic Review*, Oct 1967 [12].

not crucial to our main thesis and a great deal of mathematics is required to treat the extension into many dimensions. Nevertheless the theorem is true not only for convex regions but for many other types of P space as well. We keep this result in mind for later comment.

Returning now to the purely economic problem, we have to ask 'is there in fact a boundary to P space invalidating the theory?' The answer to this is unequivocably 'No!' It is true of course that if the wage rate were negative, that is, if the government paid businessmen to use labour and the labourer demanded no wage, then the businessman would be tempted to 'employ' an unlimited amount of labour for the sake of the subsidy, at the same time making no demands at all upon the services of his employees. But to envisage a case like this is to pervert the notion of a technique of production and hence of a cost function and thus to introduce nonsense into what began by being a sensible question.

To re-establish the rule of reason, we begin from a production function, that is a set of techniques for producing one unit of output. What we imagine is a kind of recipe book showing all conceivable methods of producing each commodity. Much depends, however, on what we mean by 'all conceivable'. Naturally we are not interested in techniques which are inefficient at any price. If for example it is possible to produce one unit of X with one unit of labour, it is equally possible to produce one unit of X with a thousand units of labour if we send nine hundred and ninety-nine labourers home for a holiday. We must suppose nonsense techniques to be ruled out of the set.

But this is by no means the end of the ambiguities. There may exist some techniques which are efficient and are minimum-cost at factor prices which cannot occur in the real world. For example, if wage rates were so low that all labourers employed at such rates must inevitably starve to death, it might be felt that any technique efficient at these wage rates is irrelevant and should be excluded from the set. Nevertheless it may still be true that there exists some technique of production which *would* be minimum-cost at such low wage rates but would never be minimum-cost for any other wage rate. We might on the one hand think it appropriate to leave low wage-rate techniques out of the set, or it might be felt that some country could be tempted to subsidise the use of labour up to the point where the wage less subsidy is as low as the impossibly low wage rate. In such a situation it would be important to include the maverick technique, for it could then occur and be observed in the real world.

Having established that there are ambiguities in the set of techniques to be included, we emphasise that this is a difficulty about the question to be put, not about the answer we have given. The question we are putting is, what properties must the set of techniques possess in order to ensure that the cost function based on that set of techniques possesses an inverse? We shall show that an answer can be given for *any* set of techniques whatever. It does not matter in the slightest whether we *include* techniques appropriate only when subsidies can be offered, or whether we *exclude* such techniques.

Of course it may matter a great deal when we come to the answer we get. One set of techniques may generate a cost function with an inverse and another may not, for one set of techniques may have different properties from another. But when we simply ask, does trade tend to equalise factor prices, it happens that the theory of the subject is the same whether we ask it of a world which admits subsidies or of a world which does not. The theoretical properties required of the cost function are the same in each case but the cost functions themselves may differ. One may possess the required property and one not.

In what follows we do not insist that techniques appropriate to subsidies should be included in the set from which we begin. We insist only that we *have* a set, a very reasonable demand in view of the fact that what we are asked is to say something about the properties of technique sets. The question 'which set?' becomes important only at a later stage when we come to the problem of testing the theory empirically.

Given a set of techniques it is easy to see that we have a cost function for *all* factor prices whether positive or negative, for it is just as simple a matter to choose minimum-cost techniques when factor prices are negative as it is when they are positive. Furthermore, the reader should not suppose that just because we might not observe negative prices in the real world, that there is any difficulty in observing which technique would be minimum-cost if there were negative factor prices. As long as the techniques themselves are observable, deciding on the appropriate a_{ij} is simply a matter of arithmetic. More will be said about this later under the heading 'Empirical Testing of the Theory.'

So far we have established that the line of criticism which rejects our principal conclusion on the ground that $|a_{ij}|$ has no meaning for negative prices is misguided. $|a_{ij}|$ has a meaning everywhere and is easily observed. On the other hand one serious weakness remains. A wide range of negative factor prices will of course imply some negative commodity prices, and as economists we can have no interest in negative commodity prices even in our wildest imaginings. Of course this is not in any way destructive of our argument. What we have proved is that if $|a_{ij}|$ is different from zero for all factor prices positive or negative, there can be no two distinct sets of factor prices yielding the same commodity price whether positive or negative. The fact that we are not interested in negative commodity prices makes no difference to the fact that we have found a condition which will ensure that the inverse $f^{-1}(q)$ to each positive commodity price is a single point.

On the other hand there are at least two reasons why it would be nice to be able to rule out the negative commodity prices. First, in any empirical test of the theory (see below) much time might be saved if we do not have to bother to compute the $|a_{ij}|$ appropriate to factor prices generating negative commodity prices. There is no difficulty about the computation itself, but there is no point in working arithmetic unless one has to.

Second, and more serious, is the fact that we could encounter cases where two or more distinct sets of factor prices generate the same negative commodity prices but where the same is not true for the positive commodity prices in which we are interested. Our condition is sufficient but not necessary for the mapping to be one to one over any restricted range of prices.

For these reasons it is desirable to extend our argument as follows. Suppose that in constructing Fig. 16.2 our interest is confined to non-negative commodity prices. Then the point q must be in the northeast quarter of Fig. 16.2(b) as drawn. The fact that we are interested only in non-negative q implies of course that we are interested only in the space P consisting of *all* points p which generate non-negative q. We must take care of course, because the reduced space P now has a boundary, say MON (Fig. 16.2(a)), and we know that boundaries cause trouble. Nevertheless we know that both p and p^0 generate a non-negative q and hence are located in P. Furthermore, if we choose the arbitrary arc connecting p and p^0, from which we began, so that it lies always in the space P,† then the loop B lies always in the space

† Readers will of course immediately demand a proof that such an arc can be constructed. Obviously it can, for raising any one factor price keeping all other factor prices constant must raise all commodity prices. Thus if we connect p and p^* (defined by selecting the highest factor price occurring either in p or p^0) by an arc which raises each factor price successively, we have an arc which generates an image in Q lying to the

Q of non-negative q. But if the whole of B lies in the north-east quarter of Fig. 16.2(b), contracting B towards q leads to a succession of arcs which lie always in the north-east quarter. Thus distortion of the arc pp^0 *cannot* be checked by the boundary of P, for if it were it could not be a boundary. Thus all our earlier argument holds as if the boundary did not exist.

To put it another way, the restricted mapping we are now considering must be boundary to boundary as required by theorem 3 above, for if some point p^* in the boundary MON (Fig. 16.2(a)) is mapped into the interior of the region of non-negative q where the loop B is located, then there must exist some point very close to p^* but outside the boundary MON which also maps into the region of non-negative q. This contradicts the assumption that P consists of *all* points generating non-negative commodity prices.

Accordingly we have

Theorem 4: If, for any cost function, $|a_{ij}|$ is different from zero for each set of factor prices generating positive commodity prices, then an inverse cost function exists and each set of commodity prices is generated by one and only one set of factor prices.

The reader should note that the non-zero $|a_{ij}|$ is not only a sufficient condition but is also (except in a few coincidental cases) a necessary one. That is, if $|a_{ij}|$ is zero at any point then there *will* exist two or more sets of factor prices yielding the same *positive* commodity prices. (See exercise 5, p. 528.)

We now draw attention to the fact that $|a_{ij}|$ might be non-zero at all positive factor prices but zero at some factor price pattern inside the region MOp_1, say (Fig. 16.2(a)). It might also be that all but one of the many points p yielding the same q are also confined to the region MOp_1. This possibility should be carefully considered, since it has been held that there is no need, indeed that we ought not to look at anything other than those commodity prices generated by positive factor prices. It has been suggested that only the region bounded by p_1Op_2 is relevant rather than that bounded by MON.

The underlying motive for this suggestion is presumably the belief that no country would ever be induced to subsidise up to the point where the net cost of a factor to the manufacturer becomes negative.

---

north-east of q, in which case the arc itself must lie in P. Joining p^0 and p^* in the same way completes an arc (between p and p^0 (via p^*)) satisfying the required condition.

As it happens, this supposition flatly contradicts the facts,† but even if it did not serious difficulties arise. One of these difficulties we discuss now; others are mentioned by implication.

It should be recalled that our basic objective is to find a condition for factor prices to be equalised by trade and not simply one which will ensure the existence of an inverse to this or that cost function. Our interest in the existence of an inverse to the cost function is simply a means to an end. We have argued that if one and only one set of factor prices generates each set of commodity prices, two countries opening trade relations must find their factor prices gravitating towards a common set of factor prices. But what happens if two such sets of factor prices exist, one with a subsidy and one without? Do we pretend that one of these possibilities is not there just because it involves a subsidy?

There are at least two reasons why we should not. First, some country might actually subsidise. Second and more important, we have no reason whatever to assume that trade cannot lead some country towards the factor price set including the subsidy just because we have chosen to assume that no country will give way to the temptation to subsidise. We can only be sure of a tendency to move towards an equilibrium A if this is the *only* position of equilibrium which exists. If another equilibrium B is possible it is one thing to assume, for whatever reason, that it will never be attained, but it is quite another to refuse even to consider the implications of its existence (see exercise 6 at the end of this chapter).

Of course it is true that if we assume that no country will ever subsidise the use of a factor, and if we further *assume* crucially that the equilibrium attained will be one in which no quantity of any factor is unemployed and in which as many commodities must be produced in common as there exist factors, then the equilibrium attained must be one of factor price equalisation as long as one and only one positive factor price pattern generates each set of commodity prices. But this once again begs the question of what is the part played by the existence of a second equilibrium (with, say, one negative factor price) in the process of inducing specialisation. It is easy to imagine cases where the opening-up of trade induces a change in factor prices towards an equilibrium in the region MOp_1

---

† In 1942, for example, in the U.K. the growing of carrots was subsidised at a price per acre in excess of the land rent of a small-holding with which the present writer was connected, on the condition that the harvest was actually gathered.

(Fig. 16.2(a)) and where the movement in factor prices in turn induces specialisation. Alternatively there could be a case where one factor price is reduced to zero in an attempt to move to the negative equilibrium, after which the problem reduces to the case of one more commodity than (effective) factor. Specialisation may be inevitable. This leads naturally into an inquiry into the problem of the consequences of further specialisation.

16.5 PARTIAL EQUALISATION OF FACTOR PRICES

So far we have dealt with the case where as many commodities are produced in common and traded as there exist factors of production. But this as we have seen is not the only possibility. Except where factor prices are equalised, specialisation must be induced up to the point where the number of commodities produced in common is not greater than the number of factors, and this may of course mean more factors than commodities. Obviously if we have fewer cost equations than we have factor prices it must be true that many patterns of factor prices yield the same commodity prices. Indeed, there will be infinitely many, so that factor prices need not be equalised by trade. But will they be partially equalised, and in what sense?

Consider the simplest possible two-dimensional case. To allow full illustration of all possibilities, at the same time keeping to a two-dimensional diagram, we forget for the moment all the restrictions to which cost functions are subject. Alternatively, the reader may think of the p_i and q_i of Fig. 16.4 as ratios p_i/p_3 and q_i/q_3 respectively, in which case no restriction is implied. For convenience we shall speak as if treating a two-factor/two-commodity case, although if prices are interpreted as price ratios the two-dimensional figure will in fact illustrate a three-factor/three-commodity world.

Suppose that two commodities and two factors of production exist but one country is induced by competition to specialise in the production of commodity 1. That is, commodity 2 is not produced. It follows that in a trading equilibrium only one price, namely q_1, is necessarily the same in both countries. The final position after trade will be one in which the points q^A and q^B, representing equilibrium price patterns in countries A and B respectively, must lie on the straight line JK in Q space (Fig. 16.4(b)). Only the q_1 element in the vectors q^A and q^B is the same.

Consider the inverse image in P of the line JK. This may be a single line FG, or two or more lines such as DE and HI (Fig. 16.4(a)).

Suppose the factor price patterns, before trade, are p^A and p^B in countries A and B respectively. If the inverse image of JK has a single component FG, then trade will shift p^A and p^B on to the *same* line FG in P, say to p^Z and p^W. If on the other hand the inverse of JK has two components DE and HI, it is possible that p^A and p^B may be attracted to different components – say the points p^X and p^Y.

Of course, when there are many factors of production it is difficult to attach any meaning to the notion of one set of prices p^1 being 'more equal' to, say, the set p^0 than some other set p^2. Some prices may be nearer and others further away. Nevertheless it may be felt that one useful definition may be to say that factor price vectors are

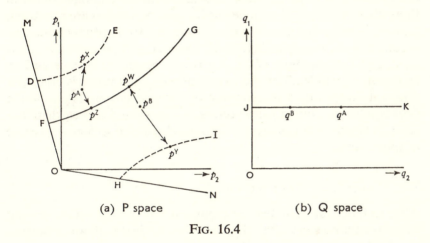

(a) P space   (b) Q space

FIG. 16.4

tending to be more equalised when they are drawn towards the same component FG than when they are drawn towards different components DE and HI which may be anywhere in relation to one another. Thus p^Z and p^W are more equal than p^X and p^Y. The justification for this is easily seen from the alternative possibilities illustrated in Fig. 16.4(a).

Naturally in the absence of any known restriction it is easy to construct oddly shaped components which make such a definition look much less sensible than it is for the case illustrated. On the other hand, the chosen definition is the only one which allows us to say anything at all about partial factor price equalisation, so we provisionally accept it. Immediately we have a condition for partial factor price equalisation for what it is worth. Clearly trade must partially equalise factor prices if the inverse of JK has only one component.

A sufficient condition for one component is clearly that $|a_{ij}|$ should be different from zero at each point p in P generating positive commodity prices, for if two components exist, their images in Q must overlap somewhere in order that JK should be a continuous line. In other words there must be at least one point in JK where the inverse $f^{-1}(q)$ consists of at least two points in P, which is impossible if $|a_{ij}|$ is different from zero everywhere.

Thus it turns out that the condition for partial factor price equalisation is exactly the same as the condition for full factor price equalisation, and this is our primary excuse for raising the problem. Any application of either theory turns on knowing whether or not $|a_{ij}|$ is zero at any point. Note especially that the analogue of JK in three dimensions is still a single line if *two* commodities are produced, that is, if only one commodity is dropped from production. The argument runs exactly as before. If, however, only one commodity is produced, the analogue of JK is a two-dimensional surface and its inverse in P will similarly be two-dimensional. Nothing is otherwise different except that less restriction (by one dimension) is put on the final equilibrium factor price vectors. As we should expect, there is a sense in which factor prices are 'less equalised' the greater the degree of specialisation.

16.6 EMPIRICAL TESTING OF THE THEORY

After so much long and tedious argument it may be as well to remind ourselves that we are after all attempting to deal with an important practical problem. We believe in the existence of a competitive mechanism common to all countries which, up to a reasonable degree of approximation, determines factor rewards wherever in the world the factor is located. It is taken for granted also that the laws of physics are everywhere the same. We have to explain why, despite these two apparent facts, factor prices differ quite remarkably according to location.

One possible explanation is that the competitive process does not work smoothly or does not exist. Another possible explanation must be that the working of the competitive process is more complicated than intuition would suggest; that is, that we have after all no reason to expect on purely logical grounds that factor prices will be everywhere equal even if the competitive process has been working smoothly.

What we have managed to isolate above is one essential ingredient of the competitive process which must be satisfied empirically before we can expect it to work. Unless cost functions in fact possess an inverse, we have no reason at all to expect factor prices to be equalised. The next step would appear to be to go to the facts and to find out whether the condition for an inverse is or is not satisfied. As we have severely criticised earlier attempts to do just this, more should be said on this point in the light of our theoretical work.

If we could actually observe cost functions, the problem would be non-existent. To see whether the cost function has an inverse, all we have to do is look at it. Unfortunately in practice we cannot observe the cost function. All that we can do is to note the techniques of production a_{ij} actually employed in various parts of the world at any given time.

Let us begin by supposing what is unlikely to the point of being impossible, namely, that the set of production techniques actually *in use* in the world constitutes the whole set we are interested in; that is, that no other techniques exist which could conceivably be used other than those we observe. Once again all our theory is quite irrelevant. A relatively simple arithmetical computation will tell us quite exactly whether two or more sets of factor prices yield the same commodity price. Indeed, it will tell us precisely what these are. We have simply to programme the computer to select the minimum-cost technique for each commodity and to record the minimum cost for each set of factor prices over any range of factor prices we like, positive or negative.

The difficulties begin when, as is bound to be the case, only a very few out of the large number of physically possible production techniques can actually be observed and hence be known. It is perhaps because of this that economists have thought it worth while to study the complicated ideas above.

Even so, to the present writer it has always seemed that the only value of the argument developed is, paradoxically, to prove that we don't need it – to prove in fact that we should not be surprised to find that trade does not equalise factor prices. The whole notion of an empirical test of the factor price equalisation hypothesis becomes a contradiction in terms as soon as we try to go beyond the simple observation that factor prices are not equalised in fact. The reason for this will become clear if we consider at length two possible ways to 'test' for the existence of an inverse to cost functions. First, we recall that we do not approach the problem with just the information implied by the observed techniques. In reality we know a great deal more. Many of us have lived in the world a long time. We have ideas about the nature of productive processes and might have some knowledge or expectation about what might happen if things were different. Indeed, information indirectly assimilated often amounts to a great deal more than the directly observed information available from measurement of the variables under consideration. As a result of this, and as a result of common experience, it is sometimes possible to conclude quite reasonably that a certain phenomenon is *unlikely* even though there is no immediate prospect of observing it.† It may be therefore that we could, without further inquiry, conjecture that it is exceedingly unlikely that $|a_{ij}|$ does not go to zero somewhere, for some commodity group (see exercise 2 to this chapter).

On the other hand the second and more obvious way to use our theory is to go to the facts. It might be thought that we could at least test whether the condition for the existence of an inverse function is *not* satisfied. To do this the following steps‡ would be necessary:

(i) Observe the techniques a_{ij} actually in use and their associated prices.

(ii) Wherever the jth input is a manufactured item, the price p_j must be eliminated from the system, as in section 15.2, to ensure that all final a_{ij} are basic inputs; that is, in the notation of Chapter 15, we have to compute α_{ij}.

(iii) If the number of basic factors is m, note whether any $m \times m$ determinant, appropriately formed from the array of a_{ij}, is positive for one set of factor prices and negative for another or is actually zero for any set.

(iv) If all are positive or all are negative for all observed prices, the set of *all* techniques *observed* must be used as the basis for the construction of a cost function defined for all factor price sets

† In case the scrupulous reader should at this point feel that we are now engaging in 'unscientific' argument, whatever that word might mean, I hasten to draw attention to the fact that many physicists and biologists, on the basis of abundant evidence that 'nature is not niggardly', are willing to place on record their view that it is *impossible* that there should not be life on some other planet than earth. If this argument from authority fails to convince, the present author thoroughly recommends a study of Prof. E. E. Harris's *Foundations of Metaphysics in Science* [4].

‡ The reader is reminded that in practice some traded factors may be present to create difficulties. To deal with this a deeper knowledge of the theory is required than that presented here. For the mathematically trained we simply remark that mobile factor prices may be treated as constants, in which case the Jacobian of the transformation drops the coefficient of the mobile factor. Except for the counting of commodities and factors the problem remains the same.

generating positive commodity prices. That is, for each set of factor prices, the minimum-cost technique is chosen from the observed set and new $m \times m$ determinants constructed for each new factor price set. The new determinants may then be examined for change of sign.

The steps (i) and (ii) above need no comment. If, at stage (iii), we note a difference of sign of any determinant, it must be supposed that somewhere the value $|a_{ij}|$ has passed through zero. If this occurs for even one selection of m commodities, no inverse cost function exists and this alone could explain the failure of the competitive mechanism to equate factor prices. Note especially that in the example of Table I (section 16.3) there is a change of sign of the determinant and that this change of sign is independent of choice of units. The divergence of factor prices due to trade in the case of section 16.3 is accordingly explained by the theory (but see also below).

Step (iv) requires extended explanation. First of all it should be noted that the theory as set out in earlier sections assumes 'continuity' of the number $|a_{ij}|$. What this means is that if, for some p^0, $|a_{ij}|$ takes the number X^0, and for some p^1 it takes the number X^1, then as p^0 passes to p^1 through all the numbers in between X^0 passes to X^1 through all the numbers in between. There are no jumps.

On the other hand there is no reason to suppose that this will be the case in practice. It is perfectly possible that only a limited, finite number of techniques of production exist. The switch from one to another is then a 'jump'. For example, we assumed in setting out Table I (section 16.3) that two and only two techniques of production exist. Either one or the other is minimum-cost in the ordinary way, but for some factor prices both techniques will ordinarily give equal costs. At these prices we have a jump in technique. Consider the following more detailed illustration.

In Fig. 16.5 we measure the input of capital up the vertical axis and the input of labour along the horizontal. There are two commodities produced, A and B, each with two possible techniques of production defined by the points A^1, A^2 and B^1, B^2 respectively; that is, one unit of A can be produced with quantities of labour and capital measured by the perpendicular distance of A^1 from the labour and capital axis and so on. Consider now the cost of production at various sets of factor prices.

Let the slope of the line RS represent the ratio of factor prices, that is, the rate at which capital and labour can be exchanged in the market. OR units of capital cost the same to hire as OS units of labour. It follows that the cost of producing one unit of A, measured in units of capital instead of money, is equal to OR when the technique A^1 is used. OR in fact is equal to the quantity of capital employed plus the quantity of labour converted at the price ratio RS into units of capital. In terms of cost equations

$$OR = q_A/p_C = a_{AC} + (p_L/p_C)a_{AL}$$

where the right-hand side is the cost of capital plus the cost of

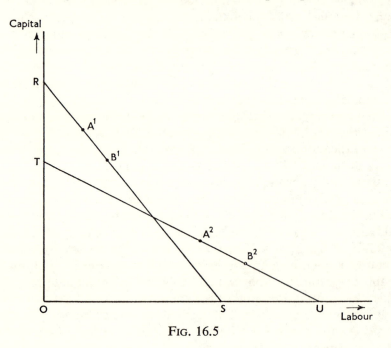

Fig. 16.5

labour divided by the price of capital to convert into units of capital.

Notice that the cost of producing A at prices RS would be greater if technique A^2 had been employed, for this would be determined by the intercept on the capital axis of a line through A^2 parallel to RS. Similarly OR is the cost of producing one unit of B at prices RS using technique B^1 which is again minimum-cost. It follows that, at factor prices RS, commodity prices are the same, that is, the commodity price ratio is $1:1$.

If on the other hand the factor price ratio changed to TU, it is clear that A^2 and B^2 now both become minimum-cost techniques.

Again the commodity price ratio is 1:1 even though factor price ratios are quite different. We might actually observe two countries in a trading equilibrium with factor prices quite different from one another, being in fact *RS* in country 1 and *TU* in country 2. What happens if we attempt to explain this disparity of factor prices in terms of the theory of this chapter?

First, we note that we can observe two 'readings' of the value of the determinant $|a_{ij}|$, one in country 1 and one in country 2. But in our example A is produced by capital-intensive methods in *both* countries. There will be no *observed* change of sign of $|a_{ij}|$ even though we might have expected it in view of the unequal factor prices. Thus the empirical worker may be tempted to say that we have failed to explain the differences in factor prices by showing that no inverse exists to the cost function.

It is important to understand that such a conclusion would be misguided. Our two 'readings' of $|a_{ij}|$ implicitly contain a lot more information than we have so far wrung out of them. We have observed the only two techniques possible, so that we have thereby discovered all techniques which could conceivably be used at *any* factor price ratio, not just for the two observed sets of factor prices. Indeed, we have enough knowledge to determine the whole cost function if we care to engage in the necessary arithmetic. In particular we note the following points.

From Fig. 16.5 we see that as the factor price ratio passes from *RS* to *TU*, it must at some time take a value equal to the slope of a line joining A^1 and A^2. At this factor price ratio both techniques A^1 and A^2 cost the same. Either can be thought of as a minimum-cost technique. As the factor price ratio passes A^1A^2 in steepness, however, A^2 becomes unambiguously minimum-cost. There is a 'jump' in technique from A^1 to A^2. Notice that the jump in technique does *not* imply a jump in cost. Since *both* A^1 and A^2 give the *same* minimum cost at the jump factor price ratio, the cost ratio proceeds smoothly through all numbers. The jump therefore does not modify any of our earlier argument relating to Fig. 16.2, but it does modify the conclusion following equation (16.4.6).

The jump from A^1 to A^2 can be seen to take place at a steeper factor price ratio than the jump from B^1 to B^2. There exists therefore a factor price ratio where A^2 is minimum-cost for A but B^1 is minimum-cost for B. This implies a value for the determinant $|a_{ij}|$ different from that observable in either of the two countries with factor price ratios *RS* or *TU*. It is moreover a price ratio at which B

is produced by more capital-intensive methods than A. There has been a change of sign of $|a_{ij}|$ even though there is no price ratio at which $|a_{ij}|$ is zero, as required by the argument relating to (16.4.6).

The reason for the apparent contradiction is simple. At the factor price ratio A^1A^2 there is no longer a unique set of a_{ij} to put in equations (16.4.1). In equation (16.4.2) there will appear, not a unique set of a_{ij}, but a weighted average of two or more distinct sets of a_{ij} which could be zero as in (16.4.3). Obviously if the two separate determinants are of opposite sign there can be a weighted average which is zero. Note that in Fig. 16.5 this occurs. It is possible to find a weighted average of A^1 and A^2 which is the technique where the straight line A^1A^2 cuts OB^1 extended. This uses capital and labour in the same proportion as B^1, thus implying a 'zero' $|a_{ij}|$. *The sign change-over of $|a_{ij}|$ has been observed implicitly even though it could not be seen explicitly, and the non-equalisation of factor prices is explained after all.*

We shall not attempt a proof here, but it is quite a simple matter to show† that this argument holds in many dimensions. Whenever, for any set of factor prices, the minimum-cost technique is not unique, we must test whether any weighted average of all techniques, which are equally minimum-cost at the given factor-prices, yields zero $|a_{ij}|$. This will clearly be the case if two or more $|a_{ij}|$ are of different sign.

The reason for step (iv) in the empirical testing procedure described above can now be fully explained. The value of $|a_{ij}|$ for various values of p may go from positive to negative and back again to positive as many times as we like. There is no reason whatever to suppose that just because $|a_{ij}|$ is positive for all values actually observed, an inverse to the cost function necessarily exists. Of course if we find the contrary, namely that changes of sign can be directly observed, then it is fairly safe to assume that no inverse to the cost function exists; but suppose that we do not observe this change of sign. We have then to try to find out whether there *would be* a change of sign if factor prices were different.

Obviously we cannot find this out for sure since we know nothing of techniques we cannot observe, but step (iv) does the next-best thing. The reader will readily accept that, if we are given a number of points on a curve but not the curve itself, a good first approximation will be a curve made up of straight lines joining the (adjacent) points given. In Fig. 16.5, for example, we might imagine that many more

† See 'More About Factor Price Equalisation', *International Economic Review*, Oct 1967, p. 269 [12] for sketch of a proof.

techniques for producing A are available forming a curve connecting A^1 and A^2. It might be thought that a straight line joining A^1 and A^2 is the nearest we can get to finding this curve. But note the following. We are in effect supposing that in addition to the techniques A^1 and A^2 any weighted average of these two is also a possible technique. To construct a cost function based upon a set of techniques including weighted averages of techniques which are equally minimum-cost for some one factor price set, as an approximation to the true set, yields exactly the same cost function as one based on the observed set of techniques alone. It follows that, in a way, our proposed empirical test is something of a waste of time. The theory tells us *a priori* that if our method of inquiry is reliable, we do not need to inquire. *We are bound as a matter of logic to find a sign change in* $|a_{ij}|$ *for the computed function if we start from observed equalised commodity prices and unequal factor prices.* The theory gives us the answer before we start.

Observe that it does not matter whether the approximating cost function is close to the true function or not. Both the true function and the approximating function must somewhere show zero $|a_{ij}|$. If we begin by observing a number of different techniques each with differing factor prices but identical commodity prices, and if at the same time we are able to confirm that each technique is minimum-cost at the existing factor prices, then theorem 4 *proves* that any cost function whatever, which 'fits' the observed data, must have $|a_{ij}|$ vanishing somewhere, and any computation we perform is bound to show this. It is for this reason that we began by arguing that the idea of testing for vanishing $|a_{ij}|$ is rather like trying to test empirically a purely logical proposition. The only sensible thing to test in the given circumstances is whether in fact each country is producing at minimum cost, given its existing factor prices and the variety of observed techniques. If this is not the case, there is no point in proceeding further. The competitive process does not work and there is no reason to expect any particular price pattern to emerge.

Of course if we could observe countries *before* trade or in circumstances where commodity prices are different, and if we wished to know in advance which factor prices would be equalised *after* trade began, then it might be valuable to test the theory by steps (i)–(iv). This might tell us, from direct observation of cost functions, whether factor prices would be equalised after the event. It has never seemed to the present writer, however, that this is the practical problem we face. Since trade does take place, we are called upon only to explain why we do not at the same time observe equal factor prices. To some economists this appears to be a surprising fact constituting something of a paradox. What the theory does is to emphasise that there is nothing surprising about the facts at all. There is nothing extraordinary about a zero $|a_{ij}|$; indeed, if one permits the kind of argument from experience referred to above (p. 514), one might almost be tempted to say that what would be surprising would be the contrary, that is, a one-signed $|a_{ij}|$.

16.7 CONCLUSIONS

There is no reason to expect trading countries with immobile factors to find that the existence of trade has equalised factor prices in the two countries; nor is there any reason to expect even a partial equalisation of factors by trade. Logically at least partial equalisation must occur if cost functions possess an inverse. A sufficient condition for factor price equalisation is that the determinant $|a_{ij}|$ of factor inputs for every selection of m commodities should be different from zero for each set of factor prices yielding positive commodity prices, where m is the number of immobile factors of production.

There is little point in attempting to test empirically whether the condition for the existence of an inverse is met if observations are confined to countries actually in a trading relation. If such countries exhibit different factor prices even though commodity prices are equalised, either the competitive process has failed to operate or some $|a_{ij}|$ is zero as a matter of logic. Testing makes sense only in cases where commodity prices are unequal.

At this point also it is worth emphasising that the controversy among economists over the problem of whether or not trade equalises factor prices is particularly deserving of the title "Much Ado About Nothing" for the following additional reason. What we usually wish to know in any particular case is the *direction* in which factor prices will move as a consequence of certain predicted commodity price changes. But once the direction and magnitude of the commodity price changes are known, the problem is *completely* solved by the straightforward observation of existing techniques a_{ij}. We need only invert

$$dq_i = \sum_j a_{ij} dp_j$$

as we do in particular cases in the following chapters. This gives the answer we want directly without any need to compute or otherwise estimate the techniques appropriate to factor prices other than those immediately observable. At bottom there is no problem provided the world can be convinced of the danger of making *a priori* generalisations on the basis of very little evidence.

One final conclusion ought to be added here, although, in a sense, it is a conclusion of a later chapter. The point has recently been made that, even if many solutions exist to cost equations, factor prices *must* be equalised between countries whose factor endowments are sufficiently alike. This is of course the purest of tautologies. The meaning of the word 'sufficiently' makes the proposition logically true without further argument. And even if we choose our words to frame an empirical proposition, it will state little more than the obvious fact that identical countries facing a common world demand would be expected to have equal factor prices; or alternatively, the more alike are factor endowments, the greater the probability that the overlap condition of Chapter 12 will be satisfied. But can anything be made of so obvious a truth?

In an attempt to do so it has been suggested that unequal factor prices will encourage factor mobility. This will have the effect of attracting resources to regions where they are scarce and hence of *equalising factor endowments*. Thus, in course of time, factor endowments will become 'sufficiently equal' for the classical factor price equalisation mechanism through trade to take over and complete the process.

The reader should be warned that this is but a new form of the old error. It is true that a *world* equilibrium is possible if all factor endowments were the same in each country, and that such an equilibrium would have equal factor prices. But this is not the only position of equilibrium *unless* each resource is always attracted from where it is abundant to where it is scarce. And to suppose that this will be the case is to invoke much the same kind of doubtful generalisation as that which gave rise to the original mistake.

Labour is not necessarily cheap where it is relatively abundant, whatever 'relatively abundant' might mean when there are many factors. The migration of labour from low-wage to high-wage regions could very well widen the gap between factor endowments. Indeed, statistics are readily available to illustrate migration of labour away from less densely populated areas to those more densely populated, even when the land left behind is of good quality.

Even more important and relevant still is the conclusion we reach in Chapter 18. Cases are there introduced where the migration of some factor in search of higher rewards actually increases the real reward of that factor in the host country rather than the opposite. Nor is there anything at all unusual about the examples quoted. If factor movements can actually raise real rewards in the region towards which migration is directed, the effect could be, presumably, to denude the country from which the factor is emigrating of its entire stock. This obviously could not have the effect of equating factor endowments, even though it would, as it must, equate factor rewards. The reader should observe also that to get back to factor price equalisation by introducing factor mobility is to do away with the whole problem of international trade (see Chapter 12).

The fact is that we are facing a problem of great complexity. The view we would wish to press here is simply that whatever may be the truth of the matter we shall come to it sooner by measurement and computation than by attempts at *a priori* argument, however ingenious that *a priori* argument might be.

APPENDIX

The Gale–Nikaidô Theorem†

For the sake of completeness it has seemed desirable to comment in this appendix upon a theorem developed in connection with the subject matter of Chapter 16 which is referred to in the literature as 'the principal theorem' but which has not been mentioned directly in the main body of the present text.

The reader will by now appreciate that, stripped of its economic content, the fundamental problem of Chapter 16 was to identify conditions under which a function possesses an inverse. As might be expected, mathematicians have already thought a great deal about this and it is already well understood that no single simple solution exists. Moreover, thanks to the mathematicians, we understand enough about the various possibilities to be quite sure that no single overall solution can *ever* be found. It will be helpful for the present discussion, and perhaps helpful in other branches of economics where the problem is relevant, to enlarge a little on this point.

† See Bibliography [3].

Any condition for the existence of an inverse function must directly or indirectly specify *two* things. These are:

(i) Something about the form of the function defining the mapping; and

(ii) Something about the *shape* and *extent* of the space mapped and/or something about the shape and extent of the image space; that is, about the shapes of *P* and *Q* in the case we are considering.

It is important to be quite clear that (i) without (ii) will ordinarily tell us nothing and vice versa. For example, if under (i) we specify, of a cost function, that $|a_{ij}|$ must be different from zero everywhere, but we say nothing about what we mean by 'everywhere', then it is clear that such a condition cannot be sufficient to establish the existence of an inverse; for if we choose a cost function with no inverse because $|a_{ij}|$ does go to zero, at the same time defining 'everywhere' as everywhere *except* those points where $|a_{ij}|$ is zero, we have an immediate counter-example to our own proposal. Conversely, if, under (ii), we specify that both *P* and *Q* must be, say, rectangles, without at the same time restricting the form of the function, examples of mappings, with and without inverses can be readily constructed. For example, a mapping of a rectangle which moves each point one inch to the right has an inverse whilst one which folds the rectangle in half has not.

In the problem of Chapter 16 we were extraordinarily fortunate. We happened to be concerned with cost functions which, from a mathematical point of view, possess two regularities which enormously simplify the problem. In the first place cost functions are 'extendable'; that is, we can determine a commodity cost for any set of factor prices whatever. Note that this does not apply to *any* function; for example consider, in one dimension, the mapping

$$q = \frac{p}{|p|}$$

where $|p|$ is a positive number taking the same numerical value as *p*. A sensible number *q* is uniquely determined for each value of *p* *except* $p = 0$. In fact $q = -1$ for $p < 0$ and $q = 1$ for $p > 0$, but no value can be assigned to *q* at $p = 0$ which will link -1 and $+1$ to yield a continuous function.

The second regularity of cost functions stems from the fact that as long as $|a_{ij}|$ is different from zero over a sufficiently wide extension, the boundary to boundary property is preserved *whatever* the shape of *P* space to be mapped.

In studying the problem of factor price equalisation, both of these important properties of cost functions seem to have been overlooked by most writers. The difficulty has been seen as one of finding conditions for an inverse when the range of the mapping is the space of all *positive or zero* factor prices; that is, under (ii) above, a rectilinear space *P* has been specified and attention concentrated upon this. But something more under (ii) is needed than this. We have to prove that the mapping is boundary to boundary (see theorem 3, section 16.4). The boundary to boundary condition ensures that the *Q* space shall have no 'hole' as in Fig. 16.3 of the main text. If we fail to recognise the extendability of cost functions and the fact that $|a_{ij}|$ different from zero over the extension *implies* that boundary points of the rectilinear region map into the boundary of its image space *Q*, then special extra conditions have to be introduced over and above the non-zero $|a_{ij}|$ to ensure that the boundary to boundary condition is satisfied. A number of proposals have been made on these lines,† only one of which still stands unretracted by its authors in the sense that it is neither wrong, superseded by something more general, or not relevant to economics. This is the Gale–Nikaidô theorem, which says, when applied to cost functions, that a cost function which maps the set of all non-negative *p* on to the space *Q* will possess an inverse if:

   (i) $|a_{ij}|$ is positive for each non-negative *p*, and
   (ii) there is some numbering of goods and factors such that every sub-determinant symmetric around the diagonal of $|a_{ij}|$ is also positive.

Condition (ii) means, in the case of a 3×3 determinant, that

$$a_{ii} > 0$$

and

$$\begin{vmatrix} a_{ii} & a_{ij} \\ a_{ji} & a_{jj} \end{vmatrix} > 0$$

for each commodity *i* and for each pair of commodities selected from the three. Notice also that $|a_{ij}|$ itself must be positive and not just non-zero. As previously indicated, this theorem has elsewhere been

† See the symposium on factor price equalisation, *International Economic Review*, Oct 1967 [12].

referred to as 'the principal theorem on factor price equalisation', so that something must be said about it.

Looked at as a piece of mathematics the Gale–Nikaidô theorem is no doubt of interest (it was published purely as a piece of mathematics with no reference to economics). But when it is presented as a theorem purporting to have relevance to the problem of factor price equalisation it is difficult to take it seriously. If as well as being an economist the present author were a physicist given to predicting the existence of life on other planets on the basis of doubtful projections of the observable on to the non-observable (see footnote, p. 514), he would at once declare himself certain that conditions as powerful as those demanded by the Gale–Nikaidô theorem are *not* met by the cost functions of the real world. Indeed, it already seems wildly improbable that even the condition $|a_{ij}|$ different from zero will be met, and what the Gale–Nikaidô theorem demands is, in the case of, say, several hundred commodities, that thousands upon thousands of extra conditions should be satisfied by the data at each value p.

Of course all this would be very much to the good if the Gale–Nikaidô condition were necessary as well as sufficient. If we knew that for factor price equalisation the Gale–Nikaidô condition *had* to be satisfied, not even the most fervent believer in factor price equalisation could expect it any longer. The difficulty really is that the Gale–Nikaidô conditions for the existence of an inverse function are so over-sufficient that one is tempted to coin the expression 'infinitely over-sufficient'. The reason for this is that for each mapping of a rectilinear region satisfying the Gale–Nikaidô condition and hence possessing an inverse, it is possible to construct an infinity of mappings *not* satisfying the conditions which nevertheless possess an inverse also.

For example, in any case where the coefficients a_{ij} are fixed and constant, the cost function has an inverse whether the Gale–Nikaidô condition is satisfied or not. Indeed, this was the assumption upon which the factor price equalisation theorem was originally founded. Notice also that fixed coefficients satisfy the demands of theorem 4, section 16.4. Now consider the following:

Suppose that a mapping $f: P \rightarrow Q^*$ is defined by

$$q_1^* = ap_1 + bp_2$$
$$q_2^* = cp_1 + dp_2$$

and suppose that this satisfied the Gale–Nikaidô condition, i.e. a, b,

c, and d are each variables dependent on p_1 and p_2 but in such a way that $a>0$, $d>0$, and $ad-cb>0$ for all non-negative p. Now let $g: Q^* \to Q$ be a mapping

$$q_1 = rq_1^* + sq_2^*$$

$$q_2 = tq_1^* + uq_2^*$$

where this time r, s, t, u are *any constants whatever* provided only that $ru-st$ is different from zero. Evidently we have defined a new mapping

$$fg: P \to Q$$

for given p we have q^* by the first mapping and given q^* we have q by the second mapping. It is also clear that the new mapping must possess an inverse for given q; then q^* is uniquely determined since r, s, t, u are constant and, given q^*, p is uniquely determined, since f satisfies the Gale–Nikaidô conditions. Furthermore, by solving the two sets of equations we may write our new mapping explicitly. Thus:

$$q_1 = (ra + sc)p_1 + (rb + sd)p_2$$

$$q_2 = (ta + uc)p_1 + (tb + ud)p_2$$

But the new coefficients clearly need not and ordinarily will not satisfy the Gale–Nikaidô conditions. In this manner we can, since r, s, t, u were any constants, construct an infinity of mappings with an inverse which nevertheless do not satisfy the Gale–Nikaidô conditions, all of which correspond to the one mapping f satisfying Gale–Nikaidô with which we began.

In particular, note that if we put $r = 1$, $s = 2$, $t = 2$, $u = -1$, $a = d = 2$ and $c = b = 1$, we have a case where $|a_{ij}|$ is negative and where one of the diagonal elements is zero, indicating that this may change sign – and all this even though the mapping has an inverse.

As economists we should take care not to allow an enthusiasm for results to lead us into making too much of over-sufficient conditions. It is one thing for mathematicians to publish an interesting piece of argument safely in a learned journal where it will be read only by other mathematicians who well understand its limitations. It is quite another thing for economists to make use of the argument in connection with a vitally important human problem in such a way as to obscure the fact that the statement made is little stronger than, say, a proposition that a sufficient condition for not drowning is never to go near the water.

EXERCISES

1. Test the contention of section 16.2 that the existence of a single-valued inverse function is the exception rather than the rule by attempting to invert a selection of the most common functions of a real variable to be found in any suitable mathematical text. In particular, show that the 'inverse' of

$$\frac{q_1}{q_2} = \left[\frac{1}{(p_1^2/p_2^2) - 1} \right]^2$$

has four branches. Show also that the inverse of

$$\frac{q_1}{q_2} = \sin\left(\frac{p_1}{p_2}\right)$$

has an infinity of branches.

2. Show that the function

$$\frac{q_1}{q_2} = \frac{(\alpha p_1^\beta + \gamma p_2^\beta)^{1/\beta}}{(a p_1^b + c p_2^b)^{1/b}}$$

where α, β, γ, a, b and c are positive constants, has no single-valued inverse. How many branches does it have? Note that this is a well-known form of cost function sometimes claimed to approximate closely to the facts of the real world suitably 'aggregated'.

3. Consider the following case with two factors and three commodities.

$$\frac{q_1}{q_2} = a\left(\frac{p_1}{p_2} - b\right)^2 \tag{i}$$

$$\frac{q_3}{q_2} = \alpha\left(\frac{p_1}{p_2} - \beta\right)^2 \tag{ii}$$

where a, b, α and β are positive constants of suitable magnitude. Show that if world prices are q_1^0, q_2^0 and q_3^0, a given country may produce all three commodities if and only if its factor price ratio satisfies either

$$\frac{p_1}{p_2} = b + \sqrt{\left(\frac{q_1^0}{a q_2^0}\right)}$$

or

$$\frac{p_1}{p_2} = b - \sqrt{\left(\frac{q_1^0}{a q_2^0}\right)}$$

according as world prices are related by the equations

$$\frac{q_3}{q_2} = \alpha \left[b - \beta + \sqrt{\left(\frac{q_1}{aq_2}\right)} \right]^2$$

or

$$\frac{q_3}{q_2} = \alpha \left[b - \beta - \sqrt{\left(\frac{q_1}{aq_2}\right)} \right]^2$$

Hence show that in spite of the fact that neither cost function (i) nor cost function (ii) possess a single-valued inverse, one and only one set of factor prices is associated with each feasible set of world commodity prices. Hence justify theorem 1 of section 16.2.

Show alternatively that any country producing two commodities only may, with the same cost functions, have different factor prices. Hence justify theorem 2 of section 16.2.

4. Using the diagram referred to in exercise 1, Chapter 12, construct a case with three commodities and two factors where factor prices become more different when two countries trade. Let one pair of commodities only show factor intensity reversal (see theorem 2, section 16.2).

5. Again using the diagram of exercise 1, Chapter 12, construct a two-commodity/two-factor case where factor intensities become equal at some one-factor price ratio but do not actually cross over; that is, $|a_{ij}|$ becomes zero but does not actually change sign. Show that in this case a global inverse cost function exists. Consider how far this case contradicts the assertion following theorem 4 of section 16.4. Show that the case where $|a_{ij}|$ becomes zero but does not actually change sign becomes more and more coincidental the greater the number of commodities and factors, given that the cost function for each commodity has no technical connection with any of the others.

6. One unit of each of commodities 1 and 2 can be produced by either of two techniques only (A and B as under):

	Technique A		Technique B	
	Factor 1	Factor 2	Factor 1	Factor 2
Commodity 1	12	2	6	6
Commodity 2	10	$1\frac{5}{6}$	6	6

With factor prices before trade at 2 for factor 1 and 3 for factor 2, show that technique A is cheapest in country A. With factor prices 3 for factor 1 and 2 for factor 2, show that B will be the chosen technique in the rest of the world. Show that if trade becomes possible, commodity 2 will be exported by country A. Assume that the rest of the world is endowed with factors 1 and 2 in equal proportions and that the rest of the world is a very large 'country', relative to country A. Show therefore that the price of commodity 2 must rise relative to commodity 1 in country A and that, accordingly, factor price 1 must fall relative to factor price 2. Show that this means that country A is moving towards a position of international 'equilibrium' where commodity prices are equal and hence where factor 1 must be subsidised if full employment is to be maintained. Hence justify the argument of section 16.4 emphasising the importance of knowing about possible equilibrium positions even though they may be unattainable without payment of a subsidy.

7. Show that payment of a subsidy to factor 1 in the circumstances of exercise 6 could improve welfare in country A by making the terms of trade more favourable than they would otherwise be.

8. Suppose, in the problem of exercise 6, that technique B had been given as

	Factor 1	Factor 2
Commodity 1	6	6
Commodity 2	6	$6\frac{1}{8}$

Show that, for both of the techniques actually observed, not only is $|a_{ij}|$ positive but the full Gale–Nikaidô condition (see appendix) is satisfied.

What computations on the observed data would you perform to satisfy yourself that factor prices could be less equal after trade than before, notwithstanding your observations?

17 Factor Taxation and Trade Union Negotiated Wage Differentials in an Open Economy

17.1 PARTIAL EQUILIBRIUM ANALYSIS – THE DANGERS OF SELF-DECEPTION

IN this chapter and that following we turn again to a general model of a trading economy and the effect upon it of certain kinds of tax or policy. Before we begin, however, it is proposed to give way once again to the temptation to introduce even more quasi-methodological comment.

Use of the more respectable collective noun 'school' rather than 'flock' poorly disguises the fact that, in the realm of ideas, scientists are often as sheep-like in their behaviour as other sections of the community. This is not a criticism; it is simply a reflection of the limitations which providence has seen fit to impose upon the human mind. Thinking is the most laborious work there is and (unlike the computer) we are permitted to think only one thought at a time. In the nature of things, therefore, a large part of what we read, or are told by others, has to be accepted without the same careful comparison of alternatives which is of necessity undertaken by the originator of the ideas under examination. The argument from authority plays a much larger part in our education that we may ordinarily be willing to admit.

At least two consequences of all this can be recognised by any student of the development of economic thought. First, it is not unknown for men of energy and self-confidence to encourage unwittingly the dissipation of a great deal of intellectual effort in directions which, to the observer at a different time or place, seem quite obviously unhelpful. Second, even in cases where some original thinker does succeed in opening up new and wider horizons, the excitement generated almost always induces naïvely exaggerated applications of the newly discovered method. Results are solemnly obtained and publicised which are so trivial, or, if not trivial, at least of such little empirical interest, that even their authors would be astonished to see anything made of them were it not for the fact that the techniques used in their development are currently fashionable.

The present writer is, of course, as deeply involved in all these difficulties as anyone else, and his prophetic utterances are backed by no special authority. Nevertheless it is possible to make out a case for supposing that future generations will note in operation at the present time both of the phenomena referred to in the previous paragraph.

Evidence of the over-enthusiastic application of particular techniques is to be found in earlier chapters of this book, where we have already commented upon the surfeit of 'theorems' developing sufficient conditions for this or that to occur which continue to be presented to students with great seriousness even though it is already known that in the real community in which we live (or any other we can imagine) such conditions cannot be and are not satisfied. Interest in theorems of this kind is most likely to be the temporary consequence of the relatively recent discovery by economists of the very real power and usefulness of the most advanced mathematical methods. In the long run, however, it will be necessary to accept that even the most ingenious mathematical tautologies are no substitute for empirical laws properly related to the subject matter we purport to study, however pedestrian these may be. It seems likely that, in the end, the real contribution of the present generation will be shown to have been the general movement towards the development of highly complex computerised models combining theory with measurement, rather than the statement and proof of certain interesting but hardly relevant propositions which currently attract more attention than their content deserves.

More important still, there is the possibility that we are only just now finding our way out of a turning in the maze into which we followed our leaders in a charge so magnificent and so unthinking that a simile more apt than flocks of sheep would be lemmings in their annual dash over the cliff to drown in the sea. Towards the end of the last century a group of scholars came to believe that it is possible to discuss the effect upon the economy of some policy change or event by concentrating upon the centre of impact of that policy, at the same time supposing that any induced secondary changes are small enough to be neglected. For example, it would probably be argued by those who favour this kind of 'partial equilibrium analysis' that the effect of a tax upon, say, motor-cars could be analysed as follows. Since the tax is paid by the producer, he will try to recoup his loss by charging a higher price for any given level of output. But a higher price means consumers will buy less, so less is produced (at a cheaper cost since reducing output is supposed to reduce costs). Hence the consequences of the tax will be reduced output and sales at lower cost, but a higher selling price. As far as the effect on the motor-car industry is concerned, this, it is felt, is all we need to know.

What is ignored (quite consciously of course) is the fact that changed aggregate expenditure on motor-cars on the part of the consumer implies changed aggregate expenditure on other commodities, and consequently changes in the prices and production of other commodities. Furthermore, changes in the pattern of production in turn imply some redistribution of factor rewards which once more implies changes in the pattern of costs and hence in selling prices. These influences all react back upon the motor-car industry itself in an unpredictable way. How can we be sure that the final result is not something quite different from that suggested in the previous paragraph? The answer is not only that we cannot be sure but also that in a disturbing number of cases precisely the contrary can be shown to hold.

It ought of course to be emphasised that criticism of the 'partial' method of analysis is not necessarily a criticism of the individuals who developed it, although it should most certainly be taken as a criticism of those who continue to employ it in our present state of knowledge. Indeed, most of the preamble of this chapter is intended to lead up precisely to this point. Partial equilibrium analysis developed logically from the attempt by earlier thinkers to proceed by tracing a chain of causation from the initial policy impact step by step as far as it could be followed. What is remarkable is not the failure of our predecessors to discover that the chain of causation had sometimes to be abandoned at a point too early to permit analysis free from error, but the very great ingenuity which enabled them to get as far as they did without the mathematical tools now available.

On the other hand it is hoped that the reader who pursues the present chapter to the end will come to share the view that even the strong words above do not in fact overstate the case against the partial approach. The present writer, himself trained in the method in common with most of his generation, has, over the years, experienced a growing and frightening realisation of the extent to which he has misled himself and perhaps others. The application of more powerful general equilibrium techniques to standard problems again and again seems to show that we do not know what we thought we knew. And little comfort can be found in the thought that a high percentage of those whose duty and privilege it is to try to frame British economic policy at the present time are directly or indirectly products of the same school.

The purpose of this chapter is to consider a class of possible policies where partial equilibrium analysis is particularly dangerous; to comment upon a special application of one such policy, reflecting upon the reason why it seems to have been thought that it would succeed; then finally to apply the techniques of this book to show that it may very well have been misapplied, or at least that it could have been applied without full knowledge of its possible consequences.

17.2 DIFFERENTIAL FACTOR TAXATION – TRADE UNION MAINTAINED DIFFERENTIALS

The recent past has seen in the United Kingdom the introduction of a 'Selective Employment Tax', that is, a tax which is imposed on labour in a selected group of industries. Not all labour is taxed in general, only that employed in one sector of the economy. It should be especially noted that this is equivalent (assuming a negligible income redistribution effect on the pattern of demand) to the successful maintenance by a powerful trade union of a permanent wage differential paid exclusively to its own members. It follows that the analysis below is applicable to a wide range of situations common to most countries.

Consider as an example the possible motives for the introduction of the British Selective Employment Tax. It is true of course that Treasury officials in any government will always welcome any revenue-raising device if the slightest excuse for it can be found; but in this instance other desirable consequences have been much emphasised. U.K. exports consist largely of manufactured products, whilst the service industries cannot in the nature of things export. To increase exports it is necessary to produce more exportables. It was argued, therefore, that a tax on labour in the service industries would

    (i) increase costs in the service industries, and hence
   (ii) increase prices, and hence
  (iii) reduce demand and hence supply, and so
  (iv) cause a reduction in the demand for labour in the service industries which accordingly
   (v) increases the supply of labour to export industries, and
  (vi) increases the supply of exportables and exports.

The word which has become fashionable is 'redeployment' of labour.

The argument above is evidently a piece of partial analysis of the worst kind. Obviously a tax on labour in one special use will cause some adjustment of all factor prices net of tax. But it is hard even to guess what will be the exact consequence of this on commodity prices and outputs without lengthy analysis of a suitably chosen general model. Furthermore, even if we suppose that the tax collected is spent just as it would have been spent by the untaxed consumer, there is bound nevertheless to be a significant change in the real terms of trade and hence of real welfare. This must in turn affect the pattern of demand and supply in a complicated and scarcely obvious way.

It is the view of the present writer that no answer can as yet be given to the question 'What will be the effect on sales and output of any kind of differential factor taxation?' and that no satisfactory answer will ever be given until a multi-sector computerised model has been constructed able accurately to simulate the precise working of the economy we are investigating.

These are strong words which need to be justified. On the other hand if the partial equilibrium view is correct, and if it is really true that secondary effects can be neglected, then it must be true also for the simplest model we might construct in general equilibrium terms, that is, the partial conclusion must hold whether secondary effects are included or not. The simplest model contradicting the partial conclusion therefore, is sufficient refutation of the method unless it can be shown that such a naïve model possesses features not typical of the real economy, the removal of which would reverse the conclusions. We shall show that a naïve model does not work and so maintain our agnostic view until such time as a more realistic analogue can be developed to supersede it.

Consider first a world with two commodities only, importables and exportables, just as in Book I. Let two countries be in a trading relation with both commodities produced in both countries. As throughout Book II, we keep the notation q for commodity prices and p for factor prices, using primes to denote 'belonging to the foreign country'. This time, however, p must denote the factor price net of factor-taxation or trade union differential. We suppose in particular that country 1 imposes a selective employment tax on factor 2 used in the production of commodity 2. Our object is to determine whether more or less labour is used in commodity 1 as a consequence. It will be of interest also to look at changes in welfare and the quantity of exports, since these are relevant to the normative argument from which we began. Once again also we emphasise that, although we have chosen to work in the context of a differential tax, results apply equally to trade union activity. We shall demonstrate implicitly the fact that the maintenance of an artificially high wage rate by collective bargaining does not after all necessarily imply reduced employment in the industry concerned. This may in some quarters be thought to be a very odd conclusion.

17.3 THE SIGN OF THE SUPPLY RESPONSE TO FACTOR TAXATION – PRICES CONSTANT

As a preliminary we investigate the properties of a new supply response. Intuitively we should now expect the rate t_2 of tax on factor 2 used in commodity 2 to appear in supply functions so that

$$S_i = S_i(q_1, q_2, t_2) \qquad (17.3.1)$$

We have therefore an important and interesting set of supply responses $\partial S_i/\partial t_2$ which measure the rate of change in supply of the ith commodity due to the tax change or change in negotiated wage differential if commodity prices remain constant. To find the properties of $\partial S_i/\partial t_2$ we need to inquire more precisely into the derivation of (17.3.1).

Consider first the cost equations

$$q_i = p_1 a_{i1} + p_2(1 + t_2)a_{i2} \quad (i = 1,2) \qquad (17.3.2)$$

Provided we have the same number of factors as commodities, as in this case, the equations (17.3.2) may be solved to give factor prices (net) as function of commodity prices and t_2.

Again we have the input/output equations

$$\left. \begin{array}{l} A_1 = S_1 a_{11} + S_2 a_{21} \\ A_2 = S_1 a_{12} + S_2 a_{22} \end{array} \right\} \qquad (17.3.3)$$

(where A_i is factor endowment) which may be solved to give supply equations

$$S_2 = \frac{\begin{vmatrix} a_{11} & A_1 \\ a_{12} & A_2 \end{vmatrix}}{|a_{ij}|} \qquad (17.3.4)$$

where $|a_{ij}|$ is the usual determinant of input coefficients.

As in earlier chapters, (17.3.4) gives supply as a function of net factor prices and the tax (or wage differential, henceforth referred to as tax), since the input coefficients a_{ij} are each functions of net factor prices and tax. Thus, since each net factor price is a function of commodity prices and tax, substitution in (17.3.4) will give the functions (17.3.1). But note especially that the $\partial S_2/\partial t_2$ which is the response from equation (17.3.4) is not the same as the response $\partial S_2/\partial t_2$ from equation (17.3.1), for the former assumes net *factor* prices constant whilst the latter assumes *commodity* prices constant. To deduce information on the sign of the $\partial S_i/\partial t_2$ of (17.3.1) is a relatively complex problem which we must now face armed with the knowledge of how (17.3.1) is derived.

Obviously the S_2 of (17.3.4) is the same as the S_2 of (17.3.1), so that we may equate changes. To find the $\partial S_2/\partial t_2$ of (17.3.1), therefore, it is sufficient to find the total change which occurs in the right-hand side of (17.3.4) whenever p_1, p_2 and t_2 change in such a way as to keep q_1 and q_2 constant. Consider therefore changes in (17.3.2) as follows:

$$dq_i = p_1 da_{i1} + p_2(1 + t_2)da_{i2} + a_{i1} dp_1 + (1 + t_2)a_{i2} dp_2 + p_2 a_{i2} dt_2$$

As in earlier chapters the minimising of cost ensures that the first two terms of the right-hand side of this equation sum to zero. Setting dq_1 and dq_2 at zero, therefore, and assuming that t_2 is initially zero we have

$$0 = a_{11} dp_1 + a_{12} dp_2$$

and

$$-p_2 a_{22} dt_2 = a_{21} dp_1 + a_{22} dp_2$$

$$(17.3.5)$$

(It will be recalled of course that t does not occur in the first equation in (17.3.5) since no factor used in commodity 2 is taxed.) (17.3.5) may be solved to obtain dp_1/dt_2 and dp_2/dt_2 as follows:

$$\frac{dp_1}{dt_2} = \frac{p_2 a_{22} a_{12}}{|a_{ij}|}$$

$$\frac{dp_2}{dt_2} = -\frac{p_2 a_{22} a_{11}}{|a_{ij}|}$$

$$(17.3.6)$$

We now have the rates of change of net factor prices required to keep commodity prices constant (i.e. zero dq_i).

To avoid confusion, let us now write ϕ for the right-hand side of (17.3.4). ϕ is of course a function of p_1, p_2 and t and is identically equal to S_2. This leads to the result

$$\frac{\partial S_2}{\partial t_2} = \frac{\partial \phi}{\partial p_1}\frac{dp_1}{dt_2} + \frac{\partial \phi}{\partial p_2}\frac{dp_2}{dt_2} + \frac{\partial \phi}{\partial t_2}$$

$$(17.3.7)$$

which may be simplified as follows. First note a property of the function ϕ as defined by (17.3.4). Each a_{ij} in (17.3.4) depends only on the factor price ratio p_1/p_2 and not upon the absolute prices. The chosen a_{ij}s are unaffected if all factor prices are changed proportionately, since they are selected to minimise cost. Evidently a minimum-cost technique (say a) for a set of prices p must also be minimum-cost for a set of prices λp, where λ is any positive constant, for if a lower-cost technique (say $\bar{a}$) existed, cost would be $\lambda p\bar{a}$ and cost at prices p using the same technique would be $p\bar{a}$, which must be less than pa, contradicting the assumption that pa is minimum-cost for prices p.

In technical terms, we say that the function ϕ is homogeneous of order zero and hence possesses the property

$$p_1 \frac{\partial \phi}{\partial p_1} + p_2 \frac{\partial \phi}{\partial p_2} = 0 \qquad (17.3.8)$$

This is a well-known mathematical result which we have had occasion to use before in connection with demand functions (section 7.5) and with which any student of economics must soon become familiar. No further explanation therefore will be offered here, the reader with doubts being referred to R. G. D. Allen, *Mathematical Analysis for Economists*, pp. 315–19[1]. One special point must be made, however. The result (17.3.8) holds equally when a tax t_2 is introduced provided the number t_2 is defined to be a proportion of the factor price p_2 and not itself a sum of money (see (17.3.2)). The reader should check for himself that the argument leading to (17.3.8) follows the same lines when the gross cost to the producer of factor 2 is $p_2(1 + t_2)$ and not simply p_2.

From (17.3.8) we note that

$$\frac{\partial \phi}{\partial p_1} = -\frac{p_2}{p_1} \frac{\partial \phi}{\partial p_2}$$

which when substituted in (17.3.7) yields

$$\frac{\partial S_2}{\partial t_2} = \frac{\partial \phi}{\partial p_2} \left(-\frac{p_2}{p_1} \frac{dp_1}{dt_2} + \frac{dp_2}{dt_2} \right) + \frac{\partial \phi}{\partial t_2} \qquad (17.3.9)$$

Using (17.3.6) in (17.3.9), we may write

$$\frac{\partial S_2}{\partial t_2} = -p_2 \frac{\partial \phi}{\partial p_2} \left(\frac{a_{22}p_2 a_{12} + a_{22}p_1 a_{11}}{p_1 |a_{ij}|} \right) + \frac{\partial \phi}{\partial t_2} \qquad (17.3.10)$$

which, in view of (17.3.2) and because initially t_2 is zero, can be reduced to

$$\frac{\partial S_2}{\partial t_2} = -p_2 \frac{\partial \phi}{\partial p_2} \frac{a_{22}q_1}{p_1 |a_{ij}|} + \frac{\partial \phi}{\partial t_2} \qquad (17.3.11)$$

It is now necessary to consider the properties of $\partial\phi/\partial p_2$. Unfortunately we have here to face a piece of mathematics more complicated than anything yet encountered. We have in fact to express the response rate $\partial\phi/\partial p_2$ in terms of response rates $\partial a_{ij}/\partial p_2$, that is, the response rates of the functions a_{ij} which are dependent on factor prices. The reader not familiar with the technique may either accept the result we are about to write direct from (17.3.4) or multiply both sides of (17.3.4) by $|a_{ij}|$ and evaluate the determinants, when the problem will reduce to one of the type previously treated in this book. What is finally obtained will be

$$\frac{\partial \phi}{\partial p_2} = \frac{\begin{vmatrix} \dfrac{\partial a_{11}}{\partial p_2} & A_1 \\[2ex] \dfrac{\partial a_{12}}{\partial p_2} & A_2 \end{vmatrix} - S_2 \begin{vmatrix} \dfrac{\partial a_{11}}{\partial p_2} & a_{21} \\[2ex] \dfrac{\partial a_{12}}{\partial p_2} & a_{22} \end{vmatrix} - S_2 \begin{vmatrix} a_{11} & \dfrac{\partial a_{21}}{\partial p_2} \\[2ex] a_{12} & \dfrac{\partial a_{22}}{\partial p_2} \end{vmatrix}}{|a_{ij}|} \qquad (17.3.12)$$

Replacing A_1 and A_2 with the right-hand side of (17.3.3) and using the fact that multiplication of a determinant by S_2 means multiplying every element in a column, terms one and two of the numerator of (17.3.12) may be collapsed into one term as under.

$$\frac{\partial \phi}{\partial p_2} = \frac{S_1 \begin{vmatrix} \dfrac{\partial a_{11}}{\partial p_2} & a_{11} \\[2ex] \dfrac{\partial a_{12}}{\partial p_2} & a_{12} \end{vmatrix} - S_2 \begin{vmatrix} a_{11} & \dfrac{\partial a_{21}}{\partial p_2} \\[2ex] a_{12} & \dfrac{\partial a_{22}}{\partial p_2} \end{vmatrix}}{|a_{ij}|} \qquad (17.3.13)$$

We also know that

$$\left. \begin{aligned} p_1 \frac{\partial a_{11}}{\partial p_2} + p_2 \frac{\partial a_{12}}{\partial p_2} &= 0 \\[2ex] p_1 \frac{\partial a_{21}}{\partial p_2} + p_2(1 + t_2) \frac{\partial a_{22}}{\partial p_2} &= 0 \end{aligned} \right\} \qquad (17.3.14)$$

and

by an argument already encountered many times (see for example (14.2.1)). Furthermore, a well-known property of determinants permits us to multiply any row by a number and add to any other row without changing the value of the determinant. Hence, remembering t_2 is initially zero, multiplying the denominator and row one of each of the terms of the numerator of (17.3.13) by p_1, at the same time adding $p_2(1 + t_2)$ times row two, yields

$$\frac{\partial \phi}{\partial p_2} = \frac{S_1 \begin{vmatrix} 0 & q_1 \\ \dfrac{\partial a_{12}}{\partial p_2} & a_{12} \end{vmatrix} - S_2 \begin{vmatrix} q_1 & 0 \\ a_{12} & \dfrac{\partial a_{22}}{\partial p_2} \end{vmatrix}}{p_1 |a_{ij}|}$$

$$= \frac{-q_1 S_1 \dfrac{\partial a_{12}}{\partial p_2} - S_2 q_1 \dfrac{\partial a_{22}}{\partial p_2}}{p_1 |a_{ij}|} \tag{17.3.15}$$

when we recall (17.3.2).

We have now to find the response $\partial \phi / \partial t_2$. As with $\partial \phi / \partial p_2$, this may be obtained direct from (17.3.4). The reader should remember in this exercise that the techniques a_{11}, a_{12} used in the production of commodity 1 are not influenced by t_2 since factors used in commodity 1 are not taxed. We have therefore, from (17.3.4),

$$\frac{\partial \phi}{\partial t_2} = \frac{-S_2 \begin{vmatrix} a_{11} & \dfrac{\partial a_{21}}{\partial t_2} \\ a_{12} & \dfrac{\partial a_{22}}{\partial t_2} \end{vmatrix}}{|a_{ij}|} \tag{17.3.16}$$

Now note that changing the tax rate t_2 must have a very similar effect on the technique chosen for commodity 2 as a change in the net factor price p_2. Since the cost of factor 2 is $p_2(1 + t_2)$, the same proportionate change in either p_2 or $(1 + t_2)$ must have precisely the same effect. Assuming t_2 is initially zero, therefore, it follows that

$$\frac{\partial a_{21}}{\partial t_2} = p_2 \frac{\partial a_{21}}{\partial p_2} \quad \text{and} \quad \frac{\partial a_{22}}{\partial t_2} = p_2 \frac{\partial a_{22}}{\partial p_2}$$

Thus, by the method already outlined, (17.3.16) can be reduced to

$$\frac{\partial \phi}{\partial t_2} = \frac{-p_2 S_2 q_1 \dfrac{\partial a_{22}}{\partial p_2}}{p_1 |a_{ij}|} \tag{17.3.17}$$

which is the same as the second term of $p_2 \dfrac{\partial \phi}{\partial p_2}$ (see (17.3.15)). (17.3.15)

and (17.3.17) can now be put in (17.3.11) to give

$$\frac{\partial S_2}{\partial t_2} = \frac{p_2 a_{22} q_1^2 S_1 \frac{\partial a_{12}}{\partial p_2}}{p_1^2 |a_{ij}|^2} + \frac{p_2 a_{22} q_1^2 S_2 \frac{\partial a_{22}}{\partial p_2}}{p_1^2 |a_{ij}|^2} - \frac{p_2 S_2 q_1 \frac{\partial a_{22}}{\partial p_2}}{p_1 |a_{ij}|} \quad (17.3.18)$$

In order to put all terms of (17.3.18) over the same denominator, it is clear that we must multiply the numerator of term three by $p_1 |a_{ij}|$. It will be more convenient, however, if we convert this before so doing. Thus

$$p_1 |a_{ij}| = \begin{vmatrix} p_1 a_{11} & p_1 a_{21} \\ a_{12} & a_{22} \end{vmatrix}$$

which, adding p_2 times row two to row one, again remembering t_2 is zero, may be written

$$\begin{vmatrix} q_1 & q_2 \\ a_{12} & a_{22} \end{vmatrix} = q_1 a_{22} - q_2 a_{12} \quad (17.3.19)$$

It can now be seen that when term three of (17.3.18) is multiplied by (17.3.19), one resulting term cancels with term two of (17.3.18), leaving

$$\frac{\partial S_2}{\partial t_2} = \frac{a_{22} q_1^2 S_1 p_2 \frac{\partial a_{12}}{\partial p_2} + a_{12} q_1 q_2 S_2 p_2 \frac{\partial a_{22}}{\partial p_2}}{p_1^2 |a_{ij}|^2} \quad (17.3.20)$$

We are now in a position to consider whether the sign of $\partial S_2/\partial t_2$ is known.

In the first place the denominator is unambiguously positive, being the square of a number. The sign therefore depends upon the sign of the numerator. All elements of the numerator must be positive except $\partial a_{12}/\partial p_2$ and $\partial a_{22}/\partial p_2$, both of which we know to be negative, for a rise in the price of factor 2 with production and all other prices constant must induce a decrease in its use both in commodity 1 and commodity 2. This is the inevitable consequence of the cost-minimisation assumption. In short, it is clear that $\partial S_2/\partial t_2$ must be negative in sign.

This looks like a new and powerful qualitative result of great significance, *but it is not*. Indeed, the whole conclusion, like so many which involve factor prices, is simply the consequence of an over-simplified model. The result does not hold as soon as we introduce more than two factors of production, and our only purpose in introducing it is to show that it is not true in any realistic case. To demonstrate this, it is convenient first to develop the result (17.3.20) in a slightly less informative way.

Consider again the two functions

$$S_2 \equiv S_2(q_1, q_2, t_2) \equiv \phi(p_1, p_2, t_2) \qquad (17.3.21)$$

Proceeding in precisely the opposite way to that used to derive (17.3.7), we may write

$$\frac{\partial \phi}{\partial t_2} = \frac{\partial S_2}{\partial q_1} \frac{dq_1}{dt_2} + \frac{\partial S_2}{\partial q_2} \frac{dq_2}{dt_2} + \frac{\partial S_2}{\partial t_2} \qquad (17.3.22)$$

where the response rates dq_1/dt_2 and dq_2/dt_2 are those which occur when t_2 is changed keeping p_1 and p_2 constant. Evidently, when p_1 and p_2 are constant there is no change in q_1 since no tax is charged on commodity 1. Furthermore, from the argument leading to (17.3.5) it is easy to see that dq_2/dt_2 is simply $p_2 a_{22}$. Thus we have from (17.3.22)

$$\frac{\partial S_2}{\partial t_2} = - p_2 a_{22} \frac{\partial S_2}{\partial q_2} + \frac{\partial \phi}{\partial t_2} \qquad (17.3.23)$$

which is a fundamental result likely to be of considerable value. We know the sign of the first term of (17.3.23) since $\partial S_2/\partial q_2$ must be positive (Chapter 15). On the other hand, from (17.3.17) we note that the sign of $\partial \phi/\partial t_2$ is unknown, depending on $|a_{ij}|$, that is, in the two-factor case, on factor intensities.

At first sight the result (17.3.23) seems to contradict (17.3.20), from which we saw that $\partial S_2/\partial t_2$ must be negative in the two-factor case. But of course this is not so. What (17.3.20) proves is simply that the magnitude of the first term of (17.3.23) must be greater than the magnitude of the second so that the sign of term two is irrelevant. We have to show in fact that this is necessarily true only in the two-factor case, and to this end we consider an alternative way of writing $\partial S_2/\partial q_2$.

It can now be revealed that most of the foregoing exercise was designed to enable us to assert, without too much irritation to the reader, that by the use of more advanced mathematical methods than we have so far explained† it may be shown that

---

† The result (17.3.24) may actually be obtained by writing

$$\frac{\partial S_2}{\partial q_2} = \frac{\partial \phi}{\partial p_1} \frac{\partial p_1}{\partial q_2} + \frac{\partial \phi}{\partial p_2} \frac{\partial p_2}{\partial q_2}$$

An expression for each $\partial \phi/\partial p_i$ can be found by taking changes in (17.3.4) as for (17.3.12), whilst $\partial p_i/\partial q_2$ comes from taking changes in cost equations as for (17.3.5). Manipulation of these results leads to the required expression (17.3.24).

$$\frac{\partial S_2}{\partial q_2} = \frac{S_1 \begin{vmatrix} 0 & a_{11} & a_{12} \\ a_{11} & \dfrac{\partial a_{11}}{\partial p_1} & \dfrac{\partial a_{11}}{\partial p_2} \\ a_{12} & \dfrac{\partial a_{12}}{\partial p_1} & \dfrac{\partial a_{12}}{\partial p_2} \end{vmatrix} + S_2 \begin{vmatrix} 0 & a_{11} & a_{12} \\ a_{11} & \dfrac{\partial a_{21}}{\partial p_1} & \dfrac{\partial a_{21}}{\partial p_2} \\ a_{12} & \dfrac{\partial a_{22}}{\partial p_1} & \dfrac{\partial a_{22}}{\partial p_2} \end{vmatrix}}{|a_{ij}|^2} \tag{17.3.24}$$

If this result, when put into (17.3.23), leads back to (17.3.20), it, and its generalisation to be introduced later, will no doubt appear more acceptable than would have been the case if the argument leading to (17.3.20) had been omitted. One further point about (17.3.24) must be added. From that part of the theory of production not treated in this book, it is generally known that

$$\frac{\partial a_{1i}}{\partial p_j} = \frac{\partial a_{1j}}{\partial p_i} \dagger \tag{17.3.25}$$

Thus each determinant in (17.3.24) may be treated in the manner of (17.3.13) (see (17.3.15)), so that, multiplying row two of the first term by p_1 and adding p_2 times row three, term one reduces to

$$\frac{S_1 \begin{vmatrix} 0 & a_{11} & a_{12} \\ q_1 & 0 & 0 \\ a_{12} & \dfrac{\partial a_{12}}{\partial p_1} & \dfrac{\partial a_{12}}{\partial p_2} \end{vmatrix}}{p_1 |a_{ij}|^2} \tag{17.3.26}$$

A further reduction of (17.3.26) can now be seen to be possible using (17.3.25). Thus multiplying column two by p_1, adding to it p_2 times column three, (17.3.26) becomes

$$\frac{S_1 \begin{vmatrix} 0 & q_1 & a_{12} \\ q_1 & 0 & 0 \\ a_{12} & 0 & \dfrac{\partial a_{12}}{\partial p_2} \end{vmatrix}}{p_1^2 |a_{ij}|^2}$$

which when expanded can be seen to be

$$\frac{-q_1^2 S_1 \dfrac{\partial a_{12}}{\partial p_2}}{p_1^2 |a_{ij}|^2}$$

† See R. G. D. Allen, *Mathematical Analysis for Economists*, pp. 502–9 [1].

Similar treatment of term two of (17.3.24) yields

$$-a_{22}\frac{\partial S_2}{\partial q_2} = \frac{a_{22}q_1^2 S_1 \dfrac{\partial a_{12}}{\partial p_2} + a_{22}q_1^2 S_2 \dfrac{\partial a_{22}}{\partial p_2}}{p_1^2 \,|\, a_{ij}\,|^2}$$

which on comparison of (17.3.18), (17.3.17) and (17.3.23) shows (17.3.23) and (17.3.20) to be equivalent as alleged. Hence use of the form (17.3.24) is justified. We note that we have shown incidentally that the two terms of (17.3.24) are both positive, a fact which immediately generalises to many dimensions. Indeed, the convenience of the form (17.3.24) is precisely that it is immediately generalisable. Thus we assert that in the three-factor case where the tax is imposed on factor 3 used in commodity 3, we should have

$$\frac{\partial S_3}{\partial q_3} = -\sum_{i=1}^{3} S_i \frac{\begin{vmatrix} 0 & 0 & a_{11} & a_{12} & a_{13} \\ 0 & 0 & a_{21} & a_{22} & a_{23} \\ a_{11} & a_{21} & \dfrac{\partial a_{i1}}{\partial p_1} & \dfrac{\partial a_{i1}}{\partial p_2} & \dfrac{\partial a_{i1}}{\partial p_3} \\ a_{12} & a_{22} & \dfrac{\partial a_{i2}}{\partial p_1} & \dfrac{\partial a_{i2}}{\partial p_2} & \dfrac{\partial a_{i2}}{\partial p_3} \\ a_{13} & a_{23} & \dfrac{\partial a_{i3}}{\partial p_1} & \dfrac{\partial a_{i3}}{\partial p_2} & \dfrac{\partial a_{i3}}{\partial p_3} \end{vmatrix}}{|\,a_{ij}\,|^2} \qquad (17.3.27)$$

We do not attempt to develop here the mathematics necessary to prove this generalisation, since it would simply add to the tedium of an already tedious section without at the same time contributing very much to our understanding of the economic problem presently concerning us. It is to be hoped that the reader will be ready to accept the result on comparison with (17.3.24),† which has been proved. The manner of generalisation is obvious.

† The reader trained in mathematical economics will observe that in each case the functions (17.3.24) and (17.3.27) consist of the weighted sum of the Hessian determinants of the production functions bordered by certain inputs a_{ij}. Minimising cost is of course equivalent to maximising production subject to a cost constraint. The Hessian determinant is therefore the discriminant of a negative semi-definite form and the borderings arise because of the constraining functions. The sign of each determinant is therefore positive. $\dfrac{\partial S_3}{\partial q_3}$ geometrically speaking is simply the weighted sum of the rate of curvature of isoproduct surfaces in a direction determined by the conditions q_1 and q_2 constant.

In the three-dimensional case we have also, corresponding to (17.3.23),

$$\frac{\partial S_3}{\partial t_3} = -p_3 a_{33} \frac{\partial S_3}{\partial q_3} + \frac{\partial \phi}{\partial t_3} \qquad (17.3.28)$$

the manner of proof being exactly the same as that used to deduce (17.3.23). We have now to show that, unlike the two-factor case, term two of (17.3.28) can, and quite ordinarily will, be as large as or larger than term one. The sign of $\partial S_3/\partial t_3$ is quite indeterminate on *a priori* grounds.

We note first that terms one and two of (17.3.27) contain only the rates of change of inputs in commodities 1 and 2, whereas term three contains only rates of change of inputs in commodity 3. To construct an example therefore with positive $\partial S_3/\partial t_3$, it is possible to choose S_1 and S_2 or some $\partial a_{1i}/\partial p_j$ or $\partial a_{2i}/\partial p_j$ appropriately so as to ensure that only the third term of (17.3.27) is significantly large numerically. Choice of these numbers does not affect the magnitude of term three, since they do not appear in term three, nor do they in any way determine the numbers which do appear in term three. With negligible terms one and two, all that is necessary for the required example is to show that term three itself need not be larger than $\partial \phi/\partial t_3$ as it was in the two-dimensional case.

Consider first the value of $\partial \phi/\partial t_3$ which may be obtained from the equation for S_3, namely

$$S_3 = \frac{\begin{vmatrix} a_{11} & a_{21} & A_1 \\ a_{12} & a_{22} & A_2 \\ a_{13} & a_{23} & A_3 \end{vmatrix}}{|a_{ij}|} = \phi$$

Taking changes in the manner described in the argument leading to (17.3.16), remembering that t_3 does not affect commodities 1 and 2, we have

$$\frac{\partial \phi}{\partial t_3} = \frac{-S_3 \begin{vmatrix} a_{11} & a_{21} & \dfrac{\partial a_{31}}{\partial t_3} \\ a_{12} & a_{22} & \dfrac{\partial a_{32}}{\partial t_3} \\ a_{13} & a_{23} & \dfrac{\partial a_{33}}{\partial t_3} \end{vmatrix}}{|a_{ij}|} \qquad (17.3.29)$$

which may be compared with (17.3.16). Evidently the sign of (17.3.29) does not now depend only on the sign of $|a_{ij}|$, for the sign of the numerator cannot be inferred from what we know. On the other hand, since

$$\frac{\partial a_{3i}}{\partial t_3} \equiv p_3 \frac{\partial a_{3i}}{\partial p_3}$$

fixing numbers for the elements of (17.3.29) will impose restrictions on the numbers we may choose for the third term of (17.3.27), so some further argument is needed.

In search of an example we reduce the third term of (17.3.27) in the now familiar manner, that is, by multiplying row and column three each by p_1 and adding p_2 row four, p_3 row five, p_2 column four, and p_3 column five respectively. This yields

$$-S_3 \frac{\begin{vmatrix} 0 & 0 & q_1 & a_{12} & a_{13} \\ 0 & 0 & q_2 & a_{22} & a_{23} \\ q_1 & q_2 & 0 & 0 & 0 \\ a_{12} & a_{22} & 0 & \dfrac{\partial a_{32}}{\partial p_2} & \dfrac{\partial a_{32}}{\partial p_3} \\ a_{13} & a_{23} & 0 & \dfrac{\partial a_{33}}{\partial p_2} & \dfrac{\partial a_{33}}{\partial p_3} \end{vmatrix}}{p_1^2 |a_{ij}|^2} \tag{17.3.30}$$

Now let

$$q_1 = q_2 = a_{12} = a_{22} = 1$$

in which case (17.3.30) reduces to

$$-S_3 \frac{\left(\begin{vmatrix} 1 & a_{13} \\ 1 & a_{23} \end{vmatrix} \right)^2 \dfrac{\partial a_{32}}{\partial p_2}}{p_1^2 |a_{ij}|^2}$$

which is positive in sign since $\partial a_{32}/\partial p_2$ is negative. In this special case, therefore, the first term (negative) of $\partial S_3/\partial t_3$ (equation (17.3.28)) consists of two terms chosen small and

$$p_3 S_3 a_{33} \frac{\left(\begin{vmatrix} 1 & a_{13} \\ 1 & a_{23} \end{vmatrix} \right)^2 \dfrac{\partial a_{32}}{\partial p_2}}{p_1^2 |a_{ij}|^2} \tag{17.3.31}$$

(17.3.31) is now negative as we would expect. Its magnitude is to be compared with $\partial \phi/\partial t_3$ which, multiplying top and bottom of (17.3.29) by $|a_{ij}|$ and reducing in the usual way, may be written

$$
\frac{\partial \phi}{\partial t_3} = \frac{-p_3 S_3 \left\{ \begin{vmatrix} q_1 & q_2 & q_3 \\ a_{12} & a_{22} & a_{32} \\ a_{13} & a_{23} & a_{33} \end{vmatrix} \right\} \left\{ \begin{vmatrix} q_1 & q_2 & 0 \\ a_{12} & a_{22} & \frac{\partial a_{32}}{\partial p_3} \\ a_{13} & a_{23} & \frac{\partial a_{33}}{\partial p_3} \end{vmatrix} \right\}}{p_1^2 |a_{ij}|^2}
$$

which in the special case chosen reduces to

$$
\frac{\partial \phi}{\partial t_3} = \frac{-p_3 S_3 (a_{32} - q_3) \left\{ \begin{vmatrix} 1 & a_{13} \\ 1 & a_{23} \end{vmatrix} \right\}^2 \frac{\partial a_{32}}{\partial p_3}}{p_1^2 |a_{ij}|^2} \tag{17.3.32}
$$

Given $q_3 > a_{32}$, (17.3.32) must be positive in sign, for $\partial a_{32}/\partial p_3$ will ordinarily be positive. For (17.3.32) to outweigh (17.3.31), leaving $\partial S_3/\partial t_3$ positive, we need in addition that the magnitude of $(a_{32} - q_3)$ $(\partial a_{32}/\partial p_3)$ should be greater than the magnitude of $a_{33}(\partial a_{32}/\partial p_2)$. This result is easily achieved by setting q_3 arbitrarily large. The fact that

$$
p_1 a_{31} + p_2 a_{32} + p_3 a_{33} = q_3
$$

does not preclude us from such a choice, for the only restrictions implied by our earlier selection of numbers is simply that p_2 should be less than unity. p_1, p_3, a_{31} and a_{33} may be any number we choose. Our example, which satisfies all known economic restrictions, is therefore a counter-example to the proposition that $\partial S_3/\partial t_3$ *must* be negative.

17.4 THE COMMON SENSE OF FACTOR PRICE DIFFERENTIALS IN GENERAL

The agnostic conclusion obtained with so much difficulty above is of such importance that it bears both repetition and some further common-sense discussion. We have shown that, when taxes on factors or other differentials exist, supply must be dependent not only on commodity prices but also on the tax rates or differentials, and this is true whether the tax is imposed upon factors used in the production of the commodity under consideration or some other. We have shown also that neither the magnitude nor the direction of the change in supply due to a tax or differential change with commodity prices held constant can be inferred on *a priori* grounds. Since many economists might take a contrary view, can we see intuitively why our result makes sense?

Let us begin by repeating the argument as it might be presented following a partial equilibrium approach. 'A tax will evidently put up costs whatever the chosen level of production. As long therefore as rising supply implies rising cost (positive $\partial S/\partial q$—see Chapter 15), only a lower supply will leave total cost including tax, i.e. prices, unchanged. Supply at constant prices *must* fall therefore when a tax on a factor is imposed, contrary to the conclusion above.'

What is wrong with this superficial argument must be obvious to the reader who has come thus far in the study of general equilibrium models. A rise in the gross price of labour in some one industry will ordinarily lead to the substitution of other factors for labour in that industry and hence to the unemployment of labour. Labour thus freed cannot be taken into any other use unless there are variations in the level of production or in techniques of production (usually both) for other commodities. Both of these consequences imply cost changes for a given output; and cost rises with supply only *when all other costs are constant*, a proviso which we have shown to be violated in the case under consideration. Furthermore, new techniques of production in untaxed industries necessarily imply some change in factor prices before tax, which in turn affects costs and commodity prices in general. It is hardly surprising that the changes in supply needed to readjust costs to their original level are numbers which depend in a complex way on the set of available production techniques (production functions), and are, moreover, numbers whose sign and magnitude cannot be inferred on *a priori* grounds. This is the sum and substance of what we have proved up to this point.

To clinch the argument finally, consider intuitively why we might expect to get a definite result in two dimensions which nevertheless breaks down in three. Suppose labour in commodity 2 is taxed. Then in production of that commodity, capital, say, will be substituted for labour. If, for the moment, we suppose that output does not change, this means that some labour must be made redundant and some capital transferred from the first industry. Assuming that all factors are to be in full employment, therefore, the untaxed industry must take up the redundant labour to replace the lost capital – precisely the reverse of the happening in industry 2. Notice, however, that no change in total production of either commodity will occur, since in competitive equilibrium the shifting of factors of production from one use to another cannot raise output of one commodity without diminishing that of the other. Or, to put it another way, shifting factors from one use to another so as to leave output unchanged in one industry, must leave it unchanged in the other. If it were not so, a greater value of output could be attained, contrary to our understanding that competition maximises the value of output (Chapter 15).

But businessmen producing commodity 1 will be satisfied to produce with a more labour-intensive technique only if the net prices of factors (untaxed in commodity 1) change so as to make labour cheaper relatively. Note that the relative cheapening of labour (net) cannot go to the point where the gross price of labour (including tax) is also relatively cheaper than it was, for the producer of commodity 2, before tax. Hence the secondary relative factor price change cannot reverse the effect of the tax. It follows that, at the new factor prices and tax rate, commodity 2 will become relatively dearer. This is easily seen if we express commodity prices in terms of units of factor 1 (capital) by dividing cost equations by p_1 as follows:

$$\frac{q_1}{p_1} = a_{11} + \frac{p_2}{p_1} a_{12}$$

$$\frac{q_2}{p_1} = a_{21} + \frac{p_2 + t_2}{p_1} a_{22}$$

As we have established that $(p_2 + t_2)/p_1$ rises and p_2/p_1 falls, and as, from the cost-minimising condition, we know that small changes in technique do not change costs, it follows at once that q_2/p_1 rises whilst q_1/p_1 falls.

What this means is that, maintaining the pre-tax output, the effect of the tax *must* be to raise the gross price of the taxed commodity relatively. But with two commodities only we may choose the price of commodity 1 as numeraire and hold it constant. In such a case the condition 'all other prices constant' is satisfied and we may expect the cost of commodity 2 to rise as output rises. To restore costs to the pre-tax ratio, therefore, it is necessary for output 2 to fall and output 1 to rise. $\partial S_2/\partial t_2$ must be negative.

But all of this argument fails with three factors. Neither the direction of movement of factor prices nor relative commodity prices, given output, can be predicted. And even if it could, only one commodity can be selected as numeraire so that the second part of the argument above equally fails. Intuition can be made to confirm the mathematical results, although, unfortunately, this is usually the case only *after* the formal mathematics have underlined the essential changes to which attention is to be directed. Attempts to use intuition before the mathematics usually result in the practitioner getting both wrong.

17.5 THE COMMON SENSE OF THE BRITISH SELECTIVE EMPLOYMENT TAX IN PARTICULAR

So far we have been concerned only with the properties of supply functions. No particular question has been put, nor has any model been developed. Indeed, the real difficulty facing anyone wishing to comment more exactly upon the desirability or otherwise of a labour tax in a particular industry is to find out precisely what proposition he is after all required to test, for those in Britain in favour of S.E.T. have been neither unanimous nor consistent in their claims. Nevertheless, we may at least seize upon the word 'redeployment' which has figured so much in recent public statements and leave aside for the moment the question why it might be considered 'desirable' to 'redeploy' labour.

To encourage the reader to suspect that even the most ordinary model will show that a tax on labour in a particular industry could bring about a situation precisely the reverse of the intended redeployment, consider the following case. Suppose that the country introducing the policy is so small relative to the rest of the world that nothing that it can do will appreciably affect world prices, that is the real terms of trade. Suppose further that production functions are such that the response rate $\partial S_3/\partial t_3$ is positive and that three classes of goods, exportables, importables and non-traded services, are to be considered. Let the tax be imposed on labour used in the non-traded goods industry (commodity 3).

From the meaning of $\partial S_3/\partial t_3$, assumed to be positive, we deduce that if prices remain constant the production of non-traded goods must rise. But with no change in the real terms of trade and no change in aggregate spending this would imply an excess supply of the non-traded commodity. Hence its price must fall relatively. One would expect the final consequence of the tax to be an increased supply of the non-traded commodity with its price slightly lower. In other words the probability is that labour will have moved *out of* the production of traded goods and *into* the production of service commodities, contrary to intention. In the same way, if the change had been induced by successful bargaining by a trade union rather than by a tax, numbers employed in the industry concerned might have increased rather than diminished.

This last piece of analysis is, of course, precisely the kind of inexact literary argument which so often leads to error and which we have been at pains to disown. It may be desirable at once, therefore, to allay any doubts by confessing that it was written *after* the development of the mathematics which is to follow and not before. As explained above, it was introduced solely to convince the sceptic beforehand that the hard work we are about to undertake is worth while.

Having now shown that the 'redeployment' might be redeployment in the wrong direction, let us return to the question of what it could have been hoped it would achieve. It is essential to do this in order to be able to select the correct question to put to any model we might choose to set out.

At least two ideas have been expressed. First, we have the belief, already noted at the beginning of this chapter, that the transfer of labour to the export industries will somehow of itself lead to more exports without any ancillary policy. Second, one of the principal architects of the British Selective Employment Tax seems to have argued as follows: 'Growth occurs through technical improvements. New and exciting technical advances occur because an industry is growing. We learn in fact by doing. Hence if we can make an industry grow we shall make it grow all the more because of technical advance'. It is further claimed that this phenomenon is to be observed only in manufacturing industry and not in the provision of services. Hence if labour can be freed by taxation from the service industries to increase production in manufacturing, then we should in consequence harvest important advantages of technical invention.

We consider the second argument first. To the present writer this seems (a) not proven and (b) to depend upon the assumption that what we want to increase is some index of industrial production measuring physical product rather than welfare. To put it another way, what seems to be suggested is that if only we can be discouraged by taxation from producing what the consumer wants and induced to produce instead what the consumer does not want, then, because of the technical advance consequent upon this action, we can have even more of the things which we don't want.

But let us not argue point (b), for this questions only what we want and is not concerned with how we might get what we want. Let us accept, for the sake of argument, that we do wish to redeploy labour into manufacturing for whatever reason and turn to point (a). Will a tax on labour in the service industry inevitably achieve the desired result?

Evidently our proof that the sign of $\partial S_3/\partial t_3$ is unknown is not of itself an immediate counter-example to the argument under consideration, for our model so far explicitly assumes that there are *no* advantages to be gained from an increase in the size of an industry, contrary to the central point above. On the other hand the claim is that technical advance takes place only to the extent that manufacturing industry grows in response to the tax. If it does not grow, the advantages cannot be reaped, and the possibility that $\partial S_3/\partial t_3$ may be positive suggests that untaxed industries may contract instead of expand.

It may, of course, be objected that an example where $\partial S_3/\partial t_3$ is positive in a model which does not allow for technical change cannot be relevant to a model which does. But this is misguided criticism. It should be intuitively obvious that, even if it should turn out that economies of growth when incorporated in a model do influence results so as to lessen the likelihood of a positive $\partial S_3/\partial t_3$, then the final result is still a question of the *extent* to which it does so. One circumstance tends to increase $\partial S_3/\partial t_3$, another tends to diminish it. In such a case it is clear that by choosing a sufficiently small technical change factor, the required counter-example can easily be constructed. There is no loss of generality involved in keeping to our well-tried model at least for the present.

Furthermore, and much more important, the work above strongly suggests that the introduction of technical advance may just as easily operate one way as another. Besides reducing overall the amount of each input required to produce *unit* output, the ratios in which factors are used will, in general, also be affected by growth. Once again outputs will need to be adjusted to take up all available factors, just as in the case where the technique changes were induced by factor price changes alone. And as before, the magnitude and direction of such changes will be determined largely by the properties of the input matrix a_{ij} about which little is known *a priori*. In short, to develop a model incorporating technical change according to output would simply teach us that, *a priori*, nothing qualitative is known about the effect of a factor tax. It is for this reason, and not because it cannot be done, that no such development is attempted here.

On the other hand it is instructive to consider in more detail the first of the two stated objectives of redeployment, namely, the increase of exports and the improvement of the balance of payments. Evidently this depends upon the supposition that all that is needed to improve the balance of payments is to increase the supply of exportables. It is to be hoped that the reader who has come this far will be able immediately to recognise the naïvety of this belief. Shifting productive resources from one use to another without at the same time operating on the pattern of demand can do nothing but harm. So long as prices and aggregate expenditure remain the same, to produce more exportables at the expense of some other commodity will contribute precisely nothing to the solution of the balance of payments problem, for consumers will demand no more and no less than they demanded and purchased before the change. The only difference will be that what was formerly produced at home will now be obtained by exchange abroad for increased exports. Exports will indeed go up but so will imports *pari passu*. Nothing can be achieved without relative price changes. Supply adjustments are not enough.

Let us look at the problem another way. Suppose a balance of payments problem exists and suppose further that world supply equals world demand. This is the classical problem treated in Book I. Two things we know at once: first, there must be excess expenditure at home over and above the value of home production, and second, no balance of payments equilibrium can ever be attained until that excess demand is removed. In addition some adjustment of relative prices will ordinarily be required. We are well aware also from our study of tariff problems that the required price adjustments are in general different according to the pattern of taxation. Just as it is not a sensible question to ask whether the imposition of a tariff will by itself correct an imbalance of payments, it is not a sensible question to ask whether a factor tax might do so. Everything depends upon the accompanying policy and/or what occurs as a consequence of the *existence* of an imbalance.

In putting questions of this kind it is important to recognise that an imbalance cannot by definition be allowed to persist. In the end it must be removed by one means or another. Furthermore, a single operation like the imposition of a tariff or tax is not necessary to its removal; nor will it ordinarily, by itself, be sufficient. There are many ways of removing excess demand, and once removed the forces of competition should adjust prices as required. All that currency depreciation or taxation policy can do is (possibly) to hasten the price adjustment or *change its nature*. In particular, any taxation policy must change the nature of the price adjustment required. Whether, and in what sense, it will hasten these adjustments calls for more extended discussion.

Price adjustment ordinarily takes place as a consequence of the competitive process, which presumably operates whether a tax is imposed or not. The only reason we have for believing that some policy (apparently) hastens the adjusting process, is simply that we sometimes envisage a situation where prices are already at the level consistent with equilibrium *after* application of the policy. In this case the policy yields immediate equilibrium. For example, in Chapters 2 and 3 of Book I we discussed at length the possibility that a deficit on the balance of payments might be observed even though aggregate expenditure did not exceed the value of production, provided that at the same time world supply and demand are not equated at the given prices. Stocks are building up in one country and running down in another. In such a case it was shown that an exchange-rate adjustment suitably chosen can bring about an immediate correction to the imbalance. This is because home prices before the depreciation are precisely those which are required for equilibrium *after* the application of the policy.

The sense in which a policy change might be said to 'hasten' price adjustment is now clear. It is indeed closely bound up with the change in the nature of the price adjustment. In the case quoted above, at one level of the exchange rate, the given prices imply disequilibrium. The currency depreciation has the effect of converting these same disequilibrium prices into those necessary for equilibrium in the new situation. There is no need to wait for the slow-acting equilibrating mechanism to work. Adjustment is 'hastened' by the policy.

Clearly the same sort of considerations apply to any kind of tariff or taxation policy. The imposition of a tax could make the new equilibrium prices more like those presently existing so that at least part of the necessary move towards equilibrium is achieved. But the reader should note two important points. First, for any given disequilibrium the pattern of taxation necessary to achieve full equilibrium is likely to be a complex one. Second, the choice of a particular pattern of taxation to achieve equilibrium implies a *different* final welfare situation from that which would be attained if market forces were allowed to operate without interference.

Short of the development of a complete dynamic model in which all the complexities of the algebra above are combined with a great deal more information regarding the actual timing of the market and profit-maximising behaviour supposed to be incorporated, there are only two sensible questions which can be put relevant to the desirability or otherwise of any tax. These are:

1. Given the present situation, which may be out of equilibrium, will the final equilibrium prices with the tax be more like present market prices than the final equilibrium without it? If the answer is 'yes', then the policy could be said to be a factor hastening the attainment of equilibrium, that is, a position of balanced overseas payments and internal demand.
2. Will the final equilibrium with the tax show greater or less welfare than the final equilibrium without it?

Note that both of these questions can be put and in part answered, at least in terms of elasticities of demand and supply, by means of the techniques developed in this book, and a model will presently be set out with this end in view. Of course there will be as many answers to question (1) as there are initial situations; nevertheless in each case an unambiguous answer can be obtained (see section 17.6). It does not matter that the initial situation is one of disequilibrium, as we saw in treating the currency depreciation problem of Chapter 3.

Before proceeding, it may perhaps be desirable to stress once again the extreme naïvety of the model to be set out below. It is not difficult to imagine with what charm and wit defenders of wrong answers to meaningless questions might draw attention to its inadequacies. Not all manufacturers produce at minimum cost, nor is all equipment the most up to date. Monopolies exist. The world consists of more than two countries producing three goods with three factors. Technical change may make nonsense of the equilibrium we are striving to reach long before we reach it and so on and so on. But all of this is no excuse for the abandonment of rational analysis or the introduction of new and important policies involving many millions of pounds of other people's money on no firmer a basis than that they accord with the incantations of currently fashionable pundits. It is essential to know that we do not know, and the work of this chapter may tell us at least that. In addition it may represent a starting point from which more work can be done. We turn therefore to the model.

17.6 THE COMPLETE FACTOR TAXATION MODEL

Obviously there can be no general answer to the problem of hastening equilibrium. Everything depends upon the disequilibrium point from which we are to begin. On the other hand there is a very relevant general problem which it is most useful and interesting to solve. We can in fact investigate the *difference* between equilibrium prices with and without any particular tax structure. Armed with this knowledge, it is sometimes easier to see whether the path from the existing situation to the new (with tax) equilibrium is shorter or longer than the path to the old. This is in fact what most economists intuitively do.

Suppose, for example, that the price of non-traded goods was too high relative to traded goods so that, coupled with an excess of spending over the value of output, we have a deficit on the balance of payments. Suppose further that analysis shows that the equilibrium position, including a selective tax on labour in non-traded goods production, has the property that non-traded goods prices are higher in relation to traded goods than is the case for the equilibrium without the tax. Then it is clear that the imposition of a tax would go some way towards helping the trade balance, that is, in attaining equilibrium. Indeed, this is essentially the method of Chapter 8 of Book I, where we investigated the power of a tariff to help the trade balance. The difference lies only in the greater complexity due to the greater realism of the model.

It follows that, as in our earlier investigation, the simplest way to proceed is to set out the equations of equilibrium without the tax and inquire into the price changes which must occur when the tax is imposed. Fortunately also this comparison of two equilibria gives us the answer to the second of our questions above as well as the first. The change in welfare may easily be computed simultaneously in the familiar manner.

Throughout the greater part of Book II it has been assumed that the reader has come to understand how to solve linear equations by the method of determinants. It is now possible therefore to introduce a much more systematic way of setting out the algebra, making the treatment of a three-commodity model much simpler. First, we set down the equations of equilibrium in full. These are:

$$B \equiv q_1 x_1 - q_2' x_2 \equiv 0 \tag{17.6.1}$$

$$x_1 \equiv S_1 - X_1 \qquad \equiv f(q_1, q_2, q_3, t, Y) \tag{17.6.2}$$

$$x_2 \equiv S_2' - X_2' \qquad \equiv j(q_1', q_2', q_3', Y') \tag{17.6.3}$$

$$q_1 \equiv q_1' \qquad \equiv \text{constant} \tag{17.6.4}$$

$$q_2 \equiv q_2' \tag{17.6.5}$$

$$Y \equiv \sum q_i S_i \qquad \equiv h(q_1, q_2, q_3, t) \tag{17.6.6}$$

$$Y' \equiv \sum q_i' S_i' \qquad \equiv k(q_1', q_2', q_3') \tag{17.6.7}$$

$$0 \equiv S_3 - X_3 \qquad \equiv g(q_1, q_2, q_3, t, Y) \tag{17.6.8}$$

$$0 \equiv S_3' - X_3' \qquad \equiv m(q_1', q_2', q_3', Y') \tag{17.6.9}$$

(17.6.1) is the balance of payments equation showing that imports and exports are equal throughout. q_1 and q_2' are home and foreign market prices, the primes indicating the foreign country in the usual way. x_1 and x_2 are exports and imports respectively, the equations (17.6.2) and (17.6.3) defining exports and imports as the difference between production and consumption in the appropriate country. This is the immediate consequence of the fact that world supply equals world demand. S_i of course stands for supply and X_i for demand. (17.6.4) and (17.6.5) show that the prices of traded goods are equal in both countries, the constant indicating that we have chosen commodity 1 as numeraire. (17.6.6) and (17.6.7) state that aggregate expenditure is equal to the value of output at market prices. Note that this is always the case if the tax proceeds are spent. (17.6.8) and (17.6.9) show that supply equals demand in the non-traded goods industry in each country.

The functions f, j, k, h, g, m, on the right-hand side of (17.6.2) to (17.6.9), where they occur, simply remind us that demand and supply are dependent on prices and aggregate expenditure as well as on the tax rate in the case of country 1. They are put in as an aid to the counting of equations and unknowns, an exercise we must now undertake.

t is the tax on labour in the home country used in commodity 3, the non-traded class. We therefore regard t as predetermined by policy. We assume in fact that it is initially zero and is to be imposed. We have to ask, given t, are the remaining variables determined? Since (17.6.4) is in fact two equations, we have a total of ten altogether. The unknowns are six prices, exports, x_1, and imports, x_2, and two aggregate expenditures, again a total of ten. The system therefore is just determined, given t. That is, we have enough equations to find all the unknowns.

The next step is to take changes in (17.6.1) to (17.6.9) and set out the resulting equations. This is most neatly done in the so-called 'matrix' form as follows:

$$
\left\{
\begin{array}{ccccccc}
q_1 & -q_2 & -x_2 & 0 & 0 & 0 & 0 \\[4pt]
-1 & 0 & \left(\dfrac{\partial S_1}{\partial q_2}-\dfrac{\partial X_1}{\partial q_2}\right) & \left(\dfrac{\partial S_1}{\partial q_3}-\dfrac{\partial X_1}{\partial q_3}\right) & 0 & -\dfrac{\partial X_1}{\partial Y} & 0 \\[10pt]
0 & -1 & \left(\dfrac{\partial S_2'}{\partial q_2}-\dfrac{\partial X_2'}{\partial q_2}\right) & 0 & \left(\dfrac{\partial S_2'}{\partial q_3}-\dfrac{\partial X_2'}{\partial q_3}\right) & 0 & -\dfrac{\partial X_2'}{\partial Y} \\[10pt]
0 & 0 & S_2 & S_3 & 0 & -1 & 0 \\[4pt]
0 & 0 & S_2' & 0 & S_3' & 0 & -1 \\[4pt]
0 & 0 & \left(\dfrac{\partial S_3}{\partial q_2}-\dfrac{\partial X_3}{\partial q_2}\right) & \left(\dfrac{\partial S_3}{\partial q_3}-\dfrac{\partial X_3}{\partial q_3}\right) & 0 & -\dfrac{\partial X_3}{\partial Y} & 0 \\[10pt]
0 & 0 & \left(\dfrac{\partial S_3'}{\partial q_2}-\dfrac{\partial X_3'}{\partial q_2}\right) & 0 & \left(\dfrac{\partial S_3'}{\partial q_3}-\dfrac{\partial X_3'}{\partial q_3}\right) & 0 & -\dfrac{\partial X_3'}{\partial Y}
\end{array}
\right\}
\left\{
\begin{array}{c}
dx_1 \\[4pt] dx_2 \\[8pt] dq_2 \\[8pt] dq_3 \\[4pt] dq_3' \\[8pt] dY \\[8pt] dY'
\end{array}
\right\}
=
\left\{
\begin{array}{c}
0 \\[4pt] -\dfrac{\partial S_1}{\partial t}\,dt \\[8pt] 0 \\[8pt] 0 \\[4pt] 0 \\[8pt] -\dfrac{\partial S_3}{\partial t}\,dt \\[8pt] 0
\end{array}
\right\}
$$

$$(17.6.10)$$

The first bracket encloses the matrix of coefficients, the second the vector of variables for which we have to solve, written column-wise. The right-hand side is a vector of constants, dt of course being the given tax change (policy). Note that in arranging (17.6.10) we have embodied equations (17.6.4) and (17.6.5), first by leaving out dq_1 and dq_1', since they are zero, and second by treating q_2 and q_2' as the same variable. The system therefore reduces to seven equations in seven unknowns.

One further point remains to be made about (17.6.10). Where appropriate we have made use of the fact that

$$\sum_i q_i \, dS_i = 0 \qquad (17.6.11)$$

This holds provided only that t is initially zero and arises from the fact, already noted in Chapter 15, that $\sum_i q_i S_i$ is maximised, given prices, by competition. By the definition of a maximum, any (small) change away will have only a negligible effect on the total. It now remains to solve the equations (17.6.10) for the variables in which we are interested.

To answer the question 'Does the tax increase welfare?', it would ordinarily be necessary to solve for each dq_i and dy. Substituting the results so obtained in

$$dX_j = \sum_i \frac{\partial X_j}{\partial q_i}\, dq_i + \frac{\partial X_j}{\partial Y}\, dY$$

gives each dX_j, and hence $\sum_j q_j dX_j$ which is the required measure of the welfare change.

But in the present case it is much easier to recall, using (17.6.6) and (17.6.11), that

$$dY = \sum_i q_i dX_i + \sum_i X_i dq_i = \sum_i S_i dq_i \qquad (17.6.12)$$

This simply says that the change in expenditure equals the change in income. From (17.6.12), given that dq_1 is zero and that X_3 equals S_3, we have

$$\sum_i q_i dX_i = (S_2 - X_2)dq_2 \qquad (17.6.13)$$

as the measure of welfare. Since $(S_2 - X_2)$ is necessarily negative, being minus imports, welfare will worsen if dq_2 is positive and improve if dq_2 is negative. That is, since q_1 does not change, there is a gain if the tax improves the real terms of trade. All that is necessary therefore is to check the sign of dq_2 by solving (17.6.10) for this variable alone.

By the usual rule, therefore,

$$\frac{dq_2}{dt} = \frac{\begin{vmatrix} q_1 - q_2 & 0 & 0 & 0 & 0 & 0 \\ -1 & 0 & -\dfrac{\partial S_1}{\partial t} & \left(\dfrac{\partial S_1}{\partial q_3} - \dfrac{\partial X_1}{\partial q_3}\right) & 0 & -\dfrac{\partial X_1}{\partial Y} & 0 \\ 0 & -1 & 0 & 0 & \left(\dfrac{\partial S_2'}{\partial q_3} - \dfrac{\partial X_2'}{\partial q_3}\right) & 0 & -\dfrac{\partial X_2'}{\partial Y} \\ 0 & 0 & 0 & S_3 & 0 & -1 & 0 \\ 0 & 0 & 0 & 0 & S_3' & 0 & -1 \\ 0 & 0 & -\dfrac{\partial S_3}{\partial t} & \left(\dfrac{\partial S_3}{\partial q_3} - \dfrac{\partial X_3}{\partial q_3}\right) & 0 & -\dfrac{\partial X_3}{\partial Y} & 0 \\ 0 & 0 & 0 & 0 & \left(\dfrac{\partial S_3'}{\partial q_3} - \dfrac{\partial X_3'}{\partial q_3}\right) & 0 & -\dfrac{\partial X_3'}{\partial Y} \end{vmatrix}}{\Delta}$$

$$\qquad (17.6.14)$$

where Δ is the determinant of the matrix of coefficients in (17.6.10).

We show first that we do in fact know a little about the probable sign of Δ. In carrying out this exercise we shall assume that the reader has progressed sufficiently far in other branches of economic theory to understand that the response rates $\partial X_i/\partial p_j$ which appear in Δ may be written in two parts, as explained in exercise 5 to Chapter 4 (Book I). Thus we have

$$\partial X_i/\partial q_j = - X_j \frac{\partial X_i}{\partial Y} + \sigma_{ij} \qquad (17.6.15)$$

Terms one and two of (17.6.15) are in fact the income effect and substitution effect of the price change referred to in section 1.2 of Book I.† Now turn to Δ as it appears in (17.6.10).

We may eliminate all the S_j which occur in rows four and five of Δ by adding S_j times columns six or seven as necessary to columns three, four and five. It will be noticed that this operation will add elements like

$$- S_j \frac{\partial X_i}{\partial Y}$$

to elements

$$\frac{\partial S_i}{\partial q_j} - \frac{\partial X_i}{\partial q_j}$$

wherever they are present. Furthermore, since exports and imports are the difference between consumption and supply, we know that

$$x_2 = S_2' - X_2' = - (S_2 - X_2) \qquad (17.6.16)$$

And this, combined with (17.6.15), permits us to write

$$\frac{\partial S_1}{\partial q_2} - \frac{\partial X_1}{\partial q_2} - S_2 \frac{\partial X_1}{\partial Y} = \frac{\partial S_1}{\partial q_2} - \sigma_{12} + x_2 \frac{\partial X_1}{\partial Y}$$

and so on. In the case of commodity three of course there are no exports or imports so that the term in $\partial X_i/\partial Y$ does not appear. For simplicity, it is convenient now to introduce the notation

$$K_{ij} = \frac{\partial S_i}{\partial q_j} - \sigma_{ij}$$

so that the result obtained by the operations described may be written

† Except that σ_{ij} is here a response rate and not an elasticity. To be quite specific, the σ_{ij} of exercise 5, Chapter 4 (Book I), is p_j/X_i times the σ_{ij} above.

$$\Delta = \begin{vmatrix} q_1 & -q_2 & -x_2 & 0 & 0 \\ -1 & 0 & K_{12} + x_2 \dfrac{\partial X_1}{\partial Y} & K_{13} & 0 \\ 0 & -1 & K'_{22} - x_2 \dfrac{\partial X'_2}{\partial Y} & 0 & K'_{23} \\ 0 & 0 & K_{32} + x_2 \dfrac{\partial X_3}{\partial Y} & K_{33} & 0 \\ 0 & 0 & K'_{32} - x_2 \dfrac{\partial X'_3}{\partial Y} & 0 & K'_{33} \end{vmatrix} \tag{17.6.17}$$

Note that having eliminated all S_j the -1s in columns six and seven may be moved to a leading position by interchange of rows and columns. The result (17.6.17) is then obvious.

The next step is to eliminate the qs in row one by multiplying rows two and three by q_1 and q_2 and adding or deducting as required from row one. Again, the 1s remaining in columns one and two are moved to a leading position by interchange of rows, leaving

$$\Delta = \begin{vmatrix} \left(-x_2 + x_2 q_1 \dfrac{\partial X_1}{\partial Y} + x_2 q_2 \dfrac{\partial X'_2}{\partial Y} + q_1 K_{12} - q_2 K'_{22} \right) & q_1 K_{13} & -q_2 K'_{23} \\ K_{32} + x_2 \dfrac{\partial X_3}{\partial Y} & K_{33} & 0 \\ K'_{32} - x_2 \dfrac{\partial X'_3}{\partial Y} & 0 & K'_{33} \end{vmatrix}$$

$$\tag{17.6.18}$$

At this point we appeal again to certain well-known propositions in economic theory not explicitly treated in this book. First, it is known that

$$\sum_i q_i \frac{\partial S_i}{\partial q_j} = 0$$

This result will at once appear acceptable to the reader on intuitive grounds, since

$$\sum_i q_i \frac{\partial S_i}{\partial q_j} dq_j = 0$$

may be written $\sum_i q_i dS_i = 0$, a fact many times noted in Chapter 15 and elsewhere. In addition it is a standard proposition of demand theory† that

$$\sum_i q_i \sigma_{ij} = 0$$

Hence by addition it follows that

$$\sum_i q_i K_{ij} = 0$$

If therefore we add q_3 times row two of (17.6.18) to row one, the

$$q_1 K_{12} + q_3 K_{32}$$

which then appears in row one column one may be written

$$-q_2 K_{22}$$

Similarly in row one column two we have $-q_2 K_{23}$. Again it is obvious that

$$\sum_i q_i \frac{\partial X_i}{\partial Y} = 1$$

for each element of the left-hand side is by definition the proportion of unit increase in income spent on the ith commodity. The total must sum to unity. Hence the $x_2 q_1 (\partial X_1 / \partial Y)$ in column one row one becomes minus $x_2 q_2 (\partial X_2 / \partial Y)$ as a result of our operation. Thus we have finally

$$\Delta = \frac{1}{-q_3^2} \begin{vmatrix} \left(x_2 + q_2 x_2 \dfrac{\partial X_2}{\partial Y} - q_2 x_2 \dfrac{\partial X_2'}{\partial Y} + q_2 K_{22} + q_2 K_{22}' \right) & q_2 K_{23} & q_2 K_{23}' \\[2ex] q_3 K_{32} + x_2 q_3 \dfrac{\partial X_3}{\partial Y} & q_3 K_{33} & 0 \\[2ex] q_3 K_{32}' - x_2 q_3 \dfrac{\partial X_3'}{\partial Y} & 0 & q_3 K_{33}' \end{vmatrix}$$

$$(17.6.19.)$$

Now we cannot be sure of the sign of this expression but something can be said. There is in fact a standard mathematical theorem‡ which tells us that if all the elements of (17.6.19) on the left-to-right diagonal are positive, and if all other elements are negative, and if at

† See for example I. F. Pearce, *A Contribution to Demand Analysis* [10].
‡ See L. McKenzie, 'Matrices with Dominant Diagonals and Economic Theory', in *Mathematical Methods in the Social Sciences*, ed. K. J. Arrow, S. Karlin and P. Suppes (Stanford University Press, 1960) [8].

the same time the sum of each column is positive, then the sign of the whole determinant is positive. Now we know that K_{33} and K'_{33} are both positive since the supply responses $\partial S_i/\partial q_i$ are positive (see Chapter 15), and it may similarly be deduced from demand theory that $-\sigma_{ii}$ is positive (see exercise 5, Chapter 4, Book I). Again from demand theory and from results in Chapter 15, we know that positive K_{ij}s, where i is different from j, are associated only with complementarity in demand and supply, that is, with the case where the two commodities i and j are closely related – say motor-cars and petrol. If commodities 1, 2 and 3 are not so related, we must expect the elements K_{ij} $(i \neq j)$ to be negative in sign. Thus since

$$\sum_i q_i K_{ij} = 0$$

and K_{13} and K'_{13} are missing from columns two and three respectively, it is clear that, on the assumption of non-complementarity, columns two and three satisfy the conditions required for the sign of the determinant to be positive.

Now consider column one. Evidently, if the K elements alone were present, column one would satisfy the conditions for reasons already given. Moreover, economists are sometimes willing to believe it probable that the substitution part of demand responses will outweigh numerically the income effect. It should also be noted that the Ks of column one will be larger than the substitution parts of demand responses since they contain supply responses of the same sign. And the $x_2 \partial X/\partial Y$ will ordinarily be at least as small as income effects since imports cannot be greater than consumption, and if the foreign country is the rest of the world its exports are likely to be small relative to its consumption of the same commodity. Thus it may be thought reasonable to expect that the conditions for the determinant to be positive will ordinarily be met.

Against this conclusion the writer should perhaps report that his own empirical investigations suggest that relatively low substitution parts, less than income effects, occur more frequently than is commonly supposed, particularly when by a commodity we mean the aggregate of a wide class of commodities. It may well be therefore that we do not know the sign of Δ. Nevertheless we shall for the moment suppose that there is some bias towards a positive value, in which case it is necessary to consider the sign of the numerator in (17.6.14). We turn therefore to this.

Evidently we may proceed exactly as before, first eliminating S_3

and S_3' in columns four and five, so reducing the whole determinant to

$$
\begin{vmatrix}
q_1 & -q_2 & 0 & 0 & 0 \\
-1 & 0 & -\dfrac{\partial S_1}{\partial t} & K_{13} & 0 \\
0 & -1 & 0 & 0 & K_{23}' \\
0 & 0 & -\dfrac{\partial S_3}{\partial t} & K_{33} & 0 \\
0 & 0 & 0 & 0 & K_{33}'
\end{vmatrix}
$$

If now the elements -1 (row three, column two) and K_{33}' (column five, row five) are moved into leading positions by interchange of rows and columns, the whole is easily seen to expand into

$$
- K_{33}' \, q_1 \left(\frac{\partial S_1}{\partial t} K_{33} - \frac{\partial S_3}{\partial t} K_{13} \right) \tag{17.6.20}
$$

Obviously we do not know the sign of this expression, for the basic results of the early part of this chapter show that we do not know the sign either of $\partial S_1/\partial t$ or $\partial S_3/\partial t$. For the sake of completeness, however, we remark that we have not yet quite exhausted the manipulative possibilities. We remind ourselves that

$$
\frac{\partial S_3}{\partial t} = - p_3 a_{33} \frac{\partial S_3}{\partial q_3} + \frac{\partial \phi_3}{\partial t}
$$

and that, by the argument leading to (17.3.28),

$$
\frac{\partial S_1}{\partial t} = - p_3 a_{33} \frac{\partial S_1}{\partial q_3} + \frac{\partial \phi_1}{\partial t}
$$

where $\partial \phi_i/\partial t$ is the response of supply of commodity i to the tax change when factor prices are held constant. By putting these results into (17.6.20), we could show that an alternative way of writing (17.6.20) is

$$
- K_{33}' \, q_1 \left(\frac{\partial \phi_1}{\partial t} K_{33} - \frac{\partial \phi_3}{\partial t} K_{13} \right) + p_3 a_{33} K_{33}' \, q_1 \left(\frac{\partial S_1}{\partial q_3} K_{33} - \frac{\partial S_3}{\partial q_3} K_{13} \right) \tag{17.6.21}
$$

But as we should expect this gets us no further forward, for the signs of the terms inside the second brackets are the same, hence the sign of the whole is unknown. And nothing at all is known *a priori* of the signs of $\partial\phi_i/\partial t$.

Before commenting further on the economic meaning of this agnostic result, it will be instructive to solve the equations (17.6.10) for dq_3/dt also. It would be tedious to write out in detail the working for this, and unnecessary, since it follows closely the steps already set out for dq_2/dt. The result turns out to be

$$\frac{dq_3}{dt} = \frac{\dfrac{1}{q_3^2}\begin{vmatrix} \Omega & \left(-q_1\dfrac{\partial S_1}{\partial t} - q_3\dfrac{\partial S_3}{\partial t}\right) - q_2 K'_{23} \\ \left(q_3 K_{32} + x_2 q_3\dfrac{\partial X_3}{\partial Y}\right) & -q_3\dfrac{\partial S_3}{\partial t} & 0 \\ \left(q_3 K'_{32} - x_2 q_3\dfrac{\partial X'_3}{\partial Y}\right) & 0 & q_3 K'_{33} \end{vmatrix}}{\Delta}$$

(17.6.22)

where omega is minus the leading element in (17.6.19). The sign of (17.6.22) is of course quite unknown. To satisfy ourselves further on this point we could, if we chose, use the result (17.3.28) and its appropriate analogue substituted in column two of (17.6.22). The numerator then breaks up into two determinants. The first will be as (17.6.22) but having the elements $-p_3 a_{33}\dfrac{\partial S_2}{\partial q_3} q_2$, $p_3 a_{33}\dfrac{\partial S_3}{\partial q_3} q_3$ and zero in column two instead of those actually appearing in (17.6.22). This is convenient since, on arguments and assumptions previously given in connection with Δ, this first determinant will have a dominant diagonal and its sign is accordingly known. Indeed, having in mind our assumptions about the sign of Δ, it is clear that the first of the two terms making up dq_3/dt will be positive in sign. Unfortunately the second term will have, in column two of the determinant in the numerator, elements $\partial\phi_i/\partial t$ whose signs and magnitudes are dependent on the nature of the input coefficients a_{ij}, and responses in these to factor price changes. Nothing can be said, therefore, overall.

We have now established that dq_1/dt is zero (since q_1 is the numeraire price) and that dq_2/dt and dq_3/dt are of unknown sign. To develop an expression for dS_3/dt – the change in supply of the commodity taxed – all that is necessary is to write

$$\frac{dS_3}{dt} = \frac{\partial S_3}{\partial q_1}\frac{dq_1}{dt} + \frac{\partial S_3}{\partial q_2}\frac{dq_2}{dt} + \frac{\partial S_3}{\partial q_3}\frac{dq_3}{dt} + \frac{\partial S_3}{\partial t}$$

$$= \frac{\partial S_3}{\partial q_2}\frac{dq_2}{dt} + \frac{\partial S_3}{\partial q_3}\frac{dq_3}{dt} + \frac{\partial S_3}{\partial t} \qquad (17.6.23)$$

and to substitute into this values for dq_2/dt and dq_3/dt already obtained. Strictly speaking this procedure should be followed and the resulting expression examined for sign. On the other hand, since we have already proved that we do not know the signs either of dq_2/dt, dq_3/dt or $\partial S_3/\partial t$, it will hardly surprise the reader to learn that nothing can be deduced. We have left this question therefore as an exercise for the student.

17.7 CONCLUSIONS

Before leaving the subject of factor taxation we sum up our agnostic conclusions and recall the analogous problem of trade union maintained wage differentials. Consider first the basic proposition that a tax on labour in the service industries will necessarily 're-deploy' labour out of that industry into some other, or the corresponding claim that a favourable union agreement will reduce employment of members, i.e. will induce redundancy. Assuming that the balance of payments is balanced before and after the imposition of the tax, we have shown both of these propositions to be false as a consequence of (17.6.23). It is true of course that less labour-intensive methods are likely to be used in the service industries following a tax or wage increase, but this effect could be offset by a positive dS_3/dt. The truth is that we do not know what will happen until we have some more realistic model and some actual *measures*, however rough, of the basic elasticities throughout the world.

Now suppose that our international payments are in a state of deficit and it is hoped that progress towards balance will be hastened by a tax on non-traded (service) commodities. As previously explained, it is necessary to consider first what changes would be needed in prices and expenditure to correct the imbalance in the absence of the tax. Fortunately there is no need to carry out this exercise in detail – an intuitive argument will do. From previous work we know that the first step towards the correction of a trade imbalance must be a cut in spending at home and an increase abroad. The cut and increase are equal so that world aggregate demand is unchanged. If, however, the foreign country is unwilling to consume the traded goods given up by the home country in precisely the proportions in which they are given up, some adjustment is necessary in prices. Again as services are not traded they must bear the whole burden of the expenditure cut. There is no compensating increase in demand from abroad since services cannot be exported. To improve the trade balance, therefore, the price of services must ordinarily fall. The direction of other price changes is unknown.

It follows that in a state of trade imbalance the price of services is too high relatively. Other prices are either too high or too low. Now suppose that dq_3/dt is positive in the exercise performed above. This means that in the presence of a tax on services the balanced trade price of services has to be higher than the balanced trade price without the tax. Hence the imposition of a tax in a position of imbalance would 'hasten' the adjustment. To attain balance without the tax would require a larger fall in the price of services than would be the case with the tax.

Unfortunately, as we have seen, we do not know for sure that dq_3/dt is positive in sign. If it were negative, the imposition of the tax would widen the necessary price adjustment and hence could not be said to help the trade balance problem. Furthermore, we know nothing *a priori* about the necessary real terms of trade changes either with or without the tax. Any belief that there is some sense in which we can be *sure* that a tax on services will help the trade imbalance is an illusion. It may or it may not.

Finally, we turn to the welfare problem. As indicated earlier a real gain accrues from the tax only if dq_2/dt is negative. Again we do not know whether it will be negative or not unless we have some knowledge of the magnitude of the relevant elasticities.

In short the only proper answer to the question 'What will be the effect of the British Selective Employment Tax or any other kind of factor taxation?' is that very little is known. What is needed is a maximum research effort, necessarily backed by a great deal of money, to develop a realistic computerised model, at the same time improving and co-ordinating available statistics so that some serious attempt might be made at measurement. The exercises of this book must be thought of as the first step towards the understanding of such a model.

EXERCISES

1. Write out in full the proof of (17.3.28) following the argument leading to (17.3.23).
2. Compare (17.3.24) and (17.3.27). What would be the corresponding expressions for $\partial S_1/\partial q_1$ and $\partial S_2/\partial q_2$ in the three-commodity case? Can you write $\partial S_i/\partial q_j$ in this form?
3. Carefully re-read section 7.11 of Book I. Show that one way to resolve the paradox referred to in paragraphs one and two of section 7.11 might be to develop the distinction drawn in section 17.5 between policies which are designed on the one hand to hasten the attainment of equilibrium, or on the other to bring about some gain in, or redistribution of, welfare. Argue that in the simple case of section 7.11 import duties and export duties are asymmetric on the first count but symmetric on the second.
4. Are the policies of section 8.3 of Book I equilibrium-hastening policies or welfare-adjusting policies? (See exercise 3 above.)
5. Prove the result (17.6.22) and show by suitable examples that nothing is known about its sign.
6. Prove that (17.6.23) set out in full must be

$$\frac{dS_3}{dt} = \frac{q_2 \left(\dfrac{\partial S_2}{\partial t} K_{33} - \dfrac{\partial S_3}{\partial t} K_{23} \right) \left[K'_{33} \dfrac{\partial S_3}{\partial q_3} + \left(K'_{33} K'_{22} - K'_{23} K'_{32} \right) \dfrac{\partial S_3}{\partial q_2} + \left(K'_{23} x_2 \dfrac{\partial X'_3}{\partial Y} - K'_{33} x_2 \dfrac{\partial X'_2}{\partial Y} \right) \dfrac{\partial S_3}{\partial q_2} \right] + \dfrac{\partial S_3}{\partial t} \varDelta}{\varDelta}$$

where $\varDelta$ has the meaning of (17.6.19). Show accordingly that even if the sign of $\partial S_3/\partial t$ were known to be negative and the sign of $\partial S_2/\partial t$ positive, as suggested by intuition, it would still not be possible to set a sign on dS_3/dt. Hence justify explicitly the central theme of Chapter 17.

7. Consider the case where three commodities are produced with two basic factors only. Let the functions

$$S_2 = S_2(q_1, q_2, S_3, t) = \phi(p_1, p_2, S_3, t)$$

correspond to (17.3.1) and (17.3.4) respectively, and let t be the tax rate on factor 2 if used in commodity 2. Prove that the result (17.3.20) still holds without modification.

18 Factor Endowment Variations – Factor Mobility, Overseas Investment and Growth

18.1 THE GENERAL PROBLEM

IN sections 12.2 and 12.9 it was explained at length that the theory of trade between countries is different from the theory of trade between regions within a country primarily because factors of production are for the most part immobile over national boundaries. The work so far has proceeded therefore on the assumption that each country has a factor endowment $A_1, \ldots, A_j$ which remains fixed. At the same time it was made clear that the assumption of a fixed factor endowment only partially reflects conditions in the real world, and it was promised that something would be said explicitly about the consequences of factor movements.

As it happens, a number of interesting practical problems arise directly in connection with changes in the factor endowment and/or the movement between countries of factors of production, all of which may be conveniently treated in much the same way. In particular, current fashion dictates that every commentator should have something to say on the subject 'economic growth', that is, on the consequences of change over time in the national stock of capital and the aggregate labour force. This is a vastly more complex problem than the superficial introduction in Chapter 10 of Book I might suggest.

Another issue attracting a good deal of attention at the present time concerns the desirability or otherwise of encouraging the private lending of capital overseas. The act of lending abroad is one which increases the foreign capital stock at the same time causing home capital stock to be less than it otherwise would be, the *quid pro quo* being the continuous receipt by the home country of a stream of profits from the capital so lent. The consequences of this naturally go far beyond the simple exchange of capital stock for profits. The balance of payments is affected and hence so are the prices of all goods and factors. By the same token losses and gains occur all of which must be considered when assessing the gain or loss from the policy as a whole. Even the effect of labour migration on the price of labour is not as obvious as might at first sight be thought.

18.2 Factor Endowment Variation in a Closed Economy

We shall begin with a model of the simplest possible kind, since this is particularly instructive and introduces in the most elementary way ideas which will be needed later. In particular, in the first instance we consider a closed economy (a country not engaged in international trade) in the hope that the surprising results obtained even in this case will condition the reader to a more ready acceptance of later conclusions.

Many economists brought up in the traditions of partial equilibrium analysis would wish instinctively to argue that an increase in the labour force in any country will, in the absence of other influences, reduce the wage rate. Similarly growth in the capital stock will, it is sometimes alleged, reduce the rate of interest. Indeed, this last observation has led to a very widespread acceptance of the general conclusion that, in the absence of restriction, countries will ordinarily lend abroad more capital than is socially desirable. The chain of deductions runs as follows.

Consider country A lending to country B. This activity will bring about a rise in the capital stock in country B and hence a fall in its interest rate $r(B)$, by the (false) proposition of the previous paragraph. The private lender in country A will naturally compare the interest rate $r(B)$ with the interest rate $r(A)$ which can be earned at home. He will in fact be willing to lend, say, £dK abroad so long as $r(B)$ is greater than $r(A)$. But suppose that other investors in A have already lent £K to B. The consequence of the action of the individual now lending £dK will be to change $r(B)$ by an amount $(dr(B))$ assumed to be negative. The return of the owners of the £K previously invested will fall by an amount equal to $Kdr(B)$. This does not matter to the individual lending £dK, but it matters a great deal to country A taken as a whole, for the country as a whole gains $rdK(B)$ but loses $Kdr(B)$. Not only might the net gain be less than the $rdK(A)$ which can be earned by investment of dK at home, it might even be negative. Moreover, it is argued, the net gain will certainly be less than $rdK(A)$ if $r(A)$ is anywhere near $r(B)$ as it is likely to be in competitive equilibrium with a relatively free flow of capital. It follows (apparently) that under free competition there will always be too much foreign lending.

On the other hand it is clear that the claim above depends crucially upon the initial assumption that $r(B)$ will fall as B's stock of capital increases. If this argument fails, the whole fails. Hence we have a powerful practical motive for a careful check upon intuition. And we shall in fact find that our intuition fails us.

The belief that $r(B)$ must fall rests probably on the instinctive feeling that there must be a demand function for capital obeying the usual rules for demand for a commodity. That is, the lower the interest rate the greater the demand for capital. If supply increases at a given interest rate, as for example when capital moves in from abroad, then the interest rate must fall.

Unfortunately, as we observed in section 18.1, a great many other things happen as a consequence of the import of capital besides the increase in the capital stock itself. There will be changes in factor prices and aggregate incomes which lead in turn to changes in commodity prices. Demand and supplies of each commodity are affected in a manner which could lead to some extra demand for capital. This extra demand could be greater than the increased supply of capital, in which case there seems no reason to suppose that the rate of interest cannot rise. Moreover, in a trading economy, we should have further complications due to changes in the real terms of trade and consequent repercussions from abroad.

If the reader could be convinced that the partial equilibrium argument is misleading even in the case of a closed economy, he would have to expect this to be so *a fortiori* where international trade is admitted. We therefore set up a model in which the endowment of one factor is supposed to be growing at a rate $\partial A_i/\partial t$, where t here means time. The ith factor may of course be capital or labour as desired. We shall inquire in particular into the sign of $\partial p_i/\partial t$, that is, whether the price of the ith factor is rising or falling over time in response to the growth of A_i. Results from this model will turn out to be informative in more than one context.

It is convenient to assume that there are three commodities and three factors of production, and that i is the third factor of production. In this case the equations of the model are particularly simple and easy to solve. We have in fact

$$
\left.
\begin{aligned}
\sum q_i S_i &= Y & (a) \\
S_1 - X_1 &= 0 & (b) \\
S_2 - X_2 &= 0 & (c) \\
q_3 &= \text{constant} & (d)
\end{aligned}
\right\} \qquad (18.2.1)
$$

(*a*) of (18.2.1) says that expenditure is equal to the value of production, which must be the case if full employment of all factors is to be maintained throughout. Equations (*b*) and (*c*) express the fact that the supply and demand for commodities 1 and 2 are always equated, and (*d*) means that commodity 3 has been selected as the numeraire commodity. Remembering that we have supply functions and demand functions in the background, the four relations (*a*)–(*d*) are four equations in the four unknowns q_1, q_2, q_3 and Y which can accordingly be found. Taking differences, therefore, in the usual way, we may write three equations in three unknowns in matrix form as under

$$\left\{ \begin{array}{ccc} S_1 & S_2 & -1 \\[2mm] \left(\dfrac{\partial S_1}{\partial q_1} - \dfrac{\partial X_1}{\partial q_1}\right) & \left(\dfrac{\partial S_1}{\partial q_2} - \dfrac{\partial X_1}{\partial q_2}\right) & -\dfrac{\partial X_1}{\partial Y} \\[4mm] \left(\dfrac{\partial S_2}{\partial q_1} - \dfrac{\partial X_2}{\partial q_1}\right) & \left(\dfrac{\partial S_2}{\partial q_2} - \dfrac{\partial X_2}{\partial q_2}\right) & -\dfrac{\partial X_2}{\partial Y} \end{array} \right\} \left\{ \begin{array}{c} \dfrac{dq_1}{dA_3} \\[3mm] \dfrac{dq_2}{dA_3} \\[3mm] \dfrac{dY}{dA_3} \end{array} \right\} = \left\{ \begin{array}{c} -p_3 \\[3mm] -\dfrac{\partial S_1}{\partial A_3} \\[3mm] -\dfrac{\partial S_2}{\partial A_3} \end{array} \right\}$$

$$(18.2.2)$$

(18.2.2) perhaps needs some explanation. In the first place, from Chapter 15 we recall that supply functions were introduced on the assumption that factor endowments were fixed. Hence, strictly speaking, whenever we write supply as dependent on commodity prices we should include also the factor endowments. That is, we should think of a function,

$$S_i = S_i(q_1, q_2, q_3, A_1, A_2, A_3)$$

where A_1, A_2 and A_3 are given constants. These 'constants' must now be included explicitly since they are henceforward to be allowed to change.

If factor endowment changes, the magnitude of the production possibility set of Chapter 15 changes and, of course, supply changes on that account. Hence we have to contend with yet another set of parameters, i.e. basic building blocks, so far left out of account, namely all $\partial S_i / \partial A_j$. Two of these now appear on the right-hand side of (18.2.2). The remainder are missing only because A_3 is the only endowment which is supposed to grow. A_1 and A_2 remain constant throughout.

One further piece of explanation is essential. Taking changes in equation (18.2.1)(a) and dividing by dA_3 yields

$$\sum_i S_i \frac{dq_i}{dA_3} - \frac{dY}{dA_3} = -\sum_i q_i \frac{dS_i}{dA_3}$$

In place of $\sum_i q_i \frac{dS_i}{dA_3}$ in (18.2.2) we have put the factor price p_3 of the factor which is growing. This is a piece of substitution which has not yet been justified. We are led accordingly into a brief but crucial digression.

First of all, consider the cost equations

$$q_i = \sum_j a_{ij} p_j \quad i = 1, 2, 3 \tag{18.2.3}$$

Evidently the equations (18.2.3) can be solved for each p_j, giving for p_3

$$p_3 = \frac{\begin{vmatrix} a_{11} & a_{12} & q_1 \\ a_{21} & a_{22} & q_2 \\ a_{31} & a_{32} & q_3 \end{vmatrix}}{|a_{ij}|} \tag{18.2.4}$$

where the denominator is the determinant of the matrix of co-efficients of the p_i in (18.2.3).

We now switch our attention to the factor usage equations

$$A_j = \sum_i S_i a_{ij}$$

solving these as in previous chapters to give

$$S_1 = \frac{\begin{vmatrix} A_1 & a_{21} & a_{31} \\ A_2 & a_{22} & a_{32} \\ A_3 & a_{23} & a_{33} \end{vmatrix}}{|a_{ij}|} \tag{18.2.5}$$

From (18.2.3) commodity prices must be constant if factor prices are constant and vice versa. If therefore we take changes in (18.2.5), keeping commodity prices (and hence factor prices) constant, all that can change is S_1 and whichever A_i is supposed to change. Thus if A_3 only changes,

$$\frac{\partial S_1}{\partial A_3} = \frac{\begin{vmatrix} a_{21} & a_{31} \\ a_{22} & a_{32} \end{vmatrix}}{|a_{ij}|} \qquad (18.2.6)$$

where $\partial S_1/\partial A_3$ is the response of supply to a factor endowment change with commodity prices constant. The reader unused to taking changes where determinants are concerned should first expand the numerator of (18.2.5) down column one and apply the techniques explained in Book I to check (18.2.6).

If now the numerator of (18.2.4) is expanded down column three, it will be observed on comparison with (18.2.6) that its first term is simply

$$q_1 \frac{\partial S_1}{\partial A_3}$$

And on finding expressions for $\partial S_2/\partial A_3$ and $\partial S_3/\partial A_3$ corresponding to (18.2.6) the reader will easily satisfy himself that

$$\sum q_i \frac{\partial S_i}{\partial A_3} = p_3 \qquad (18.2.7)$$

by (18.2.4). The common sense of this important result is obvious. It says simply that if the endowment of any factor is increased by one unit, then the value of aggregate output at the original prices will change by the price of the factor. Indeed, were it not for the fact that we shall need to make further use of (18.2.4), (18.2.5) and (18.2.6) as they stand, it would have been easier to prove (18.2.7) by taking changes (all prices constant) in the identity

$$\sum_i p_i A_i \equiv \sum_i q_i S_i$$

which gives expression to the equality of the value of input and the value of output.

Now let us reconsider the changes

$$\sum_i q_i \frac{dS_i}{dA_3}$$

which occur when we take changes in equation (18.2.1) (*a*) of the model. These may be split up as follows:

$$\sum_i \sum_j q_i \frac{\partial S_i}{\partial q_j} \frac{dq_j}{dA_3} + \sum_i q_i \frac{\partial S_i}{\partial A_3}$$

into the total value of the changes due to commodity price changes (term one) and the value of the changes due to the increase in factor endowment. And we have repeatedly noticed that, when the economy is in a position of free competitive equilibrium, changes simply due to price movements have zero sum value. This is because competition maximises the value of output so that small changes in the pattern of output leave total value unchanged. Hence from (18.2.7) we are justified in writing $-p_3$ on the right-hand side of equations (18.2.2).

Before concluding this digression, we shall need one further result from (18.2.6) as hinted above. In earlier chapters we have had occasion to take changes in the cost equations (18.2.3) and to write

$$dq_i = \sum_j a_{ij} dp_j \qquad (18.2.8)$$

(The reader is reminded that by the minimum cost condition $\sum_j p_j da_{ij}$ is zero.) Now consider a special case of (18.2.8), namely, that when dq_2 and dq_3 are both zero. Solving (18.2.8) in this case for dp_3, we have

$$dp_3 = \frac{\begin{vmatrix} a_{11} & a_{12} & dq_1 \\ a_{21} & a_{22} & 0 \\ a_{31} & a_{32} & 0 \end{vmatrix}}{|a_{ij}|} = dq_1 \frac{\begin{vmatrix} a_{21} & a_{22} \\ a_{31} & a_{32} \end{vmatrix}}{|a_{ij}|}$$

Dividing both sides by dq_1 and recalling that dp_3 is the change with q_2 and q_3 constant, we have

$$\frac{\partial p_3}{\partial q_1} = \frac{\begin{vmatrix} a_{21} & a_{22} \\ a_{31} & a_{32} \end{vmatrix}}{|a_{ij}|} \qquad (18.2.9)$$

Comparing (18.2.9) with (18.2.6) yields the fundamental result

$$\frac{\partial S_1}{\partial A_3} = \frac{\partial p_3}{\partial q_1} \qquad (18.2.10)$$

which we shall later use. Similar results may be obtained of course for any commodity/factor combination by parallel argument.

We are now in a position to consider solutions to the equations (18.2.2). In particular, we have an interest in the factor price p_3. Thus we write

$$\frac{dp_3}{dA_3} = \frac{\partial p_3}{\partial q_1}\frac{dq_1}{dA_3} + \frac{\partial p_3}{\partial q_2}\frac{dq_2}{dA_3} + \frac{\partial p_3}{\partial q_3}\frac{dq_3}{dA_3}$$

which, remembering (18.2.10) and the fact that commodity 3 is our numeraire, reduces to

$$\frac{dp_3}{dA_3} = \frac{\partial S_1}{\partial A_3}\frac{dq_1}{dA_3} + \frac{\partial S_2}{\partial A_3}\frac{dq_2}{dA_3} \qquad (18.2.11)$$

Solving (18.2.2) for dq_i/dA_3 and substituting in (18.2.11), it follows that

$$\frac{dp_3}{dA_3} = \frac{\begin{vmatrix} 0 & -\dfrac{\partial S_1}{\partial A_3} & -\dfrac{\partial S_2}{\partial A_3} & 0 \\[2ex] -p_3 & S_1 & S_2 & -1 \\[2ex] -\dfrac{\partial S_1}{\partial A_3} & \left(\dfrac{\partial S_1}{\partial q_1} - \dfrac{\partial X_1}{\partial q_1}\right) & \left(\dfrac{\partial S_1}{\partial q_2} - \dfrac{\partial X_1}{\partial q_2}\right) & -\dfrac{\partial X_1}{\partial Y} \\[2ex] -\dfrac{\partial S_2}{\partial A_3} & \left(\dfrac{\partial S_2}{\partial q_1} - \dfrac{\partial X_2}{\partial q_1}\right) & \left(\dfrac{\partial S_2}{\partial q_2} - \dfrac{\partial X_2}{\partial q_2}\right) & -\dfrac{\partial X_2}{\partial Y} \end{vmatrix}}{\varDelta}$$

$$(18.2.12)$$

where $\varDelta$ is the determinant of the matrix on the left-hand side of (18.2.2). The principle for the construction of (18.2.12) is easy to see. The determinant set out should be expanded along row one, when it will be noted that the two terms of the expansion correspond with the two terms of (18.2.11), having in view the solution of (18.2.2) for dq_1/dA_3 and dq_2/dA_3. We have now to inquire into the probable sign of (18.2.12).

First, examine the denominator $\varDelta$. As in the previous chapter, S_1 and S_2 may be eliminated from row one and the determinant expanded to give

$$\varDelta = -\begin{vmatrix} K_{11} & K_{12} \\ K_{21} & K_{22} \end{vmatrix}$$

where K_{ij} has the meaning of the previous chapter.

In this form $\varDelta$ is easily seen to be negative in sign when account is taken of standard results in the theory of demand and supply.†

The numerator of (18.2.12) may be similarly reduced to the form

† See for example I. F. Pearce, *A Contribution to Demand Analysis*, pp. 163–4 [10]. Refer also to exercise 5, Chapter 4, Book I.

$$\begin{vmatrix} 0 & -\dfrac{\partial S_1}{\partial A_3} & -\dfrac{\partial S_2}{\partial A_3} & 0 \\[2.2ex] -p_3 & 0 & 0 & -1 \\[2.2ex] -\dfrac{\partial S_1}{\partial A_3} & K_{11} & K_{12} & -\dfrac{\partial X_1}{\partial Y} \\[2.2ex] -\dfrac{\partial S_2}{\partial A_3} & K_{21} & K_{22} & -\dfrac{\partial X_2}{\partial Y} \end{vmatrix} \qquad (18.2.13)$$

If this determinant is expanded along row two, it will be seen to be equivalent to the sum of two 3×3 determinants in convenient form. One of these will be minus the determinant $|K_{ij}|$ bordered by $-\partial S_i/\partial A_3$. The sign of this is known to be positive since it is the bordered discriminant of a positive definite quadratic form.[†] If this were all, therefore, and in view of the known sign of Δ, we could say that the sign of dp_3/dA_3 is unambiguously negative in accordance with the intuitive idea from which we began. Unfortunately, however, we are left with another term equal to $+p_3$ times the determinant $|K_{ij}|$ with the row bordering $-\partial S_i/\partial A_3$ and the column bordering $-\partial X_i/\partial Y$. Since we know nothing of the sign or magnitude of $\partial S_i/\partial A_3$ on *a priori* grounds (see (18.2.9) and (18.2.10)), there is no reason to suppose that the extra term may not be both negative and large enough to turn dp_3/dA_3 positive. Indeed, it is easy to choose numbers quite consistent with all that we know about the theory of supply and demand to achieve this result. Nor do these numbers have to be in any way extreme or unlikely or unusual. We conclude that both the sign and magnitude of dp_3/dA_3 is unknown.

18.3 POPULATION GROWTH AND THE REAL WAGE – A MODEL

We are now in a position to reflect upon what the results of section 18.2 might imply in terms of the intuitive ideas set out at the beginning of this chapter. Two common topics for debate were referred to – labour growth and capital growth. We shall find these two to be subtly different, each with a special characteristic interesting for its own sake. Suppose, first, that factor 3 is labour and that p_3 is the wage rate. Why, in the face of the results above, should some economists believe that an increase in the aggregate labour supply

[†] See R. G. D. Allen, *Mathematical Analysis for Economists*, pp. 485–92 [1].

must reduce the 'real' wage rate; that is, why might they be tempted to think, imprecisely, of a demand function for labour with a negative response rate (i.e. a downward-sloping demand curve)?

Before we try to answer this, consider what we have proved. In order to get any result at all it is necessary to choose a numeraire commodity, in this case commodity 3. When we then show that dp_3/dA_3 may be positive, we have proved only that p_3 might rise *relative to the numeraire price q_3* which of course remains constant. We have not established that it does not fall relative to all or any other price whether of a factor or a commodity. Furthermore, if some other commodity or factor price had been chosen as numeraire rather than q_3, the result obtained for dp_3/dA_3 would ordinarily be numerically different. Indeed, it would have been a simple matter to bias the model towards a negative dp_3/dA_3 by selecting as numeraire any commodity or factor whose price rises relatively.

Note especially that it is *not possible* to answer the question 'What happens to the wage rate as a consequence of immigration?' *unless* we assume or infer something about the general level of prices. There are simply not enough equations if (18.2.1) (*d*) is omitted without anything put in its place. In order to do justice to those economists whose views we are inquiring into, we have to examine what is implicitly assumed.

In a world with only one commodity produced, no doubt what would be meant is that the wage rate must fall *relative* to the price of that commodity, so that labour will be unambiguously worse off. But in a world with many commodities the whole question must be reframed. One obvious way to be more precise would be to ask whether the wage rate falls relative to some average of all commodity prices. But this simply poses a new problem in place of the old, namely, 'What kind of average?' If we have three commodities, food, clothing, and toy trumpets, and if the wage rate remains constant, with food and clothing prices rising 2 per cent and toy trumpets costing 50 per cent less, then, when equal weight is given to each price, wages will have risen relative to the average. Nevertheless, many people might be worse off in a real sense. It would almost certainly be protested that more weight ought to be given to some commodity prices than to others. What we have to decide is how much.

The difficulty over choice of weighting would not arise of course if the wage rate could be shown to fall relative to *every* price. But our example makes it clear that this is not necessarily the case, for we have proved in section 18.2 that the wage rate can rise relative to commodity price 3. Indeed, this is precisely why we went to so much trouble to work the problem. It cannot be true in general that immigration of labour must lead to a fall in the wage rate relative to any arbitrary index of commodity prices.

Against this, however, it can properly be objected that to claim the necessity of a fall in the wage rate relative to *any* commodity price index is a very powerful statement, much stronger perhaps than that implied by the loose contention that the 'real' wage rate must fall. A weaker theorem which said simply that the welfare of each unit of labour must fall would be interesting and useful if true, and such a theorem could easily be true even in the face of the results of section 18.2. We proceed to show therefore how this possibility might be tested, at the same time proving it to be not true in general. For it to be wholly true, additional very powerful assumptions are needed.

First, we have to say what we mean by a fall in the real income of each unit of labour. Strictly speaking of course we cannot do this without a great deal more knowledge than that which is implicit in the observed aggregate demand and supply response rates. To be accurate, we should need to know the change in consumption, valued at original prices, of each individual wage-earner; for if wage-earners have different tastes and if commodity prices change, it could well be that one gains whilst the other loses even though both receive the same money wage. Following the procedure of an earlier chapter, however, we might make the broad assumption that all individuals buy commodities in the same proportion in order to attempt a first approximation. Thus we could estimate the change in welfare of the community as a whole and afterwards consider the share of each unit of labour in that change (see section 14.5).

Stage one is very simple. Indeed, it is easy to see intuitively that the only change in aggregate welfare will be that accruing to the newly arrived labour force dA_3, for small changes in the neighbourhood of competitive equilibrium, given existing resources, can make no appreciable difference to welfare if welfare is already maximised. To obtain the result formally, however, we recall that consumption is identically equal to production in this model so that

$$\sum q_i dX_i = \sum q_i dS_i = p_3 dA_3 \qquad (18.3.1)$$

by (18.2.7) above. And this is of course the aggregate wage bill of the newly arrived labour.

It follows that the original community taken as a whole will neither gain nor lose after a *small* amount of immigration provided there is no international trade as in the present model.† To test for a gain or loss on the part of the *original* labour force, A_3, we need only test whether the share of labour of the aggregate real income less that part accruing to newly arrived labour rises or falls. One way to carry out the necessary test would be to solve the equations (18.2.2) as they stand for dY, deducting $p_3 dA_3$ to give the new money income available for distribution to the original population. The share of the original labour force is $(p_3 + dp_3)A_3/(Y + dY - p_3 dA_3)$ which is to be compared with the previous ratio $p_3 A_3/Y$.

In practice, however, it will be much simpler to choose a new numeraire. Notice that choice of a different numeraire will not affect the real wage-rate change although it will of course affect the money-wage change. It is easiest in fact to suppose that the general level of prices changes in such a way that

$$dY = p_3 dA_3 \qquad (18.3.2)$$

In such a case it can be seen that labour will gain or lose according as the aggregate wage bill $(p_3 + dp_3)A_3$ paid to the original labour force is greater or less than $p_3 A_3$, that is, labour will gain or lose according as dp_3 is positive or negative.

Choice of the new numeraire means that we replace equation (18.2.1)(d) of the model by (18.3.2) and proceed, as before, solving for dp_3/dA_3. Remembering (18.3.2) and the fact that dq_3 now changes, the equations (18.2.2) become

$$
\begin{bmatrix}
S_1 & S_2 & S_3 \\[2mm]
\left(\dfrac{\partial S_1}{\partial q_1} - \dfrac{\partial X_1}{\partial q_1}\right) & \left(\dfrac{\partial S_1}{\partial q_2} - \dfrac{\partial X_1}{\partial q_2}\right) & \left(\dfrac{\partial S_1}{\partial q_3} - \dfrac{\partial X_1}{\partial q_3}\right) \\[3mm]
\left(\dfrac{\partial S_2}{\partial q_1} - \dfrac{\partial X_2}{\partial q_1}\right) & \left(\dfrac{\partial S_2}{\partial q_2} - \dfrac{\partial X_2}{\partial q_2}\right) & \left(\dfrac{\partial S_2}{\partial q_3} - \dfrac{\partial X_2}{\partial q_3}\right)
\end{bmatrix}
\begin{bmatrix}
\dfrac{dq_1}{dA_3} \\[2mm]
\dfrac{dq_2}{dA_3} \\[2mm]
\dfrac{dq_3}{dA_3}
\end{bmatrix}
=
\begin{Bmatrix}
0 \\[2mm]
\left(-\dfrac{\partial S_1}{\partial A_3} + p_3 \dfrac{\partial X_1}{\partial Y}\right) \\[2mm]
\left(-\dfrac{\partial S_2}{\partial A_3} + p_3 \dfrac{\partial X_2}{\partial Y}\right)
\end{Bmatrix}
$$

$$(18.3.3)$$

† Great care should be taken not to interpret this to mean that in a general way immigration is a 'neutral' policy. The result (18.3.1) holds only approximately, so that if dA_3 is large and continuing, the original community might lose welfare.

and the solution for dp_3/dA_3 is

$$\frac{dp_3}{dA_3} = \frac{\begin{vmatrix} 0 & S_1 & S_2 & S_3 \\ 0 & \dfrac{\partial S_1}{\partial A_3} & \dfrac{\partial S_2}{\partial A_3} & \dfrac{\partial S_3}{\partial A_3} \\ \left(-\dfrac{\partial S_1}{\partial A_3}+p_3\dfrac{\partial X_1}{\partial Y}\right) & \left(\dfrac{\partial S_1}{\partial q_1}-\dfrac{\partial X_1}{\partial q_1}\right) & \left(\dfrac{\partial S_1}{\partial q_2}-\dfrac{\partial X_1}{\partial q_2}\right) & \left(\dfrac{\partial S_1}{\partial q_3}-\dfrac{\partial X_1}{\partial q_3}\right) \\ \left(-\dfrac{\partial S_2}{\partial A_3}+p_3\dfrac{\partial X_2}{\partial Y}\right) & \left(\dfrac{\partial S_2}{\partial q_1}-\dfrac{\partial X_2}{\partial q_1}\right) & \left(\dfrac{\partial S_2}{\partial q_2}-\dfrac{\partial X_2}{\partial q_2}\right) & \left(\dfrac{\partial S_2}{\partial q_3}-\dfrac{\partial X_2}{\partial q_3}\right) \end{vmatrix}}{\varDelta}$$

$$(18.3.4)$$

where $\varDelta$ is the determinant of the matrix on the left-hand side of (18.3.3). It is not hard now to show that the sign of (18.3.4) is uncertain. As a first step, we prove that $\varDelta$ will ordinarily be positive. Consider the general term

$$\frac{\partial S_i}{\partial q_j} - \frac{\partial X_i}{\partial q_j}$$

of $\varDelta$. Breaking $\partial X_i/\partial q_j$ into income and substitution parts and using the notation K_{ij} of Chapter 17, we have

$$\frac{\partial S_i}{\partial q_j} - \frac{\partial X_i}{\partial q_j} = K_{ij} + S_j\frac{\partial X_i}{\partial Y} \qquad (18.3.5)$$

Writing $\varDelta$ in this new notation we may now multiply row three by q_2 and row two by q_1, deducting both from row one. Since

$$\sum_j q_j K_{ji} = 0 \qquad (18.3.6)$$

and

$$\sum_j q_j\frac{\partial X_j}{\partial Y} = 1 \qquad (18.3.7)$$

it is clear that $\varDelta$ is equal to

$$q_3\left| K_{ij} + S_j\frac{\partial X_i}{\partial Y} \right| \qquad (18.3.8)$$

where the notation $|\ |$ means a determinant with general element as indicated within vertical lines. Furthermore, in Chapter 17, it was explained that K_{ii} must be positive and $K_{ij}(i \neq j)$ will ordinarily be negative. This, together with (18.3.6), implies that the matrix $|K_{ij}|$

has quasi dominant diagonal and is in the so-called 'diagonal form' (see footnote relating to (17.6.19). This property is known (loc. cit., footnote relating to (17.6.19)) to be sufficient to ensure that each co-factor of $|K_{ij}|$ is positive (the ijth co-factor is the determinant obtained by eliminating from $|K_{ij}|$ the ith row and the jth column with the sign which would be attached to the ijth element if $|K_{ij}|$ were being expanded along the ith row).

Now notice that the determinant in (18.3.8) may be written

$$| K_{ij} | + \sum_i \sum_j \left(S_j \frac{\partial X_i}{\partial Y} \right) \text{(co-factor } ij)$$

Thus, since $|K_{ij}|$ is zero,† $S_j \, \partial X_i / \partial Y$ is positive and co-factor ij is positive, (18.3.8) must be positive; hence Δ is positive. But note that this depends upon the assumptions made about K_{ij} (see section 17.6).

We now show that the numerator of (18.3.4) is of uncertain sign whatever assumptions are made about K_{ij}. Consider the following numerical example.

Let $$p_1 = p_2 = p_3 = 1$$

and let production techniques be given by

$$\{a_{ij}\} = \left\{ \begin{matrix} 6 & 2 & 50 \\ 12 & 2 & 90 \\ 40 & 40 & 1 \end{matrix} \right\} \tag{18.3.9}$$

A simple computation using (18.2.6) and summing columns of (18.3.9) to obtain q_i, remembering $p_i = 1$, shows that,

$$\frac{\partial S_1}{\partial A_3} = \frac{80}{5588} \quad \text{and} \quad q_1 \frac{\partial S_1}{\partial A_3} = \frac{4640}{5588}$$

$$\frac{\partial S_2}{\partial A_3} = \frac{60}{5588} \quad \text{and} \quad q_2 \frac{\partial S_2}{\partial A_3} = \frac{2640}{5588}$$

and $$\frac{\partial S_3}{\partial A_3} = -\frac{12}{5588} \quad \text{and} \quad q_3 \frac{\partial S_3}{\partial A_3} = -\frac{1692}{5588}$$

This example demonstrates that on quite ordinary assumptions $\partial S_1 / \partial A_3$ and $\partial S_2 / \partial A_3$ may lie between zero and $+1$. Suppose that these supply responses do in fact take the values of the example in (18.3.4). Note that if elements of (18.3.4) are written, where appropriate, in the form (18.3.5), terms in $(\partial X_i / \partial Y)$ may be eliminated everywhere except in column one by multiplying row one by $\partial X_1 / \partial Y$

† If a solution is to exist for the equations (18.3.6).

or $\partial X_2/\partial Y$ as required and deducting from rows three and four. We may therefore select values of $\partial X_1/\partial Y$ and $\partial X_2/\partial Y$ at will without affecting the value of any element in columns two, three and four. Suppose that we choose $q_1(\partial X_1/\partial Y)$ greater than $q_1(\partial S_1/\partial A_3)$, which is possible since both numbers lie between zero and one. It follows that $q_2(\partial X_2/\partial Y)$ must be less than $q_2(\partial S_2/\partial A_3)$, since marginal propensities to consume must sum to a number equal to unity. Suppose that with the chosen marginal propensities the whole determinant is negative in sign. Clearly we could make it positive by changing $q_2(\partial X_2/\partial Y)$ to a number greater than $q_2(\partial S_2/\partial A_3)$, at the same time making $q_1(\partial X_1/\partial Y)$ less than $q_1(\partial S_1/\partial A_3)$, for this would change the sign of every element in column one without changing anything in the rest of the determinant.

Evidently dp_3/dA_3 may be of either sign. *There is no reason to suppose that an increase in the endowment of any factor must necessarily cause the real reward per unit of that factor to fall. It may just as easily cause it to rise.* And this is true even for a closed economy. On the other hand it is worth noting that if we had chosen to operate with a two-factor/two-commodity model, a definite result *could* have been obtained. This is easily seen by eliminating the fourth row and column in (18.3.4), reading A_3 as A_2 and expanding the resulting 3×3 determinant. Note first that not every supply can rise as a result of an increment in one factor endowment (prices constant), for with unchanged technique this would imply an increased total usage of some factor whose endowment has not increased (see excercise 4 at the end of this chapter). If therefore $q_1(\partial S_1/\partial A_2)$ is positive in sign, it must be greater than p_3 by (18.2.7), for $q_2(\partial S_2/\partial A_2)$ must be negative. But $q_1(\partial X_1/\partial Y)$, being a marginal propensity to consume, must be less than unity, so that the sign of the single element in column one of the reduced 3×3 determinant now being expanded must be

    (*a*) opposite to that in row one column two, and
    (*b*) the same as that in row one column three.

Since S_1 and S_2 are both positive, it follows that the whole determinant is necessarily positive. Now note that in the 2×2 case Δ is negative, since only one row interchange is necessary to put it in the form where it can be seen to be positive instead of two interchanges as in the 3×3 case. Hence in the 2×2 case dp_2/dA_2 is necessarily negative. The real reward of factor 2 must fall.

The 2×2 case of course has no intrinsic interest. There are two reasons, however, for introducing it. The first is to show precisely where the argument breaks down when there are many factors and commodities, and the second is to provide yet another example of the danger of self-deception by over-aggregation. We need not of course dwell upon point two. And on point one it is sufficient to remark that with more than two commodities it ceases to be possible to find any correspondence between the signs of elements in column one and row two of the determinant forming the numerator of (18.3.4), as evidenced by the numerical example quoted.

18.4 THE COMMON SENSE OF GROWTH OF THE WORK FORCE IN A CLOSED ECONOMY

The frequent appeals to the reader (which take up far too much space in this book) never to rely, even partially, upon 'common sense' unsupported by rigorous argument should not be taken to mean that there is no place in science for intuition. On the contrary it is probably true that progress in any subject is directly proportional to the degree of imagination and intuition brought to it. It is often the case that intuitive argument, even where it is strictly false, contains a substratum of truth. The power of the algebraic method of this book is revealed as much by its success in uncovering what is right about common sense as by its success in uncovering what is wrong. Consider for example why many economists might be very reluctant indeed to abandon the idea that an increase in the labour force must reduce the real wage.

Once attention is drawn to the fact that growth in the work force implies increased aggregate demand, it would be readily accepted that this must imply an increase in the demand for labour over and above that originally existing. It is likely, however, that the well-brought-up economist would feel 'in his bones' that this extra demand must be more than matched by the extra supply of labour. Why should we suppose this? Good reasons do in fact exist.

First, we might feel that we begin with an economy which has a certain pattern of demand met by the use of its given productive resources whatever those might be. The appearance of an addition to the work force would be expected to give rise to extra demand in much the same proportions, commodity by commodity, as that previously existing. No bias is imparted on the demand side. On the supply side, however, an immediate and powerful bias can be noted. Productive resources are increased but not in proportion factor by factor. The only factor endowment which has grown is labour. The demand for factors might be expected to be increased roughly in proportion, but the supply increase occurs only in the case of labour. Intuition cries out that this asymmetry should induce a weakening in the bargaining power of labour and hence of its real earnings. Why is this not reflected in the algebra?

The answer is that it *is* so reflected, at least in part. Consider one hidden assumption of the verbal argument above. We have quite naturally supposed that increased demand must arise in proportion to existing demand. In terms of the model of section 18.3 this would mean that the increment in aggregate expenditure dY of (18.3.2) will be spent on commodities 1, 2 and 3 in the proportion $S_1 : S_2 : S_3$. Inspection of the model (18.2.1) and equations (18.3.3) now reveals that the consequence of this assumption must be that each $\partial X_i / \partial Y$ of column one of the determinant in (18.3.4) will be proportional to S_i. This is because the dY of (18.3.2) is not made up of increments of income accruing to the existing labour force but is, on the contrary, the whole of the expenditure of the increment in the labour force. On the other hand it should be noted that the $\partial X_i / \partial Y$ which occur in (18.3.8) come from demand elasticities relating to the work force as a whole and do therefore measure changes in expenditure due to an added increment of expenditure for all. With these thoughts in mind, consider again the sign of the numerator of (18.3.4).

If each $\partial X_i / \partial Y$ in column one is proportional to S_i we may, by multiplying row one by p_3 times the factor of proportionality and adding to row two, introduce into row two terms like $p_3(\partial X_i / \partial Y)$ so that row two and column one become symmetric. Furthermore, if the procedure leading to (18.3.8) is followed for the numerator of (18.3.4), the zero in row one column one is replaced by $(-(\partial S_3 / \partial A_3) + p_3(\partial X_3 / \partial Y))$ when use is made of (18.3.7) and (18.2.7). Interchange of rows now introduces still greater symmetry. The numerator of (18.3.4) may be seen to be the denominator bordered symmetrically. Furthermore, the argument following (18.3.8), used to prove that Δ is positive, may equally be used to prove that any subdeterminant of Δ which is symmetric around the left/right diagonal (that is, any principal minor of Δ) is positive also. Thus if Δ were fully symmetric it would be possible to say at once by a standard mathematical theorem† that dp_3 / dA_3 is necessarily negative.

† See R. G. D. Allen, *Mathematical Analysis for Economists*, pp. 487–9 [1]. Δ would be the discriminant of a positive definite form, and the numerator would be the discriminant of the same form under constraint.

Now note that the asymmetry of Δ is due only to the presence of the general term

$$S_i \frac{\partial X_j}{\partial Y}$$

which occurs in each ith column and jth row (see (18.3.8)). If we again had S_j proportional to $\partial X_j / \partial Y$ for each j, these elements would be symmetric also. On the other hand we have already noted that there are no grounds for supposing that the $\partial X_j / \partial Y$, which come from demand elasticities, should be proportional to S_j. We take up this point again below.

In short, the verbal argument requires that, for all individuals, marginal and average propensities to consume each commodity must be the same. That is, we must have

$$q_i \, \partial X_i / \partial Y = q_i S_i / Y$$

for each i.

Having now isolated the precise assumption necessary to support the intuitive argument, we are in a position to consider how plausible an assumption it is. The reader may feel that, having found a proof for the case where $\partial X_i / \partial Y$ are proportional to S_i, considerable deviation from proportionality will be necessary to falsify the proposition that the real wage must fall. But is this really so and, even if it were, is such a deviation unlikely? Consider again the numerical example (18.3.9). Observe that the difference

$$\sum_{i \neq 3} \frac{q_i}{p_3} \frac{\partial S_i}{\partial A_3} - \sum_{i \neq 3} q_i \frac{\partial X_i}{\partial Y}$$

is always numerically equal to or less than

$$\left| \frac{q_3}{p_3} \frac{\partial S_3}{\partial A_3} \right| + \left| q_3 \frac{\partial X_3}{\partial Y} \right| \tag{18.4.1}$$

where $|\;|$ means modulus (i.e. without sign), for both summations including $i = 3$ equal unity. Suppose (18.4.1) to be quite small. Let us suppose for example, to simplify the figures of (18.3.9), that we have

$$q_1 \frac{\partial S_1}{\partial A_3} = \frac{9}{11} \quad \text{and} \quad q_2 \frac{\partial S_2}{\partial A_3} = \frac{4}{11}$$

which is not too different from the values calculated. It would then be possible to have

$$q_1 \frac{\partial X_1}{\partial Y} = \frac{6}{11} \quad \text{and} \quad q_2 \frac{\partial X_2}{\partial Y} = \frac{4}{11}$$

At the same time we could assume

$$\frac{\partial X_i}{\partial Y} = \lambda S_i \quad \text{(all } i)$$

which would ensure a negative dp_3/dA_3. Obviously now a change of $3/11$ in $q_1(\partial X_1/\partial Y)$ is all that is necessary to turn the sign of dp_3/dA_3.

This may at first sight seem rather a lot, but this is not so when we recall that we have only three commodities. If there were many commodities over which the difference (18.4.1) could be spread, each $q_i(\partial S_i/\partial A_k)$ could be set very close indeed to its corresponding $q_i(\partial X_i/\partial Y)$. Only very slight changes would then be necessary to turn the sign of dp_3/dA_3.

Again, the reader should reflect that the assumption that the income accruing to the new increment of the growing factor will be spent on each commodity in precisely the same way as the community spends as a whole is a very powerful one. There are bound to be considerable deviations in practice, particularly if the factor concerned is capital rather than labour. It is highly improbable that income from profits is used to buy the same pattern of commodities as income from employment. The reader is referred also to section 10.2 of Book I, where it is argued that, if the increment dA_3 of the work force arises because of natural population growth, the increment of aggregate spending may well be disbursed in quite a different way from extra spending arising out of immigration. In the former case there is an increment in family income, whereas immigration introduces extra families.

Finally, and most important, the suggestion that for each consumer the increment of income will be used to increase consumption on each commodity proportionately is immediately refuted by the very concept of a luxury commodity, the idea of which implies that a higher proportion is consumed by the wealthy. Indeed, by now the reader will have come to understand that the model of this section really requires further disaggregation to deal properly with the questions put. Our whole approach so far has been based upon a single demand function for the community as a whole when, as part of the problem, expenditure is supposed to increase, not as a result of an increase accruing to each individual, but because the number of persons in the community has increased.

It would of course be perfectly possible to set up a model with two distinct demand functions, one for labour and one for expenditure by owners of other factors. In such a case the problem of measuring the welfare of 'labour' would be more complicated, but there is no difficulty in principle. The reason we have not done this is that it is already clear that we shall get the answer 'don't know' (see exercise 6 at the conclusion of this chapter). Since the work above shows the sign of dp_3/dA_3 to be uncertain when $\partial X_i/\partial Y$ is not proportional to S_i, as it will not be with separate demand functions, it is clear that the welfare effect will *a fortiori* remain uncertain in cases where the measure of welfare is more complicated. It is not worth while to work the disaggregate model except perhaps as an exercise or as the prelude to a serious attempt at computation. The reader looking for intuitive confirmation of these results may find the following approach helpful.

We began this section with an appeal to common sense. Let us try the common-sense approach once more. The argument really is that if we produce and demand goods and factors in a certain proportion and then if, suddenly, there appears in the economy an increased supply of some one factor, a bias is introduced. To use up the increased supply some mechanism must induce substitution out of factors now in relatively short supply into greater use of the growing factor. To achieve this substitution, prices must move appropriately. Note that this is an argument about *substitution* and about the signs of price changes necessary to achieve substitution. But all that we know about substitution in demand concerns the sign of the substitution part of demand elasticity with real welfare constant. And all that we know about the signs of supply elasticities concerns substitution with the value of the national product constant at constant prices, i.e.

$$\sum q_i dS_i = 0 = \sum q_i dX_i.$$

If there is any change in real welfare, or departure from competitive equilibrium, other effects intervene whose signs we do not know. *It is the income effect, wherever it occurs, which our intuition fails to take into account.*† What we have proved is that these real income effects can be important enough to destroy intuitively based results however small such income effects may seem to be.

To illustrate even more exactly the real welfare effect, suppose we

† To put this in terms more familiar to economists trained in partial equilibrium analysis, we know only that demand curves slope downwards (real income constant) and supply curves slope upwards in competitive equilibrium. Real income changes cause shifts in demand schedules of uncertain sign and magnitude, and these shifts turn out to be crucial.

had begun from a position where there existed a tax t on the production cost p_3^* of, say, the third commodity. In such a case the first equation of (18.3.3) becomes (see exercise 5 at the conclusion of this chapter)

$$\sum_i S_i \frac{dq_i}{dA_3} = -tq_3^* \frac{dS_3}{dA_3}$$

provided the convention (18.3.2) is retained. tq_3^* is tax revenue per unit, and dS_3 is the total change in production of S_3 (see exercise 1 of this chapter). A new term has appeared on the right-hand side which may be in part transferred to the left-hand side when we recall that

$$\frac{dS_3}{dA_3} = \sum \frac{\partial S_3}{\partial q_i} \frac{dq_i}{dA_3} + \frac{\partial S_3}{\partial A_3}.$$

Accordingly, the first equation of (18.3.3) now reads

$$\sum_i (S_i + tq_3^*) \frac{dq_i}{dA_3} = -tq_3^* \frac{\partial S_3}{\partial A_3} \qquad (18.4.2)$$

(see again exercise 5 at the conclusion of this chapter).

Clearly it is not now possible to sustain the argument of p. 584. Notice particularly that the tax terms in (18.4.2) arise precisely because the existence of a tax gives rise to a loss or gain in real welfare per person as a direct consequence of the growth in the labour force. Indeed, we have

$$\sum q_i dX_i = \sum q_i dS_i = dY - \sum S_i dq_i$$
$$= p_3 dA_3 - (-tq_3^* dS_3) \qquad (18.4.3)$$

which is different from the no-tax case where the total welfare change is $p_3 dA_3$, that is, the amount accruing to the newly appeared units of factor 3. The reader should confirm, however (see exercise 5 at the end of this chapter), that if the $\partial X_i / \partial Y$ of the demand responses were proportional to S_i it would still in fact be possible, even in the presence of the tax, to show that dp_3 / dA is necessarily negative. The element of truth underlying the intuitive approach is again laid bare and shown to be not more than an element of truth.

The change in total welfare due to the presence of the tax does moreover draw attention to yet another ambiguity. It is not clear whether writers who suggest that growth in the labour force induces a fall in the real wage rate mean a fall in labour's *share* of real welfare (which may occur even if the absolute real wage rises) or a fall in the absolute real wage. The work above in fact confirms only that the change in the *share* of labour in total real welfare is of uncertain sign assuming that every individual in the original community spends in the same proportion on each commodity, for it tests only whether labour's share in aggregate money spending rises or falls. The reader should therefore attempt exercises 6 and 7 at the end of this chapter to satisfy himself that the absolute real wage rate is equally of uncertain sign. Our agnostic conclusion, which arises *a fortiori* in the most general case, is not due to any confusion between the share of total welfare and the absolute real wage, a fact which should be obvious without working exercises 6 and 7, for we can already be sure that the sign of dS_3 in (18.4.3) is uncertain.

Clearly the failure of our intuition is due to two causes. The first is that changes in demand patterns, due to changes in real welfare, can lead to secondary price changes which offset those needed to bring about substitution, in the productive process, of the growing factor for those not growing. Partial analysis directs attention to the substitution effect, ignoring the income effect. The second cause is that intuition fails to register the crucial importance of the probable divergence between the adjustment $\partial X_i/\partial Y$ due to incremental changes in real welfare and the average purchase X_i/Y per unit of total expenditure.

If we attempt to defend our intuition by plausible assumptions we lose both ways. If we assume a closed economy, growth in the labour force can be due only to natural population growth. Hence, for reasons given in Chapter 10, incremental changes in consumption due to growth will not be proportional to average. If on the other hand, we assume that growth in the labour force is due to immigration, where the assumption of proportionality between $\partial X_i/\partial Y$ and S_i is more plausible, then it is illogical to assume no trade. And if there is trade, the real terms of trade must change. There will be a welfare gain or loss and the uncertainty returns. Above all, of course, it is never plausible to assume that the real welfare effects of price changes give rise to proportional changes in the consumption of each commodity.

We conclude this section with what it is hoped represents a few more common-sense remarks. It could be that some economists would wish to argue that their belief, if they hold it, that population growth must reduce the real wage is not entirely based upon the supply/demand arguments which have been reviewed above. At least two other approaches are possible. First, there is the so-called 'law of diminishing returns' which deems it to be self-evident that the greater the quantity of labour applied to given natural resources, the smaller will be the product of the last unit of labour employed. And since no producer will pay in wages to any labourer more than the value of the product produced by that labourer, the wage rate must fall as the ratio of labour to resources increases. The second possible argument is the argument from observation. It might be claimed as a matter of fact that over-populated countries are poor countries. We consider these suggestions in turn.

The 'law of diminishing returns' as applied in the present context is particularly naïve. It rests upon the incorrect supposition that, except for an 'index number problem' which can be ignored, all commodities can readily be aggregated into one commodity called 'production' irrespective of the problem under review. If only one commodity is produced by, say, capital and labour, then it must be true that the labour/capital ratio in its manufacture must grow as the work force grows. But a moment's reflection shows that, as soon as we have three or more items in production, the labour/capital ratio for each separate industry need not rise even though it rises for the country as a whole, for the ratio of all labour to all capital is simply a weighted average of the separate industry ratios, the weights being the levels of production. Everything depends upon what happens to the weights as prices change. Furthermore, if there exist three or more factors of production it is not even true any longer that a rise in the labour/resources ratio necessarily implies a fall in the productivity of labour, even though for each separate industry the law of diminishing returns continues to hold. As we saw in Chapter 16, the 'index number problem' is sometimes precisely the problem we are interested in. To aggregate is simply to lose the baby with the bath water. All that our algebra has done is to reflect this fact.

On the argument from observation there are at least two points to be made. First, one wonders whether the observation has not been rather more casual than is desirable, or indeed in what sense observation is even possible in present circumstances. It may be little more than the unconscious absorption of constantly repeated dogma which leads us to feel intuitively that Indian labour is poor because of India's 'teeming millions', for her labour/land ratio is much less than that of Belgium or even the United Kingdom. Again Australia is (or was before the most recent discoveries) relatively poor in what is commonly called 'natural resources', yet its wage rates are high. The Congo on the other hand is unbelievably rich in natural resources yet its wage rates are low. If one is tempted to wonder whether wage rates run in proportion to capital per head, there is always the case of Abu Dhabi, whose total resources consist of no capital, one oasis and a hole in the ground exuding oil, yet whose citizens are well set to become the richest in the world next to those of Kuwait.

The second argument against casual observation is that even if it were true that a high labour/resources ratio necessarily implied low wage rates, this would not entirely contradict the results obtained from the algebra. What the model proves is that, when the labour force grows, real wages can conceivably rise *over a certain range.* If we observe a country A, with a low labour/capital ratio, whose labour is rich, and another, B, with a high labour/capital ratio and poor labour, this is not in itself sufficient to enable us to infer that the growth of labour in A will cause the real wage *immediately* to fall. It does of course suggest that if we continue the process until the two labour/capital ratios are identical then real wage rates must be the same and A's wage rates will accordingly have fallen. But there is no reason to suppose that A's wage rates must fall continuously until they are the same as B's. They may rise first and then fall.

Even more important, we have to remind ourselves once more that there are in the real world many more than two kinds of resources (factors of production). Nothing has ever been established either empirically or theoretically to suggest that the same labour/other resources ratio will give rise to the same wage rate if the composition of 'other resources' is different. Nor in the present state of know-ledge can we be quite sure what 'other resources' mean. In ordinary language we may be quite willing to say that 'labour' is paid less in the Congo than it is in the United States. But for the more exact purpose of *explaining* these differences and their concomitant differ-ences in commodity prices, it may be incorrect to identify educated labour with uneducated labour. Differences in the wage rates of Congolese and U.S.A. citizens might well persist even if Congolese were allowed to live and work in America with full rights and privileges (except education). It may be that in observing that low real wages are (apparently) associated with a higher labour/resources ratio we are observing no more than that those with less educational advantages tend to earn less than those with better.

Our final conclusion is that it would be exceedingly dangerous to assume, on the basis of intuition or over-simplified theory, that growth in the labour force necessarily reduces the real wage rate. There is no substitute for careful empirical inquiry. We have dis-covered in an earlier chapter that trading in commodities cannot be shown to, and in many cases very probably does not, tend to equalise the rewards of factors. We have now learned that the same could be true even of the migration of factors. It is true of course that labour will tend to leave countries where rewards are low for those where rewards are high. But it does not by any means follow that by this act the wage rate is reduced in the host country, as the algebra shows. Nor, in view of the work of the present chapter and Chapter 16, have we the right to expect, without empirical inquiry, that labour should necessarily come from a country where the labour/resources ratio is low and go to one where it is high.

We do not dispute of course that, as a matter of logic, a long-run stationary equilibrium exists where techniques of production are the same in every country for commodities produced in common and where accordingly every factor receives the same real reward wherever it is located. But is this equilibrium stable? What the algebra suggests is that there may *not* be an automatic economic regulator carrying us to such a position either through migration or through trade. And is this really surprising? It is commonly said that disparities in real welfare are growing greater rather than less in the present century. We observe migration from the subcontinent of India to the United Kingdom despite the lower land/labour ratio of the last country. Can it be supposed that some Congolese might not wish to settle in Belgium, where almost certainly real rewards are greater, despite the fact that in the Congo there is a lower ratio of labour to real resources by any reasonable measure? Again, who would wish to hold that white settlers arriving in South Africa necessarily reduce the real wage of the white population relative to the (on the average) less well-educated black? It may be that the algebra above represents the beginning of a bridge between over-simplified theory and some of the apparent anomalies observable in the real world.

18.5 CAPITAL ACCUMULATION IN A CLOSED ECONOMY

A great deal has been written about problems of growth, ranging from visionary projections of the course of human history to academic inquiry into the circumstances in which imaginary and barely possible models of non-existent communities might, at an infinite time hence, reach a state of 'equilibrium'. All of these studies are valuable in their way and give important insight into the real problems and choices which modern governments are bound to face. On the other hand it is the view, at least of the present writer, that what we have so far learned about growth confirms the impossibility, even in principle, of saying anything very useful about the actual or desirable course for any economy beyond a relatively short period ahead. Accordingly we shall confine our interest to this kind of study. Indeed, it is not proposed to look ahead at all in the strictest meaning of the words 'look ahead'. We shall examine only the current direction and rate of change of certain variables in the economy as it is, an inquiry which calls for nothing new in the way of mathematical techniques. That there really is nothing new should in fact be obvious, since we shall find that at least one classical problem of growthmanship is already solved implicitly in the previous two sections, and this is our excuse for the present remarks.

If one were asked to sum up the difference in attitude towards growth displayed by economists of the nineteenth and twentieth centuries respectively, it would be tempting to say that the former had an interest in the evolution of society whilst the latter seem more concerned with growth of productive power, that is, getting more for less effort. The present writer has an uncomfortable feeling that there is something less dignified about the newer interest than the old despite very proper intentions in regard to underdeveloped territories. It is to be hoped therefore that the reader will excuse the following brief incursion into the history of economic thought.

Classical writers of the last century fall into two groups, characterised by pessimism and optimism respectively. The pessimists† observed the growing labour and capital stock applied to what was understood to be limited natural resources. For reasons very close to, but perhaps less coherent than, the supply/demand argument of section 18.4, it was believed that the final outcome must be a secular decline in the real wage rate. People must, in the long run, be made worse off by growth. Optimists‡ on the other hand agreed the logic of the pessimists but disputed the premises. It was felt that the lesson of the declining wage rate would be quickly learned and the population growth accordingly voluntarily checked. A stationary state or 'equilibrium' would eventually be reached with no further growth except perhaps that generated by minor technical change. One or two super-optimists§ among the optimistic group attached more importance to what we should now call either technical advance or the productive power of capital and foresaw some part of the

† e.g. West or Ricardo.
‡ John Stuart Mill would be the archetype.
§ Carey and List might be classed as super-optimists.

extraordinary growth in real wealth which in the event actually
occurred in some areas of the world.

Well-meaning attempts to classify thinkers into tidy groups is of
course always bound to fail, so that there is no room for Karl Marx
in either of the categories above. Marx believed above all in the
productive power of capital and clearly foresaw its vast potentialities.
On the other hand he looked forward to both a falling real wage rate
and, paradoxically, a falling rate of profit. The productivity of
capital in the Marxian scheme would be directed in the main simply
to the production of still more capital, at least until the system
destroyed itself. One might add that almost all the writers above
consistently or inconsistently took for granted a falling rate of profit,
since this seemed at the time an obviously observable phenomenon.
The only difference lay in their explanations of the observed facts.

If we were asked, in the light of our work above, to comment upon
nineteenth-century disputations, what would we say? It would be
necessary, of course, to defend our belief in the forces of competition
and argue that we are not too far wrong when we suppose that
commodity prices are always equal to cost, including the reward of
capital. Given this fundamental assumption, however, the model of
growth of sections 18.2, 18.3 and 18.4, properly interpreted, give
some answers. The rate of change dA_i/dt per unit of time measures
the growth of the ith natural endowment where i may be capital or
labour. The rate of change of price, p_3, of the third factor of production, that is dp_3/dt, is immediately given by (18.2.12) or (18.3.4)
multiplied by dA_3/dt. Similarly we may work out the rate of change
over time of any variable of the system (18.2.1).

Suppose first that factor 3 is capital and we are witnessing growth
of capital at the rate dA_3/dt. What of the rate of interest? The reader
should note carefully that dp_3/dt cannot be the rate of change in the
money rate of interest. To suppose that it is is inconsistent with the
notion that capital is real and that accumulation demands an act of
saving (see appendix to Chapter 15). The rate of interest r is the
rental for money, whereas A_3 represents an aggregate of the timing or
roundaboutness of all production processes in the economy which is
independent of money.

If the money measure of 'roundaboutness' rises because, say, of a
rise in the general level of prices, the total money rental of a given
quantity of 'roundaboutness' rises even though the rental of money,
r, remains constant. To put the matter more specifically, a given
machine may embody a certain amount of 'roundaboutness' priced

at £100. If now there is a rise in the price of the machine, the money rental for the machine will rise even though the rate of interest remains constant. It follows that observation of dp_3/dt tells us nothing by itself about the movement of the money rate of interest. In order to solve for r with complete accuracy it would be necessary to turn to the formula in the appendix to Chapter 15 and to separate any change in p_3 due to growth into its constituent parts. Since p_3 depends upon r and upon all other factor prices (in this case p_1 and p_2), changes in p_3 will break up into changes in r, p_1 and p_2. Hence if we solve the system (18.2.2) for dp_1, dp_2 and dp_3, the value of dr may be obtained by substitution.

Inspection of the formula for p_3 (appendix to Chapter 15) reveals the following property. Doubling p_1 and p_2, keeping r constant, doubles p_3 which in turn doubles q_1, q_2 and q_3. This suggests that the money rate of interest will be independent of our chosen numeraire and this accords with common sense. r is a number of pounds money per pound money, that is, it is the money cost of renting money. If all prices double and hence the money value of real wealth doubles, the rental of money should stay constant. Thus we should find that in seeking to solve for the change in the money rate of interest it will not matter which price we hold constant. Whether we keep q_3 constant or Y in the model (18.2.1), we shall get the same answer for dr/dt in contrast to the problems raised in our discussion (sections 18.3 and 18.4) of the effect of growth on the real wage rate.

This conclusion saves us a good deal of trouble, for it is now intuitively obvious that in view of earlier results we shall not be able to say whether r rises or falls as saving takes place. We have already shown that we do not know the sign of dp_3/dt. *A fortiori* we do not know the signs either of dp_1/dt or dp_2/dt. Hence we do not know the sign of dr/dt. This must be the case whether we take q_3 or Y or any other variable as numeraire.

Remembering that p_3 is a rental price for real capital, the algebra of sections 18.3 and 18.4 also demonstrates that we do not even know whether the rental for real capital falls, either relative to any commodity price (since commodity 3 may be any commodity) or relative to aggregate money income Y. Even if we knew that the rental did fall, say, relative to Y, it still would not follow that r must fall, for r could rise provided some index of factor prices fell relatively more than p_3. Once again we have an agnostic conclusion – and this for much the same reasons that we reached a similar conclusion in the case of real wages. Changes in the structure of demand may easily increase the demand for 'money capital' by an amount greater than the increased supply generated by the act of saving.

Our comment on the falling rate of interest controversy must therefore be that, on their one point of agreement, nineteenth-century economists were wrong. The money rate of interest could fall but it might not. It is obvious also that if we allow the labour force to grow as well as capital, the position is even less certain than would be the case if capital alone were the growing factor. If we wish to know whether the money interest rate will rise or fall *next year*, we have first to predict the expected *rate* of growth of labour, capital and any other natural resource. Given then some knowledge of the response rates of demand and supply, etc., to prices, and given information on optimal techniques a_{ij} we could, after considerable calculation, reach a conclusion. But even this would depend upon the development of a much more realistic and complex model than that described here. And we emphasise again that the answer we get will depend upon the numerical values of the fundamental response rates which may themselves change over time.

The work so far also makes it clear that both the pessimists and the optimists of the nineteenth century missed a great deal of the point in other respects as well. No one would wish to dispute that if world population ever reached the point where standing-room only was available, then in some sense the consumption of commodities per individual would have to be a great deal lower than it is today. But equally it is obvious that such a statement has little meaning. Taken literally, the situation could never exist. Either some revolutionary way must be found to contain the imagined population, by building upwards or downwards or other means, or a check to population growth must occur. That is, either the new way of life will be so different as to render meaningless any idea of comparison of real wage rates, or population growth will be controlled to an extent sufficient to raise doubts about the validity of the assumption that a reduced standard of living is necessarily implied.

All of this focuses attention upon the twentieth-century view of growth. Capital accumulation and population growth are now no longer thought of as acts of God but as instruments of policy. The rates of change dA_i/dt of the algebra should be looked upon as numbers under the control of government whether they are so in fact or not. If they are not they must become so, as the nineteenth-century optimists foresaw. What we have learned from our inquiries, therefore, is that simple arguments based upon some notion of a very long-run final state of evolution towards which society is supposed to be progressing will not do. Examination of the direction of movement of the variables of even the relatively simple model of this chapter suggests that the economy need not necessarily be moving in the direction to be expected from any special view of the long-run evolutionary trend. Whether the labour force is growing more rapidly than the capital stock or vice versa, it is impossible to predict either absolute or relative wage/interest rate changes without statistical inquiry.

From this it should be understood also that when rates of growth of labour and capital are looked on as instruments of policy, it is again impossible to say what is the 'best' rate of growth of each without statistical measurement. The number $\sum q_i \, dX_i/dt$, which is the change in welfare over time, will clearly be dependent on all the fundamental response rates which appear in our model. We could, if we chose, easily find what policy maximises welfare growth by the usual methods of this book. But we know enough already to be sure that the direction of the welfare change and hence proper choice of policy will depend upon both factor and commodity price changes, which in turn depend upon the values taken by the K_{ij} and a_{ij} of our model. No *general* rule is available which will apply to all economies in all situations. There is no point therefore in engaging in algebraic exercises simply to obtain the answer 'don't know'. What is needed is a realistic computerised model of the economy to which all questions may be put using essentially the techniques of this book in an infinitely more complex framework.

The reader is now reminded that so far in this chapter our model has been of a closed economy without international trade. Partly as an exercise and partly because we have already raised in Chapter 10 the problem of growth and the terms of trade, applicable only to a trading economy, we shall how develop the model in this direction.

Again, at the beginning of this chapter reference was made to an argument purporting to prove that under conditions of competition individuals will ordinarily lend overseas more money than is socially desirable. It will be recalled that this was based upon the intuitive belief that capital accumulation must lead to a fall in the rate of interest, a proposition we have now shown is not necessarily true. It is desirable therefore to re-examine the whole question of the welfare effects of overseas lending, and this also will be one of the tasks of the present chapter.

18.6 GROWTH AND THE TERMS OF TRADE

In Chapter 10 it was shown that in a world where each country produces only one commodity, that country which is growing faster will ordinarily lose some of its gains to the rest of the world. The product of growth is spread throughout the world by a movement against the growing country of the real terms of trade. This section is intended to serve as a warning to those who might be tempted to suppose that this reflects a general rule which can be applied at all times to any kind of economy. In fact, wherever two or more commodities are produced the conclusions of Chapter 10 may quite ordinarily be reversed. Gains from growth may lead to still further gains from improvements in the real terms of trade.

The common sense of this is obvious. Growth leads to growth in demand which in turn implies a greater consumption of importables. If importables cannot be produced at home, the growing country must compete, with its own good, for more importables in a world market where the supply of importables is no greater than before. Obviously the price of importables will rise relative to exportables. On the other hand if the home country actually produces some of its own importables, some growth will occur in this sector. Furthermore, relative market prices will change with consequent changes in the pattern of production. It is accordingly easy to see that the increased supply of importables might well exceed the increased demand so that importable prices could fall. It is our purpose now to trace these changes more exactly with our usual algebraic techniques.

First we set up the equations of the model. With two countries, each exporting one commodity but producing two, we have the following system:

$$q_1 x_1 - q_2 x_2 = 0 \qquad \text{Balance of payments balanced}$$

$$x_1 = X_1' - S_1' \qquad \text{Exports equals foreign consumption less foreign supply}$$

$$x_1 = S_1 - X_1 \qquad \text{Exports equals home supply minus home consumption} \qquad (18.6.1)$$

$$Y = \sum_i q_i S_i$$
$$Y' = \sum_i q_i S_i'$$

Aggregate expenditure equals value of production at home and abroad

All symbols have the usual meaning, except that with all commodities traded and with no taxes or tariffs there is no need to distinguish between home and foreign commodity prices. The economic meaning of the equations (18.6.1) set out above serves also as a sufficient reminder of definitions. If S_i is taken to be a given function of prices and if X_i is again a function of prices and Y, we have in the system (18.6.1) five equations in six unknowns, two q_i, Y, Y', x_1 and x_2. Thus, taking q_1 as a given numeraire, it is possible to solve for the remaining unknowns.

For greatest generality we suppose two factors of production, capital and labour, which we assume to be growing at the rates dA_1/dt and dA_2/dt respectively. Thus, taking changes, we have the following equations in matrix notation:

$$
\begin{Bmatrix}
\begin{bmatrix}
-x_2 & q_1 & -q_2 & 0 & 0 \\
K'_{12} + X'_2 \dfrac{\partial X'_1}{\partial Y} & 1 & 0 & 0 & -\dfrac{\partial X'_1}{\partial Y} \\
-K_{12} - X_2 \dfrac{\partial X_1}{\partial Y} & 1 & 0 & \dfrac{\partial X_1}{\partial Y} & 0 \\
-S_2 & 0 & 0 & 1 & 0 \\
-S'_2 & 0 & 0 & 0 & 1
\end{bmatrix}
\begin{bmatrix}
\dfrac{dq_2}{dt} \\[1mm]
\dfrac{dx_1}{dt} \\[1mm]
\dfrac{dx_2}{dt} \\[1mm]
\dfrac{dY}{dt} \\[1mm]
\dfrac{dY'}{dt}
\end{bmatrix}
\end{Bmatrix}
$$

$$
= \begin{Bmatrix}
0 \\[2mm]
0 \\[2mm]
\dfrac{\partial S_1}{\partial A_1}\dfrac{dA_1}{dt} + \dfrac{\partial S_1}{\partial A_2}\dfrac{dA_2}{dt} \\[2mm]
\sum_i q_i \dfrac{\partial S_i}{\partial A_1}\dfrac{dA_1}{dt} + \sum_i q_i \dfrac{\partial S_i}{\partial A_2}\dfrac{dA_2}{dt} \\[2mm]
0
\end{Bmatrix}
$$

$$(18.6.2)$$

In this model we have assumed no growth in the rest of the world The symbols K_{ij} have the usual meaning. We recall also that

$\sum_i q_i\, \partial S_i/\partial A_j$ is equal to p_j, a fact we shall make use of in writing solutions to the equations (18.6.2), and we remind the reader that

$$\Sigma\, q_i \frac{\partial S_i}{\partial q_j} = 0.$$

Obviously, if q_2 rises in consequence of growth, the terms of trade move against country 1, for q_1 is constant. In order therefore to accord with the results of Chapter 10 it would be necessary to be able to show that dq_2/dt is always positive in sign. In fact we shall discover that this need not be the case.

Solving (18.6.2) in the usual way, we are able to express dq_2/dt as the ratio of two determinants, namely, the determinant of the matrix on the left-hand side of (18.6.2) divided into the same determinant, with the vector on the right-hand side of (18.6.2) replacing column one. It is convenient to reduce the denominator of this expression by multiplying column four by S_2 and column five by S_2', adding both to column one. In view of the 1's in rows four and five, this operation yields a 3×3 determinant which easily expands to give an expression

$$- q_2 \left[K_{12}' - x_2 \frac{\partial X_1'}{\partial Y} + K_{12} + x_2 \frac{\partial X_1}{\partial Y} \right] \qquad (18.6.3)$$

Note that we have replaced $X_2' - S_2'$ by $- x_2$ and $S_2 - X_2$ by x_2, which we are entitled to do by definition of x_2.

Strictly speaking the sign of (18.6.3) is uncertain. On the other hand there is a very strong bias towards a positive sign. If units are chosen so that all commodity prices are unity, $\partial X_1'/\partial Y$ and $\partial X_1/\partial Y$ will in ordinary cases be less than unity, being the proportion of an increment of expenditure directed towards commodity 1 abroad and at home respectively. Moreover, they will ordinarily be not so very different numerically. On the other hand K_{12}'/x_2 and K_{12}/x_2 are certainly negative in sign and in sum seem likely to exceed the difference between $\partial X_1'/\partial Y$ and $\partial X_1/\partial Y$. We suppose therefore that (18.6.3) is positive.

Accordingly to sustain the argument that dq_2/dt is necessarily negative it would be sufficient to show that the numerator of our solution for dq_2/dt is negative wherever the K_{ij}s of (18.6.3) outweigh the income effect in (18.6.3) as indicated.

Straightforward expansion of the numerator leads to an expression

$$q_2 \left[\Pi' - \Pi \frac{\partial X_1}{\partial Y} \right] \qquad (18.6.4)$$

where
$$\Pi' = \frac{\partial S_1}{\partial A_1}\frac{dA_1}{dt} + \frac{\partial S_1}{\partial A_2}\frac{dA_2}{dt}$$

and
$$\Pi = \sum_i q_i \frac{\partial S_i}{\partial A_1}\frac{dA_1}{dt} + \sum_i q_i \frac{\partial S_i}{\partial A_2}\frac{dA_2}{dt} = \sum_j p_j \frac{dA_j}{dt}$$

Obviously Π is positive as long as each natural resource is growing rather than diminishing. Everything therefore depends upon the sign and magnitude of Π'. But inspection of equation (18.2.6) above, reduced to take account of the fact that we have now only two factors of production, reveals that $\partial S_1/\partial A_1$ and $\partial S_1/\partial A_2$ *must* be of opposite sign. It is easy in fact to choose values of dA_i/dt so that Π' is positive whatever the magnitudes involved. It is equally easy to see that Π' may be less in magnitude than $\Pi(\partial X_1/\partial Y)$, thereby turning the real terms of trade in *favour* of the growing country rather than against.

Indeed, in this case the condition for a favourable movement of the terms of trade may be put quite simply in words. Recalling that commodity prices are assumed to be unity by choice of unit, Π' can be seen to be the increase in the value of output of commodity 1 which would have occurred if prices had remained constant. Similarly Π is the change in the value of *all* output which would have been observed in country 1 if prices had remained constant. Hence $\Pi(\partial X_1/\partial Y)$ is the change in the value of aggregate expenditure which would have been directed towards commodity 1 if prices had remained constant. Clearly this could be either greater or less than the increased value Π' of output of exportables.

Notice that crucial determinants of sign and magnitude are first the determinant $|a_{ij}|$ of optimal factor techniques and second the 'mix' of growth rates of resources $\partial A_i/\partial t$. Much depends on whether, say, capital is growing faster than labour or vice versa.

18.7 DEPLETION OF NATURAL RESOURCES

Throughout this book so far we have assumed that natural resources and/or the capital stock are either growing or are constant. It is perhaps worth remarking, if only because the point is so seldom noted in economic theory, that the act of production by itself may and ordinarily does lead to the depletion of the stock of some resources. Indeed, the fact is so much discussed in other contexts that it is surprising that it has received so little formal attention. It is also true that the *rate* of depletion might well depend upon prices, since it could depend upon the rate of production.

None of this, however, will make any difference to our conclusions, for the only amendment called for to our argument would be the introduction of negative $\partial A_i/\partial t$ or the inclusion in the system of new equations relating A_i to prices or production or both. Obviously this would serve only to lessen the possibility of reaching *a priori* conclusions. We see no point therefore in working at this stage even more complicated algebra only to show what can be shown at a more simple level. Useful answers, as usual, await numerical analysis.

18.8 OVERSEAS LENDING

The question of the desirability of international investment is currently a political issue and should not therefore pass without comment. It is convenient to include some account of this in the present chapter since the whole argument is closely allied to problems of growth and is in any case concerned with variations in the stock of national capital exactly as we have studied them.

The point is a simple one. Any country where citizens are willing to save has a measure of choice open to it. An act of saving is an act of waiting and, as we saw in Chapter 5 of Book I, whenever saving takes place, if full employment of resources is to be maintained, it is necessary to use up in some other way factors of production which would otherwise be employed to create consumer goods. Either the government must increase its own spending or the timing of inputs must be reorganised so as to increase the capital stock. If the capital stock is to be increased, one more choice is open. We might increase our exports to create a balance of payments surplus, thus transferring the 'waiting' abroad, at the same time lending the foreign country sufficient funds to pay for their excess imports. This might make possible an increase in the capital stock abroad. Alternatively the waiting may be used to increase our own capital stock. The question is, which is better, or alternatively, how much good do we do by lending abroad in this way?

Of course the activity described may not be, and usually is not, the consequence of some conscious government action. The result may be achieved by direct government lending, but more usually it would be the consequence of individuals, or businessmen acting on behalf of their firms, either lending money abroad or building productive equipment abroad in pursuance of their own private interests. Nevertheless it is possible by direct banning or by other means to control private lending abroad and attention is currently being paid to the question whether this should be done.

One apparently obvious reason why it might be desirable to discourage investment abroad is that foreign lending imposes a strain upon the balance of payments. Even though the value of exports may be equal to the value of imports, the actual balance of payments will be in deficit by the amount of foreign lending. Individuals in the U.K. cannot lend dollars to America unless they have first been bought from America by exports. Alternatively if pounds rather than dollars are lent, these can be spent in the last analysis only in the U.K. In other words we have a transfer problem exactly as described in Chapter 6 and this may of itself be an embarrassment.

Against such a view it is often pointed out that lending overseas creates a continuous stream of interest payments in the reverse direction which favours the balance of payments. Indeed, a once-for-all act of lending affects the balance of payments only in the single period when the lending takes place. On the other hand the stream of interest payments helps the balance indefinitely afterwards. The case against foreign lending based on balance of payments difficulties is not clear-cut and in the long run is no case at all, for in the long run all the money lent and more must be returned.

But this is by no means the whole of the story. We have already referred to an argument (section 18.2) which claims that private individuals will always lend too much abroad, since they will tend to lend wherever the rate of profit (interest) is highest. It is then, as we have noted, assumed that the act of lending will reduce the profit rate causing a loss of revenue on the existing *stock* of capital held abroad. This loss must be deducted from the rate earned on the new capital to measure the true social return, and there is no automatic mechanism to ensure that this will be done (see above, section 18.2).

We have now assembled the apparatus needed to show how imperfect this argument is. In the first place it is not at all clear what the 'rate of profit' which the individual investor is supposed to look at really is. Is it r, the rate of interest on money, or is it p_i, the *rental* of the real work in progress which is the ith input in our model? It is easy in fact to think of circumstances in which it might be either. If the lender is simply offering money for which he is to receive a fixed rate of interest, then the price in which he is interested will be the rental of money r. But if the lender is a businessman intent on setting up a productive process to be owned by himself but operated in the foreign country, he will have a very considerable interest in the actual quantity of work in progress that can be acquired for any given sum of money expressed in his own currency. It could be that some of the objects reflecting this work in progress can be acquired in the home country and exported, in which case the businessman is exporting *real* capital and may wish to compare goods rentals p_i in the two countries.

To put the problem another way, as long as some factors of production are not traded and hence may have different prices at home and abroad, the price of 'real' capital (see appendix, Chapter 15) may be different at home and abroad. A given sum of money whether expressed in terms of home or foreign currency would create a different amount of real capital according as it is invested at home or abroad; that is, the same act of saving at home is capable of producing different amounts of capital in different locations. If we are to compare accurately the effects of capital creation at home or abroad, and if the capital creation is expressed in money, then we have to compare the effects of a *different* change in real capital stock in each case. If on the other hand *real* capital is lent, then we have to compare the welfare effects of the *same* change in capital stock.

We emphasise that there is no difficulty in principle in treating either case. We have in Chapter 15 (appendix) developed an unambiguous definition of the price of capital which permits exact computation of the difference in capital creation which we need to solve the problem. The theoretical inquiry, however, is much more complicated if we assume that it is money which is transferred, for we have a model in which commodity prices are identical in both countries so that factor prices in the two countries are related and can be worked out once the structure of capital is known. That is, they can be worked out in terms of common production possibilities and the capital structure. It follows that for a complete test of our conjecture that nothing is known *a priori* about welfare effects, it would be necessary to check whether the complex relation between capital prices implied by the argument above does not impose a constraint upon our choice of numbers in a counter-example.

Because of this difficulty and because we need only a counter-example to make our point, we shall confine our attention to the lending of real capital. That is, we shall consider the case where, for example, the home country undertakes a large piece of construction work abroad, say a dam and a power station, providing both the machinery and a labour force from home. This is not a totally unrealistic possibility and in any case the reader may, if he so chooses, check for himself that the introduction of the complications mentioned above makes no difference whatever to the principal conclusions we shall reach.

We now recall that we have already proved that the rental of real capital need not fall as a result of an increase in the capital stock, at least in a closed economy. It would therefore be very surprising if it turned out that we could show that it must fall in every case when the economy is supposed to be engaged in international trade. Trade opens up possibilities which make a positive result less likely rather than more. It seems probable therefore that the argument against foreign lending will fail on this account, although of course foreign lending *may* still be socially undesirable *if* capital rental abroad does fall in consequence of capital creation. Once again everything depends on measurement.

Nor is this all. In a open economy, with international trade, growth leads, as we have seen, to a change in relative commodity prices. This means a change in the real terms of trade suggesting, from earlier work, that there will be a social gain or loss on this account to be added to or to offset other losses or gains. No simple answer to the problem posed is available. We have no alternative but to develop a model on the usual lines. Before we begin this, however, we digress on a methodological point.

It is particularly tempting in the present case to wonder whether the loan of, say, £1 million worth of capital by Britain to the United States could possibly make any difference to the real terms of trade. Many economists would say that the effect would be insignificant and can accordingly be neglected. This is a grave error. Much depends on what one is trying to measure. It is true of course that the effect of the loan expressed as a percentage change in the real terms of trade is likely to be very small indeed. But that very small percentage change, when applied to the full £5,000 million of British trade abroad, will give a very significant number compared with the modest £100,000 worth of rental we should expect to get from our £1 million worth of loan.

If one wishes to argue that numbers of the magnitude of £100,000 are small enough to be neglected, the proper thing to do would be to forget the whole problem altogether and to say that whether we invest overseas or not will have little effect upon the value of our national income; therefore we need not be concerned. If on the other hand £100,000 looks like a large enough sum for us to worry whether it is £100,000 or nothing, then we must work the problem properly. It is utterly inconsistent to use the relative size of the sums involved as an excuse to neglect the difficult part of the problem and at the same time to be sufficiently concerned about the issue to work the simple part.

It is of course possible sometimes legitimately to neglect certain items as small. But it is not usually possible to do this unless we have first worked the problem in all its complexity to decide whether or not the effect really is small relative to the numbers we are interested in. We shall proceed therefore to develop a full model.

18.9 OVERSEAS LENDING – THE COMPLETE MODEL

The question we have now to put must be carefully defined before we can proceed. We are supposing that some part of the home country's production in the present period is to be set aside for capital creation either at home or abroad. The choice is simply, shall the investment be at home or abroad?

If the investment is to be abroad, the home country will experience temporarily a transfer problem (see Chapter 6 of Book I.). The real capital to be lent must be exported in the form of commodities, otherwise there can be no real act of saving on the part of the home country taken as a whole. On the other hand the transfer problem created is transient only. Once the real loan has been made, the value of exports can be allowed to fall back to their original level, indeed to something less than their original level since the flow of interest payments from abroad will have increased. In the case of investment abroad, therefore, we shall compare the situation *before* the loan with the final *equilibrium* situation after the loan, that is, after the transfer has been effected and when exports have fallen back appropriately. The transfer problem itself is left out of consideration. The reader will be able to follow more exactly what is meant here when he examines the equations specified below.

If the investment takes place at home we should have a situation very like that considered in the previous section. There will be growth due to capital accumulation which necessarily improves welfare. In addition, there would be a secondary change in welfare due to any resulting change in the real terms of trade. What we have to compare are the welfare changes generated by each of the alternative policies. We invest at home or abroad according as the welfare change is greater in the one case than in the other.

First we compute the welfare change if the increase in the capital stock takes place at home. The model here is essentially that set out in (18.6.1) except for one important modification. In order to be able to put our question at all, it is necessary to assume that country 1 holds a stock of capital abroad as well as at home. Let K' be this stock and let p_2' be the rental of capital abroad. The aggregate expenditure in country 1 will therefore be the value of output in country 1 *plus* the revenue $p_2'K'$ from rental of its foreign-based capital stock. Similarly the balance of payments equation must be amended to take account of the inflow of $p_2'K'$ from abroad. Hence equations one, four and five of (18.6.1) become:

$$q_1 x_1 + p_2' K' - q_2 x_2 = 0$$

$$Y = \sum q_i S_i + p_2' K'$$

and

$$Y' = \sum q_i S_1' - p_2' K'$$

Note that we must deduct profit payments from aggregate expenditure of country 2 just as we add it to country 1.

What we wish actually to compute is the welfare change $\sum q_i dX_i$ in country 1, and to this end we make the following simplification:

$$dY = \sum q_i dS_i + \sum S_i dq_i + K' dp_2' = \sum q_i dX_i + \sum X_i dq_i \quad (18.9.1)$$

This comes from taking changes in the expenditure equation and in the identity

$$Y = \sum q_i X_i$$

Note that K' is constant since the increase in capital stock occurs in the home country. From (18.9.1), making use of the fact that q_1 is our numeraire and of the definitions of exports and imports x_i, we find that the welfare change dW is given by

$$dW = \sum q_i dX_i = \sum q_i dS_i - x_2 dq_2 + K' dp_2'$$

We know also that $\sum_i q_i \dfrac{\partial S_i}{\partial q_j}$ is zero when competition prevails, so that

$$\sum q_i dS_i = \sum q_i \frac{dS_i}{dA_2} dA_2 = p_2 dA_2$$

where dA_2 is the increment of capital invested in country 1 and p_2 is the home rental of capital. Hence

$$dW = p_2 dA_2 - x_2 dq_2 + K' dp_2' \quad (18.9.2)$$

The result (18.9.2) is open at once to economic interpretation. Term one is the increased value of output (valued at the original prices) due to the increment dA_2 of capital. Term two is the loss or gain due to the change in the real terms of trade and term three is the loss or gain in profit receipts due to the change in the foreign rental price of capital.

We now recall from the work of Chapter 14 that it is possible to solve for dp_2' in terms of price changes dq_1 and dq_2 and the foreign inputs a_{ij}'. Thus we have

$$dq_1 = a_{11}' dp_1' + a_{12}' dp_2' = 0 \text{ (numeraire)}$$

and
$$dq_2 = a_{21}' dp_1' + a_{22}' dp_2'$$

or
$$dp_2' = \frac{a_{11}'}{J'} dq_2 \qquad (18.9.3)$$

where J' has the usual meaning, $|a_{ij}'|$. Putting (18.9.3) in (18.9.2) we have

$$dW = p_2 dA_2 + \left(\frac{a_{11}'}{J'} K' - x_2\right) dq_2 \qquad (18.9.4)$$

This form of dW is particularly convenient since it holds for both cases we are to examine. Even if the capital stock is invested abroad, it turns out that we arrive at an expression for dW formally the same as (18.9.4). The basic model is of course the same. The equivalent of (18.9.1) becomes

$$dY = \sum q_i dS_i + \sum S_i dq_i + K' dp_2' + p_2' dA_2' = \sum q_i dX_i + \sum X_i dq_i \qquad (18.9.5)$$

The added term on the left-hand side appears because the capital stock K' held abroad is increased by the amount dA_2' of the investment. Hence

$$dW^* = \sum q_i dS_i - x_2 dq_2 + K' dp_2' + p_2' dA_2'$$

where the * is added after dW to indicate that a different welfare effect is implied. In case two, the changes dS_i are the price-generated changes only since there is no change in the capital stock at home. Hence $\sum q_i dS_i$ is zero by (15.4.14), so that we now have

$$dW^* = p_2' dA_2' - x_2 dq_2 + K' dp_2'$$

$$= p_2' dA_2' + \left(\frac{a_{11}'}{J'} K' - x_2\right) dq_2^* \qquad (18.9.6)$$

This is of the same form as (18.9.4) but we have again starred dq_2 to remind the reader that this real terms of trade change will in general be quite different from that which occurs in case one. Obviously the relative magnitudes of the changes dq_2 and dq_2^* will be crucial. We shall therefore compare the two solutions for these variables. Taking changes in the equations (18.6.1), modified as explained to take account of capital held abroad by country 1, we have:

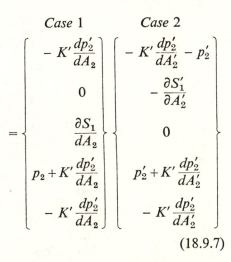

$$
\left\{
\begin{array}{ccccc}
-x_2 & q_1 & -q_2 & 0 & 0 \\
K_{12}' + X_2' \dfrac{\partial X_1'}{\partial Y} & 1 & 0 & 0 & -\dfrac{\partial X_1'}{\partial Y} \\
-K_{12} - X_2 \dfrac{\partial X_1}{\partial Y} & 1 & 0 & \dfrac{\partial X_1}{\partial Y} & 0 \\
-S_2 & 0 & 0 & 1 & 0 \\
-S_2' & 0 & 0 & 0 & 1
\end{array}
\right\}
\left\{
\begin{array}{c}
\dfrac{dq_2}{dA_2} \\[2mm]
\dfrac{dx_1}{dA_2} \\[2mm]
\dfrac{dx_2}{dA_2} \\[2mm]
\dfrac{dY}{dA_2} \\[2mm]
\dfrac{dY'}{dA_2}
\end{array}
\right\}
$$

$$
=
\underbrace{
\left\{
\begin{array}{c}
-K' \dfrac{dp_2'}{dA_2} \\[2mm]
0 \\[2mm]
\dfrac{\partial S_1}{dA_2} \\[2mm]
p_2 + K' \dfrac{dp_2'}{dA_2} \\[2mm]
-K' \dfrac{dp_2'}{dA_2}
\end{array}
\right\}
}_{\text{Case 1}}
\underbrace{
\left\{
\begin{array}{c}
-K' \dfrac{dp_2'}{dA_2'} - p_2' \\[2mm]
-\dfrac{\partial S_1'}{\partial A_2'} \\[2mm]
0 \\[2mm]
p_2' + K' \dfrac{dp_2'}{dA_2'} \\[2mm]
-K' \dfrac{dp_2'}{dA_2'}
\end{array}
\right\}
}_{\text{Case 2}}
$$

$$(18.9.7)$$

The two sets of equations (18.9.7) which are generated have the same left-hand side so that the left-hand side has been written out once only. The separate vectors on the right-hand side are listed under case 1 and case 2 respectively.

Obviously the denominator for the solution for dq_2/dA_2 or dq_2^*/dA_2' is the same and is the same as that computed in the previous section for dq_2/dt, i.e.

$$- q_2 \left[K_{12}' - x_2 \frac{\partial X_1'}{\partial Y} + K_{12} + x_2 \frac{\partial X_1}{\partial Y} \right]$$

The numerators are likewise conveniently calculated as in the previous section. In fact, we have, cancelling $-q_2$, the following results:

$$
\left.
\begin{aligned}
\frac{dq_2}{dA_2} &= \frac{-\dfrac{\partial S_1}{\partial A_2} + p_2 \dfrac{\partial X_1'}{\partial Y} + K' \dfrac{dp_2'}{dA_2} \left(\dfrac{\partial X_1'}{\partial Y} - \dfrac{\partial X_1}{\partial Y} \right)}{\varDelta} \quad \text{Case 1} \\[2em]
\frac{dq_2^*}{dA_2'} &= \frac{-\dfrac{\partial S_1'}{\partial A_2'} + p_2' \dfrac{\partial X_1}{\partial Y} + K' \dfrac{dp_2'}{dA_2'} \left(\dfrac{\partial X_1}{\partial Y} - \dfrac{\partial X_1'}{\partial Y} \right)}{\varDelta} \quad \text{Case 2}
\end{aligned}
\right\} \quad (18.9.8)
$$

where $\varDelta$ is that part of the denominator above in the square bracket.

To develop an instructive counter-example, it is convenient to consider a special case. We suppose therefore that trade between the two countries has equalised factor prices and that accordingly the techniques of production in use are the same in both countries.

It follows at once that

$$\frac{\partial S_1}{\partial A_2} = \frac{\partial S_1'}{\partial A_2'}$$

for we know that

$$\frac{\partial S_1}{\partial A_2} = -\frac{a_{21}}{J} \qquad (18.9.9)$$

and by assumption production techniques and hence a_{21} and J are the same in both countries. Equalisation of factor prices also implies

$$p_2 = p_2'$$

Consider now the case where J is negative and where the income responses $\partial X_1'/\partial Y$ and $\partial X_1/\partial Y$ are sufficiently alike to ensure that the first two terms of the numerators in (18.9.8) outweigh the third term in each case. The same assumption will of course ensure that $\varDelta$ is negative in sign. Since the first two terms in the numerators of (18.9.8) are positive, it follows that both dq_2/dA_2 and dq_2^*/dA_2' must be negative in sign.

A particularly interesting example, which the reader will recognise as contradicting much of the intuitive argument earlier referred to, would be one where investment abroad brings greater welfare *even though capital rentals are equal in both countries*, that is, where

$$\frac{dW}{dA_2'} - \frac{dW}{dA_2} > 0$$

which by (18.9.4) and (18.9.6) means

$$\left(\frac{a_{11}'}{J'} K' - x_2\right)\left(\frac{dq_2^*}{dA_2'} - \frac{dq_2}{dA_2}\right) > 0 \qquad (18.9.10)$$

since dA_2' equals dA_2 by assumption.

As J' is negative by assumption and both a_{11}' and x_2 are positive, (18.9.10) means that we have to find a case where

$$\frac{dq_2^*}{dA_2'} - \frac{dq_2}{dA_2} < 0$$

Using (18.9.8), a sufficient condition would be

$$\frac{p_2\left(\frac{\partial X_1}{\partial Y} - \frac{\partial X_1'}{\partial Y}\right) + K'\left(\frac{dp_2'}{dA_2'} + \frac{dp_2'}{dA_2}\right)\left(\frac{\partial X_1}{\partial Y} - \frac{\partial X_1'}{\partial Y}\right)}{\Delta} < 0$$

since $p_2 = p_2'$. And as by assumption dq_2/dA_2 and dq_2^*/dA_2' are both negative, and since J' is negative both dp_2'/dA_2' and dp_2'/dA_2 are positive by (18.9.3). It is clear therefore that by choosing $\partial X_1/\partial Y$ greater in magnitude than $\partial X_1'/\partial Y$ we have the required example. Note especially that our initial selection of the case where $\partial X_1/\partial Y$ and $\partial X_1'/\partial Y$ are sufficiently alike to keep the magnitude of

$$\left(\frac{\partial X_1}{\partial Y} - \frac{\partial X_1'}{\partial Y}\right)$$

sufficiently small does not in any way inhibit freedom of choice of sign for the same term.

18.10 CONCLUSIONS

The reader is reminded that the work above is constrained by the need to choose the simplest possible counter-example in a context where the problem of finding any example is very complicated. It is not legitimate simply to assign numbers to the various parameters without regard to the interrelations between them. Numbers assigned must satisfy all the sign conditions and relationships which we should expect to hold according to the theory of demand and supply. We emphasise therefore that all the oddities of the above example were included for the sake of simplicity and not because all possible counter-examples are odd. Many of the constraints disappear if we have three factors and three commodities. Nor would it be too difficult to find many more ordinary examples even in two dimensions. It is quite generally true that the chance of a gain from transferring capital overseas is just as likely as the chance of a loss.

We conclude that there is no possibility of saying on *a priori* grounds whether or not competition leads to an undesirable level of capital exports. The question put cannot be answered without knowledge of the numerical values of the relevant parameters.

It is certainly true of course that competition does not lead to an optimal level of overseas lending at least from the point of view of the lending country. Some control may be desirable. But we have no means of knowing, except after careful measurement, either the direction or magnitude of the required interference with the competitive process.

No extensive comment is needed on the common-sense reasons for our result. The classical argument that the individual looks only at his rental in reaching his decision and not at the important welfare effects of price changes is substantially correct. It is wrong, however, for reasons already given to suppose that we can tell the direction of these price changes without empirical inquiry.

EXERCISES

1. Show that (18.3.1) does not hold if taxes on production exist before immigration occurs.
2. From the equation system (18.3.3) find expressions for

$$\frac{dp_2}{dA_3} \quad \text{and} \quad \frac{dp_1}{dA_3}$$

   Prove that

$$\sum_i A_i \frac{dp_i}{dA_3} = 0$$

   Hint: Recall that

$$\sum_i A_i \frac{\partial S_j}{\partial A_i} = S_j$$

   since doubling factor endowment, prices constant, doubles supplies.

Hence show that the welfare of at least one factor of production must fall as a consequence of the growth of any factor even though the factor which loses may not be that which is growing.

3. Show that the result

$$\sum_i A_i \frac{dp_i}{dA_3} = 0$$

of exercise 2 is a condition of equilibrium and not an identity. Show that it does not hold if sales taxes are in existence.

4. Prove from the two commodity analogue of (18.2.6) that if $\partial S_1/\partial A_2$ is positive, $\partial S_2/\partial A_2$ is negative and vice versa. Show further that, no matter how many factors or commodities, if $\partial S_i/\partial A_j$ is positive at least one $\partial S_k/\partial A_j$ must be negative. In other words prove that not every co-factor of a non-zero determinant with all positive elements can be of the same sign. Hence show for the three-factor/three-commodity case that if $\partial S_3/\partial A_3$ is zero, at least one of $\partial S_2/\partial A_3$ and $\partial S_1/\partial A_3$ must be negative.

5. Refer to section 18.4. Hence show that even if a tax on production exists, a change dA_3 in A_3 will reduce the share in real wealth of factor 3 if each $\partial X_i/\partial Y$ is proportional to S_i whether $\partial X_i/\partial Y$ measures changes arising out of an increment of spending or an increase in the number of individuals in the community.

Hint: Write equation one of (18.3.3) as

$$\sum_i S_i \frac{dq_i}{dA_3} = dY - \sum_i q_i \frac{dS_i}{dA_3}$$

$$= p_3 - \sum_k \sum_i q_i \frac{\partial S_i}{\partial q_k} \frac{dq_k}{dA_3} - \sum_i q_i^* \frac{\partial S_i}{\partial A_3} - tq_3^* \frac{\partial S_3}{\partial A_3}$$

or

$$\sum_i \left(S_i + tq_3^* \frac{\partial S_3}{\partial q_i} \right) \frac{dq_i}{dA_3} = p_3 - \sum_k \sum_i q_i^* \frac{\partial S_i}{\partial q_k} \frac{dq_k}{dA_3} - \sum_i q_i^* \frac{\partial S_i}{\partial A_3} - tq_3^* \frac{\partial S_3}{\partial A_3}$$

which, using

$$\sum_k \sum_i q_i^* \frac{\partial S_i}{\partial q_k} \frac{dq_k}{dA_3} = 0$$

and

$$\sum_i q_i^* \frac{\partial S_i}{\partial A_3} = p_3$$

reduces to

$$\sum_i \left(S_i + tq_3^* \frac{\partial S_3}{\partial q_i} \right) \frac{dq_i}{dA_3} = - tq_3^* \frac{\partial S_3}{\partial A_3}$$

Thereafter proceed as in section 18.4 to show that both the new Δ and the new numerator to the analogue of (18.3.4) can be made symmetric.

Hence justify the claim in section 18.4 that it is the real wealth effects which cause the trouble when the increment of consumption is different from the average.

6. Set up a model of labour growth in a closed economy. Let

$$X_i^1 = X_i^1(q_1, q_2, q_3, Y^1)$$

and

$$X_i^2 = X_i^2(q_1, q_2, q_3, Y^2)$$

be demand functions for factor 1 (labour) and factors 2 and 3 together (the rest) respectively. Hence let

$$Y^1 = \frac{p_1 A_1}{\sum p_i A_i}$$

and

$$Y^2 = \frac{p_2 A_2 + p_3 A_3}{\sum p_i A_i}$$

be aggregate expenditure of 'labour' and 'others' respectively.

Following the principles of section 14.5 and Chapter 18, find the change in real welfare of labour due to an increase dA_1 in the work force. Assuming that all labourers have the same tastes in consumption, that all take each commodity in fixed proportions and that each new labourer again spends his income in the same way, show that it is still impossible to say whether labour gains or loses unless the demand functions 1 and 2 above are identical.

7. Carry out the same exercise as in exercise 6, except let a tax on production of some one commodity exist. Prove that once again the real income effect on labour is of uncertain sign. Hence justify the claims in section 18.4.

8. Introduce into the problem of section 18.6 a class of non-traded commodities in both countries. Find the conditions under which growth in the home labour force will cause the price of non-traded goods at home to fall relative to the prices of both traded commodities.

9. Construct a model with two countries each producing exportables, importables and non-traded items with three factors of production, land, labour and capital. The political situation in country 1

is such that any loss of welfare by labour will provoke an immediate revolution. An earthquake occurs in country 2 which destroys an amount dA_1' of that country's capital stock. Find the conditions under which this will be the cause of a revolution in country 1.

19 The Final Lesson – A Model for the Computer

19.1 WHAT NOW?

THE concluding chapter of any book ought to be its most important. Whatever message the work is intended to convey should be found in the closing sections in its clearest and most persuasive form. At such a point the reader will be armed with all the techniques and should have attained a sufficient degree of understanding to leave to the author who has something to communicate no excuse for failing to communicate. The words which follow therefore have been chosen with some care.

Again and again we have found in earlier chapters that the question put has had to be answered 'don't know'. Unlike the fool in the proverb we do at least understand that we do not know. But this offers little comfort, for none of our problems was trivial. Each case studied represents our best effort to discover the consequences of some policy which has been, or very well might be, the subject of actual legislation in the real world. Why is it that we seem always to have to answer 'don't know' to questions which, whether they are or are not crucial to human well-being, are at least widely believed to be crucial? The truth is that we have tried to do too much on the basis of *a priori* reasoning alone. Too little effort has been put into fact-finding, measurement and sophisticated analysis of observed data.

The time has long since passed when the individual thinker working alone in his armchair could make any significant contribution to positive economics. It may still be possible for the unaided philosopher to say something new about what is, or ought to be, regarded as 'good', but it is highly unlikely that he would ever be able to settle the direction and magnitude of the practical steps required to attain the proposed 'good' result without the assistance of a highly organised team of applied economists backed by very considerable financial resources and powers to require the production of data.

Conversely it seems, at least to the present author, that the problem of achieving given desired objectives is not difficult in principle provided the necessary financial and statistical resources can be made available. The major difficulties are political and practical. These difficulties arise first because the research effort now needed is both gigantic and expensive, and second because the need itself for purposeful research is not sufficiently widely accepted. The need is not accepted for a complex of reasons.

On the one hand there are those who continue to be influenced by the nineteenth-century belief that the economy is a self-regulating mechanism which will run itself with maximum efficiency if only the individual, suitably provided with 'proper incentive', is allowed 'freedom of action'. In other quarters it seems naïvely to be thought that all that is necessary to control economic forces is a government order. The only difference between King Canute and the Prices and Incomes Board is that the P.I.B. presumably believes that its various orders have some real (as distinct from apparent) effect, whereas King Canute's celebrated order to the waves was given precisely to demonstrate that there are after all some things which government exhortation cannot change.

Finally and above all, appeals for a large-scale, sophisticated and properly organised effort to solve the economic problem are scarcely to be heard above the cries of the numerous purveyors of the 'Wonderful Peppermint Cure'.† The Cure has many names, often ending in 'ism' but almost as frequently insidiously disguised as new and exciting economic policies understood at last to yield the final solution. The history of economic thought is littered with examples. *Laissez-faire*, the Single Land Tax, Social Credit, Free Trade, the Gold Standard, the Keynesian Revolution – all of these refer to ideas presented (not usually by their originators) as the one thing to solve everything. It is perhaps a reflection upon the sameness of human nature to observe that there is no lack of panaceas on current offer; 'productivity' or 'growth' or the 'Common Market' or 'technological advance' are the latest formulae for the Wonderful Cure which in fact does not exist.

The truth is that control of the economy is a highly complex technical task at present only partially understood. We can be sure, however, that no single simple method of control will ever be found. Economic institutions evolve in response to new technical discoveries and new ideas about what is desirable, and in response to new

---

† All we want is the six-hour day
And the five-day week and twice the pay
And for all the ills man must endure
The wonderful 'Wonderful Peppermint Cure'.

opportunities for international co-operation. As institutions and behaviour change, so will the problems and so will the methods of control. We have to contend with an organic entity full of new tricks and surprises. Even so we repeat, given the resources, the task is not impossible or even difficult in principle.

It may be thought perhaps that this is a large claim and that whoever makes claims ought properly to defend them; and this is the purpose of the present chapter. In one sense the work so far completed has served only to prove that deductive thinking by itself does not really get us very far. In another sense, however, the various exercises undertaken constitute an essential preliminary to the next step which, sooner or later, society must take. This will become clear as we proceed.

So far we have been manipulating a model which is 'dead'. Our attention has been concentrated upon 'equilibrium'. Either we have been concerned to compare the welfare of one equilibrium position with another or we have sought to explain why equilibrium might not automatically be attained and what steps should be taken to set this right. At the same time we have had to make do with a numeraire commodity the price of which has been assumed to remain constant. That is, we have had to opt out of any discussion of the way in which policies designed to achieve one purpose may in fact influence the economy in quite another direction. In the same way the section (Chapter 5) on employment problems stands uncomfortably on its own. Apart from warnings here and there, no systematic account has been given of the way in which taxation, say, affects the level of employment or what subsidiary policies are necessary to maintain full employment when, for other reasons, taxation is imposed. Similarly we have had to argue that currency depreciation is not a policy by itself since its consequences can be known only if it is assumed that some other policy (unspecified) maintains full employment and prevents inflation.

Remarkably enough, only a relatively few additions are needed to make the 'dead' model come alive. Using very much the same notation and not more than one or two extra ideas, we shall discover the living entity referred to above. Our model of the economy will change and grow of its own accord and require constant control to prevent matters getting out of hand in one or another sector. No longer shall we need a numeraire to study the consequences of policy. Employment, inflation, the balance of payments and relative prices are inextricably linked. We shall find ourselves able to study all the ramifications of any type of interference with the mechanism quite free of any kind of assumptions about 'other things held constant'. The more sophisticated reader with access to a computer should be able to experiment with the system to be described in order to discover for himself some of the tricks of which it is capable. The behaviour of the model will be found to parallel quite closely some of the contortions of the real economy which have been observed at different times in the past. We need to learn first to control the model. At the same time the model may be used as a framework for measurement. Finally, we learn through the model to control the economy itself, all the time carefully noting and measuring the basic changes which occur so that methods of control might keep pace with change and growth.

The purpose of the remainder of this chapter is limited but none the less ambitious. By describing a dynamic model and its uses, we hope to be able to bring the reader to an understanding

(*a*) that something can be done;

(*b*) of the way in which it can be done; and

(*c*) of the truth of our claim that sooner or later society must abandon the pretence that it can control what elementary observation reveals that it cannot yet control and that, accordingly, it must give the problem up or make up its mind to do whatever is necessary to solve it.

Research on the right lines is beginning, but only upon a microscopic scale. What is at present a trickle must become a flood.

19.2 A DYNAMIC MODEL

We proceed by formulating and numbering the equations of the model, following up the statement of each equation with a few words of explanation. The undermentioned conventions will be observed.

Where there are many equations of the same form we shall write only a representative example. Thus only one consumer demand equation will be included, it being taken for granted that if the model is to have n commodities then n equations of the specified form will be required. This makes it possible to use the notation, X, without any subscript for consumption of the representative commodity. If a *single* subscript is used, this implies a vector. For example, q_i no longer means the market price of ith commodity. It now represents the set of *all* market prices for all commodities 1 to n. If a symbol has a double subscript it means a matrix. Thus a_{ij} is the array of inputs of each factor required to produce unit output of each commodity. Where appropriate, equations may be written in matrix form, sometimes with a partitioning,† the meaning of which will be obvious from the context.

Certain new variables will appear which might be termed 'out of equilibrium' variables. For example, we shall now have excess profits and stock variations which are by their nature foreign to the concept of equilibrium. Variables of this kind we shall denote always with Greek symbols. Superscripts are used where necessary to identify variables, that is, we now write X^c for consumer demand to distinguish this from X^i which is demand by firms for the same commodity. Finally, we have in some equations to bring in unknown parameters which play a part similar to the familiar response rates, measuring the basic behaviour of the economy. For these we reserve the symbol α. We shall in fact put α^{ij} for the *j*th parameter in the *i*th equation. In all other respects every effort will be made to retain notation and conventions already familiar from earlier chapters. The model consists of the following equations:

$$X^c = X^c(q_i^h, Y) \tag{19.2.1}$$

(19.2.1) is simply the ordinary demand equation to be treated in the usual way except that Y is now aggregate expenditure on final consumer goods alone. Expenditure by firms on commodities for use as inputs and purchases by government will be identified later by the use of separate suffixes. The suffix c in (19.2.1) means 'consumers'.

At this point we comment also upon one of the host of difficulties which are universally encountered as soon as an attempt is made to associate equations like (19.2.1) with actual recorded data. Suppose that the commodity X is a durable item like refrigerators or grand pianos. Is the quantity X^c the number of units sold by the shops per year or per week, or is it the number of units actually in use by consumers? It is essential to be quite sure what the theory refers to before any attempt at measurement is made.

In the case of equation (19.2.1) there is no alternative to defining X^c as the quantity in use. Accordingly, q is a rental and Y is the total cost of renting all commodities. If the item concerned is one like, say, food, which is used up in one single act, then the quantity in use is

† See Almon, *Matrix Methods in Economics*, pp. 1–22, for an account of matrix notation and partitioning [2].

the same as the quantity used up and the rental is the same as the selling price. Thus there is no need to distinguish between the two types of commodity. Commodities used up are those 'in use' with a life of one time period only.

It is true of course that it is much easier in practice to get hold of actual statistics of quantities sold than it is to find out what commodities are in use in consumers' homes at any one time, but this is no excuse for fitting into a theory information other than that for which the theory calls. A consumer who buys a motor-car buys it for use not only in the current time period but also for use in future time periods. On the other hand a function like (19.2.1) makes sense only if it refers to one time period.

To put the problem another way, the reason why we write a function like (19.2.1) is to give expression to what we believe to be consistencies in human behaviour; that is, we believe that given the same prices and given the same expenditure the consumer will always demand the same quantity X^c. But if the commodity concerned is a motor-car and if the number X^c refers to actual purchases and the prices q refer to market prices, then we should not expect consistency. At given prices and with given aggregate expenditure, whether or not the consumer buys a motor-car must depend heavily upon whether or not a motor-car was purchased in the previous period. What is consistent in each time period is not the amount purchased but the amount held for use.

There is of course no difficulty in principle in all this. What is purchased and what is held in use are intimately bound up with one another and the one can be computed from the other. Thus if we write Q for purchases we should have

$$Q = (X^c(t) - X^c(t - 1) + \gamma(X^c(t - 1))$$

as a possible relation. This says that the quantity sold is equal to the change in the desired stock between period t and period $t - 1$ plus a factor γ times the stock in period $t - 1$ which represents replacement of stock wearing out. In practice our model should specify relations of this kind and attempts should be made to compute the value of γ. Naturally this would call for observation of data on both X^c and Q for many time periods, and the fact that information about X^c is hard to come by presents difficulties. But we repeat that this is a practical and not a theoretical problem. If society wishes to be able to control the economy, society must provide the data.

On the other hand for ease of comprehension we have not explicitly included a variable Q in the model. We do, however, have a variable D^h which is total home sales. This is shown in equation (19.2.5) below as dependent on some function $\phi(X^c)$. The function Q above may be thought of as a possible form of ϕ. Also for simplicity we have in the model intended q to be interpreted as a rental wherever it occurs. We shall comment upon this later. A model with rentals only is much easier to comprehend than one with market prices. It may be a fact that businessmen have a rule for setting market prices rather than rentals, but since one can be computed from the other the two amount to the same thing (see appendix, Chapter 15).

The next equation of the model is

$$S^h = S^h(\Pi, \Sigma^u) \tag{19.2.2}$$

which says that home production S^h is dependent upon excess profits, Π, and unplanned stock changes, Σ^u. Note that S^h here means actual production in the period. It is not, as in earlier sections of the book, where equilibrium is presumed, the output required to sustain a stock S^h of consumer goods in use (see appendix, Chapter 15). Note also that (19.2.2) is not a supply function in the ordinary sense of the word. On the contrary the presence of the 'out of equilibrium' variables Π and Σ indicate that it is one of the new dynamic equations designed to turn the dead equilibrium model into the moving analogue of the real economy that we are seeking to construct. In equilibrium both Π and Σ^u will be zero. On the other hand S^h will not be zero but should, with both Π and Σ^u zero, be the equilibrium level of supply.

One way of writing (19.2.2) to incorporate these desired properties would be

$$S^h(t) = \alpha^{21} \Pi + \alpha^{22} \Sigma^u + S^h(t - 1)$$

where α^{21} and α^{22} are constants to be determined by observation of actual experience. This form of (19.2.2) assumes that businessmen will manufacture the same quantity in period (t) as they manufactured in period $(t - 1)$ unless they observe either that something more than normal profit may be earned, or that they are able to sell more or less than they had planned. α^{21} should be positive, indicating that high profits induce extra output. α^{22} should be negative, implying that failure to sell the planned output will lead to a cut in production. When Π and Σ^u are both zero, supply is the same as in the previous period.

The reader should, however, be quite clear that the equation specified is just one proposal for the form of (19.2.2) out of many possible. The exact nature of the dependence is not as yet known. Nor are we able to deduce as much about the form of (19.2.2) from the assumption of human self-interest as we were about (19.2.1). On the other hand there is again no difficulty in principle. We have simply to study the reactions of businessmen to various situations, perhaps even by inducing them to play 'business games' with the very model we are now describing as well as by analysis of actual behaviour in the real world. It may then be found that it would be better to write Π squared or Π cubed instead of Π, or for that matter any other expression with Π in it, and similarly with Σ^u. Or it may be found desirable to introduce different forms of time lags, that is, $\Pi(t-1)$ and $\Sigma^u(t-1)$ may be important in determining businessmen's plans. The final selection of a function form will depend upon which best fits the facts. In the meantime the linear form is proposed partly on the principle of Occam's Razor and partly to allow the reader to conduct experiments as explained below.

Next we have

$$\Pi = q^h - a_j p_j - a_k q_k - T^p - T^c \qquad (19.2.3)$$

This is a very straightforward definition of abnormal profits Π. As in the main text, each 'a_j' measures the input required to be *in use* to produce one unit of output, and q_k or p_j is its rental according as a_k or a_j is an intermediate manufactured input or import or a basic factor. Note that the rental of an input contains *normal* profit on the money capital tied up (see appendix to Chapter 15). T^p is taxation on production, that is, on profits (direct taxation of firms), and T^c is taxation of sales (indirect taxation on commodities). Of course taxation on profits is sometimes expressed as a percentage of profits and taxation on commodities as a percentage of selling price; but for simplicity we have written all taxation as a deduction from abnormal profits per unit produced and sold. T^p and T^c are assumed to be determined by government policy. Note that in the model as presented the act of selling is counted as 'production' in the same way as the actual manufacturing process. In practice, when data is to be fitted it is a simple matter to assume that the government sets tax rates only and to allow the total tax collected to be dependent on actual profits and actual selling price. Fewer symbols are required, however, and the model is easier to comprehend if T^p and T^c are treated as in (19.2.3).

Notice particularly that in equilibrium, if it is ever attained, Π will be zero, in which case (19.2.3) reduces to the familiar cost equations

$$q_i = \sum a_{ij} p_j$$

of earlier chapters when due allowance is made for taxation.

Equation four of the model is even more easily recognised. In matrix notation we write

$$\{A_j : X_k^i\} = \{S_i^h\}\{a_{ij} : a_{ik}\} \tag{19.2.4}$$

The only way in which this differs from the 'equilibrium' equations (17.3.3) is that A_j is to be interpreted as the *usage* of factor endowment including items of fixed capital – machines and buildings, etc. – rather than the actual fixed endowment, and X_k^i is the vector of total demand for single-use intermediate inputs. The matrix a_{ij} is partitioned to separate out those inputs j which are basic non-produced factors and fixed capital items from those inputs k which are intermediate manufactured items or imports. Notice that this implies that the a_{ij} are of the unreduced kind (15.2.1) and (15.2.2) and not of the type (15.2.3) and (15.2.4). Hence we have no capital stock as such, only many items of fixed equipment. The symbol $\bar{A}_j$ is reserved for the vector of basic fixed factor endowments and actual stock of fixed capital items. The equations (19.2.4) therefore tell us, given the production vector S_i^h, what proportions $A_j/\bar{A}_j$ of the fixed factor endowment and capital stock will actually be in use in the time period and at the same time determine the demand X_k^i for intermediate products.

At a later stage it will be found that the usage of the factor endowment and commodity rentals together determine basic factor rentals and the demand for intermediate products helps to determine commodity prices. If ever, therefore, both basic factor and commodity prices settle to an equilibrium level, factor usage would become fixed and (19.2.4) would reduce to a set of equilibrium equations like (17.3.3). In such a case we have (implicitly) the static supply equations (17.3.4) which played such a large part in the equilibrium model. But notice that on the present formulation we have no difficulty over the number of factors and commodities since we are never required actually to solve for S_i^h. The econometrician is not asked to estimate some elasticity which might be infinite or indeterminate as explained in Chapter 15. It will, however, be necessary to find the a_{ij} (see equation (19.2.12) below).

Equation five simply adds total home demand D^h for commodities from all sources. Thus

$$D^h = \phi(X^c) + \alpha^{51}A + X^i + X^g + X^k \qquad (19.2.5)$$

The reader is first reminded that this is a demand equation for the representative commodity and not the aggregate demand for all items. It may be therefore that some terms will not be present for some commodities. $\phi(X^c)$ is consumer demand which has already been commented on. Term two represents sales between firms to replace capital items wearing out. A is the total usage of the representative commodity in all productive processes taken together as determined by (19.2.4), and we have assumed that a fixed proportion α^{51} of A is to be replaced in each time period. X^i is intermediate demand for the representative commodity when it is used up in a single time period (equation (19.2.4)). Thus $\alpha^{51}A$ and X^i will not ordinarily exist together in the same commodity equation, for the same item used in production cannot simultaneously be durable and consumable in a single act. X^g is government demand, assumed to be arbitrarily determined by government policy. X^k is new construction of fixed capital (real investment) determined by equation (19.2.15) below.

Notice that we might very well have made demand by firms for durable commodities symmetric with consumer demand ϕ as follows. Suppose we assume that the demand $\{A_j : X_k^i\}$ of (19.2.4) is the producer's equivalent of X^c, that is, it is the quantities of input in use in the period. To preserve symmetry with consumers, we then might write for sales to firms

$$A(t) - A(t - 1) + \alpha^{51}A(t - 1)$$

or $\qquad X^i(t) - X^i(t - 1) + \alpha^{51}X^i(t - 1)$

according as the commodity concerned is durable or consumed in a single act. The difference between the first two terms might then be interpreted as new investment X^k, and α^{51} would be unity for single-use commodities. On this interpretation we arrive at something very like (19.2.5).

We have not, however, followed this procedure since it is known that the commodity usage equations (19.2.4) do not fully reflect the demand of producers for durable commodities. It frequently happens that, unlike consumers, producers wish to have at their disposal some spare manufacturing capacity so as to be able to meet unexpected fluctuations in output. For this we introduce equation (19.2.15) below, which determines investment X^k according to a rule quite distinct from (19.2.4).

We now have

$$x = S^h - D^h - \Sigma \qquad (19.2.6)$$

where Σ measures changes in stocks of the representative commodity. In the usual notation, x is either imports or exports of the representative commodity. Clearly (19.2.6) is just an identity, for any change in stocks can only come about because production plus imports (net) is greater than or less than sales. Accordingly x will be imports if negative and exports if positive. We observe also that in equilibrium (i.e. with zero Σ) x equals production minus demand exactly as in other parts of this book.

Notice further that, given (19.2.6) we should have no need of an equation to 'explain' exports and imports were it not for the stock changes Σ. (19.2.5) determines home demand and (19.2.2) fixes supply, so that imports and exports and hence the balance of payments appear simply as a by-product, given stock changes. It is well worth while to reflect at length upon this point, since a great many attempts have been made in the past by economists and econometricians interested in balance of payments problems to measure something called the 'elasticity of demand for imports'.

The ordinary approach is to make the apparently eminently reasonable assumption that imports depend upon the terms of trade and aggregate expenditure at home, that is, to assume the existence of a function

$$x = x(q^h, q^f, D^h)$$

and so to attempt to find, by analysis of observed data, the response rates with respect to the variables postulated. But the reader should observe that when we write (19.2.6) we have something very different from an ordinary function expressing the way in which a variable, say x, is in some causal sense *determined* by the independent variables S^h, D^h and Σ. There are in fact no parameters specifying the nature of the dependence to find. All response rates are just unity. Given S^h, D^h and Σ, finding x is simply a matter of addition and subtraction.

Of course we could, if we chose, solve the whole system of equations to find S^h, D^h and Σ in terms of prices and expenditure or any other variables we decide not to eliminate and so obtain an apparent dependence of x on these variables by substitution in (19.2.6). But the response rates associated with an identity of this kind will not reflect any new basic uniformity of the real world. Rather they will be numbers dependent upon the response rates of all the other equations of the model. Indeed, more than once in earlier chapters of this book our inquiries actually required us to express some response rate of our import equation as a function of other response rates (see, for example, equation (4.4.16)). The right-hand side of (4.4.16) is a function measuring the reaction of exports to a change in the terms of trade when all the equations of the model are solved (on the assumptions specified) to give imports as a function of the terms of trade alone.

In short, the concept of the elasticity of demand for imports has a meaning only when we can agree upon a complete model, for it is a composite of other elasticities in the model and may even depend upon the values taken by policy-determined variables such as the exchange rate or the level of money expenditure. The difference between, say, the demand equation (19.2.1) and our import equation is that the demand equation exists because of the postulated behaviour of a body of consumers whose actions depend in a consistent way on prices and available expenditure whatever the circumstances. This is not true of 'imports', since imports come into existence only when some commodity, not especially different from any other, is actually imported rather than purchased at home. Clearly we cannot study the behaviour of an import as if it were an object with some kind of uniform activity in its own right rather than a reflection of the activity of other elements in the system. On the other hand importers and exporters do exist in the sense of people who engage in the activity of importing and exporting and their behaviour is important. The next equation is needed to describe this.

The remarks above are intended to emphasise that the import/ export equation we are about to develop has nothing directly to do with consumer demand for exportables or importables. The response rates (parameters) of (19.2.7) below measure the uniform reactions of exporters to the selling opportunities they face. They do not purport to explain how these selling opportunities arise in the first place. From some points of view in fact it is better to think of the problem as one of determining who holds world stocks rather than what determines exports, and our final equation will be set out in this form. This is consistent with the argument above that, but for the existence of stocks, exports would already be determined and no equation would be necessary.

On the other hand it is clear from casual observation that there have been times in the recent past where importers have found it desirable to use up their stocks temporarily rather than buy abroad, or where exporters have found their stocks building up because of some adverse price movement, foreign demand being met out of stocks abroad. It is this kind of phenomenon we wish to explain.

It is to be expected that exporters will be most successful

(*a*) when they have much to sell;
(*b*) when there is excess demand abroad (i.e. some unplanned stock diminution); and
(*c*) when good profits are to be earned, that is, when the foreign price net of transport cost and duty is higher than the home market price.

The amount available for sale abroad for each commodity, assuming no unplanned encroachment upon stocks or unplanned building-up of stocks, must be

$$S^h - D^h - \Sigma^p$$

that is, home production less home sales less the planned increase in stocks designated Σ^p. Excess demand abroad may be written

$$S^w - D^w$$

if we assume that the rest of the world demand, D^w, includes planned stock changes. It is convenient to adopt this convention since D^w is given from outside the model. Finally, the price ratio will be

$$\frac{eq^f}{q^h - T^t} = v$$

where e is the exchange rate, q^f is the foreign price net of foreign import duty and transport costs. T^t, the home duty is deducted from the home market price to cover the case where the commodity is an import. In the case of an export T^t will of course be zero (see below). For simplicity, we use the symbol v for the price ratio as defined.

Following this line of thought, we should naturally put

$$x = x((S^h - D^h - \Sigma^p), (S^w - D^w), v)$$

which says that exports are determined by planned exports, foreign demand and profits from exporting. But it would be wrong to leave the matter here, for a proper export function ought to have certain properties consistent with (19.2.6). It ought to be true in fact that when v is unity, that is. when normal profits only are earned on exports and when world supply equals world demand, then stock changes should be planned stock changes only. One form of function which will satisfy this requirement is

$$x = \alpha v^{\beta(1)}(S^h - D^h - \textstyle\sum^p) - (\alpha - 1)v^{\beta(2)}(D^w - S^w)$$

where α, $\beta(1)$ and $\beta(2)$ are response parameters to be discovered by statistical analysis. Note that when $v = 1$ and

$$(S^h - D^h - \textstyle\sum^p) - (D^w - S^w) = 0$$

then $$x = (S^h - D^h - \textstyle\sum^p) = D^w - S^w$$

Hence by (19.2.6) unplanned stock changes, $\sum^u$, must be zero as required.

Notice also that the equation proposed serves equally well for imports. This is best seen by observing that imports must be minus the rest of the world's exports. If therefore we write an export equation for the rest of the world on the principles already outlined, all that is necessary is to change its sign. And the only difference between the equation above and a similar equation for the rest of the world will be

(a) v will appear as $1/v$ in the rest of the world equation if we remember to introduce taxes on trade, T^t (see above); and

(b) demands and supplies are reversed.

It follows that we can achieve the required sign reversal for the home import equation by leaving demands and supplies as written. And the inversion of v simply means that for import equations we should expect each $\beta(i)$ to be of opposite sign to the $\beta(i)$s which occur in export equations. The form remains precisely the same.

Consider now whether the proposed form is plausible. First of all, note that we need not consider more than the first term; for, if x is an export, term one is the home export element and term two the foreign import element. But if x is an import, term one is the home import element with precisely the same properties as term two when x is an export, except that term two refers to the rest of the world instead of the home country.

Suppose therefore that x is an export. Term one is the product of a positive number $\alpha v^{\beta(1)}$ and the planned amount available for export. It seems natural to suppose that the larger the planned exports the larger will be the attained level of exports, other things being equal, and this is reflected in term one. In addition, however, we should expect the export effort to be greater the greater the profits of exporting, so that attained exports should be greater the higher is v. If more profits can be earned abroad than at home, v will be greater than unity so that $v^{\beta(1)}$ is greater than unity and attained exports will be greater on that account.

Term two is of course the influence due to unsatisfied demand abroad. As previously indicated it is more informative to look at this as equivalent to term one with x an import. In this case.

$$S^h - D^h - \Sigma^p$$

will be negative measuring planned imports. If demand at home is unusually high, planned imports will be high giving rise to high attained imports. Notice also that if attained imports are not high enough so that stocks begin to fall at home, then, by the price-fixing equation (19.2.10) below, home price will rise and v will fall. But for an import equation $\beta(i)$ is negative so that $v^{\beta(i)}$ will rise as v falls. Hence imports rise on this account.

In fact the proposed form of equation allows for a phenomenon, often noticed by casual observation, sometimes called 'import spillover'. If aggregate demand rises rapidly to the point where all productive capacity is in use and consumer demand is still unmet, almost all the excess demand will be channelled into imports. The effect is a sudden and marked increase in imports, the proportion of the increment of expenditure directed to imports being very much higher than the proportion of total imports to total product. If $\beta(i)$ is large and negative, this will be observed in the present model provided the increased demand for imports is accompanied by the rise in price which is to be expected as stocks run out.

One more difficulty remains. The chosen form of function is not very convenient since it is non-linear and may, because of this, be difficult to use in statistical analysis. We proceed therefore as follows. The inconvenient function

$$v^{\beta(i)}$$

wherever it occurs is replaced by a linear function tangential to the original function at the point (1, 1). That is, we write

$$\beta(i)v - \beta(i) + 1$$

instead of

$$v^{\beta(i)}$$

in each case and our import/export function accordingly becomes

$$x = \alpha(\beta(1)(v-1)+1)(S^h - D^h - \Sigma^p)$$
$$-(\alpha-1)(\beta(2)(v-1)+1)(D^w - S^w)$$

which may be manipulated to the form

$$x = \alpha(S^h - D^h - \Sigma^p - D^w + S^w) + (D^w - S^w) +$$
$$\alpha\beta(1)(v-1)(S^h - D^h - \Sigma^p) - (\alpha-1)(\beta(2)(v-1)(D^w - S^w))$$

One more brief manipulation is instructive. From (19.2.6), dividing Σ into its planned and unplanned elements, we have

$$\Sigma^u = (S^h - D^h - \Sigma^p) - x$$

Substituting for x in this result gives in an obvious notation

$$\Sigma^u = (1-\alpha)(S^{(w+h)} - D^{(w+h)} - \Sigma^p) - \alpha\beta(1)(v-1)$$
$$(S^h - D^h - \Sigma^p) + (\alpha-1)(\beta(2)(v-1)(D^w - S^w))$$

Notice that this can conveniently be thought of as an equation determining the home country's share of world changes in stocks. Term one is evidently a positive fraction (less than unity) of the unplanned change in world stocks. As long as v remains at its equilibrium value of unity, terms two and three remain zero and unplanned stock changes at home represent the home country's normal proportion $(1-\alpha)$ of world changes. If, however, v is greater than unity so that extra profits can be made by exporting, less than the normal share of world stock increases will be retained at home. This effect will be offset in some degree if S^w is greater than D^w so that unplanned stocks are building up abroad and so on. The reader should check for himself that the equation obtained is consistent with all the other possibilities.

Finally, to obtain equation (19.2.7) of the model we add back planned stock changes. Thus

$$\Sigma = \Sigma^p + \alpha^{71}(S^{(w+h)} - D^{(w+h)} - \Sigma^p) - \alpha^{72}(v-1)$$
$$(S^h - D^h - \Sigma^p) + \alpha^{73}(v-1)(D^w - S^w) \qquad (19.2.7)$$

Note that α^{71}, α^{72} and α^{73} are independent numbers to be estimated from observed data. Note also that

$$\alpha^{71} = (1-\alpha)$$
$$\alpha^{72} = \alpha\beta(1)$$

and
$$\alpha^{73} = (\alpha-1)\beta(2)$$

so that the original αs and βs can be computed from α_{ij}s. Hence (19.2.7) may, if we choose, be used for statistical analysis only. Once parameters are determined, the linear approximation could be dropped. Better forecasts might be obtained by reverting to the original non-linear form of function.

The next pair of equations is designed to separate observed stock changes into their planned and unplanned components. We need to discover in fact the principles upon which businessmen plan their holdings of stocks. It is natural to suppose first of all that the larger the scale of the industry the more stocks it is necessary to maintain. Again, for most commodities there is likely to be a big seasonal element present. More stocks may be held in winter than summer or vice versa. Technical change also will have some influence. Newer and better methods of stock control are constantly being devised. Finally, expectations can be an important determinant. For example, casual observation suggests that, in the past, balance of payment crises have arisen because currency depreciation is *expected*. Foreign buyers hold up purchases in the expectation of a price fall, depleting their stocks to meet immediate needs. Stocks build up at home as a counterpart to foreign reserves which would have been earned. As soon as the crisis is over, however, a foreign buying spree to replace diminished stocks abroad restores the *status quo*.

One way to proceed might be to set down a function in the usual way, relating planned stocks and the variables mentioned above. The difficulty however, is, that, as things are at the moment, it is impossible to observe planned stock changes so that we have no statistical data upon which to work. Of course, businessmen could be asked to indicate what part of their actual stock changes are planned and what part unplanned, and it is to be hoped that one day this information will be forthcoming. In the meantime, however, all that we have are figures recording the aggregate of both planned and unplanned stocks.

Fortunately the very notion of the distinction between planned and unplanned changes implies that planned changes are systematic following a rule or rules whereas the unplanned changes will be more random in their incidence. It is true of course that even unplanned changes have their explanation somewhere and indeed it is the purpose of the model to explain them. On the other hand unplanned changes will be generated by responses of the whole model to more or less random policy shocks, whereas planned changes are likely to follow a regular trend or cycle.

Statistical techniques are readily available which will separate the trend and cyclical components of a series of figures from the more random variations, and what is now proposed as a first approximation is that the systematic components should be treated as planned stock changes and the unsystematic part as unplanned. The model will then predict the unplanned part whilst the planned part must be assumed to continue through time as before.

This gives us two 'equations' as under:

$$\Sigma^u = \Sigma - \Sigma^p \tag{19.2.8}$$

$$\text{and } \Sigma^p = \text{systematic component of } \Sigma \text{ in previous} \atop n \text{ time periods} \tag{19.2.9}$$

It is to be supposed that among the systematic components would be those referred to above which arise out of expectations of price changes. Thought should be given to whether these should be treated as planned or unplanned. If the speculation is in stocks, that is, if stocks are held in the expectation of selling later at a higher price, then the stock changes are planned. If on the other hand the speculation is in money, that is, if buyers refrain from buying in the expectation of falling prices, then the stock changes are unplanned.

We now come to the equations which determine prices. Commodity prices are set by sellers so as to yield the desired level of profit. If, however, unplanned stocks are rising, businessmen will be less willing to raise prices for fear they will not be able to sell the whole of their output. When unplanned stocks are negative, however, both prices and production will be increased. The following price function therefore should reflect behaviour in this sector.

$$dq^h = \alpha^{10.1}(Z^{-1}) + \alpha_i^{10.2} \, dp_i + \alpha_j^{10.3} \, dq_j + \alpha^{10.4} \, dT^p$$
$$+ \alpha^{10.5} \, dT^c \tag{19.2.10}$$

This says that price changes are determined by the reciprocal of the level of stocks Z (or Z^{-1} may be interpreted as orders in hand if the commodity is not one where stocks are ordinarily held), by basic factor price changes and by changes in the prices of intermediate products. The two final terms measure the reactions of producers and wholesalers to changes in taxes on profits and sales respectively. The reader is reminded that subscripts i and j are used to indicate that dp_i and dq_j are vectors of all factor and commodity price changes which enter into the representative commodity price q^h.

The level of stocks Z may of course be obtained by adding

changes in stocks period by period to some initial figure. We do not therefore record a separate equation for Z.

Next we have

$$dp = \alpha^{11.1}(\bar{A} - A)^{-1} + \alpha_i^{11.2}\, dq_i \qquad (19.2.11)$$

indicating that the change in rentals of basic factors depends upon the extent to which that factor is used and changes in the cost of living. For example, one basic factor may be labour, so that p is the wage rate. $\bar{A}$ is the work force and A is labour employed as determined by (19.2.4). $(\bar{A} - A)^{-1}$ is the reciprocal of the level of unemployment. When unemployment is very low the wage rate will rise more rapidly through competition for scarce labour. The wage rate depends also upon 'cost push' as well as 'demand pull', so that term two of (19.2.11) is introduced to take care of this. The greater the rise in the price of commodities dq_i, the more insistently will trade unions demand higher wages.

Notice particularly that not all elements in the vector A_j refer to basic factors. As previously explained, the factor endowment on present conventions includes stocks of capital equipment in use, and capital equipment is of course a manufactured item whose rental is determined by (19.2.10). (19.2.11) determines the price of non-produced basic factors only.

Before we turn to the next equation, it is perhaps worth remarking on the connection between the price equations (19.2.3), (19.2.10), (19.2.11) and the corresponding price equations of the equilibrium version of the model. Clearly in equilibrium abnormal profits are zero so that (19.2.3) reduces to the ordinary cost equations (15.2.1) and (15.2.2). Again, in equilibrium $(\bar{A}_j - A_j)$ would be zero. In this case (19.2.11) should be the inverse of (19.2.3). This imposes important restrictions upon the form which (19.2.11) can take when considered in conjunction with (19.2.12) below, that is, there must be a relation between the αs in (19.2.11) and the as in (19.2.3). (19.2.10) looked at together with (19.2.3) may be recognised as no more than an equation determining abnormal profits.

It is now necessary to know something about the technical production possibilities underlying the various manufacturing processes. It is relatively easy of course to observe the matrix a_{ij} of input coefficients at each moment of time. What is difficult is to predict the way in which they will change. We do know, however, that techniques change when rentals change, for the producer will always try to choose the technique which minimises cost or, more properly, maximises profit. We know also that new inventions continuously appear to add to the set of techniques from which the manufacturer may select. Accordingly we write

$$a = \alpha_i^{12.1} q_i + \alpha_j^{12.2} p_j + \alpha^{12.3} t \qquad (19.2.12)$$

for the quantity of the representative input required to produce one unit of the representative output. αs $^{12.1}$ measure changes in a due to manufactured input price changes, while αs $^{12.2}$ measure those due to the changes in prices of basic factors. t is a time variable, the co-efficient $\alpha^{12.3}$ reflecting changes in a (with the passage of time) due to technical changes. Notice that the problem of finding αs from observed data is not unlike the problem of finding elasticities of demand for consumer goods. It is important also to write all prices q_i and p_j as price *ratios*, so that a will not change as long as price ratios remain constant.

Two identities now follow which are easily explained. First, we have

$$\bar{A}(t) = \bar{A}(t - 1) + \Delta L + X^k \qquad (19.2.13)$$

which simply states that the factor endowment at time (t) is equal to the factor endowment in the previous time period ($t - 1$) plus the amount added to it. ΔL is the change in the work force which is itself when $\bar{A}$ is labour and zero when $\bar{A}$ is any other factor. ΔL is a variable determined by influences outside the model. X^k is new investment in capital items which is itself where $\bar{A}$ is the capital item concerned. X^k is determined by (19.2.15) below.

The next identity is written

$$\text{Unemployment} = \bar{A} - A \qquad (19.2.14)$$

when $\bar{A}$ is the work force and A is labour employment. (19.2.14) is included as an equation only for ease of reference to Fig. 19.1 below.

New investment in capital items will be high when profits and expected profits are high and when $\bar{A} - A$, the quantity of fixed capital not in use, is low. A high rate of interest r on money will perhaps discourage investment. We propose therefore equation (19.2.15):

$$X^k = \alpha^{15.1} \Pi + \alpha^{15.2} (\bar{A} - A)^{-1} + \alpha^{15.3} r \qquad (19.2.15)$$

for the relation determining fixed capital formation of the representative item. We should naturally expect $\alpha^{15.1}$ and $\alpha^{15.2}$ to be positive with $\alpha^{15.3}$ negative.

Government income is simply the sum of all tax revenue. Thus

$$I^g = T^c + T^i + T^p + T^t \qquad (19.2.16)$$

where c, i, p and t indicate taxation on commodites (sales), income (direct tax), profits (production), and trade respectively. For convenience we have retained the notation T for total tax collected, even though elsewhere it has meant 'per unit'.

Personal incomes must equal the value of the national product less taxation less profits retained by firms. That is,

$$I^p = q_i S_i - T^c - T^i - T^p - \Pi^r \qquad (19.2.17)$$

We assume that retained profits Π^r is given exogenously and is not explained by the model. In equilibrium, retained profits should be zero. In a more realistic model of course it would be necessary to bring in all the equations required to determine retained profits, but this would enormously complicate the system here described, for dividend policy is closely bound up with banking policy which in turn is closely controlled by the government. For present purposes it is not necessary to go into this.

Only one more equation with behavioural parameters is needed to complete the system. This is the so-called consumption function, which determines what proportion of total personal incomes will be spent. The fact that we encountered this equation in (5.3.4) and nowhere else in the whole book testifies to the unifying property of the dynamic model. In other contexts books have been written about the consumption function, as indeed they have about other equations of the model, so that for present purposes we content ourselves with the claim that expenditure depends upon income, total wealth held, the rate of interest and prices. Thus

$$Y = \alpha^{18.1} I^p + \alpha^{18.2} W + \alpha^{18.3} r + \alpha_i^{18.4} q_i \qquad (19.2.18)$$

Notice that, on the principles of Chapter 5, we have an equilibrium level of employment when money spent out of the stock of wealth accumulated in previous periods is equal to titles to wealth added to the stock, that is, when private saving plus retained profits plus government saving is equal to new investment in fixed capital items – in other words, when

$$(I^p - Y) + \Pi^r + I^g - q_i X_i^g = q_i X_i^k$$

Substituting (19.2.17), (19.2.18) and (19.2.16) into this gives

$$Y - T^t = q_i S_i - q_i X_i^k - q_i X_i^q$$

that is, private expenditure less tariff revenue is equal to the total value of all output for consumption as opposed to investment less the government share in consumption. This is strictly in accord with the principle of the equilibrium model of earlier chapters where total expenditure on private and government consumption and investment was required to exceed the total value of production just and only just by the value of tariff revenue for equilibrium employment and no balance of payments surplus or deficit.

The following identities define the remaining symbols. The balance of payments is

$$\beta = eq_i^* x_i \tag{19.2.19}$$

where q_i^* is q_i adjusted for tariffs; government budget surplus is

$$I^g - q_i X_i^q \tag{19.2.20}$$

and personal titles to wealth at time t, $W(t)$, is naturally

$$W(t) = W(t - 1) + I^p - Y + \Pi^r \tag{19.2.21}$$

that is, last-period wealth plus savings plus profits retained by firms.

19.3 USING THE MODEL

A system of twenty-one equations is not by any means an easy thing to make sense of. It is moreover utterly impracticable to attempt to manipulate so many equations in the manner of the earlier work of this book; nor would any useful purpose be served by this even if it were possible. The inexperienced reader will find, however, that a surprising amount can be learned from the construction and study of a flow chart.

Figure 19.1 is a flow chart for the model of section 19.2. Each box represents a variable, the symbol for that variable being inscribed within it. Connections entering the box, as indicated by an arrowhead, are made with those variables determining the variable named in the box entered. The number of the functional equation or identity defining the form of the dependence appears in a circle near the arrowhead, and corresponds with the numerals assigned to each of the equations set out and described in section 19.2.

It will be noted that the connection between certain variables is broken by a wavy line, which is the usual symbol for a resistance in the diagram of an electrical circuit. This is to indicate that the determining variable acts upon the determined variable only after a

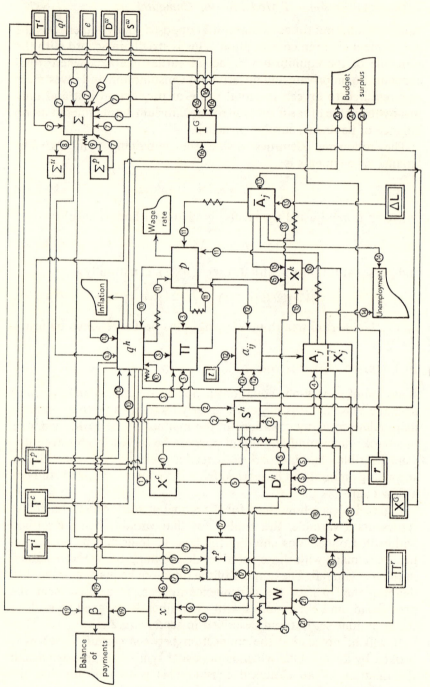

FIG. 19.1

time lag. Boxes which contain determining variables (connections leaving) which are themselves given outside the model (no entering connections) have a double border for ease of identification. These are the exogenous variables, that is, they are either the instruments through which the economy may be controlled or the outside influences (objective facts) with which the controller of the economy has to contend.

As a further aid to recognition, those variables which have connections entering but none leaving, that is, those which are determined but do not determine, have been assigned to a box of the irregular shape commonly used to signify computer output. In addition the full name of the variable has been printed within the box. This is to draw special attention to those elements of the economy over which we ordinarily wish to maintain the closest control.

Of course, there is a powerful sense in which we wish to control every variable, and indeed the control of any one usually implies the control of many others. Thus the computer output symbol is no more than a device to highlight those items which make news when they get out of control in the real world. Indeed, the reader will observe that in some cases we have connected an ordinary variable to an output variable when the two really amount to the same thing. No equation number appears on such a connection. For example, 'inflation' is really the same thing as commodity prices q^h. The expository nature of the output device is especially clear in this case. This completes the description of the chart which enables the equation system to be looked at as a whole.

Consider now how the model will 'work'. We assume that we are given a set of values of the exogenous variables, taxation, the interest rate, demand and supply for the rest of the world and so on. In addition we need some initial conditions, that is, wherever a time lag appears in a connection it is necessary to know some 'starting' value of the determining variable before we can begin. The starting variables are prices, the stock of titles to wealth, the level of production, and capital stock and usage.

Assume that we know the values of demand elasticities and of all other parameters, α, of each equation of the model. A simple count of equations and unknowns reveals that we can now solve for the twenty-one unknowns. Indeed, there is no need to count, for the flow diagram itself will reveal any shortage or surplus either by the presence of some box without an entering connection or by the presence of two or more differently numbered entering connections to the same box.

Notice that the solution of equations yields a new set of values for the starting variables, prices, production, titles to wealth, etc. These new values will not in general be the same as the starting values with which we began. The starting values should in fact be interpreted as the values taken at time period (say zero) whilst those obtained by solution of equations are those for the next time period (one).

The new values for the lagged variables (period one) now give us new starting values which together with values for exogenous variables whatever they may be in period one enable us to solve the system again for values of all variables in period two, and so on indefinitely. The economy will change and grow.

Consider now what is meant by a state of equilibrium. It could be the case that a point is reached in the process described above where the solution of the equation system yields values for the variables precisely the same as those given for the previous period. Clearly, if this occurs once it will occur for ever, so that the economy will cease to change. Equilibrium is reached.

It is obvious, however, that no such equilibrium can ever be attained with the model of section 19.2. All that is necessary to confirm this conclusion is to look at equation (19.2.11). dq_i here means $q(t) - q(t - 1)$, the difference between prices at time t and prices in the previous period. If commodity prices are not changing, as they cannot be in equilibrium, then factor prices must be changing, for the reciprocal of the difference between factor endowment and factor usage can never be zero. Equilibrium is possible only if $\alpha^{11.1}$ is zero, that is, only if trade union pressure to increase wages is completely absent even when full employment is reached. Such an assumption would be quite unrealistic at the present time.

The reader may now ask why, if equilibrium can never be attained, was so much time spent in earlier chapters discussing states of equilibrium. The answer is that another kind of quasi-equilibrium *is* possible. With a suitable choice of parameters, α, and with suitable assumptions about the movement of the values of exogenous variables, a point may be reached where all prices increase at a constant rate. Thus all *relative* prices remain constant. And we have seen again and again that constant relative prices can mean that all other variables remain constant. The real situation may be static even though inflation continues at possibly varying rates.

The study of any dynamic system begins with a study of its

stationary states. Our earlier work has been precisely this. We have been looking at and comparing the properties of situations where the dynamic model might eventually settle down to a state of constant rate of growth of all prices and a static real situation. The continual use of a numeraire price was a device to avoid talking about changing absolute prices. It is also a fact that control of the economy will ordinarily mean guiding the economy into something very like a stationary state, for if one real situation is better than another the object must be to attain the best situation and stay there. Of course 'staying there' may mean accommodating to outside influences which are changing, e.g. population growth, but the principle is the same.

The step forward we are now in a position to take is the examination of the actual path to equilibrium in the broadest sense. Obviously a computer is a necessary tool, so that readers who have no access to a computer can hardly expect to make much further progress. Where a computer is available, however, a great deal of work remains to be done.

First of all it is instructive to take a simple system such as that of section 19.2 and carry out exercises in simulation. It is not difficult to program a computer to perform the calculations required to operate the model and so to provide a running set of figures for the 'output' variables of Fig. 19.1 through time. This opens the possibility of playing a 'government game'. Movements of the key variables may be watched as they come off the computer just as they are watched by the government in real life. If at any moment some variable is judged to be getting out of hand, that is, if the balance of payments is too much in deficit or unemployment is too high or if moderate inflation is turning into galloping inflation, the machine may be stopped and a policy adjustment made. The currency may be devalued or taxation or tariffs increased. Or government spending may be adjusted or the rate of interest raised. Policy changes are of course made by altering the exogenous variables appropriately. The computer is then restarted to discover whether the 'policy' has been successful and how quickly the control operated.

Of course it will sometimes be necessary to run the program with and without the policy change in order to find out to what extent the economy would have righted itself and to what extent any favourable change was due to the policy, but this again is a simple matter. With a more sophisticated program and with properly designed terminal equipment, it is even possible in principle to introduce manual control of the exogenous variables and so to learn to 'fly' the economy, keeping the endogenous variables steady in the same way that an aircraft pilot maintains course and stability. Clearly a great deal might be learned from experiments of this kind by anyone who has some idea of what goes on inside the 'works'.

The next stage is to introduce more complicated systems. In section 19.2 the rest of the world demand and supply are given. In the real world, however, these two variables will be determined by another system independently controlled by some other government. Very little more work is needed to link two or even three countries together to form a joint model. Thus an exact mirror image of Fig. 19.1 with 'home' and 'world' interchanged would have two of its exogenous variables labelled D^h and S^h and two endogenous variables labelled D^w and S^w. The same applies to q^f and q^h when allowance is made for tariffs. These six variables of the mirror image link with their six counterparts in Fig. 19.1 itself to give a two-country model in which all demands, supplies and prices are endogenous. Parameters must of course be chosen so that x in Fig. 19.1 appears as minus x in the mirror image, but this will be no more than a natural restriction on (19.2.7) and its mirror image, as will appear obvious when the construction of (19.2.7) is studied.

If in an analogous way a three-country model with three commodities is built up, the scope for simulation exercises is enormously increased. All the work of this book may be re-examined in dynamic form. We now have three countries and three governments in control, with three sets of internal and external problems. Tariff wars may be fought out on the computer with the machine programmed to give a running commentary on welfare effects. Common markets may be created and the effect on factor prices studied. And all without annoyance to anyone more important than the unfortunate head of the department providing the computing service.

Of course, the value of all this work will be in proportion only to the extent to which the model is 'like' the real world. Likeness has two elements. First, the model must be complete and the form of the equations properly specified. Second, the values of the parameters α must correspond more or less exactly to those of the real world.

One of the principal objects of simulation is to discover points where the model is obviously misbehaving when compared with the real world. This can be due to a wrong function form or to incompleteness as well as to wrong values of parameters. It is feasible to experiment with many function forms, beginning with simple models and proceeding to the more complex. This process should go on side by side with attempts to find values of parameters which fit the data. Techniques for 'fitting' functions have been developed and improved with extraordinary rapidity in recent years, and progress continues in this field. All that is needed is data, equipment and a properly organised team – in short, money wisely spent.

It is perhaps worth reminding the reader also that among all the difficulties economists have one enormous advantage. It is possible in principle to achieve maximum welfare by proceeding in small steps from the given situation to one better. It follows that there is no more than one essential question to be answered about any policy, namely, 'Is it good?' The corollary to this is that we ordinarily need to be able to predict not the actual value of a variable but only whether it will change in a positive or negative direction. It seems quite likely that answers to this kind of question may be obtainable with only the crudest estimates of the relevant parameters. A wide margin of error may, and indeed almost certainly will, be quite admissible. This is a comforting and encouraging thought.

19.4 A Last Word

It is to be hoped that the limited objective of this work has now been attained. If the reader is not yet convinced that something should be done and that something can be done, or if he does not yet know how to begin, then it is beyond the power of the present writer to convince him.

The task before us is not an easy one. The model of section 19.2 has twenty-one equations or identities if all commodities are aggregated into one. With a reasonable and probably desirable disaggregation to, say, 400 commodity groups and, say, twenty basic factors, the number of equations would be close to 10,000. With a model of ten countries in a trading group it would approach 100,000. The computing problem is formidable. On the other hand it is currently possible to perform in less than one second calculations which fifty years ago would have been deemed to be impossible beyond our wildest imaginings. If it should prove necessary to build a special-purpose computer at a cost of £10 million to save 1 per cent of the national product by better control of the economy, we shall have made a profit of £300 million pounds at the end of the first year of operation. We leave the reader to calculate the return after fifty years.

Again progress is frustrated, at least in some quarters, by lack of data. We implore anyone who retains vestigial beliefs in the self-regulating nature of a modern economy to try the simplest experiment with the model of section 19.2. Once it is accepted that control is necessary, it is axiomatic that data necessary for control should be made available. Yet at the present time it is impossible to discover with any accuracy an economic fact as elementary as the quantities of intermediate products sold by firms to firms. In fact what is extraordinary is how little we know and not how much.

Curiously enough, however, all the information which could conceivably be required must, in the nature of the case, already be written down somewhere. Furthermore, for a minute fraction of the probable saving due to better control, it is already technically feasible to transfer to a central information bank all this data in such a way that it could be extracted quite anonymously in any form in which it might be needed. Immediate and massive attention should be given to this.

It seems appropriate to conclude this book with the same words used at the end of section 19.1. Research on the right lines is beginning, but only upon a microscopic scale. What is at present a trickle must become a flood.

Selected Bibliography

I Books and Articles Referred to in the Text

[1] ALLEN, R. G. D., *Mathematical Analysis for Economists* (Macmillan, 1938).

[2] ALMON, C., *Matrix Methods in Economics* (Addison–Wesley, 1967).

[3] GALE, D., and NIKAIDÔ, H., 'The Jacobian Matrix and Global Univalence of Mappings', *Mathematische Annalen*, CLIX (1965).

[4] HARRIS, E. E., *The Foundations of Metaphysics in Science* (Allen & Unwin, 1965).

[5] KOOROS, A., *The Elements of Mathematical Economics* (Houghton Mifflin, 1965).

[6] MARSHALL, A., *Principles of Economics*, 7th ed. (Macmillan, 1916).

[7] MCKENZIE, LIONEL W., 'Equality of Factor Prices in World Trade', *Econometrica*, XXIII (July 1955).

[8] ——, 'Matrices with Dominant Diagonals and Economic Theory', in *Mathematical Methods in the Social Sciences*, 1959, ed. K. J. Arrow, S. Karlin and P. Suppes (Stanford University Press, 1960).

[9] PEARCE, I. F., 'The Factor Price Equalisation Myth', *Review of Economic Studies*, XIX(2) (1952).

[10] ——, *A Contribution to Demand Analysis* (Oxford University Press, 1964).

[11] ——, and GABOR, A., 'The Place of Money Capital in the Theory of Production', *Quarterly Journal of Economics* (Nov 1958).

[12] ——, MCKENZIE, L. W., and SAMUELSON, P. A., 'Symposium on Factor Price Equalisation', *International Economic Review* (Oct 1967).

[13] RADFORD, R., 'The Economic Organisation of a Prisoner of War Camp', *Economica*, XII (1945).

[14] STOLPER, WOLFGANG F., and SAMUELSON, PAUL A., 'Protection and Real Wages', *Review of Economic Studies*, IX 1 (Nov 1941).

II Surveys

[15] BHAGWATI, J., 'The Pure Theory of International Trade: A Survey', *Economic Journal* (Mar 1964).

[16] CAVES, R., *Trade and Economic Structure* (Harvard University Press, 1960).

[17] CHIPMAN, J. S., 'A Survey of the Theory of International Trade': Part I, *Econometrica* (July 1965);

Part II, *Econometrica* (Oct 1965);
Part III, *Econometrica* (Jan 1966).

[18] CORDEN, W. M., 'Recent Developments in the Theory of International Trade', *Princeton Special Papers in International Economics*, no. 7 (Mar 1965).

[19] HABERLER, GOTTFRIED, 'A Survey of International Trade Theory', *Princeton Special Papers in International Economics*, rev. ed. (1961).

[20] METZLER, LLOYD A., 'The Theory of International Trade', in *A Survey of Contemporary Economics*, ed. Howard S. Ellis (Blakiston, for the American Economic Association, 1948).

III FOR GENERAL READING AND REFERENCE

[21] CHALMERS, HENRY, *World Trade Policies* (University of California Press, 1953).

[22] ELLSWORTH, PAUL T., *The International Economy: Its Structure and Operation* (New York: Macmillan, 1950).

[23] ENKE, STEPHEN, and SALERA, VIRGIL, *International Economics* (Prentice-Hall, 1957).

[24] HABERLER, GOTTFRIED, *The Theory of International Trade with its Applications to Commercial Policy*, trans. Alfred Stonier and Frederick Benham (William Hodge, 1936).

[25] HARROD, ROY, *International Economics* (University of Chicago Press, 1958).

[26] KEMP, M. C., *The Pure Theory of International Trade* (Prentice-Hall, 1964).

[27] KINDLEBERGER, C. P., *International Economics* (Irwin, 1958).

[28] LEFEBER, LOUIS, *Allocation in Space* (North Holland, 1958).

[29] MACHLUP, FRITZ, *International Trade and the National Income Multiplier* (Blakiston, 1943).

[30] MARSH, DONALD B., *World Trade and Investment: The Economics of Interdependence* (Harcourt, Brace, 1951).

[31] MARSHALL, ALFRED, *Money, Credit and Commerce* (Macmillan, 1923).

[32] ——, *The Pure Theory of Foreign Trade*, Reprinted, together with *The Pure Theory of Domestic Values* (London School of Economics and Political Science, 1930).

[33] MEADE, J. E., *The Theory of International Economic Policy*, vol. I: *The Balance of Payments* (Oxford University Press, 1951).

[34] ——, *The Theory of International Economic Policy*, vol. II: *Trade and Welfare* (Oxford University Press, 1955).

[35] ——, *A Geometry of International Trade* (Allen & Unwin, 1952).

[36] MEIER, G. M., *International Trade and Development* (Harper & Row, 1963).

[37] MOSAK, JACOB L., *General Equilibrium Theory in International Trade* (Principia Press, 1944).

[38] NEISSER, HANS, and MODIGLIANI, FRANCO, *National Incomes and International Trade* (University of Illinois Press, 1953).

[39] OHLIN, BERTIL, *Interregional and International Trade* (Harvard University Press, 1933).

[40] SCAMMELL, W. M., *International Monetary Policy* (Macmillan, 1961).

[41] SCHELLING, THOMAS, *International Economics* (Allyn & Bacon, 1958).

[42] VANEK, JAROSLAV, *International Trade Theory and Economic Policy* (Irwin, 1962).

[43] VINER, JACOB, *International Economics: Studies* (Free Press, 1951).

[44] ——, *Studies in the Theory of International Trade* (Harper & Bros, 1937).

[45] YEAGER, L. B., *International Monetary Relations* (Harper & Row, 1966).

IV THE BALANCE OF PAYMENTS AND THE EXCHANGE RATE MECHANISM

[46] ALEXANDER, SIDNEY S., 'Devaluation versus Import Restrictions as an Instrument for Improving Foreign Trade Balance', *International Monetary Fund Staff Papers* (Apr 1951).

[47] ——, 'The Effects of Devaluation on a Trade Balance', *International Monetary Fund Staff Papers*, II 2 (Apr 1952).

[48] ——, 'The Effects of Devaluation: A Simplified Synthesis of Elasticities and Absorption Approaches', *American Economic Review*, XLIX 1 (Mar 1959).

[49] BICKERDIKE, C. F., 'The Instability of Foreign Exchange', *Economic Journal*, XXX 1 (Mar 1920).

[50] BLACK, J., 'A Savings and Investment Approach to Devaluation', *Economic Journal* (June 1959).

[51] BLOOMFIELD, ARTHUR I., 'Foreign Exchange Rate Theory and Policy', in *The New Economics: Keynes' Influence on Theory and Public Policy*, ed. Seymour E. Harris (Knopf, 1948).

[52] BRONFENBRENNER, M., 'Exchange Rates and Exchange Stability', *Review of Economics and Statistics*, XXXII 1 (Feb 1950).

[53] BROWN, A. J., 'The Rate of Exchange', in *Oxford Studies in the Price Mechanism*, ed. T. Wilson and P. W. S. Andrews (Oxford University Press, 1951).

[54] COPPOCK, J., *International Economic Instability*, Economic Handbook Series (McGraw–Hill, 1962).

[55] EINZIG, PAUL, *A Dynamic Theory of Forward Exchange* (Macmillan, 1961).

[56] FRIEDMAN, MILTON, 'The Case for Flexible Exchange Rates', in Milton Friedman, *Essays in Positive Economics* (University of Chicago Press, 1953).

[57] HABERLER, GOTTFRIED, 'The Market for Foreign Exchange and the Stability of the Balance of Payments', *Kyklos*, III 3 (1949).

[58] HAHN, F. H., 'The Balance of Payments in a Monetary Economy' *Review of Economic Studies*, XXVI (2) 70 (Feb 1959).

[59] HOLMES, ALAN R., *The New York Foreign Exchange Market* (Federal Reserve Bank of New York, 1959).

[60] JONES, RONALD W., 'Depreciation and the Dampening Effects of Income Changes', *Review of Economics and Statistics*, XLII 1 (Feb 1960).

[61] ——, 'Stability Conditions in International Trade: A General Equilibrium Analysis', *International Economic Review*, II 2 (May 1961).

[62] KEMP, MURRAY C., 'The Rate of Exchange, the Terms of Trade and the Balance of Payments in Fully Employed Economies', *International Economic Review*, III 3 (Sep 1962).

[63] KINDLEBERGER, C. P., 'Speculation and Forward Exchange', *Journal of Political Economy*, XLVII 2 (Apr 1939).

[64] LAURSEN, SVEND, and METZLER, LLOYD A., 'Flexible Exchange Rates and the Theory of Employment', *Review of Economics and Statistics*, XXXII 4 (Nov 1950).

[65] MACHLUP, FRITZ, 'Relative Prices and Aggregate Expenditure in the Analysis of Devaluation', *American Economic Review*, XLV 3 (June 1955).

[66] ——, 'The Terms-of-Trade Effects of Devaluation upon Real Income and the Balance of Trade', *Kyklos*, X 4 (1956).

[67] MEADE, J. E., 'The Case for Variable Exchange Rates', *Three Banks Review*, XXVII (Sep 1955).

[68] METZLER, LLOYD A., 'Exchange Rates and the International Monetary Fund', in *Postwar Studies*, no. 8 (Washington: Board of Governors of the Federal Reserve System, 1947).

[69] MORGAN, E. V., 'The Theory of Flexible Exchange Rates', *American Economic Review*, XLV (June 1955).

[70] MUNDELL, ROBERT A., 'The Monetary Dynamics of International Adjustment under Fixed and Flexible Exchange Rates', *Quarterly Journal of Economics* (May 1960).

[71] ——, 'The Appropriate Use of Monetary and Fiscal Policy for Internal and External Stability', *International Monetary Fund Staff Papers*, IX (Mar 1962).

[72] PEARCE, I. F., 'The Problem of the Balance of Payments', *International Economic Review* (Jan 1961).

[73] ——, 'Note on Mr Spraos' Paper', *Economica*, new series, XXII 86 (May 1955).

[74] ROBINSON, JOAN, *Beggar-My-Neighbour Remedies for Unemployment: Essays on the Theory of Employment* (Blackwell, 1947).

[75] ——, 'The Foreign Exchanges', in *Essays in the Theory of Employment* (Macmillan, 1937).

[76] SOHMEN, EGON, *Flexible Exchange Rates: Theory and Controversy* (University of Chicago Press, 1961).

[77] SPRAOS, JOHN, 'The Theory of Forward Exchange and Recent Practices', *Manchester School*, XXI 2 (May 1953).

[78] ——, 'Speculation, Arbitrage and Sterling', *Economic Journal*, LXIX 273 (Mar 1959).

[79] ——, 'Consumers' Behaviour and the Conditions for Exchange Stability', *Economica*, N.S., XXII 86 (May 1955).

[80] STUVEL, GERHARD, *The Exchange Stability Problem* (Leiden: H. E. Stenfert Kroese, 1950).

[81] SWAN, T. W., 'Longer-Run Problems of the Balance of Payments', in *Readings in the Theory of International Trade*, ed. H. W. Arndt and W. M. Corden (Blakiston, 1949).

[82] TSIANG, S. C., 'The Role of Money in Trade Balance Stability', *American Economic Review*, LI 5 (Dec 1961).

V THE ROLE OF MONEY

[83] COMMITTEE ON THE WORKING OF THE MONETARY SYSTEM (The Rt. Hon. The Lord Radcliffe, C.B.E., Chairman), *Report* (H.M. Stationery Office, 1959).

[84] KENEN, P. B., 'International Liquidity and the Balance of Payments of a Reserve-Currency Country', *Quarterly Journal of Economics*, LXXIV (Nov 1960).

[85] MACHLUP, F., *Plans for Reform of the International Monetary System*, Special Papers in International Economics, no. 3 (International Finance Section, Princeton University, 1962).

[86] ——, 'The Need for Monetary Reserves', *Banca Nazionale del Lavoro* (Sep 1966).

[87] ——, 'World Monetary Debate: Bases for Agreement', *The Banker*, CXVI (Sep 1966).

[88 NURKSE, RAGNAR, *International Currency Experience: Lessons of the Inter-War Period* (League of Nations, 1944).

[89] WILLIAMS, JOHN H., *Postwar Monetary Plans and Other Essays* (Knopf, 1947).

VI TARIFFS, QUOTAS AND CUSTOMS UNIONS

[90] BALDWIN, ROBERT E., 'The Effect of Tariffs on International and Domestic Prices', *Quarterly Journal of Economics* (Feb 1960).

[91] BHAGWATI, J., 'Protection, Real Wages and Real Incomes', *Economic Journal*, LXIX (Dec 1959).

[92] ——, and RAMASWAMI, V. K., 'Domestic Distortions, Tariffs and the Theory of Optimum Subsidy', *Journal of Political Economy*, LXXI (Feb 1963).

[93] BLACK, J., 'Arguments for Tariffs', *Oxford Economic Papers* (June 1959).

[94] CORDEN, W. M., 'The Calculation of the Cost of Protection', *Economic Record*, XXXIII (Apr 1957).

[95] ——, 'Tariffs, Subsidies and the Terms of Trade', *Economica*, N.S., XXIV (Aug 1957).

[96] FLEMING, M., 'The Optimal Tariff from an International Standpoint', *Review of Economics and Statistics* (Feb 1946).

[97] GEHRELS, FRANZ, 'Customs Unions from a Single-Country Viewpoint', *Review of Economic Studies* (June 1958).

[98] GORMAN, W. M., 'The Effect of Tariffs on the Level and Terms of Trade', *Journal of Political Economy* (June 1959).

[99] ——, 'Tariffs, Retaliation and the Elasticity of Demand for Imports', *Review of Economic Studies*, xxv(3) 68 (June 1958).

[100] GRAAF, J. DE V., 'On Optimum Tariff Structures', *Review of Economic Studies*, xvii(1) 42 (1949–50).

[101] GRAHAM, F. D., 'Some Aspects of Protection Further Considered', *Quarterly Journal of Economics* (Feb 1923).

[102] HEMMING, M. F. W., and CORDEN, W. M., 'Import Restriction as an Instrument of Balance of Payments Policy', *Economic Journal* (Sep 1958).

[103] HORWELL, D. J., and PEARCE, I. F., 'A Look at the Structure of Optimal Tariff Rates', *University of Southampton Discussion Papers*, no. 6704 (1967).

[104] JOHNSON, H. G., 'Discriminatory Tariff Reduction: A Marshallian Analysis', *Indian Journal of Economics*, xxxviii (July 1957).

[105] ——, 'Optimum Welfare and Maximum Revenue Tariffs', *Review of Economic Studies*, xix (1951–2).

[106] ——, 'The Cost of Protection and the Scientific Tariff', *Journal of Political Economy* (Aug 1960).

[107] ——, 'Optimum Tariffs and Retaliation', *Review of Economic Studies* (1953–4).

[108] JONES, RONALD W., 'Comparative Advantage and the Theory of Tariffs: A Multi-Country Multi-Commodity Model', *Review of Economic Studies*, xxviii (June 1961).

[109] KAHN, RICHARD F., 'Tariffs and the Terms of Trade', *Review of Economic Studies*, xvi(1) (1947–8).

[110] KEMP, MURRAY C., 'Tariffs, Income and Distribution', *Quarterly Journal of Economics*, lxx 1 (Feb 1956).

[111] LERNER, ABBA P., 'The Symmetry between Import and Export Taxes', *Economica*, N.S., iii 3 (Aug 1936).

[112] LIPSEY, R. G., 'The Theory of Customs Unions: A General Survey', *Economic Journal*, lxx (Sep 1960).

[113] ——, 'The Theory of Customs Unions: Trade Diversion and Welfare', *Economica*, N.S., xxiv (Feb 1957).

[114] LITTLE, I. M. D., 'Welfare and Tariffs', *Review of Economic Studies*, xv(2) (1949–50).

[115] MANOILESCO, MICHAEL, *The Theory of Protection and International Trade* (King, 1931).

[116] MEADE, J. E., *The Theory of Customs Unions* (North Holland, 1955).

[117] ——, 'The Balance of Payments Problems of a European Free Trade Area', *Economic Journal* (Sep 1957).

[118] METZLER, LLOYD A., 'Tariffs, the Terms of Trade, and the Distribution of National Income', *Journal of Political Economy*, lvii 1 (Feb 1949).

[119] ——, 'Tariffs, International Demand and Domestic Prices', *Journal of Political Economy*, LVII (Aug 1949).

[120] MUNDELL, R. A., 'Tariff Preferences and the Terms of Trade', *Manchester School*, XXXII (Jan 1964).

[121] SCITOVSKY, TIBOR, 'A Reconsideration of the Theory of Tariffs', *Review of Economic Studies*, IX 2 (Summer 1941).

[122] ——, *Economic Theory and Western European Integration* (Allen & Unwin, 1958).

[123] VINER, JACOB, *The Customs Union Issue* (New York: Carnegie Endowment for International Peace, 1950).

VII TRADE AND ECONOMIC GROWTH

[124] BHAGWATI, JAGDISH, 'Immiserising Growth: A Geometrical Note', *Review of Economic Studies* (June 1958).

[125] ——, 'Growth, Terms of Trade and Comparative Advantage', *Economia Internazionale*, XII (Aug 1959).

[126] CORDEN, W. M., 'Economic Expansion and International Trade: A Geometrical Approach', *Oxford Economic Papers* (June 1956).

[127] HABERLER, G., 'Terms of Trade and Economic Development', in *Economic Development for Latin America*, ed. H. S. Ellis (Macmillan, 1961).

[128] JOHNSON, H. G., 'Effects of Changes in Comparative Costs as Influenced by Technical Change', in *International Trade Theory in a Developing World*, ed. R. Harrod and D. C. Hague (Macmillan, 1963).

[129] KEMP, MURRAY C., 'Technological Change, the Terms of Trade and Welfare', *Economic Journal*, LXV 3 (Sep 1955).

[130] MYINT, H., 'Protection and Economic Development', in *International Trade Theory in a Developing World*, ed. R. Harrod and D. C. Hague (Macmillan, 1963).

[131] NURKSE, R., *Problems of Capital Formation in Underdeveloped Countries* (Blackwell, 1953).

[132] POSNER, M. V., 'International Trade and Technical Change', *Oxford Economic Papers*, XIII (Oct 1961).

[133] PREBISCH, R., 'Commercial Policy in Underdeveloped Countries', *American Economic Review: Proceedings*, XLIX (May 1959).

[134] SCHLESINGER, EUGENE R., *Multiple Exchange Rates and Economic Development* (Princeton University Press, 1952).

[135] VINER, JACOB, *International Trade and Economic Development* (Clarendon Press, 1953).

VIII PRICE FORMATION AND COMPARATIVE ADVANTAGE

[136] ARROW, K. J., CHENERY, H. B., MINHAS, B. S., and SOLOW, R. M., 'Capital–Labor Substitution and Economic Efficiency', *Review of Economics and Statistics*, XLIII (Aug 1961).

[137] BALASSA, B., 'An Empirical Demonstration of Classical Comparative Cost Theory', *Review of Economics and Statistics*, XLV (Aug 1963).

[138] BALDWIN, ROBERT E., 'Equilibrium in International Trade: A Diagrammatic Analysis', *Quarterly Journal of Economics* (Nov 1948).

[139] BALOGH, T., 'Factor Intensities of American Foreign Trade and Technical Progress', *Review of Economics and Statistics*, XXXVII (Nov 1955).

[140] CHENERY, HOLLIS B., 'Comparative Advantage and Development Policy', *American Economic Review*, LI (Mar 1961).

[141] ——, and TSUNEHIKO, WATANABE, 'International Comparisons of the Structure of Production', *Econometrica*, XXVI (Oct 1958).

[142] DANIERE, ANDRE, 'American Trade Structure and Comparative Cost Theory', *Economia Internazionale* (Aug 1956).

[143] DIAB, M., *The United States Capital Position and the Structure of the Foreign Trade* (North Holland, 1956).

[144] EDGEWORTH, F. Y., 'The Theory of International Values', *Economic Journal*, IV (Mar, Sep and Dec 1894).

[145] GRAHAM, FRANK D., *The Theory of International Values* (Princeton University Press, 1955).

[146] HABERLER, GOTTFRIED, 'Real Cost, Money Cost and Comparative Advantage', *International Social Science Bulletin*, III, (spring 1950).

[147] ——, 'The Relevance of Classical Theory under Modern Conditions', *American Economic Review: Papers and Proceedings* (May 1954).

[148] HEILPERIN, MICHAEL A., *The Trade of Nations* (Knopf, 1957).

[149] ISARD, WALTER, and PECK, MERTON D., 'Location Theory and International and Interregional Trade Theory', *Quarterly Journal of Economics* (Feb 1954).

[150] JOHNSON, H. G., 'Gains from Freer Trade with Europe: An Estimate', *Manchester School of Economic and Social Studies*, XXVI (Sep 1958).

[151] ——, 'Factor Endowments, International Trade and Factor Prices', *Manchester School* (Sep 1957).

[152] JONES, R. W., 'Factor Proportions and the Heckscher–Ohlin Model'. *Review of Economic Studies*, XXIV 1 (Oct 1956).

[153] KEMP, MURRAY C., 'The Relation Between Changes in International Demand and the Terms of Trade', *Econometrica*, XXIV 1 (Jan 1956).

[154] ——, 'Gains and Losses from Trade', *Canadian Journal of Economics and Political Science*, XXVII 3 (Aug 1961).

[155] ——, 'The Gain from International Trade', *Economic Journal*, LXXII 4 (Dec 1962).

[156] ——, 'The Mill–Bastable Infant Industry Dogma', *Journal of Political Economy*, LXVIII 1 (Feb 1960).

[157] KRAVIS, I., 'Wages and Foreign Trade', *Review of Economics and Statistics*, XXXVIII (Feb 1956).

[158] ——, ' "Availability" and Other Influences on the Commodity Composition of Trade', *Journal of Political Economy*, LXIV (Apr 1956).

[159] LAND, A. H., 'Factor Endowments and Factor Prices', *Economica*, XXVI (May 1959).

[160] LAURSEN, SVEND, 'Production Functions and the Theory of International Trade', *American Economic Review* (Sep 1952).

[161] LEONTIEF, WASSILY, 'Factor Proportions and the Structure of American Trade: Further Theoretical and Empirical Analysis', *Review of Economics and Statistics*, XXXVIII 4 (Nov 1956).

[162] ——, 'Domestic Production and Foreign Trade: The American Capital Position Re-examined', *Economia Internazionale*, VII 1 (Feb 1954).

[163] ——, 'An International Comparison of Factor Costs and Factor Use', *American Economic Review*, LIV (June 1964).

[164] LERNER, ABBA P., 'Factor Prices and International Trade', *Economica*, N.S., XIX 1 (Feb 1952).

[165] ——, 'The Diagrammatical Representation of Cost Conditions in International Trade', *Economica*, XII (Aug 1932).

[166] ——, 'The Diagrammatical Representation of Demand Conditions in International Trade', *Economica*, N.S., I (Aug 1934).

[167] LOVASY, GERTRUD, 'International Trade under Imperfect Competition', *Quarterly Journal of Economics* (Aug 1941).

[168] MACDOUGALL, G. D. A., 'British and American Exports: A Study Suggested by the Theory of Comparative Costs':
Part I, *Economic Journal*, LXI (Dec 1951);
Part II, *Economic Journal*, LXII (Sep 1952).

[169] MASON, EDWARD S., 'The Doctrine of Comparative Cost', *Quarterly Journal of Economics* (Nov 1926).

[170] MCKENZIE, LIONEL W., 'On Equilibrium in Graham's Model of World Trade and Other Competitive Systems', *Econometrica*, XXII (Apr 1954).

[171] ——, 'Specialisation and Efficiency in World Production', *Review of Economic Studies*, XXI (June 1954).

[172] ——, 'Specialisation in Production and the Production Possibility Locus', *Review of Economic Studies*, XXIII (1955–6).

[173] MEIER, G. M., 'The Theory of Comparative Costs Reconsidered', *Oxford Economic Papers* (June 1949).

[174] METZLER, LLOYD A., 'Graham's Theory of International Values', *American Economic Review* (June 1957).

[175] MICHAELY, M., *Concentration in World Trade*, Contributions to Economic Analysis, no. 28 (North Holland, 1962).

[176] ——, 'Factor Proportions in International Trade: Current State of the Theory', *Kyklos*, XVII, fasc. 4 (1964).

[177] MINHAS, B. S., *An International Comparison of Factor Costs and Factor Use*, Contributions to Economic Analysis, no. 31 (North Holland, 1963).

[178] MOOKERJEE, SUBIMAL, *Factor Endowments and International Trade: A Study and Appraisal of the Heckscher–Ohlin Theory* (Asia Publishing House, 1958).

[179] MORGAN, E. V., and REES, G. L., 'Non-traded Goods and International Factor Price Equalisation', *Economica* (Nov 1954).

[180] MORISHIMA, MICHIO, 'A Reconsideration of the Walras–Cassel–Leontief Model of General Equilibrium', in *Mathematical Methods in the Social Sciences*, 1959, ed. K. J. Arrow, S. Karlin and P. Suppes (Stanford University Press, 1960).

[181] MUNDELL, R. A., 'The Pure Theory of International Trade', *American Economic Review*, L 1 (Mar 1960).

[182] MYINT, H., 'The "Classical Theory" of International Trade and the Underdeveloped Countries', *Economic Journal* (June 1958).

[183] ——, 'The Gains from International Trade and the Backward Countries', *Review of Economic Studies* (1954–5).

[184] ONIKI, H., and UZAWA, H., 'Patterns of Trade and Investment in a Dynamic Model of International Trade", *Review of Economic Studies*, XXXII (Jan 1965).

[185] PEARCE, I. F., 'A Note on Mr Lerner's Paper', *Economica*, N.S., XIX (Feb 1952).

[186] ——, 'A Further Note on Factor–Commodity Price Relationships', *Economic Journal*, LXIX (Dec 1959).

[187] POLAK, J. J., *An International Economic System* (University of Chicago Press, 1954).

[188] REITER, STANLEY, 'Efficient International Trade and Equalisation of Factor Prices', *International Economic Review*, II 1 (Jan 1961).

[189] ROBINSON, R., 'Factor Proportions and Comparative Advantage': Part I, *Quarterly Journal of Economics* (May 1956); Part II, *Quarterly Journal of Economics* (Aug 1956).

[190] ——, 'Factor Proportions and the Structure of American Trade: Further Theoretical and Empirical Analysis. Comment', *Review of Economics and Statistics*, supplement, XL (Feb 1958).

[191] RYBCZYNSKI, T. N., 'Factor Endowments and Relative Commodity Prices', *Economica*, N.S., XXII 4 (Nov 1955).

[192] SAMUELSON, PAUL A., 'Prices of Factors and Goods in General Equilibrium', *Review of Economic Studies*, XXI 1 (Oct 1953).

[193] ——, 'The Gains from International Trade', *Canadian Journal of Economics and Political Science*, V 2 (May 1939).

[194] ——, 'Equalisation by Trade of the Interest Rate along with the Real Wage', in *The Collected Scientific Papers of P. A. Samuelson* (Cambridge, Mass.: M.I.T. Press, 1966).

[195] ——, 'The Gains from International Trade Once Again', *Economic Journal*, LXXII 4 (Dec 1962).

[196] STERN, ROBERT M., 'British and American Productivity and Comparative Costs in International Trade', *Oxford Economic Papers*, N.S., XIV (Oct 1962).

[197] TATEMOTO, M., and ICHIMURA, S., 'Factor Proportions and Foreign

Trade: The Case of Japan', *Review of Economics and Statistics*, XLI (Nov 1959).

[198] UZAWA, HIROFUMI, 'Prices of the Factors of Production in International Trade', *Econometrica*, XXVII 2 (July 1959).

[199] VANEK, J., 'The Natural Resource Content of Foreign Trade, 1870–1955, and the Relative Abundance of Natural Resources in the United States', *Review of Economics and Statistics*, XLI (May 1959).

[200] ——, 'Variable Factor Proportions and Inter-Industry Flows in the Theory of International Trade', *Quarterly Journal of Economics*, LXXVII (Feb 1963).

IX INTERNATIONAL CAPITAL FLOWS AND OTHER FACTOR MOVEMENTS

[201] BALOGH, T., and STREETEN, P. P., 'Domestic Versus Foreign Investment', *Bulletin of the Oxford University Institute of Statistics*, XXII 3 (Aug 1960).

[202] BLOOMFIELD, ARTHUR I., *Capital Imports and the American Balance of Payments, 1934–1939: A Study in Abnormal International Capital Transfers* (University of Chicago Press, 1950).

[203] FANNO, M., *Normal and Abnormal International Capital Transfers* (University of Minnesota Press, 1939).

[204] IVERSON, C., *Some Aspects of the Theory of International Capital Movements* (Levin & Munksgaard, 1936).

[205] JASAY, A., 'The Choice Between Home and Foreign Investment', *Economic Journal*, LXX (Mar 1960).

[206] JOHNSON, HARRY G., 'The Transfer Problem and Exchange Stability', *Journal of Political Economy* (June 1956).

[207] KEMP, MURRAY C., 'The Benefits and Costs of Private Investment from Abroad: Comment', *Economic Record*, XXVI 1 (Mar 1962).

[208] ——, 'Foreign Investment and the National Advantage', *Economic Record*, XXVIII 1 (Mar 1961).

[209] ——, 'Unilateral Transfers and Terms of Trade', *American Economic Review*, XLVI 1 (Mar 1956).

[210] KEYNES, J. M., 'Foreign Investment and National Advantage', *The Nation and Athenaeum*, XXXV (9 Aug 1924).

[211] ——, 'The German Transfer Problem', *Economic Journal* (Mar 1929).

[212] KINDLEBERGER, CHARLES P., *International Short-Term Capital Movements* (Columbia University Press, 1937).

[213] LITTLE, I. M. D., and CLIFFORD, J. M., *International Aid* (Allen & Unwin, 1965).

[214] MACDOUGALL, G. D. A., 'The Benefits and Costs of Private Investment from Abroad: A Theoretical Approach', *Economic Record*, XXVI 1 (Mar 1960).

[215] MCDOUGALL, I. A., 'Non-Traded Goods and the Transfer Problem', *Review of Economic Studies*, XXXII (Jan 1965).

[216] METZLER, LLOYD A., 'The Transfer Problem Reconsidered', *Journal of Political Economy*, L 3 (June 1942).

[217] MUNDELL, R. A., 'International Trade and Factor Mobility', *American Economic Review*, XLVII 2 (June 1957).

[218] NURKSE, RAGNAR, 'The Problem of International Investment Today in the Light of Nineteenth-Century Experience', *Economic Journal*, LXIV 4 (Dec 1954).

[219] OHLIN, BERTIL, 'The Reparation Problem: A Discussion', *Economic Journal* (June 1929).

[220] PEARCE, I. F., and ROWAN, D. C., 'A Framework for Research into the Real Effects of International Capital Movements', in *Essays in Honour of Marco Fanno* (Padova: Cedam, 1966).

[221] ROBERTSON, DENNIS H., 'The Transfer Problem', in *Essays in Monetary Theory* (Staples Press, 1940).

[222] SAMUELSON, PAUL A., 'The Transfer Problem and Transport Costs', *Economic Journal*, LXII 2 (June 1952); LXIV 2 (June 1954).

[223] THOMAS, BRINLEY, *Migration and Economic Growth: A Study of Great Britain and the Atlantic Economy* (Cambridge University Press, 1954).

X MEASUREMENT AND METHODOLOGY

[224] BALOGH, THOMAS, 'Static Models and Current Problems in International Economics', *Oxford Economic Papers* (June 1949).

[225] ——, and STREETEN, P. P., 'The Inappropriateness of Simple "Elasticity" Concepts in the Analysis of International Trade', *Bulletin of the Oxford University Institute of Statistics*, XIII (Mar 1951).

[226] DE GRAAF, J., *Theoretical Welfare Economics* (Cambridge University Press, 1957).

[227] JOHNSON, H. G., 'The Taxonomic Approach to Economic Policy', *Economic Journal*, LXI (Dec 1951).

[228] LEONTIEF, WASSILY W., 'Implicit Theorising: A Methodological Criticism of the Neo-Cambridge School', *Quarterly Journal of Economics*, L (Feb 1937).

[229] MORGAN, D. J., and CORLETT W. J., 'The Influence of Price in International Trade: A Study in Method', *Journal of the Royal Statistical Society*, Series A (General), CXIV(3) (1951).

[230] ORCUTT, GUY H., 'Measurement of Price Elasticities in International Trade', *Review of Economics and Statistics*, XXXII 2 (May 1950).

[231] SAMUELSON, PAUL A., 'Evaluation of Real National Income', *Oxford Economic Papers*, N.S., II 1 (Jan 1950).

[232] ——, 'Welfare Economics and International Trade', *American Economic Review* (June 1938).

[233] VANEK, J., 'A Rehabilitation of "Well-Behaved" Social Indifference Curves', *Review of Economic Studies*, XXXI (Jan 1964).

Index